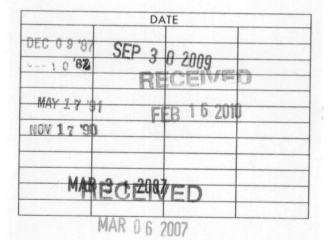

THE
ENGLISH CATHOLIC
COMMUNITY
1570–1850

the interior of the new catholic chapel

A. W. N. PUGIN

'The Interior of the New Catholic Chapel'

Drawn by Pugin in 1840 for the second edition of his *Contrasts*, in which mediaeval and modern civilisation were visually compared to the latter's disadvantage. Not included in the published version. Intending to caricature the early nineteenth-century Catholic congregation and its worship from his standpoint of romantic Gothicism, Pugin proved a good deal sharper about the post-Reformation English Catholic community than he did about the Middle Ages; but he was right about the contrast. The word 'chapel' should be emphasised.

JOHN BOSSY

THE
ENGLISH CATHOLIC
COMMUNITY
1570–1850

Oxford University Press
New York

© John Bossy, 1976

ISBN 019 519 847-6

Printed in Great Britain

'S'il n'y avoit en Angleterre qu'une Religion, le despotisme seroit à craindre, s'il y en avoit deux, elles se couperoient la gorge; mais il y en a trente, et elles vivent en paix heureuses.'

VOLTAIRE, *Lettres Philosophiques* (ed. G. Lanson, 2 vols., 1924), i, p. 74.

CONTENTS

II THE MISSION AND THE MISSIONER

PART THREE   BIRTH OF A DENOMINATION, 1770–1850

MAPS, TABLES AND FIGURES

PREFACE

IN writing this book I have incurred a variety of debts. First, to
those who one way or another encouraged me to write it: the
President and Fellows of Queens' College, Cambridge; the late
H. O. Evennett, Professor Lawrence Stone and John Todd, who has
been an extremely patient publisher; colleagues and superiors at
Goldsmiths' College, University of London, and the Queen's University of Belfast, above all Professor Michael Roberts.

Second, to all those on whose work I have drawn; to the Catholic
Record Society and the editors of *Recusant History* for their continuing
and essential labours; to those whose theses, wholly or partly unpublished, I have used—Thomas H. Clancy, Joan M. Connell, Eamon
Duffy, Keith Lindley, Albert J. Loomie, D. M. Lunn, J. L. Miller,
Marie Rowlands, Richard Schiefen, C. M. F. J. Swan, F. X. Walker
and A. D. Wright. I have a particular debt to three people who have
allowed me to make considerable use of work prepared for publication
but not yet published: M. J.-A. Lesourd of the University of Nancy for
the analysis of the Papist Returns of 1767, and Map 3, drawn from his
thesis 'Les Catholiques dans la société anglaise, 1765–1865'; Mr
Donald Steel of the Society of Genealogists for the account of
Catholic births, deaths and marriages in his introduction to volume 3
of the *National Index of Parish Registers*;[1] and Dr David Miller of the
Carnegie-Mellon University, Pittsburgh, Pa., for his work on Catholic
religious practice in early nineteenth-century Ireland. I have received
valuable help in the shape of documents, material and advice from
Dr A. F. Allison, Mr P. Knell, Miss K. M. Longley, Dr Lunn, Miss
Rowlands and Rev. W. Vincent Smith. May I add an apology to those
on whose work I have failed to draw, or drawn inadequately? I should
be glad to be told.

Third (although I did not set out to write this book from the docu-

---

[1] Now published in D. J. Steel and Edgar R. Samuel, *Sources for Roman Catholic
and Jewish Genealogy and Family History* (London/Chichester, 1974).

ments upwards), to the owners, keepers and staff of a number of archive collections, to whom I am most grateful for access, helpful guidance and permission to quote: in particular the Archives of the Archbishop of Westminster (and Miss Elizabeth Poyser), the Archives of the English Province of the Society of Jesus (and Rev. Francis Edwards, S.J.), of the Old Brotherhood of the English Secular Clergy (most helpfully made available in microfilm), of Ushaw College, Durham (and Rev. David Milburn); and the County Record Offices of Lancashire at Preston (for the archives generously deposited by the Archbishop of Liverpool), and of Northumberland at Jesmond. I have a further debt to the Catholic Record Society for access to the Gillow Library, now in the Jesuit house in Farm Street, London, and to the kindness of its custodian, Mr Ronald Browne; and to Fr Frederick Turner, S. J., librarian of Stonyhurst College.

Fourth, to Mr Brian Magee and Messrs Burns and Oates, for permission to use the material on which Maps 1 and 2 are based; and to the Trustees of the British Library for the illustration used as a frontispiece.

My warmest thanks, finally, to friends who have read drafts of the book or parts of it, and to whose criticisms and comments it owes a great deal: to Dr J. H. Whyte in particular, who had to grapple with it in its least attractive form, to Professor J. C. Beckett, Dr Christopher Haigh, Dr Peter Jupp and Deborah Lavin. The dedication, which is to my sister and my brother, may also serve to indicate the greatest debt of all.

Belfast, January 1975   JOHN BOSSY

NOTE

I HAVE made no attempt to regularise the spelling of quotations. I have tried to give full and comprehensible references, but to keep them reasonably concise I insert at p. 434 a short alphabetical list of abbreviations used, full titles of works frequently cited, and details of volumes used from the Catholic Record Society's publications and the Victoria County Histories, which will normally be referred to by volume number and date.

FOR MARJORIE AND MICHAEL

INTRODUCTION

THE English Catholic community has bred some great historians, but they have not contributed much to its own history. Their reluctance is understandable, but a pity; for it has left the community uneasily related to its past, uncertain where to look for it and what to make of it, embarrassed or over-devout, unable to draw on the kind of sustaining tradition which, whatever else he may lack, a Catholic ought presumably to have at his disposal. Thirteenth-century scholastics, sixteenth-century martyrs or nineteenth-century potato-fields are artificial substitutes for this tradition; they distort perspective when venerated singly, and cannot be related to form a convincing whole. Even the second of them will, of necessity, lie at a tangent to the continuous history of the community as such. This, or a part of it, it was my ambition to recover, in the hope that, through this recovery, what is after all a sizeable part of the population of England might move a little more securely in its environment than it has found it possible to do so far. I put this large proposal in the past tense; historians are probably unwise to bare their souls so far, and had better be content to decline the role of saviours of the nation. Still, one must have some motive in starting to write a book and this, I confess, was mine.

Needless to say I did not, even in my first ignorant enthusiasm, suppose that I would be starting from scratch, and in so far as I had had ambitions to make all things new, the attempt to realise them would have taught me a more fruitful modesty. One cannot do without a historiographical tradition even where, as in this case, it may not be a particularly strong one; in any event, to write a book of this scope in something less than a lifetime is to depend enormously on the work of others. On those, in the first place, who have tried to do the thing before: there have not been many of them, and none of them has been a Lingard, an Acton or a Knowles, but one of them at least has been a historian of distinction. It may be said that David Mathew had every qualification for writing this book except the vulgar pertinacity inseparable from largish projects. Many or most of the ideas which have helped, I hope, to give its presentation of the community a certain originality will be found somewhere or other in his writings on the subject. Sometimes I have borrowed them consciously, sometimes discovered them when I thought I had invented them myself; so far as they may emerge more forcibly here, it is mainly because I have pursued them more obsessively than he did. All the same, I think I was entitled to believe that *Catholicism in England* had not really done the job I wished to do.[1] Episodic in structure, ungenerous with references, written as from sources of information not accessible to the general public, it had the air of a series of snapshots in a family album. This was not very good for the Catholics to whom it was primarily directed, since it was likely to encourage that sense of being a peculiar people which was one of the things inhibiting them from seeing themselves in a genuine historical perspective. It was also likely to sustain the inherited conviction of outsiders that a Catholic community was a foreign body with which—even if they were historians, perhaps especially if they were historians—they were not required to bother. More recent attempts to draw attention to the Englishness of English Catholicism have been too slight,[2] or too full of special pleading, to make much difference to this conviction.

None of the other predecessors or contemporaries to whom I am most indebted has attempted a treatment of the subject as a whole. One group consists of historians working in the first twenty years of this century, who produced a body of work on the earlier and later phases of the period whose virtues help to explain why it is easier to get a grasp of the Catholic community in 1600 or 1800 than, say, in the reign of James II. Most of them—the exception was the German historian A. O. Meyer—were members of one or other branch of the English Catholic clergy; the Jesuit J. H. Pollen, the seculars Edwin Burton and Bernard Ward. They lived with the documents, and wrote with balance and sympathy on subjects which generated disturbance in others.[3] When they ceased to write, around 1920, there was a distinct hiatus. This was partly the result of a number of accidents: Meyer, for reasons of his

1. David Mathew, *Catholicism in England. The Portrait of a Minority: its Culture and Tradition* (London, 1936; 2nd edn, 1948).
2. e.g. M. D. R. Leys, *Catholics in England, 1559–1829. A Social History* (London, 1961); none the less a rather useful book.
3. Cf. J. H. Whyte, 'Historians of Nineteenth-Century English Catholicism', *Clergy Review*, n.s. lii (1967), pp. 791–801; and, on Meyer, my own introduction to his *England and the Catholic Church under Queen Elizabeth* (London, repr. 1967).

own, decided to abandon a book on the seventeenth century which would have done a great deal to close the gap between the two ends of the subject; Pollen died rather early; Benedictines preferred the Middle Ages. But there were more fundamental difficulties: martyrology pointed the subject, historiographically speaking, up a cul-de-sac; a lack of contact with universities left too much scope for imitation of Hilaire Belloc and too little for influences which might have enlarged an over-clerical conception of the community and its history. Detached from wider perspectives, clerical history tended to degenerate into clerical backbiting. Philip Hughes, the most serious contributor from this period if one excludes the unclassifiable Mathew, gave the impression of battling with problems which required a reformulation he had neither the time nor the equipment to achieve. Since my own first steps in the subject were made against this background, I had better give notice that my judgment may have been warped by a prevalence of influences deriving from one party to the arguments in question, the Society of Jesus.

By the 1950s it was clear—at least it was clear to one or two outside observers—that a change of perspective was a good while overdue. It was in fact under way, as the point of vantage began to shift from the centre, national or corporate, to the locality, following the revolution in English local archives; here it became possible to make contact with an antiquarian tradition which had been doing indispensable work since the mid-nineteenth century. In the nature of the case, the cultivation of this broader field has been the work of many hands, but the hand that has mattered most has been that of John Aveling.[4] In deciding to investigate the history of the Catholic community in Yorkshire from the accession of Queen Elizabeth to the relief act of 1791 rather than, as he might presumably otherwise have done, the history of the English Benedictine congregation, Aveling gave a decisive shift to the subject. Without his work it would no doubt have been possible to envisage in rough outline what this book ought to look like, but impossible to fill the outline with anything like adequate substance. This is not merely a matter of submitting general conceptions to the test of local detail; it is also, and perhaps more profoundly, a matter of the dimension of time. For the capacity, such as it may turn out to have been, to substantiate

4. I have discussed Aveling's work at greater length in 'The Catholic Community of Yorkshire, 1558–1791', *Ampleforth Journal*, lxxviii, part 2 (1973), pp. 27–32, from which I have borrowed a sentence or two here.

an idea that the Catholic community existed in real life continuously throughout the period I have been concerned with, and that its history has been a cumulative process to which every generation, every decade, has had its part to contribute, I am indebted to him; and also to those who, fired by his example, have gone and done likewise in Stafford-shire, in Wiltshire and elsewhere. It is offering a modest return for what they have contributed to this book to say that, where the trend of the times is towards a localisation of the field of study, someone who seeks to make general sense of what everyone else is doing has a reasonably useful function to perform.

   In seeking to make that general sense I have insinuated a good deal of my own. By the time the general intention to write the book had begun to be translated into practice I had delimited the subject in ways that need to be explained. They followed from some historical choices and assumptions which are expressed, one way and another, in my title and the quotation which accompanies it. The first was that the period from roughly 1570 to roughly 1850 formed an 'intelligible field of study'; that is to say that the dates at either end were associated with dis-continuities in the historical sequence which caused grave distortion if one tried to ignore them; that no discontinuities of this order were to be found between them; and that it was therefore proper, indeed essential, to treat the intervening period as a whole. This conclusion had fairly important implications at either end. On the side of the *terminus a quo* it represented a departure from the view taken by Mathew, and gener-ally implied in existing treatments of the subject, that the proper place to begin a history of the English Catholic community was the reign of Henry VIII. For reasons which will emerge, I do not consider the lives of Thomas More or John Fisher, of Queen Mary or Reginald Pole, or of the average Englishman of conservative instincts during, say, the half-century which followed the breach with Rome, as forming part of the history of the English Catholic community. If pressed, I would admit to regarding them as part of the history, the posthumous history if you will, of 'mediaeval' or 'pre-Reformation' Christendom in England; that, in my view, is so far a different thing from the history of English Catholicism that anyone who tries to conflate the two is in for trouble. Broadly speaking, my *terminus a quo* is the erection of the seminary at Douai. On the side of the *terminus ad quem*, 1850 is meant to refer to the 'restoration of the hierarchy', to the climax of Irish immigration into England, and most of all to a combination of both these events with other developments which between them produced a critical discontinuity in the history of the community. Anyone gifted with precognition looking forward from a date before 1568 would have been gazing from the standpoint of a universal *Christianitas* in the direction of something markedly different, whose frequent similarities to what he was familiar with would only have puzzled him the more. Anyone looking back across the events of the mid-nineteenth century is looking from a new Catholic community at an old one, whose ways may be equally hard to understand. In neither case, of course, are the barriers watertight; it has always been my view that the second was less so than has often been supposed, and on reflection I am not sure that the first is quite as high as I thought it was. I have also come to the conclusion that a crux of considerable importance may be detected about halfway between the two. All the same, I am willing to stand by the conviction which my title expresses, that what one may call the old Catholic community in England was launched on its career about 1570, fundamentally transformed about 1850, and had between those dates a continuous history which we do well to take as a whole.

A second implication of my title is that I am dealing with a 'community'. One of the ways of explaining the difference between this book and Mathew's is to notice that he spoke of his subject not as a community but as a minority. This does more than account for the difference in *termini*. A minority is by definition one of a pair; a community may be one of several. To claim the status of a minority for English Catholics is I think to claim too much. It is important to the general argument of the book that I consider Englishmen, between the sixteenth and the nineteenth centuries, as being divided for religious purposes not into Protestants and Catholics but into Anglicans, Presbyterians, Independents, Baptists, Fifth-Monarchy men, Quakers, Unitarians, Methodists of various colours, Jews and a good deal more. I do not think any account of a single religious body in post-Reformation England can make much sense if it does not take notice of the baffling fertility of the religious imagination of Englishmen. What, one may well enquire, was a Catholic community among so many? It also follows that I am not primarily concerned with the relation of minority to majority, considered either as state or as church, but with the body of Catholics as a social whole and in relation to itself, with its internal constitution and the internal logic of its history. Hence, and contrary to a recent trend whose origins may be found in the growth of admini-

strative history, I do not speak of 'recusants' or 'recusancy', for men
who were recusants in the eyes of church and state were Catholics in
their own. More generally, I have not been directly concerned with the
politics of English Catholicism, meaning by that the active or passive
status of it or of any of its members in the political or constitutional
history of England, or in the history of relations between the states of
Europe, including the papacy. If by the phrase one means the history
of the distribution of power within the community itself, I have certainly been concerned with that. I have also been concerned, so far as
my evidence will take me, with the community in all its members, and
consequently with the laity in the first place and the clergy in the second.
There is of course a great deal about the clergy in the book: two of its
four sections are almost exclusively devoted to them. But I have tried
to see them in the context of the community, as part of a social whole,
and not the only part which may have a history. I hope I have done this
without falling into an anti-clericalism which must be self-defeating for
a historian of Catholicism; to put the point in perspective, I should add
that I have also tried, among the laity, to keep a balance between
the gentry and the rest of the community. In the end, what I
have been after is the religious and social experience of the average
Catholic.

Finally, my title implies that the geographical field of my subject is
England. It is not possible, in the period I am dealing with, to exclude
Wales from this field, but my comments on things Welsh are valid only
to the degree that Welsh history may be incorporated with English; in
so far as there is a Welsh Catholicism distinct from English I am not
competent, and have not sought, to talk about it. My field of view does
not include Scotland, and only includes Ireland in so far as some
knowledge of the background of Irish Catholic emigrants is necessary
to account for what happened when they came to England; as I have
indicated, I touch on that subject only in the short term, and from outside. I have felt it important to affirm that there is an English Catholic
history as well as an Irish one, and that it is not a good idea to conflate
them. Similarly, it has been necessary for my purposes to mark English
Catholicism off from the Catholicisms of the continent, to the extent
that English Catholics who expatriated themselves, individually or as
members of religious communities, have as such no part in the book.
The continental side of English Catholicism, important as it was from
the reign of Queen Elizabeth to the French Revolution, is only con-

sidered in so far as, in the seminaries for instance, it contributed directly to the history of the community in England.

These are negative delimitations, and some may seem rather drastic; but they are meant to define a field within which an advance in historical understanding may occur. As a rule, such advance as this book may claim has come from trying to follow what historians have been saying about English history at large, and seeing to what degree it might apply to Catholics. I am of course especially indebted to those who have written about English religious traditions with an eye to their place in English society as a whole; some of their names will appear in the footnotes, others will not. I hope that here too it may be possible for the book to give something in return for what it has received, and offer it as a contribution to the synthetic view of English religious experience since the Reformation whose achievement seems to me still some way in the future. In this context I present the last and, I suppose, the most radical of my assumptions; it may seem the least convincing, but it does no more, really, than put in a nutshell what I have said so far. At almost every point of the book I have been guided by a conviction that, speaking historically and for the centuries with which I am concerned, the Catholic community ought properly to be considered a branch of the English nonconforming tradition. If the book has one particular thing to say, that is it.

These were the notions with which I began the book; by and large I am still satisfied with them now that I have ended it. The reader may judge whether they were the right ones or not.

PART ONE

DEATH OF A CHURCH, 1570–1688

'It is my opinion that we always had a *church*, incomplete, it is true, since the death of the last bishop, but ever remaining a society of true believers . . . holding communion with the centre of unity, the Roman see. The words *mission*, then, and *missionaries* have been improperly applied to us, which always designate a society recently converted to Christianity . . .'

Joseph Berington, *The Memoirs of Gregorio Panzani*
(Birmingham, 1793), Introduction, p. 42.

A MISSION AND A CHURCH

THE origins of the community were overshadowed by a problem which it found extremely difficult to solve. How could the religious tradition and institution of pre-Reformation England adapt themselves to the conditions of a society which had been so drastically transformed? Could they indeed be so adapted at all? Seen in a European perspective, from a distance of four centuries, the chances of a successful adaptation do not strike one as very good. If we set aside the exceptional case of Ireland, it was to be accomplished in only one other country through which the winds of Reformation had blown; and against the case in question, that of Holland, one must weigh that of Scandinavia, where circumstances which might have seemed rather favourable to Catholic survival entirely failed to guarantee it.

Yet in England the adaptation was achieved. In face of a variety of exterior obstacles, a body which had some right to claim continuity with the past but was nevertheless in most respects a new creation, which had come to some sort of *modus vivendi* within itself and with the overwhelmingly Protestant society it lived in, came into existence and proved able to endure. We need not be surprised that the community which finally emerged was a small one, for this conclusion was difficult to reach and painful to accept. To reach it required something like a century of almost continuous self-scrutiny and shattering internal conflicts. These conflicts have been variously interpreted, and will bear a variety of interpretations. If I propose to envisage them here as the death-throes or posthumous convulsions of a church it is not because I wish to deny validity to other interpretations. It is because the death of the mediaeval English Church—in the sense of a final recognition that it had ceased to live on the part of those Englishmen who hankered after it most—seems to me a principal condition for the emergence of a viable Catholic community in a non-Catholic England. Readers of this book will no doubt divide into those who think the tradition it represented worth preserving for its own sake, and those who do not. To those who do, it may speak for itself; to those who do not a word may be added. The experience I have sketched was in some respects unique; yet, seen from the middle distance, it had its immediate counterpart among Englishmen of other and more widely-held persuasions, whose dilemmas it may help to clarify; and taking the longest view it was no more than a particularly sharp demonstration of what was in store for all forms of European Christianity in its passage from the mediaeval to the modern world. It is worth some attention on either score.

In suggesting that the emergence of the English Catholic community was associated with a long and painful agony I do not wish to repudiate the traditional starting point of its history, the foundation of the English college at Douai in 1568, but to place this in a certain context. Given the tradition and the institution which required adaptation, it was practically inevitable that the initiative in adapting them should lie with members of the clergy: the first and probably the most important step towards this end was to grasp and apply to post-Reformation English conditions the idea of the missionary priest. Much of the credit for this departure should certainly go, where it has traditionally gone, to an Oxford don from a family of minor gentry in Lancashire, William Allen; yet the process which resulted in it was a complicated one, in which elements of the old regime were mixed with something new. The appearance of Douai as an institution for the training of a missionary priesthood was the consequence of two distinct movements, and Allen had some reason to regard their convergence as providential. Only one of these originated among men who, like himself, had been members of the Catholic establishment as it had stood at the death of Queen Mary; and the only branch of that establishment which made any contribution to it was the staff of its universities, and notably of Oxford. Something over a hundred fellows and other senior members left Oxford during the first decade of Elizabeth's reign; between 1559 and 1566 New College appears to have lost twenty-seven.[1] Many went abroad, and settled down in the Netherlands university of Louvain, where they resumed their careers and inaugurated a long controversial battle with their

---

1. C. M. F. J. Swan, 'The Introduction of the Elizabethan Settlement into the Universities of Oxford and Cambridge, with particular reference to the Roman Catholics, 1558–1603' (Cambridge University Ph.D. thesis, 1955), pp. 15–17, 76 ff., and Appendices C and E; A. C. Southern, *Elizabethan Recusant Prose* (London/Glasgow, 1950), p. 23, etc.

former colleagues. They give the impression of having accepted the change of scenery without much surprise or dismay; it had little effect on their manner of life, confirmed if anything their existing preconceptions, and did not necessarily prove a barrier to their advancement in the conventional sense. Among a group of men which included the more prominent names of Thomas Harding, Thomas Stapleton and Nicholas Sanders, Allen was in no sense distinguished; Thomas Fuller, using as he did the traditional criteria of his profession, was perfectly right to complain that Allen's merit did not justify the advancement which came to him. Fuller depicted him as a natural activist; yet Dr Rowse's 'mild, scholarly, rather dull man' gets nearer to his character and instincts.[2] His activism was achieved, not born, and while he has more claim than anyone else to be remembered as the founder of the English Catholic community, his claim rests on an initiative which turned out quite differently from what he had intended. This he would have been the last to dispute: it is just because he was himself so explicit about the origins of the college at Douai, that we are able to see how closely the motives which led him to establish it conformed to an inheritance of assumptions which he shared with his fellow émigré clerks. He agreed with them that the object in view was the restoration of the English ecclesiastical establishment as it had existed in 1558; that this restoration would come about in God's good time; and that in the meanwhile they must get on with their work of clarifying and defending its belief and practice, 'nothing more being proper to men of their profession, or possible as long as a heretical government held sway in their country'. He did not even, as yet, differ from them as Sanders came to do in believing that, since Providence was proving very slow in procuring the downfall of this government, they should step out of their academic posture and see what could be achieved by forcible action. His difference was merely to suggest that, since it all seemed to be going to take longer than they had anticipated, it was their academic responsibility to see that younger men were bred up competent for the task of restoration which, when the day came, they themselves might no longer be there to carry out.[3]

2. Southern, op. cit., pp. 44 f.—quoting Fuller, Worthies, iii (1840), pp. 261 f., at p. 46; A. L. Rowse, The England of Elizabeth (London, 1951), p. 461.
3. The essential texts are Allen's An Apologie and true Declaration of the Institution and Endevours of the two English Colleges (Mons, vere Reims, 1581), ff. 21v and ff., also in Southern, Elizabethan Recusant Prose, pp. 18–20; and Vendeville to Viglius, November–December 1568, and Allen to Vendeville, 16 September 1578, in Letters

This modest provision for 'a perpetuall feede and supply of Catholikes, namely of the Clergie' seemed unwarrantably pessimistic to his colleagues who, by his own account, regarded the institution as superfluous and did little to assist it.[4] It was not a missionary foundation, or indeed a seminary, and it seems clear that Allen had not only not yet grasped the idea of a mission, but had had the idea suggested to him and, in effect, rejected it. In 1567 he shared a trip to Rome, with his friend Jean Vendeville, professor of law in the new university at Douai. Vendeville, whose reading as a layman had been historical rather than theological, had concluded that the only solution for the problems of the Church in both England and the Netherlands lay in a renaissance of the missionary spirit which had achieved their conversion to Christianity in the first place. The seven or eight mature students who came together under Allen's direction at Douai in the summer of 1568 were the outcome of this proposal; the funds were raised by Vendeville, and some of the students were Netherlanders. The experiment misfired: Allen does not seem to have grasped what Vendeville had in mind, and the institution rapidly retreated within his own more conventional frame of reference.[5] This, even when somewhat expanded, remained purely academic.

According to his published account of the origins of the college, he thought that the Elizabethan settlement had provoked in the English clerical order, and in the universities in particular, a malaise transcending the categories of Catholic and Protestant, and proposed to use the new foundation to exploit it. He hoped that Douai would attract the 'best wittes out of England', and not only those who were 'Catholickly bent'; others, he thought, would be drawn over by declining intellectual standards in the English universities, by distaste for the Oath of Supremacy, by unwillingness to enter a profession as unattractive as the ministry of the Church of England, or by a general state of mental uncertainty and a wish to explore alternatives to the established regime.[6] This account was written thirteen years later, and I doubt if anything so clear or so subtle was in Allen's mind in 1568. As a description of what

---

and Memorials of William Cardinal Allen, ed. T. F. Knox (London, 1882), pp. 22 f., 52 ff. For Sanders, Patrick McGrath, *Papists and Puritans under Elizabeth I* (London, 1967), pp. 61 f.

4. Southern, *op. cit.*, p. 19.

5. Knox, *Allen Letters*, pp. 22, 54; M. Haile, *An Elizabethan Cardinal: William Allen* (London, 1914), pp. 71–76.

6. Southern, *Elizabethan Recusant Prose*, p. 19.

had happened in the meantime, it was most penetrating; but everything suggests that the response to the foundation of the college went far beyond what Allen had expected, and perhaps we may take his remarks as revealing rather more about the attitudes and aspirations of Allen's new recruits than about his own.

It might be argued that the inauguration of an English mission, and so of an English Catholic community, owed more to these men, taken as a group, than it did to Allen himself. For this demanded an openness to new departures, and a degree of spiritual enthusiasm, which were equally foreign to the bluff and sceptical conservatism of Queen Mary's church, and certainly did not come naturally to Allen. The simplest way of explaining why Gregory Martin, Edmund Campion and Robert Parsons—the most distinguished of the new men—possessed these characteristics, is to point out that they were Elizabethans, formed by the institution they rejected. None of them had entered Oxford before 1559; they had no ties with the Marian establishment, and treated it with some contempt; in their intellectual background, which was predominantly humanistic, and in their outlook on the university, the church and the world, they had more in common with many of their colleagues who stayed behind than they did with the émigrés of Louvain. From generally humanist or specifically Protestant motives, they had shared the hope that the new ecclesiastical order could be made the vehicle of a reforming idealism. Campion was a product of the Christian humanism taught in the London schools, as was his contemporary, the Puritan William Fulke; William Reynolds, another of the group, was the brother of John Reynolds, who had a distinguished career before him as a leader of the Puritan movement, and he had himself occupied a benefice in the Church of England; Parsons admitted to having passed through a phase of Protestant conviction of which it is tempting to detect traces in his mature activity. Anthony Wood recorded an Oxford story that William and John Reynolds, the first as a Calvinist and the second as a Catholic, argued themselves into each other's position; the story was no doubt untrue, but indicates the similarity of motives and assumptions inspiring all whose original hope in the Elizabethan Church turned, however unreasonably, to disillusion.[7] All of these men illustrate the sharpness of Allen's observa-

7. To the indications in my 'Character of Elizabethan Catholicism', in T. Aston (ed.), *Crisis in Europe, 1560–1660* (London, 1965), p. 231, add, for Parsons, C.R.S. xxxix (1942), pp. 30, 36, and C.R.S. ii (1904), pp. 15, 19; for Reynolds, *D.N.B.*,

tions, and their experience had probably provided him with much of his insight.

What they found lacking in the Church of England was precisely those characteristics which they sought to employ as partners in a missionary enterprise. At the risk of being too schematic, one might present their mental procedure somewhat as follows. In the first place they jibbed at the royal supremacy. They did this, not so much because it was in conflict with traditional belief and practice, but because they felt it an affront to the high ideal of the clerical vocation which they held. Roughly speaking, they saw it not from an institutional or political, but from a sociological point of view: as the culmination of a social process by which the secular aristocracy had come to impose its will on the English Church. Naturally enough, they tended to think first of the universities, noting with alarm how their curriculum and atmosphere were shifting to accommodate the aspirations of the gentry. On this point their view lacked breadth, and they had possibly misunderstood the facts; but what they saw was a triumph of 'proud ignorance' and the advent of a 'kingdom of grammarians and unlearned ears'. It was probably a consequence of a humanist upbringing that they were able to envisage this movement in a long historical perspective. In this connection Parsons developed a version of the 'Norman Yoke' theory which he applied with some plausibility to Henry VIII's reformation, the failure of the Marian regime and the present condition of the Church of England.[8]

Yet their complaint about lay supremacy was not simply a defence of a clerical caste, but also, in their minds, an assertion of the primacy of the spiritual. A zealous, learned and independent clergy was required because it seemed to them the only conceivable vehicle of a religion of

William Rainolds. Two less familiar cases are those of Richard Stephens, who had been one of John Jewel's assistants: *The First and Second Diaries of the English College, Douai*, ed. T. F. Knox (London, 1889), pp. 103, 311, and cf. John E. Booty, *John Jewel as Apologist of the Church of England* (London, 1963), p. 113; and of the Anglo-Irishman and later Jesuit, Henry Fitzsimon: E. Hogan, *Distinguished Irishmen of the 16th Century* (London, 1894), pp. 200 f.

8. Parsons, 'Storie of Domesticall Difficulties', in C.R.S. ii, pp. 50–57, and see below, p. (32); Campion's 'Challenge', in Southern, *Elizabethan Recusant Prose*, p. 154. Cf. T. H. Clancy, 'Political Thought of the Counter-Reformation in England' (London University Ph.D. thesis, 1960), p. 67, more briefly in his *Papist Pamphleteers* (Chicago, 1964), p. 37; J. E. Neale, *The Elizabethan House of Commons* (London, 1949), p. 305; H. Kearney, *Scholars and Gentlemen* (London, 1970), pp. 15–33.

the spirit. Their use of the term 'spirit' seems distinctly contemporary, and I doubt if it would have come very easily to Catholics of Allen's vintage. It was of course contrasted with the religion of exterior observance, as in Parsons's criticism of the Marian regime for not 'renewing the Spirit' and being content—the image may recall Puritan comments on a similar theme—with 'a stage-play, where men do change their Persons and Parts, without changing their minds or Affections'. But it was also contrasted with the purely scholastic or intellectual, and here they found themselves, when they went abroad, unsympathetic to the attitude of the original academic émigrés at Louvain. For these men, correctness of doctrine was what mattered, and controversial writing intended to uphold it was all that should be expected of men in their position. The newcomers were concerned with the reformation of behaviour, with interior conversion and 'godly discipline'; they were not very keen on learned controversy, and thought it on the whole a distraction from Christian living. 'The things a man hath to believe'—to quote Parsons once again—'are muche fewer, than the thinges he hath to doe.' The spirit, for them, was active, and conveying it to others was the supreme task of the active life.⁹

Arrived at from this angle, a fully consistent repudiation of the royal supremacy was almost obliged to take the form of a spiritual counter-action, in short, of a mission. Most of the later émigrés went abroad with the instincts of the missionary already latent in them; yet the instrument for turning them to their most appropriate use was not quite fully developed. Some, like Martin, found the atmosphere of Douai congenial, and stopped there. To others, in the early 1570s, it still looked rather staid and unexciting: looking for something to give scope to their ambitions, they found the institution which was most obviously designed to accommodate them, the Society of Jesus. At the time, this seemed to mean that England could not be the scene of their activity: Campion went off to Poland, another of the group, Thomas Stephens, to a notable career in India. Parsons was keen to go to 'the Indies' too, but did not get the chance.¹⁰

9. Parsons, *Memorial for the Reformation of England*, ed. E. Gee, as *The Jesuit's Memorial* (London, 1690), pp. 20 ff., and *The First Booke of the Christian Exercise, appertayning to Resolution* ([Rouen], 1582), p. 6; William Reynolds, *A Refutation of sundry Reprehensions* (Paris, 1583), Preface, quoted in Southern, *Elizabethan Recusant Prose*, p. 257.
10. E. Waugh, *Edmund Campion* (London, 1936), pp. 58–77; for Stephens, brother of Richard, mentioned above, n. 7, B. Basset, *The English Jesuits* (London, 1967),

Meanwhile Allen's tortuous progress towards the notion of an English mission was slowly reaching its conclusion. It was partly that his limited initiative had been so successful that he found he had far more people on his hands than he could find funds to support, and the only way of keeping his head above water was to have them ordained and send them off to England. But he was obviously undergoing some kind of conversion to the idea himself, and this extraordinary response was clearly one of the things which provoked it. It seemed to him, understandably enough, a direct intervention of Providence, and one which demonstrated that Providence had in mind something nearer to Vendeville's idea of the college than to his own: 'in this whole business', he wrote later, 'God himself decided otherwise than we had foreseen'.[11] Under the impact of this revelation Allen came to make what was probably the most radical of the mental adjustments required of him: the change from a notion of Providence fulfilling itself by mysterious dispositions wholly external to man, to one which proposed tasks which could only be accomplished by human co-operation and activity. Here Allen, as we have been told that Queen Mary never did, 'discovered the counter-Reformation'; perhaps he discovered the Renaissance at the same time. Increasingly intimate relations with Jesuits, English and foreign, clarified the practical implications of his discovery, and made him anxious to recover the men he had lost. All these influences fused to convert him from the 'scholastical attempts' with which he had begun to the active ideals of the younger generation, and to persuade him to enter with enthusiasm on the task of transforming the college into a seminary for missionary priests. One may take the transformation as having been completed somewhere in the mid-1570s, when Allen introduced the Jesuit Spiritual Exercises as part of the discipline of all students.[12]

With the despatch to England of the first priest with missionary faculties in 1574, the new foundation in Rome which followed shortly

pp. 457–459; for Parsons, C.R.S. xxxix, p. 4, and T. Hughes, *History of the Society of Jesus in North America: Documents*, i, part 1 (London/New York, 1908), p. 5. The general state of missionary excitement among the English Jesuits is well conveyed in Parsons to William Good, then in Sweden, 1579: C.R.S. xxxix, pp. 5 ff. Martin was widely expected to become a Jesuit, but did not: *ibid.*, p. 2; Basset, *English Jesuits*, p. 20; letters to Campion in Knox, *Douai Diaries*, pp. 308–320.

11. Knox, *Allen Letters*, p. 54.

12. *ibid.*, pp. 33, 35, 54, 57 f., 62 f.; C.R.S. ix (1911), pp. 68, 69; C.R.S. xxxix, p. 28; L. Hicks, 'Cardinal Allen and the Society', *The Month*, 1932, ii, pp. 343–344; A. G. Dickens, *The English Reformation* (London, 1964), p. 280, for the remark about Queen Mary; Rowse, *The England of Elizabeth*, p. 461.

after and the recovery of the English Jesuits in 1580, the English mission was fully launched. As it gathered way, Allen visibly shed his earlier inhibitions and emerged as a prophet of the active missionary ideal. When he was told in Rome that it was wrong to send such splendid priests into England only to be executed, and that he ought to keep them back for better times, he replied, with what was rightly remembered as his most penetrating remark, that better times were achieved by working, not by waiting. He had had farther to come than, say, Campion; bits of an older world clung to him all his life. Perhaps because of this, he showed a grasp of common reality more solid than Campion in what were in substance identical statements about the common enterprise in which they were now engaged. Campion is precise, lapidary, but abstract and excessively optimistic: 'The expense is reckoned, the enterprise is begun; it is of God, it cannot be withstood. So the faith was planted, so it must be restored.' Allen shows the marks of the long sequence of unforeseen events which had finally excluded him from the scholarly haven he had come abroad to seek: 'The quarrel is God's: and but for Hys holy glory and honour I might sleepe at ease, and let the world wagge and other men work . . .' Neither of them can have imagined just how unpromising was the prospect before them. Parsons lived long enough to see it more clearly, and it was no doubt in his mind when, talking to Sir Tobie Mathew in Rome a quarter of a century later,

> he took occasion from somewhat which was said of Savoy to speak much to me of the hideous rocks and mountains of that country, and with how extreme hazard and pains men were glad to climb, or rather indeed to creep up by inaccessible ways, to pick out handfuls of earth which they might either plant or sow for the getting of a miserable poor subsistence. And if this (said he) be discreetly done for such a poor kind of life, as this is, how well must it deserve another manner of labour and care, when there is question of acquiring another kind of life, which is to be infinite and eternal.[13]

The clergy had found the breach through which an English Catholic community, distinct from the historic past, would ultimately emerge;

13. Knox, *Allen Letters*, pp. 367, 37; Campion's 'Challenge', in Southern, *Elizabethan Recusant Prose*, p. 155, and Waugh, *Campion*, p. 222; *Relation of the Conversion of Sir Tobie Mathew*, quoted in David Mathew, *Catholicism in England* (London, 1948 edn), p. 48.

but they were at the same time the people least likely to appreciate that this was what had actually occurred. For as a permanent condition the status of a missionary priest could scarcely prove attractive to anyone who had received from the pre-Reformation Church, directly or indirectly, a high doctrine of the public role of the clergy. The contrast might well have been conveyed even with the blunt weapons of sixteenth-century caricature. On one side, the priest as governor, judging, determining, ordering a uniform Christian society regulated by the comprehensive machinery of the canon law; on the other—the terms were to become familiar to missioners in England—the priest as a 'merchant' doing 'business' with 'customers', a commercial traveller for an old-established firm offering to the householder, in competition with new and vigorous rivals, a commodity for whose consumption there was a limited demand.[14] The contrast was all the more dispiriting, since it was not only a matter of comparing the present with the past, but of confronting the missionary condition with a reinvigorated hierarchical order gathering confidence throughout the Catholic continent, and also with the hierarchical order of the Church of England, which survived in so much more impressive a condition than the émigrés had anticipated.

In this environment it was only to be expected that most of the clergy should see the launching of the English mission not as the inauguration of a totally new phase in the history of English Catholicism, but as an emergency measure to bridge a temporary hiatus in the continuous history of the English Church.[15] This was true of those who were most committed to the mission, and among them even of the Jesuits, who should more than anyone else have been capable of envisaging the missionary condition as permanent. Allen never put down what he supposed the English Church would look like after the hiatus was over, and it seems significant that he never saw this as presenting a problem. But Parsons did: in the *Memorial for the Reformation of England*, written after Allen's death in 1596, circulated in manuscript, but never published from the Catholic side, he created the one clear image of an English Church to emerge from the Elizabethan Catholic clergy.

14. For this language, see my 'Postscript' to H. O. Evennett, *The Spirit of the Counter-Reformation* (Cambridge, 1968), p. 129, n. 3; P. Caraman, *Henry Garnet* (London, 1964), pp. 61, 63; Basset, *English Jesuits*, p. 5; G. Anstruther, *Vaux of Harrowden* (Newport, Mon., 1953), p. 187; B. Hemphill, *The Early Vicars-Apostolic of England* (London, 1954), p. 101.
15. Thus, e.g., Allen to Campion, 5 December 1579: Knox, *Allen Letters*, pp. 84 f.

Parsons's vision of the restored English Catholic Church had a certain grandeur, and though one could not call it revolutionary it revealed a willingness to make drastic innovations in what were more than matters of detail. It was in many ways a genuine attempt to mediate between ecclesiastical tradition and the contemporary world, and frankly I doubt if Allen would have liked much of it. It is notable that Parsons waited until Allen was dead to put his thoughts on paper although, as he said, he had been thinking about the problems involved for the best part of twenty years beforehand. It was of course to be a uniform Church, coextensive, like Hooker's, with the commonwealth: Parsons expressly said that he did not believe in religious liberty as a principle, but thought that a limited period of coexistence and open argument under a Catholic government would be sufficient to bring truth to light for all but a hard core of the irreclaimable. He showed some desire that his Church should not persecute, and was clearly hoping for something like the relatively painless restoration of Catholicism which had occurred in the southern Netherlands under the Duke of Parma; how this was to be achieved without the opportunity of emigration, available to an intransigent Protestant in Ghent or Antwerp, he did not explain. For all that he wanted it to prevail by conviction rather than by force or terror, Parsons's Church would ultimately have been an institution of which membership was compulsory.[16] It was also to be closely connected with the secular authority: in Parliament members of the clergy would sit with the Commons as well as with the Lords, and in its early years the new dispensation was to be supervised by a widely competent Council of Reformation, reminiscent of the Anglican ecclesiastical High Commission. The episcopal hierarchy would be redistributed, with three provinces instead of two (including a Western province centred at Bristol) and three universities instead of two (including a northern university, perhaps at Durham); there would be more bishops with smaller dioceses, modestly endowed by comparison with the past, as unprelatical as possible, and dedicated to the supervision of a variety of social institutions. The clergy in general were to carry great weight in the society envisaged, but were to deserve it by the godly discipline in which they would be trained and the public services they were to perform; to ensure that they lived up to their profession,

16. *Memorial for the Reformation of England*, pp. 32 ff.; there is a valuable synopsis and commentary in T. H. Clancy, 'Notes on Parsons's *Memorial*', *Recusant History*, iv (1959), pp. 17–34.

the parish clergy would lose the freehold of their benefices, and be promoted, demoted or dismissed according to their merits.[17]

Many of the public services required of the clergy—in education, instruction and welfare—would be performed by religious orders, and here Parsons made the sharpest breach with the past. At least in its early years the new Church would have little room for contemplative orders, and regulars would have to justify their existence by active service. This meant that monasteries, as such, would be low on the list of priorities, and further that the resources which in the mediaeval Church had been locked up in supporting them would have to be diverted to other uses. Monastic impropriation of parishes would be abolished, and impropriated tithes restored to the secular clergy; former monastic property would be subject to wholesale redistribution to support the multiple activities of the new Church. Here of course Parsons was obliged to face the fact that monastic property, whether in lands and buildings or in impropriations, had been for over half a century in the hands of the crown, and now formed a sizeable part of the wealth of the English landowning class. He believed that the economic problems of his Church could only be solved if something were done about this. He did not propose a total restitution, which would in any case have been questionable in view of the papacy's recognition of laymen's titles during the reign of Queen Mary; but he thought that impropriations should be passed to the parish clergy without compensation to the lay impropriator, and proposed for church lands a compounding system, giving security of tenure in return for a rent payable to the Church, with provision that 'undeserving' landowners would be expropriated altogether, and poor landowners with a good record on religion relieved in cases of hardship. Former owners were to have no title to this revenue, which was to be administered and distributed by the Council of Reformation in accordance with the general needs of the Church: much of it, by implication, to religious orders and others who undertook work of social utility.[18]

These were extremely drastic proposals, and it is not surprising that they raised virulent objection in several quarters; all in all, they amounted to a compulsory re-endowment which, the monastic order excepted, would have put the church in a far better financial position than it had held before the Reformation. They would also have implied

17. *Memorial*, pp. 70 ff., 90–92, 102 f., 128, 133–135.
18. *Memorial*, pp. 49–57, 68 f.; cf. below, n. 30.

something like a social counter-revolution, a redistribution of wealth and power back from the gentry to the clergy much more substantial than Archbishop Laud was to attempt forty years later.[19] It is perhaps fair to add that Parsons strikes one as having had a more generous idea of what the Church might do with its money than Laud did.

It would be a little unfair to leave Parsons's platform of a church reformed at the point where it appears most bluntly as a counter-revolution. For, to put the point crudely, Parsons was not a mediaeval man but a Renaissance activist. The Church he tried to design was all-comprehending, stable and hierarchical as, in theory, the mediaeval Church had been; but at the same time its whole justification was to lie, not in what it was but in what it did. These requirements, if not perhaps in absolute contradiction, pointed in quite different directions: Parsons was applying the instincts of a missionary to the rebuilding of a church on the traditional pattern. One proposal shows him conscious of the difficulty, and seeking an exit. He thought that the Church, once re-established in England, should become the springboard for a further and vaster missionary enterprise which would have the whole of the Protestant North for its field. Seminaries ought to be set up in London as the source of missions to 'Denmark, divers parts near to us of Germany, Poland, Gothland, Sweedland, Scotland (*sic*), Muscovy and the Isles of Zeland; from all which places store of youth might be had, by reason of the concourse and contraction of Merchants that daily come to London from those parts'. The reconstruction of the English Church, even according to his own vision, was something he would rather leave to others; what he would really have liked to do himself was to run this seaborne mission to the North.[20]

Here, you feel, Parsons was both offering a solution of some merit to the general dilemma, in the form of a safety-valve through which an excess of activist energy might blow itself off without threatening the new Church with permanent revolution; and also indulging in a personal dream of escape from conflicts and contradictions he was not really prepared to face. Of course the whole conception may well be regarded as a fantasy, a vision the more powerful because it had no ties with reality; yet anyone who dismisses it entirely on this ground will have to contend with a worrying sense of the kinship between Parsons's

19. Christopher Hill, *Economic Problems of the Church from Archbishop Whitgift to the Long Parliament* (Oxford, 1956), chs. xii and xiv.
20. Parsons, *Memorial*, pp. 149–151.

ideal reformation and the problems and efforts of those, bishops and Puritans, who had on their hands the real job of trying to reform the English Church. For the most part, the *Memorial for the Reformation of England* strikes me, not as a daydream, but as a respectable attempt to square the circle.

Those who were responsible for founding the English mission, who worked tirelessly for it and guided its destinies for thirty years, were nevertheless men in whom the ideal of an all-embracing English Catholic Church remained a reality; in so far as they were the founders of the English Catholic community they were, to borrow a term from Arthur Koestler, sleepwalkers. Time was to bring awakening, but some woke sooner than others; differences of formal profession and individual taste, which had disappeared in the euphoria of the early decades, re-emerged as it became clear that the emergency was destined to last for a very long time. In particular Jesuits and secular priests began to discover that they were constitutionally disposed to react to this situation in opposite ways. For the Jesuits, the problem was relatively simple: they did not stand for the mediaeval Church; they had not committed them-selves to Parsons's modernised version of it, which could plausibly be presented as an individual aberration; the missionary profession was their specific *métier*. As their position in England began to come under attack, they inclined more and more to take the line that England was a Protestant country where their skills were specially needed and the restrictions on their activity obtaining in Catholic countries did not apply. They might well have been advised to take this line from the start, as they did in the United Provinces; in any case, it was firmly established during the early seventeenth century, and fell neatly into a pattern of Jesuit policy in this period which we shall be discussing in due course.[21] The change of position seems to have taken scarcely more time to complete than the decade 1610–1620; one might roughly date the beginning and end of the process as coinciding with the death of Parsons and the constitution of the English province of the Society under Richard Blount. It would probably be going too far to say that by

21. The first to adopt this point of view seems to have been Henry Garnet in a letter to Parsons, November 1603: Caraman, *Garnet*, p. 315; L. J. Rogier, *Geschiedenis van het Katholicisme in Noord-Nederland in de 16e en de 17e Eeuw*, ii (Amsterdam, 1946), p. 55, for the position in the Netherlands, which explains the divergence between Oliver Manare, who was responsible for the Dutch mission, and Parsons in 1597: Tierney-Dodd, *Church History of England*, iii, p. xcv.

this latter date (1623) the English Jesuits had definitively accepted that their mission was to a minority sect; but though they might in some sense still regard their position as a provisional one, they had certainly by this time become firmly *installé dans le provisoire*.

The secular clergy was in a very different case; since it took the professional missionaries so long to extricate themselves from a churchly nostalgia, we can hardly be surprised that many of the seculars never escaped from it at all. There were, in the first place, those of Allen's generation who had simply frowned on the missionary notion, even as a short-term expedient. He had himself remarked on the unsympathetic attitude to Douai of many of his colleagues in the Netherlands, and their presence gives weight to his well-known letter to Maurice Chauncy, prior of the émigré Carthusians, to whom he sent in 1577 a moving defence of its alumni against carpers from the traditionalist side.[22] But as a practical issue the question only came into the open with the foundation of a comparable institution in Rome.

The English College in Rome dated from 1576, and the main agent of its erection, in premises formerly occupied by the hospice for English pilgrims, was the Welsh canonist Owen Lewis, a former colleague of Allen at Oxford and in the Netherlands who was making for himself a successful career in the papal administration. Before achieving its final settlement in 1579, the infant college went through a series of convulsions from which it emerged a very different institution from what had been originally planned.[23] These were partly a consequence of national differences between Welsh superiors and a body of predominantly English students transferred from the overflowing college at Douai; it would be unwise to underestimate the reality of this division, or the importance of the antagonisms it generated for the future of the mission. But this was not the only or perhaps the principal issue in the 'stirs' at Rome. They had revealed an irreconcilable difference of opinion about what the foundation was for. The majority of the students took one view, and had cautious support from the Jesuits, notably from Parsons who was then at an early stage in his Jesuit career; Lewis, his nominee as rector of the college Morys Clynog, and the Roman estab-

22. Knox, *Allen Letters*, pp. 53, 31–37.
23. Earlier accounts are superseded by Anthony Kenny, 'From Hospice to College', in *The English Hospice in Rome : the* Venerabile *Sexcentenary Issue* (vol. xxi, 1962), pp. 218–273; that in J. H. Pollen, *The English Catholics in the Reign of Queen Elizabeth* [to 1580] (London, 1920), pp. 271–282, remains very useful.

lishment in general took another. For the students, it was to be a replica
of Douai as they had left it; for Lewis, who was never to go through
Allen's conversion to missionary activism, 'a house of studies to secure
academic'—and perhaps also non-academic—'employment for exiles
who awaited abroad the inevitable return of England to Rome': very
much, that is, what Douai had been when Allen first conceived it.[24] In
1579 it was transformed, as Douai had been, into a missionary college,
not however by evolution but by revolution. By a mass walkout and a
conduct of public relations so skilful that it is difficult to believe Parsons
had nothing to do with it, the students converted Pope Gregory XIII to
their view; he took the foundation into his own hands, imposed on all
entrants an oath to serve on the English mission if required and
handed the college's government over to the Jesuits.

The Elizabethan Catholic movement had been started by a group of
conservative academics; the events at Rome were a defeat for academic
conservatism, but the bias towards it remained. During much of the
Roman college's earlier years, it suffered from a further dispute between
the Jesuit authorities and a new set of English academic exiles. Rectors,
they complained, took no account of their degrees and accorded them,
in the college, none of the precedence these should have ensured them;
they resisted the rigorous discipline of the institution as something
designed for boys; and they complained that they met obstruction if
they wanted to proceed to a university doctorate after leaving it, which
all alumni were finally prohibited from doing without written approval
from the rector in 1597.[25] These may seem petty arguments, but they
arose from a general difficulty. The requirements of a college for training missionary priests were simply not the same as those of a traditional
European academic institution, with its leisurely progress to a doctorate
through a hierarchy of degrees, and its total subordination of practical
to intellectual values. And this was not only an academic issue: 'degrees
in schools' were inextricably part of the larger hierarchical structure of
the traditional Church, and no doubt to many, as to Shakespeare's
Ulysses, of a traditional universe. Those who tried to water down the
effects of the decision made in 1579 to turn the Roman college into a

24. Kenny, art. cit., p. 244.
25. For the seminary regime, A. O. Meyer, England and the Catholic Church under
Queen Elizabeth (London, 1967 edn), pp. 100–114; complaints, ibid., pp. 502, 506,
and Humphrey Ely, Certaine briefe notes upon a Briefe Apologie (Paris, ?1603), pp.
84–94; text of prohibition in Tierney-Dodd, Church History of England, iii, pp.
cii–iv; see also C.R.S. xli (1948), pp. 109–111, 141–143.

missionary institution, like those who had resisted it in the first place but perhaps more self-consciously, were standing up in general for the claim that an English Catholic clergy must embody and represent the traditional order as it had stood, or theoretically stood, at the death of Queen Mary, and that the first principle of this order was a God-given hierarchy. The issue was most clearly seen, and the argument came to be most firmly advanced, by one of these mature students, Christopher Bagshaw, who had had in any case a score to settle with Parsons ever since they had been fellows of Balliol together. He forms the closest of many connections between this intramural dissension and the wider rift of the Archpriest controversy.

It would however be wrong to give the impression that the idea of a church as it persisted among the English secular clergy was a purely traditionalist one. In late sixteenth-century Italy, as later in early seventeenth-century France, Englishmen were in contact with a revised version of the traditional ecclesiastical order which maintained and indeed intensified its legal claims and hierarchical characteristics, but sought to utilise them to achieve a more devoted pastoral care and a more penetrating social influence. This in general was the ideal of the Council of Trent, of Charles Borromeo whose decisive episcopate in Milan straddled the dates of foundation of the two English colleges, and of a long succession of Italian and French bishops for whom he served as a pattern. As a conception of the Church this had obvious attractions for Elizabethan secular priests beginning to wonder whether the missionary enthusiasm of Allen and the Jesuits might not be endangering the long-term interests of their order. The Borromean tradition stood for the inviolability of established hierarchies, the supremacy of bishops and the rights of the secular priesthood; while prepared to use the Jesuits in their place, it was extremely hostile to institutional and other experiments associated with them, and determined to resist the extension of their influence in the Church as a whole.[26] At the same time it was a reforming ideal, not open to the charges of obstruction, legalism, spiritual unconcern and sheer laziness to which the extreme conservatives among the English secular clergy were vulnerable. It could then serve, as unadulterated traditionalism could not, as a light to priests who had genuinely embraced and embodied the missionary ideal.

26. Cf. Evennett, *Spirit of the Counter-Reformation*, pp. 138–140, and references there cited; C. Orsenigo, *Life of St Charles Borromeo* (St Louis/London, 1945), pp. 113 f.

How far it did so is not entirely clear. Owen Lewis came into close relations with Borromeo especially after his defeat over the Roman college, when he withdrew to Milan and filled a prominent niche in the Milanese ecclesiastical establishment; William Gifford—an important figure among the younger generation of secular anti-Jesuits whose attitude we shall be considering in a moment—claimed to take Borromeo as his model and mentor, and had probably been introduced to him by Lewis; traces of a later connection may be seen during the regime of Borromeo's nephew and successor Federico, around and after 1600.[27] One instance deserves mention, since it comes from a priest the progress of whose feelings is of particular interest. John Mush had been one of the leaders of the student revolution in the Roman college and proved, back in England, to be a dedicated and effective practitioner of the missionary life; but he turned out to have second thoughts about the Jesuits, and we find him, twenty years after they had been installed in the college, suggesting that it was time they were removed. His immediate reason was that as long as they governed it the best students would tend to be drawn away from the secular clergy and into the Society, and he appealed to Borromean precedent to justify the step. 'This only reasone weyghed so much with Card[inal] Borromeo of holy memorie that he for this cause only discharged the Jesuites of the government of his seminaries att Milane; saying yt was more necessarie for Godes Churche to have learned pastoures then learned religiouse men.'[28] This suggests acquaintance with a Borromean ideal of the Church, and indicates roughly what an equivalent of Parsons's *Memorial* would have looked like if Mush had stopped to write one. All the same, there is no convincing sign that Borromeo provided the English secular clergy with an image of a reformed church which had for them the determining power which Parsons found in his Jesuit environment. The

---

27. G. Anstruther, 'Owen Lewis', in *The* Venerabile *Sexcentenary Issue* (above, n. 23), pp. 278–294; Pollen, *The English Catholics in the Reign of Queen Elizabeth*, p. 276, n. 2; J. Gillow, *Bibliographical Dictionary of English Catholics*, ii, pp. 458, 460; J. McCann and C. Cary-Elwes (eds.), *Ampleforth and its Origins* (London, 1952), pp. 86–87; Richard Smith to Thomas More, 30 September 1610 (A.A.W. Main series, ix, no. 77). For Lewis's career in Milan see A. D. Wright, 'Post-Tridentine Reform in the Archdiocese of Milan under the Successors of St Charles Borromeo, 1584–1631' (Oxford University D.Phil. thesis, 1973), pp. 55 f., 75 f.
28. Comments by Mush on a Letter of Parsons to Garnet, 12/13 July 1598, in T. G. Law, *The Archpriest Controversy* (Camden Society, 2 vols., 1896, 1898), i, p. 47; likewise [J. Bennet], *The Hope of Peace* (Frankfort, *vere* London, 1601), p. 21.

influence, if any, strikes one as superficial; in much the same way, in France a little later they had a good deal to do with Pierre de Bérulle, a counter-Reformation figure of similar calibre and general inclinations to Borromeo's, but his ideal of the priest and the Oratory he founded to embody it seem to have passed them by.[29] When all the evidence is assembled, it may appear that these new continental models provided, for the English secular clergy, only a few trimmings to a notion of the Church which depended for its substance on an appeal to the inviolable tradition of the past, and was accordingly insular as well as extremely conservative: even the Council of Trent does not seem to have impinged on them much until the seventeenth century. To illustrate the point, one need for the moment do no more than draw attention to the part some leaders of the secular clergy played in conjuring up another spectre from the mediaeval Church.

Parsons's vision of a reformed English Catholic Church had broken with a pre-Reformation tradition most sharply in its treatment of the monastic order. If he did not envisage English Benedictinism as totally defunct, he certainly saw it as playing a very minor role in the future, and considered that whatever monastic institutions were to emerge would have to start again from scratch, without continuity or legal claims deriving from the pre-Reformation monks. It is unlikely that he expected his proposals to attract much opposition on this score, yet it proved the point on which conservative opposition coalesced. Laymen, anti-Jesuit seculars, émigré monks and continental prelates united to defend the inviolability and legal continuity of Benedictine rights as a test case for the inviolability and legal continuity of the pre-Reformation church order. This was more plausible than it might have been in other countries, owing to the fusion of monastic houses and cathedral chapters in the mediaeval English Church.

It proved possible to embody this continuity in something more tangible than abstract legal argument, since a single member of the pre-1559 monastic establishment survived in 1600, in the person of Sigebert Buckley, a monk of Westminster Abbey as refounded by Queen Mary. This 'venerable peice of antiquity' was at the time a prisoner in Wisbech Castle, along with various other members of the English Catholic priesthood, including Christopher Bagshaw, by then a leading member of the anti-Jesuit reaction among the secular clergy in England; it seems to have been Bagshaw who first drew attention to the use to

29. Evennett, *Spirit of the Counter-Reformation*, pp. 139 f., 141, and n. 3.

which Buckley could be put. Shortly afterwards a Welsh common lawyer from Abergavenny, who later became a Benedictine himself and is best known under his religious name of Augustine Baker, elaborated the legal case on which the claim for Benedictine continuity was to turn. This was that the pre-Reformation English Benedictine order constituted a legal corporation; that its rights would inhere in any surviving member; and that such a member could transmit them to others by admitting them to membership of the body. Buckley was persuaded to enact this transmission and so, if the argument was sound, to secure the continuity of the English Benedictine body and the maintenance of all its rights. There are two different stories about how this was done, and the argument itself had several flaws; what matters here is that Parsons's *Memorial* had inspired his conservative antagonists to add to their antiquarian baggage, burdensome enough already, a trunkful of monastic claims which shortly became embodied in a resuscitated English Benedictine congregation.[30]

This is not all there is to be said about the English Benedictine revival. A version of the Benedictine ideal proved attractive to students at the seminaries, and notably at the newer foundations erected by Parsons in Spain from 1589 onwards. The Spanish form of monasticism they received was activist and 'modernistic' in character, not utterly removed from the Jesuit ideal, which indeed it had played some part in forming;[31] most of them remained by instinct missionaries rather than conventuals and, bearing in mind the example of Augustine of Canterbury as Vendeville and Parsons had those of Boniface and Willibrord, launched after 1600 an English Benedictine mission which proved permanent and substantial. This was not at all what the revivers of the English Benedictine congregation had had in mind. When they finally joined it, after negotiations of extreme complication, the missioners had to undergo stiff criticism from those who saw as its object the revival and maintenance of the conventual life abroad, and those like Augustine Baker who put contemplative values before active ones. In the end, and

---

30. David Knowles, *The Religious Orders in England*, iii (Cambridge, 1959), pp. 444-455; *Ampleforth and its Origins*, pp. 81-106; P. Guilday, *The English Catholic Refugees on the Continent* (London, 1914), pp. 215 ff. The most recent and fullest account of the Benedictine revival is D. M. Lunn, 'The Origins and Early Development of the Revived English Benedictine Congregation, 1588-1647' (Cambridge University Ph.D. thesis, 1970), on which my discussion in the next paragraph depends: especially chap. ii, and pp. 320 ff.

31. Evennett, *op. cit.*, pp. 53, 58 f., 127.

almost without noticing it, the English Benedictines of the seventeenth century, missioners and conventuals, actives and contemplatives, passed from the status of a notional fragment of a ghost-church, preserving paper claims against some providential day, to that of a large and enriching participant in the English Catholic community as it actually existed, modest but alive. In so far as the secular-clergy conservatives had sought to raise an ally in the monks, they were to be rather disappointed.

One might well object, to this evidence of a ghost-church persisting among the English Catholic clergy, that no reasonable person could have expected anything else. Besides, up to perhaps 1603 a Catholic restoration was not quite inconceivable. It had after all happened in much of the Netherlands, from a point of departure not much more promising than it was in England; the example was, we have seen, present at least in Parsons's mind. When he wrote, a more limited version of the process he envisaged was about to get under way in France. And whether this vision of a restoration was fantastic or not, it is probably true that without it the mission could not have been launched or an English Catholic community have come into existence. All this may be conceded. Yet if we can understand why the mirage persisted, the fact remains that that was what it was, and in anything but the shortest run it led into a sterile wilderness of unreality. The failure to grasp reality lay at two quite separate points. There was first the obvious failure to recognise the definitive reality of the Reformation in England, as an ecclesiastical structure and as a way of life, and to draw the consequences of these facts in establishing the external conditions in which English Catholicism would be obliged to survive, if it was to survive at all. There was, in addition and perhaps more serious, the failure to admit that behind the visible facts of religious and ecclesiastical change in sixteenth-century England, there lay a more fundamental and even less reversible alteration in the balance of power between the constituent elements of English and, taken as a whole, of European society: a passage of authority from the clergy to the lay aristocracy, taking the term in its widest sense. This was a fact about English society in general, not simply about Protestant England, though of course it did as much as anything else to dish the prospects of a Catholic restoration. It would probably, in any event, have survived a Catholic restoration if one had occurred; and it would certainly be true, in the foreseeable future, of any minority Catholic body. Members of the lay aristocracy, who claimed the right to live as Catholics, did not do so because they hankered after the *status quo ante*, still less after the revived clericalism of the continental counter-Reformation. Titles to church property, repugnance to prelatical government, moved them as deeply as anyone else, and they came to see how decisively their status was enhanced where plurality of religion became a condition of life. All in all, they were better off controlling the destinies of a minority sect in a country dominated by their Protestant counterparts, than playing second fiddle in a uniform society of the Catholic clergy's devising. Upon this rock nobody was going to build a church.[32]

The drama of clerical ideals and action, agonising readjustment and mutual recrimination, occupies the stage in the century of English Catholic history which followed the launching of the mission; but it was played in an atmosphere of stress between clergy and laity, which its *dénouement* reflected: the audience invaded the scene. In view of its importance for the interpretation of English Catholic history which will be offered in what follows, this point of view will need some illustration here. It is borrowed once again from Parsons, who was the first to try and put what he called the 'domestical difficulties' of English Catholicism into a historical perspective:

> If we caste back our eyes unto the former times in England [he wrote], we shall finde that for above five hundred yeares, even from the Conquest and entrance of the Normans and Frenche Governours over our Countrey, they hath ever continued a certaine faction and emulation of the Laitye (especially those that were great men) against the Clergie, which did make the path by little and little unto that open schisme, heresye and Apostacie, whereunto at length it fell.[33]

We have seen that he applied this view widely to the events of English sixteenth-century history; he also applied it to the conflicts which, by the time he wrote in the 1590s, had become rampant among the English Catholic émigrés.[34] It governed a great deal of his political

---

32. Cf. the discussion in W. K. Jordan, *The Development of Religious Toleration in England*, ii (London, 1936), pp. 505–521, on the growth of a 'sectarian' attitude among the English Catholic laity, which seems to me to combine real penetration with a good deal of misunderstanding.

33. Parsons, 'Storie of Domesticall Difficulties', in C.R.S. ii, pp. 50 f.; see also his *Brief Apology or Defence of the Catholic Ecclesiastical Hierarchy* (?1601), ff. 1–2.

34. Parsons, 'Punti per la missione d'Inghilterra', in C.R.S. iv (1907), pp. 62 ff.; R. Lechat, *Les refugiés anglais dans les Pays-Bas espagnols, 1558–1603* (Louvain,

activity, and accounts for the more startling proposals of the *Memorial for the Reformation of England*. The pcint was well understood by his enemies, among whom the émigré priest William Gifford, a self-conscious member of a family which had come over at the Conquest, showed the clearest grasp of the issue. He attacked Parsons for 'contemptus nobilitatis', and told his family to keep clear of people who 'vainly promise reformation or rather subversion of the state'; he hoped for a reconciliation between the Catholic gentry and the Elizabethan government which would obstruct 'the subversion of her Majesties estate and the utter ruining of all our families without any regard of religion'.[35] The attitude was shared by a representative member of the southern Catholic gentry like Sir Thomas Tresham, who withdrew from an association with the Jesuits which had been very close in the early days of their mission, and by 1600 was being roundly dismissed by them as an 'atheist'.[36] It was relevant, one way and another, to many aspects of late Elizabethan Catholicism: it helped to provoke schism between the students of the college in Rome, with whom Gifford had a good deal of influence, and their Jesuit superiors;[37] it helps to explain the success of the Benedictine revival, which Gifford again did a lot to further.[38]

Yet here a misconception should be avoided. It was not only in the form in which Parsons presented it that the clerical vision of a church restored aroused the hostility of the gentry. Parsons suffered, in this case, because he had had the courage or imprudence to consign his dream to paper. If they had revealed their secret thoughts with the same

1914), pp. 157–197, followed in L. von Pastor, *History of the Popes*, xxiv (London, 1933), pp. 12 f.; on two of the lay émigrés concerned, Thomas Morgan and Charles Paget, L. Hicks, *An Elizabethan Problem* (London, 1964). His suggestion that in opposing the clerical leadership they were acting directly on behalf of the English authorities seems to me unconvincing; cf. my 'Character of Elizabethan Catholicism' (see above, n. 7), pp. 238 ff.

35. Law, *Archpriest Controversy*, i, pp. 14, 15; ii, pp. 277–278; Gifford to Walsingham, 18 April 1586, in Knox, *Allen Letters*, pp. 262–263. On Gifford in general, *Ampleforth and its Origins*, pp. 137–160.

36. T. G. Law, *Jesuits and Seculars in the Reign of Queen Elizabeth* (London, 1889), p. 143; Anstruther, *Vaux of Harrowden*, p. 257.

37. Meyer, *England and the Catholic Church*, p. 102, n. 2; Foley, *Records of the English Province S.J.*, vi, pp. 8 f., 24, 28, 58 (visitation of 1596); Law, *Archpriest Controversy*, i, pp. 7–15 (extracts from Gifford's correspondence with the students).

38. *Ampleforth and its Origins*, pp. 82, 86–87; Guilday, *English Catholic Refugees*, p. 219; note the connection with Henry Constable, for whom see my 'Character of Elizabethan Catholicism', pp. 243 f., 246.

frankness, secular priests and Benedictines would perhaps not have fared much better. Before long, when the religious orders had come to terms with their situation, it was the secular clergy who were to be left on their own, straining after the receding vision. This was the penalty of their victory, such as it was, in the Archpriest controversy.

2

THE ARCHPRIEST CONTROVERSY

'BEHIND the Archpriest Controversy, which at first sight exhibits nothing but a drama of personal animosities and quarrels to gain the upper hand, great differences on matters of principle lay concealed.' So far it is easy to agree with its most influential interpreter, Arnold Oskar Meyer; but it is possible to take a different view of what the matters of principle were, or at least of the order of priority which, for the participants, existed among the variety of questions it raised. Meyer was a political historian, and saw the controversy, from a viewpoint determined by the German *Kulturkampf*, as a political issue. The great matter of principle concerned the birth of the modern state, and the conflict lay between those English Catholics who welcomed and those who resisted it. The conclusive document in his case was the Protestation of Allegiance to Queen Elizabeth made by a number of Catholic secular priests shortly before the queen died, on 30 January 1603; in this they repudiated the political claims of the papacy so far as they had been or might be used against her, and rejected the tradition of hostile political involvement, practical and theoretical, which had become associated with Allen and Parsons during the 1580s and 1590s. Meyer saw this as proof of a culminating victory on the moral front, for Elizabeth and for the modern state, of the same order as the physical victory over the Spanish Armada in 1588; it provided an apposite and dramatic conclusion to his account of the relations between England and the Catholic Church during the Elizabethan period, and a model, as he saw it, for the future.[1]

It is very difficult not to be carried away by the force of Meyer's argument, and I think it is generally regarded as correct; so I must explain why and how far I disagree with it. It is not, in my view, totally wrong or irrelevant, but it treads rather heavily where delicacy is

1. Meyer, *England and the Catholic Church under Queen Elizabeth*, pp. 420, 456 f., and *passim*; fuller comments will be found in my 'Introduction' to the 1967 reprint.

needed, fails to make some important distinctions, ignores one or two obvious facts, and puts the whole weight of interpretation on a question which was important, but secondary, to most of those concerned. Perhaps, in any case, it is only to be expected that the same events will present themselves in a different light to a writer whose subject is the external relations of two institutions, than they do to another who seeks to chart the interior history of a community.

To begin with one of the obvious facts. Professor Elton, who seems to be in general agreement with Meyer about what constitutes a modern state, has found much support for his view that the founding charter of English national self-sufficiency was the statute of 24 Henry VIII prohibiting appeals to Rome.[2] Is he not at all surprised to find, portrayed as inspired by a primary sense of national loyalty, men who appeal to Rome so frequently as to go down in history under the title of Appellants? This is not simply a verbal point, since it helps to draw attention to the further fact, equally obvious and sometimes equally neglected, that on the face of it the Archpriest controversy was an ecclesiastical, not a political argument: a dispute, between men who all accepted that the Roman Curia had without question authority to settle it, about the ecclesiastical organisation of a missionary territory; a dispute which disguised the more fundamental argument about whether England ought properly to be considered a missionary territory at all. As Meyer himself remarked, it was an argument almost entirely conducted by clerics,[3] and in 1600 clerics were primarily concerned with clerical problems.

Which brings us to the important distinction Meyer failed to make. His Catholicism, like his English nation, was monolithic: he never really got to grips with the distinction between the clerk and the layman. The result was that, while noting that the dispute was a predominantly clerical one, he put all the weight of his interpretation on a point where the clergy had, for once, got involved in a problem which primarily concerned the Catholic laity, the problem of allegiance. This was a shaky foundation. I am not suggesting that the problem of political allegiance was of no significance in the Archpriest controversy; I am

2. G. R. Elton, *England under the Tudors* (London, 1955 edn), pp. 160–162, and *The Tudor Constitution* (London, 1960), pp. 344–349. The Appellants would in fact appear to have been infringing section v of the complementary statute for the Submission of the Clergy, 25 Henry VIII, cap. 19: *ibid.*, p. 341; the penalties here were those of *praemunire*. Cf. Mush's remark in Meyer, *op. cit.*, p. 424.

3. Meyer, *England and the Catholic Church*, p. 377.

suggesting that, in the manner already indicated, it lies among the general problems of clergy–laity relations which were still, at this time, only in the background of the visible conflict. It was one of the more salient features of that background, and as such deserves consideration, if only because it reveals among the gentry an attitude of mind hostile to all clerical pretensions, not simply to those of political activists among them.

Except in the wilder parts of the North, the Catholic gentry had never given much credence to Pius V's Bull of 1570,[4] and the more prominent of them had proffered a collective declaration of allegiance to Elizabeth as early as 1585; this had been an unsuccessful effort to dissuade her from giving the royal assent to a Bill which would make it a treasonable act to 'harbour' a Catholic priest ordained since her accession.[5] Composed by Sir Thomas Tresham, and presented to the queen in his own name and in those of Lord Vaux and Sir John Arundell, it was an attempt to work out some kind of acceptable division between the spheres of influence which might be covered by a Catholic gentleman's relation to his queen and his relation to his priest. Tresham assumed, in all relevant circumstances, an overriding loyalty to Elizabeth and her successors; but a variety of tensions between the two relationships had now emerged, and he hoped to relax them by removing misunderstandings he believed to prevail.

The implied relation between a gentleman and a priest is a profoundly patriarchal one: in the principal case envisaged, a Catholic gentleman or nobleman employs a priest, much as he might employ a lawyer, to provide him with 'spiritual counsel', and with the sacraments without which he believes he cannot save his soul. Despite the impending statute, it never really entered Tresham's head that a gentleman's autonomous choice in this matter was open to question, and by and large it was not. The difficulty was that, having claimed the right to choose his spiritual counsellors among Catholic priests, a gentleman could not continually refuse to do as they counselled him. What

4. The latest discussion of the subject, P. McGrath, *Papists and Puritans under Elizabeth I*, pp. 68–71, suggests that they were not really obliged to do so; cf. Parsons's commentary of 1606 in T. Clancy, *Papist Pamphleteers*, p. 92.

5. *H.M.C. Various Collections*, iii, pp. 37–43 (Supplication), and 34–37 (Tresham's reasons for and against making it); discussed in W. K. Jordan, *Development of Religious Toleration*, i (London, 1932), pp. 399–401; G. Anstruther, *Vaux of Harrowden*, p. 154; J. Lecler, *Toleration and the Reformation* (trans. T. L. Westow, 2 vols., New York/London, 1960), ii, p. 377

Tresham and the others were anxious to say to the queen was that there were two separate questions here, of which one was a genuine problem and the other not. They were sorry to say that they could no longer find priests who would answer for their salvation if they attended from time to time the services of the Church of England, though they would most gladly do this if her own clergy could persuade their priests to change their minds. They felt that this refusal might be interpreted as a denial of due service, and did not believe it ought to be so understood. Here they felt a genuine difficulty which they hoped Elizabeth would appreciate: the idea that their priests might be counselling them to abandon their allegiance altogether struck them as fantastic, and they were irritated by the supposition that they would take any notice of what priests might have to say in this matter. They had never met a priest, they said—no doubt with some poetic licence—who had not recognised Elizabeth as undoubted queen both *de jure* and *de facto*, and if they came across one who so much as hinted that he held a contrary opinion, they would smartly turn him over to the authorities. In accordance with his patriarchal presuppositions Tresham did not find it necessary that the priests should make a declaration of this kind themselves: it was quite enough if the gentry made it for them.[6]

These presuppositions were even more clearly expressed in a similar declaration made twenty years later, shortly after the accession of James I, in the hope of securing formal toleration from the new regime. It was probably again composed by Tresham; it is not clear that it was actually presented to James, but it was put into print and so achieved a certain amount of publicity. This *Petition Apologetical*, as it was described, offered in return for toleration of Catholicism that the number of Catholic priests in the country should be reduced to so many as the gentry required; that every gentleman who kept a priest in his house should take absolute civil responsibility for his behaviour; and that priests themselves should now take an oath of allegiance 'before they shall be admitted to our houses, otherwise they shall not have relief of us'.[7]

6. *H.M.C. Various Collections*, ii, pp. 40, 35; cf. my 'Character of Elizabethan Catholicism' (see above, ch. 1, note 7), p. 228.
7. The printed version, *A Petition Apologeticall, presented to the Kinges most excellent Maiestie by the lay Catholikes of England in Iuly last* (Douai(?), 1604)—B.M. C.26.l.7—especially pp. 33–35, where an important passage is omitted, which will be found in the version printed from ms. in Tierney-Dodd, *Church History of England*, iv, pp. lxxxii f.—it promises to procure the withdrawal from the country

Since this was the chief statement relative to political allegiance to have emanated from the Catholic gentry during the years when the Archpriest controversy was in full swing, its implications for those involved in the controversy are worth pondering. It made explicit earlier indications that the clergy, in whichever direction their larger ambitions might lie, were not going to get much scope for realising them if the gentry had anything to do with it. If the Catholic clergy became, as Tresham seems to have envisaged it, a learned profession dedicated to the service of the gentry, neither prelacy nor missionary zeal would have much place in it. In so far as the Appellant priests hoped to gather the gentry behind their own programme by bringing to the fore the question of allegiance, they were on very doubtful ground. The more perceptive of them did not take long to realise this.

The Protestation of Allegiance of January 1603, as a purely clerical production in a genre normally appropriate to the gentry, bears a relation whose ambiguity Meyer failed to grasp to the series of similar efforts into which it falls. To put the issue crudely, both the Appellant priests and gentlemen like Tresham were by this time anxious to affirm allegiance and to get rid of the Jesuits; but while the gentry proposed to get rid of the Jesuits as a means of affirming allegiance, the priests offered declarations of allegiance in the hope of getting rid of the Jesuits. Except for a few *exaltés*, the Appellants were not prepared to advance any further along the road of political allegiance than would be compatible with their ecclesiastical status and programme. These hesitations emerged during the pre-history of the Protestation itself, which Meyer had little opportunity of exploring: they account for the important factor that what was offered was, precisely, a 'protestation' and not an oath.[8]

This does not seem to have been the original idea. It appears from Elizabeth's proclamation of 5 November 1602, in which the existence of the Appellants as a distinct body of opinion among the English Catholic clergy was for the first time publicly recognised, that some of them had

---

of any priest for whom a satisfactory lay surety cannot be found. Jordan, *Development of Religious Toleration*, ii, p. 519, uses the first text and misdates the event, which occurred in July 1604, to 1603; for the circumstances, see J. Bossy, 'Henri IV, the Appellants and the Jesuits', *Recusant History*, viii (1966), pp. 95 f.

8. Text in Tierney-Dodd, *Church History of England*, iii, p. clxxxviii, to which it is important to add the 'explanatory declaration' in *H.M.C. Salisbury*, xii, p. 632. For the events leading to its presentation Bossy, 'Henri IV, the Appellants and the Jesuits', pp. 89 f.

indeed offered to take an oath to 'be the first that shall discover . . . traiterous intentions against us and our state, and . . . the foremost by arms and all other means to suppress it'.[9] William Watson, the chief Appellant in contact with the government at this time, was probably the author of the idea, and it appears to have been cast in a form resembling the statutory oath finally imposed in 1606: a 'corporal oath' of individual loyalty and allegiance to be sworn in person by each individual priest. His colleagues, the more important of whom did not return from Rome until some time after conversations about it had begun, held in general that an oath of this kind was more appropriate for laymen than for priests and, taken individually, would lead to the disintegration of the secular clergy as a body and in many cases to the abandonment by a priest of his priestly character. This turned out to be exactly what the Privy Council was after: declaring allegiance, as at least the majority of the councillors envisaged the case, would protect a priest from molestation only if, for the future, he ceased to exercise his functions as a priest in England. At this point the Appellants refused to proceed, Watson and Thomas Bluet dissenting, and negotiations broke down some time in January 1603.[10] What happened after this was for practical purposes mainly a postscript. More because they wished to make their position clear, than for any result they expected of it; speaking as much to their fellow-Catholics, who were entitled to some reassurance about what they had been up to, as to the government; and in a spirit which mingled defiance with submission, they produced their Protestation at the end of the month. In it, while affirming their allegiance and repeating earlier declarations about the defence of the realm, they made it perfectly clear that they intended to go on exercising their priestly functions, and stood out for the organic unity of their body in lawful submission to the see of Rome. They neither offered to take an oath, nor suggested a formula for one, but cast their protestation in the form of a written text, signed by all those assenting to it—which excluded Watson and Bluet—and presented it to the government through deputies.

9. Tierney-Dodd, *Church History of England*, iii, p. clxxv; 'Henri IV, the Appellants and the Jesuits', p. 89; this seems to be the 'juramentum' referred to in Rome during the appeal of 1602: Law, *Archpriest Controversy*, ii, pp. 150 f.

10. 'Henri IV, the Appellants and the Jesuits', p. 89; Bancroft to Cecil, 1 February 1603: *H.M.C. Salisbury*, xii, pp. 631–632, misreading 'Benet' for 'Bluet'; for possible divergences of view in the Privy Council, Meyer, *England and the Catholic Church*, p. 458 and n. 1; further evidence of last-minute stiffening of the text in Law, *Archpriest Controversy*, ii, p. 246, though his comments should be disregarded.

Neither the contents of the document, nor the form adopted in presenting it, were considered acceptable by the Council; the deputies were sent to jail.

That was the end of the Appellants' only attempt to come to terms with the government on the matter of political allegiance. It was a fiasco, and they never tried again.[11] Three years later, in the backwash of the Gunpowder Plot, they were confronted with a statute which required them, under the penalty of *praemunire*, to do what they had refused to do in 1603: to take individually an oath of offensive character, which implied no toleration for their priesthood if they took it. The demand put them in some disarray. Most of them seem to have changed their minds about the oath at some time or other, and to have been willing to advise gentlemen to take it in order to preserve their estates; but after the pope had condemned it they would have nothing to do with it themselves. Two signatories of the Protestation were executed after refusing it. Despite a great deal of confusion, some resounding clerical surrenders like that of George Blackwell the Archpriest, and widespread acceptance of the oath among the gentry, this decision of the responsible Appellants preserved the overall unity of the clergy and enabled the Catholic community to survive a difficult period without grave damage.[12] The Appellants accepted the papal ruling against James I's oath of allegiance, partly because it accorded with their own priestly instincts as revealed in 1603, and partly because they could not afford to antagonise the papacy, from which alone the fulfilment of their ecclesiastical ambitions could come.[13] In either case, their action at this point must surely indicate that Meyer had got their values wrong: that their Protestation, far from being the central statement of their belief,

11. A further formula offered in 1604, in conjunction with the gentry's *Petition*, was not an Appellant production: 'Henri IV, the Appellants and the Jesuits', pp. 95 f.
12. Text of the statute imposing the oath (3 James I, cap. 4) in Tierney-Dodd, *Church History of England*, iv, pp. cxiii–cxxi. There are two different accounts of the crucial meetings of the clergy leaders in July 1606 at which Blackwell announced his conversion to it; one by Mush, *ibid.*, p. cxxxvii, another by Parsons's agent John Sweet, in W. K. L. Webb, 'Thomas Preston *alias* Roger Widdrington', *Biographical Studies (Recusant History)*, ii (1953), pp. 222–223. As in 1603, it seems to have been mainly Mush who kept the Appellants on a steady course; cf. J. H. Pollen's very just remarks in *The Institution of the Archpriest Blackwell* (London, 1916), pp. 31 f. The executed signatories to the *Protestation* were Robert Drury and Roger Cadwallader: Philip Hughes, *The Reformation in England*, iii (London, 1954), p. 394.
13. See the examination of William Bishop. 4 April 1611, in *Calendar of State Papers, Domestic, 1611–18*, p. 28.

was the result of a short and unsuccessful excursion into alien territory.

Historians ought to beware of dividing sixteenth-century Europeans into progressives and conservatives. But since the Appellant priests have been mainly presented to the modern reader by nineteenth-century liberals who thought they shared their views, it may be a useful corrective to argue that their party was a conservative product of a conservative decade. 'The old approved paths of our forefathers . . .,' said Watson, the only one of the Appellants who aspired to literature, 'will always prove the best. Novelties and fine devices of busy and unquiet heads are but as May-flowers that are gone in June; they may carry a fair show, but they will not continue.'[14] It is true that they were not always, indeed not often, all of one mind: as a movement of opposition to Jesuits they drew in members for a variety of reasons. One might roughly divide them into practical Appellants, that is, missionary priests upset by Jesuit preponderance in the actual organisation of the mission during the regime of Garnet and Parsons; theoretical Appellants, who had little or no experience of the mission but objected to Jesuits on principle; some cranks; and some opportunists. The best example among their leaders of the first category was John Mush, though there were others; of the second, Christopher Bagshaw. William Watson was a mixture of the second and third, Thomas Bluet in the third category and John Cecil in the fourth.[15] There must then be some degree of artificiality in trying to offer an ideology which would equally represent them all, and in particular a tendency for the view of the second category to be over-represented. None the less all the Appellants held in some degree or other four points of ecclesiastical doctrine, which expressed their claim to represent the true ideal of an English Church.

The first was a point about continuity: the English Church was not dead, and England could not be treated as a *tabula rasa* for missionary purposes like, say, Japan. 'Our country had from the beginning of these chevesies [*adulteries*: meaning presumably since Henry VIII] sundry prelates with the laity that *nunquam ante Baal*, etc., *ergo*,' said Watson, it had been 'continually *ex parte catholica*'.[16] The body of English Catholic clergy—by which they meant secular clergy—now existing in

---

14. [William Watson?], *Important considerations* (London, 1601), p. 2.
15. On Cecil, see Pollen, *Institution of the Archpriest Blackwell*, pp. 67 ff., 98; Bossy, 'Henri IV, the Appellants and the Jesuits', *passim*.
16. Law, *Archpriest Controversy*, i, p. 90 f.; cf. Pollen, *op. cit.*, p. 37.

England and abroad was the same body as the pre-Elizabethan and pre-Henrician Church. It is most significant that Bagshaw should have organised the scenario intended to ensure the legal perpetuity of the pre-Reformation monastic establishment;[17] for just as Sigebert Buckley was supposed to embody this himself, so the Appellant priests claimed to be the body of pastors and doctors of the English secular clergy as it had stood on the day King Henry sinned or Queen Mary died.

The second was an almost obsessive concern about hierarchical order. J. H. Pollen remarked with his usual sharpness that the Appellants felt themselves to be a 'priestly aristocracy', and their programme contained large elements of what has been termed 'aristocratic constitutionalism'.[18] The England of their imagination consisted of clearly defined orders of clergy, laity and religious, each in its clearly defined role, each with its hierarchy embodied in visible degree, the clergy's at least God-given and unalterable. On the whole they were not very concerned about the secular social order; but they were occasionally prepared to point out that without the support of a clerical hierarchy the other orders, which enjoyed no such divine guarantee—meaning those of both laity and religious—would be washed away by the tides of time and circumstance.[19]

The third was a consequent rejection of one of the most characteristic features of the counter-Reformation Church, the widening of the 'religious' ideal by which new forces and energies were harnessed to a traditional vehicle. *Regularia regularibus, saecularia saecularibus* meant for them that the proper place for religious was the cloister, and the whole worldly business of the Church the sphere of the 'secular' priesthood. This was of course a doctrine principally directed against the Jesuits, but its implications could be wider. Here one must certainly distinguish one Appellant from another, but by and large they were

17. Above, pp. 29 f.
18. *loc. cit.*, n. 16.
19. William Watson, *A Decacordon of Ten Quodlibeticall Questions* (London, 1602), is the most comprehensive statement of Appellant doctrine; the same position was put more moderately by Matthew Kellison, *A Treatise of the Hierarchie and Divers Orders of the Church against the Anarchie of Calvin* (Douai, 1629). There are briefer statements in Watson's preface to *Important Considerations* (above, n. 14); the General Preface, probably by Bagshaw, to H. Ely, *Certaine briefe notes* (above, chap. 1, n. 25), pp. 6–10; Bagshaw's 'Letter to a Norfolk Gentleman [William Wiseman]', Wisbech, 1595, in C.R.S. li (1958), pp. 14 f.; and the *Refutatio responsii P. Personii*, Rome, 1602, in Law, *Archpriest Controversy*, ii, p. 142.

inclined to suggest that the beauty and significance of the Church lay in its just proportions, and not in anything the clergy might be doing. The contrast with Parsons and his *Memorial* speaks for itself; but the Appellants were also in danger of unlearning Allen's painful lesson, and of simply relapsing into the attitude of the unquestioning conservatives who had criticised his action in the first place. 'God doth seldom bless their enterprises with good success, who run before he send them' was a comment which might have come from that earlier period.[20]

Finally the Appellants had a strong general conviction that the forces of order and disorder in the Christian Church at large, or at least in England at large, did not divide along the confessional frontier. Among Elizabeth's clergy, they could see the 'pseudo-bishops', intruders as they might be, trying to maintain something not unlike the true cause; they felt they had found in Richard Bancroft an ecclesiastical ally as well as a political friend. On the other side, they saw an ultimate kinship, and no doubt a common origin, between the assault on God's church order being mounted by Puritans in the Elizabethan Church, and the standing defiance of it which the Jesuits represented in their own. Later, when James I had given publicity to it, this view became something of a platitude; for the Appellants, it was a fresh and penetrating discovery. The parallel lay not only, and not mainly, in alleged similarities of political ideas and conduct; it lay in their offensive claim to be the vehicle of a superior religion of the spirit, in their formation of groups and conventicles among clergy and laity, in their relativist and instrumental view of ecclesiastical order, in the 'tyrannical' or 'Japponian' forms which they sought to impose. The charge that Jesuits were 'Puritans, precisians, Genevans and synhedrical brethren' began as a jeer thrown over the dinner table at Wisbech; but the more the Appellants thought about it, the more convincing it became.[21]

Trouble seems to have been brewing on the mission from about 1590; what precipitated it were the so-called 'stirs at Wisbech', a running dispute among the clergy living in custody in Wisbech Castle. Like the somewhat similar 'troubles at Frankfort', they had a comic side, which

20. Ely, *Certaine briefe notes*, General Preface, pp. 9–10; comments in Meyer, *England and the Catholic Church*, p. 416; cf. H. O. Evennett, *Spirit of the Counter-Reformation*, pp. 67–88.

21. Watson, *Decacordon*, pp. 26 ff. and *passim*; numerous comments in Law, *Archpriest Controversy*, i, pp. 8, 97 f., 121, 209, 213; ii, 161; Bagshaw, in C.R.S. li, p. 326. Cf. C. H. McIlwain (ed.), *The Political Works of James I* (Cambridge, Mass., 1918), p. xxii.

arose from the application of large principles to matters of domestic detail. They were in most respects a repetition of earlier difficulties in the college at Rome, and Christopher Bagshaw played a prominent part in both; a mental picture of the younger members of an Oxbridge combination room interned for the duration, trying to turn it into an evangelical community and a light to the Gentiles, will give a fair idea of the position. Most of the prisoners were in favour of reform; but the old regime remained invincibly in occupation of the hall, which had been the object of bitterest contention. The reformers had proposed that at meals people should, for edification, sit as they came, irrespective of status: 'a thing', Bagshaw protested, 'not practised in any ordered place in the world; a disgrace to all degree and learning and fit for Anabaptists; a seditious mutiny and confusion against the several orders of the Church; a contempt of reverend age', and so on for half a page. He opposed the new regime as popular and demagogic in form, 'things passing by faction of voices' with no regard to seniority, and as 'without example in the habitable world except the synhedrical congregations of Geneva and the like'.[22]

Had it not found an echo in the experience of secular priests working on the mission, this ludicrous controversy could hardly have reverberated as it did; as it was, the troubles at Wisbech turned out to be a working model for a dispute engulfing the English Catholic clergy, or at least those members of it who did not feel they had something better to do. To stake out their claim against Jesuit encroachment, the independent seculars outside Wisbech took steps to produce out of their own body the hierarchical order which, in their view, they virtually embodied; they formed an association, and began to organise an election of officers designed for early conversion into a hierarchy. As in the case of Sigebert Buckley and the monastic order, they, as the *digniores* among the English secular clergy, claimed to be the receptacle of all rights traditionally inhering in their body: in this case, of the right of canonical episcopal election by dean and chapter. Accepting the need for Roman confirmation, and toning down their proposal in the hope of getting it through, they sent off to Rome to ask that 'a hierarchy, approved by the free votes of the seminary priests and by them alone, should be instituted'.[23] They made no progress. Rome, which was never very willing to swallow the claim to monastic continuity, was certainly

22. Letter to a Norfolk Gentleman (see above, n. 19), pp. 14–17.
23. J. H. Pollen, *Institution of the Archpriest Blackwell*, p. 36.

not going to swallow a much more far-reaching and dubious claim on the part of the secular clergy; Parsons, now a successful rector of the college in Rome, was strategically placed in the way; and 'the wisest lay Catholics' were alleged to have taken fright at the idea of an association because they saw it as an instrument of clerical power.[24] The papacy had in any case already propounded its own solution by appointing George Blackwell as archpriest in April 1598.

The practical implications of this step will be discussed later; on the theoretical plane it was evidently a grave affront to anyone who held the views which have been described. The archpriest's office was without precedent in the English Church; he did not exercise his functions within a framework of canon law, whose applicability, in some sense, to England was a consequence of the Appellant claim to continuity; he had a kind of propulsive power, but no real jurisdiction, over the seminary clergy, and none whatever over regulars or the laity.[25] It was almost impossible for men of Appellant instincts to conceive that a responsible ecclesiastical authority could have instituted this regime, and inevitable that they should see it as another step in a Jesuit conspiracy to overthrow legitimate ecclesiastical order. How much part Parsons and Garnet had actually had in Blackwell's appointment, and how far, if at all, they continued to guide his hand, are questions which remain obscure and do not much matter here.[26] The Appellants were certainly right to see in it a challenge to their whole conception of the Church.

In the spring of 1598, they rejected Blackwell's authority; in the autumn of 1602, Clement VIII brought the consequent dispute to a close. These four and a half years of bitter, tangled and verbose argument have been admirably dealt with by J. H. Pollen from a constitutional point of view, and we may pass over them here.[27] The effect of Clement VIII's decision was that the Appellants gained most of their negative objects, while failing to get recognition for their positive ones. The change most acceptable to them was that the Archpriest should

24. ibid., pp. 23, 31; Law, Archpriest Controversy, i, p. 205.

25. Text of letter appointing him and detailing his faculties in Tierney-Dodd, Church History of England, iii, pp. cxx–cxxiii; further instructions requiring him to consult Garnet in Law, Archpriest Controversy, ii, p. xvii. See below, p. [207].

26. The point is discussed in Pollen, Institution of the Archpriest Blackwell, pp. 25–29, the work referred to below; and see below, p. 208.

27. Brief Venerunt nuper, 5 October 1602, concluding the dispute, in Tierney-Dodd, Church History of England, iii, pp. clxxxi–clxxxiii.

not, in the execution of his office, consult or co-operate with Jesuits;
this had important practical consequences for the mission, and represented a large concession to the Appellant idea of a traditional segregation of functions. This segregation did not, admittedly, confine the
regulars to their cloisters; on the contrary, it inaugurated half a century
of dramatic expansion by self-contained Jesuit and Benedictine missions. But, at whatever cost, segregation had been achieved, and it was
now possible to envisage the existence in England of a body of secular
clergy free to try and illustrate the Appellant ideal .

During the years of negotiation the Appellant representatives in
Rome showed a good deal of flexibility. Ultimately, their claim was for
continuity, electivity and an episcopal hierarchy exercising ordinary
jurisdiction. Since all these objects were more or less unacceptable in
Rome, and most of them would have been even more unacceptable in
England—not least to Bancroft—they showed good sense in concentrat-
ing for the time being on complaints against the *status quo*; after the
original rebuff in 1598, it was not until 1605, well after the argument
about the Archpriest had been settled, that a formal request for the
appointment of bishops was made.[28] In the interval the positive side of
their case was distinctly weak: they were in the position of asking the
pope to replace the Archpriest regime by a more conventional hierarchical structure which did not include bishops. They came up with a
scheme of extraordinary complication involving two visitors, for north
and south, and six provinces, each with an Archpriest and two assistants;
these, in the first instance, to be chosen by the pope from the 'senioribus
et doctioribus sacerdotibus', and then by annual or triennial election.
It was designed to operate chiefly as a system of traditional canon-law
jurisdiction, and this was to extend to the laity in the important matter
of bequests and donations for pious uses, that is to say for religious and
charitable purposes.[29] The scheme, which was no doubt tossed off in
something of a hurry, is of interest as a precedent for the future; as a
proposal for the present, Parsons had little difficulty in ripping it to
shreds. What they settled for was something significantly less than this,
in that it entailed no jurisdiction, in particular no jurisdiction over the
laity. Clement VIII maintained the Archpriest regime as it stood, but

28. Law, *Archpriest Controversy*, ii, p. 118; Tierney-Dodd, *Church History*, vi,
pp. 8–12, xiii–xx; Bossy, 'Henri IV, the Appellants and the Jesuits', p. 104.
29. *Considerationes quaedam*, in Law, *Archpriest Controversy*, ii, pp. 118–122;
Pollen, *Institution*, p. 86.

took steps to ensure that the Appellants should take it over themselves. Blackwell received instructions to appoint members of the party among his twelve assistants; by the time he was removed after taking the Oath of Allegiance, in 1607, they had come to constitute a majority firm enough to carry his successor, George Birkhead, with them.[30]

With this takeover of the Archpriest regime by priests of the Appellant temper the first phase of ecclesiastical conflict in the English Catholic community reached an ironical denouement. It was certainly a *volte-face* on the part of men whose original standpoint had been that this was an inadmissible constitutional novelty, a Japponian tyranny and an invention of the devil. Yet, by an instructive contrast with the evolution of their views on allegiance, their attitude to it in no way changed: it was always, for them, a sham and a monstrosity.[31] They thought of it less as an instrument for running the mission than as a convenient base from which to pursue their campaign of ecclesiastical restoration. Here it gave them the immense advantage of vindicating, in a form acceptable to Rome, their claim to represent the English secular clergy; the fight for bishops, and for the elimination of Jesuit influence, could now be pursued through the proper channels, and began to prosper. Shortly after Birkhead's appointment, and with mild encouragement from Rome, the new administration began collecting votes among the secular missioners for a new petition for conventional order and jurisdiction, forwarded in 1611.[32] In 1610, the year of Parsons's death, it sent to Rome the first of a succession of agents of the English clergy to act as spearhead of the campaign; three years later it achieved its second important success when the college at Douai was pulled out of the pro-Jesuit camp and put into the capable and friendly hands of Matthew Kellison.[33] Absorbed in this flurry of invigorating activity, buoyant, and relatively disinclined to attend to practical problems of the missionary field, the secular leaders in London were in no mood to listen to those of their provincial subordinates who from time to time reported forces assembling which would, just when the march of ecclesiastical legitimacy seemed to be reaching its goal, bring it to a conclusive halt.

30. Tierney-Dodd, *Church History*, iii, p. clxxxii; v, pp. 12 ff.
31. John Bennet, 'Narrative', in C.R.S. xxii (1921), pp. 137, 144.
32. Tierney-Dodd, *Church History*, v, pp. cxlii–clii.
33. *ibid.*, v, p. 47, and see below, p. 201; the early phases of the movement are documented in C.R.S. xli (1948) *passim*.

3

BISHOPS AND GENTRY

THE most eventful years in the posthumous history of the *Ecclesia Anglicana* were those between 1623 and 1631, when, in partial fulfilment of decades of agitation by the secular clergy, William Bishop and Richard Smith exercised episcopal rule in England as successive Bishops of Chalcedon. They saw themselves as symbols and agents of a church restored, in spirit if not in physical possession,[1] and Smith in particular acted so as to bring smartly to the boil a problem which had been simmering for decades. In the ensuing crisis he and his cause were defeated. His defeat was certainly inevitable, but it came with a swiftness and a totality which are staggering if one considers the indefinite proliferation of earlier disputes. What had happened was that, beneath the continuing surface of ecclesiastical argument, a decisive shift in the structure of the problem had taken place. Three intimately related developments had occurred. The two independent regular missions, Jesuit and Benedictine, had emerged, expanded and achieved formal organisation; the regulars had abandoned the notions of ecclesiastical restoration which had been prevalent among them around 1600, and come to treat the missionary state as acceptable in itself; and the core of the Catholic gentry, which during the Archpriest controversy had been on the whole too diffident to intervene but sympathetic to the Appellants, had by now become friendly to the regulars, conscious of a community of interest, determined to intervene if they saw those interests threatened, and aware that nothing could really prevent them getting what they wanted. To put the point crudely, the Jesuits and the Benedictines had given up for lost the ideal of an English Catholic Church, and gone to join the gentry on their own sectarian ground. What was emerging was something which closely resembled the pattern of a gentry-dominated

1. See in particular Bishop's Brief erecting the Chapter, 10 September 1623: Tierney-Dodd, *Church History*, iv, p. cclxxx.

Catholic body outlined in the *Petition Apologetical* of 1604, except that its sanctions, which Tresham would have seen as operating against the Jesuits and their allies, would now be operating in their favour.

A number of converging influences worked to secure this reversal of alliances. Some arose in the practical development of the mission, and will be more fully considered in due course. But without trespassing very deeply on that ground, it is not difficult to explain how and why the change should have taken place. It was of course the Jesuits who, from the gentry's point of view, had most to live down; the charge of 'contemptus nobilitatis' had stuck to Parsons, and there would always be a query about the Jesuits' attitude to the gentry as long as he was alive. Yet even he had gone a considerable way before he died to reduce apprehensions. After 1600 he prudently left political theory alone, as indeed did the Society in general, and in the major writings of his last years, the *Treatise tending to Mitigation* and the *Judgement of a Catholic Englishman*, he took a distinctly moderate point of view on the question of allegiance and seemed prepared to envisage the minority status of Catholics in England as a permanent one. He also rather neatly turned to advantage his principal gaffe, the proposals about church property in the *Memorial for the Reformation of England*, when he suggested that Catholics might come to terms with the government by formally surrendering all claims of this nature in return for household toleration. This was not a very practical suggestion so far as the government was concerned, but it was well designed to appease the Catholic gentry.[2] It may seem odd to suggest that the Gunpowder Plot contributed to the same end, but from the point of view of a Catholic gentleman, concerned that his communications with his spiritual adviser should remain confidential, Garnet had acted rather creditably, and among Catholics his pursuit and execution probably did the Jesuits more good than harm.[3] In any event, with Parsons and Garnet dead, the Jesuit authorities were in a position to institute a new regime, and acted

2. Jordan, *Development of Religious Toleration*, ii, pp. 499 f.; Clancy, *Papist Pamphleteers*, p. 94. For the general Jesuit change, *ibid.*, pp. 105, 196 f.; P. Blet, 'Jésuites gallicans au XVIIe siècle?', *Archivum historicum Societatis Jesu*, xxix (1960), pp. 64 ff.
3. This is perhaps suggested by the rather desperate way in which some of the seculars, notably Richard Smith, tried to discredit John Gerard as an actual participant in the Plot: A. F. Allison, 'John Gerard and the Gunpowder Plot', *Recusant History*, v (1959), pp. 43–63.

prudently, so far as the gentry were concerned, in picking Richard Blount as superior in England and Thomas Fitzherbert as rector of the college in Rome.[4]

Under Blount's regime, missionary practice rapidly evolved towards a close accommodation with the gentry, as the typical Jesuit missioner tended to leave the circulating role of the earlier period for permanent quarters in the household of a single family.[5] In this new environment a point which had cropped up during the Archpriest controversy but made little impression at the time, began to assume considerable importance. Gentlemen who supported the Jesuits in the earlier controversy, like John Gerard's host William Wiseman, had pointed out—no doubt under advice—that a great advantage of the missionary regime was that parochial divisions and jurisdiction ceased to exist, and that in consequence a layman became free to choose his pastor as he pleased. In sticking out for a traditional church order the Appellants, it was suggested, were seeking to deprive the laity of this new freedom, and subject them compulsorily to interference from priests whom they had had no hand in choosing.[6] For anyone, at least, who was rich enough to have a choice, the argument was perfectly correct; and the more intimate and stable grew the relation between gentleman and priest, the more necessary it appeared to the gentry to ensure that the choice was absolutely theirs. Since there was, during these decades, an increasing surplus of priests on the mission, the gentry were in a buyer's market and could hardly fail to carry their point. But in carrying their own point they were also carrying a point for the religious orders, in that any version of a parochial system would be likely to hand the mission over bodily to the secular clergy. A number of other practical reasons tended to encourage the growth of special relationships between gentry families and religious orders: their influence and contacts, for example, in seminaries and religious houses abroad, at a time when it was becoming a headache for a Catholic gentleman to know what to do with his children; above all, for the Jesuits, the existence of the school at St Omer. But none of them seems so important, in the long run, as the

---

4. For Blount, see P. Caraman, *Henry Morse, Priest of the Plague* (London, n.d.), pp. 28 ff.; for Fitzherbert, my 'Character of Elizabethan Catholicism' (see above, ch. 1, n. 7), pp. 244 f.
5. See below, pp. 255 f.
6. Law, *Archpriest Controversy*, i, p. 54; also pp. 93, 95 (Watson), and p. 195 (Holtby).

gentry's claim to liberty in the choice of their pastors, and the feeling that they would get short shrift in this respect if the seculars had their way.

A great deal hung upon this point, since the gentry's attitude implied a degree of *laissez-faire* in the affairs of English Catholics as a whole which was not compatible with the claims to pastoral authority and hierarchical order advanced by the secular clergy: 'hos', said their petition to Pope Paul V in 1611, meaning bishops, 'constituit Christus Dominus principes super omnem terram'.[7] This authority they were seeking to impose on men whose outlook in this respect did not seriously differ from that of other members of the English gentry and aristocracy. Richard Smith and William Laud were contemporaries, and their episcopates raised similar problems in the smaller field of English Catholicism and in English society as a whole.[8] Compared with their Protestant neighbours, the English Catholic gentry had no greater incentive to accept prelatical episcopacy in their midst and no political obstacles to overcome before they could get rid of it. Of course it would be wrong to give the impression that they all held identical views, either in the 1590s or in the 1620s, but the general change of atmosphere between the two periods is unmistakable, and one case may perhaps suffice to illustrate it. It seems fair to take Sir Thomas Tresham as representing the more substantial Catholic gentry of the reign of Queen Elizabeth; Tresham's views on political allegiance got him into bad odour with the Jesuits, and led him to work, if not exactly with the Appellants, at least on a parallel course. Considering the part of the country he came from, his wealth, position and general views, one might well have chosen Sir Thomas Brudenell of Deene as a fairly exact counterpart of Tresham, twenty-five years later, even if he had not been his son-in-law and sought in his building operations to follow Tresham's example and enshrine his memory.[9] Yet if any layman may be said to have led the movement which defeated the secular clergy's programme in the 1620s, it was Brudenell. These were unpromising circumstances in which to try to revive episcopacy among English Catholics.

7. Tierney-Dodd, *Church History*, v, p. clxviii.
8. Cf. H. R. Trevor-Roper, *Archbishop Laud* (London, 2nd edn, 1965), preface, pp. viii f.
9. Joan Wake, *The Brudenells of Deene* (London, 1954 edn), pp. 101 ff. ; for relations with Tresham, pp. 104–105, 109. Miss Wake does not refer to Brudenell's role in internal Catholic affairs during this period.

The ensuing conflict was extremely involved in detail, but may perhaps most conveniently be described as an argument about whether the English Catholic community should be governed according to the disciplinary decrees of the Council of Trent or not.[10] This in itself was something of an advance, since it indicated a certain shift of attention from the jurisdictional and historical claims of the Appellants towards practical problems of pastoral care; but the change was a very relative one. In claiming to restore 'ordinary' episcopal government to England, Bishop and especially Smith continued to think mainly of its jurisdictional implications, and they made sure that the claim to historical continuity was provided for. Pastoral needs and realities, though they did not ignore them, seem still to have taken second place among the objects of their concern: like much else in the controversy, the point is certainly open to discussion, but my own feeling is that in the 1620s there were still some decades to go before this order of priorities was reversed.

In the few months which intervened between his consecration in 1623 and his death William Bishop was able to erect a structure of vicars-general, archdeacons and rural deans, and to fulfil the first ambition of the Appellants by setting up a Dean and Chapter to give formal representation to the hierarchical body of the English secular clergy, maintain its claim to continuity with the past, and express its elective will in the choice of future bishops.[11] He also came to an agreement with the Benedictines which gave them a status of loosely supervised autonomy. Whether this represented in Bishop's mind the first stage of a compromise with the regulars as a whole, or an attempt to secure Benedictine neutrality in an impending battle with the Jesuits, Bishop died too soon for one to tell; Blount and Fitzherbert were certainly preparing for the worst, and the latest opinion suggests that they may have been right.[12]

10. The main treatment of the case is Philip Hughes, *Rome and the Counter-Reformation in England* (London, 1942), pp. 322 ff., who takes a pro-Smith point of view; the other side is represented by Thomas Hughes, *History of the Society of Jesus in North America: Text*, vol. i (London, 1907), pp. 202 ff.; A. F. Allison, 'Richard Smith, Richelieu and the French Marriage', *Recusant History*, vii (1964), pp. 148–211, is an important contribution, mainly on the political side. A series of important texts is printed in C.R.S. xxii (1921), pp. 146–186.
11. Tierney-Dodd, *Church History*, v, p. cclxxx.
12. P. Hughes, *Rome and the Counter-Reformation in England*, pp. 326–328; Allison, 'Richard Smith, Richelieu and the French Marriage', pp. 156 f.; D. M. Lunn, 'The Origins and Early Development of the Revived English Benedictine Congregation' (Cambridge Univ. Ph.D. thesis, 1970), p. 312.

One clause of the agreement, which incidentally tends to confirm this view, is rather startling in an otherwise down-to-earth document. It provided that neither party should occupy any church property except what belonged to it, and must imply both a continuing concern, on either side or both, with their historical claims, and a feeling that Prince Charles's Catholic marriage, then in train, might ultimately give these claims a more than historical reality.[13]

If Bishop had conciliatory intentions they were not shared by Smith, who arrived to succeed him in April 1625; Smith was a doctrinaire hierocrat, who had no doubts of his position as 'spiritual father and pastor' of all English Catholics,[14] and took a broad view of what the term 'spiritual' covered. His effective episcopate lasted for four years, though he remained in England a little over six. The first two were occupied by a technical dispute about pastoral administration, in which he failed to preserve Benedictine goodwill and was soon faced with solid opposition from them and the Jesuits combined, since he appeared to be threatening the existence of the regular missions. Smith chose to open his assault with the perfectly correct claim that according to the decrees of Trent on the sacrament of penance, no priest other than a parish priest might exercise what was called the 'jurisdiction' of confession, the power to bind and loose sins, unless he had received the approval of the bishop of his diocese, and that if he purported so to exercise it his exercise would be invalid: God, that is, would not forgive the sins which his penitents had confessed to him.[15] There is some doubt as to what precisely had moved Smith to take this course, but it is fairly obvious that he wished to make episcopal authority felt at the most intimate point of the relationship between priest and layman; he gives the impression of working up anxiety among the gentry as to whether, if they chose their priests themselves, they might not die with their sins unforgiven. It does not strike one as a very creditable way to go about

---

13. P. Hughes, *loc. cit.* (n. 12)—item 5 in the agreement; the Benedictines were still putting in claims to the monastic cathedral chapters: Lunn, thesis *cit.*, p. 314.

14. P. Hughes, *Rome and the Counter-Reformation in England*, p. 353.

15. *ibid.*, pp. 336, 347 ff., *passim*; *Canons and Decrees of the Council of Trent*, ed. and trans. H. J. Schroeder (St Louis/London, 1960 edn), p. 173. Smith's primary concern with confession as a jurisdictional rather than a pastoral problem emerges from his *Treatise of the best kind of confessors* (?Paris, 1651), where he argues that it is better to confess to a priest possessing parochial jurisdiction than to one without it, and does not imply that other qualifications might be needed in a confessor; cf. C.R.S. xxii, p. 150.

the institution of a parochial system, which was no doubt what Smith had ultimately in mind.[16]

He was at least more straightforward in attacking the independence of the regular missions at its financial roots. The laity, which meant predominantly the gentry, supported the mission in two ways: by direct payment to individual priests, and by making endowments;[17] Smith sought to bring both of these resources under his control. Both he and Bishop claimed the right to a contribution from the laity towards their own support, which was reasonable enough, though they were unwise to press it as a legal obligation.[18] The burning question was the support of the local clergy, and on this point Smith appears to have got from Propaganda, the relevant authority in Rome, a decision to the effect that 'alms' must not be paid directly to individual priests, but to the local superior of the secular clergy, the archdeacon, who would redistribute them as he saw fit.[19] It is possible that there was a genuine misunderstanding here, since the Jesuits at least used the term 'alms' to cover a priest's regular salary, and Smith may perhaps only have intended the ruling to apply to alms properly speaking, or occasional donations. There is, as far as one can see, no justification for the charge that he proposed to introduce a compulsory tithe; but since he had already made a claim for compulsory payments to support himself and his administration, it was not unreasonable to suppose that this would shortly follow. Something of the sort must presumably have resulted from the institution of a parochial system.

Smith also claimed control of all missionary endowments, as custodian and supervisor of pious bequests. Bishop, in his agreement with the Benedictines, had asserted his right to be informed of all such bequests, so that he could make sure their provisions were properly carried out; Smith, more aggressively, required that they should be presented to him for confirmation before they took effect.[20] The claim, which again

16. P. Hughes, *Rome and the Counter-Reformation in England*, pp. 384, 359; cf. Allison, 'Richard Smith, Richelieu and the French Marriage', p. 157 (Jesuit complaints against Bishop).

17. See below, pp. 229 ff.

18. Philip Hughes, *op. cit.*, p. 326; Allison, *art. cit.*, p. 157; M. J. Havran, *The Catholics in Caroline England* (London, 1962), p. 78.

19. Philip Hughes, *op. cit.*, p. 338; cf. the Benedictine Codner's objections, *ibid.*, p. 369.

20. *ibid.*, pp. 327, 396; cf. H. G. Schroeder (ed.), *Canons and Decrees of the Council of Trent*, pp. 156 f.

was grounded on the legislation of the Council of Trent, was for several reasons a very important one; it was also impractical in the extreme. The law which would keep English missionary funds safe was English, not Roman; and it would do this, if at all, only by means of the most complicated trusteeship arrangements which would ensure that their purpose was not visible to the naked eye. Smith was now requiring the gentry to reveal to him, as of right, arrangements which, if they were to have any hope of fulfilling their object, must remain a secret between the donor, his legal counsel, and his most intimate friends, and must probably at some point involve a member of the Church of England, whose position had some claim to consideration too. One really cannot be surprised that most of the gentry thought Smith should mind his own business in this matter. No reasonable person will claim that the arrangements made for financing the English mission in the earlier seventeenth century were at all satisfactory, and in theory there was a great deal to be said for Smith's attempt to reform them. It would, as he claimed, have had a redistributive effect in favour of poorer Catholics, something, as we shall see, which was urgently needed at this point; it should also have helped to prevent the disappearance of missionary funds, which was another serious problem.[21] But it did not correspond to the external situation or internal social balance of the Catholic community in the seventeenth century, and it was foolish to suppose that episcopal legislation could alter these realities overnight.

During the first two years of Smith's episcopate, he was mainly at grips with the religious orders, and the interests of the gentry figured vicariously in the dispute; but by the middle of 1627 it had come perilously close to fundamental matters of property right, and it was time for the gentry to speak for themselves. Brudenell and his brother-in-law Sir Basil Brooke, along with Sir Tobie Mathew who was in fact a Jesuit anyway, appear to have taken the lead by asking Smith whether, in claiming ordinary ecclesiastical jurisdiction, he was claiming to exercise 'as much authority over the Catholic laity of England and Scotland as the Ordinaries of old exercised, when the Catholic religion was established here, and as much as they now possess in Catholic countries', and in particular whether in that case he was proposing to set up courts of 'spiritual' jurisdiction in the traditional sense: courts, that is, which would deal with causes testamentary and matrimonial, of tithe, defama-

21. See below, pp. 244 f.

tion and so on. They warned him that, if he was, there would be trouble.[22]

This was, all told, the heart of the matter. In approaching it, it is advisable to distinguish the question whether Smith actually exercised such jurisdiction during his episcopate, from the question whether he claimed to exercise it, and to stick to the second. The answer to this is that Smith certainly claimed to exercise an exterior jurisdiction which covered a wide range of the matters mentioned, and some other things as well.[23] On his own showing he claimed matrimonial jurisdiction over all English Catholics: after his withdrawal he argued this on the pragmatic ground that the Anglican church courts were no longer willing or able to enforce jurisdiction over them, which was partly true,[24] but at the time he showed no doubt that this was a right inherent in his office. He also claimed to exercise testamentary jurisdiction over any will made by a Catholic containing a charitable bequest, and whether or not he actually proved wills there was really no difference between this and a general claim to probate jurisdiction. He also claimed jurisdiction in defamation, and finally 'in all cases which cannot be brought before a heretical tribunal [an Anglican Church court] either because of the scandal or because they involve priests'.[25] These phrases might have been construed to extend the jurisdiction practically at pleasure; all in all about the only thing on the gentry's list which Smith does not seem to have claimed was jurisdiction in tithes, and if he had got his way in financial matters the result would have been much the same as if he had. An ecclesiastical court as operated by Smith would no doubt have been a reformed version of those of pre-Reformation England; but for that

22. Thomas Hughes, *History of the Society of Jesus in North America : Text*, i, pp. 203–206; Philip Hughes, *Rome and the Counter-Reformation in England*, pp. 353 f.; text of letter in C.R.S. xxii, pp. 159 f. See also J. Berington, *Memoirs of Gregorio Panzani* (Birmingham, 1793), pp. 121 f., and p. 178 for a further protest by Sir Basil Brooke in 1635.

23. The essential text here seems to be the *Praecipua quaedam puncta*, of which Philip Hughes presents a summary in *Rome and the Counter-Reformation*, pp. 395–396; this is a petition to Propaganda, probably dated 1631, in which Smith asks for confirmation 'that he is the lawful judge in England for ecclesiastical causes and that the Catholics in England must take their cases to him, especially marriage cases, cases concerning pious legacies, calumnies and' as follows in quotation later in this paragraph.

24. *ibid.*, p. 421; cf. H. Aveling, 'The Marriages of Catholic Recusants', *Journal of Ecclesiastical History*, xii (1963), p. 81.

25. See n. 23.

reason it would probably have been more, not less, effective as an instrument of clerical supremacy.

Smith could hardly have chosen a worse ground than this to fight on: church courts were an object of general distaste in seventeenth-century England, and Catholics, who after a long struggle had reached some kind of armistice with those of the Church of England, were in no mood to start all over again with a new system of their own, where traditional restraints and compromises would not operate. If he was misunderstood and misrepresented on particular points, that was his own fault; for by continually harping on jurisdiction, and by appearing to set more store by his juridical claims than by his pastoral functions, he had raised the spectre of prelacy in a society which was unwilling, and a community which was not obliged, to stand for it. Even those among the gentry and nobility who stood up for him, like the Montagus with whom he had had long and close personal relations, do not seem to have understood him. 'The generality of the laity,' wrote the papal agent Gregorio Panzani, who was a vigorous supporter, 'from the very beginning desired nothing more than to be governed by a bishop, and many persons of distinction offered to take the whole concern upon themselves, not only in providing for his subsistence, but in answering for his behaviour, and engaging he should appear when the king or ministry required it.'[26] This lumbering patronage was precisely what Smith was trying to get rid of.

By comparison with Tresham, who had had considerable difficulty in putting his petition to Queen Elizabeth in 1585, the English Catholic gentry had ready enough access to the government of Charles I. In the autumn of 1628, when they had waited something over a year since their enquiry to Smith and got no satisfaction in the meantime, one of them, probably Brudenell, in the name of an impressively long list of nobility and gentry, presented to the Privy Council a statement refusing to admit Smith's exterior jurisdiction as contrary to their allegiance, and evidence, in the form of nine probates of wills, of the type of jurisdiction which he had been exercising.[27] Smith said they had forged them, and perhaps they had; from the present point of view it does not greatly matter. The coup was entirely successful: early in December a

---

26. J. Berington, *Memoirs of Gregorio Panzani*, p. 182: the phrasing of the translation is of course Berington's.

27. Philip Hughes, *op. cit.*, pp. 372–373, 382; Thomas Hughes, *op. cit.*, i, p. 206 and n. 1, where the names of the peers are given.

proclamation was issued for his arrest on a charge of high treason which would of course involve anyone harbouring him. This did not quite mean what it said, but it meant enough to persuade Smith to retreat into the French embassy early in 1629, and from there, when Rome had decided against him, he only emerged two years later in order to go back to France.[28] On the date of his departure, 24 August 1631, one might have said that he took the idea of a Catholic Church in England with him, had not an essential constituent of it remained behind.

28. Philip Hughes, *op. cit.*, pp. 370 f., 389.

4

THE END OF A CHAPTER

AFTER 1631 gentry supremacy was ensured for an indefinite time; the regular missions were entrenched; the Catholic community began to settle down into the position of what has been fairly accurately called an upper-class sect,[1] without any hierarchy of pastors. When, after half a century, it finally received bishops, these were missionary bishops who made no claim to represent the historic English Church, exercise ordinary jurisdiction or, in anything but the long run, upset the *status quo* in the community. In that long run these vicars-apostolic managed to do everything useful and possible that Smith had tried to do, without precipitating any crisis. By 1685 at least the secular clergy had emerged from the mental revolution which had proved so much harder for them to accomplish than for the religious orders; indeed the terminal point might probably be put somewhat earlier, in the first years of the Restoration.[2]

Whenever one dates it, there were certainly several decades between it and the departure of Smith: an interlude of uncertainty and confusion among the secular clergy, characterised by an intensity of mutual recrimination among them which put the more traditional disputes rather in the shade. In English history as a whole, the period was dominated by the Civil War and the Interregnum; in English Catholic history it was dominated by the Chapter of the English Secular Clergy.[3]

1. Lawrence Stone, *The Crisis of the Aristocracy* (Oxford, 1965), p. 731.
2. See below, p. 211.
3. Apart from John Sergeant's *Account of the English Chapter*, ed. William Turnbull (London, 1853), which is hardly a substitute, there is no comprehensive account of the Chapter's activity or constitutional history; for one aspect of its activity, see T. A. Birrell, 'English Catholics without a bishop, 1655–72', *Recusant History*, iv (1958), pp. 142–178; and for its constitution, J. A. Williams, *Catholic Recusancy in Wiltshire, 1660–1790* (C.R.S. monograph series, i, 1968), pp. 96 ff. See also below, pp. 211 f.

Nothing could have been better designed than the Chapter to ensure a long and difficult transition. It had been brought into existence to represent the body of pastors of the English Church, and it had little choice but to seek to revive a true ecclesiastical hierarchy. Hence, up to and after Smith's death, which did not occur until 1655, it continued to press the claim for ordinary episcopal government, and to reject all substitutes. It was also a self-perpetuating oligarchy, and developed a constitution in which change was easy to resist. Since its programme proved quite unrealistic, and under the stress of the general political conflict in England, its members fell out with one another; its proposals became more unconvincing, and its actions more desperate, until the ideal it embodied had fallen into discredit even among its natural supporters. In the end it began to come to terms with the real existence and problems of the Catholic community, and finally made way with something like good grace for the new regime. The history of the Chapter remains to be written, and this cannot be done here. But three points in it will help to illustrate the general view put forward: the emergence of parties among its members; the production, by one of these parties, of the last and certainly the most imaginative of schemes for a restored Catholic Church in England; and the dogged defence conducted over thirty years by the last genuine proponent of the original secular-clergy cause, John Sergeant.

In the present state of knowledge, there is not much sign of grave division in the Chapter until after the outbreak of the Civil War. The division was not however, or not principally, a direct consequence of this conflict, though the parties did tend to take different sides in it, and to be either royalist émigrés or London-based Cromwellians afterwards. The principal question appears to have been whether or not the Chapter should drop what had been almost the first article of the secular-clergy programme from the beginning: that the hierarchy of pastors could not be brought into visible existence without an act of the supreme authority of Rome. Those who refused to drop it were in the first place men who had been close associates of Smith, and who held for the 'old way of our ancestors, for the old clergy'; they were also royalists. Apart from the oldest members of this party, like Anthony Champney, a late survivor of the original Appellants and Dean of the Chapter during the 1630s, the most prominent among them was George Leyburn, who behaved with remarkable commonsense during a mission to the Irish Catholic confederacy in 1647, and was president of Douai for eighteen years from 1652.[4] From him the tradition was handed down to his nephew John Leyburn, who ultimately launched the new style of episcopacy in 1685. Hence it was those who had been Smith's most loyal supporters, who regarded themselves as seculars of the old school, who finally proved willing to abandon impracticable visions, and settle for what was possible. Precisely how they came to make this transition seems at present unclear, though one can see what general influences were operating on them. Respect for papal decisions was one; accessibility to influences from the nobility and gentry, and also probably from the monarchy, was another; but what was perhaps more persuasive than anything else was the caricature of their ideal presented by their opponents in the Chapter.

These came to be known as Blackloists, after Thomas White *alias* Blacklo, the one first-class intellect produced by the English secular clergy during the seventeenth century; he had begun his career as professor of philosophy at Douai, and later spent a period as head of a new secular-clergy college at Lisbon, founded in 1626. From the 1630s he lived in Paris and London the life of a scholar and writer of wide-ranging interests, connected with a variety of the movements and personalities of a period of peculiar intellectual excitement, and notably with Hobbes. He was a member of the Chapter from 1638, and in 1650 finally settled in London, where he collected around him a group of Catholic priests and laymen, former pupils and friends, 'who made'— wrote the historian Charles Dodd—'a kind of Junto in the way of learning', and were later known to their enemies as Blacklo's Cabal. Professor Bradley, in a brief but fundamental essay, has presented him as a reformer, who saw the Chapter as a 'providential beachhead for the eventual overhauling of the Church Universal'; he looks to me, as he did to Dodd, rather a pure intellectual, not greatly concerned with the practical consequences of his ideas.[5] The views are probably not as incompatible as they may appear at first sight.

His general theological position puts him close to the mainstream of English secular-clergy ideology, despite a tone, and some practical

---

4. Birrell, 'English Catholics without a bishop', pp. 142 ff., 161; Gillow, *Bibliographical Dictionary of English Catholics*, iv, pp. 220 f.; R. Bagwell, *Ireland under the Stuarts*, ii (London, 1909), pp. 140–143.

5. R. I. Bradley, 'Blacklo and the Counter-Reformation', in C. H. Carter (ed.), *From the Renaissance to the Counter-Reformation: Essays in Honour of Garrett Mattingly* (London, 1966), pp. 348–370, quotation at p. 365; Charles Dodd, *Church History of England* (Brussels, 1742), iii, pp. 285 f., 256 f.

applications—as to the doctrine of Purgatory[6]—which most of them found risky, if not scandalous. It was a modernised Aristotelianism, a special kind of rationalism which took the form of identifying reason with tradition, and interpreted tradition in a rigorously antiquarian sense. Except for some implications which were difficult to reconcile with papal sovereignty, this was on the whole only a more complicated and more self-conscious way of saying what the seculars had been saying all along, and it had obvious relevance to the themes of ecclesiastical continuity and clerical collectivity embodied in the Chapter as an institution. So, when applied to the construction of a church, it inspired a plan which certainly contained some surprises, but only differed in principle from the received ideas of the secular clergy in being more resolutely antiquarian than they were. This dates from 1647, and was designed by one of Blacklo's former pupils, Henry Holden, in his rooms at the Sorbonne.

There were good reasons why it should have appeared just at this time. Charles I had lost the Civil War, and the ecclesiastical scene in England was in a state of unprecedented confusion. The Church of England, as it had stood since 1559, had been pulled down by Parliament in the previous year; its hierarchy had gone, its property had been confiscated; anyone who thought it had gone for good was in for a disappointment, but things would certainly never be the same again. An attempt to substitute a new Presbyterian establishment for the old episcopal one had collapsed against the resistance of the Army, where sectarian forms of Protestantism prevailed, and the army's Independent leaders were now trying to devise a pluralist form of Church settlement. It did not seem inconceivable that the proposed tolerance of dissenting opinions might extend to Catholics: from a social point of view, there was a good deal of common ground between the Independent officers and the Catholic gentry, many of the largest of whom had estates in regions which had always been controlled by Parliament, had avoided compromising themselves with the king, and were anxious to come to terms with the victors. An approach, led once again by Brudenell, now a peer, and encouraged by a number of the clergy, including the Jesuit provincial Henry More, had been made to see whether a tolerated

---

6. In *The Middle State of Souls* (London, 1659); Dodd, *Church History*, iii, p. 286, reports the general resentment among the clergy against this attack on Purgatory as seriously prejudicing their income. Cf. Keith Thomas, *Religion and the Decline of Magic* (London, 1971), pp. 590 f.

sectarian status for Catholics could not be secured in exchange for some affirmation of allegiance to the new regime.[7] This alliance of gentry and regulars was much the same team as had defeated Richard Smith, and one of the things they obviously had in mind was that the *status quo* in the Catholic community might well be more secure under the Independents, than under a monarchy now in relatively close relations with Smith and his chief supporters. It was this attempt—which proved in fact as abortive as earlier efforts—and the refusal of the older Chaptermen to have anything to do with it, which inspired Holden to put in a counter-bid.[8]

His idea was so brilliant that he was himself rather dazzled by it: his and Blacklo's friend Sir Kenelm Digby, to whom he sent the scheme, told him that it had been dictated by the Holy Ghost, and I do not think he meant this as a joke.[9] His first suggestion was that the only sort of Catholicism which the Independents could afford to tolerate was an episcopal Catholicism in total control of its own laity and absolutely loyal to the new settlement. This was a version of an argument which had been put forward by earlier defenders of the secular cause, including Smith, who had suggested, on the evidence of the Gunpowder Plot, that 'No bishop, no king' might apply to Catholic bishops too.[10] Except for the regime it was directed to, Holden's proposal had no originality here. This was not true of his next idea, that nothing could better solve the Independents' entire ecclesiastical problem than putting this episcopal Catholicism back in possession of its ancient sees: they would block the Presbyterians and knock out the Church of England with one devastating blow. It is difficult to blame Holden for assuming that anyone who was presented with this idea would be bowled over by its stunning force. It was clear to him that Oliver Cromwell and his fellow officers had to want to tolerate Catholics, to want Catholics so tolerated to be governed by ordinary episcopal jurisdiction, and to want

7. K. J. Lindley, 'The Lay Catholics of England in the Reign of Charles I', *Journal of Ecclesiastical History*, xxii (1971), pp. 219 f.; T. H. Clancy, 'The Jesuits and the Independents, 1647', *Archivum Historicum Societatis Jesu*, xl (1971), pp. 67–89.

8. R. Pugh (ed.), *Blacklo's Cabal Discovered in Several of their Letters* (?Liège, 1680), pp. 26–30, 48–51; also Thomas Hughes, *History of the Society of Jesus in North America: Text*, ii (London, 1917), pp. 613–617.

9. Holden's scheme in *Blacklo's Cabal*, pp. 30–40; Digby's remark *ibid.*, p. 53.

10. e.g. Smith's letter to the lay Catholics of England, 16 October 1627: C.R.S. xxii, pp. 151–152; John Bennet to Edward Bennet, 10 October 1622: Tierney-Dodd, *Church History of England*, v, p. cclii.

the bishops who governed them to sit in the ancient sees; everything the secular clergy had fought for for fifty years would be achieved at one glorious stroke. 'I conceive,' wrote Holden to Digby without waiting for empirical justification, 'you may freely give out [in Rome that] the Independents intend us an absolute toleration . . . and that they will let Catholics have their bishops, and the rather to counterpoint the Protestant bishops, and therefore [they] desire they may be titular of the Kingdom: that less than six will not be sufficient in England . . .'[11]

Fully developed, the scheme went as follows. Parliament was to design an oath of allegiance, which would be taken by all Catholics, clerical or lay; anyone refusing it would be banished. It would then 'let the Catholics have, or rather oblige them to have, six or eight bishops more or less', bearing 'some of the ancient national titles of the Kingdom'. As such, they would be 'successors to the Apostles, and have their authority immediately from Jesus Christ'; the pope would have no power to remove them, or modify their jurisdiction, and they would receive no messages or instructions from Rome without the knowledge and consent of the state. If the pope refused to appoint them on these terms, they would have to explore the possibility, canvassed already on the secular side, of getting themselves consecrated in France or Ireland, or 'whether some priests may not be appointed in the interim, whose power may be equivalent to this effect'. Parliament would of course want to know whether these bishops would lay claim to the temporalities of their sees, and whether they would want to exercise exterior spiritual jurisdiction. The first claim they would renounce by solemn oath; the second was a difficult one for Holden, since if he maintained the claim he would alienate the government, and if he abandoned it the bishops would not have a proper and effective superiority over the Catholic laity; he left it for negotiation. 'It will be easy to limit their jurisdiction in these occasions, as it may be thought fit in the discussion of these particulars.'[12]

Once erected, this hierarchy would proceed to bring law and order to the Catholic community. Regulars and other priests claiming missionary faculties from the pope would have to renounce them and take an oath to depend wholly on the bishops, and to exercise no faculties except those they should receive from them or their officers; anyone refusing to do either of these things or claiming to have faculties from any other

11. *Blacklo's Cabal*, p. 31.
12. *ibid.*, p. 34; he later altered this to 'as the state shall think fit . . .': *ibid.*, p. 39.

person whatsoever was to be expelled from the country. That took care of the regulars, and left only the laity to deal with:

> The lay Catholics of the Kingdom will be subject in matter of religion and conscience to these ordinaries, who are their true and lawful Pastors (according to the doctrine of the Catholic Church), and this by Christ's institution and express command (as all Catholics do believe) and are therefore answerable for souls: and bishops are obliged, both by the principles of their religion, and by their particular interests, to be watchful over the persons and actions of the priests whom they appoint under them, to guide the consciences of the laity.[13]

The bishops would therefore exercise their power to nip in the bud and reveal to the government any movements in the Catholic community against it; Holden did not feel it necessary to add that they would exercise it in other ways too.

Plausible or not—and one need hardly add that its logic was not found convincing in England—Holden's 'Catholic government of England' was the last in a series of church-systems constructed in the imagination of the English Catholic clergy after the launching of the mission. It was not a monstrous aberration: most of it, as I have suggested, stood fairly firmly in the centre of the secular-clergy tradition. It modified the tradition in two ways, one superficial and one important. The superficial modification lay in the regime to which it was addressed. Since the Blackloists were not the only Catholics trying to come to terms with the Independents in 1647 one cannot regard this shift from loyalist tradition as the really distinctive characteristic of the scheme: though it does help to illustrate a point already made, that for the Appellants and those who succeeded them ecclesiastical objects were more important than political ones. The more important modification was effectively to sever the connection between the envisaged English Catholic Church and the pope: Holden complained that the anti-Blackloists in the Chapter would 'never dare to go to the close-stool without a Breve from Rome'.[14] Here he was defying the whole conception of hierarchical order in the Church as it had been maintained by the secular clergy since the days of the Appellants, since that order depended on the papacy at its head. On the other hand: sitting in their

13. *ibid.*, p. 39.
14. *ibid.*, p. 27.

ancient sees, elected by the qualified representatives of a clerical corporation surviving from the indefinite past, bearing an authority divinely ordained because warranted in a tradition the light of whose majestic rationality outshone the feeble glimmers of individuals, popes or others [15] —Holden's Blackloist bishops may caricature the programme of the English secular clergy, or its successive spokesmen, but do so with some sharpness, because they expose the undergrowth of half-conscious fantasy from which it had never, so far, been wholly extricated. His 'Catholic government' makes, in its way, an appropriate pendant to Parsons's *Memorial for the Reformation of England*.

From about 1650 the 'Blackloists' were in control of the Chapter, though the effective leader of the party was not Blacklo himself, who remained fully occupied with his writing, but John Sergeant, a Cambridge graduate who had been converted to Catholicism during the Civil War and became secretary of the Chapter in 1653.[16] Sergeant's career, which lasted for another half-century, was a long, skilful, but increasingly desperate rearguard action against the inevitable: a defence of the vanishing secular-clergy vision, and of the historic and constitutional claims of the Chapter, which combined absolute rigidity about ends with reckless flexibility of means. He did in fact make one contribution to the party ideology, by claiming that the clergy was essentially collegiate in structure, from which he deduced that chapters existed *jure divino* and that, equally by divine right, episcopal authority reverted to them in the absence of a bishop.[17] But here he is worth a little attention, not for this piece of theoretical opportunism, but as an example of the aberrations which may ensue from sticking to an *idée fixe* in the face of contradictory fact. His achievement, which was to put off the time for facing facts by two decades or more, seems a totally destructive one.

Under his leadership the Chapter became a machine, less for demanding ordinaries from Rome—it continued to send missions for that purpose, but nobody now believed that they would be successful—than for

15. Cf. Bradley's analysis of Blacklo's position in 'Blacklo and the Counter-Reformation' (see above, n. 5), pp. 364 f.

16. For Sergeant, see Birrell, 'English Catholics without a bishop' (see above, n. 4), *passim*; and his edition of John Warner's *History of the English Persecution of Catholics and the Presbyterian Plot* (C.R.S. xlvii–xlviii, 1953, 1955), pp. x f., 79 f.; M. V. Hay, *The Jesuits and the Popish Plot* (London, 1934), pp. 10 ff., etc.

17. See his *Encyclical Epistle sent to the Brethren by the venerable Dean and Chapter of the Catholic Clergy in England* (?London, 1660), p. 1, and *Account of the English Chapter* (see above, n. 3), pp. 65 ff., 76.

obstructing any effort to introduce a different kind of regime. For this purpose consistency of tactics was not required. He himself was in charge of the Chapter's policy for some fourteen years, and carried out the Blackloist programme of co-operation with the Cromwellian and other interregnum regimes until 1660, when he performed a smart about-turn, and tried to outbid the rest of the community in offering allegiance to Charles II. This did not go down very well, either with the king, or with the Catholic nobility and gentry, who had now the odour of republicanism to add to their existing reasons for finding the Chapter and its programme distasteful. It shows Sergeant's tenacity that he was able to survive a crisis which blew up in the Chapter immediately after the Restoration; the immediate reason for it was that the agent of their current request to Rome for ordinaries had abandoned the cause and settled for a vicar-apostolic, but it was no doubt as much political as ecclesiastical in character.[18] The Chapter's constitution was not hard to manipulate, and despite the growing strength and savagery of Leyburn and the opposing party, Sergeant remained in the saddle for another seven years. At the Chapter's General Assembly of 1667 he was forced to resign his secretaryship;[19] as will be suggested later, this alteration marks the beginning of a new and altogether more fruitful period in the activity of the Chapter. It is fairly clear what influences had been brought to secure his dismissal. The rising power in the Catholic community was now Philip Howard, who represented in himself a grand coalition of all the forces which made Sergeant an anachronism: the gentry, the monarchy, the papacy and the religious orders. His family, recently restored to Catholicism, felt entitled to a primacy in the community and had a strong resistance to clericalism; he himself had been a royalist agent during the 1650s and was now a chaplain to Charles II's Catholic queen, Catherine of Braganza, in charge of a motley collection of clergy at court; he was a religious of the Dominican Order; he had close relations in Rome, dating from the lifetime of his art-collecting

18. Birrell, *art cit.* (n. 4), pp. 148–151.
19. *ibid.*, pp. 152–155; Hay, *The Jesuits and the Popish Plot*, pp. 116 f.; *Blacklo's Cabal*, pp. 108–125. George Leyburn's tart analysis of the membership of the Chapter in 1667 (C.R.S. xi, pp. 532–539) seems to have been compiled in preparation for the coup, perhaps for Howard's benefit. See also J. L. Miller, 'The Catholic Factor in English Politics, 1660–1688' (Cambridge University Ph.D. thesis, 1972), p. 22; this thesis contains, among other valuable things, an excellent survey of Restoration Catholicism (pp. 1–76). (Now published as *Popery and Politics in England, 1660–1688* (Cambridge, 1973).)

grandfather the Earl of Arundel, with whom he had been brought up, and was shortly to become a cardinal.[20] Since the anti-Blackloist party in the Chapter were willing to co-operate with Howard, Sergeant hardly had a chance, and John Leyburn succeeded him as secretary. This coup was meant to pave the way for Howard's appointment as vicar-apostolic, but the project did not come off, partly because of obstruction in the Chapter, but mainly because Charles II failed to carry his second Declaration of Indulgence and was forced to withdraw his support for the proposal.[21] Howard retired to Rome, taking Leyburn with him, and it was not until 1685 that Leyburn returned to complete the operation and inaugurate a new regime.

Sergeant meanwhile had allowed his animosities to get the better of him, and become sadly mixed up in the revelations of the Popish Plot. His contribution, offered in the autumn of 1679, was a ludicrous story that John Gavan, one of eight English Jesuits recently executed on the evidence of Titus Oates and others, had given an opinion permitting the killing of Charles II on the grounds of his unfaithfulness to his wife. Sergeant had some contact with the Whig leadership, and presented them with a scheme for reforming the English Catholic body on lines similar to Holden's; but this was hardly more than a gesture, and by this time I doubt if he was much interested in anything except pursuing a vendetta against the Jesuits and the Catholic aristocracy. He offered his services as an informer, and accepted a good deal of money from the Secret Service fund.[22] This sordid episode came to an end with the collapse of the Whigs and the Exclusion movement; Sergeant lived on for a quarter of a century, and died in the reign of Queen Anne, long after the Chapter had resigned its powers into the hands of the vicars-apostolic. He was for many years its senior member, and disappears from view vigorously defending his right to preside over its meetings in the absence of the Dean.[23]

In the history of English Catholicism the reign of James II may be

20. C. F. R. Palmer, *The Life of Philip Thomas Howard, O.P., Cardinal of Norfolk* (London, 1867), pp. 114 f., 128 f., 163–165; Hay, *The Jesuits and the Popish Plot*, pp. 104–108; *Downside Review*, xvii (1898), pp. 144 ff.
21. Hay, *op. cit.*, pp. 109 f.; Birrell, *art. cit.*, pp. 156–158.
22. Hay, *The Jesuits and the Popish Plot*, pp. 149 f., 159 f., 163 f.; Warner, *History of the Presbyterian Plot* (C.R.S. xlvii–xlviii), pp. 122 f., 277 f., 357 f., 456 f. J. P. Kenyon, *The Popish Plot* (London, 1972), is a fine account, but does not add much on Sergeant.
23. Birrell, in C.R.S. xlviii, pp. 531 f.

regarded as the end of an old story or the beginning of a new one. It is
proper to conclude these preliminaries by trying to view what little is
known of the conduct of English Catholics between 1685 and 1688, in
the light of the preceding discussion. Four points seem worth noting.

The year in which James, Duke of York, ascended the English throne
was also the year in which, institutionally speaking, the ghost of the
mediaeval Church was laid by the erection among English Catholics of
a new and this time lasting ecclesiastical regime with no historic and few
jurisdictional claims, that of the vicars-apostolic. The events were
related, how closely is not entirely clear. James, who had been lobbied
by the Chapter on the subject, would in the first place apparently have
preferred an ordinary episcopate as more dignified and less dependent
on Rome; he certainly, however, offered no real objection to the course
taken, and collaborated with it to the extent of ensuring that the single
bishop appointed in the first place should be, not Cardinal Howard, but
John Leyburn. By 1688, when it was decided that one was not sufficient,
he was happy enough to request the pope to set up the four districts
into which English Catholics were divided for the next 150 years, and
to arrange for the consecration of the new bishops, with considerable
pomp, in three royal palaces.[24] As has been pointed out, this conduct
implies that James was contented with a sectarian status, however
favoured, for his own community; a penetrating recent study of his
reign confirms this conclusion and puts it into a convincing perspective.[25] My own impression is that it is probably correct, though it is
hard to believe that this long-controverted question will ever be entirely
closed; I do not conclude that a continuance of Jacobite rule would
have been good for the country.

In any case James and the Catholic community were two different
things, and I do not think there can be much doubt about the general

24. B. Hemphill, *The Early Vicars-Apostolic in England* (London, 1954), pp. 6 f.—
an account drawn almost entirely from the Chapter records, and probably a little
one-sided; *ibid.*, p. 16.
25. J. P. Kenyon, *The Stuart Constitution* (Cambridge, 1966), p. 455 and n. 6, which
seems to represent a change of view since his *Robert Spencer, Earl of Sunderland*
(London, 1958), p. 122; J. R. Western, *Monarchy and Revolution: the English State
in the 1680s* (London, 1972), esp. pp. 185 f. Cf. also Maurice Ashley, 'King James II
and the Revolution of 1688: Some Reflections on the Historiography', in H. E. Bell
and R. L. Ollard (eds.), *Historical Essays, 1600–1750, presented to David Ogg*
(London, 1963), pp. 185–202; and J. G. Simms, *Jacobite Ireland* (London/Toronto,
1969), pp. 86–89. J. R. Jones, *The Revolution of 1688 in England* (London, 1972),
pp. 66 f., 81–83, takes a marginally more conservative view.

attitude of the community as such. Millenarian expectations may still
have persisted at a popular level, but they were not shared by those who
were responsible for its destinies. It has always been clear that the
leaders of the Catholic laity—inevitably, in this period, the aristocracy
—maintained the position they had held at least since the beginning of
the century: that any sort of revival of a Catholic establishment would,
quite apart from its effect upon Englishmen of other persuasions, involve a dangerous increase in clerical power which they were not prepared to contemplate. Their ranks had been markedly thinned by the
conformity—temporary in the first two cases, permanent in the third—
of the heads of the Howard, Talbot and Somerset families, and they
had been shaken by the consequences of the Popish Plot. As a result,
their voice was not heard as strongly as it might otherwise have been.
But, modest figures as they were, William Herbert Earl of Powis, Lord
Bellasis and Lord Arundell of Wardour spoke up for a prudent consolidation of existing positions and conciliation towards the rest of the
country.[26] In falling in with the new ecclesiastical regime, in which they
took the places due to them, the leaders of the secular clergy expressed
clearly enough their repudiation of ancient ambitions and their submission to the social and ecclesiastical *status quo* in England. In the pastoral
letter which he issued on the occasion of the first Declaration of Indulgence early in 1687, Leyburn exhorted his flock to take due advantage of the opportunities it offered, the clergy 'contribut[ing] their
labour in a more than ordinary measure', the gentry by 'inlarg[ing] their
charityes so far as may be necessary for a decent maintenance of those
who undergoe it'. The Catholic Church in England, its historic resources 'being fallen into other hands than those they were intended
for', was 'reduced . . . unto its prime [i.e. primitive] condition, and
accordingly may by the rules of justice, as well as pietie, require to be
maintained after the prime method'. This was as warm-hearted an
embrace of the sectarian condition as could well have been expected in
the circumstances, and when Leyburn protested to James against the
intrusion of one of his colleagues, Bonaventure Gifford, into the headship of Magdalen College, Oxford, he showed that he meant what he
said.[27] As for the regulars, the Benedictines took the opportunity to

26. Kenyon, *Sunderland*, pp. 125, 141 f., 145, etc.; Kenyon, *The Popish Plot* (London, 1972), pp. 29 f., etc.
27. Hemphill, *Early Vicars-Apostolic*, pp. 13 f.; A. C. F. Beales, *Education under
Penalty* (London, 1964), p. 244.

revive the conventual life in London, and one of their members became a vicar-apostolic; he preached a sermon repudiating, on their behalf, all claims to former monastic property. Meanwhile the Jesuit provincial, John Keynes, and his local subordinates were extremely busy, in the spirit of Leyburn's pastoral, setting up a network of town chapels, and of schools which, on the face of things, made a remarkable submission to the principle of religious plurality.[28] Looked at as a whole, the impression left by the conduct of the community during these three and a half years is that it had learnt the principal lesson imposed upon it by the first century of its history, and that it was anxious to act responsibly within the limits of the situation given, and to consider the long term as well as the short. It has been suggested that this behaviour did a good deal to reconcile the country to its continued existence.[29]

At the same time, it is necessary to come to grips with the historiographical tradition which ascribes the breach of this painfully achieved consensus, the advocacy of a 'forward policy' designed to secure the disestablishment of the Church of England and a full Catholic restoration, to 'the Jesuits'. If the term is meant to refer to the official authorities of the Society, whether in Rome or in England, I cannot see any justification for the claim. If it is meant to refer to two individual Jesuits, neither of whom, at the time, seems to have held an official position in the order, though both were fairly prominent members of it, the case is more obscure. One of them, it need hardly be said, was Edward Petre, and the other John Warner. Petre's case, though much the more notorious, is the less interesting. James was evidently very attached to him: on his accession he made him priest of the royal chapel in St James's palace; later he petitioned the pope, without success, to make him, first a bishop, then a cardinal; he appointed him an official of his household, and finally a member of the Privy Council. This advancement is not easy to explain: it was certainly not due to Petre's talents, or to his position in the English province, both of which were modest; the suggestion that it was a return for services performed for James, before his accession, in the upbringing of his illegitimate children, seems the most plausible one. He was not pushed into the position by his superiors: Keynes acquiesced in his entrance to court—he was scarcely in a position to refuse it—but does not seem to have been specially interested in

28. *Downside Review*, xviii (1899), pp. 97 f.; Beales, *Education under Penalty*, pp. 247, 248–254.
29. Kenyon, *Stuart Constitution*, pp. 455 f.

what he did thereafter; the General in Rome found it all most embarrassing. Petre's political influence, if he had any, was very probably bad, but it is hard to believe that it was governed by any general or independent views whatever.[30] Totally exposed to influence as he seems to have been, it is likely that he was in some degree under that of Warner, for whom he procured the appointment of the king's confessor early in 1687. Warner was a very different, and a much more imposing, figure, who had been, from abroad, an effective provincial during the difficult years after the Plot, and was at the time of James's accession rector of the college at St Omer. Although there seems to exist practically no evidence about his activity in England in 1687 and 1688, we know three relevant things about him. First, he was on very bad terms with his provincial, whom he fairly obviously regarded as a lesser man occupying a position which he would have filled much better himself; if Keynes was consulted about the appointment he may very well have regarded it as a means of getting Warner effectively out of the province. Secondly, he seems to have been obsessed by a feud with John Sergeant which had already lasted more than ten years. In his history of the Popish Plot, finished just before he came to England, he had made the most of Sergeant's contribution; earlier, in 1680, he had published, with the object of discrediting him, a volume of Blackloite documents dating from the 1640s and 1650s and including Henry Holden's scheme for a 'Catholic government of England', which he considered to be still in the party programme. It may well be that so lasting an obsession with this topic had inspired him with similar thoughts of his own. He was certainly, at the same time, entertaining comparable notions about the disestablishment of the Church of England. Lastly—and, if true, perhaps most pertinently—he may have brought with him, when he came over in 1687, the copy of Parsons's *Memorial for the Reformation of England* which was published by Edward Gee to damn the Jesuits after the Revolution.[31] All this is very far from convincing evidence; and

30. Bernard Basset, *The English Jesuits* (London, 1967), pp. 261 ff., for the Jesuit tradition about Petre, which seems on the whole convincing; Kenyon, *Sunderland*, p. 122; and now Miller, *Popery and Politics* (see above, n. 19), p. 235.
31. Kenyon, *Sunderland*, p. 155; Birrell, in C.R.S. xlvii, p. vi (Warner's appointment: Birrell describes him as chaplain); Warner's Letter-book, Cambridge University Library Ms. Ll.i.19, ff. 50v, 54 ff.; C.R.S. xlviii, pp. 524, 526 (difficulties with Keynes); C.R.S. xlvii, pp. ix–xiv (Warner and Sergeant: the work referred to is *Blacklo's Cabal*, for which see above, n. 8, etc.); C.U.L. Ms. Ll.i.19, f. 25, Warner to nuncio at Cologne, 2 September 1680 (disestablishment). Gee described his copy of Parsons's *Memorial* as having been 'presented to . . . James II', though this is

it may be added that Warner, after their flight, accompanied James to Ireland, where there is no sign that he influenced the king's religious policy, which was moderate, in this sense. However, three things may finally be said: it may well be that the opportunity of James's reign did produce, from among the English Catholics, a last appearance of the ghost of an English Catholic Church restored; if the ghost did walk, John Warner is the man most likely to have conjured it up, and Warner was certainly a Jesuit; there is nothing to suggest that this was in any genuine sense the policy of the English Jesuits as such, and a good deal —not least from Warner himself—to suggest the contrary.

What is in any case more obvious than that Petre and Warner were advocates of a policy of Catholic restoration, is that their position was a consequence of the relation of patron and client in which James and the English Jesuits stood to one another. The relation must have been well established by that fateful date in April 1678 when the triennial assembly of the professed fathers of the mission was held in the Duke of York's apartments in Whitehall.[32] The exact circumstances in which it had been entered into remain unclear, but it is in general perfectly intelligible as a case, no doubt the classic case, of the growth of aristocratic patronage among the English Catholic clergy visible since the Restoration, and of the relation between such aristocratic influence and the advance of the regular establishments. Dryden's hostility to Jesuit activity under James had profound ideological roots, but it was surely due in part to his own position as a client and kinsman of the Howards, whose predominance in the community James had, not unwittingly, eclipsed.[33] In this respect the brief years of James's rule, which may have permitted the final flicker of the dream of a Catholic Church restored, and certainly prefigured the more modest, yet prosperous future still a century ahead, were likewise a witness to the existence, in the intervening present, of an actual Catholic community whose principal social characteristic was the intensity with which it was dominated by a secular landowning class.

---

hardly evidence in itself; since he also possessed the manuscript of Warner's history of the Plot it seems quite likely that the copy of the *Memorial* had been found among Warner's books and papers: T. H. Clancy, 'Notes on Persons's *Memorial*', *Recusant History*, v (1959), p. 18; C.R.S. xlvii, p. xix.

32. Kenyon, *Popish Plot*, p. 56; C.U.L. Ms. Ll.i.19, ff. 40, 45*v*.

33. C. E. Ward, *The Life of John Dryden* (Chapel Hill, 1961), pp. 230 f., 248; G. Anstruther, 'Cardinal Howard and the English Court, 1658–1694', *Archivum Fratrum Praedicatorum*, xxviii (1958), pp. 353, 356 f.

PART TWO

THE COMMUNITY IN THE AGE OF THE GENTRY, 1600–1770

I

SEPARATION AND CONGREGATION

'Sister Mall, I pray you Sister Mall, will not knowledge of cockle bread and turning the cat in the pan
bring a body to Heaven?'
'Oh, by no means, love.'

William Blundell, 'An Exercise . . . for to
embolden [the children] in speaking'
(see p. 166).

5

NORTH AND SOUTH:
THE DISTRIBUTION OF CATHOLICS

A T this point we begin a journey of exploration inside the community as such, as it existed from roughly 1600 to roughly
1770. Two guiding assumptions may be mentioned for a start.
The first is that I have treated this period, speaking very broadly and
excluding the original period of construction, as a period of stability
and continuity. Notably in the first section, I shall be taking the liberty
of bringing illustrations from any date between the late sixteenth and
the mid-eighteenth century; in so far as this procedure can be justified
by statistics about the community's size, I shall try to justify it in a
brief concluding chapter. This is not to say that I do not think that anything of moment was happening to the community in the meanwhile—
on the contrary, my intention is to offer an account of its coming into
existence—but that to find out what was happening we must abandon
the comparatively rapid time-scale of the kind of event which has so far
been discussed, and adjust ourselves to a very much slower movement:
to changes often barely perceptible, and not least to those who participated in them, since it might have been difficult even for a keen observer
in the course of a long lifetime to make out what was going on. In the
first half of what follows I shall try to deal with aspects of the community's life which were characterised either by stability or by such
practically unconscious change. In the second, I shall consider other
processes which, though they were the result of a conscious effort of
transformation, were reduced by the stability or rigidity of their environment to a pace which makes them observable on much the same time-
scale as those I shall deal with first. The chapters which follow are intended to tell a story, as well as to describe a situation, but the reader
should be prepared for a story unfolding in slow motion. Although I do
not propose to resort to geological or other metaphor, and although the
matters dealt with are not often, and sometimes not happily, dealt with
by himself or those whom he has inspired, it should be clear that what

has just been said would hardly stand as it does if the doctrine of the *longue durée* had never been preached or practised by Fernand Braudel.[1]

The second assumption is that the primary sociological division in a Catholic population is that which separates its laity from its clergy. Since the point will be somewhat enlarged in due course, I shall simply state it here: adding however that the division between laity and clergy has been treated here as also dividing the two types of aspect of the community's existence mentioned above—those, that is, which tend more, and those which tend less towards the stationary. I do not propose this as a universal law of Catholic communities, or indeed for the English Catholic community during the whole period to be covered by this book; but for this community, for this time, and for the matters to be dealt with here, I think it will do. Hence it has seemed correct to treat the laity first and the clergy afterwards, even though this is inevitably, in some respects, to put the cart before the horse.

I shall approach the lay community by exploring successively: the geographical distribution of its members, and what explanations can be offered for it; such aspects of its religious behaviour as seemed particularly helpful in charting the process of its detachment, as a community, from the body of Englishmen in general; some of the social bonds which subsequently held it together; and finally its numbers and what happened to it, numerically speaking, from about 1600 to about 1770. Whether this sequence of topics has any more general validity I find it impossible to say: it is certainly not exhaustive, and I do not think I should be able to defend it by reference to any generally accepted view of why things happen in history or human society. All I can say is that it seems to work here fairly well: to present, that is, some of the more promising topics in an order which helps to extend the implications of what may be discovered in any one of them.

To consider the English Catholic community as a geographically defined entity is in the first place to consider it in terms of the primary geographical distinction of the English landscape, the distinction of highland and lowland, of—to oversimplify for a moment—North and South.[2] It is offering a cliché to allege that these categories have some

---

1. As in 'History and the Social Sciences', in P. Burke (ed.), *Economy and Society in Early Modern Europe* (New York, 1972), pp. 11–42.
2. Before proceeding, the reader may care to consult Maps 1–4 (below, pp. 404–410), on which this chapter may be regarded as a commentary. John D. Gay, *The*

relevance to our case, since Catholicism was at the time and has since been held to be a feature of the 'dark corners of the land'. In the end, the cliché may not satisfy; but the closer we examine it, the more likely it is to turn into something more illuminating. Seen from the established centres of English authority and civilisation, the North has often appeared irritatingly out of step. In the late Middle Ages it was understood to harbour primitive forms of social organisation and authority; in the industrial age it gave birth to unpleasantly novel types of economic activity. Between these two epochs, when problems of religious difference dominated the scene, the North was perhaps most commonly envisaged as breeding Catholics in numbers often overestimated, but sufficient to add a discordant undertone to what, by and large, the South would have wished to be a more conventional harmony. People, then and now, have felt that there was some connection between the northern character and the northern landscape. Defoe, having taken his readers across the Trent, introduced them in the High Peak of Derbyshire to 'the beginning of the mountains [whose] continuance . . . is such that we know no bounds set to them'; such transitions in nature frequently mark transitions in belief. The Catholic establishments of Mediterranean lands, Braudel has remarked, had comparatively little success in the mountains, and allowing for differences of scale one might say somewhat the same of the Anglican Church in England. Yet we should be careful to avoid too simplified dichotomies. Upland geography has no doubt been the chief condition of northern originality in religion, as in other respects; yet historians of the North have been rightly anxious to explain, as Defoe did, that 'the North' is a large place, and that many things may happen there. Its landscape has made it more, not less, various than the South, and Pope's 'Ask where's the North?' is a useful question for explorers of its religious experience to bear in mind.[3]

Geography of Religion in England (London, 1971), chap. 5, is a useful introduction to the subject, though better for the period after 1800.

3. Daniel Defoe, *A Tour through England and Wales, 1724–4* (ed. G. D. H. Cole, Everyman's Library, 2 vols., n.d.), ii, p. 179; F. Braudel, *La Méditerranée et le monde méditerranéen a l'epoque de Philippe II* (2nd edn, Paris, 1966), i, pp. 30 ff. (English translation, 2 vols., London, 1972–1973, ii, pp. 34 f.); A. G. Dickens, *The Marian Reaction of the Diocese of York*, ii. *The Laity* (Borthwick Institute: St Anthony's Hall Publications, no. 12, London/York, 1957), p. 3; B. W. Beckinsale, 'The Characteristics of the Tudor North', *Northern History*, iv (1969), pp. 67 ff.

This said, it is evident that, between the sixteenth century and the eighteenth, people who lived in certain sectors of the northern landscape were particularly susceptible to a persistence of Catholic feelings. One of these was the band of hills and dales running continuously along the eastern side of the Pennines from the vicinity of York to the Scottish border, and repeated on the seaward side of the Vale of York in Cleveland and around the moorlands of north Yorkshire. One might take Coquetdale as typical of this relation between environment and religious opinions: a valley unusual in its comparative breadth, and in being enclosed by moorland not only on its mountain side, where it adjoins the Cheviots, but on the seaward side as well, where the Coquet runs through a narrow gorge into the coastal plain of Northumberland. Sir Walter Scott, who was no novice in these matters, so took it. It was here that he sited Osbaldistone Hall, from which Sir Hildebrand Osbaldistone—not, one may add, a likely Christian name for an English Catholic gentleman—stood out against book-learning, Hanoverians and the advance of the turnip. Biddlestone Hall, the house which he is supposed to have taken for his model in *Rob Roy*, has been demolished, but next to where it stood one may see a nineteenth century chapel perched on top of half a square Northumbrian tower house, standing by itself on a little ridge where a stream comes out from the Cheviots into the valley. Plainfield, the hill in the middle of Coquetdale where the Catholic gentry of Northumberland assembled on a wet afternoon in October 1715, is a few miles away; the remains of Cartington Castle, home of a memorable north-country Catholic and connoisseur of the Borders in the early seventeenth century, Roger Widdrington, stand on top of a hill on the other side of the valley; at the bottom of it, the chapel and priest's house which served the Coquetdale farmers have stood discreetly in the main street of the village of Thropton, beside the Coquet, since they were moved from Thropton Hall in 1811.[4] The Catholics of Coquetdale were not short of neighbours: to speak only of the gentry, to the north they had the rugged Northum-

---

4. N. Pevsner, *The Buildings of England: Northumberland* (Penguin Books, 1957), p. 95; Sir Walter Scott, *Rob Roy* (Everyman's Library, repr. 1963), pp. 117, etc.; D. D. Dixon, 'Notes on the Jacobite Movement in Upper Coquetdale 1715', *Archaeologia Aeliana*, ii series, xvi (1894), 93-112; M. H. Dodds (ed.), *Northumberland County History*, xv (Newcastle-upon-Tyne, 1940), pp. 339 ff., 370 ff.; J. Bossy, 'Four Catholic Congregations in rural Northumberland, 1750-1850', *Recusant History*, ix (1967), pp. 88 ff. On Roger Widdrington, see A. M. C. Forster, *ibid.*, x (1972), pp. 196 ff.

brian *gentes* of Collingwood and Clavering; eastwards, a string of Catholic families, like Swinburne's forefathers at Capheaton, occupied manor-houses on the sea-facing side of the moors. To the south-west, there were wilder country and few friends in Redesdale, but beyond that were the waters of Tyne, where people were like-minded, and Charltons, Ratcliffes, Widdringtons and others dominated the valley in each of its phases from the bare pastures above Bellingham and the steep woods around Hexham to where the coal-pits began just short of Newcastle. A history of northern Catholicism in our period might well begin with Dorothy Lawson's missionary base at St Anthony's, sited for the reception of priests from ships dropping anchor in the mouth of the river, and proceed upstream to Dilston, the house of the Ratcliffes whose shell still stands overlooking the valley near Corbridge, with a chapel beside it built in 1616. It would register the execution of James Ratcliffe, Earl of Derwentwater, after the 1715 rebellion, and the passage of leadership among Catholics of the valley to men like the farmer Jasper Gibson of Stonecroft, near Hexham, whose twenty children included two bishops, and the Silvertops, who made their money by managing pits at Stella-on-Tyne and built a house at Minsteracres, in the uplands south of the river. It might conclude with the building of Ushaw College, over the border in Durham.[5]

It would be tedious to pursue this enquiry all the way down the northern uplands to the Peak: roughly the same conditions prevailed throughout, and some comments on the region as a whole will be offered in a moment. But we may take advantage of the full and precise inventory which Aveling has made of the Catholicism of Yorkshire to follow its distribution in the territory of the largest and most important county in the North: taking as our point of departure the pattern as it stood around 1600, and observing its persistence through the best part

5. A guide to Catholicism among the Northumbrian gentry may be found, for the beginning of this period, in C.R.S. liii (1961), pp. 150–153, and for the end in A. M. C. Forster, 'Catholicism in the Diocese of Durham in 1767', *Ushaw Magazine*, lxxii (1962), pp. 79–92); there are some valuable, though probably over-pessimistic, comments on the intervening period in Edward Hughes, *North-Country Life in the Eighteenth Century: the North-East, 1700–1750* (Oxford, 1952), pp. xvi f., etc. Details in W. Palmes, *Life of Mrs. Dorothy Lawson* (ed. G. B. Richardson, Newcastle-upon-Tyne, 1851), pp. 26 f.; Pevsner, *Buildings of Northumberland*, pp. 111, 137, 170; David Mathew, *Catholicism in England* (London, 1948), p. 161; M. D. R. Leys, *Catholics in England* (London, 1961), p. 173. An introduction to the otherwise ill-surveyed Catholicism of county Durham will be found on pp. 71–79 of Miss Forster's article cited above.

of two centuries.[6] The northern extremity of the county, the valley of the Tees, resembled that of the Tyne in the relative density of its attachment of Catholicism. In the early seventeenth century it was alleged that the gentry on both sides of the river were recusants all the way up 'from the haven mouth to the source', and unlike other such remarks this was no great exaggeration. With Aveling's guidance we can illustrate it precisely from the case of the Conyers of Sockburne, 'with their mansion in the loop of the river [below Darlington] in county Durham and most of their manor in Yorkshire', or that of the Wycliffes at Wycliffe, where the Tees was at the bottom of the garden.[7] In its lower reaches the valley led into Cleveland and the northern fringes of the Yorkshire moors; in its upper reaches to Richmondshire, a large and remote region of uplands, moors and dales tenuously connected with the rest of the shire. Both areas were justly reputed to breed an attachment for Catholicism. Towards the sea, the barely accessible coastal dales behind Whitby nurtured a popular variety of it which maintained an Elizabethan missionary base at Grosmont abbey and kept priests busy through the seventeenth and eighteenth centuries. Among the gentry, Catholicism persisted strongly around the northern and western fringes of the moorlands, and came to a halt on the edge of the plain of York, where the more substantial families of Bellasis and Fairfax, building up house and property at Newburgh and Gilling, moved prudently towards it during the seventeenth century, and finally provided a site for the monks at Ampleforth.[8]

Across the Great North Road in Richmondshire, the bellicose traditions which had inspired its participation in the Northern Rising were settling into a more pacific consensus by 1600. The Tees from Darlington to Barnard Castle, and the edge of the Pennines to the south, en-

6. Hugh Aveling, *The Catholic Recusants of the West Riding of Yorkshire, 1558–1790* (Leeds, 1963); *Northern Catholics* (London, 1966). The earlier studies of A. G. Dickens—'The First Stages of Romanist Recusancy in Yorkshire, 1560–1590', and 'The Extent and Character of Recusancy in Yorkshire, 1604', *Yorkshire Archaeological Journal*, xxxv (1941), 157–182, and xxxvii (1948), 24–48—are still worth consulting, though some of their conclusions (about, for example, the distinction between 'survivalism' and 'seminarism') can probably not be maintained in the form in which Dickens proposed them. See also J. T. Cliffe, *The Yorkshire Gentry from the Reformation to the Civil War* (London, 1969), chaps viii–x.

7. P.R.O. S.P. 14/88/94; Aveling, *Northern Catholics*, pp. 129, 171, 178 f.

8. *ibid.*, pp. 23 f., 178 ff., 183 f., 189 and *passim*; Leys, *Catholics in England*, pp. 120–123, 161 f.; C.R.S. lvi (1964)—papers of Meynells of North Kilvington, ed. with introduction by Aveling.

closed a territory where practically all the gentry were Catholics; it became something of a refuge for families anxious to move from more exposed parts. So it did for bishops: from 1689, when James Smith retired from York to Wycliffe, the bishop of the Northern District usually lived there, often hardly distinguishable from the local gentry. To the south, around Richmond, in Swaledale and along the edge of the uplands towards Ripon, Catholicism remained strong: about half the gentry were more or less Catholics in 1600. This was also, like Cleveland, a region where it had roots, independent of the gentry, among the upland farmers: no gentry seem to have resided in Swaledale, but the dale parish of Grinton produced a long list of recusants in 1603 and later the Restoration lawyer and M.P. Sir Solomon Swale, whose vanity Defoe remarked on. Robert Rider, a farmer of Coverdale, a small valley to the south of Wensleydale, made a will in 1678 in which he left money to support a priest 'except that the Catholic religion come in, in which case the Revenew is to be applied to some priest to Catechize and Instruct the people of that tract of Coverdale'.[9]

Southwards again, the edge of the uplands, from Ripon to Knaresborough and the Wharfe, and the dales and moors behind them, were to the West Riding what Richmondshire and Cleveland were to the North. The area had been the most southerly to give support to the Northern Rising, and at the end of the sixteenth century the allegiance of something like two-thirds of the gentry was held together by the Inglebys, a large and energetic family with wide connections, from their house at Ripley at the bottom of Nidderdale. At this time, the dale was notorious for Catholicism, a place, like Northumberland, for pipers, and the scene of one classic instance of northern traditionalism: the interlude of the Bible and the Cross, played at Gowlthwaite Hall one Christmas around 1610 by players from Egton in Cleveland. This featured a dispute, moderated by a fool, between a priest and a minister: when the minister lost, the fool 'did clapp [him] on the shoulder, and said: "Well, thou must away anon" ', and he was carried off by the Devil in a flash of fire, 'whereat all the people greatly laughed and rejoiced a long time together'. It was no doubt an expiring genre, if only because the gentry who had fostered it got into trouble and decided to conform. But Catholics, gentry and otherwise, remained comparatively numerous in

9. Aveling, *Northern Catholics*, pp. 170 ff., 344, 100, 175, 343; C.R.S. liii, pp. 89 f.; Aveling, *Catholic Recusancy in the City of York, 1558–1791* (C.R.S. monograph series, ii, 1971), p. 92; Defoe, *Tour through England and Wales*, ii, p. 223.

the area through the seventeenth and eighteenth centuries: Celia
Fiennes, on her travels, met some of them in 1697 at St Mungo's well
near Harrogate, kneeling up to their chins in the 'exceedingly cold'
water of the spring to say their prayers, and was much impressed by
their fortitude.[10] On this properly rugged note we may pause, since the
continuity of upland Catholicism was broken at this point, though it is
possible, around 1600, to detect a fragmentary example of it farther
south, in some of the Derbyshire dales.[11] What lay between were, of
course, the industrious dales of the West Riding, which never supported
Catholics. They marked a frontier which had revealed its importance
in English history at the retreat of the northern rebels in 1569,
and was to do so again when Charles I was defeated at Marston
Moor.

In the 1620s one Protestant Northumbrian considered 'papist rogue'
and 'highland fellow' equivalent terms of abuse.[12] He had, one will
readily concede, some reason on his side. The northern lowlands sustained plenty of Catholic gentry, from the Haggerstons facing Holy
Island on the Northumbrian coast, to the Bellases and Fairfaxes,
Constables and Langdales, Gascoignes and Stapletons around the
Yorkshire plain. But the religion of these prosperous squires, many of
whom entered the peerage during the seventeenth century, was much
more clearly a Catholicism of the gentry and of individual choice (often
not made until well into the seventeenth century), not different in its
character or effects from that which prevailed south of the Trent. It did
not reflect, and scarcely determined, a consensus in the regions where
they lived, which were hardly less conformist or Protestant than
anywhere else in the country.[13] In the regions I have been describing,

10. Aveling, *West Riding*, pp. 210 f., 221 f., 275–280; Christopher Howard, *Sir
John Yorke of Nidderdale, 1565–1634* (London, 1939), pp. 17–25; Christopher
Morris (ed.), *The Journeys of Celia Fiennes* (London, 1949), pp. 81–82, and cf.
J. C. Cox, 'The Household Books of Sir Miles Stapleton, Bart., 1656–1705', *The
Ancestor*, ii (1902), p. 36.
11. Mathew, *Catholicism in England*, p. 52, partially supported by list of recusants
printed by J. C. Cox in *Journal of the Derbyshire Archaeological and Natural History
Society*, x (1888), pp. 60–70; P. Caraman, *Henry Garnet* (London, 1964), pp. 72 f.—
reported about 1590 as an area of refuge 'where the papists have their harbours in
the stony rocks, and are relieved by shepherds'.
12. P.R.O. S.P. 14/185/43 ii—incident at Morpeth Quarter Sessions, described by
Roger Widdrington in March 1625.
13. Bossy, 'More Northumbrian Congregations', *Recusant History*, ix (1969), 12 ff.;
Aveling, *Post-Reformation Catholicism in East Yorkshire* (E. Yorks. Local History
Society, 1960), pp. 44 f., 52 f., etc.; *West Riding*, pp. 225 f., 255, etc.

this was not the case, at least not until after the middle of the seventeenth century, and a variety of reasons have been offered to explain why it was not. They boil down to two: that the uplands were protective, and that they were primitive. The first would I think be the traditional explanation among Catholic historians, more sensitive perhaps than others to what a sixteenth-, seventeenth- or even eighteenth-century Catholic might want to be protected from; the second has in various forms been implicit in the main stream of English historiography, and in recent decades has lent itself to formulation in more or less Marxist terms.

There is a good deal to be said in favour of the first approach: it is obvious that Catholic gentry families felt a lot safer with a good stretch of moorland coming down to the back of the house, and that if they had property so situated, they would often choose to live on it rather than in more comfortable houses elsewhere. The Ratcliffes of Dilston offer a classic example: they were lords of the manor of Derwentwater in the Lake district (from which they later took the title of their peerage), and when things began to get warm in Northumberland during the 1590s retired, temporarily, to live on the King's Island in the middle of the lake. The Widdringtons abandoned Widdrington Castle on the Northumberland coast, and lived at Great Swinburn in north Tynedale thereafter; the Claverings preferred Callaly in the uplands to Duddo in the Tweed valley; the Lawsons moved from Newcastle to Brough in Richmondshire, the Maires from Hardwick, in a rather exposed position in Durham, to Lartington, high up in Teesdale above Barnard Castle; a group of Elizabethan Yorkshire families retired to the far west of Craven, putting the Pennines between themselves and York. During the decades around 1600, the pressure of recusancy investigation urged a velocity of circulation on the northern Catholic gentry in which de-campings of this sort were barely noticeable; they must have made life difficult or impossible for Catholics among the rest of the population, who stayed behind.[14] To move into the uplands was also, very often, to put a variety of administrative barriers between oneself and hostile authority. Jurisdictional liberties still prevailed widely there, though much diminished since pre-Reformation times; more important, the tight parochial machinery of the lowland Church ceased, in effect, to

14. C.R.S. liii, pp. 63, 340; J. C. Hodgson (ed.), *Northumberland County History*, iv (Newcastle-upon-Tyne, 1893), pp. 279 f.; Aveling, *Northern Catholics*, pp. 92, 100, 336, cf. *Catholic Magazine*, ii (1832), 119 (Maires); *West Riding*, pp. 215, 225.

operate at the edge of the uplands, and the Reformation almost certainly retarded its advance.[15]

All this may give one pause before concluding that, if Catholics were often to be found in dark corners of the land at the time of the Civil War, it was because these were their natural habitat; it may help historians to avoid treating varieties of religious belief as if they were types of vegetation. It is also true that at least one of the arguments for regarding upland Catholicism as socially primitive will not stand up to investigation, since, whatever may have been the case before 1569, it was scarcely thereafter an effect of the influence of northern magnates of the traditional sort. Such influence was in fact markedly absent in the North-east at the close of the sixteenth century. The power of the Percies had gone from Northumberland; that of the Nevilles in Durham was a feeble ghost, conjured up, if at all, by daughters. The only cases where magnate influence may at all plausibly be supposed to have affected the geography of upland Catholicism in the North are the marginal instances of the Earls of Shrewsbury in the Peak district, and of the Cholmleys in Whitby Strand; and the argument for the second of these, which has looked on the surface much the more impressive, turns out to be a weak one, since the Cholmleys went over to the Church of England about 1600 without much effect on the Catholicism of the region.[16] In so far as the northern Catholic laity had leaders at this time, they were gentry, and commonly enterprising younger sons of gentry, like David Ingleby in Yorkshire and Roger Widdrington in Northumberland.

This does not however exhaust the possibilities of establishing a genuine connection between the geography of northern Catholicism and the incidence of relatively backward social forms. If Catholics retired for protection to the uplands, this might also be because they found the state of opinion there more congenial; where it was not, as around Derwentwater, the settlement of a gentry family from outside

---

15. A. G. Dickens, *The English Reformation* (London, 1964), pp. 212–213; Aveling, *Northern Catholics*, p. 19—an example in *West Riding*, p. 226.

16. Aveling, *Northern Catholics*, pp. 62 f.; J. Morris, *Troubles of Our Catholic Forefathers* (London, 1877), iii, pp. 186 f.; F. X. Walker, 'The Implementation of the Elizabethan Statutes against Recusants, 1581–1603' (London Univ. Ph.D. thesis, 1961), p. 313; Mathew, *Catholicism in England*, p. 34; Dickens, 'First Stages' (see above, n. 4), p. 176, cf. Aveling, *op. cit.*, p. 181. On Northumberland see now M. E. James, 'The Concept of Order and the Northern Rising of 1569', *Past and Present*, no. 60 (1973), esp. pp. 69 ff., 83.

was unlikely to make it so. And there seems to be some sort of a case for suggesting that Catholic opinions were likely to prevail in upland communities whose chief occupation was stock-raising. Edward Charlton remarked in the nineteenth century of his own part of Northumberland that the absence of cultivation, and the continued practice of stock-raising, had preserved the original features of the country, and the comment seems relevant to its attitude in religion.[17] In Cleveland, as elsewhere, the enforcement of recusancy laws did not mean the sequestration of land but more hazardous attempts to seize cattle. 'It is of great difficulty to perform a search in that country,' wrote a York administrator in 1599, after a series of savage incidents, 'for the Recusants keep scouts and watches day and night, that their cattle should not be seized, as they pretend, and they rid all with calivers, petronels and French pistols; very miserable is the case of poor ministers and Protestants in that place.'[18] The notorious hostility of stockbreeders and cultivators is, at least at the beginning of our period, a factor to bear in mind in charting the religious divisions of the North.

Catholic feelings were almost uniformly absent in those parts of the North which followed a different way of life. The case of the West Riding clothing districts needs no emphasis, and to this one must add extensive parts of upland Derbyshire, and the high Pennines round Alston Moor, where the chief activity was the mining of lead and other minerals. The Eyres made their fortune out of Derbyshire lead, but Catholicism remained entirely alien to the mining communities.[19] Coal-mining communities do not seem to have been quite so impervious. I am not sure whether it is relevant to our enquiry that coal-miners were noted for an attachment to traditional habits like the observance of saints' days;[20] but several of the Catholic gentry owned and exploited mines in the West Riding and on Tyneside, and social

17. Edward Charlton, *Memorials of North Tynedale* (2nd edn, Newcastle-upon-Tyne, 1871), p. 7.
18. John Ferne to Sir Robert Cecil, 5 July 1599: J. J. Cartwright, *Chapters in the History of Yorkshire* (Wakefield, 1872), p. 175; cf. Morris, *Troubles*, iii, p. 144; Foley, *Records of the English Province S.J.*, vii part 2, pp. 981, 989, 990; C. Howard, *Sir John Yorke of Nidderdale*, p. 52.
19. List of Derbyshire Recusants above, n. 11 (none in mining area); for the miners, see Defoe, *Tour*, ii, pp. 159, 161–165; R. Meredith, 'A Derbyshire Family in the Seventeenth Century: the Eyres of Hassop', *Recusant History*, viii (1965), 14; another case in Aveling, *Northern Catholics*, p. 266.
20. Christopher Hill, *Society and Puritanism in Pre-Revolutionary England* (London, 1966 edn), p. 147.

relations in the industry were sufficiently seigneurial for this to have some effect on the behaviour of those who worked in it. At Stella-on-Tyne, where the pits belonged in succession to the Tempests and the Widdringtons, there was always a congregation of Catholics, and in 1780 this was one of the largest in the North-East.[21] But coal-mining was not before this date a large-scale activity in the uplands, and with this exception one must agree that in the sixteenth and seventeenth centuries any sort of sustained industrial development in the North was a practically absolute barrier to the persistence of Catholicism.

On this ground alone there could have been no uniformity in the religion of the northern uplands; but if the economic explanation, entirely valid so far as it goes, is to be taken as implying that where there was no industrial development the people were Catholics, it must certainly be rejected. Upland Catholicism was in fact an even patchier phenomenon than has perhaps been so far implied, and I suspect that the reason for this will be found to lie in the very structure of traditional society in the North. If, ignoring the mining and clothing valleys, one takes a bird's-eye view of the sequence of northern dales around 1600, and tries to gauge their predominant religious flavour, what seems to emerge is a pattern not of uniformity but of alternation. Put very broadly indeed, the sequence runs: Coquetdale, Catholic; Redesdale, Protestant; Tynedale (north Tyne and main valley from Hexham), Catholic; South Tynedale (the home of the Ridleys), Protestant; Weardale, Protestant; Teesdale, Catholic; Swaledale, Catholic; Wensleydale, Protestant; Nidderdale, Catholic; Wharfedale, Protestant. In some degree this alternation must reflect the more or less accidental presence of local magnates, like the Bishop of Durham in Weardale and Lord Scrope of Bolton in Wensleydale;[22] but it would surely be taking positivism too far to reject from the constituents of this pattern the inbuilt contentiousness of traditional northern society. Problems of religious choice had entered a territory where instinct counselled people, in kindred, clientage or local community, to practise the peace in the feud, and they seem to have dealt with them by the methods they were familiar with. Nowhere in England were the principles of feud

21. Leys, *Catholics in England*, p. 173; E. Walsh and A. Forster, 'The Recusancy of the Brandlings', *Recusant History*, x (1969), 34–65; Aveling, *Northern Catholics*, pp. 263 f., 266; *West Riding*, pp. 246, 255 and Dickens, 'Extent and Character' (see above, n. 4), p. 40 (Gascoignes); House of Lords, Returns of Papists 1780, Diocese of Durham: 334 Catholics in parish of Ryton, which includes Stella.

22. Aveling, *Northern Catholics*, pp. 81 f., 175.

better understood than in Northumberland, where one may find the clearest examples of the continuity suggested. The Halls and the Charltons, kindreds traditionally dominant in the adjacent border valleys of Redesdale and Tynedale, differed in no material respect in their manner of life, but the first were Protestant and Parliamentarian, the second Catholic and Royalist.[23] This is no doubt an extreme case; yet far to the south, in Nidderdale and the adjoining parts, the Inglebys, their kinsmen, clients, friends and enemies, fall into a not dissimilar pattern.[24] The mark which distinguishes north-country Catholicism of this kind from that of other regions, that it reflected local or collective options rather than individual ones, accounts in itself for a lack of uniformity. Where we find something more solid, we should seek an explanation, not in general social or economic conditions, but in the particular efforts of individuals, usually priests.

The idea that the northern uplands were a region where missionary effort might prove especially productive was, as we shall see, one which dawned rather slowly on the seminary priests and, taken as a whole, they were not very enthusiastic about working there. William Allen was no uplander and, in his only reference to the problem that I know of, remarked defensively that he established his less brilliant priests 'only in uplandishe places wher ther is no better learned then themselves'.[25] Parsons took a more positive view, but nothing of much moment seems to have been done until the emergence of the scene of Richard Holtby, to whom more than to anyone else is due the building of a resilient Catholic community in the North-east. He came from a family of minor landowners settled near Hovingham in the North Riding, returned there after his ordination at Douai, and seems to have made the arrangements for Campion's brief stay in the district in 1580. After this he left for the continent again, entered the Society of Jesus, and landed

---

23. Charlton, *Memorials of North Tynedale*, pp. 85 f.; J. Hodgson, *History of Northumberland*, ii part 1 (Newcastle-upon-Tyne, 1827), pp. 113 f. John Hall of Otterburn, head of the family, was executed for joining the rebel forces in 1715, but it is not clear that his presence was voluntary: Dixon, *art. cit.*, above, n. 2, pp. 101, 109. A smaller Tynedale kindred, the Robsons, were Protestant, no doubt by opposition to the Charltons: *Northumberland County History*, xv, p. 259. For another case (Selbys *v.* Collingwoods), *ibid.*, xiv, pp. 516 f.; C.R.S. liii, pp. 152 f. The effect of this alternating pattern may still be seen (or suspected) in the map of Catholicism in Northumberland and Durham in 1851 in J. D. Gay, *The Geography of Religion in England* (London, 1971), p. 280.

24. Howard, *Sir John Yorke of Nidderdale*, pp. 12 f., 37.

25. Knox, *Allen Letters*, p. 34: the problem is discussed more fully below, chap. 10.

a second time on the coast near Whitby in January 1591. From this time he devoted his grasp of the geography of his native region to constructing a system of passage and distribution for priests, and to developing general rules for their work. The system was no doubt fairly fluid, but when it can be seen in operation priests were being landed, by collusion with a Newcastle merchant trading to the Netherlands, at South Shields, and passed via Hebburn on the Tyne to Thornley near Durham, where Holtby normally stayed, and from there along a chain of missionary centres set up at Grosmont in Cleveland, at Upsall on the western edge of the moors, and across the vale of York to houses in Nidderdale, perhaps also in Swaledale, and in the Peak district. Very noticeably, Holtby made no attempt to found an establishment in the clothing district of the West Riding: the Derbyshire house was approached via two houses, one—significantly perhaps—in the Shambles at York run by the butcher's wife Margaret Clitheroe, and one at Osgodby, near the crossing of the Ouse at Selby. From these and similar centres, a circulating priesthood served the northern uplands during the half-century before the Civil War, helping, within the limits already indicated, to convert geographical data into conscious unity.[26]

The assumption that the upland North-east was, during the later sixteenth and earlier seventeenth centuries, one of the 'dark corners of the land', seems in general well founded. But what its various backwardnesses made of it was not so much a region naturally predisposed to Catholicism, as a *pays de mission* which would respond to almost any sort of serious and sympathetic proselytising. In spite of shining examples to the contrary, like Bernard Gilpin, the clergy of the Church of England were ill-equipped with the instincts and flexibility of organisation which would have made this possible; at the Puritan end, less inhibited in these respects, they surely laboured under the handicap of

26. L. Hicks (ed.), *Letters and Memorials of Robert Persons*, i (C.R.S. xxxix, 1942), p. 108; Morris, *Troubles of our Catholic Forefathers*, iii (Holtby's narrative), pp. 105 ff.; Aveling, *West Riding*, pp. 218 f.; *Northern Catholics*, pp. 55 f., 166, 172; and his *Catholic Recusancy in the City of York, 1558–1791* (C.R.S. monograph series, ii, 1971), pp. 4, 23, for general prevalence of Catholicism among butchers in York. For some light on Holtby's operations in the Tyne valley, which are less well documented than those farther south, see P.R.O. S.P. 14/20, nos. 13, 14, 45–47 and 14/87/3. Cf. B. W. Beckinsale, 'The Characteristics of the Tudor North', *Northern History*, iv (1969), p. 77, for a judgment on the importance of missionary communications for the geography of northern Catholicism, picking up a suggestion put forward in my own 'Rome and the Elizabethan Catholics: a Question of Geography', *Historical Journal*, vii (1964), p. 140.

approaching the people they proposed to convert as inhabitants of
'another Achaldema and the valley of Hinnom', where the spirits of
wickedness dwelt in the high places. Such maladjustments left scope to
the seminary priests, and by exploiting them they were able to create a
chain of viable Catholic communities. But the Catholic mission had its
limitations too, and by the middle of the seventeenth century it had
become clear that the greater benefits of Anglican incapacity in the
northern uplands were falling, not to Catholicism, but to various other
forms of nonconformity, and notably to the Quakers.[27]

What is true in the North-east is truer still of Craven, a large and
out-of-the-way district of Yorkshire straddling the main passages
through the Pennines into Lancashire and the North-west. This was
archetypal upland country, and had given evidence of strong attachment to traditional ways in society and religion in the Pilgrimage of
Grace and the Northern Rising. It was also a direction where Catholics
of the North-east, obstructed in their external relations by the industrious West Riding and the administration at York, were accustomed
to look for congenial spirits. Among the gentry, relations of kinship
extended through it across the Pennines, as the movements of the
Yorkshire gentry show. The family connections of William Allen ran
from his home at Rossall on the Fylde coast, up the Ribble, down the
Wharfe and northwards to the Tees: they provided the skeleton for his
own tour of the North in the 1560s and for Campion's later. Yet the
record of recusancy in Craven suggests little success, and perhaps little
effort, on the part of gentry or clergy in developing Catholic communities during the seventeenth century. In the heart of the region, only
the Tempest family, at Broughton near Skipton, managed the transition; down the Ribble, the allegiance of some of the gentry left little
permanent impression until the point where the river flows into
Lancashire, the domain of the Shireburns, and later of the Jesuits, at
Stonyhurst.[28]

If one compares the situation of Lancashire Catholicism with that of

27. Christopher Hill, 'The Puritans and the Dark Corners of the Land', *Transactions of the Royal Historical Society*, 5 series, xii (1963), pp. 77–102; G. Carleton, *The
Life of Bernard Gilpin* (1633), cf. D. L. W. Tough, *The Last Years of a Frontier*
(Oxford, 1928), p. 61; E. Hughes, *North-Country Life in the Eighteenth Century*
(Oxford, 1952), p. xiv; N. Penney (ed.), *The Journals of George Fox* (London, etc.,
1924), pp. 45–93, 163–166, 215–245, cf. Aveling, *Northern Catholics*, pp. 343 f.
28. Aveling, *West Riding*, pp. 203–204, 210 f., 280–284; cf. examination of Robert
Aske, 1537, in A. Fletcher, *Tudor Rebellions* (London, 1968), pp. 133 f.

the North-east, one is struck immediately by two similarities and two differences. They were alike in that the parochial structure with which Lancashire Catholics were confronted was in as primitive a condition as in the remotest uplands; and in that here, as east of the Pennines, the progress of the textile industry in south-east Lancashire had thrown up a community as impervious to Catholic influences as their neighbours in the West Riding of Yorkshire. They were different in that the degree of concentration of Catholicism in those parts of Lancashire where it existed at all was of a quite different order from anywhere in the North-east: it was certainly true in the eighteenth century, and would probably have been true in 1600, that there were more Catholics in this relatively small area than in the rest of the North put together. It was also different in the character of its economy and society. In parts of the Ribble valley Catholicism, as in the North-east, was a religion of up-land gentry; but these were a little out of place in what was essentially a lowland community. At the close of our period, and so far as one can see at the beginning, the boundaries of the sort of Catholicism that was characteristic of Lancashire were fairly well defined, and only on the South were they identical with those of the county. Here it stopped more or less abruptly at the Mersey, from whose shores the Blundells and their neighbours gazed across at the resolute conformity of Cheshire;[29] on the North it did not extend much beyond Lancaster, despite the presence farther north of some important Catholic gentle-men, like the Prestons in Furness and the Stricklands in Westmorland; on the east, except in the Ribble valley, it was contained within a line which ran along the edge of the moorlands and by Wigan and Warring-ton to the Mersey. It thus occupied an area practically equivalent to the hundreds of West Derby, Leyland and Amounderness.[30]

29. Cf. K. R. Wark, *Elizabethan Recusancy in Cheshire* (Manchester, Chetham Society, 1971), *passim*, esp. pp. 130 ff.—there were admittedly some recusants among the gentry of the Wirral, but they seem to have had no popular support.
30. A. L. Rowse, *The England of Elizabeth* (London, 1950), pp. 440, 446–451; F. O. Walker, *Historical Geography of South-West Lancashire before the Industrial Revolution* (Manchester, Chetham Society, 1939), p. 71 (map of early seventeenth-century recusancy), and *passim*. These are the only two accounts which offer any sort of explanatory suggestions; the second is valuable and rather neglected. T. E. Gibson, *Lydiate Hall and its Origins* (n.p., 1876), pp. 193–213; W. A. Shaw, in *V.C.H. Lancashire*, ii (1908), pp. 54–94; and J. S. Leatherbarrow, *The Lancashire Elizabethan Recusants* (Manchester, Chetham Society, 1947), all provide useful in-formation, but anyone wishing to get a grasp of Lancashire Catholicism should proceed direct from the above accounts to the various published records of the

These are very much the boundaries of Lancashire's agrarian plain, one of the distinctively lowland regions of the North. Like the uplands it was predominantly stock-raising country, its coastal fringes exclusively so; but taken as a whole it had developed into an area of complex husbandry, in which arable farming played a considerable part. It was relatively prosperous: the process of improving its naturally rather waterlogged soil had begun, rather late, in the high Middle Ages, and went ahead steadily through the following centuries, as observers of the Blundells will be aware. Among its other resources it counted excellent and easily available coal. These would seem to be signs of a safely conforming community: no region with a similar geography and economy —neighbouring Cheshire, for example, or coastal Northumberland— showed reluctance to accept the Reformation. Why should this part of Lancashire have differed?

One may suggest that it was by comparison a bit off the map, encircled by moorland, peatmoss, marsh, sand-dune and mud-flat, easily accessible only at a few narrow passages, and lacking in maritime connections until Liverpool began to develop during the seventeenth century. It supported a fairly numerous gentry whose interests, except perhaps for the wider family connections which have been indicated, seem to have been distinctly confined to their own territory. It was an area of marked social continuity, and also—which may well be more to the point than anything so far mentioned—of marked social harmony. It had little or no tradition of feud, and the relations of landlord and tenant were exceptionally amicable: there was land to spare, and enclosure never presented any problems. Apart from its recusancy, southwest Lancashire was best known to the rest of England about 1600 for its addiction to country sports and country pleasures: this strikes one, here, as an indication of a harmonious society.[31]

Blundell family, below, n. 34. The map in J. D. Gay, *The Geography of Religion in England* (London, 1971), p. 278, relates to 1851, but is relevant to this period. Lord Burghley's map (published in C.R.S. iv) is worth looking at; for the parochial structure of Lancashire, see W. K. Jordan, *The Social Institutions of Lancashire* (Chetham Society, 1962), pp. 75 f. The present state of knowledge about early Catholicism in Lancashire is about to be transformed by Dr Christopher Haigh of the University of Manchester, to whose comments on this passage I am particularly indebted.

31. J. Thirsk (ed.), *The Agrarian History of England and Wales*, iv (Cambridge, 1967), pp. 80–89; *ibid.*, pp. 82 f., and Walker, *op. cit.*, pp. 49 ff., for landlord–tenant relations, and cf. William Blundell's case of conscience about tenant right in

I do not wish to claim that these considerations amount to an explanation of why Catholicism should have been, overall, so much more prominent here than anywhere else in the country. One must, in any case, clearly add to them the fact that William Allen was a member of the community, and in many ways a rather typical one; one may note the importance, at least to his widespread kinship among the Lancashire gentry, of his residence in the area during the 1560s, and speculate, without much evidence, on the implications of his provenance for the distribution of missionary priests. It has been suggested that the Elizabethan authorities, secular and ecclesiastical, were particularly lax here, though I wonder if they were more so than in several other regions;[32] no doubt other factors will emerge when the subject is fully investigated. If, so far, they do not seem quite to account for the existence of so comparatively large a Catholic community in Lancashire, they do perhaps account for some of its distinctive characteristics: notably that, by comparison with the North-east, it was relatively uniform—by which I do not mean that Catholicism was at any point the religion of a majority of people in the region as a whole—and that it was comparatively pacific. The instincts and discontents which made northeastern Catholics, on the whole, a rather aggressive body found little echo here: the Catholics of south-west Lancashire seem by and large to have practised coexistence with their immediate Protestant neighbours, less so no doubt with the hotter Protestants of the South-east; throughout this period they joined no armed rebellion, and on the one occasion when they appeared in arms they did so in the Civil War, under the banner of the king and in (unsuccessful) defence of their own territory.[33] If one may take successive masters of Little Crosby to represent them, they were a comfortable, well-established body, not incurious or unwilling to experiment, but satisfied with the pattern of their lives, intent on country concerns, and convinced that the world would get on all

---

A Cavalier's Notebook (below, n. 34), pp. 254, 250, and some comments by Christopher Hill, *Society and Puritanism*, p. 488. For sports, *ibid.*, p. 191; D. H. Willson, *King James VI & I* (London, 1959), p. 401. One case of feud (Molyneuxes *v.* Blundells) lasting most of the sixteenth century: *Cavalier's Notebook*, pp. 9 ff.; the Molyneuxes do not seem to have become Catholics until it was over: Gibson, *Lydiate Hall*, p. 186.

32. Rowse, *England of Elizabeth*, pp. 440 f.

33. Walker, *South-West Lancashire*, pp. 63, 101, 125; Fletcher, *Tudor Rebellions*, pp. 26, 96; some signs of military preparation for Elizabeth's death in Leatherbarrow, *Lancashire Elizabethan Recusants*, p. 146.

right if only people would let it alone. [34] With these characteristics they were not badly equipped for survival.

Lancashire and the North-east were thus in some ways ill-assorted yoke-fellows to the English Catholic community. Possibly, their sense of having, from a religious point of view, something in common which transcended their differences did not predate the work of the seminary priests. How it was consolidated during the seventeenth century one may guess from the experience of William Blundell. In 1635, then aged fifteen, he rode north to Haggerston to marry; the marriage was a great success, and after it Blundell visited Haggerston quite often and corresponded with his Northumbrian relations. In 1650 he wrote a long letter to his young nephew, Thomas Selby of Biddlestone, asking him to 'think often . . . that the time will come when you shall sit like an oracle in the Highlands of Northumberland, giving counsel and assistance to all your friends and neighbours', and suggesting that he take as a model his 'late neighbour and kinsman', Roger Widdrington. [35] This implies a degree of interest and sympathy which one would not automatically expect from a Lancashireman, whose home conditions were so different; one wonders whether it would have been forthcoming except under the influence of a shared religion. Though this was not one of them, there were certainly some regional boundaries which even religious sympathy found it difficult or impossible to penetrate.

In the North-east, even in Lancashire, Catholicism may have failed to achieve the regional predominance which the state of opinions at the beginning of this period seemed likely to indicate; but, however modest its dimensions, a Catholic community was established which proved capable of survival. There was one part of the North where this was not the case; and if we widen our view of the 'dark corners of the land' to embrace the western uplands, which have normally been treated as falling equally into this category, we shall find that it was hardly the case there either. Despite what is suggested by a well-known but hastily-

---

34. The available Blundell records consist of: T. E. Gibson (ed.), *Crosby Records: A Cavalier's Notebook* (London, 1880); T. E. Gibson (ed.), *Crosby Records* (Chetham Society, 1887); M. Blundell (ed.), *Cavalier: Letters of William Blundell to his Friends, 1620–1698* (London, 1933)—extracts from correspondence with commentary, and some other papers; M. Blundell (ed.), *[Nicholas] Blundell's Diary and Letter-Book, 1702–28* (Liverpool, 1952)—extracts; full text in F. Tyrer (ed.), *The Great Diurnal of Nicholas Blundell*, i: 1702–1711; ii: 1712–1719; iii: 1720–1728 (Record Society of Lancashire and Cheshire, 1968, 1970, 1972).
35. *Cavalier's Notebook*, p. 59; M. Blundell, *Cavalier*, pp. 3 f., 50 f., 69 f.

constructed map of English Catholicism in 1603, the extreme North-west displayed throughout these centuries an imperviousness to Catholicism so uniform as to indicate the lack of some essential pre-condition in the make-up of Cumbrian society. It seems to have been peculiarly self-contained; partly, perhaps, through lingering racial differences, and more certainly because it was extremely short of gentry. In this respect it stood in stark contrast to Northumberland: in the nineteenth century, of all the counties of England, Northumberland had one of the highest proportions of acreage in estates of over 1,000 acres, Cumberland all but the lowest. No doubt it would be wrong to read this contrast directly back into the Elizabethan period, but it surely has some relevance to the differing religious history of the border counties east and west of the Pennines. We have already seen that the Ratcliffes failed to exert around Derwentwater anything of the influence they possessed along the Tyne; somewhat the same conclusions might be drawn from the case of Lord William Howard of Naworth, who inherited the Dacre estates at the beginning of the seventeenth century but failed, as an outsider, to make any appreciable impact on the people of the North-west. There was possibly a more simple reason for this failure: there seems to have been still in his time a fair amount of quasi-religious traditionalism in the region, but he was probably, like many of his family, too much of an anti-clerical to seek to convert this into something more positive by encouraging an influx of priests. Probably, had they come, they might have found this an un-grateful territory for missionary operations; but the experiment was not tried, and by the Civil War, except for one or two isolated house-holds of the Howards and a couple of more firmly seated gentry families like the Curwens at Workington and the Stricklands at Sizergh, it had lost all connection with Catholicism.[36]

36. Map reprinted from R. G. Usher, *The Reconstruction of the English Church* in P. McGrath, *Papists and Puritans under Elizabeth I* (London, 1967), p. 402, which gives a figure of 80% 'open or secret' Catholics in Cumberland and Westmorland in 1603; how Usher arrived at this from the figures of recusants which he himself printed (*ibid.*, p. 399) would be hard to say—this shows 74 recusants in the diocese of Carlisle in 1603 (cf. 2,482 in the diocese of Chester). F. M. L. Thompson, *English Landowning Society in the Nineteenth Century* (London/Toronto, 1963), pp. 32, 113-117, esp. p. 115; C. M. L. Bouch and G. P. Jones, *A Short Economic and Social History of the Lake Counties, 1500-1800* (Manchester, 1961), pp. 75, 91, 174-176; *Household Books of Lord William Howard* (Surtees Society, lxvii, 1877), p. 424, etc.; M. E. James, *Change and Continuity in the Tudor North* (Borthwick Institute: St

The Welsh borders, or part of them, present a very different picture. A blanket association of Catholicism with the upland north and west may not be universally acceptable, but it corresponds fairly enough to the position at the southern end of this region, including Monmouth and part of Hereford, at least until the Civil War. In 1641 there seem to have been proportionally more recusants in Monmouthshire than in any northern county: the position at the beginning of the century cannot have been very different, since the county then produced about a quarter as many recusants as Yorkshire did. The Catholicism of this region resembled that of the North-east in its upland topography, its contrast with industrious Gloucestershire, its aggressive tendencies. It extended northwards into the valleys of south-west Herefordshire, and was particularly strong in the Golden Valley, where in 1605 the forcible burial of a Catholic woman led to a summer of general disturbance. Fresh from an attempt to cope with similar conditions in Northumberland, Lord Eure remarked four years later that 'few cases arise [in Monmouthshire] which are not made into a question between the Protestant and the Recusant'; during the early years of the Civil War the region appears to have been more or less under Catholic control. By this time, the predominant local magnate, the Marquess of Worcester, was certainly the main force behind the Catholicism of the area, and his home at Raglan Castle provided a centre for it; but this had not been the case much before about 1620. The Catholicism of the Earls and Marquesses of Worcester was itself in some sense a consequence of the state of opinion in the countryside, since it only seems to have come into the open after marriages with the local gentry, in particular the Morgans of Llantarnam, whose Catholicism was of much longer standing. Families at this level had been responsible for establishing the seminary priests in the region, and they were fortunate in acquiring two local men of particular competence: the secular Roger Cadwallader, whom we shall see at work later, and the Jesuit Robert Jones. Jones was a missionary technician of the same order as Richard Holtby: having spent some time prospecting the ground, he established his headquarters at The Cwm, a strategic house overlooking the Monnow five miles north of Monmouth which remained the base of Jesuit operations in the area for over half a century.[37]

Anthony's Publications, no. 27, London/York, 1965), pp. 9 f., etc. (Curwens and Stricklands).
37. B. Magee, *The English Recusants* (London, 1938), pp. 201, 47; F. Pugh,

It would be a little surprising if this well-established Catholicism at the southern end of the Welsh border did not have its counterpart farther north, but for the moment the region remains something of a blank. After the Restoration the Herberts, Earls of Powis, occupied much the same position here as the Marquesses of Worcester to the south and, though they changed religion in the early eighteenth century, priests continued to work in and around Powis Castle, near Welshpool. Presumably, too, the continuing popularity of Holywell as a place of pilgrimage implies some degree of religious continuity at the northern end of the border; yet one's provisional impression would be that Catholicism here was a feeble plant, with little in the way of popular roots, and had not been much more since the reign of Queen Elizabeth.[38]

No doubt it had its share of the problems which were to lead, at the other end of the border, to the precipitous decline which began in the last decades of the seventeenth century. Some of these will be more usefully discussed elsewhere, but two ought to be mentioned here. In the first place, though it was relatively strong in the border uplands, Catholicism had little or no following in the highland interior of Wales. Even where the two types of country came closest to each other, the social frontier held, as one may gather from Augustine Baker's account of his upbringing: 'He was norsed in a mountainous country not far from Abergavenny [where he was born], called Blainey Guent, his nourse a healthful woman, and more than ordinary discreet, for a mountanier . . .' The mountains of south Wales had produced no recusants by 1603, and recusancy would in any case have had little meaning there; and while narratives of seventeenth-century priests appear to show efforts being made after this date, they may well have exaggerated the wildness of the territory penetrated. It seems unlikely the Jesuit and secular missioners would have differed much in the area

---

'Monmouthshire Recusants in the Reigns of Elizabeth and James I', *South Wales and Monmouthshire Record Society Publications*, no. 4 (1957), pp. 59–110—quotation from Lord Eure at p. 60; R. Mathias, *Whitsun Riot* (London, 1963); Foley, *Records of the English Province, S.J.*, iv, pp. 334, 441 f., 472, and see below, chap. 10; K. J. Lindley, 'The Lay Catholics of England in the Reign of Charles I', *Journal of Ecclesiastical History*, xxii (1971), p. 217. For the survival of Catholic–Protestant feud in Monmouthshire through the seventeenth century see J. P. Kenyon, *The Popish Plot* (London, 1972), pp. 213, 226 f.

38. Mathew, *Catholicism in England*, pp. 106, 131; C.R.S. xiv, p. 342; cf. however Wark, *Elizabethan Recusancy in Cheshire*, p. 132.

of their operations; and the Jesuits reported quite explicitly in the middle of the century that the effect of the parliamentary occupation of Monmouthshire in 1645 had been to drive them into the Welsh mountains, where they had never been before. Making the best of a bad job, they said they would take the opportunity to start work there, but there is not much sign that they did.[39]

Obviously, there was a language problem here. There is a fairly well-established view which would put down the relative failure of the Catholic mission in Wales, by comparison with the north of England, to the exclusion of Welshmen from a determining role in missionary planning, and this in turn to national conflicts among the Elizabethan émigrés, especially in connection with the founding of the English College in Rome. Although these conflicts may be otherwise interpreted, I am sure there is a lot of truth in this view: the aim of the seminaries was very distinctly to train priests for missionary work in English. It is true that the early leaders of the mission in south Wales, Cadwallader and Jones, were both bilingual, and Jones is reported as preaching alternately in Welsh and English; one assumes that this was the case with most of the priests who worked under their direction. But there are signs that early in the seventeenth century Welsh-speaking priests were becoming hard to find. Around 1610 the archpriest, George Birkhead, was attacked by a Welsh priest for neglecting missionary opportunities in Wales, and his comments are revealing:

> Strange to me it is that he beinge but ignorant, and dwellinge in the mountains of Wales, shold have so hautie a spirit as to censure so ruggedly the doinges wherewith he is not acquainted . . . What should English men do there which have not the languadge?

Perhaps Birkhead's attitude was not always as contemptuous as this letter would suggest, and there seems no convincing sign of priest-starvation in Wales before the Civil War. By then, the English orientation of the seminaries must have been beginning to tell, and what seemed at one time a likely organ of Welsh Catholic revival, the Benedictine congregation, failed to inspire it: had Augustine Baker been an active, not a contemplative, the case might have been different. It

39. C.R.S. xxxiii (1933), p. 55 (Baker); F. H. Pugh, 'Glamorgan Recusants, 1577–1611', *South Wales and Monmouthshire Record Society Publications*, no. 3 (1954), p. 51; 'Monmouthshire Recusants', p. 61; Foley, *Records*, iv, p. 472, and see below, chap. 11, for Cadwallader.

would appear that such blows as the defection of the Marquesses of Worcester after the Restoration and the destruction of the Jesuit mission network in 1679 fell on a community which had already become too weak to recover from them.[40] The South Wales borderlands continued to breed Catholics, but they were no longer of much weight in the community at large and there was no question of a second Lancashire surviving in this region. A lot has been said of Catholicism as a religion of 'North and West'; one might equally well think of it as incorporating a conflict of North *versus* West, from which the West emerged in very poor shape. Some comments on its much more radical failure in the extreme south-west of England will be offered in a moment.

At this point we have left behind regions where Catholicism might in any sense be said to be popular; until 1700 at least, it would be true enough to say that in the rest of the country Catholicism was a nonconformism of the gentry. That being so, it might well be assumed that its distribution would, from a geographical point of view, have been more or less random, but this does not quite turn out to be the case. In the Midlands, there was a marked disparity between the western shires, notably Staffordshire, Warwickshire, Worcestershire and perhaps Shropshire, where the gentry had fairly strong leanings towards Catholicism (variously employed in the Gunpowder Plot and the escape of Charles II from the battle of Worcester), and the eastern shires, where this was an eccentric choice.[41] South of the Thames, there is also a fairly clear pattern: there were very few Catholic gentry in the South-East (Kent, Surrey, east Sussex), and fewer still in the South-West, from Gloucestershire and Wiltshire to Land's End. Between these extremely barren areas, in west Sussex, Hampshire and the adjoining fringes of Wiltshire and Dorset, they were comparatively numerous, and the region was in particular exceptional for the number

40. C.R.S. liii, p. 133 (Jones preaches in Welsh and English); George Birkhead to Thomas More, 7 January 1611 (A.A.W. series A, x, no. 3); Pugh, 'Monmouthshire Recusants', p. 64. Miller, 'The Catholic Factor in English Politics' (see above, chap. 4, n. 19), p. 30, notes that the Somerset family continued to protect popery after its conversion.

41. For this and the following paragraph see in the first place Magee, *English Recusants*, pp. 199, 201 and Maps 1–3 (below, pp. 404–408); far the best study of Catholicism in the west Midlands is M. Rowlands, 'Catholics in Staffordshire from the Revolution to the Relief Acts, 1689–1791' (Birmingham Univ. M.A. thesis, 1965); for the earlier period, *V.C.H. Staffordshire*, iii (1970), pp. 99 ff. Cf. below, chap. 10, pp. 223 ff.

of Catholic magnate families which were settled there during some or all of these centuries: Welds at Lulworth, Arundells (Lords Arundell of Wardour) at Wardour, Paulets (Marquesses of Winchester) at Basing House, Viscounts Montagu at Cowdray, Dukes of Norfolk at Arundel.[42] The west Midlands and this south-central district were the only regions of lowland England where the gentry chose Catholicism in sufficient numbers to influence in any real way the general tone of the area. But there were two other regions where the choice was sufficiently common to have an impact on the economy of the Catholic community, though it made little difference outside it: these were East Anglia and the Thames valley.

The Catholic gentry families of East Anglia formed a well-established and wealthy body which of all these regional groups is the only one whose origins seem unequivocally pre-Elizabethan: the Norfolk rebellion of 1549 had probably more influence in determining their views than any subsequent event. John Gerard, who began his missionary career in their midst, remarked that they had little or no popular support, and during the seventeenth century, in a region where people were more enthusiastically Protestant than anywhere else in the country, they were more than usually exposed to popular violence at moments of crisis. But in the end, their wealth and continuity of tenure imposed respect on their neighbours, and though they remained a little cut off from the rest of the Catholic gentry until the latter began to frequent London, this proximity also ensured them a fairly prominent voice in the counsels of the community: in the Petres they possessed the one family of cast-iron landed magnates to remain invincibly Catholic from the sixteenth century onwards, and one in a very advantageous position for making its wealth felt.[43] No other considerable branch of the Catholic

42. Lindley, 'The Lay Catholics of England in the Reign of Charles I', p. 201; R. B. Manning, *Religion and Society in Elizabethan Sussex* (Leicester, 1969), pp. 151–165; J. E. Paul, 'Hampshire Recusants in the Time of Queen Elizabeth', *Proceedings of the Hampshire Field Club*, xxi (1959), pp. 61–81; J. A. Williams, *Catholic Recusancy in Wiltshire, 1660–1791* (C.R.S. monograph series, i, 1968), pp. 82 f., 182 ff. and *passim*.

43. Mathew, *Catholicism in England*, p. 28; Rowse, *England of Elizabeth*, pp. 454–457; P. Caraman (ed.), *John Gerard: the Autobiography of an Elizabethan* (London, 1956 edn: hereafter *Autobiography of John Gerard*), pp. 18 ff., esp. p. 32; R. Clifton, 'The Popular Fear of Catholics during the English Revolution', *Past and Present*, no. 52 (1971), pp. 31, 41, 49; for the Petres, L. Stone, *The Crisis of the Aristocracy* (Oxford, 1965), index under name, and C. Clay, 'The Misfortunes of William, 4th Lord Petre (1638–1655), *Recusant History*, xi (1971), pp. 87–116.

gentry was so relatively detached from the main body as this: a fairly sizeable group of families and houses in the Thames valley—Talbots, Webbs, Fermors, Stonors north of the river in Oxfordshire, Englefields, Blounts and others south of it in Berkshire—made for a congenial passage between the west Midlands and the far South. For this reason the Catholics of the region had had an important role in the Elizabethan mission, especially for Campion and Parsons; and in the quite different circumstances of 1700, when the woods had ceased to be a protective screen and become a pastoral environment, the milieu in which Pope found himself when his father moved to Binfield played a similar role, integrating the Catholic gentry among themselves, and mediating between them and the metropolitan civilisation of London—functions memorably enacted in 'The Rape of the Lock'.[44] Yet there were limits to integration. It is in every sense a long way from Hampton Court, where Pope's catastrophe occurred, to Osbaldistone Hall; Arabella Fermor, who lost her lock, would have been much of an age with Sir Hildebrand's sons, but she would scarcely have married one of them.

What influences, other than random choice, may be said to have governed the distribution of Catholic opinions among the landowning peers and gentry of lowland England? Without too sanguine expectations, we may see how they respond to the factors indicated by the survey of remoter parts: the influence of the local environment, the consequences of prudent withdrawal, and the activity of priests. Try as one may, one cannot quite escape from the prevailing notion that a choice of Catholicism must have corresponded to some more general sluggishness of spirit, and that in turn to some lack of stimulus in the regional environment. In the Midlands it would be hard to deny some relevance to the contrast of a high-farming gentry in the East, all but unanimously Protestant, and a pastoral gentry in the West with Catholic leanings; a contrast, also, between a region where there were enclosure problems, and one where there were not.[45] In the South, we should be equally unwise to ignore the information that, before the

44. Mrs B. [M. H. A.] Stapleton, *A History of Post-Reformation Catholic Missions in Oxfordshire* (London, 1906); R. J. Stonor, *Stonor* (Newport, Mon., 1951); Waugh, *Campion*, pp. 150 f.; Mathew, *Catholicism in England*, p. 51; G. Sherburn, *The Early Career of Alexander Pope* (Oxford, 1934), pp. 36 ff. and *passim*. See also C.R.S. lx (1968), pp. 211-245, for a good list of Oxfordshire recusants for the early seventeenth century.

45. J. Thirsk (ed.), *Agrarian History of England*, iv, pp. 99-112—note the remarks on the ecology of religious dissent, pp. 111-112.

Civil War, the area comprising Sussex and east Hampshire was the least accessible and least populated in the whole of lowland England;[46] here, too, there was an obvious contrast with the west-country clothing districts on one side, and the London-centred home counties on the other. As in Lancashire, a relative remoteness, a relative lack of social tension were obviously among the conditions in which a Catholic gentleman might feel more at home than elsewhere, and other members of the community would be relatively undiscouraged from following his example.

A glance at the Maps (below, pp. 403 ff) should indicate that there is some truth in these assumptions, yet they must certainly be handled with extreme caution, if only because we are not dealing with regional or local communities as a whole, but, in effect, with men of a single class. It must also be said that Catholic opinions among the gentry were perfectly compatible with an entrepreneurial approach to agriculture or anything else. The west-Midland gentry may not have been high farmers, but they might be ironmasters, sometimes, like Sir Basil Brooke and Sir John Winter during the reign of Charles I, very considerable ones.[47] It seems, on the whole, true to say that in regions of intense socio-economic readjustment or stress landowners were not Catholics; yet on the other hand one might guess from some cases that popular disorder arising from tensions of this kind might sharpen or revive in a landowner Catholic inclinations which might otherwise have remained dormant or painlessly disappeared. Apart from the Catholic gentry of East Anglia, to whom I have suggested that this pattern may be applicable *en bloc*, there are more or less well-known cases of the Markhams in Nottinghamshire, the Treshams in Northamptonshire and the Englefields at Wootton Basset in Wiltshire to illustrate it.[48] With these the question was evidently not whether a Catholic landlord would have the

---

46. H. C. Darby, *Historical Geography of England before 1800* (Cambridge, 1936), pp. 342, 438–439; cf. J. C. Mousley, 'The fortunes of some gentry families of Elizabethan Sussex', *Economic History Review*, 2 series, xi (1959), 478 f., for economic situation of Catholic gentry in Sussex.

47. Stone, *Crisis of the Aristocracy*, pp. 344–351; Leys, *Catholics in England*, p. 173; Christopher Hill, *Reformation to Industrial Revolution* (London, 1967), p. 88.

48. M. E. Finch, *The Wealth of Five Northamptonshire Families, 1540–1640* (Northants. Record Society Pubs., Oxford, 1956), pp. 66–99, esp. pp. 87 f.; H. R. Trevor-Roper, *The Gentry, 1540–1640* (Econ. H. R. Supplement, 1953), pp. 40 f.; G. Anstruther, *Vaux of Harrowden* (Newport, Mon., 1953), pp. 215–217; R. H. Tawney, *The Agrarian Problem in the Sixteenth Century* (New York, repr. 1967), pp. 148, 251–252.

gumption to enclose, but whether a landlord who was also a Catholic could be a radical encloser and survive the repercussions. On this point the evidence seems inconclusive. The case of the Treshams suggests that they could not, that of the Englefields that they could; and even they, after successfully battling with their tenants for decades in Star Chamber and elsewhere, finally moved to Whiteknights near Reading, where Pope found them.[49] While it was clearly possible for a well-established Catholic gentry family to withstand any amount of popular hostility around them, they were, for business and other reasons, foolish to provoke it; it was perfectly possible, as the Petres showed in Essex, the Bedingfelds in Norfolk and the Brudenells in Northamptonshire, for a Catholic to get along successfully in a competitive agricultural environment, without inviting trouble of this kind.[50]

Lowland gentry were more stable than uplanders, and even in the heat of Elizabethan recusancy pressure did not move so much. It therefore seems unlikely that the distribution of Catholicism here had been as much affected by evasive movements as in the North. There is however at least one important exception to this, which is worth a little notice because it helps to explain why the far South-west, which had come out in rebellion against the prayer book of 1549 and might have been expected to form a region of upland Catholicism similar to the North-east or the Welsh border, did not do so. Humphrey Arundell, the main leader of the rebellion, belonged to a family which was widely influential throughout the South-west and had a solid record of Catholicism thereafter. During the 1570s, it seemed that its family relationships, landed interests and social influence, given a sharper religious tone by the import of seminary priests, were about to entrench a Catholic interest in Cornwall of similar importance to that, say, which centred on the Ingleby family in Yorkshire. Dr Rowse has traced the process by which this interest was evicted and destroyed by a hostile coalition of sea-faring gentry led by Sir Richard Grenville. The Arundells retreated to Chideock in Dorset, failed to produce heirs and were succeeded by their cousins of Wardour in Wiltshire; meanwhile two successive disastrous captures had led Lady Arundell to break off

49. J. A. Williams, *Catholic Recusancy in Wiltshire*, p. 238.
50. Trevor-Roper, *The Gentry*, pp. 12, 54; Joan Wake, *The Brudenells of Deene* (2nd edn, London, 1954), p. 113; P. J. Bowden, *The Wool Trade in Tudor and Stuart England* (London, 1962), p. 9.

relations with the seminary priests, and though the breach may not have lasted very long it seems to have been serious enough to destroy any prospect that an effective missionary network in the South-west would survive the withdrawal of the family.[51] One may suspect that something of the same process operated, in the opposite direction, on the second Viscount Montagu, who abandoned Battle Abbey in east Sussex, which his mother had made into a well-documented stronghold of Catholicism before her death in 1608, and returned to less exposed quarters at Cowdray, far to the west of the county. Behind what by the mid-seventeenth century had become a certain concentration of Catholic landowners in the central South, we may detect the repellent force of hostile pressure in more exposed areas, as well as the positive pull of a neighbourly environment and a certain density of mutual support; things such as these gave sharpness to what, on the bare geographical facts, could not have been much more than a feeble tendency.

How far, finally, was the distribution of Catholic gentlemen across the English lowlands determined by the activities and requirements of the missionary priests? We should not, certainly, consider the priests, especially not the Elizabethan priests, as passively adjusting themselves to a distribution over which they had no influence. Yet altogether the evidence that they had any very important effect in modifying this part of it is rather slender. It is true that, for perhaps two decades at the close of the reign of Queen Elizabeth, when direct passage through London and the South-east was extremely difficult, access to and from the coasts of East Anglia and west-Sussex–Hampshire was probably essential to the functioning of the mission in southern England, and this may have helped to direct missionary attention to their respective hinterlands. One could plausibly adduce in support of this connection John Gerard's career in Norfolk and Suffolk, and evidence of joint action by priests and gentry to ensure access to the sea on the Sussex–Hants border.[52] In the west Midlands, Henry Garnet chose his mis-

---

51. Fletcher, *Tudor Rebellions*, pp. 49 ff.; A. L. Rowse, *Tudor Cornwall* (London, 1941), pp. 342–378, esp. pp. 361 f.; R. Lloyd, *Dorset Elizabethans* (London, 1967), pp. 72–86. The situation from the later seventeenth century onwards is excellently described in G. Oliver, *Collections illustrating the history of the Catholic Religion in the counties of Cornwall, Devon, Somerset, Dorset, Wiltshire and Gloucestershire* (London, 1857); it improved slightly after the conversion of the Cliffords in 1672.
52. F. A. Gasquet, *Hampshire Recusants* (London, n.d.), pp. 37 f., 44; C. Devlin, *Robert Southwell* (London, 1956), pp. 127 ff., etc.; Manning, *Religion and Society in Elizabethan Sussex*, pp. 156 f.

sionary headquarters—Hinlip House in Worcestershire—first, and converted its mistress later.[53] But in none of these cases does one really have a firm impression that missionary strategy did much more than intensify existing dispositions; if we leave aside one or two regions, particularly in the east Midlands, where missionary successes proved singularly barren in the long term, we are left with hardly more than the gentry of the Thames valley among whom it may reasonably be felt that the needs of missionary communication enforced an unusual intensity of priestly attention and maintained a higher proportion of Catholics than one might otherwise have expected.[54] In general, the nearer one got to London, the less scope there was for the priests.

Before concluding this chapter I think I had better raise a question of method which has some wider implications. It will have been noticed that in attempting to account for the geographical distribution of the English Catholic community during the period we are now concerned with, I have confined myself to environmental and other factors operative from the later sixteenth century, and failed to pursue what may seem the more promising method of seeking its origins in the geography of genuine attachment to Catholicism in earlier sixteenth-century and pre-Reformation England. My justification for this course is not that it is in principle impossible to measure this attachment: a number of indices exist which lend themselves to statistical and distributional treatment, and they have been at least partially exploited.[55] It is that, so far, they have not revealed any predisposition in the religious make-up of early sixteenth-century England to produce the pattern of the English Catholic community as it subsequently emerged. It is reasonable to suppose that a readiness, relative to one's wealth and other interests, to invest money in Mass-foundations was some kind of index of autonomous attachment to Catholicism. One can discover from W. K. Jordan's volumes on English philanthropy how much is known to have been invested in such foundations in a number of English counties between 1480 and (effectively) 1560, expressed as a percentage of the total investment in the country for charitable and related purposes

---

53. *Autobiography of John Gerard*, p. 44; Caraman, *Henry Garnet*, pp. 91 ff.
54. e.g. *Autobiography of John Gerard*, p. 169, cf. p. 40; Devlin, *Southwell*, p. 113.
55. Preambles of wills: Dickens, *The English Reformation*, pp. 191 f.; seasonality of marriage, see below, chap. 6, pp. 145 f.

between 1480 and 1660.[56] The figures are as follows: Yorkshire, something over 10%; Somerset, 9%; Norfolk, 6%; Lancashire, 5%; Hampshire, 1%; Buckinghamshire, less than 1%. They are not in every respect contradictory to what might have been expected, and one may certainly gain from Jordan's analysis information which is illuminating from our point of view. It is worth knowing that in Yorkshire and Lancashire chantry foundations were cut off in full spate by the Reformation, and our sketchy account of the background to Lancashire Catholicism is strengthened by the knowledge that in chantry foundations, as otherwise, the country was a late developer, launching only in the fifteenth century a movement which was evidently unsatisfied when brought to a halt. It would be helpful to know whether this was true in northern counties which Jordan has not dealt with: to cite at random a Northumbrian case, Robert Collingwood, the founder of the family fortunes, founded a chantry in his parish church at Whittingham at almost the last possible moment, in 1556; the vigour of the family's later attachment to Catholicism suggests that they were anxious to get value for money.[57] It seems however obvious from Jordan's figures that this sort of explanation can have no general validity: taken as they stand, they shed next to no light on the distribution of the post-Reformation Catholic community. Of his three most chantry-minded counties, it was practically unrepresented in one and notoriously weak in another. His three least chantry-minded (so far as his published figures extend) include the only county where it was really well entrenched and one of the few southern counties in which it had any strength at all. The study of sixteenth-century wills may have other results in store for us than this, but as things stand the implication is that there was a very fragmentary continuity between the distribution of the post-Reformation Catholic community and the distribution of traditional devotion in pre-Reformation England. One justification for the length of this discussion may be to have indicated that the continuities we are concerned with proceed forwards rather than backwards from the close of the sixteenth century.

56. W. K. Jordan, *Philanthropy in England* (London, 1959), p. 307; *The Charities of London* (1960), p. 273; *The Charities of Rural England* (1961), pp. 63, 176, 366 ff.; *The Social Institutions of Lancashire* (Chetham Society, 1962), pp. 5, 77 f. I have left Jordan's figures for London out of account.
57. *Northumberland County History*, xiv, p. 491.

6

SEPARATION: TYPES OF RELIGIOUS BEHAVIOUR

To view a religious tradition, as a social historian must, as a continuum of behaviour rather than of belief, is generally to renounce the facility of a ready-made corpus of evidence: it is not easy to grasp the experience of being a Catholic Christian in England as it appeared to the average layman between the close of the sixteenth and the middle of the eighteenth century. In presenting what is nevertheless a lengthy chapter on the subject, I have made no effort to be comprehensive. As the title of the chapter indicates, I have taken as theme the idea that the principal characteristic of this experience, seen as a whole over nearly two centuries, was that it involved a process of separation: a severance of bonds of collective behaviour which would once have united them to other Englishmen; a movement from the habit of performing religious and sacramental acts as members of a uniform society, to that of performing them as members of a small nonconforming community; an experience parallel on its own less self-conscious level to the one which we have envisaged, among the clergy, as the 'death of a church'. This theme has governed the choice of topics for investigation: we shall be concerned with religious acts of a social not an individual character, with the obligatory not the optional. This choice excludes, on the one side, such more or less archaic or 'magical' features of Catholic feeling and behaviour as have recently been explored by Keith Thomas and Jean Delumeau,[1] and on the other side the field of voluntary or individual piety or 'devotion' to which I propose to return at a later stage.

However restrictive this choice may be it does not, as may at first appear, exclude the treatment of properly religious behaviour as such. In reconsidering the theme and content of this chapter as they have developed, it has been borne in upon me that the word 'separation' has

---

1. Keith Thomas, *Religion and the Decline of Magic* (London, 1971); Jean Delumeau, *Le Catholicisme entre Luther et Voltaire* (Paris, 'Nouvelle Clio', 1971), pp. 237 ff.

another and perhaps a deeper meaning here than the one which was at first intended: a ritual, as well as a social, signification. To be separate, or set apart, is one of the attributes of the holy. In deciding to begin with the topic of fasting and abstinence, I had in the first place purely social considerations in mind: that as a domestic observance it was probably the feature of traditional religious practice most readily capable of transposition from the practice of a multitude to that of a minority; and that, since it implied the least degree of external separation from the rest of the population, it could be treated logically and also chronologically as the first in a series of stages, extending through the practice of public worship and of the *rites de passage*, through which this separation was accomplished. But it has dawned on me that fasting and abstinence, before they are anything else, are acts of ritual separation, the separation of meats, and are as such perhaps inherently better adapted to the circumstances of a sectarian community than to that of a religious multitude. In such circumstances, they are well calculated to support a caste-like consciousness of superior purity. Once one has seen fasting and abstaining in this light one gets a more penetrating view of why they were important to English Catholics in this period; one also begins to see in the same light the whole series of acts through which I have tried to trace the process of their separation. I find, for example, that I have quoted, when dealing with the experience of Catholics in public worship, a passage which treats their withdrawal from the services of the Church of England as a case of the separation of meats.[2]

The chapter has not been constructed with these considerations in mind, and holiness may seem a little remote from some of the matters discussed in it; but, if one takes it as a whole, the social and the ritual senses of separation seem not to conflict, but to reinforce one another. I think the theme will emerge more sharply, the pattern suggested achieve a greater exemplarity, if both are borne in mind. I leave until the close of it to broach some related questions which may emerge.

2. Below, p. 126. For what is said above I am much indebted to Mary Douglas, *Purity and Danger* (London, 1966).

(i)

SEPARATION OF MEATS AND DAYS: FAST AND FEAST

It is noticeable that the features of pre-Reformation Christian practice to which conservatively-minded people held most strongly were those which offered fewest opportunities of conflict with the established church order, since they belonged to a region of private social practice which in effect lay outside the field of legislation. On the occasions when Elizabethan secular legislation did attempt to enter it, as in the act of 1563 imposing abstinence on Wednesdays, it did so in support of traditional practice. English Protestantism, it has been argued, contributed much to developing in Englishmen the rhythm of life, founded on a regular six-day working week, on which modern society depends; and though it may be that the counter-Reformation performed much the same function on the Continent, it is obvious that the social rhythms of pre-Reformation Christianity took a far more seasonal or cyclical form. The year, natural and liturgical, turned on a sequence of festivals, and these in turn were balanced and prepared by periods of collective abstinence. For those for whom abstinence was not a permanent condition, the life of the household was an alternation of frugality and hospitality, fasts and feasts. There were considerable differences in local custom, but by and large over a third of the days in the year were days of fasting or abstinence from meat. About a hundred were fast days: all Fridays, except during Christmas- and Eastertide, all the forty weekdays of Lent, the twelve Ember days, so far as they were not already accounted for, and the vigils of feasts that were locally felt to be important. One ate a single meal, which could not be taken before midday and must not include meat; the prohibition was widely interpreted, especially in the north of England, as also applying to 'whitemeats', i.e. cheese and eggs. Another forty days or so—the Sundays in Lent, all Saturdays except at Eastertide, the Rogation days (Monday, Tuesday and Wednesday before Ascension day) and, for some reason, the feast of St Mark (25 April)—were the days of abstinence, on which no meat was eaten.[3]

3. J. E. Neale, *Elizabeth I and her Parliaments*, i (London, 1965 edn), pp. 114-116, 225; Christopher Hill, *Society and Puritanism in Pre-revolutionary England* (London, 1966 edn), esp. chap. 5—'The Uses of Sabbatarianism'; Aveling, *West Riding*,

There is fairly unanimous testimony that this ascetic regime was the branch of pre-Reformation religious practice held on to most firmly by Elizabethan Catholics; it seems likely that it was what chiefly distinguished them from their neighbours in the days between the death of Queen Mary and the arrival of the seminary priests. It was the first thing to strike the less rigorous Catholics of the Netherlands about the behaviour of English Catholic émigrés, and the only pre-Reformation practice of which traces survived to the mid-seventeenth century in a place unvisited by seminary priests, the Isle of Man.[4] How instinctive an avoidance this was, how far outside the region of ordinary ecclesiastical discipline, we may gather from the case of Lady Montagu, as recorded by her confessor Richard Smith about 1600. Well beyond the age at which she was no longer required to fast (60), she 'did piously observe all the fasts of Lent, the Ember days, and whatsoever other were either commanded by the Church, or introduced by the pious custom of the country, to which of her own devotion she added some Wednesdays'. When she was dying, Smith and her doctor united, to her intense disgust, in forcing her to eat meat on Ash Wednesday, 'which she never did in her life before'; even then she made them take care that the family did not catch her doing it.[5] Smith's experience in trying to moderate a lay enthusiasm for fasting and abstinence which he obviously found excessive and superstitious reflected that of the missionary priests in general, though because of their anti-ascetic tradition Jesuits probably felt it more sharply than others. Parsons spoke strongly on the subject, accusing the English Catholics of ignoring the interior man while they 'relied on such external practices as living on bread and water on Fridays, vigils and most of Lent, and things like that'.[6] The phrasing suggests a mildly satirical intention, but Parsons was a diplomat, which his successor Jasper Heywood was not. In East Anglia, where he was working, he issued a set of instructions on the subject at

p. 255; B. Hemphill, *The Early Vicars-Apostolic in England* (London, 1954), pp. 185 f. For some relevant comments on the traditional regime of eating in Europe, see J. R. Hale, *Renaissance Europe* (London, 1971), pp. 19–21.

4. A. J. Loomie, 'Spain and the English Catholic Exiles, 1580–1604' (London Univ. Ph.D. thesis, 1957), p. 16; Blundell, *Cavalier*, p. 97.

5. A. C. Southern (ed.), *An Elizabethan Recusant House* (London/Glasgow, 1954), pp. 48, 35; note the case of the student at the Inns of Court about 1600 who was converted by his room-mate, a Catholic, during Holy Week, after having agreed, 'as a kind of joke', to fast Lent with him: C.R.S. liv, p. 172.

6. C.R.S. xxxix, pp. 330, 340.

which, wrote the old priest Alban Dolman, 'all the Chatholique howsholders were greatli scandalized . . . *et merito*, for thei conteined erronius doctrine'. It is annoying not to know more about this incident: the trouble was in any case serious enough for Heywood to be withdrawn from the mission because of it.[7] For all their efforts, the missionaries made little or no impression on the instincts of lay Catholics in this matter; the customary regime remained in force for another two centuries. So important was the practice of abstinence in the lives of Catholics, that it tended to provide a model for other experiences of life. 'I lost patience,' wrote one young lady to her sweetheart in the seventeenth century, 'to fast all Lent from the lov'd dainties of your letters, but Easter brings an expectation of such feasts again. I therfor now bring in the first corse of an ordinary homly dish . . .' Less trivial instances developed an instinct for self-denial which was appropriate enough in the circumstances.[8]

Three remarks may be made at this point. The first is that a way of life in which fasting and abstinence played so prominent a part could have little meaning for anyone who lived more or less permanently at a level of bare subsistence. This was surely one of the more obvious reasons why the Catholic community, as the seminary priests found it and for the next century at least, was most strongly represented among the gentry.[9] The second is that what a family was to eat fell into the area of the household activity for which a wife or womenfolk generally were responsible: the ritual importance of making correct decisions about it does something to explain the role of women in Elizabethan Catholicism. The third is that a choice to fast or abstain was something which had to be made not by individuals, but by households, and problems arose where a household contained members of different religious persuasions. There was in general a strong pressure for household conformity to which it seems likely that Catholics submitted so long as they or their children were in Protestant houses.[10] On the other side,

---

7. C.R.S. li, pp. 208, 210; Waugh, *Campion*, pp. 117, 119.
8. A. Clifford (ed.), *Tixall Letters* (2 vols., London, 1815), ii, p. 71; cf. i, p. 157 and esp. 158: sonnet of Catherine Aston to her small daughter Catherine, Ash Wednesday, 1654, 'finding her weeping at her prayers because I would not consent to her fasting'; cf. Aveling, *West Riding*, p. 262—Stephen Tempest on Self-Denial.
9. Cf. R. Mandrou, *Introduction à la France moderne* (Paris, 1961), p. 21: 'pour les plus pauvres, le carême dure toute l'année'.
10. Cf. below, chap. 7, pp. 161 f; a possible example in G. Sherburn (ed.), *Correspondence of Alexander Pope* (5 vols., Oxford, 1956), i, p. 81—'In this point of

Catholic doctrine was extremely firm that those in charge of a Catholic household were obliged to see that all its members, individually Catholic or not, followed the rules of fasting and abstinence. We may find it hard to explain why the Hampshire secular clergy decided in 1691 that Catholics might not serve meat on Fridays and other fast-days to Protestant guests and servants; but their ruling seems to have been in line with some general decision of the clergy at this time. For the gentry it was practicable, if unhelpful to neighbourly relations, but James Smith, the new bishop of the Northern District, had to face an outcry from the substantial farmers of the North or somebody claiming to speak on their behalf. It was very well, they said, for the gentry, and would make little difference to those who lived of their own labour and were used to 'faring hard'. But they needed farm labourers, who must often be Protestants, and would not work if they were not fed: how were they to get their ploughing done in Lent? The law, they complained, was hard enough on Catholic labourers, and intolerable for Protestants; if it were not changed they could not continue in farming. Smith sympathised with their point of view, and though the ruling does not seem to have been revoked it was perhaps evaded by a liberal use of dispensations.[11]

The argument is interesting for a number of reasons. It reveals a persisting sense of the discipline as an objective discrimination of the holy, rather than a practice worth keeping up because self-denial was good for the soul. More mundanely, it was a sign of the emergence of a farming interest in the Catholic community about 1700. It may imply that fasting habits traditional among the gentry had recently been transplanted to a social environment for which they were not designed; otherwise one might take it as evidence for a shift in lay feeling which may safely be dated to about this time.

The first signs appeared towards the end of Charles II's reign. In 1676 the General Assembly of the Chapter complained that people in the North were slacker than they used to be and had come round to eating eggs on Fridays in Lent; it blamed the regulars for allowing this

---

Praying, I am an Occasional Conformist. So just as I am drunk or Scandalous in Town according to my Company, I am for the same reason Grave and Godly here.'
11. Leys, *Catholics in England*, p. 111, quoting C.R.S. xliii, pp. 9 ff.; Ushaw Mss. iii, no. 498, undated but must be *c.* 1701 if the obviously related petition of James Smith to Propaganda cited by Hemphill, *Early Vicars-Apostolic*, p. 183 (from A.A.W. Main series xxxviii, no. 8) is rightly dated.

and asked them to tighten up. Eight years later it confessed failure, and took advantage of complaints from the northern gentry about a shortage of fish in their parts to unify the regimes north and south of the Trent.[12] By 1700 people were beginning to claim relief on medical grounds; and there is a new feeling in Pope's letter of January 1711 to John Caryll, who had sent him oysters, that he would now fast the coming Lent, 'which'—at 22—'I have not done many years before', or in his complaint the previous Holy Week that the penitential season kept you so busy that it was hard to get on with writing poetry.[13] His was of course a metropolitan point of view, and the persisting difference of feelings in the North may be gathered from a *contretemps* which occurred in Lent 1727. Bishop Gifford in London had been obliged by lay demand to allow flesh three days a week, and make concessions over eggs and cheese. The Midland and Western districts had followed suit. In the North, for which he was responsible since the district was vacant, Gifford gave no dispensation for flesh on the grounds that people were stricter there and would be scandalised. The Jesuits however made what looks like the deliberate mistake of taking his faculties to apply to the North as well, and the result was a culinary schism in Lancashire. Lady Molyneux, while roasting chicken for dinner at eleven o'clock on Sunday morning, was told that she was not entitled to eat it, and forced to change to red-herring. It appears that lay opinion was genuinely divided, but that the chief upholders of the old regime were by now the secular clergy, convinced that any concession was one more victory for the Flesh over the Spirit.[14] In 1743 the northern vicar-apostolic rejected another hint from the Jesuit superior in Lancashire that the time had come to moderate the severities of Lent; this, he said, 'would amount to a revocation of our Master's commands, and encourage among the Rich the disorders he chiefly intended to remedy'.[15] From now on the bishops give the impression, which may well be exaggerated, of being snowed under by requests from the gentry for dispensations, on grounds which they regarded as frivolous; and there were probably

12. Hemphill, *Early Vicars-Apostolic*, pp. 186–187.
13. M. Rowlands, 'The Education and Piety of Catholics in Staffordshire in the 18th Century', *Recusant History*, x (1969), p. 70; G. Sherburn (ed.), *Correspondence of Alexander Pope*, i, pp. 81, 144; the first remark must have been meant as a joke since no one was required to fast before the age of 21.
14. Anon., 'Abstinere cum Abstinentibus', *Ushaw Magazine*, lxii (1952), pp. 21–40.
15. Dicconson to Cornelius Morphey, 21 January 1743: Lancs. C.R.O., RCWB, Dicconson Papers, i, 347.

other priests than the *bon viveur* Pierce Parry of the clergy mission at Oscott who, as the parson reported, 'has been known sometimes to forget that it was fish-day; a circumstance I must not tell to his bishop though I may to my own'.[16]

Although the inevitable process of installing a reformed regime was long drawn-out, and not complete until the end of the eighteenth century, it may be dealt with here. After a running battle between the metropolitan gentry and aristocracy and the London vicars-apostolic during the 1770s and 1780s, the Friday fast was converted into abstinence and the Lenten fast, though retained in theory (and in the Catechism), was abolished in practice by automatic dispensation and retained only for Ash Wednesday and Holy Week; Saturday abstinence seems to have disappeared shortly after. Reduction of the festal calendar disposed of most of the fasting vigils.[17] This was certainly a memorable date in the history of the community, and we might well suppose that the instinct of stern if crude asceticism with which the Catholic gentry had confronted the Elizabethan age had now been entirely lost. This is probably true in the sense that fasting and abstinence were no longer consciously felt as practices of ritual character, and that Catholics, if called upon, would now have defended them on moralistic grounds. Otherwise the tradition had been successfully modified and conserved. The essentials of the new regime, Friday abstinence and a Holy Week fast, were a little more than token survivals, and far from presaging extinction of the practice, reduction to these more manageable proportions seems to have revived its vigour and equipped it for survival in a new age. The anonymous Catholic who, in the middle of a public controversy about the method of appointing vicars-apostolic, looked forward in 1790 to the prospect that 'when bishops shall be chosen dependently on [the votes of the female sex] their lordships will make rules for the lenten season more suitable with domestic economy', was making a successful joke about something he was fond of. So was Lady Jerningham when she reported her Gallicised brother-in-law, who had come to stay at Costessey for Easter 1799, as going away on Maundy Thursday because 'the fasting and praying this week was

16. M. Rowlands, 'Staffordshire Papists in 1767', *Staffordshire Catholic History*, no. 6 (1965), p. 39.
17. Hemphill, *Early Vicars-Apostolic*, pp. 184–186; E. H. Burton, *The Life and Times of Bishop Challoner* (2 vols., London, 1909), ii, p. 179; Ward, *Dawn of the Catholic Revival*, i, pp. 32 f., 117; J. A. Williams, *Bath and Rome : the Living Link* (Bath, 1963), pp. 53 f.

too much for him'.[18] Beneath some conventional eighteenth-century opinions, Catholics remained attached to something which was peculiarly theirs, the longest-established feature of their way of life, and one of the few for which they were not indebted to the seminary priests.

As with fasting, it requires some stretching of the imagination to grasp the importance of feast-days in the pattern of life which English Catholics had inherited from the pre-Reformation past. There were, in the first place, a very large number of them: getting on for forty, though practice differed from one part of the country to another until, in the middle of the seventeenth century, Pope Urban VIII imposed the uniformity of the Roman calendar. Until that date their festal cycle was something English Catholics had invented for themselves, and it attracted as much spontaneous loyalty as the fasting cycle did; here, too, they had successfully resisted Jesuit criticism.[19] The festal instinct in the community was so strong as to override considerations of security, and greatly simplified the task of its enemies. As John Gerard remarked, it was at festal seasons that pressure on priests' services was most acute, and the chances of their capture highest; numerous instances at Easter, others at Candlemas, confirm his judgment. Christmas seems to have been safer, though it was perhaps at this time the feast of greatest importance to Catholics; it may be that it was thought a general period of truce, or that Protestant gentlemen were unwilling to be disturbed at this season.[20]

Feast-days were days apart, holydays; like fast-days they were, for Catholics, incidents of the domestic cycle, predominantly of the gentry. Catholics did not work or, more to the point for the gentry, allow others to work for them: the prohibition cannot have applied very rigorously to ordinary domestic service, though it must have been

---

18. Ward, *Dawn*, i, p. 229; E. Castle (ed.), *The Jerningham Letters, 1780–1843* (London, 1896), i, p. 150.
19. Aveling, *West Riding*, p. 255; Hemphill, *Early Vicars-Apostolic*, pp. 162 f., 183 f.; Leander Jones, in *State Papers collected by Edward Earl of Clarendon* (3 vols., Oxford, 1767–1786), i, p. 205; Rowlands, 'Catholics in Staffordshire from the Revolution to the Relief Acts, 1689–1791' (Birmingham Univ. M.A. thesis, 1965), p. 218; R. Parsons, *The Jesuit's Memorial* (ed. E. Gee, London, 1690), pp. 85 f.
20. *Autobiography of John Gerard*, pp. 17, 58; Tierney-Dodd, *Church History of England*, iii, pp. 90 f.; P. Caraman, *Henry Garnet* (London, 1964), p. 185; *Calendar of State Papers, Domestic, 1595–7* (ed. M. A. E. Green, 1869), p. 183; Foley, *Records of the English Province S.J.*, ii, p. 572; v, p. 996; C.R.S. liv, pp. 243, 245; A. C. F. Beales, *Education under Penalty* (London, 1963), p. 158.

respected to some extent, since John Gother accused the gentry of over-working their servants on the evenings before feast-days in order to make up for it.[21] The space thus made free was to be given to ritual celebration; but there were in 1600 widely different interpretations of what that meant, and much of the seventeenth century was spent in achieving an acceptable compromise between them. There was of course an obligation to hear Mass, and this was celebrated with as much pomp as possible. There was normally a good deal else of a strictly religious nature besides: vespers on the vigil, confession and com-munion, sermon and catechism in devouter households. But so rigorous a Catholic as Dorothy Lawson 'solemnized [the major feasts] in both kinds . . ., corporally and spiritually'; inviting those who had come to Mass to break their fast with Easter lamb or Christmas pie, and seeing that there was dancing after dinner, and games of chance on which, at Christmas, she was prepared to have a modest flutter.[22] Lawrence Vaux had taken a sterner view. 'If we mispende the holy day,' he wrote in his *Catechism*, 'in unthrifty games, as cardes and dise for covetousness . . ., or if we use daunsing for wantonness . . . we breake the holy day and so offende God.'[23] In spite of this, anarchic folklore was probably still the predominant tone of Christmas in the community around 1600. There is a fine example from about 1620, when some servants of Lord William Howard left their feasting and invaded the church at Bampton in Westmorland while the parson was trying to conduct his Christmas service; they waved banners, fired pistols, whistled sheepdogs, 'sport[ed] with pies and puddings in the church, using them as bowls in the church allies', and parodied the service with toasts and a collection. Established a little earlier than this, the Benedictine school at Douai maintained a full traditional Christmas, under a boy elected as Christ-mas king, until the eighteenth century. It was an occasion of this kind, when some of the more traditionally-minded priests in captivity in Wisbech castle came in to Christmas dinner in 1594 with morris-dancing and a hobby-horse, which set off the schism in the company

21. Cf. below, chap. 7, pp. 171 f; *Great Diurnal of Nicholas Blundell*, i, p. 65—8 September 1704: 'James Addison came to geld my Stoned Hors but being Holy day (Nativity of Our Lady) I would not let him.'
22. W. Palmes, *Life of Mrs. Dorothy Lawson* (ed. G. B. Richardson, Newcastle-upon-Tyne, 1851), pp. 38–40; cf. *Autobiography of John Gerard*, pp. 174 f.; A. C. Southern, *An Elizabethan Recusant House*, pp. 47 f.
23. Lawrence Vaux, *A Catechisme or Christian Doctrine* (ed. T. G. Law, Chetham Society, 1885), p. 36.

known as the 'Wisbech stirs', and may be said to have launched the Archpriest controversy.[24] Interludes, as in the Yorkshire case already mentioned, plays, music and dancing remained essential ingredients of a Catholic Christmas until after the middle of the seventeenth century. Thus William Blundell wrote at least two Christmas plays, one for the coming of civil peace played in 1647, and a comedy of domestic manners played by himself and his children in 1663; dancing was his great enthusiasm, and in his unregenerate days before the Civil War he had written a sort of jig, to be sung to the music, which was a barely disguised invitation to bed. Even Vaux conceded that it was allowable 'to sing, or to play upon instruments' on holydays; partly for this reason, there was a powerful musical tradition in the community, though it did not survive the middle of the seventeenth century.[25]

Resistant to frontal attack from Elizabethan priests, the traditions of ritual folklore yielded to gentler pressure in the course of the seventeenth century. Upon this uncertain foundation had been built by 1700 a sober structure of sacramental practice known as the indulgences: a cycle of eight feast-days, distributed through the year at intervals of about six weeks—Christmas, the first Sunday in Lent, Easter, Whitsun, SS Peter and Paul (29 June), the Assumption (15 August), Michaelmas (29 September) and All Saints (1 November)—on which members of the community would be expected to prepare themselves diligently to go to confession and receive communion. The evolution is not easy to trace, but one can see it happening among the Blundells. Somewhere about 1650 William Blundell began to register embarrassment and remorse at the memory of his earlier Christmas excitements; in his grandson's time Christmas Day was treated in the family as a day of religious observance and recollection. Overnight or early in the morning, the household of Little Crosby went to confession; at ten o'clock they went to Mass, after 1709 in the chapel of the priest's house in the village, then

24. B. Magee, *English Recusants* (London, 1938), p. 49; T. G. Law, *Jesuits and Seculars in the Reign of Queen Elizabeth* (London, 1889), pp. liv, 18 f.; cf. Hill, *Society and Puritanism*, pp. 187 f. See above, pp. 44 f.

25. Above, chap. 5, p. 83; M. Blundell, *Cavalier* (London, 1933), pp. 5 f., 28, 298 f., 304 ff.; Clifford, *Tixall Letters*, i, p. 91; Alan Davidson, in *Worcestershire Recusant*, no. 15 (1970), p. 17, quoting Richard Carpenter, *Experience, Historie and Divinitie* (1642) on the 'great Christmasses' kept by the Catholic gentry. J. C. Cox, 'The Household Book of Sir Miles Stapleton, Bart., 1656-1705', *The Ancestor*, iii (1902), pp. 148 f., for plays, etc., at Carlton (Yorks.) at Christmas 1662 and 1664.

came back to dinner. After dinner, Nicholas Blundell remarks on three occasions that he 'read in a spiritual book', which was not a thing he did very often; there is little sign of festivities, though the atmosphere was perhaps relaxed a little after supper. The household kept up its tradition of 'merry nights', at home and with its neighbours, but it celebrated them on other days of the twelve in the season.[26]

The impression may have been given that this festal cycle, even more than the fasting cycle, was chiefly a possession of the gentry, and impinged on others only as much as they did. This would not be quite true: as we may see from the life of the Benedictine Ambrose Barlow, a Lancashire farming congregation of the 1630s could celebrate Easter with a degree of collective passion not inferior to that of the gentry.[27] Nevertheless by 1700 it would appear that most other members of the community had come to regard the cycle of feasts, like the cycle of fasts, as an irritating hindrance to work. The 'servile work' which was to be abstained from on the holy day had been glossed by Vaux as 'any servile labour, that properly perteyneth to servantes: as plowghing, carting, digging, and such like, or . . . handy craftes'. Before 1600 Parsons had pointed out, with a sharpness worthy of Christopher Hill, that this was grossly unfair to the industrious poor, and recommended a general reform; his suggestions were not made public, and I have found no explicit echo of them before the 1680s, when William Blundell came to much the same conclusions. Partly inspired by his reading in the new science of political arithmetic, and partly by the fact that, since Christmas Day 1683 fell on a Tuesday, there were then eight consecutive feast days in a row, he mused glumly on the economic effects of the prohibition. 'If there be four million of working people in a country who are each able to earn 6d. *per diem*, the work of one day will amount to £100,000; so that the difference of working and not working . . . is no small matter as to civil and political respects.' He went on to contrast the effects of industry and idleness as exemplified by the state of France, Holland and Flanders on the one hand (he rightly thought that French Catholics observed far fewer feast-days than English Catholics did), and that of 'Spain and the lazy old Irish' on the other; 'a thowsand

26. Ward, *Dawn of the Catholic Revival*, i, p. 13; Blundell, *Cavalier*, pp. 298 f.; *Great Diurnal of Nicholas Blundell*, i and ii *passim* at Christmas; for what appear to be the signs of the transition at Carlton, Cox. 'Household Book of Sir Miles Stapleton', *The Ancestor*, ii (1902), pp. 21 f.
27. See below, chap. 11, p. 262.

weighty matters may be considered pro and con on this occasion'.[28] A Catholic as faithful as William Blundell could hardly have said more plainly that it was time the Church reformed its festal system. Meanwhile pressure from farmers and others was intensifying, and priests had evolved an elaborate casuistic practice in dispensations for work, which the Yorkshire clergy attempted to codify in 1686, with bizarre results. 'St James's day (25 July) to be easily dispensed with, but not so if it falls on a Wednesday or Thursday; unless the season be very hazardous. And that to be counted a hazardous season when there has been in the forepart of the week such rains or showers as are enough to spoil the greatest part of a hay-day . . .'; and so on through the year.[29] A calendar as complicated as this had evidently fallen out of step with the real life of the community and was, like Ptolemy's system of the universe, ripe for supersession by something simpler; by the end of the century even the bishops had become anxious to reform it. In 1701 James Smith in the North, who must have been under the greatest pressure, asked Propaganda for authority to modify the prohibition of servile work on feast-days, and suggested that it might in future be confined to fifteen feasts, of which six were among the twelve days of Christmas and none fell in harvest-time; this reasonable proposal seems to have been generally adopted by the vicars-apostolic, and in 1715 the same request was made for the Midland district. Rome appears to have taken no notice for sixty years, and in the meantime the vicars-apostolic, certainly in the Midlands and presumably elsewhere, had brought in the new regime on their own authority. Finally in 1777 Rome reduced the holydays 'of obligation' to twelve, and leave was given to the vicars-apostolic to permit working on two of them, SS Peter and Paul and the Assumption.[30] Of the rest, it seems likely that only four (Ascension, Corpus Christi, Annunciation and All Saints) were not generally considered holidays in England; so that English Catholics were formally subject to effectively the same regime of work as the rest of the population, as they had no doubt already been for some time in practice. The

---

28. Vaux, *Catechism*, p. 35; Parsons, *loc. cit.*, above n. 19; T. E. Gibson (ed.), *Cavalier's Notebook* (London, 1880), pp. 121–123.
29. Aveling, *West Riding*, p. 256, where more to the same effect may be found; Rowlands, 'Catholics in Staffordshire from the Revolution to the Relief Acts', p. 219.
30. Hemphill, *Early Vicars-Apostolic*, pp. 183–185; Rowlands, 'Education and Piety' (see above, n. 13), p. 70; E. H. Burton, *Life and Times of Bishop Challoner*, ii, p. 179.

point seems still to have been in the future when, save for a vestigial
Mass obligation on a handful of weekdays, their festal calendar would
have become wholly assimilated to that of English Protestants, Guy
Fawkes' Day not excluded.

This assimilation has become so natural that it calls for an effort to
visualise how much, originally, the distinctiveness of the community
depended on its possession of a peculiar calendar, and how compre-
hensively that calendar governed, not simply the liturgy, but the facts
of everyday life. Gabriel le Bras has characterised some modern types
of Catholic life as 'seasonal conformity'; English Catholicism, so far as
the laity was concerned, had its origins in a seasonal nonconformity.

(ii)

SEPARATION IN WORSHIP: RECUSANCY AND THE MASS

Seasonal nonconformity, the separation of meats and days in accordance with tradition or instinct, was not, however extensive its implications, sufficient to constitute a separated Christian community: this
called for exclusiveness in the practice of the principal act of worship,
the Mass, and here instinct and tradition were not assistants but
obstacles which required to be overcome. In considering the progress
of this exclusiveness, the history of recusancy, we are on well-trodden
ground; but it may not be amiss to repeat that a recusant of the first
generation was not simply a man who would not attend the services of
the Church of England, but a man who had once attended them, and
had ceased to do so. For twenty years after 1559 almost every person
whose domestic life was conducted in the way which has been described,
saw this as compatible with some degree of church attendance; for
another sixty this feeling persisted, though in steady decline. Practically
all Elizabethan Catholics, and some until the Civil War, must have been
familiar with a good deal of Cranmer's liturgy; although this experience
may technically fall outside the history of the community, some grasp
of it is necessary for a comprehensive view of the milieu from which the
community was largely drawn.

Naturally enough, the more eccentric incidents in this experience
have left the most trace: most of them come from uplandish places,
where audible barracking was not uncommon. In Cornwall, when his

parson rose to preach, John Trevelyan got up, invited him to dine with him when he had done, and left; in Yorkshire, Christopher Moorhouse of Keighley 'said to Laurence Deane the minister then reading the [Thirty-Nine] Articles'—evidently with a commentary—'Sir Laurence rede on your articles and leave your talke for the day is nere spent . . .'; Sir Richard Shireburn ostentatiously 'stop[ped] his ears with wool'; and 'coughing and unquiet behaviour' were heard in York Minster, admittedly on the part of recusants who had been forcibly brought there to hear a sermon. More devout gentlemen from more orderly regions took their prayer-books with them, and read them to themselves, like Sir Thomas Cornwallis who 'all service time when others on their knees are at praiers will sett contemptuously reading on a book, most likely some Lady Psalter or portasse which have been found in his pue'. But most church-papists probably made no gesture of either sort: it should be remembered that in many cases this would be neither necessary nor appropriate. The Inner Temple church, where legal Catholics spent the service time walking around the Roundel and discussing the legal news, was no doubt an unusual case, but there was hardly yet a tradition of reverent silence to be broken. Most cases of disturbance or dissociation seem to be connected with sermons, as in the case of John Earle's model 'Church-Papist' who 'if he be forced to stay out a sermon, . . . pulls his hat over his eyes and frowns out the hour; and when he comes home thinks to make amends . . . by abusing the preacher'; but in the Elizabethan parish avoiding sermons cannot have been as difficult as all that.[31]

Allen, in his classic account of their attitude, implied that church-papists found other features of the Anglican liturgy quite attractive, enjoyed having scripture and psalms in English, and saw no harm in joining in. Communion was another matter. The Elizabethan communion service was not a very frequent event, and would often occur on feasts which Catholics were celebrating at home. Allen had the impression that on such occasions Catholics might first hear Mass at home, and then go to church and communicate there; but at this point he probably had more clearly in mind priests who were prepared to cele-

31. G. M. Trevelyan, *English Social History* (London, 1946 edn), p. 180; Aveling, *West Riding*, p. 210; F. X. Walker, 'Implementation of the Elizabethan Statutes against Recusants' (London Univ. Ph.D. thesis, 1961), pp. 18, 27 f., 315, 99 f.; P. McGrath, *Papists and Puritans under Elizabeth I* (London, 1967), pp. 106 f.; J. Earle, *Microcosmography, or a piece of the world discovered* . . . (ed. H. D. Osborne, London, n.d.; original edn 1628), p. 25.

brate in both rites, and it seems unlikely that a gentleman who had gone
to the trouble of procuring a priest for, say, Easter would attend his
parish church as well, far less communicate twice in different rites on
the same day.[32]

How far a seasonal nonconformity of this kind was felt to be compatible with communicating in church at other times seems a matter of
some doubt. It was obviously possible to take the simple view of the
Yorkshireman who 'after he had receyved the Communyon saide he had
receyved nothing but bread and wyne, and that he wold bringe it with
hym next tyme and soe save his money'; taken at their face value, the
earliest statistics of recusants and non-communicants in the county
imply that virtually everybody who went to church communicated.
This does however seen unlikely: the Elizabethan bishops, who presumably knew what they were doing, believed that communion was
something genuine Catholics would jib at, and that a repressive system
which used it as a test would be much the most efficient method of
reducing their numbers. Their advice was not followed, but the Yorkshire recusancy figures over the next quarter of a century, which are
probably typical, suggest that they had a good case. During the 1580s
the number of recusants returned in Yorkshire went up rapidly to
about 600, while non-recusants who avoided communion accounted for
half as many more; in 1604, when hopes of a new deal raised the number of Yorkshire recusants to 1,800, the number of non-communicant
attenders stood at 600. These figures suggest a fairly strong inhibition,
though we have no figures of communicants to compare them with.
By the 1620s, when these were disappearing, the non-communicant
church-papist was still a common enough figure to rate as a 'character'
in Earle's *Microcosmography*; Earle makes the plausible suggestion that
the excuse generally offered for avoiding communion was that one was
'out of charity' with a neighbour. Possibly the willingness of a church-
papist to take communion from the parson was in inverse proportion to
his opportunity of receiving it from a priest. With some qualifications
it seems legitimate to treat non-communicating as a 'first sign' of
recusancy; without exactly saying so Allen seems to have indicated to
the first generation of Douai priests that they might be prepared to
accept it as a step in the right direction.[33]

32. Knox, *Allen Letters*, pp. 55 f.; Walker, 'Implementation', p. 29.
33. Aveling, *West Riding*, p. 210; Dickens, 'First Stages' (see above, chap. 5, n. 4),
pp. 169–170 and 'Extent and Character', pp. 30 f. and see below, chap. viii, n. 23, for

Since going to church was obviously, for most Catholics, an irritating and disagreeable experience, one may ask why they did it. This may seem a simple-minded question: Allen said that Catholics went because they were afraid of the consequences of not going, and this would normally be accepted as a sufficient answer to the question. But the clerical inventors of the mission believed on principle that the Elizabethan government was a brutally repressive one, and were also inclined to save the faces of the laity by claiming that they did things under constraint which actually they did from choice; if a fully satisfying answer to the question is to be found, it will certainly be a complex one. The chronology is hard to adjust to a motivation in which fear would figure predominantly: the heyday of the church-papist evidently came before 1580, and discussions of the topic by Allen and others refer to this period; but the major constraining force, fear that a gentleman's recusancy would shatter the family property, did not arise until after the statute of 1581. Before this date, it has been suggested, the chief legal deterrent was excommunication, and this would imply that what then held Catholics back from recusancy was less a fear of the consequences of breaking the law as a positive attachment to the general life of the community.[34] For the gentry this motive had particular force, and Catholic gentry, probably more strongly than others, felt in their bones that differences of religious practice were extremely bad for social order and political stability; that since at least the middle of the century forces had been at work towards the lower end of English society which were threatening to bring in an anarchic congregationalism; and that in face of this danger it behoved them to do what they could to strengthen parochial discipline. In these circumstances, to cease to attend one's parish church must appear, to oneself and to neighbours whose opinions one respected, a grave dereliction of social duty and a shocking example to sectaries and separatists. As such, if for no other reason, it also suggested a neglect of the obligations of one's allegiance.

On this point, and before the seminary priests arrived to give them second thoughts, the Catholic gentry had a position that was perhaps so axiomatic to them that they scarcely felt the need to put it into words.

figures from Hampshire and Lancashire; Walker, 'Implementation', pp. 33 ff., 124, 13; *Microcosmography*, p. 25—examples in W. R. Trimble, *The Catholic Laity in Elizabethan England* (Cambridge, Mass., 1964), p. 124 (being 'out of charity' an excuse for not going to church), and K. R. Wark, *Elizabethan Recusancy in Cheshire* (Chetham Society, 1971), pp. 6 f.; Knox, *Allen Letters*, pp. 31 f.
34. Knox, *Allen Letters*, p. 56; Walker, 'Implementation', p. 12.

It depended on a distinction, which the religious history of sixteenth-century Europe was almost everywhere tending to present with a clarity unknown to the mediaeval Christian, between the public and the private life. Like landowners throughout Europe, they had no real doubt that, whatever the statute-book might say, they were entitled to 'liberty of conscience': to observe, that is, whatever form of Christianity appealed to them, and to cause it to be observed by others with the orbit of their private or domestic authority. They might also have fairly expansive ideas about how far such an authority might extend; but they all seem to have thought that it ended somewhere. Beyond it was a sphere of public religious activity in which the Queen had the right to take such steps as she saw fit, and here it was their duty to comply with her wishes by physical presence at public worship as and when she required it. They were aware that this presence might be regarded as sinful but that, they felt, was the Queen's problem, not theirs. Parsons, in the book he wrote while in England to change the gentry's attitude on this point, pictured them as 'saying, that al which is done amisse shal not be layed uppon them at the daye of iudgment, but upon the Prince and the Magistrats, which compel them to doe the same against their owne willes'. This point of view was only disingenuous in so far as it implied the presence, at this time, of really coercive constraints; otherwise, we ought to give it the weight appropriate to its having convinced, if only temporarily, so serious a Catholic as Sir Thomas Cornwallis, and reduced Sir Thomas Tresham to acute embarrassment when he found himself forced to renounce it.[35]

Historians have paid more attention to the withdrawal of Catholics from the worship of the Church of England than to the evolution of their experience of the Mass. Here we must try to redress the balance, for their separation was a positive as well as a negative act. Its traumas were easiest to face for anyone who could feel that a whole community was seceding with him, but not many Catholics were in this fortunate case. There were certainly parts of the country where the missionary priests inherited something like a ready-made congregation from the past, and could even, from among the remote chapels which had sometimes been left high and dry by the Reformation, find a consecrated building to house it. Cases of this appear on the Welsh borders, revealed by the investigation which followed an outbreak of religious

35. Parsons, *Brief Discourse why Catholics refuse to go to Church* ('Doway', 1580), f. 23; McGrath, *Papists and Puritans*, pp. 106 f.; cf. above, chap. 2, pp. 37 f.

rioting in 1605; in 1618 the Catholics of Great Singleton in the Fylde actually bought one such chapel and used it thereafter for Mass. But spare chapels were hard to come by in Lancashire and this seems to have been unique; for the most part one hears of Mass being said and sermons preached in barns and farmyards. This did not necessarily imply a makeshift organisation or modest claims; a member of parliament in the 1620s thought that Lancashire Catholics chose times and places for Mass which would ensure that on their way home they met the Protestants coming out of church. This may not have meant that they were spoiling for a fight, as he supposed; but it suggests some consciousness of a claim to constituting the genuine parochial or congregational community which survived in parts of the uplands until the mid-seventeenth century, and later perhaps in Lancashire: we hear, during the Restoration, of a Mass-centre at Kirkham in the Fylde 'whither visibly and ordinarily do resort some hundreds'. Such large-scale secessions were a rarity, and confined to weakly parochialised parts of the country; despite a certain amount of nostalgia, few of the Catholic laity were by this time concerned to argue with the Anglican clergy who put their Mass-assemblies down under the general heading of non-conformist 'meetings' or 'conventicles'.[36]

In either of the social forms which these now took, they were clearly sectarian in character. Such of the gentry as had sooner or later made up their minds 'never', as Francis Tregian had written, 'to eat profaned/ The lamb without thy house' had made arrangements to secure a permanent provision at home; by somewhere about the mid-seventeenth century, for reasons which will be discussed later, the usual arrangement was the simple but rather extravagant one of keeping a priest permanently in the house. It may help us to grasp the extent of the accompanying domestication of the Mass if we remember that it was for a long time unusual for it to be offered in anything that was architecturally speaking a chapel. The idea that gentry families in any significant number had Mass said more or less continuously in their chapels from before the Reformation to modern times has been found attractive by some and irritating by others, but is in any case not true; of three

---

36. Dickens, *English Reformation*, pp. 212 f.; Pugh, 'Glamorgan Recusants' (see above, chap. 5, n. 37), p. 51; R. Mathias, *Whitsun Riot* (London, 1963), pp. 22 f., 49; C.R.S. liii, pp. 133, 135 f.; Leys, *Catholics in England*, p. 63; Foley, *Records of the English Province S.J.*, vii part 2, p. 1108; Magee, *English Recusants*, p. 46; *V.C.H. Lancashire*, ii, p. 92; J. Rogan, 'Episcopal Visitations in the Diocese of Durham, 1662–71', *Archaeologia Aeliana*, 4th series, xxxiv (1956), p. 96.

suggested cases, two will not stand up to investigation and the third (Stonor in Oxfordshire) seems extremely hypothetical. In general it appears that families which possessed a pre-Reformation chapel attached or adjacent to their houses avoided using it; partly for security, but mainly so as not to fall foul of the ecclesiastical authorities. In two West Riding cases discussed by Aveling—Hazelwood (Vavasours) and Carlton (Stapletons)—the chapel had also Anglican parochial functions; during the seventeenth century the families contented themselves with sabotaging these by appointing absentee parsons or none at all; during the eighteenth, significantly enough, they felt safe enough to take the offensive, and tried to recapture the chapels for their own, and Catholic, use. In the first case they were successful and in the second they were not.[37]

There are also some early instances of new chapels being built: we are told that Lady Montagu, Sir Everard Digby and others did this, and as late as 1616 Francis Ratcliffe built an unpretentious but solid one at Dilston which is still standing, though it has been used for Anglican worship since 1715.[38] But with these exceptions Mass on Sunday, or more often, was as domestic as fish on Friday. It followed a well-marked itinerary around the house, from the halls and 'fair, large chambers' where the congregations of the Elizabethan pioneers assembled, like Campion's before his arrest at Lyford; up to the less vulnerable attics where many of the first generation of chaplain-missioners sat 'like sparrows upon the house top' and most of the earliest special Mass-chambers were fitted up; thence, as the seventeenth century drew to a close and houses perhaps grew larger, tentatively down to the first floor, where a suite of rooms accommodated priest, chapel and sacristy; and finally back to ground level by the middle of the eighteenth century —though scarcely as yet to the new generation of outdoor chapels which began to go up a decade or so after it.[39]

Mass in this environment was, in reality as in theory, very much a private Mass for a private congregation; outsiders came to it by invita-

37. A. L. Rowse, *Tudor Cornwall* (London, 1941), p. 353; Aveling, *West Riding*, pp. 264 ff.; R. J. Stonor, *Stonor* (Newport, Mon., 1951), pp. 356 f.
38. Southern, *An Elizabethan Recusant House*, p. 43; *Autobiography of John Gerard*, pp. 168 f.; P.R.O. S.P. 14/89/31, cf. above, chap. 5, p. 81.
39. Aveling, *West Riding*, pp. 249 f.; *Northern Catholics*, pp. 388 f.; Waugh, *Edmund Campion*, p. 157; Rowlands, 'Catholics in Staffordshire' (see above, n. 19), p. 175; below, chap. 11, p. 255. On special occasions the Blundells had Mass 'on the stairs' at Little Crosby: *Great Diurnal of Nicholas Blundell*, i, p. 67.

tion. This posed a number of missionary problems, which will be discussed in due course; but since, in that context, the conduct of the gentry may come in for criticism, it seems worth pointing out, in the present one, that Mass was so domestic an occasion that an invitation to attend it seems to have been generally understood as an invitation to breakfast as well—with the family, or the servants, according to rank—and one may spare an occasional thought for the gentry in this position.[40] The domestic context added a distinctive tone to the event, though not by any means a uniform one. One may find it in the classic portrait of the domestic counter-reformation at its height in the south Yorkshire household of the Babthorpes at Osgodby in the 1620s, described by one of the priests who served there:

> Our house I might rather consider a religious house than otherwise . . . On the Sundays we locked the doors and all came to Mass, had our sermons, catechisms and spiritual lessons every Sunday and Holyday. On the workdays we had for the most part two Masses . . . one for the servants at six o'clock in the morning, at which the gentlemen, every one of them without fail and the ladies if they were not sick would, even in the midst of winter, of their own accord be present; and the other we had at eight o'clock for those who were absent from the first.

The average household of this date is probably better represented by the suggestion that on weekdays members would take turns to come to the priest's early-morning Mass in the attic, as much to keep him company as for any reason of devotion. The sacred and the domestic might mingle in various proportions. At the end of the century John Gother complained of those who came to communion 'in such a disrespectful undress that it would be an affront to the meanest Friend . . . which can be called nothing less than stepping out of Bed to the Altar'. He was equally censorious of those who dressed up too much, and 'approach[ed] the Holy Table powdered, patch'd, perfumed, bare-necked, or any other ways so set forth as seems more suitable for a Ball . . .' Neither of these alternatives sounds as disquieting as an incidental reference among the instructions for grooms in the Petre household at Ingatestone in the mid-eighteenth century: they were to get up at five to wash and

---

40. Good examples in J. Gillow and A. Hewitson (eds.), *The Tyldesley Diary, 1712–14* (Preston, 1873), pp. 26, 74 and *passim*; and see above, p. 117, and below, p. 328.

feed the horses, and 'by half-past eight . . . will have a good stomach themselves and may be allowed an hour and a half to hear Mass and eat their breakfast'.[41] It was certainly a universal assumption, visible at Osgodby as well as at Ingatestone, that servants could not be expected to appreciate the finer points: but if each had been typical of its time we should have to recognise a sad falling-off in the intervening century or so. But each was an extreme case of tendencies which were undoubtedly there; between the two, most houses seem to have maintained a steady level of devotion.

To describe the domestic Mass-going of the gentry as nonconformist or sectarian in character may seem wrong in tone, however justified in principle; but the tone is perfectly appropriate to the alternative environment of Mass-attendance, which emerged later but grew more common as the other tended to contract, the independent Mass-house, located in a farmhouse, or in a building specially designed but similarly constructed. There were not many of these before 1700, and there seems to be no full description of their *mores* for a century after that. At this time the country Mass was almost more of a social event than it was for the gentry in their houses. Those who were communicating, no doubt a small minority on ordinary Sundays, came separately to chapel at 8 a.m. and went home to breakfast; everyone dressed in their Sunday suits and came to Mass at ten, and those who came from a distance stayed to dinner with those who lived nearby; after dinner the children were sent off to catechism, and the rest followed shortly after for rosary and evening prayers before going home. Probably arrangements had become more formal in the course of the eighteenth century; but Nicholas Blundell's diary reveals this pattern of Mass-going at Little Crosby around 1720, and we have a vivid account of something almost identical, also from Lancashire, which dates from before the Civil War.[42] We may then take it as characteristic of country missions as soon as they existed.

41. Morris, *Troubles of our Catholic Forefathers*, iii, pp. 467 f.; Aveling, *East Riding*, pp. 33 f. (Osgodby), cf. the Montagu household at Battle in Southern, *An Elizabethan Recusant House*, p. 47; Foley, *Records of the English Province*, ii, p. 4; John Gother, *Instructions for Confession, Communion and Confirmation* (London, 1744 edn), pp. 112 f.; J. Stephan, 'Notes on a Petre Household Book', *Notes and Queries*, cciii (1958), p. 98.
42. Aveling, *Northern Catholics*, pp. 387 f.; Robert Gradwell, in Ward, *The Sequel to Catholic Emancipation*, i, p. 187; Rowlands, 'Catholics in Staffordshire', p. 210; *Great Diurnal of Nicholas Blundell*, ii, pp. 247, 278; and below, chap. 11, p. 262. The last two references are not however to ordinary Sundays, but to feast days.

Another characteristic of such missions was that a priest might not be available every Sunday, sometimes not more than once a month or less; in such cases Catholics would say their prayers at home, or improvise a service for themselves, as they seem to have done fairly widely in the later eighteenth century.[43] In so far as regular as well as exclusive Mass-going was essential to the construction of a Catholic community, it is obvious that this took a great deal longer to achieve than withdrawal from the services of the Church of England. Taking a weekly attendance as the norm, we may judge that the gentry and their dependants exceeded it and the rest of the community fell short of it; it was perhaps mainly in the town chapels which emerged in the course of the eighteenth century, and united in various ways the experience of both *milieux*, that weekly Mass-going became habitual for all.

We may finally enquire, from the point of view of the layman, what Catholics actually did when they went to Mass; from the date we have reached, it is possible to look back and see an evolution which may be partly understood in the light of the social background just described. In its earliest phase the attitude of congregations retained, as one would expect, several of the more doubtful features of pre-Reformation practice. Among these, the cultivation of feasts and saints' days at the expense of the ordinary Sunday has already been noticed;[44] to it one may add the urge towards multiple Mass-hearing which one finds in a woman of old-fashioned religious sensibilities like Lady Montagu, who normally heard three Masses a day, one from each of her three chaplains, 'and more would willingly have heard if she might'.[45] Circumstances were however against the survival of the second practice, and though to some extent they encouraged the first, we have seen that the festal cycle gradually lost its compelling power. What survived more strongly than either, no doubt because it was less obviously open to criticism, was the idea that Mass-time was mainly a specially aus-

43. J. Gother, *Instructions and Devotions for Hearing Mass* (?London, 1744 edn), pp. 34, 113 ff.; Aveling, *West Riding*, p. 250; Stonor's *Exercise of Devotion . . . for the use of such neighbourhoods and families, as have not the opportunity of assisting at Church-service* (below, chap. 11, p. 274); S. Leslie (ed.), *From Cabin-boy to Archbishop: the Autobiography of Archbishop Ullathorne* (London, 1941), p. 9—Scarborough, *c.* 1820.

44. Also R. Howell, *Newcastle-upon-Tyne in the Puritan Revolution* (Oxford, 1967), p. 74—Hebburn and Thornley 'frequented by the Papists in greater multitudes on their Saints' Days and Festivals than divers parish churches in the county by the Protestants and the Lord's Day'.

45. Southern, *An Elizabethan Recusant House*, p. 47.

picious time for exercises of interior devotion. When Sir Thomas Cornwallis read his psalter in church, he was probably doing much what he
would have done if he had been at Mass. At the end of the seventeenth
century John Gother's *Instructions and Devotions for Hearing Mass*
assumed that most Catholics had only a very vague idea of what actually
went on at Mass; the object he set himself, of getting the people to
'accompany' the priest, as he put it, would be a new departure even for
the best of them. Most people, he thought, assumed that what went on
at the altar was purely the priest's business; theirs was to be present and
reap its fruits by meritorious prayer in the meantime. 'For this End we
see some saying their Beads all the time of Mass, others their Morning
Prayers, others the Offices of the Day, or some private Devotion, and
but with little regard to what the priest does'; he made the modest
suggestion that they might 'spare so much time from their private devotions, as to comply with [the] greater duty' of offering the sacrifice with
the priest. He provided a brisk translation of the ordinary of the Mass
and, as a mode of Mass-attendance, following the priest through a
vernacular text in a missal or something similar must have gained
currency from the diffusion of his *Instructions* during the eighteenth
century. It did not, admittedly, become general practice in quite the
form which Gother had recommended; after 1740 most Catholics went
to Mass with Challoner's *Garden of the Soul*, which represented a compromise between the two positions. Neither Gother nor Challoner were,
of course, any help to members of a congregation who could not read,
a fairly high proportion at this date; they were still recommended to say
the rosary.[46]

One may probably associate individualistic and participatory forms
of Mass-devotion with the different *mores* of the gentry and what one
may term the 'third estate', and justifiably see the movement from one
towards the other after 1700 as a consequence of social changes in the
community which will be discussed in due course. Yet even so this
movement was generally appropriate to the situation of a community
which needed strong congregational bonds but would not find much

---

46. Gother, *Instructions and Devotions for Hearing Mass*, pp. 7–8, 9; cf. the ?sermon
notes of Mary Middleton of Stockeld, written on the flyleaf of an Office of Our Lady,
undated but ?Restoration: 'When the faythfull go to masse they ought to ioyne with
the Priest and offer up the Body and Blood of Christ . . .' (Aveling, *West Riding*,
p. 250); discussion in Aveling, *Northern Catholics*, p. 252, of Richard Lascelles's
Little Way How to Heare Mass with Profit and Devotion (1644); *West Riding*, p. 266;
and see below, chap. 14, pp. 369 f.

warrant for them in Catholic doctrine at large. In his *Instructions* Gother placed just before the Consecration a short prayer, which may strike a modern reader as reactionary or over-optimistic, but was pertinent and proper at the time:

> Behold, O Lord, we all here, tho' of different conditions, yet united by Charity, as members of that one Body of which thy dear Son is head, present to thee in this Bread and Wine, the Symbols of our perfect Union . . .

Gother, we may observe, had grown up a Presbyterian, and as such may have had a particularly clear view of the needs of a body which remained universalist in theory but had had to adjust to separatism in practice.[47]

(iii)

THE RITES OF PASSAGE

The rites of passage—baptism, marriage and burial—do not often figure very largely in studies of Christian behaviour, perhaps because they appear simply to reinforce existing forms of social relation, which may be regarded as an inferior thing for Christianity to be doing.[48] Yet just for this reason they may be felt as of special importance in a threatened community whose continuing existence they protect. I therefore propose to consider briefly how they were experienced by English Catholics in this period, and specifically how they were involved in the process of separation. It seems proper to treat them last, partly because in some respects separation took longer to accomplish here than elsewhere, and partly because, as fundamental elements in the constitution of the community, they have an obvious connection with the subject of the following chapter. I have not been concerned with the substance of the rituals themselves; but I should add that, if full account were to be taken of the ritual as well as the social senses of the word separation,

47. *Instructions and Devotions*, p. 63; cf. Gradwell's comment on the rural congregations (*loc. cit.*, above, n. 42): 'This common assembling of all together has good effects. It forms the whole congregation into one family . . .'; *D.N.B.*, Gother.
48. But cf. A. Macfarlane, *The Family Life of Ralph Josselin* (Cambridge, 1970), pp. 81 and ff.; also my own 'Counter-Reformation and the People of Catholic Europe', *Past and Present*, no. 47 (1970), pp. 56 f.

two subjects would call for attention. The first arises from the fact, observed by van Gennep in the work whose title I have borrowed here, that the sacrament of baptism as practised by Catholics included a ritual of separation (exorcism) as well as a ritual of incorporation (water, the sign of the cross).[49] This was not the case among Protestants; hence it might be possible to observe in the baptismal practice of Catholics traces of the claim to superior purity which has been visible in other features of their religious behaviour. The second is the subject of mixed marriage. I find myself embarrassed by not having dealt with this important topic here, but it would be hard to dispose of at tolerable length; roughly speaking, in this period the clergy opposed it and the gentry avoided it, but there seems to have been little prejudice against it in the rest of the community.[50] It is difficult to know which of these attitudes to regard as a token of sectarian status.

In the teaching of the seminary priests, baptism, marriage and burial were as much as church attendance matters in which there could be no communicating with heretics, and though this may sometimes seem a hard doctrine one cannot easily envisage a distinct Catholic community continuing in existence which did not control its own means of survival. There is also very little sign, at least until a new problem was created by the Marriage Act of 1753, that anyone really objected to it, either among the gentry or in the rest of the community. On the part of the gentry this may seem a little surprising: a Protestant baptism, for example, was generally understood to be valid; a statute of 1606 added a £100 fine to the ecclesiastical penalties already in existence for clandestine baptism, and the church courts maintained until the Civil War a fairly heavy pressure on this point. One might also have expected the gentry to be affected by the feeling generally abroad in sixteenth-century Europe that orderly societies required as watertight a system of parochial registration as could be devised.[51]

What seems to have weighed heavier than all this was an overriding sense of the importance of family, and that public authority had no

49. A. van Gennep, *The Rites of Passage* (London, 1960), pp. 10 f., 63, 93 ff.; Macfarlane, *op. cit.*, p. 88.

50. A good guide to the subject is the section on Roman Catholics in D. J. Steel and Edgar R. Samuel, *Sources for Roman Catholic and Jewish Genealogy and Family History* (National Index of Parish Registers, iii, Society of Genealogists, London/Chichester, 1974), pp. 870–875. (Cited hereafter as 'Steel, *Sources*'.)

51. Dickens, 'First Stages', p. 170; 'Extent and Character', pp. 37, 40 (see above, chap. 5, n. 4); Leys, *Catholics in England*, p. 60; Steel, *Sources*, p. 851.

claim to obedience in respect of acts and occasions where it was most intimately concerned. From an outsider observing the Northumbrian Catholic gentry in the 1580s we get a glimpse of vigorous life in this region: 'themselves or their kindred, being papists, have diverse conferences and conventicles amongst them; and the women also have like conversing and meetings at gentlewomen's labours, children's christenings, and by such other means'. More than a century later Nicholas Blundell records such an occasion at Little Crosby for the birth of his first daughter: they must have been universal.[52] Home baptism fitted very naturally into these surroundings, especially after most of the houses of the gentry had a resident priest; they seem to have been told that baptism as soon as possible was a consequence of Catholic sacramental teaching, and to have diffused throughout the rest of the community a habit of promptitude in this respect.[53] On the other hand they were anxious to avoid any legal tangles or grounds for alleging illegitimacy which might follow failure to have their children entered in parish registers, and missionaries were prepared to sanction a variety of methods for ensuring this: including bribing the parson to enter children as baptised by himself or, where he was adamant, allowing him to baptise the child a second time. What was probably more typical than either was the entry of the vicar of Pyrton in Oxfordshire, in 1635, to the effect that, 'at the request of Mr Shepherd, Mr William Stonor's curate'—that is, the priest resident at Stonor—he had entered the christenings of the Stonor children in his register, though none of them had been baptised in the parish church, and he professed not to know when, where and by whom they had been baptised. In most cases, provided the fee was paid, parsons were willing to make some compromise of this kind.[54] What seems implied in all this is that baptism was a field where practically no one was really prepared to question paternal authority; in a decision which recalls their views about fasting, the missionaries conceded that, if a Catholic couple gave birth while living in the household and under the guardianship of a Protestant

52. Report of Robert Arden to Earl of Huntingdon, 1578, printed by M. Claire Cross, *Archaeologia Aeliana*, 4th series, xli (1963), p. 133; *Great Diurnal of Nicholas Blundell*, i, p. 67.
53. Steel, *Sources*, p. 849; Rowlands, 'Catholics in Staffordshire', p. 214; Bossy, 'Four Catholic Congregations in rural Northumberland', *Recusant History*, ix (1967), pp. 100 f., and 'More Northumbrian Congregations', *ibid.*, x (1969), p. 23.
54. Aveling, *West Riding*, p. 250; Steel, *Sources*, pp. 852 f.; Leys, *Catholics in England*, p. 63; *V.C.H. Oxfordshire*, ii, p. 45, n. 1.

relative, it would be proper for the child, if so demanded, to be baptised in church.[55]

In the rest of the community views do not seem to have been so firm: it must have been difficult, especially before the days of settled congregational life in the eighteenth century, to get one's children baptised by a Catholic priest without unreasonable delay, and sooner than leave them heathens parents were probably willing to go to the parson. One may ask why, in these perfectly legitimate circumstances, people did not baptise their children themselves; and I can see no answer to this question, other than that, before the general diffusion of catechism in the eighteenth century, they were not aware that they could baptise, or in any case did not know how to do it. Where signs of lay-baptism appear in the seventeenth century, they usually point to midwives rather than to parents; at Little Crosby in 1705 we find a newborn child of a tenant being baptised by the landlord's wife.[56] There seems no firm evidence that this ignorance or lack of self-confidence had been overcome before the middle of the eighteenth century; after this, mission registers often refer to conditional baptism by the priest of children who had presumably been baptised by their parents already, in case they died.[57]

It is obvious that the appearance of a separate, congregational register of baptisms marks an important concluding step in the process of separation. I am not suggesting that without a distinct baptismal register you cannot have a distinct community, and there were fairly convincing reasons of prudence for not starting one before the middle of the eighteenth century; but the recording hand may here have been less far behind the social event than might be supposed. Perhaps the statutes of William and Mary, and of Anne, which required incumbents to enter in a separate register the births of dissenters' children, are nearer the true terminus in this respect; the instruction seems to have been understood as including those of Catholics, and to have been fairly widely observed in the North-east, if not elsewhere.[58]

55. Aveling, *West Riding*, p. 251.
56. Steel, *Sources*, p. 853; Aveling, *East Riding*, p. 27; *Great Diurnal of Nicholas Blundell*, i, p. 84. Challoner printed the form of baptism in a prominent place at the beginning of the *Garden of the Soul*.
57. e.g. at Biddlestone, Northumberland: C.R.S. xiv, pp. 254 f.
58. Steel, *Sources*, pp. 853 f.; D. D. Dixon, 'Notes on the Jacobite Movement in Upper Coquetdale', *Archaeologia Aeliana*, ii series, xvi (1894), p. 110 (Rothbury parish); Aveling, *Catholic Recusancy in York*, pp. 118 f.

Of all the acts which marked their separation from the Church of England, the withdrawal from Anglican marriage was the one which disturbed Catholics least, and this although a statute of James I claimed, among other penalties, to invalidate the common-law rights of recusant partners in a clandestine marriage. In this case social instinct and precedent were more than usually explicit: Catholics had on their side a long, powerful and not yet exhausted tradition that marriage was the effect of private contractual agreement between individuals or families and that the presence of a priest or parson was essential neither to its legal validity nor to its status as a sacrament. For continental Catholics the position had been radically altered by the Council of Trent, which for the first time made publicity a condition of both; substantially the same change was to come in England in 1753. In the meantime there was little to alarm recusants in the prospect of marrying without the parson; they do not seem to have been particularly concerned to get him to put their marital record in his register; and the church courts gave up trying to get them to conform at an early date.[59] For the gentry, at any rate, marriage remained almost as safely entrenched in the domestic environment as fasting and abstinence: the processes of exploration, of courtship, betrothal, negotiation and marriage in the house of the bride or her relations, pursued their course unchanged from the reign of Elizabeth to that of George II. In the 1570s Edmund Lord Sheffield and Ursula Tyrwhitt were betrothed in the 'great dining chamber' of her father's house, Thornton College in Lincolnshire, and the following day, when a priest had arrived, less publicly 'married with a Mass' in the steward's room. In 1799, after the Marriage Act had added one new element to the scene, Sir Thomas Webb and Fanny Dillon were married at the London house of her relatives, the Jerning-hams: the (Anglican) Bishop of Exeter officiated 'in the Dining Room' at 10 a.m.; the (Catholic) Archbishop of Narbonne, a Dillon, arrived at 11 and 'performed with great dignity below in the Parlour . . . We all then went up again and there was a large table with tea, coffee and chocolate.' In between we have Nicholas Blundell's laconic entry for 17 June 1703, when he was with the Webbs at Hatherop: 'I was married to Lord Langdale's Doughter by Mr Slaughter a Clergyman [i.e.

59. Aveling, 'The marriages of Catholic Recusants, 1559–1642', *Journal of Ecclesiastical History*, xiv (1963), pp. 68 ff. and 68–93 *passim*; cf. my own 'Counter-Reformation and the People of Catholic Europe', *Past and Present*, no. 47 (1970), pp. 56 f.

secular priest].'[60] Before the Civil War, and especially in the hardier North, it was often thought safer to perform the actual marriage ceremony outside the house. The Northumbrian gentry tended to slip across the Border; and from various parts of the North one hears of couples married 'in a field', 'under a tree' or 'in a close . . . by the light of a lanthorn' and that in the middle of a January night.[61]

By contrast with baptism, it seems to have been clear to most people that a valid, and lawful, sacramental marriage could take place without the presence of a priest: in the seventeenth century Jesuit missioners at least were at pains to explain the point. The secular clergy, who never quite gave up hope of seeing the Council of Trent in force in England, were possibly less forthcoming at the time and seem to have become evasive on the question in the eighteenth century.[62] There was therefore less reason why Catholics below the gentry should have found any difficulty in marrying, or have resorted to the parson, and they do not seem to have done so before 1753. Some at least of the numerous clandestine marriages of labouring Catholics from Cleveland and the Pennines which turn up in the church courts in the early seventeenth century seem to have been performed without a priest. By the time of Nicholas Postgate, who worked in this area somewhat later, this was probably no longer true: beginning in the 1630s, he was said to have married 226 couples in 34 years. One Saturday in January 1708 Nicholas Blundell records what must have been a very typical case: 'John Kerpy and Elizabeth Py come to be married but Mr Aldred [the priest] being gone to Lidiat [Lydiate Hall] . . . they stay'd till he came after supper, and then were Maryed.'[63]

About this time, as with baptism, a point of equilibrium seems to have been reached: the ordinary Catholic had become incorporated into a fairly effective congregational structure, and would normally be married by the priest in charge, though there was nothing to prevent the couple from picking any priest they chose. In the Midland district the vicars-apostolic were now requiring priests to report marriages to

60. Aveling, 'Marriages', p. 72; E. Castle (ed.), *Jerningham Letters* (London, 1896), i, p. 151; Leys, *Catholics in England*, p. 192, cf. the case of Mrs Fitzherbert and the Prince of Wales, December 1785, in S. Leslie, *Mrs Fitzherbert* (London, 1939), pp. 23 f., 52; *Great Diurnal of Nicholas Blundell*, i, p. 37.
61. Aveling, *art. cit.*, pp. 74, 77; *West Riding*, p. 251; Surtees Society, xxxiv, p. 69.
62. Aveling, *art. cit.*, p. 70; Burton, *Challoner*, i, p. 343 and n.
63. Aveling, *art. cit.*, pp. 77, 83; Steel, *Sources*, p. 858; *Great Diurnal of Nicholas Blundell*, i, p. 160.

them, and those who married people from another mission to inform the priest who served it. On the other hand the Anglican clergy had, with very occasional exceptions, given up the attempt to treat couples married before a Catholic priest as fornicators, and one might have foreseen that as a result of the 1695 Act the claim to parochial marriage would shortly settle into a service of parochial registration.[64] Neither of these was a novel position: the relevant case at ecclesiastical law had been decided, during the Wentworth regime, at York in 1637, when the archbishop's Chancery Court had accepted as valid a marriage admitted to have been celebrated by one seminary priest and witnessed by two others; this precedent seems to have been maintained. In 1653, the Commonwealth had brought in a system of civil marriage and registration, and the Chapter had decided that this was perfectly acceptable, though Catholics should see their priest beforehand, receive his nuptial blessing afterwards and not consummate the marriage before they had done so.[65] This reform, which would have prevented a great deal of trouble in future, was abolished at the Restoration, and Catholics enjoyed a century of almost complete immunity until the passage of the Marriage Act in 1753.

There is some question as to whether they used it wisely or not,[66] but it seems probable that in their case the Act did not regularise a disorderly situation, but disturbed a satisfactory one: except for Quakers and Jews, it invalidated marriages not celebrated publicly, in the parish church or elsewhere with licence, according to the rites of the Church of England, and made the celebration of marriage in other circumstances a felony carrying, for the officiating party, a penalty of transportation for fourteen years. Assurances were eventually given to Catholics that the ceremony should be treated as a purely civil affair, but the Act was none the less for them a reversal of the normal evolution of things. It says a lot for the power which the Tridentine ideal still had over the vicars-apostolic that they made so embarrassed an opposition to it.

64. Rowlands, 'Catholics in Staffordshire', pp. 33, 216; Steel, Sources, pp. 859, 861.
65. Aveling, 'Marriages', p. 81; West Riding, p. 251; Steel, Sources, p. 861, cf. Archives of the Old Brotherhood, Mss. ii, f. 332—decision of Chapter, 1653.
66. Evidence of matrimonial misbehaviour may be found in the polemical account of Peter Fitton (1632), in P. Hughes, Rome and the Counter-Reformation in England (London, 1942), pp. 421–422; Aveling, 'Marriages', pp. 72, 82 f.; an Anglo-Irish case in B. Jennings (ed.), Wadding Papers, 1614–38 (Irish Manuscripts Commission, Dublin, 1953), pp. 337 f.

Provided that couples did not actually participate in the Anglican service by kneeling or prayers, they were prepared to agree that Catholics should now go through two marriage ceremonies, and contented themselves with trying to ensure that the Catholic one came first. On the whole this strikes one as an unnecessarily feeble position, and it was certainly untenable.[67] For the gentry, who were in any case accustomed to paying fees to two sets of clergy, it was an invitation to get their money's worth, and for some time they seem generally to have followed the bishops' advice: thus in 1780 Thomas Whitgreave of Moseley in Staffordshire was married at home by his chaplain; the following day everybody, priest included, proceeded to Saredon parish church for the parson's marriage, and the whole party came home to dinner.[68] It seems a pity to carp at such genuine displays of good feeling, but they were hardly relevant in the rest of the community, who were at the same time advised that they must pay two sets of marriage fees, and given the impression that either sort of marriage would do. The Catholic clergy were put in the absurd position of trying to dragoon unwilling couples to go through a second ceremony in the parish church. Cases have been found where this advice was followed; but on the whole common sense seems to have told people that once was enough. In Wiltshire two congregations whose behaviour has been investigated reacted in opposite ways. At both Stourton and Wardour, everyone had been married by the priest before 1753; afterwards, most of the Stourton congregation went to church, but only a quarter of those who married at Wardour. No doubt the presence of a resident Catholic magnate made them bolder; it would appear that it was more usual for poorer Catholics simply to marry in church, and by the time the Act had been amended the clergy had changed their position so far as to require couples seeking marriage from them to have gone through the Anglican ceremony first.[69] The gentry had already moved to this position, and it was not until 1836 that the Catholic community recovered possession of this part of its social machinery. Had its bishops been less impressed by the dangers of clandestine marriage, the community might have

---

67. My discussion is based on Burton, *Challoner*, i, pp. 325–345.
68. Rowlands, 'Catholics in Staffordshire', p. 218.
69. Burton, *Challoner*, i, 333, 340, 344 f.; Leys, *Catholics in England*, pp. 127 f.; J. A. Williams, *Catholic Recusancy in Wiltshire* (C.R.S. monograph series, i, 1968), pp. 90–92; *Report on the State of the Irish Poor in Great Britain* (Parliamentary Papers, 1836, xxxiv), pp. 3, 23—refusal of Irish immigrants to follow the now recommended practice of Church-marriage first, or indeed at all.

come better out of what seems a rather messy episode in its evolution.[70]

The burial of Catholics added to the tensions arising over baptism and marriage an extra degree of emotional intensity and the material problem of what to do with the body. We need not be surprised that it gave rise to more lively incident than any other step in the passage of the Catholic community to separate existence. It had another distinctive feature. From the sixteenth to the eighteenth century, the burial of Catholics in consecrated ground meant almost invariably burial in the parish churchyard, and the Catholic clergy had no objection to this in itself; in the typical burial case, by contrast with those arising out of baptism and marriage, Catholics were trying to get in to the parochial premises, and parsons were trying to keep them out. If the dead person had been a recusant, he or she had in principle died excommunicate, and so was not entitled to parish burial; in any event Catholics were not very willing to let the parson read the Anglican burial service over their dead.[71]

Incumbents were therefore on strong ground in refusing to accept Catholics in their churchyards, and fairly often did so. In December 1584 Richard Lumbye of Leeds was 'by his kynsfolk and neighbours brought towards the churche to be buried, but at the churchyard gate stopped by the curate and churchwardens, where his corps remained' for the next four days, before apparently being buried somewhere else. In 1603 there occurred in Wiltshire the sensational affair of Thomas Gawen, where legal and religious difficulties were multiplied by family feud, provoking exhumation, riot and a case in Star Chamber. The best known case dates from 1611 and arose in Sefton in Lancashire, where the rector, surrounded as he was by Catholics, none the less determined to take a strong line, and corpses turned away from the churchyard were 'laid, some . . . in the fields, some in gardens, and others in highways as

70. My interpretation of Challoner's attitude depends a great deal on a passage from his letter to Thomas Gibson of Newcastle-upon-Tyne, 4 April 1754, in Burton, *Challoner*, i, p. 333: 'As for our countenancing marriages *absolutely clandestine*, which the Church has always detested, [it] is what should not be thought of.' This seems to be an answer to a query from a northern layman whether Catholics might not get round the act by marrying without a priest at all; and I take it that Challoner's response is related to what appears to have been his private sentiment that the priest was the minister of the sacrament.
71. General discussions in Aveling, *West Riding*, p. 252; Steel, *Sources*, pp. 875–893.

it chanced . . . One of these . . . being interred in a common lane, was
pulled out by the hogs, and used accordingly.'[72]

Few rural communities, one suspects, were prepared to stomach this
kind of clerical intransigence: even in Sefton, where the exclusion was
maintained for eighteen years, it lapsed under the next incumbent.
Sometimes a parson might simply be ignored or overawed by a powerful
landlord; but the usual response, especially in the days before the Civil
War, was for Catholics to bury their dead at night, in circumstances
which according to the views of the parson and the habits of the region
would approximate more nearly to discreet agreement or forcible entry,
and where the most distinctive visual feature of a Catholic funeral, the
carrying of candles or tapers, must often have proved both useful and
picturesque. As one would expect, most of the more exciting occasions
are reported from uplandish parts. Katherine Hodgson of Egton died
in childbirth in 1595, and her brother-in-law John, 'together with all
or most of the recusants of that chapelry did come with the corpse of the
said Katherine in the dawning of the day, having gotten the church key,
into the church, and buried her without any minister'. Mrs Katherine
Ingleby of Lawkland, in Craven, was buried in Clapham church in 1600,
'at sunset', by nine women; Howell Thomas was carried to Caerleon
churchyard by 'a large concourse of persons' early one morning in 1603,
after the Jesuit Robert Jones had said the burial service over his body.
At Allensmore in Herefordshire, in May 1605, the body of a yeoman's
wife was brought to the churchyard at five o'clock in the morning
with cross, bell and candles, and fifty armed men stood round while she
was buried, fending off the parson, who had woken up in the meantime,
and sparking off a general commotion in the region. Accounts of nocturnal burial continue at a steady rate until at least 1630: thirteen are
reported from Hathersage in the High Peak of Derbyshire between
1629 and 1631, and they come from most parts of the south as well as
from the uplands. Here, though, the person buried was most likely to
be from the gentry, and the parson would often be in collusion, as in the
case of Mrs Horseman, of Holton near Oxford, who died on New Year's
Eve, 1630. On the morning of Epiphany it was discovered that the
door of the parish church had been broken open in the night, a grave
dug under the communion table, and Mrs Horseman buried in it.

72. *ibid.*, pp. 74, 77 f., 87; Williams, *Catholic Recusancy in Wiltshire*, p. 223;
Blundell, *Cavalier*, p. 244; T. E. Gibson (ed.), *Crosby Records* (Chetham Society,
1887), p. 41.

Investigation revealed that there had been a wake at her house the night before; when they were questioned, the servants said that so as not to spoil the supper they had put the body in the garden, from which it had unaccountably disappeared.[73]

By this time, the ecclesiastical courts were beginning to give up resistance on this front; a case before the Durham High Commission in 1635, when two men were proved to have attended the burial of a recusant in St Oswald's churchyard in the city, but acquitted, looks like a test case of the same kind as the marriage case at York mentioned above.[74] As President of the Council in the North, and probably the person really responsible for these ecclesiastical decisions, Wentworth offered a positive solution, by which parsons would admit to burial recusants who had entered into his arrangements for fine-compounding, provided the kinsmen applied for a special licence, which would be granted after some conventional acknowledgment that the party had repented of his recusancy at the hour of death. A precedent for this procedure has been found in a case from Essex in 1594, and Aveling implies that it was quite commonly resorted to in the West Riding during the 1630s, which seems surprising, even if the declaration suggested was open to various interpretations; in the case of Mrs Horseman, the lady's relatives had failed to get a licence from the archdeacon because they had refused to make it.[75] In any case, undermined by Wentworth's compounding policy, Anglican resistance to Catholic burial seems to have largely collapsed before the Civil War broke out, and by the Restoration it was far too late to revive it.

Normally, Catholics were now given parish burial by agreement, though the burial service seems to have been said by the priest before the departure of the corpse, and burial at night was perhaps still usual until about 1700. Undisputed local supremacy accounts for Richard Shireburn's success in burying his chaplain at Stonyhurst in Mitton Church, apparently with the Catholic rite performed in broad daylight, in 1677; this would be abnormal at this date. About 1700 the position

---

73. C.R.S. liii, p. 32; Aveling, *West Riding*, p. 252; Steel, *Sources*, pp. 878, 880; R. Mathias, *Whitsun Riot* (London, 1963), pp. 2 f.; *V.C.H. Oxfordshire*, ii, p. 45. Other cases of nocturnal burial in F. A. Gasquet, *Hampshire Recusants* (London, n.d.), p. 52; *V.C.H. Leicestershire*, ii, p. 66; Leys, *Catholics in England*, p. 63; Williams, *Catholic Recusancy in Wiltshire*, pp. 70, 88 f.
74. Steel, *Sources*, p. 882; cf. above, p. 138.
75. Aveling, *West Riding*, p. 252; Steel, *Sources*, p. 876; *V.C.H. Oxfordshire*, ii, p. 45.

at Little Crosby was that everyone, except the priests, was now being buried at Sefton in the daytime, probably without a priest. By 1750 a public Catholic burial in daytime, providing fees were paid, seems to have been acceptable to most parsons; and in parishes where Catholics were strong it was common for a part of the churchyard to be reserved by custom for their use, as at Egton in Yorkshire, or at Tisbury, in the precincts of Lord Arundell of Wardour. Open parish burial was also by this time quite common for priests.[76]

Views may obviously differ about where exactly lay the optimum line of separation for the Catholic community: one which would provide the maximum of self-determining capacity and the minimum of destructive isolation. My own feeling is that while the marriage practice of the community after 1753 lay rather off the optimum line, its burial practice lay fairly exactly on it, and it may well be that one of the reasons was that this was a field in which, broadly speaking, the laity had been left to work out an answer for themselves. It was certainly arguable that it would better suit a separated community to bury its dead in graveyards of its own, and after 1791 this seems fairly soon to have become the sense of the community. The practice was not entirely new. At a very early date a disused graveyard outside Winchester had been taken over by the local Catholic gentry, and it seems to have remained peacefully in Catholic possession and use ever since. At the height of the burial crisis in Sefton, William Blundell enclosed a piece of his own demesne which had vague religious associations, known as the Harkirk; on Sunday morning, 7 April 1611, one of his tenants was buried in it, having first been carried to church and refused burial there. During the next eighteen years over a hundred people were buried in Blundell's graveyard, 'and amongst them some had stones on their graves with crosses, according to the Catholic manner, which were put there by their relations'; some were buried there who had not previously been refused burial at Sefton, like William Tarleton, another Blundell tenant, who 'wish[ed] his wife to bury him after his death in the said burial place, [and] was accordingly there buried'. On the whole, though, instinct seems to have been against it; the burial ground was disturbed by the sheriff in the 1620s, and after the parochial veto had been with-

76. Aveling, *loc. cit.*; Gibson, *Crosby Records*, p. xviii; *Great Diurnal of Nicholas Blundell*, i, pp. 215, 211, 106, etc.; Steel, *Sources*, p. 885; Williams, *Catholic Recusancy in Wiltshire*, p. 88; Leys, *Catholics in England*, p. 123; *Northumberland County History*, xv, p. 214.

drawn in 1629 was used only for priests. In Staffordshire two similar grounds were used, and some advantage may have been taken of the grant of independent burying rights to Protestant nonconformists in 1689; but these are marginal exceptions to the rule that before 1791 the separation of the Catholic community had not yet extended to its dead.[77]

(iv)

TWO SIMPLE QUESTIONS

I have considered the emergence of the English Catholic community as the withdrawal of a separating body from the Church of England. We have seen it as launched by a phase of seasonal nonconformity determined by the anxiety to maintain a traditional and irregular calendar; as crossing the threshold of separation by withdrawing from Anglican worship and adopting an exclusive practice of the Mass; as completing it by developing an exclusive discipline of the *rites de passage*. Incidentally—the point might have been more firmly underlined—we have observed the religious practice of the separated community moving towards a pattern of systematic regularity at variance with the habits of its primitive phase. Except for the first, which may be regarded as our primary datum, these processes were accomplished slowly. A fully developed Catholic community can scarcely be said to have come into existence until they were completed, perhaps about 1700.

This description may help us to answer two simple but serious questions with which I conclude. First, taking as generally correct the assumption that Catholic differed from Protestant nonconformity in being conservative not progressive in character, is it possible to measure the backwardness of Catholics? How far, to be precise, were they behind their contemporaries in maintaining allegiance to a traditional calendar? Second, was the religion of members of the new community the same as or different from, continuous or discontinuous with, the Christianity of the mediaeval church? To try and answer the first question I should

77. Gasquet, *op. cit.*, p. 56; *Crosby Records*, pp. 41, 45 f., 70—register of burials, pp. 69–87; Rowlands, 'Staffordshire', pp. 214 f.; Williams, *Wiltshire*, p. 88; Steel, *Sources*, p. 891.

like to consider the implications of a piece of recent research which does, I think, shed light on both of them.

Between 1538, when they begin, and 1812, the parish registers of the city of York have been investigated to discover changes in the seasonal incidence of marriage. The relevance of this is that it was part of the discipline of the pre-Reformation Church, as it has continued to be part of modern Catholicism, severely to discourage, if not absolutely to forbid, marriage in Lent and Advent; beneath this discipline there may have lain an ascetic instinct associating collective abstinence from food with collective abstinence from sexual relations. Like fasting by the calendar, this prohibition was regarded by Reformers as superstitious, and in England attacked with vehemence by Puritans, though the Church of England sought half-heartedly to maintain it. There was in any case nothing to oblige couples to do violence to their feelings in this respect, and by discovering how far people fought shy of these seasons for marriage we may get some light on the persistence in the collective consciousness of Englishmen in general—perhaps one should say, in their unconsciousness—of a complex of seasonally determined compulsions and taboos.[78]

The marriage statistics at York show that seasonal inhibitions about marriage were still solidly entrenched in 1600 and had largely disappeared by 1750. The change is specially clear in regard to Lent: the percentage of an average monthly total of marriages occurring in March, which one may take as roughly equivalent, was less than twenty in 1538–1601, about thirty-five in 1602–1651, about forty-five in 1652–1701, about seventy-five in 1701–1752 and about seventy in 1752–1812.[79] Taken with the figures for April, which show little or no departure from the average after 1650, they suggest that instinctual or traditional inhibitions ceased to carry much weight after that date. For Advent, which had probably never had the same place as Lent in

---

78. Ursula M. Cowgill, 'The People of York, 1538–1812', *Scientific American*, vol. 222, no. 1 (1970), pp. 104–112; M. M. Knappen, *Tudor Puritanism* (London, 1939), pp. 251–252, 453; K. Thomas, *Religion and the Decline of Magic* (London, 1971), pp. 620 f. Thomas points out that, in theory, the discipline of the Church of England was more restrictive than that of the counter-Reformation Church; this seems, on the whole, to strengthen the case for taking Dr Cowgill's figures as an index of popular instinct, though differing attitudes among the clergy must also have some part in explaining them. Vaux, *Catechisme*, p. 73.

79. One wonders whether the slight relapse after 1750 was due to the entry of Catholic marriages after 1753.

popular feeling, the figures speak less clearly. December was throughout these centuries a month in which people married as much as in other months; it is not of course unlikely that a high proportion of these marriages occurred in the week between Christmas and New Year, and the shadow of a winter close-season seems to be cast forward by the popularity of November as a marrying month, overwhelming until 1600 and considerable afterwards. Only during the second half of the seventeenth century, when for some reason it lost its place to May, was it not the most popular of all months. But though this primacy was maintained until the end of the eighteenth century, there had in the meantime been a radical change from a regime of enormous seasonal variation to one of virtual consistency throughout the year, which may be most simply indicated by giving the ratio, for each half-century or so, between marriages in March and marriages in November. In 1538–1601 it was a good deal higher than 1:10; in 1602–1651, 1:4; in 1652–1701, 1:3; in 1701–1752, 1:2; in 1752–1812, slightly less than 1:2.

It is possible to make a rough comparison in this respect between English Protestants and French Catholics. Pierre Chaunu has assembled a number of tables of seasonality of marriage in France for a period which is not exactly specified but appears to be roughly the seventeenth century. These seem to give, for marriages in Paris, a ratio between March and November of 1:4 or 5, and something rather higher in examples from rural France.[80] Crude as it is at the moment, this comparison may give us some kind of perspective. Without attempting precision I am prepared to take the population of York as roughly representative of the population of England, and also to assume that, for present purposes, marriage-behaviour may be taken as an index of all social acts of religion. If so, we may conclude that a seasonal pattern of religious behaviour had still a powerful hold on Englishmen as a whole in 1600; that it essentially collapsed, mainly no doubt under Puritan pressure, during the first half of the seventeenth century; and that after about 1650 it exerted little or no influence. Thereafter we may assume as a model that acts of religion in England moved in something

80. P. Chaunu, La civilisation de l'Europe classique (Paris, 1966), pp. 205 ff. These tables also show that in France, unlike in England, Advent was as much a close season as Lent; and they also present some evidence from the seasonality of conceptions for sexual abstinence during these seasons. The only place where the effect was really dramatic was in French Canada, where the population appears to have abstained more or less totally during Lent.

resembling a clockwork motion in which Sunday marked the hours and all Sundays were roughly equal.[81]

From what has been said in this chapter, I think it is safe to affirm that during this period the religious practice of English Catholics underwent the same kind of sea-change as that of the great majority of Englishmen who had accepted the Reformation: how much one may attribute this to influences from the English environment, how much one should treat it as a normal effect of the counter-Reformation, is a delicate question which it would be foolish to try and answer here. I think one can also speak with reasonable firmness about the chronology of the change. It had obviously occurred some time before official reform of the calendar began around 1780; at the other end, William Blundell's reflections on the economic consequences of holydays, dating from 1683, are perhaps somewhere near the beginning of the process. On the whole it would seem that the instincts of the English Catholic laity, if not entirely their practice, went over to the clockwork system during perhaps half a century centred on 1700.[82] They may thus be regarded as lagging some three-quarters of a century behind their Protestant countrymen, and a little behind their fellow-Catholics in France.

So simple an answer cannot be given to our second question. We cannot simply regard post-Reformation English Catholicism, in practice, as a continuation of mediaeval English Christianity; on the other hand we evidently cannot regard it as something totally different. What we can do, in the light of the process I have tried to analyse, is to distinguish some continuous from some discontinuous elements, and indicate a relation between them. What was most evidently continuous in the community's pattern of life was the foundation of seasonal observance; but on this foundation, and in various ways against it, were built the structures of separation and regularity which were essentials of the new community. Perhaps we should do better with a Freudian metaphor, and envisage these as disciplines which con-

81. Hill, *Society and Puritanism*, pp. 147 ff.; Thomas, *Religion and the Decline of Magic*, pp. 621–623, who dates the change somewhat later.
82. Note also Gother's 'Instructions for keeping Sunday', in *Instructions and Devotions for Hearing Mass*, pp. 130–151. Gother's teaching is not only rather strict in itself, but (unlike that of Laurence Vaux, above, p. 117) Sabbatarian in Hill's sense; see *ibid.*, pp. 143–145, where the six-day working week is assumed. Gother died in 1704, and his 'Instructions' were probably written during the 1690s: Gillow, *Bibliographical Dictionary of English Catholics*, ii, pp. 540 f.

fronted a primitive material, repressed its abundant energies, diverted them through unfamiliar channels and harnessed them to the setting in motion of a body equipped to survive in the modern world. Separated, scarcely pioneers—except perhaps in separation—Catholics were all the same participants of the civilisation they lived in.

7

CONGREGATION: THE ROLE OF THE GENTRY

We have seen the separative process conclude in the formation of Catholic congregations which possessed a continuing existence: on a large scale, I have suggested, this had hardly occurred much before 1700. How, we need to enquire, had such bodies come to be? The answer given here—that they came into existence by a process of accretion which originated in the family life of the English landowning classes—will rightly seem a partial one. It ignores the role of the priest and the community-forming effects of religious behaviour as such; it ignores the cementing factor of local consensus, and (except among the gentry) those of kinship and irreducible individual decision; it ignores whatever effect external persecution or pressure may have had in the consolidation of groups; it has little to say about the formation of congregations in towns. In defence, I may claim that some of these matters have been touched upon already and others will be dealt with later; besides, to date the process of congregational crystallisation to somewhere around 1700 is, in effect, to ascribe to the gentry the function of principal catalyst. It is time, in any case, to try and grasp the role of the gentry in the formation of the community; and the best way to do this seemed to be to take as model an extreme interpretation of that role, and see how it would fit. This attitude may have the drawback, if it is one, of overemphasising the less heroic moments in the community's construction; it has the advantage of helping to test at least one assumption about the structure of English society in this period. I therefore examine, first, the constitution of the Catholic gentry family itself (meaning husband, wife and children) and, second, the widening circles of dependence through which its influence was felt.

(i)

MAN, WOMAN AND CHILD

Pre-industrial England, we are told, was a patriarchal society, in which all decisions that mattered were made by members of a small group of *patresfamilias* who exercised the authority of fatherhood over all—wife, children, servants and others—who lived beneath their sway. Decisions about religion were decisions where rules of patriarchy might specially have applied, since they determined so much in a family's way of life; it seems advisable to look for the social foundations of the English Catholic community in autonomous decisions made by English patriarchs and mainly, since they were the patriarchs *par excellence*, by patriarchs from the landowning classes.[1]

There is certainly ample evidence that such decisions were made, and at all times in the community's history. Although Catholicism was, generally speaking, a hereditary allegiance, there was nothing fatal about family continuity: the way of life of a 'family' was not really determinable for more than one generation at a time. The remorseless constancy of a family like the Blundells ought not to disguise the fact that in principle every successive head of a family chose its regime anew. Domestic revolutions at the point of succession were in fact frequent, particularly towards the beginning and end of the period. The history of both the two families of classic English nobility—Howard and Talbot—in which Catholicism was most prevalent, are full of them; it would be superfluous to do more than cite the first.

Between 1570 and 1850, there were thirteen heads of the Howard family. Thomas, 4th Duke of Norfolk, executed 1572, was a Protestant; his son Philip (1st Earl of Arundel, who died in the Tower 1595) was brought up a Protestant and converted to Catholicism in 1584; his son Thomas (2nd Earl, connoisseur and traveller, died 1646) was brought up a Catholic by his mother, but turned Protestant in 1615; his son Henry Frederick (3rd Earl, died 1652) was a Protestant too. Of his sons the eldest, Thomas, to whom, as 5th Duke, was restored the dukedom of Norfolk in 1660, was insane; several of the others turned Catholic, following the example of the youngest, Philip, who entered the

1. P. Laslett, *The World we have Lost* (London, 1965), pp. 19 f., etc.; Stone, *Crisis of the Aristocracy*, p. 591.

Dominican order in Italy and eventually became a cardinal; among them Henry (6th Duke, 1677–1684), whose son, also Henry (7th Duke, 1684–1701), returned to the Church of England and helped to bring in William of Orange; he was succeeded in turn by two Catholic nephews (8th and 9th Dukes, 1701–1777), who produced no heirs, and they by an ancient country cousin, also a Catholic (10th Duke, 1777–1786). He was followed by his son Charles (11th Duke, 1786–1815), who had turned Protestant, and died without issue; his cousin and successor Bernard (12th Duke, died 1842) was a Catholic, though his father had not been; his son Henry (13th Duke, died 1856) just managed to remain a Catholic, though he went over to the Church of England for a few years in support of the Ecclesiastical Titles Bill. His son Henry (14th Duke, died 1860) opposed the bill; he had been brought up a Protestant and become a Catholic in 1840 under the influence of Montalembert. So in three hundred years of male succession, the Howards provide only one firm exception to the rule that every son succeeding his father in the headship of the family adopted a different religion.[2]

It would be misleading to give the impression that this was a typical family but what makes its case appear absurd is that it illustrates in practice what was always possible in theory. In framing anti-Catholic legislation, Parliament bore in mind the moment of succession, as in modifying recusancy laws in the first year of James I to establish that a conforming heir was not obliged for any debt to the Exchequer which might be outstanding on account of his father's recusancy; and especially in the act of 1700, which claimed (without much effect) to debar a Catholic heir who succeeded to an estate without conforming, in favour of the nearest Protestant relative who should claim it.[3] But through this period individual choice seems to have had more weight than legal threats, which were rarely as impressive as they appeared. If, with Aveling's help, we look at the gentry of the West Riding of Yorkshire between 1570 and the Civil War, we find plenty of instances of what the Howards did on a more spectacular scale. William Hawkesworth of Otley was a keen follower and kinsman of William Allen, but his sons conformed and Catholicism disappeared from the family. Between 1570 and 1600 there were three successive Thomas Watertons of Walton, of whom the first was a Protestant, the second a recusant and

2. D.N.B., *passim* under Howard; other cases among the aristocracy in J. P. Kenyon, *The Popish Plot* (London, 1962), p. 30.
3. C.R.S. lvii (1965), p. xli; Leys, *Catholics in England*, p. 114.

the third a conforming Catholic. The Inglebys of Ripley, one of the most energetic supporters of Catholicism in Elizabethan Yorkshire, were transformed by the accession in 1617 of Sir William, who had married a Protestant and established the family thereafter as Anglicans; his kinsman William Mallory of Studley did exactly the same when he succeeded his father some eight years later.[4] The eighteenth century is also strong in examples of domestic revolution: in 1753 Lord Teynham, head of the family of Roper, turned up at Douai and told the college authorities he was meditating a long stay in France because his son and heir had just married a Protestant girl and abandoned the Catholic faith. Sir Thomas Gascoigne, a large Yorkshire landowner whose father had died when he was small in 1750 and left him in the care of three Catholic trustees, conformed when he came of age. Sir John Swinburne of Capheaton in Northumberland, who had imbibed ideas of liberty and equality in the course of an education in France, abandoned Catholicism when he inherited in 1786 and cleared it off his land.[5] One case, where the outcome was not the same as these, sheds as clear a light as any on patriarchal assumptions. When Alexander Pope's father died, his Anglican friends delicately suggested that there was now no obstacle to his changing his religion; Pope replied that he would stay as he was, because he had no social ambitions and did not want to grieve his mother.[6]

Patriarchal choice of household regime did not necessarily imply arbitrary government during it; but here one must give their due weight to indications of anti-feminism which crop up in a variety of contexts throughout our period, and might have been anticipated in a body among whose strongest instincts had been from the beginning the instinct for a celibate priesthood. 'Women'—so Clancy has expounded the views of recusant writers like Thomas Fitzherbert—'are poor weak creatures who are prone to heresy (and) do untold harm when they fall on evil ways.' Lord Vaux encountered an instance of something similar when he was sent into custody with a neighbour, whose wife tried to make a Protestant of him. When he got away, he persuaded his friend Sir Thomas Tresham to compose a stiff letter to her complaining 'for that you, being of such modesty and withal so often reading the Scriptures, would so deeply reason with me, and that in the presence of your

4. Aveling, *West Riding*, pp. 226, 227, 243–244.
5. C.R.S. xxviii, p. 293; Aveling, *West Riding*, pp. 261 f.; C.R.S. xiv, pp. 237 f.
6. G. Sherburn, *Early Career of Alexander Pope* (Oxford, 1934), p. 214.

husband', and went on to quote St Paul on the virtues of womanly silence 'and that in their houses they themselves should learn by demanding of their husbands'. From the close of our period we may cite a second time the spoof *Ladies' Address* submitted to the Catholic Committee in 1790. This was an attempt to reduce *ad absurdum* the proposal that the laity should participate in the choice of bishops by claiming the right to vote, if they did, of 'Ladies, Widows, Wives and Spinsters, Housekeepers, Cooks and other Female Persons', who 'constitute[d] one half of the body, and have given birth to the whole' but had hitherto been 'excluded from every duty of the sanctuary except that of sweeping it'.[7] Bearing these comments in mind, we would hardly suppose that the Elizabethan *paterfamilias* who answered so confidently for the behaviour of his household, in one sense to the government and in another sense to the missionary priests, should have had any difficulty in keeping his promises.[8]

There is however plenty of evidence that they had great difficulty in meeting them: so much difficulty that it has been possible to present the community, in its early days, as in effect a matriarchy. In *The England of Elizabeth* A. L. Rowse has advanced the view that English Catholicism was founded not in legitimate decisions made by responsible men but in a series of conjugal *coups d'état* mounted by aggressive wives, and allowed to take root because of the feeble resistance offered to their spouses by too many henpecked husbands.[9] Rowse's portrait of a class victorious on the Narrow Seas but defeated in the kitchen and the nursery is a comic invention of some power; it is surely also to a large degree true.

On few points in the early history of English Catholicism is there such a unanimous convergence of evidence as on the importance of the part played in it by women, and specifically by wives. The administrative and parliamentary record is here exceptionally strong. As early as 1580, before Parliament had really entered the field of recusancy, the

7. T. H. Clancy, *Papist Pamphleteers* (Chicago, 1964), p. 39; Anstruther, *Vaux of Harrowden*, p. 118; Tierney-Dodd, *Church History*, iv, pp. ccxxvii–ccxxxiii; Ward, *Dawn of the Catholic Revival*, i, pp. 228 f.; Leys, *Catholics in England*, p. 141. Cf. Barbara Charlton, *Recollections of a Northumbrian Lady* (ed. L. E. O. Charlton, London, 1949), p. 134: 'My son, remember, only married you because you looked to be a good breeder.'
8. For cases of either, J. Wake, *The Brudenells of Deene* (London, 1954 edn), p. 81; W. R. Trimble, *The Catholic Laity in Elizabethan England* (Cambridge, Mass., 1964), p. 101; C.R.S. xxxix, pp. 337 f.
9. Rowse, *The England of Elizabeth*, pp. 430, 453, 456 f., 458.

Privy Council and the bishop of Winchester were struggling with the legal and psychological problems thrown up among the Hampshire gentry by a high incidence of conformable husbands with recusant wives; the bishop said he had made them give bonds for their wives' good behaviour, and imposed a weekly fine on them for as long as their wives continued absent from church, which the husbands had thought 'something strange'.[10] This was one of the many points at which the heavy-footed intervention of a Puritan-led House of Commons in 1581 did more harm than good, since it transferred recusancy jurisdiction to the courts of Common Law, whose principles could hardly have been less helpful in coping with the problem.[11] In the first place, at common law a wife was a 'femme covert': her property was vested in her husband, and it was therefore useless to indict women recusants directly under the act. At the same time, common law made a distinction between a wife's 'temporal debts', for which a husband could be held responsible, and her 'corporal acts', for which he could not; and this was held to mean that a husband could not coerce his wife's conscience nor be held responsible for her decisions in conscientious matters. It was further held by some interpreters to mean that a wife could not be punished by imprisonment, which the act could possibly be construed to permit, since this would be to punish the innocent husband by upsetting his housekeeping and depriving him of services to which he was entitled.[12] It was some time before a serious attempt was made to undo the damage; the Earl of Huntingdon, as President of the Council of the North, got a reputation for trying to solve the difficulty by prerogative action, including the separation of wives from husbands, either for instruction from Anglican clergy or for imprisonment.[13] A combination of clamour from husbands and a generally unfavourable climate of opinion brought Huntingdon's drive to a halt and in 1593 the Council tried to put a bill through Parliament with a clause which would have imposed on hus-

10. F. A. Gasquet, *Hampshire Recusants* (London, n.d.), pp. 39 f.; cf. Aveling, *Catholic Recusancy in York*, p. 59, etc.
11. Walker, 'Implementation of the Elizabethan Statutes against Recusants' (see above, chap. 6, n. 31), p. 131.
12. Trimble, *Catholic Laity in Elizabethan England*, pp. 151-152; cf. J. D. Hanlon, 'These be but Women', in C. H. Carter (ed.), *From the Renaissance to the Counter-Reformation* (New York, 1965), p. 394, for a story that Elizabeth objected to the imprisonment of women.
13. Aveling, *West Riding*, p. 213; Claire Cross, *The Puritan Earl* (London, 1966), pp. 234 f.; Morris, *Troubles of our Catholic Forefathers*, iii, p. 168; Trimble, *op. cit.*, pp. 152-153.

bands a fine of £10 a month—half the recusancy fine—for having a recusant wife. At the same time they went to some lengths to conceal from Parliament that this was what they were doing: the original clause made no mention of a wife, but spoke merely of harbouring a recusant in one's house. There were, said a diarist of the Parliament, many M.P.s 'who had a special eye to . . . statutes of recusants, that no such thing might be inserted';[14] yet in the end their vigilance was evaded, and such a thing was in fact inserted. A number of prosecutions were brought under the act, but the victory, like so many parliamentary victories in the sixteenth century, was largely on paper; in 1610 a new act succeeded, where that of 1593 had failed, to the extent that a husband whose wife had been imprisoned for recusancy would have to pay half a fine, or an equivalent in seized property, before he could get her home again. But J.P.s seem to have refused to collaborate by imprisoning, and the whole problem was in any case soon overtaken by the progress of the technique of compounding for recusancy.[15]

From all this, two facts become clear: that a lot of Protestant or conformist gentlemen had Catholic wives around 1600; and that husband–wife relationships in this matter constituted an area of intense sensitivity into which government would enter at its peril. What does not necessarily become clear is whether, as Rowse assumes, this sensitivity concealed a weak-kneed evasion of patriarchal responsibility, or a patriarchal determination that governors and legislators should keep out of what was not their business. But most of the evidence suggests that Rowse is correct. Around the turn of the sixteenth century there seem to have been plenty of recusant wives like Bridget Baskerville, wife of Sir Roger Bodenham of Rotherwas in Herefordshire, 'an imperious dame of high stomach and stirring humour', who despised the mercantile origins of her conforming husband, and conforming husbands like Sir Ralph Gray of Chillingham, allegedly the richest landowner in Northumberland 'but because he is a man of no action he is not set by', who put up no opposition to a wife who received seminary priests at Chillingham and maintained a largely Catholic household. Such cases emerge from wholly different types of source, and do not

14. J. E. Neale, *Elizabeth I and her Parliaments*, ii (London, 1957), p. 293.
15. *ibid.*, pp. 281 f., 283 f., 287, 293 f.; the solution to Neale's puzzle about the act will be found in H. Bowler (ed.), *Recusant Roll no. 2, 1593–4* (C.R.S. lvii, 1965), introduction, pp. xlvi–xlviii; Walker, 'Implementation', pp. 337 ff.; Aveling, in C.R.S. liii, pp. 295, 293.

seem untypical. From the recusancy records we may take another
Northumberland case, that of Margaret, wife of Thomas Swinburne of
Capheaton, suspected as a receiver of seminary priests, with a recusant
son, daughter and son-in-law in the household, and understood to
proselytise among the servants and neighbours. John Gerard tells the
story of the married sister of one of his Norfolk hosts, who turned
recusant under his influence and was punished by her husband for it;
she was pregnant at the time, and later had a very difficult birth, and
when she seemed to be going to die her husband relented and allowed
Gerard to bring her an old Marian priest. He gave her extreme unction;
she recovered; and he was so staggered and delighted by this that he
became a Catholic also. From the *responsa* of the students entering the
English College at Rome, from which numerous similar examples could
be selected, we may take the case of Edmund Hastings of Braunston in
Leicestershire, who entered the college, aged twenty-three, in 1623, and
lost no time in telling the authorities about the sterling qualities of his
mother Dorothy Huddleston, and the feebleness of his father, Sir
Henry, whom he dismissed as a schismatic and a time-server.[16]

If we leave aside widows like Lady Montagu or Elizabeth Vaux, the
best documented story is that of Dorothy Lawson. She was almost a
second generation matriarch, for her mother, Margaret Dormer, had
been one of the wives imprisoned by the Earl of Huntingdon in the
1590s; her father, Sir Henry Constable of Burton Constable in Holderness, one of the wealthiest men in the North and M.P. for Yorkshire,
though not during the parliament of 1593, seems to have let his wife
have things fairly well her own way at home. She was able to take over
one of the outlying family estates in the North Riding and use it as a
base for priests, and to bring up all her children as Catholics; perhaps
it is significant that Dorothy was born, in 1580, at her mother's family
house at Wing in Buckinghamshire. In 1597 Dorothy married Roger
Lawson of Brough, eldest son of the Sir Ralph who had just migrated
there from Newcastle, and within a short space of time succeeded in
turning a reluctant mother-in-law and most of the family into recusants.
Her husband did not follow, and though after some years she moved
north with her own rapidly increasing family to settle on one of their
numerous estates around Newcastle, he spent most of his time in

16. Mathias, *Whitsun Riot*, pp. 33 f.; Surtees Society, vol. lxvii, p. 434; C.R.S. liii,
pp. 150 f., 55; *Autobiography of John Gerard*, pp. 19-21; *V.C.H. Leicestershire*, ii,
p. 58; C.R.S. lv, p. 372.

London practising the law; they do not seem to have seen very much of each other until he was dying in 1613, when he asked her to come down to London and is supposed to have been converted on his deathbed. All this time she had been energetically proselytising, and the new house at St Anthony's, on the north bank of the Tyne below Newcastle, where she lived from 1616 to her death in 1632, was apparently built to Richard Holtby's specifications as a centre for the Jesuits in the far north-east.[17] As in other cases, one has the feeling that at this period husbands had few functions in the Catholic community beyond that of begetting children.

This is of course an exaggeration: if we seek statistical confirmation from the domestic histories recorded by boys who entered the college in Rome, we shall find reason to suppose that only about a quarter of them were similar to those described above.[18] But if paternal authority is the norm, this is surely a very significant departure from it. We may possibly be victims of an optical illusion: it is possible that most of these differences between wife and husband could be explained as a devolution of power on the part of a *paterfamilias* who felt it necessary, for reasons of property, good example or access to local or other office, to go to church himself, but required his wife to maintain Catholic practice at home. The view however would not stand up well to most of the cases mentioned, and it is also hard to reconcile with the type of Catholicism practised by many wives, which was active and proselytising rather than merely domestic. It seems more in accord with the facts to accept the difference as genuine, and to look for reasons which, in the English landowning class of the late sixteenth century, would make Catholicism more attractive to women than to men.

There seems a good deal of evidence that religious nonconformity is in general, or at least was in this period, specially attractive to women;[19]

17. Aveling, *East Riding*, pp. 25 f.; Hanlon, 'These be but Women', pp. 374 ff.; Palmes, *Life of Mrs. Dorothy Lawson, passim.*
18. C.R.S. liv–lv (1962–1963). On the assumption that domestic uniformity means paternal authority, domestic division female emancipation (cf. Keith Thomas, 'Women and the Civil War Sects', in T. Aston (ed.), *Crisis in Europe, 1560–1660* (London, 1965), pp. 331–333), I have investigated the *responsa* up to the end of 1647; of the 433 which survive, 212 give an answer about the religion of parents. In 156 cases both were given as Catholics, in 56 there was a division of belief or practice; the Catholic party was the wife in 47 of the latter cases. There are some differences between my results and those of Beales, *Education under Penalty*, pp. 85 ff., but they do not seem to affect the point at issue here.
19. Thomas, *art. cit.*, pp. 320 ff., 330.

it is not hard to suggest why this should have been true of Catholic nonconformity at this time. The average woman of the upper classes might reasonably feel that the Reformation had not been designed with her in mind. If she was married, a whole sequence of ritual functions had been removed from her jurisdiction by the decline of fasting and abstinence and the desacralisation of holydays; if she was not, she had lost the chance of an honourable and possibly useful life in a religious order. She was also put at a disadvantage by the heavy implications in church-Protestantism (as distinct from sect-Protestantism) that literacy was a condition of salvation; in an age when the average gentleman had achieved a reasonable education while the average gentlewoman still got by on very little, this was likely to make for genuine differences of feeling between man and wife. Finally, the priesthood of all believers carried, in practice, implications of domestic authoritarianism, and just as in the political community the clerical estate might be considered a barrier to the sovereignty of monarchs, so in the domestic community a wife might find a useful ally in an authoritative priest.[20] All in all, I think the evidence entitles us to conclude that, to a considerable degree, the Catholic community owed its existence to gentlewomen's dissatisfaction at the Reformation settlement of religion, and that they played an abnormally important part in its early history.

This matriarchal era, if one may call it so, seems to have come to an end about 1620. Two reasons may be given for this. The first was a change in the administration of recusancy laws: by this date the risk of fines and sequestration of property, erratic as it may have been, was rapidly declining. Admittedly James I's suspension of the statutes proved temporary, but methods of more or less amicable composition for recusancy were being evolved which would become general practice during the following reign. The exterior reasons which would dictate a difference of conduct between husband and wife were therefore losing their force.[21] More intimately, the posture of the church-papist was something which could hardly be maintained for longer than a single generation, since it was not a line of conduct which children could be educated or even recommended to follow. Heirs would have to choose

20. D. M. Stenton, *The English Woman in History* (London, 1957), pp. 105–109; Thomas, *art. cit.*, pp. 321 f., 327, cf. the cases in Foley, *Records of the English Province*, vii part 2, pp. 1109, 1143 (which admittedly concern the poor); L. S. Schucking, *The Puritan Family* (London, 1969 edn), pp. 28–36.
21. Aveling, in C.R.S. liii, pp. 291–303.

one way or the other, enforcing their own conformity on their families or giving it up altogether; they would also probably find it increasingly difficult to marry girls whose religion differed from their own. The difficulty arose because religious divisions were clarifying at the same time as ideals of conjugal behaviour were rising and pressure for the spiritual unity of the household intensifying on all sides. That a couple, as was said in the 1640s, 'who lie in the same bed and in the eye both of God's Law and Man's are both one, should yet be of two churches, it is such a solecism, such an absurdity in Christianity, as . . . the world never saw practised . . .' So it had already seemed to the first Lord Falkland, who had the bad luck to marry, in 1601, Elizabeth Tanfield, 'a woman of most masculine understanding, allyed with the passions and infirmities of her sex', and one of the very few among the sixteenth-century crop of learned women, if not the only one, to convince herself by reading of the truth of the Catholic faith. Shortly after her marriage Lady Falkland changed her religion, but somehow kept the change a secret from her husband for twenty years; when it got out, in 1625, he separated from her and tried to stop her having anything to do with the children.[22] It is hard to know whether such general pressure for domestic uniformity worked to the advantage of Catholicism or not; on the whole it probably had an inhibiting effect, though several cases to the contrary could be produced from the Roman *responsa*.[23] What is more obvious is that it worked to entrench or restore the authority of the *paterfamilias*, in Catholic families as elsewhere. Besides, the more the energies of the Catholic *paterfamilias* were withdrawn by recusancy from the politics and administration of the country, the freer he was to bring the full weight of his authority to bear inside the Catholic community itself. Altogether, it is not difficult to see why, from about 1620, there was a patriarchal revival among the Catholic gentry. In so far as this had consequences for the clergy, they are noticed elsewhere; its

22. Hill, *Society and Puritanism*, pp. 443 ff.; Stone, *Crisis of the Aristocracy*, pp. 662 ff.; Schucking, *The Puritan Family*, pp. 37 ff.; J. Brinsley, *A looking-glass for good women* (London, 1645), qu. Thomas, *art. cit.*, p. 332; Stenton, *English Woman in History*, p. 137: for the children, see below, p. 163.

23. Thus *responsa* nos. 757, 784, 787; note also the cases where conversion precedes or accompanies marriage, e.g. nos. 1066, 1086. Fitton's report to Propaganda in 1632 (see above, chap. 6, n. 66) claimed that some priests, especially Jesuits, were causing domestic dissension by backing the *paterfamilias* against wives and children: A.A.W., films from Propaganda Archives, Scritture Riferite: Anglia I, f. 118v (volume reference from Philip Hughes, *Rome and the Counter-Reformation in England*, pp. 409 ff., where the document is summarised).

consequences for the women of the Catholic community call for comment here. They may be illustrated by the history of the *Institute of the Blessed Virgin Mary* invented by the Yorkshirewoman Mary Ward.[24]

The *Institute* was an attempt to carve out for unmarried women a missionary role, which would differ from that of the Jesuit or other active regular only in that its members would not be priests, and that their apostolate would be principally directed towards women. Mary Ward was the daughter of an obscure gentry family from the Pennine fringes around Ripon, brought up with her richer relatives the Babthorpes at Osgodby, one of the bases of missionary operations in Yorkshire. She had good offers of marriage and could have become a matriarch like Dorothy Lawson, whose age and background were otherwise much the same as hers; but at the age of about 20, in 1605, she went over to the Netherlands to seek an outlet for her active ambitions in a religious vocation. Failing to find satisfaction in any existing order, she launched into an enterprise of her own which was under way by 1610. Since there were numbers of young women in much the same position and with much the same ambitions as herself, she gathered recruits very quickly, and for about a dozen years her *Institute* flourished in spite of much hostility. Much of its work on the continent lay in girls' education, and she tried to establish a girls' equivalent of the school at St Omer. In England, in the immediate context, the *Institute* was intended to guide and stimulate the efforts of married women, help in the religious instruction of their households, and in general to bring a skilled female hand to the work of domestic reformation. It also took over some of the outside work which the progress of domestication was preventing the clergy from doing. It was thus both a product of the matriarchal era in the community and an attempt, if not exactly to prolong its existence, at least to ensure some permanent readjustment of the roles of man and woman. As such it had appeared at an unfavourable juncture, and in response to a wave of hysterical agitation had been suppressed by the papacy before the close of the 1620s. From this point onwards there is little to suggest that Catholics differed from the norm in their estimate of paternal authority.

24. General accounts in Guilday, *English Catholic Refugees on the Continent*, pp. 163–214; L. Hicks, 'Mary Ward's Great Enterprise', *The Month*, cli (1928), 137–146, 317–326; clii (1928), 40–52, 231–238; cliii (1929), 40–48, 223–236. Details from Aveling, *West Riding*, pp. 238 f.; Hanlon, 'These be but Women', p. 375; Tierney-Dodd, *Church History*, iv, pp. ccxxvii–ccxxx; M. C. E. Chambers, *The Life of Mary Ward* (ed. H. J. Coleridge, 2 vols., London, 1882–1885), ii, pp. 27 ff.

Whether its true author was a husband or a wife, nothing could stop a decision to follow a Catholic way of life, taken by one of the country's natural governors, from reverberating in widening circles through the population. With an unexpected sense for nuances, Richard Smith once wrote of Lady Montagu that she 'commanded her children, encouraged her servants, and importunately exhorted' others, to maintain the Catholic faith. It was part of the unwritten law of early modern England, more binding than almost any statute, and certainly more binding than the statutes which sought to interfere with it, that parents should absolutely determine the religion of their children, so long as they were children: in preparation for a mixed marriage, whole treaties were drawn up to regulate the fate of children yet unborn.[25] There seem to be only two exceptions to the rule, and in different ways an investigation of both of them tends on balance to support it. Until the early seventeenth century, it seems to be generally agreed, family upbringing was not the rule among the upper classes, and children spent comparatively little of their time under the parental roof: they spent their earliest years with a wetnurse—as did Augustine Baker in the case mentioned earlier—and shortly after that were sent off, either to gain experience and connections in some other and usually grander household, or else to some form of apprenticeship.[26] The effect of this was that, at least until the early seventeenth century, Catholic parents continued to send their children to be brought up in houses that were Protestant or conformist, in the knowledge that they would have to conform to the practice of the house. The early *responsa* of the Roman students are full of cases where children had during their upbringing successively conformed to two or more different regimes; it is not surprising that some grew up extremely confused about which religion they belonged to. Two cases, both dating from 1600 or so, may be cited: George Morgan, a boy from Abergavenny sent to London to be apprenticed to a merchant, lived with him for six months, during which time he 'went unwillingly to the Protestant church'; Ferdinand Poulton, similarly apprenticed in London, was after five years persuaded by John Gerard to refuse to go to church, and so dismissed.[27] Universal

25. Southern, *An Elizabethan Recusant House*, p. 40; Steel, *Sources*, p. 873.
26. P. Ariès, *Centuries of Childhood* (London, 1962), pp. 365 ff.; Stone, *Crisis of the Aristocracy*, pp. 590 ff.; cf. above, chap. 6, p. 112.
27. *Responsa*, nos. 409, 558; cf. nos. 453, 464, 499, 550, 568, etc.; Aveling, *Northern Catholics*, p. 238.

recusancy was not reconcilable with this manner of upbringing, and pressure for it reinforced a movement towards family upbringing which was going on in any case.

A second qualification is that until the 1650s a variety of attempts was made to secure the removal of children from recusant parents by legislation or prerogative action. Much the most successful of these was Lord Burghley's use of his Mastership of the Elizabethan Court of Wards to improve the state of religious conformity among the peerage. Henry Wriothesley, 3rd Earl of Southampton, succeeded his father in 1581, at the age of eight; both his parents were Catholics, but as one of the Queen's wards he was removed from his mother and brought up in Burghley's household. The poor child stuck out against conformity for a time, but eventually succumbed; he never seems quite to have recovered from this disastrous experience. In other cases Burghley achieved his object without apparent ill-effects. Yet it would be very misleading to take such cases as evidence of any general policy of securing conformity by removing children from their parents: as Lawrence Stone very properly remarks, among the peerage 'only the early death of a father allowed the Government to interfere in the educational process by the exercise of the powers of wardship', and this itself was about as much as the mainstream of opinion in the English governing class was prepared to tolerate.[28] Although there was at least one very important case of religion changed by wardship during the early seventeenth century, that of James, later Duke of Ormonde, by 1640 it was at least as common for the wardship of Catholic peers who succeeded as minors to be successfully acquired by their Catholic friends and relations.[29] Outside the peerage, the prospects for successful intervention were very limited.

Not that the idea was not thought of or tried. During the 1580s a scheme was devised, attributed to Lord Burghley, for extending the royal prerogative to a general segregation of children from recusant parents in order that they should be brought up Protestants, and the idea was certainly current in the Privy Council at the time. The original

28. Stone, *Crisis of the Aristocracy*, p. 740, and in general pp. 739–741; J. T. Cliffe, *The Yorkshire Gentry from the Reformation to the Civil War* (London, 1969), pp. 184–186; the more drastic view of A. C. F. Beales, *Education under Penalty* (London, 1963), pp. 57 ff., is unconvincing.

29. Beales, *op. cit.*, p. 102; [Winifred Gardner,] Lady Burghclere, *The Life of James, first Duke of Ormonde* (2 vols., London, 1912), i, p. 32 f.

government bill of 1593, mainly concerned with recusant wives, also contained a clause providing for statutory removal of a recusant's children at the age of seven; this seems to have been due to Lord Chief Justice Popham, who thought that the legal problems of separating children from parents were easier to get over than those of segregating wives from husbands.[30] In almost every Parliament of James I a similar attempt was made, though it was by now the opposition, not the government, which made them: the last and best thought out, a bill of 1624, would have required all recusant parents to send their children off at the age of nine to be brought up as an apprentice, servant or scholar in a Protestant household or school, at their own choice if they collaborated, at direction if they did not.[31] None of these bills was enacted; only the last gives the impression that its framers knew what they were doing, and they were probably several decades behind the times. Government and local authorities did take sporadic action of this kind, especially during the last twenty years of the reign of Elizabeth, and during the Interregnum; but without any clear legal warrant they were not very successful. A variety of methods were tried on the four Worthington boys, seized with their uncle Thomas, later President of Douai, in Lancashire in 1584—upbringing in the bishop's household, putting out to reliable Protestants in Manchester, prison, forcible Protestant schooling—but none of them made any difference, and all the boys eventually got away to the continent. So, half a century later, did the four daughters of Lady Falkland, sent to be brought up with their brother under William Chillingworth after their parents' separation.[32] Both cases were a gift to the martyrologist; and in neither of them was there a Catholic father to contend with. Where there was, attempts went off at half-cock, as with the two sons of Sir Henry Jerningham, arrested in London in January 1593 on their way to school abroad: some kind of attempt seems to have been made to turn them into Protestants, but when Sir Henry asked for them back, he got them, along with a tame letter from the Privy Council to say that 'we doe look that [they] bee brought up and instructed by a schoolmaster known to

---

30. Beales, *op. cit.*, pp. 58, 61, 62; J. E. Neale, *Elizabeth I and her Parliaments*, ii (London, 1957), pp. 281, 284, 285; Walker, 'Implementation of the Elizabethan Statutes against Recusants', pp. 337–338.
31. Beales, *op. cit.*, pp. 92–95.
32. *ibid.*, p. 59; Leys, *Catholics in England*, pp. 47 f.; C. Hole, *English Home Life*, *1500–1800* (London, 1949), pp. 86 f.

be well affected to Religion'.[33] So far as I can see, the few cases where children of Catholics were successfully brought up Protestants before the Civil War were all cases of wardship following a father's death, though it seems possible that the notion of wardship was occasionally stretched so as to cover them.[34]

The parliamentary regime of the 1640s was a little more active than this: though it abolished the Court of Wards it continued to use its powers in this respect on an emergency basis. It also passed the only statute which made any kind of impression on the problem. The act for confiscation of the property of delinquents left a sizeable portion of it to the landowner for the maintenance of his wife and children, but only on condition that they were brought up Protestants: the threat does seem to have persuaded some Catholic landowning families to surrender some of their children for a Protestant upbringing. Thus Alethea Anderton, when she became a nun at Louvain at the end of the 1650s, reported that when the family property (Euxton Hall, near Wigan) was sequestrated, three of the fourteen children (one son and two daughters) were taken away by the commissioners, and part of the estate assigned to their support.[35] This does not seem to have been common, but more pressure was probably exerted at this time than at any other. If so, it was not given much time to take effect, since from 1650 or very shortly after the sequestration system, like the recusancy system before it, had subsided into a system of compounding and no longer offered any threat to the religion of children. After some time the Anderton children were restored to their family, and though they had been effectively proselytised and held out against a return to Catholicism for some time, eventually they came round.[36] This was the end of all efforts at statutorily preventing the upbringing of children as Catholics, and since the Court of Wards was not revived in 1660 the Crown could no longer, had it wished to do so, use its prerogative in this field. But even before 1660, with some exceptions when a father died prematurely, Catholic parents had in effect been free to bring up their children as they liked.

What this meant was that those parents who could afford it sent

33. Beales, *Education under Penalty*, p. 63; cf. the slightly different story in Leys, *Catholics in England*, p. 46.
34. Cases in Beales, *op. cit.*, pp. 60, 107.
35. P. Hardacre, *The Royalists during the Puritan Revolution* (The Hague, 1954), pp. 60–61; Beales, *op. cit.*, pp. 107–108. It seems possible that this was another case where there was no father.
36. Beales, *op. cit.*, p. 108.

their sons to be educated abroad at St Omer, Douai and other continental establishments; the practice got really under way in the early
1590s, when St Omer was founded, and had probably become the
norm by about 1620. For girls, if they were not themselves destined
for a convent life, it seems to have come a good deal later, and to have
been less effective and even more restricted in social class; the failure
of Mary Ward's *Institute* was never entirely compensated for in this
field. Perhaps there is room for some surprise that Catholic gentry
couples, having successfully defended their rights in the bringing up
of their children, did not show more concern to bring them up themselves. But really they had little choice. If seventeenth-century England
had possessed a system of undenominational public education, there is
not much reason to suppose that Catholic parents would not have
availed themselves of it, and kept their children at home; as things were
it was probably not until some time after 1600 that children given a
Catholic education on the continent became more numerous than those
educated in the ordinary grammar schools in England, and it may well
be true that the change occurred relatively late in the North, where
people were less well off and access to the continent harder. Here again
the seminary *responsa* are helpful: forty-four of the Roman entrants
between 1598 and 1621 said that they had two Catholic parents but had
got their education, or some of it, at a local grammar school.[37]

The difficulty of this, of course, was that it involved, theoretically at
least, a good deal of participation *in sacris*, ranging from prayers to
supervised church attendance.[38] Where this could not be evaded, it was
probably in the early days acceptable to parents, on much the same
principle as applied in the case of apprentices. As ideas of differential
conformity lost ground before the advance of recusancy, the situation
of a Catholic boy in a grammar school became more uncomfortable.
Two of the *responsa* show the problem in contrasting regions and
through contrasting temperaments. Around 1610 Ralph Salvin was

37. *ibid.*, p. 85; cf. David Mathew, *The Age of Charles I* (London, 1951), p. 148.
38. See the grammar school statutes assembled in Foster Watson, *The English
Grammar Schools to 1600* (Cambridge, 1908). However, reality did not always
correspond: in 1605 there was a new master at Wolverhampton grammar school who
insisted that all papist boys attend church, including those with recusant parents;
these—no doubt mainly from the gentry of the surrounding countryside, among
whom Catholicism was strong—objected, on the grounds that this was an innova-
tion, and managed to have the master dismissed in 1610: *V.C.H. Staffordshire*, iii
(1970), p. 104.

going to school in Durham from his home at Croxdale nearby; he had no trouble for three years, but then a couple of his fellow-schoolboys—one of them the bishop's son—started to follow him around calling him a papist. He hit one of them, and was expelled. Robert Rookwood, at school in Brentwood in Essex a few years later, was evidently a more sensitive boy. He said he had sometimes skipped church and got a beating for it, but had usually gone 'out of cowardice', and because he had been told, inaccurately as it turned out, that his father had conformed. Pressure from the Catholic clergy at home was no doubt added to difficulties at school: in the 1650s we hear of a boy of nine, the only Catholic in a school in Northumberland, who was not allowed to make his first communion.[39] Perhaps, outside the gentry, there were more of such children than one supposes, but it seems a fairly reliable rule of thumb that, from a fairly early period, Catholic parents who wanted a respectable education for their children would have to send them away to get it. This had obvious implications for the level of education in the community at large; in the present context it means that, when we are considering a family of Catholic gentry as a congregational nucleus we have to envisage a group of children the eldest of whom would probably not be more than fourteen. Whatever one generation was to learn directly from its predecessor, without the intervention of clergy or religious, would have to have been absorbed before that age. In speculating on what may have been so transmitted, two moments stick in one's mind.

The first of them was at Christmas 1663, when William Blundell wrote for his three daughters, Mary (Mall), Frances (Franke) and Bridget—who were then nine, seven and four years old—a little play, or 'Exercise . . . for to embolden them in speaking', which they managed, 'in part', to recite. It begins with William intending to beat Mall for 'uncivil' behaviour; she argues that when she goes to confession her sins are forgiven by a promise to amend, and he should follow this example. After some argument, her father lets her off and goes away. She congratulates herself that she 'never came off thus in all [her] life', and decides to 'pray and mend'. At this point the two smaller girls come in; Franke is driving Bridget like a horse 'with a string in her mouth'. Mall says primly that they must stop this and do something

39. *Responsa*, nos. 608, 612; Foley, *Records of the English Province*, iii, p. 124; a much later case (William Ullathorne, Pocklington, *c.* 1800), in S. Leslie (ed.), *From Cabin-boy to Archbishop* (London, 1941), p. 5.

more civil. Franke jeers at her change of heart, and they have a discussion about what civility has to do with virtue, with interjections from Bridget, who wants them to stop arguing and 'knead cockle bread' or 'turn the cat in the pan' [do somersaults]. 'Sister Mall, I pray you, Sister Mall, will not knowledge of cockle bread and turning the cat in the pan bring a body to Heaven.' 'Oh, by no means, love.' Eventually Mall's resolution cracks and they all dress up their father's bass viol as himself, and abuse it for not giving them a tune to dance to.[40]

The other refers to a childhood spent a century later, when civility had won through, recollected some sixty years later still by Charlotte Jerningham. Her husband had just died, and she wrote of the 'dreary Independence' she now felt. She had always identified happiness with security, and thought back to her childhood as a model of both, governed by feelings of 'deference' and 'affectionate respect' for her parents, elder relatives and for the elderly in every walk of life. Childhood, she thought, 'is often ignorant of its happiness, but I was born, I believe with an instinctive feeling upon the Subject . . . On my 7th Birthday I remember the tears I shed, because I was come to the "Use of Reason" and consequently answerable for my Conduct.' She recalled the joy she had felt later, at ten or twelve, when her mother identified her with her younger brothers as 'the Children'. At thirteen, she was sent for three years to the Blue Nuns in Paris, and here she was extremely happy, apart from the thought that she would soon be 'grown up'. All this may sound mawkish, unhealthy, and a dubious augury for her future: in fact she grew up into a talented and intelligent woman and married very happily at twenty-four. One can see why from her final thought, which follows naturally enough from her account of her childhood, but puts it in a different light. Now, her parents, her husband, many of her relatives were dead. 'What then makes me wish to linger behind? The same dread of change! The same clinging to what is—the same attachment to *persons* and *places*.'[41] These two glimpses of childhood among the Catholic gentry convey so powerful a sense of reality that it seems

40. Blundell, *Cavalier*, pp. 304–312; for 'cockle bread', see Germaine Greer, *The Female Eunuch* (London, 1971 edn), p. 89, quoting John Aubrey. Another description of the impact of formal religion on childhood folklore will be found in M. C. E. Chambers, *The Life of Mary Ward* (ed. H. J. Coleridge, 2 vols., London, 1882–1885), i, pp. 19 f.

41. *Jerningham Letters*, ii, pp. 320–321; see also M. Norman, *Recusant History*, xi (1972), p. 314, for an extract from Gother's instructions for children, which I have not seen.

trivial to ask whether, sociologically speaking, they ought to be regarded as typical. It may, of course, be of some significance that both of them concern girls.

(ii)

SERVANTS AND TENANTS

The 'family' of early modern England included not merely parents and children, or other blood-relations, but all members of the household in which they lived; for the gentry, it included a number of household servants which in cases of affluence might rise to fifty or more, but would probably in a normal case be something more than a dozen. It seems obvious that to some degree these were not considered autonomous individuals in respect of a choice of religion, but hard to be sure just what the degree was. On one side we have plenty of Elizabethan evidence that ecclesiastical and secular authorities considered the head of a 'family' answerable for the conformity of all its members, and that this responsibility was accepted.[42] Against this we should bear in mind the insufficiency of similar assurances about wives, and take note of Richard Smith's distinction in the power wielded by Lady Montagu over her children and her servants; as Peter Laslett has explained, the early-modern family consisted of associations of various kinds.[43] In fact there was perhaps no very satisfactory social theory on the matter; the head of a household was, in respect of his servants, partly a father and partly an employer. We should not be surprised that in matters of religious uniformity the households of Catholic gentlemen had a rather fluctuating career; nor that—considering both the social and the economic factors involved—the tendency of household servants to conform to the Catholicism of their masters was on the whole very strong.

The signs are that in the pre-missionary era of Elizabethan Catholicism household solidarity was the rule; so long as the principal mark of Catholics was adherence to the cycle of fast and feast, it is hard to see how it could have been otherwise. In 1562, commissioners investi-

---

42. Examples in Hughes, *Reformation in England*, iii, pp. 430, 431, 433; cf. Trimble, *Catholic Laity in Elizabethan England*, pp. 101, 109 f.
43. *The World we have Lost* (London, 1965), p. 2, and in general pp. 1–4.

gating a clandestine Mass offered in such a household found that 'neither the priest, nor any of his auditors, not so much as the kitchen maid will receive any oath before us [and they] say also they will neither accuse themselves nor none other', one may take Lady Montagu's large household at Battle, where 'a visible church or company of Catholics' numbering eighty or more, was 'assembled and preserved', as carrying this tradition into the early seventeenth century.[44] The first effect of the missionary priests seems to have been to upset it, partly because the priests themselves were often chary of becoming enmeshed in domestic functions and sought to pursue their activities in a wider field;[45] and partly because the increase of tension between the Catholic gentry and the government put their servants in a very difficult position. The gentry were often prepared to make things easier by sending their servants to church, or having a Prayer Book service for them in the house; some of them appear to have agreed to dismiss recusant servants.[46] It seems at least to have been fairly usual, during the early decades of the mission, for a distinction to be drawn between senior and more intimate servants, who would be Catholics, and the rest, who would not. Early in the seventeenth century, the Jesuits reported the typical small gentry household, where missioners were beginning to settle as chaplains, as likely to contain some Protestants; 'since they were his servants, and under many obligations to him' the head of the household would, they suggested, feel some confidence in their discretion, but the position did not strike the Jesuits as a very happy one.[47] It would be hard to say how much their unease reflected fears about security, and how much the ideal of a godly household; but at least from the time of John Gerard's missionary operations in the 1590s, a drive had been under way for household conformity, which ought probably to be distinguished from the more instinctual solidarity of the earlier decades. 'Catholic gentlefolk,' Gerard wrote bluntly, 'must have Catholic servants'; and he described in some detail how he went about establishing conformity in the household of Elizabeth Vaux. When he came, he says, she had a house full of ill-disciplined servants, who were either Protestants or nominal Catholics; after sermons and indivi-

44. Hughes, *op. cit.*, iii, p. 255, n. 4; Southern, *An Elizabethan Recusant House*, p. 39.
45. e.g. C.R.S. xxxix, pp. 321–323.
46. Cases above, n. 42; Trimble, *Catholic Laity*, p. 93.
47. Foley, *Records of the English Province*, ii, pp. 3 f.; cf., among other examples, *Autobiography of John Gerard*, pp. 58 f., 145; Waugh, *Campion*, p. 134.

dual talkings-to, the Catholics mended their ways, and the Protestants were in effect given a choice between conversion and dismissal. 'Some' were converted, and 'a few' dismissed.[48]

At least two obstacles had to be overcome before the drive for household conformity could be generally successful. There were obvious dangers in sending away discontented servants at a time of national tension: one Lancashire servant who 'was required to go, as did his master and mistress, to hear a Jesuit preach, which he did not', and presumably dismissed as a consequence, naturally enough turned informer; 'as these times go', Lord Brudenell was told by his son in similar circumstances under the Commonwealth, 'all servants are masters, and we their slaves'.[49] But this was in fact merely to deplore the premature dismissal of a man on whose evidence the family might be convicted of 'delinquency' in the Civil War, on the grounds that if Lord Brudenell had waited a year he could not have failed to find a convincing excuse for getting rid of him. Even in difficult times, an employer who was prepared to exercise a little patience could always get his way. The other difficulty was that in 1606 Parliament finally imposed on heads of households a statutory fine of £10 a month for keeping a recusant servant. This was certainly enforced in some cases, but it seems possible that the act helped to precipitate the progress of the movement it was designed to prevent. According to the French ambassador, it led mainly to the dismissal of Catholic servants from Protestant households, which can only have helped to encourage uniformity all round.[50] With the labour market as overcrowded as it was in this period, Catholic masters and mistresses cannot have had too much difficulty in persuading servants that a job was worth a Mass.

The matriarchal period of English Catholicism was in some ways particularly favourable for the progress of household conversion, and it seems clear that it was practically complete by the close of the matriarchal regime. Dorothy Lawson, with her intention 'to prepare a house for God, which she did in a decent garbe', her stealthy filling of her household with Catholic servants, one at a time so her husband would not notice, her 'relating Saints' lives to the maids, and reading

48. *Autobiography of John Gerard*, pp. 33, 145 f., 150.
49. Leatherbarrow, *Lancashire Elizabethan Recusants*, p. 90; J. Wake, *The Brudenells of Deene*, p. 142.
50. C. Hole, *English Home Life, 1500-1800* (London, 1949), p. 85; Southern, *An Elizabethan Recusant House*, pp. 44, 54; A. le Fèvre de la Boderie, *Ambassade de M. de la Boderie en Angleterre (1606-11)* (5 vols., n.p., 1750), i, pp. 230 ff.

pious books in their company', would serve as an equally good example; there were less exceptional matrons like Margaret Swinburne, busy converting the servants at Capheaton.[51] In so far as one can grasp the short-lived activity of the *Institute of Mary* in England, it seems to have been directed to much the same end. John Donne envisaged the situation in his own way, remarking in one of his sermons that 'there may be examples of women, that have thought it a fit way to gain a soul, by prostituting themselves . . . with a purpose to convert a servant, which is somewhat a strange Topique to draw arguments of religion from'.[52] No doubts the methods were often crude enough. In any case, when the Catholic *paterfamilias* began to come into his own, he was likely to have a solidly Catholic household to govern, whose days were framed in a rigorous sequence of communal religious observance. The life of the servants at Osgodby, with their Mass at six o'clock in the morning and their evening prayers before bed, was an early example; by perhaps 1630, when a very normal household like that of Thomas Meynell had become a closed shop, this was probably the life of servants in most Catholic families, and continued to be so for at least a century and a half.[53] About 1700 John Gother's spiritual instructions and Nicholas Blundell's diary show the institution in its best days; so does Richard Challoner's account of his mother Grace who after the death of her husband, a 'rigid Dissenter' from Lewes, went into service with the Gages at Firle and turned Catholic.[54]

Gother's view of the Catholic household, whose uniformity he took for granted, was in some respects a stern one; but it was redeemed by a genuine concern that servants should not be deprived by their duties in it of access to the spiritual and sacramental resources it possessed. He had strong views on Sunday observance, and regarded Sunday games as a barely permissible evil, but he also realised that servants deserved a bit of recreation, and thought that masters ought to make time for this out of their own six days, not out of God's one. ' 'Tis almost

51. W. Palmes, *Life of Mrs. Dorothy Lawson* (ed. G. B. Richardson, Newcastle-upon-Tyne, 1851), pp. 17, 42—she also 'gave her servants more than was due in temporalls'; C.R.S. liii, p. 55.
52. Sermon at St Paul's Cross, Christmas Day, 1622, in *Complete Poetry and Selected Prose* (ed. John Hayward, London, 1929), p. 584.
53. For Osgodby, see above, chap. 6, p. 128; C.R.S. lvi (1964), p. xxiv (Meynells); another case *V.C.H. Leicestershire*, ii, p. 68 (Sir Fras. Englefield of Shoby recusant 'with all his household', 1634).
54. Burton, *Challoner*, i, pp. 1 f.

impossible to conceive how [servants] can save their souls, if they abuse the Sundays, and neglect to employ them for [exercises of piety]. For if we look at them all the week, they are engaged in a continual Slavery, such as hinders them from Praying and Reading; so that if they begin and end the day with a short Prayer, 'tis as much as they generally do; and God knows how often, thro' Hurry and Drowsiness, they omit even them too.' He also wrote of the heavy labour which servants had to put in on the vigils of feast-days, kept up till all hours of the night preparing house, clothes and food for the family, when they ought to have been preparing themselves for the feast by going to confession and otherwise; masters and mistresses, he reminded them, would answer at the Day of Judgment for treating the superficial order of their households as more important than their servants' souls.[55]

In most gentry households the servants seem to have remained under firm religious discipline throughout most of the eighteenth century: in the 1770s John Hornyold, bishop of the Midland district, told all his priests who lived in them to see that all the servants attended regularly to say their evening prayers and examine their consciences.[56] But it is probably significant that by this time the clergy were being expected to take the initiative; Hornyold complained that heads of households were themselves no longer regular attenders at prayers. Possibly we should date from about this time the beginning of the end of the Catholic household in its classic form. As an ideal of religious community it was certainly being replaced by others; on the other hand the parsons of 1767, when they approached Catholic gentlemen for a religious census of their households, still came away monotonously with a list of family, priest and a dozen or so Catholic servants.[57] The institution evidently had some life left in it.

A policy of converting the servants may well seem a modest one, and it obviously received emphasis to the degree that wider missionary operations were difficult or impossible. None the less it had exterior

55. 'Instructions for Keeping Sunday', in *Instructions and Devotions for Hearing Mass* (London, 1740 edn), pp. 130-135, esp. pp. 143-145; *Instructions for Confession*, etc. (London, 1744 edn), pp. 83 f., 85 f. Cf. above, chap. 6, p. 117.
56. Leys, *Catholics in England*, p. 209.
57. Aveling, *East Riding*, p. 56; *Catholic Recusancy in York*, pp. 133 f. Stephen Tempest, *Religio Laici* (n.p. 1764), p. 121: heads of households to attend to the religion of their servants, 'including if different from yours'. Examples of 1767 returns in my 'Four Catholic Congregations in rural Northumberland', pp. 93 f., and 'More Northumbrian Congregations', p. 12 (see above, chap. 6, n. 54); Williams, *Catholic Recusancy in Wiltshire*, p. 197 (31 Catholics in Arundell household).

consequences, if only because domestic service was probably not in this period considered so much a career in itself as a step towards advancement in general; this will also help to explain the general success of the Catholic gentry in transmitting their religion to their servants. There might be more at stake for a servant than the prospect of good references within the community, like Nicholas Blundell's recommendation of a housemaid as 'a Catholick and a brisk Mettled workwoman'.[58] Towards the end of the eighteenth century Joseph Berington claimed that all rural Catholics below the gentry were 'servants, or the children of servants, who have married from those families, and who chuse to remain round the old mansion, for the conveniency of prayers, and because they hope to receive favour and assistance from their former masters'.[59] This was certainly a great exaggeration, though it may have roughly represented the position in much of the South and Midlands; but it is obvious from Stephen Tempest's advice, dating from half a century earlier, that it was not wholly misleading. He advised the gentry to choose for principal servants young people who 'are come of Honest Parents, who have long behaved creditably in the Neighbourhood', and who showed signs of possessing 'good Blood'; 'if [later] they marry, and you have farms fall in convenient for their circumstances, they ought to be preferred before new tenants'.[60] Examples of the practice, alleged and real, may be found in complaints against the Petres, who were supposed to ensure the conversion of Protestant servants by, among other things, 'marrying them and settling them out in the world', and from the practice of Catholic families up and down the country.[61] It was no doubt at the bottom of the prosperity of numerous Catholic farmers. Gentry households were not detached from their neighbourhoods, and a Catholic way of life followed inside one of them was bound to spill over outside it.

In testing the assumption that in the Catholic community the

58. *Great Diurnal of Nicholas Blundell*, i, p. 69.
59. J. Berington, *State and Behaviour of English Catholics* (Birmingham, 1780), p. 115.
60. *Religio Laici*, pp. 69, 121.
61. Rector of Ramsden Bellhouse, Essex, to Gibson, Bishop of London, 11 September 1723 (Bodleian Library, Rawlinson C. 233, ff. 70, 71); J. A. Williams, 'Some Eighteenth-century Conversions', *Essex Recusant*, iii (1961), p. 133; *Wiltshire*, pp. 194–195 (Arundells); 'More Northumbrian Congregations', p. 14 (Haggerstons); W. Price, 'Three Jesuits at Plowden Hall', *Recusant History*, x (1969), p. 169 (Plowdens, Actons, Blounts); David Mathew, 'The Approach to Recusant History', *Dublin Review* (1959), p. 29 (Langdales).

characteristic agent of transition between a domestic nucleus and a genuine congregation was the exercise of a landlord's prerogative within the boundaries of his estate, we shall be advised not to envisage this prerogative too crudely. It had no legal embodiment, since English landlords did not possess seigneurial jurisdiction and with marginal exceptions Catholic landlords were not justices of the peace. If we see it in economic terms, we may recognise that the buying power of a gentry household would always be enough to invite a variety of tradesmen to consider the advantages of the religion it professed; [62] but the central question, what was the relation between a Catholic landlord and those who held and worked on his land, is not reducible to quite such simple terms as this, and it is probable that too sweeping judgments have been made about it. Both John Earle, who claimed in the seventeenth century that a countryman's religion was 'part of his copyhold, which he takes from his landlord and refers . . . wholly to his discretion', and Christopher Hill, who has recently written of the effect of the Reformation as having been to introduce into England a form of the principle *cujus regio ejus religio* operative at the manorial level, strike one as overdoing things a good deal. [63] The power of an English landowner over his inferiors, though considerable enough, was not that of the landlords of France or central Europe, where the regime described did indeed obtain fairly widely during the post-Reformation period; [64] if it had been, the English Catholic community would have been a good deal larger than it was.

All the same, there seems no reason to apologise for having used the word 'seigneurial' to describe its social pattern, even if its seigneurialism was by continental standards a diluted one. [65] 'I look upon every man possessed of a great landed estate,' wrote on of the most representative Catholic gentlemen of his age, 'as a Kind of Petty Prince, in regard to

62. e.g. Dickens, 'Extent and Character', p. 40; 'Four Catholic Congregations in rural Northumberland', pp. 93–94; Williams, *Wiltshire*, p. 219.

63. *Microcosmography*, p. 53; Hill, *Society and Puritanism* (1958 edn), p. 44; Rowse, *Tudor Cornwall*, p. 378. Contemporary opinions to the same effect in Mathew, *Catholicism in England*, p. 43; *V.C.H. Staffordshire*, iii, pp. 99 f.

64. There seems to be no proper general treatment of the question, but see J.-H. Mariéjol, in E. Lavisse, *Histoire de France*, vi part i (Paris, 1911), p. 418; O. Chadwick, *The Reformation* (London, 1964), p. 148; B. J. Kidd, *The Counter-Reformation* (London, 1933), p. 9; H. Kamen, *The Rise of Toleration* (London, 1967), pp. 119–122.

65. 'Character of Elizabethan Catholicism', in T. Aston (ed.), *Crisis in Europe, 1560–1660* (London, 1965), p. 223, etc.

those that live under him.' He should look to their contentment, but also to their faith and morals: 'a wicked abandoned set of Tenants who frequent no Place of Worship, who serve God nowhere, will never do their duty to their lord'.[66] Even if they had not been influenced by considerations of security and prestige, landlords who thought the Catholic religion good for themselves could hardly have failed to think it would be good for their tenants.

The assumption might be demonstrated almost by statistics alone: from the Recusant Rolls of Elizabeth to the Returns of Papists of the later eighteenth century, every attempt to count Catholics reveals them as coagulated in local groups at the centre of which a gentleman's household will usually be found. If we take, at random, a list of Derbyshire recusants taken from the first thirteen rolls (1592–1604), we find that it contains the names of some 160 people, 125 of whom came from five localities. The village of Longford, in the Trent valley, provided twenty recusants: seven yeomen, two husbandmen, eight spinsters, two widows and Nicholas Langford, Esquire, lord of the manor. The village of Hathersage and its environs, high up the Derwent valley towards the High Peak, provided no less than sixty-five; it had been inherited from the Eyres by one branch of the Fitzherberts, in whose house at Padley nearby priests had recently been arrested. Over the next twenty years, Norbury on the Staffordshire border, which belonged to the other branch of the Fitzherberts, provided forty-five.[67] In 1606 Edward Morgan, the largest landowner in the parish of Llantarnan in Monmouthshire, was convicted for recusancy along with sixty of the parishioners; in the 1650s the Meynells at North Kilvington in the North Riding had thirty recusant tenants on their not very large estate; in 1676 there were 152 recusants in the Kesteven division of Lincolnshire, and 56 of them lived in the parish of Irnham, where the landlords were the recusant Thimelbys; in 1706 twenty-five male Catholic householders were returned from the Northumberland village of Netherwitton, which belonged to the Thorntons and had the reputation of a closed shop.[68] From soon after the middle of the eighteenth century

66. Stephen Tempest, *Religio Laici*, pp. 61 f.
67. *Journal of the Derbyshire Archaeological and Natural History Society*, x (1888), pp. 60–70; cf. Trimble, *Catholic Laity in Elizabethan England*, p. 163, for Langford and his subsequent conformity.
68. Pugh, 'Monmouthshire Recusants' (see above, chap. 5, n. 35), p. 60; C.R.S. lvi, pp. xxiv f.; Stone, *Crisis of the Aristocracy*, p. 733; Northumberland C.R.O., Quarter Sessions Papers, 88 and below, p. 178.

reliable lists of Catholics coexist with systematic inventories of Catholic estates which give tenants' names, and it becomes possible to establish the relations of tenancy and religion with some precision. I have looked in this light at the estates of half-a-dozen Northumberland families around 1770: on three of them all or practically all the farmers seem to have been Catholics, on two something less than half, on one none at all. The last case (Hesleyside, which belonged to the Charltons) strikes one as exceptional, at least in the North and at this date; the family was in some disarray at this time.[69] Altogether these accumulated instances suggest a fairly high level of tenant conformity, and that there were more closed villages than Little Crosby, where 'William Blundell is the lord or owner of one small lordship or manor consisting of forty houses or thereabouts, and there are not . . . any other but Catholics in it, except peradventure one or two day labourers which being born in other places, are come to live there for work.'[70]

It may have been noticed that the most impressive cases are from the North and the upland fringes; as a rule Catholic landowners in the South and Midlands were far less likely to have Catholic farmers on their estates. One should not over-estimate the difference: Somerton in Oxfordshire, as the incumbent wrote in the 1730s, 'has always been remarkable for a great many papists, which I suppose proceeds from most of the inhabitants being tenants to Mr Fermor, a Roman Catholic gentleman who lives at Tusmore'.[71] From Staffordshire, where the relation has been investigated at a slightly earlier date, it has been calcu-lated that, out of thirty-four tenants on the Draycott estate at Paynsley, where there was an endowed priest, ten were certainly and eight more possibly Catholics; of fifteen on the Macclesfield estate at Maer, there were four certain and three possible; of fifty-seven on the Fitzherbert estate at Swinnerton, no more than seven certain and two possible. The Gifford estate at Chillington is said to have contained mainly Catholic farmers until after 1800, when the family had already changed its religion for some time, though there seem to be no figures to support

69. 'Four Catholic Congregations', pp. 94–97; 'More Northumbrian Congrega-tions', pp. 12–14.
70. Blundell, *Cavalier*, p. 250; *Cavalier's Notebook*, p. 55. See below, chap. 11, p. 260, for priests maintained specifically to serve tenants.
71. Leys, *Catholics in England*, p. 102; similarly for Eyre estate at Warkworth: Mrs B. [M. H. A.] Stapleton, *Post-Reformation Catholic Missions in Oxfordshire* (London, 1906), pp. 37–42.

this.[72] At Coughton in Warwickshire, which belonged to the Throck-mortons though they did not live there very much, no more than a fifth of the population were given as Catholics in the 1670s.[73] Coming as they do from the west Midlands, these figures are likely to represent the greatest degree of landlord influence outside the North; leaving aside a few magnates, a Catholic family living in the east Midlands, South or South-West was very likely to be isolated in a population more or less totally Protestant. This was very noticeably the plight of Sir Thomas Tresham, surrounded at Rushton in Northants by an angry Protestant tenantry in the years around 1600; that of a number of families in Essex and elsewhere who suffered from popular rioting in the troubled times at the outbreak of the Civil War in 1641–1642; of the Carringtons and other recusant gentry in Leicester and Nottinghamshire under the Restoration; and also, to skip a century, of the Welds at Lulworth in Dorset, if one may judge from the tone of the farmer who wrote to Thomas Weld apropos of some dispute that he was 'unwilling to turn informer, but if we let this pass you will at the next opportunity come with your Jesuit priest and cut all our throats'.[74] Provided one does not take the distinction too far, it seems to me legitimate to think of the magnetic powers of a household of Catholic gentry as acting compara-tively strongly on their tenants in the North, and likely to evoke little or no response, if not a positive repulsion, in the South.

How exactly are we to account for the degree of tenant conformity which was achieved? There are one or two signs of strong-arm action to be found: from Nidderdale in the early seventeenth century we hear of one William Joye asking his brother to retract an information for priest-harbouring against Sir John Yorke of Gowlthwaite, 'for if thou doest not, I dwell upon Sir John his land and shall be . . . put out of [my] farm'; and Elizabethan recusant landlords were occasionally charged with instructing their tenants not to go to church. Proselytism as active as that of Dorothy Lawson on her lands at Heaton may have

72. Rowlands, 'Catholics in Staffordshire', pp. 140–144; V.C.H. Staffordshire, iii, pp. 111, 100 and n. 17.

73. V.C.H. Warwickshire, ii, p. 45; E. A B. Barnard, A Seventeenth-Century Country Gentleman: Sir Francis Throckmorton, 1640–80 (Cambridge, 1948), pp. 4 f., 53 ff.

74. 'Character of Elizabethan Catholicism', p. 227 and references; above, chap. 5, n. 43; R. Meredith, 'The Eyres of Hassop', Recusant History, viii (1965), p. 63, cf. small figures for Catholics in Leicestershire. V.C.H. Leicestershire, ii, p. 69; Row-lands, 'Catholics in Staffordshire', p. 178.

amounted to much the same thing: there were said to be one Catholic family when she arrived and no Protestants when she left; far from leaving the business of instruction and conversion to her priest, she did it herself, baptised their children, and had a hundred converts at the end of it.[75] But I know of no case where a tenant was actually turned off a farm for failing to conform to his landlord's religion. Some degree of positive discrimination in favour of Catholic tenants, prospective or actual, is a different matter, though here again there were more and less vigorous ways of exercising it. In the extreme case, John Thornton of Netherwitton was alleged in the 1660s to 'let no land unless they revolt to Popery'; if the seventeenth-century practice on the estate was the same as the eighteenth, this seems to have meant that a Protestant proposing to take a farm would be expected to marry a Catholic girl and change his religion, if not immediately, at least with the minimum of delay. At Everingham, Sir Marmaduke Constable certainly exercised religious discrimination in charity to poor tenants, and possibly also in allowing latitude for arrears of rent.[76] More usually, one gets the impression that encouragement of Catholicism on an estate was effected by a slightly favourable leasing policy and, where the neighbourhood was mainly or wholly Catholic already, by encouraging so far as possible security of tenure; though where a family had decided to build up a Catholic estate from scratch, as the Haggerstons did at Ellingham during the eighteenth century, something more energetic was required.[77] Beneficial leasing to Catholics could only be convincingly established by intricate investigation of particular estates; here one can only report a certain number of signs which point to its existence. Some action of this sort seems to have been taken by the Arundells under Elizabeth. In 1642, at the outbreak of the Civil War, according to Clarendon, Parliament was informed that Catholic landlords 'used their Protestant tenants worse in the raising their rents than they did those of their own religion', and issued an order against the practice which led to com-

75. C. Howard, *Sir John Yorke of Nidderdale* (London, 1939), p. 34; Dickens, 'First Stages', p. 163; Palmes, *Life of Mrs. Dorothy Lawson*, pp. 18, 23, 40, 51.
76. 'Survey of the Archdeaconry of Northumberland, 1663', *Archaeologia Aeliana*, 2nd series xvii (1895), p. 247; 'Four Catholic Congregations', p. 119, n. 81; 'More Northumbrian Congregations', p. 24; Forster, 'Catholicism in the Diocese of Durham in 1767' (see above, chap. 5, n. 2), pp. 82 f.; P. Roebuck, 'Absentee Land-ownership in the late 17th and early 18th Centuries', *Agricultural History Review*, xxi (1973), p. 6.
77. 'More Northumbrian Congregations', pp. 12–13.

pulsory rent-fixing in some cases; from just before this date we have one indication from Cumberland of heavy fining of Protestant tenants, and from a little later, under the parliamentary regime, an offer of a beneficial lease to a Catholic tenant, prudently declined.[78] This was however at Little Crosby, where all the tenants seem to have been Catholics anyway; yet what we know of the Blundells' relations with their tenants does seem suggestive of what went on elsewhere. In general, a well-established tenant family on the Little Crosby estate was in a remarkably secure and favourable position: copyhold leasing for three lives at a moderate fine continued to a late date, and leasing for years at an economic rent was not introduced until towards the end of the eighteenth century, though William Blundell had worked out that leasing for lives was unfavourable to himself in 1663.[79] When the lives expired, the heir of a good tenant got strongly preferential treatment; according to Blundell, he would pay for a new three-life lease something like £50 for a tenure which would have fetched £100 on the open market, five- or six-years' value instead of ten.[80] Blundell said this was no more than the custom of the country, which seems more or less true; even so, he strikes one as an exceptionally scrupulous observer of it, and he was at the same time given to making special concessions for tenants who he thought deserved it. One we have already noticed; on another occasion he gave a lease to a man *gratis* 'for the great service he had done to his late Majesty [Charles I] in time of war'; in 1663, he left a memorandum to his heirs to 'regard the heir of John Howard according as he regardeth or ought to regard his ancient tenants [and] to show sometime unto the said John and his children some marks of particular favour, which may be known to be chiefly done in memory and gratitude for the long and faithful service of his uncle Edward

---

78. A. L. Rowse, *Tudor Cornwall*, p. 378; [Edward Hyde, Earl of Clarendon], *The History of the Rebellion and Civil Wars in England*, i (ed. W. D. Macray, Oxford, 1888), p. 595—though the (unlikely) implication here was that Catholic landlords charged higher rents than their neighbours; *H.M.C. Portland Mss.*, iii, p. 69; Blundell, *Cavalier*, p. 16. In the late seventeenth century Lady Clifford, at Ugbrooke in Devon, was alleged to be 'cruel' to her Protestant tenants and to have forced some to turn Papist: Oliver, *Collections illustrating the History of the Catholic Religion in the counties of Cornwall [etc.]*, p. 23.
79. *Cavalier's Notebook*, pp. 144 f.; for cases similar to that of the Blundells, see Meredith, 'The Eyres of Hassop', pp. 30, 64; Tempest, *Religio Laici*, pp. 61 f.
80. See Blundell's general case of conscience about tenant right in Lancashire, 1654, in *Cavalier's Notebook*, pp. 253–259; Blundell seems to have been a good deal more scrupulous in these matters than the priest whom he consulted.

Denton, performed to my grandfather and myself'.[81] In his grandson's time the beneficiary of this instruction seems to have been Edward or Ned Howard; when it was decided that the priest would have to leave the manor house because he could not get on with Nicholas's wife, he was set up in lodgings in Howard's cottage and part of it was turned into the village chapel.[82] We need not, on the other hand, idealize conditions at Little Crosby. Just because, perhaps, he did not squeeze his tenants economically, William Blundell expected a proper degree of deference as landlord, and knew the difference between 'deserving' and 'undeserving' tenants; 'by *undeserving* I understand all great misdemeanours or notable disrespect to his landlord for which the landlord would punish him'.[83] But even here, admittedly at a time when drastic action would have been unwise, he was prepared to admit an heir for a fine not more than £10 higher than for the heir of a deserving tenant and still substantially below the economic rent; when he put the question as a case of conscience, he was careful to specify that the discrimination must be 'for example's sake, and not for revenge'. It is easy to see how religious conduct could enter into a judgment of what was 'deserving' behaviour and what was not; so far as one knows, all the tenants at Little Crosby were Catholics, deserving and undeserving alike, but given less careful attention they would probably have been less uniform. Nicholas 'discoursed' his tenants pretty frequently, especially when there was a question of adding lives to leases; possibilities of marriage were bound to come up on these occasions, and it was probably at this point that the landlord's influence was strongest. Thus on 24 June 1709 Blundell 'discoursed John Tickley about his Courting and about adding his [future] Wives Life to his Leas'.[84] I see no evidence that, at Little Crosby, this influence was used to ensure that Protestant partners changed religion; probably there were enough Catholics in the neighbourhood to make it unnecessary to look outside them; but in other respects what happened here seems rather like what happened at Netherwitton. Probably it is an exaggeration to suggest, as I have done elsewhere, that landlord influence was a, or the, principal factor in preventing mixed marriage among Catholics during this period;[85] but

81. *Cavalier*, p. 16; *Cavalier's Notebook*, pp. 49, 250.
82. *Great Diurnal of Nicholas Blundell*, i, p. 63.
83. *Cavalier's Notebook*, p. 255.
84. *Great Diurnal*, i, p. 220; cf. p. 95: 'I proposed Richard Bryanson for Ellen Tickley' (13 October 1705).
85. 'Four Catholic Congregations', pp. 112–114.

I think it would be unrealistic not to give it a good deal of weight in the relation of landlord and tenant. If, after all, the families of landlord and tenant were to live as neighbours for the decades, indeed centuries, which tenurial arrangements like the Blundells' imply, a landlord was entitled to be interested in whom the tenants married; if he was giving them as good a deal as the Blundells seem to have been doing, he was entitled to have his advice taken very seriously.

At this point, to avoid misunderstanding, I should repeat that the purpose of this chapter has been to outline the role of the gentry in the formation of the community, and not to explain why people became Catholics. I do not wish to argue that, at any time between the reign of Queen Elizabeth and that of George III, Catholicism outside the gentry was invariably an expression of deference towards Catholic members of that class. If, for example, we were to take a more rounded view of the relation of landlord and tenant, we should have to look at it from the point of view of the Catholic farmer, who must have faced stronger pressure from Protestant landowners than Protestant farmers did from Catholic ones, and have had much less freedom of choice: there was a push- as well as a pull-effect involved.[86] Even so, the decision in the end belonged to the landlord: hence one may take the incidence of Catholic tenants on Catholic estates as representing, in its regional variations, a point of equilibrium between what the landlord wanted and what the neighbourhood would stand. There were probably also variations in time: during the eighteenth century Catholic landlords seem to have exercised a greater influence over the religion of their tenants than they had done before. I think it would be implausible to deny that, however explained, this influence was the principal factor which ensured that the process of separation was followed (at some distance) and completed by a process of congregation. Without the gentry there would certainly have been Catholic recusants—for how long?—but I find it very difficult to believe that there would have been a Catholic community.

86. cf. Forster, 'Catholicism in the Diocese of Durham in 1767', p. 70; the two effects are nicely distinguished in Aveling, *Catholic Recusancy in York*, p. 134.

8

HOW MANY CATHOLICS?

H ow large was the community whose creation I have tried to describe? Some may feel that the question might have been raised at an earlier point; and so perhaps it should have been, had it been possible to offer any meaningful answer to it which did not demand some knowledge of the community's history and structure, and on these grounds there would be a good case for postponing discussion of it still further. Nevertheless, it would be a strange attempt to estimate the contribution of the laity to the community's history which did not seek to find out how many of them there were. This is however easier said than done. Not, one may add, because there is a shortage of statistical or quasi-statistical information—quite the contrary; but there are two important problems involved in making use of the information that exists. The first and probably less serious one is that until the very close of this period the information needs very careful handling and interpretation: more careful, perhaps, than it will be possible to give it here.[1] A larger and more deeply rooted obstacle to understanding has been a presupposition which has been taken as so axiomatic as not to need discussion.

The axiom, on which I have offered some critical comments already, is that English pre-Reformation Christianity and English post-Reformation Catholicism are the same thing, or that one is a continuation of the other. The statistical implications of this view are roughly as follows: it is assumed that, at some notional point and barring a few obvious exceptions like Lollards—at say 1520—all Englishmen were Catholics; it is further assumed that, at some later point and ignoring some other exceptions—say 1750—all Englishmen were Protestants. The task of the statistician is to construct two symmetrical curves which will show

1. See most recently Aveling, 'Some Aspects of Yorkshire Catholic Recusant History, 1558–1791', in G. Cuming (ed.), *Studies in Church History: iv, The Province of York* (Leiden, 1967), pp. 107 ff.

at what rate this change occurred, and where the crucial crossing-point is to be found. Naturally enough Catholics and Protestants have differed as to the general shape to which these curves should conform. On the Catholic side the preferred shape has been comparatively straight: without too much exaggeration one might say that the Catholic percentage of the population of England was regarded as having been divided by two in the course of each successive half-century, reaching say 50% in 1570, 25% in 1620, 12½% in 1670 and declining towards vanishing-point during the eighteenth century. To a surprising degree this position of the problem has proved acceptable to Protestant historians, though most of them would have shifted the dates a good deal further forward. But these differences do not affect the main point, that posed in these terms the statistics of English Catholicism are statistics of steady decline and the history of the community that of a 'dwindling minority'.[2]

I do not think much progress will be made in the statistical description of English Catholicism during this period until this axiom is abandoned, until indeed it is replaced by the opposite one: that, to put the point in its crudest possible form, statistically speaking one starts in the Elizabethan period, and not from 100 but from nil. I am aware that this is an assumption as arbitrary as the first, and I hope I have shown that I am not presenting it as a historical fact; my point is that, of two arbitrary axioms, this one is statistically operable and the other is not. Two respectable attempts have been made to count the English Catholic community in this period, one by A. O. Meyer sixty years ago, and the other by Brian Magee in the 1930s.[3] Magee, whose effort is a very serious one and still valuable, built on the first assumption and came to conclusions which are in many ways remote from reality. Meyer, who made a very rough stab at the problem but started from the second assumption, got much nearer the truth.

Some consequences follow from the use of this axiom. We are not trying to calculate a body of opinion, but membership of a community; and I should define community membership in this case as meaning habitual, though in view of physical difficulties not necessarily very frequent, resort to the services of a priest and, from at least the later

2. See, e.g., P. Hughes, *Reformation in England* (London, 1954), iii, pp. 48 f., 239 f.; Magee, *English Recusants*, pp. 23–31, etc.; David Mathew, *The Jacobean Age* (London, 1938), pp. 11, 230; and now J. P. Kenyon, *The Popish Plot* (London, 1972), pp. 21, 236.
3. A. O. Meyer, *England and the Catholic Church under Queen Elizabeth*, pp. 55 ff.; Magee, *The English Recusants* (London, 1938).

seventeenth century, a degree of continuous congregational participation. These are positive criteria and the onus of proof must lie on establishing them. To me, this means that no figure for the size of the community, or of any of its parts, is admissible which does not preferably arise from an actual positive count of heads of people whom one may assume from the nature of the act counted to have been members of the community in one of the senses defined. If it is an estimate, or dependent upon a combination of estimates, no notice should be taken of it unless the informant shows himself to share, in practice, the general conception of the community defined above, to have some grasp of its structure and workings, and to be using something like the criteria of membership which have been suggested. This will eliminate nearly all the vague guesses which have commonly been used as evidence of Catholic numbers in the sixteenth and seventeenth centuries; one or two of these estimates do fulfil the criteria and will be used, with caution, to help interpretation. But the main burden must fall on the head-counting operations which in various ways and at various times were applied to the community between the reign of Queen Elizabeth and that of George III—recusant-counting, statutory and ecclesiastical, in the first century of the community's history, official papist-counting and the statistical efforts of its own authorities during the second. Among these head-counting operations we shall be advised to proceed from the more to the less reliable, from those which need less to those which need more interpretation; which means proceeding backwards in time.

In 1767 Parliament mounted a papist-counting operation which was generally and rightly thought to be a great improvement on any of its predecessors: it produced a figure of 69,376.[4] This figure seems to have been the result of a fairly painstaking count of individuals by the parochial clergy, and included children, but given the conditions of eighteenth-century statistical enquiry it was bound to be something of an underestimate. From my own experience it seems realistic to suppose that, taken as a whole, returns from country parishes underestimated by about 15%;[5] so far as I know nobody has tried to assess the accuracy

4. Magee, *op. cit.*, p. 197; Aveling, *art. cit.*, p. 108; Williams, *Wiltshire*, pp. 256 f. and references to printed extracts in n. 14. Those for the diocese of Chester are in process of publication by the Catholic Record Society.

5. *Recusant History*, ix, pp. 101 f.; x, pp. 16 f. For reasons explained here I concluded that the best procedure for getting something like full parochial returns of Catholics was to take, for each parish, whichever of the two successive returns of

of returns from larger towns, where counting may have been more difficult, but in default of such investigation we may reasonably take the rural underestimate as generally applicable, giving a total of 80,000 Catholics in England and Wales about 1770. This figure would probably exclude a fair number of people who were in some sense Catholics but not congregational participants, but it seems a fairly accurate guide to the real membership of the community at this point. It is supported by an estimate, based on a survey of their congregations by the four vicars-apostolic in 1773, of 59,500; this seems to have been meant to exclude children of non-communicating age, and the bishops at the time were inclined to minimise the numbers of their flock, but it also includes a figure of 20,000 Catholics in London which was only offered as a guess and cannot be accepted as a genuine figure of congregational members.[6]

1767 and 1780 gave a larger figure, add these up, and attribute to the result an inter-mediate date. In the two sets of congregations investigated this gave results respec-tively 19·5% and 16·8% above the figures for 1767, but this proved somewhat larger than was characteristic of rural Northumberland as a whole. Applied to the four rural deaneries of Northumberland, the results of this procedure are as follows:

Deanery	1767	1780	'1776'	Actual increase on 1767	% increase on 1767
Alnwick	655	694	768	113	17·2
Bamburgh	446	469	517	71	15·9
Corbridge	326	334	381	55	16·9
Morpeth	411	367	448	37	9·0 *
Total	1,838	1,864	2,114	276	14·2

* Six out of the fifteen parishes made no return in 1780, and though none of them contained large numbers of Catholics, the figure here would no doubt be somewhat higher if they had made returns; enough, anyway, to justify the use of a more con-venient allowance of 15%.

Figures from House of Lords Mss., *Returns of Papists*, 1767 and 1780.

6. J. H. Whyte, 'The Vicars Apostolics' Returns of 1773', *Recusant History*, ix, pp. 205 ff.—for London figure, p. 207 and cf. below, chap. 12, p. 312; T. G. Holt, 'A note on some eighteenth-century Statistics', *ibid.*, x, pp. 3 ff. It seems evident from Rowlands, 'Staffordshire', pp. 102, 112, that all figures given here are intended as figures of communicants; but cf. my own comments on some individual figures for Northumberland, *Recusant History*, x, p. 17, which would seem exaggerated if treated in this way. Cf. John Chadwick to Bishop Matthew Gibson, 3 February 1783 (Ushaw Mss. ii. 129), for an informed opinion that the northern returns only in-cluded communicants, and minimised numbers. In 1787 Gibson made a return of 33,685 communicants in the North, a figure 50% higher than what has been deduced from the rather vague indications given by his predecessor in 1773: Eamon Duffy, 'Joseph Berington and the English Cisalpine Movement, 1772–1803' (Cambridge Ph.D. thesis, 1973), p. 13. This suggests that the overestimation for London may be balanced by underestimation in the North.

As usual, the foundations of this internal estimate seem shakier than those of the external one, but so far as they go they give it a reasonable degree of confirmation, and I think the figure of 80,000 in 1770 may be accepted as a fairly firm starting-point.

As we proceed backwards from 1767 we run into increasing difficulties. There were several previous censuses of Catholics during the eighteenth century, but none of them seems at all satisfactory; the reason, it was alleged in 1767, was that what had been counted on earlier occasions was not individuals but heads of families.[7] This seems too sweeping, but true to some degree, and probably the main reason why these returns have so far proved of little value. In fact, to find anything at all comparable to the figures for 1770 we must go back more than a century to the eve of the Civil War, and try to make use of the much more difficult recusancy statistics. The most convincing attempt to use these as the basis for an estimate of the total size of the English Catholic community was made by Magee in his *English Recusants*,[8] and though his conclusions seem obviously wrong much of his argument remains sound and valuable. He took, so far as they were available, what appear to be reliable figures of recusants convicted in twenty-eight southern counties of England during the reign of Charles I up to 1640–1641, from which, after sampling, he deducted $12\frac{1}{2}\%$ to account for people who would have been convicted more than once during this period. He added disparate but fairly well-substantiated totals of recusants from four northern counties dating from the same period; made up for a lack of information about three other northern counties by giving figures similarly based to those of the southern counties but dating from thirty years later; and finally put in a notional figure for six other counties and Wales, for which he could find no relevant statistics. From all this he concluded that in 1641 the number of people in England and Wales who had been convicted for recusancy was something like 27,000. His procedure was open to some objections, and on the whole I think his figure was something of an underestimate: in the most important case, that of Lancashire, his figure of 5,496 recusants is one of those supplied from the Restoration period and so particularly

7. Aveling, *art. cit.*, p. 108; see Rowlands, 'Staffordshire', for examples.
8. Pp. 94–112. K. J. Lindley, 'The Part played by Catholics in the English Civil War' (Manchester Ph.D. thesis, 1968), pp. 19–42, has a survey of the strength and distribution of Catholicism in 1641 which adds something (from subsidy rolls) to the evidence used by Magee, and generally confirms it; he attempts no estimate of overall numbers.

suspect; it ought obviously to be replaced by that of 9,000, the figure for recusants convicted in 1641; similarly in Staffordshire, the same alteration would give a figure of 1,069 instead of 678.[9] In fact, the period from 1640 to the outbreak of the Civil War saw a very determined drive to convict recusants, and higher numbers were reached than at any other time; if it were possible to offer a total for recusants convicted in the whole country during this period it would probably give us a sounder basis than Magee's; but since this does not seem to be practicable I think we shall do well to accept his figure with the modifications suggested above, giving us a total of 31,000 recusants in England and Wales in 1641.

Magee was certainly correct in supposing that a total of convicted recusants was not the total membership of the English Catholic community; he was equally certainly far too lavish in his additions.[10] He proposed to add to his total on four grounds; first, that not all members of the community were recusants; second, that many recusants avoided presentation for recusancy through influence, neglect of churchwardens, etc.; third, that many recusants who were presented were not convicted; and fourth, that no child below communicating age could be presented for recusancy. He assumed that half the 'recusant' population consisted of non-recusant children, which gave a total of 54,000; he further supposed that three or four times as many recusants existed as were actually convicted, and that there were perhaps as many churchpapists as recusants. From all this he came to the conclusion that a Catholic population at this time of 200,000 was 'reasonably well established', and that it 'might have been' as high as half a million.[11] Most of these last additions are indefensible, and can only be explained as a mistaken attempt to reconcile the figures with the axiom mentioned above. Of Magee's four suggested grounds for addition, the first may be rejected, since church-papists were a virtually extinct race in 1641. The third ought probably to be rejected as well, since, by an amendment

9. *V.C.H. Staffordshire*, iii, p. 104—the figure appears to be one of recusants indicted rather than convicted, and not to include anyone under 16: *Staffordshire Catholic History*, no. 5 (1964), pp. 1 ff.; Magee, *op. cit.*, pp. 93, 200. The Yorkshire figures, on the other hand, seem rather exaggerated in the light of those offered by Aveling, *art. cit.*, p. 110, n. 1; cf. John Miller, *Popery and Politics* (see above, chap. 4, n. 19). p. 12. Miller remarks that these Restoration figures contain a high proportion of Protestant recusants.

10. cf. Steel, *Sources* (see above, chap. 6, no. 50), pp. 831 f.

11. Magee, *op. cit.*, pp. 111 f., 116 f.; cf. Miller, *Popery and Politics* (above, n. 9), pp. 11 f.

of 1587 to the original act of 1581, conviction for recusancy followed more or less automatically upon indictment unless particular action was taken by the recusant, which by this time it very rarely was.[12] The second and fourth grounds are serious, though Magee has probably made exaggerated use of both of them. The age of conviction, which was sixteen in the original act and remained so in the amending act of 1587 which Magee cited, was reduced to nine by a further statute of 1606.[13] It seems to me most unlikely that children of this age were commonly presented as recusants; but in the light of this it would seem excessive to multiply by two for recusants' children, and even the conventional figure for non-communicant children in a seventeenth-century population, 40%, sounds rather high. If we start from a figure of 31,000 recusants, something under 50,000 seems a reasonable guess at a total for them and their children. Finally, as in 1767, we have an allowance to make for sheer administrative inadequacy. It seems fairly safe to say that a larger allowance must be made here than in 1767, but considering the span of time covered by most of the county returns and the intense activity of 1641–1642 I should be sceptical of a figure much above 25%.[14] This would give us a total Catholic community in England and Wales in 1641 of about 60,000 men, women and children.

To anyone coming to the subject without preconceptions, these estimates for 1641 and 1770 would lend each other a certain degree of plausibility, and something can be done to bridge the gap between them. In 1687 John Leyburn, the first of the vicars-apostolic and the first Catholic bishop functioning in England for fifty years, toured his entire flock administering the sacrament of confirmation, and we know that in the northern counties he confirmed 20,859 people. Eleven years earlier Archbishop Compton's census had reached a figure of 11,871 Catholics in the province of Canterbury.[15] The later was a figure for

12. Bowler, introduction to C.R.S. lvii, pp. xxxix–xl; Walker, 'Implementation of the Elizabethan Statutes against Recusants' (see above, chap. 6, n. 31), pp. 239 f.
13. Aveling, *art. cit.*, p. 107.
14. cf. Magee's suggestion (p. 107) that only one recusant in 'three or four or five' was convicted; the only real evidence he cites, a comment on the position in Northumberland in 1625 (*ibid.*, p. 48), was probably fairly well-informed, though it actually only claimed a difference of something over twice. But Northumberland was not a typical country.
15. Magee, *op. cit.*, pp. 112, 219; A. Browning (ed.), *English Historical Documents*, viii, *1660–1714* (London, 1953), pp. 413–416; Williams, *Wiltshire*, pp. 254–256, for Wiltshire figures of Compton census and valuable evidence of the general conformity of these with recusant figures taken over a period; it is clear that they were meant

communicants, and it seems reasonable to double both these figures to get some idea of the size of the community about 1680, which would again give a total of some 60,000. It seems fairly certain that the number of Catholics being served by Jesuits in 1710 was 20,000 or somewhat less, and since at this time they formed between a quarter and a third of all missionary priests this would suggest much the same figure for the whole community.[16] With due regard to the fallibility of these conjectures I think one may draw three fairly reliable conclusions. The first is that the English Catholic community was reasonably stable in size from before the middle of the seventeenth century to after the middle of the eighteenth, a conclusion hard to reconcile with the traditional assumption that Catholics were a 'dwindling minority'. The second is that during the seventeenth century it was a great deal smaller than has usually been supposed; perhaps one-third as large as the 200,000 considered by Magee as 'reasonably well established' and accepted by Meyer on the basis of repeated estimates of this order.[17] The third is that in so far as it showed a general tendency, this was not to decline but to increase; or, to be more specific, it was more or less static during the second half of the seventeenth century and on the increase, perhaps to the extent of some 30%, thereafter.[18] I am aware that this last conclusion may be felt to be forcing the evidence to give a far more precise meaning than it can bear, and must ask the reader to

to represent communicants. Miller, *Popery and Politics* (above, n. 9), pp. 9–11, notes that the area covered by the confirmations included some counties in the province of Canterbury but accepts a total of 60,000 Catholics at this date. William Penn, who thought there were 30,000 Catholics in England in the reign of James II, was presumably relying on these figures: Alan Cole, 'The Quakers and the English Revolution', in Aston (ed.), *Crisis in Europe, 1560–1660*, p. 357.

16. Foley, *Records*, v, p. 161—the figure of 12,476 returned would seem from *ibid.*, pp. 513, 783 f., to be a figure for adults; it was compiled from serious-looking returns from the districts. It could possibly be deduced from the annual total of 500 baptisms returned by the Jesuits around 1670 that the figure for that date, children included, would have been about 15,000. Steel, *Sources*, p. 832, n. 143, tentatively estimates some 85,000 Catholics in 1675 and some 72,000 in 1705, on what basis I am not clear.

17. Magee, *op. cit.*, p. 112; Meyer, *England and the Catholic Church*, pp. 64 f.; Kenyon, *The Popish Plot*, pp. 24 f.

18. For the present state of discussion on this point, see Steel, *Sources*, pp. 829 ff. Hitherto Meyer (*op. cit.*, p. 65) had been the only historian to adopt this general point of view (for the seventeenth century); Lecky, quoted by Steel, p. 832, seems to have thought it possible for the eighteenth. See Aveling, *art. cit.*, p. 110, n. 1, for a set of Yorkshire figures, 1580–1780, which provide a model for the general view taken here.

accept it as plausible but speculative for the moment. One must add that an absolute increase of this order might, if established, still mean some decline in the number of Catholics relative to the rest of the population, though not a very marked one.

Difficulties in enumeration get larger as we proceed backwards from 1640. Problems of definition increase. Even supposing that we exclude the indeterminate mass of 'conservative' religious opinion which either did not want, or failed, to enter the clientele of the missionary priests—such, for example, as one may dimly see it outlined in the York marriage figures of Dr Cowgill—we are still left with a proportion of non-recusant members of the community of whom little of any statistical content can be said, except that it must be assumed to increase steadily as we move backwards from 1640 towards 1570. As for the recusants themselves, I think one may take it that recusant returns become more arbitrary and problematical as one approaches their source, though not to a degree which makes them totally useless.

The best of them date from shortly after the accession of James I in 1603, so we may try a calculation at that date. Before we do, one of the very few general estimates which meets most of the criteria suggested above is worth a little notice. In 1613 the papal nuncio in the Spanish Netherlands, Guido Bentivoglio, forwarded to Rome information which he had evidently received from some English source to the effect that there were some 600 priests then working in England, and it was reckoned on the mission that a priest would have about 30 families to serve.[19] What is striking about this attempt is that it is the only one, so far as I know, to approach the problem in a way which was in principle capable of arriving directly at a more or less reliable answer. Meyer, who seems to have been the first to spot it, counted 6·5 individuals to a family and deduced a Catholic population, defined by our criteria, of 120,000. The only thing wrong with this calculation, so far as I can see, is that each of its steps incorporates an element of exaggeration, though these are not individually very serious; but since the final figure depends on multiplying them all by each other, the final error is large. It seems fairly safe to say that the number of priests actually working on the mission at this time was not 600 but something like 400.[20] What underlies the figure of thirty families for every priest is the idea of a missionary circuit in which the priest would stay overnight with each of the families

19. Meyer, *England and the Catholic Church*, p. 63.
20. See below, chap. 10, pp. 215–223.

he served and get round the whole in about a month. There is no doubt that this *was* the pattern of operations of many priests at this time, and it was probably the nearest anybody could have got to an abstract model of what a missionary priest would be doing. But I am sure that, even if we take it as an average clientele for a circulating priest at this time, we cannot take it as an average clientele for all the priests on the mission; many were already in effect private chaplains to one gentry household, or a small group of them, and the largest of these would scarcely involve the cure of more than 100 souls; some appear to have been unemployed. Altogether it would seem reasonable to reduce the average figure of families per priest to twenty, and even this might be a little on the generous side. Finally, his family multiplier seems too high: admittedly an exceptionally large proportion of the 'families' in question would have been large families of the gentry; but religious uniformity was as yet by no means the rule in these, and it seems more credible to multiply by five.[21] Thus modified, Bentivoglio's figures give us a community of 40,000 people.

When we come to the diocesan returns of recusants of 1603, we find a total of 8,590 compared with an Anglican communicant population of $2\frac{1}{2}$ million.[22] As far as I can see this was the only general 'census' made at the time, though a number of local ones were made shortly afterwards, usually based on a fairly energetic use of the secular recusancy machinery; it is obvious from these that the bishops had not been putting themselves out.[23] However their return did cover the country, and

21. cf. Laslett, *The World we have Lost*, pp. 64 f.; Magee, *op. cit.*, p. 104. For the system of operations of priests at this time, see below, chap. 11, pp. 252 f; estimated ratios of priests to Catholics, chap. 10, p. 223.

22. Magee, *op. cit.*, p. 83; McGrath, *Papists and Puritans*, p. 399, prints the same table from R. G. Usher, *Reconstruction of the English Church* (2 vols., New York/London, 1960), i, p. 158, but gets 8,630 because of a difference of 40 in the figure from Chester diocese.

23. Here are some comparisons between diocesan returns and local county investigations:

Winchester diocese	398 (actually 447)	Hampshire	437
Lincoln diocese	295	Oxfordshire	556
Chester diocese	2,442	Lancashire	3,516
York diocese	720	Yorkshire	1,839

The Hampshire figure is a total of recusants convicted, 1598–1603; the figure for Winchester diocese appears to be in effect a figure for Hampshire alone, but there would have been few recusants in Surrey (J. H. Paul, 'Hampshire Recusants in the Time of Queen Elizabeth', *Proceedings of the Hampshire Field Club*, xxi (1959), pp. 77–81). The Oxfordshire figure is a total of individual recusants indicted from

I propose to use it as a basis. To proceed from it to an estimate of the total size of the Catholic community in 1603 calls for three steps, which I present in crude form.

1. *Recusant total as returned :* 8,590

2. *Add* for non-communicants and church-papists, an equal number.[24]

TOTAL 17,180

3. *Add* for inefficiency, etc. (compare the 15% of 1767 and the 25% of 1642), 50%—i.e. 50% of recusants and non-communicants, since I do not think we can make an allowance for inefficiency in respect of people whom the machinery was in principle unable to discover; and further assuming non-communicants to be half the total of non-communicants and church-papists: i.e. 50% of 12,885 = 6,443.

TOTAL 23,623

4. *Add* for children, assuming them to be 40% of the total community, since the statutory age for secular conviction was still 16, and the ecclesiastical figure is specifically compared to one of Anglican communicants: 15,749.

TOTAL 39,372

July 1604 to January 1613; it is obviously somewhat inflated by this time-span, but the territorial discrepancy is much more serious (A. G. Petti, *Recusant Documents from the Ellesmere Mss.*, C.R.S. lx (1968), pp. 211–245). The Lancashire figure is from a diocesan visitation in 1604; I am indebted for it to Dr Christopher Haigh, as also for valuable comments on an earlier version of this calculation. The Yorkshire figure is from Dickens, *Yorks. Archaeological Journal*, xxxvii (1948), pp. 30–31; it represents a survey of 1604, and is particularly valuable in that it distinguishes recusants who had emerged since the previous year (400 or so). On this basis I assume that an addition of 50% will be appropriate to bring the ecclesiastical figures up to the level of efficiency of a good local survey; theoretically one should then make a further allowance for inefficiency in the latter, but since most of these local figures reflect the boom in recusants which occurred immediately after 1603 (most of them presumably former non-communicants and church-papists, for whom an allowance will already have been made) I think it would be dangerous to do this, and have used an addition of 50% in the text.

24. There can obviously be no figure for communicating church-papists; as for non-communicants, the sources used in the previous note give one for every two recusants in Hampshire, one for every three in Yorkshire and one for every seven in Lancashire; in 1613 rather more non-communicants than recusants were returned from Lancashire (2,393 and 2,075 respectively: Magee, *English Recusants*, pp. 87 f.). I think it would be excessive to go beyond the suggestion made in the text.

The suggestion is, then, that if we multiply the returns by four or five we shall get a fair idea of the real size of the Catholic community at that date. I would not claim too much for the methods used at this point, but I think the result requires serious consideration. The likeliest errors in it seem to be that it makes too much allowance for children, considering what has been said about the history of household conformity, and possibly also for non-communicants and church-papists; on the other hand it probably makes too little allowance for inefficiency, especially in Lancashire, and these errors may perhaps cancel one another out. If we take the figure for the diocese of York, and compare it with the Catholic population proposed by Aveling for Yorkshire, we shall find some support for a multiplier of four.[25] Finally, of course, the figure given is almost the same as that of 40,000 already suggested for 1613. Personally I find it plausible (a little on the high side if anything), as I do the consequent conclusion that the Catholic community, as here understood, increased by something like a half between 1603 and 1641.

I doubt if it is profitable to pursue the problem beyond this point. If, of course, we define the Catholic community as the number of people making habitual use of the services of a *missionary* priest, the position is an extremely simple one: the number of such people rose from nought in 1570 to some 30,000 to 40,000 in 1603, which seems the most plausible figure for the harvest of the Elizabethan mission.[26] According to whether one considers the English Catholic community a survival or a new arrival, this will seem a more or less acceptable answer to questions about its size during the Elizabethan period; acceptable or not, it—or something on the same lines—is the only one available. Beyond this point, judgments about quantity seem purely arbitrary. Not, as we have seen, that the religious opinions of sixteenth-century Englishmen are wholly resistant to quantification; but it would be optimistic to suppose that any available index of them could shed much light on the two categories of Elizabethan Englishmen and women

25. Compare the figure for York diocese above, n. 23, with Aveling, *loc. cit.*, above, n. 18, *c.* 3,000 Catholics in Yorkshire in 1603. Aveling's figure would seem to exclude children; on the other hand the diocesan figures exclude those parts of the country which were in the diocese of Chester. These two considerations may roughly balance out. For the general figure, cf. Steel, *Sources*, p. 814, suggesting that the largest possible figure for the Catholic community in 1603 is 50,000.

26. Meyer started from much the same premises as those used here, but supposed that by 1585 the mission had 'converted' 100,000 people, a figure based on the feeblest of literary evidence (*England and the Catholic Church*, p. 496).

whom it would be relevant here to know about: those who used the services of the premissionary Catholic clergy after 1558; and those whose idea of Catholicity meant principally fasting and feasting, and who may not, as Patrick McGrath has observed, have had any contact with priests at all.[27] The fact that we cannot count such people is, I think, some indication that we cannot really consider them, in themselves and in their unmodified state, as genuinely forming part of the history of the community as such.

The attempt made here to give a statistical account of its first two centuries would hardly satisfy the professional standards of the historical demographer, and may well prove suspect to experts in the history of recusancy administration; it seems to me sufficiently convincing to support two conclusions. The first is that the correct approach to this phase of English Catholicism is not to see it as an originally massive body subject to continuous erosion, but as a small community gradually getting larger, except perhaps in the late seventeenth century when it seems to have been stationary and may possibly have contracted a little. The second brings us back to where we started. While the history of a Catholic community is in the first place the history of a laity, and the history of a laity is something which has meaning and structure in itself, none the less the source of its dynamics must, given the general character of the counter-Reformation Church, mainly be looked for among its clergy. The mission did not by itself suffice to create the community, but without the mission no community could have been created.

27. McGrath, *Papists and Puritans*, pp. 57, 59.

II

THE MISSION AND THE MISSIONER

'Jesuits are like Apricocks, heretofore one suckled here and there in a great man's house, and cost dear; now you may have them for nothing in every cottage.'

John Donne, *News from the Very Country*

9

LAYMAN INTO PRIEST

In passing from the laity to the clergy we are crossing a threshold which had a more awesome character for Catholics than it did for any of their contemporaries. Hence it is proper, in presenting the Catholic body as a whole, to treat clergy and laity as being of roughly equal weight. This may seem to be putting it mildly. Yet, as I have tried to show, we should not be misled into exaggerating the formative functions of the Catholic clergy to a degree which would reduce the laity to the status of a passive recipient of clerical initiatives or instructions; if this has ever been the case, it was certainly not so in England between the sixteenth century and the eighteenth. The object of the following chapters is to isolate the clerical contribution to the construction of an English Catholic community: to investigate how, during the two centuries which followed the institution of the college at Douai, the seminary priests and their colleagues from religious orders fulfilled their missionary task; to look at the mission as a whole, and as an individual calling.

By way of introduction I should like to say one or two things about the seminaries themselves. The institutions as such lie outside our field of vision: I consider them here simply as the passage through which the clergy recruited itself from the laity, with a view to detecting, at this point of entry, some characteristics of the relationship between the clergy and the community as a whole. Specifically, I have tried to find out from what sectors of the community the clergy were recruited, what changes happened in the pattern of recruitment over these two hundred years, and when they happened. Properly speaking, such changes can only be explained by the whole contents of the chapters which follow: I confine myself to asking one obvious question. Even so, what emerges is something like a miniature version of the general story: a further reason for presenting it by way of introduction. One more reason, to end with. The evidence that we have for the social origins of the Catholic clergy, while far from complete, seems unusually full and reliable; it should therefore be of interest to historians who, in a sociological age, have been grappling more generally with problems about the relationship of clergy and society in England which are of some importance.[1] Was the clergy—is the clergy—a category by itself, or a derivative of other categories? A load of social cement or a tool of social transformation? Perhaps the formal situation of the Catholic priest is too particular, his tradition of separate status too strong, for evidence about him to be admissible in the general case: perhaps not.

First, the bare facts. For the best part of a century, the Jesuit authorities of the seminary in Rome required an intending student to furnish them with details of his previous history; among other questions (the answers to which have proved useful in other contexts), they asked him to state whether his parents were *nobiles*, or *plebei*, or *mediae sortis*. None of the other colleges did this so continuously, but those at Douai and Valladolid collected the same information for periods of differing length, and the biographical details available for students at Douai in the eighteenth century may be used to similar effect.[2] I do not think we need enquire too closely here what the categories were intended to mean: the first meant sons of the landed gentry, and since few students described their parents as *plebei* we may employ a simple division between the sons of gentry and the sons of commoners. Considered from this point of view, the recruitment of the Catholic clergy went through three well-marked phases. The first went up to about 1610: during it, the gentry and the rest of the community appeared in almost equal numbers, with a slight predominance of the latter. We know the origins of 124 Roman students during this period, and of 222 at Valladolid: at Rome, 58 (47%) were from the gentry, and 66 (53%) not; at Valladolid, 109 (49%) and 113 (51%). These figures are very similar to those for Catholic laymen of known social origins executed for their religion under Elizabeth,[3] and suggest a well-defined general phenom-

1. Most recently Hugh Kearney, *Scholars and Gentlemen* (London, 1970), e.g. p. 33. For the history of the seminaries in general, see P. Guilday, *The English Catholic Refugees on the Continent* (London, 1914), pp. 63-120, 307-345; A. C. F. Beales, *Education under Penalty* (London, 1963), pp. 115-157; P. R. Harris, 'The English College, Douai, 1750-1794', *Recusant History*, x (1969), 79-95.
2. What follows is compiled from C.R.S. liv-lv (Roman *responsa*, 1598-1685); C.R.S. xxx, 20-142 (Valladolid *Liber Primi Examinis*, 1592-1624); C.R.S. x, pp. 269-314 (details of Douai students, 1628-1633); C.R.S. xxviii, pp. 10-266 *passim* (details of Douai *alumni*, 1692-1750). See Table I (below, p. 415).
3. P. Hughes, *Reformation in England* (London, 1954), iii, p. 339.

enon. The next phase began rather sharply around 1610 and continued until somewhere after the Restoration: during this period the clergy was overwhelmingly recruited from sons of the gentry. Already between 1610 and 1620 some two-thirds of the students at Rome and Valladolid described their parents as *nobiles*, and though Valladolid ceases to provide information after 1623, at Rome this proportion remained practically constant for half a century; in the 1650s the proportion of sons of gentry among students at Rome was higher than at any other time, nearly three-quarters. At Douai this information was only elicited between 1628 and 1633, and it is harder to interpret because not all students here were intending to be ordained. But so far as it goes it agrees with that from the other colleges: 125 students were accepted, of whom 95 were sons of gentry; the proportion of sons of gentry who stayed in the college to become priests was somewhat lower than this: eleven out of eighteen.[4] This is not very strong evidence to go on, but it does suggest that during this period differences of recruitment between colleges were marginal, and gentry predominance common to them all. The beginning of the third phase is harder to pin down exactly, but it started somewhere between the restoration of Charles II and the departure of James II, continued to the close of our period, and was characterised by a gathering decline of priestly vocations from the gentry. The Roman *responsa* are much less complete after 1660, and disappear altogether in 1685, but evidence for 65 students survives from these years (something under half the number of students accepted), and only 24 of them (37%) described themselves as sons of gentry; of the remaining 41, all but two gave *mediae sortis* or something equivalent. This is imperfect evidence, and the college at Rome may have been different from others: it drew most of its students from the Jesuit school at St Omer, and it is quite likely that sons of the gentry who had gone there and proposed to become priests tended to enter Society instead.[5] But some change was evidently happening, as we can tell by the origins of intending missioners or *alumni* in the college at Douai, which are known from 1691 to 1750. During this period there were 202 of them: 75 of their fathers (37%) seem to have been landowners

4. Those given as taking the mission oath in T. F. Knox (ed.), *The First and Second Diaries of the English College, Douay* (London, 1878), pp. 44 f.; others were no doubt ordained elsewhere.
5. cf. Beales, *Education under Penalty*, pp. 167 f.—*c.* 300 Jesuit vocations from St Omer, 1660–1700.

describing themselves as 'esquire' or something better, those of the remaining 127 not.[6] Except for a short boom after 1715, which is not difficult to explain, the gentry provided a steady 40% of the *alumni* until about 1740, when a further decline seems to have begun. There is no available information about the origins of the 137 Douai students who became *alumni* between 1751 and 1780, but judging by their names I should be extremely surprised if more than about 30 of them were sons of gentry.[7] We emerge with a fairly clear picture of the social origins of priests: during the first forty years after the foundation of Douai they came about equally from the gentry and the rest of the community; during much or most of the seventeenth century the clergy was largely recruited from the landowning classes; from somewhere after the Restoration to about 1740 sons of the gentry were in a minority, though a large one; after that the clergy was substantially recruited from other sectors of the community.[8]

As I have said I am not proposing to offer a full explanation of these developments. I should like at the moment simply to explore how far this changing pattern of recruitment was a consequence of the cost of seminary education, and of changes in the degree to which it could be borne by someone other than the parents of the intending priest. I confine myself to Douai, since we have fairly adequate information for this college. Not long after its foundation, the college (then at Reims) was endowed by the pope, and this and other subsidies made it accessible to poorer students. Until the end of the sixteenth century Allen

6. A few sons of the gentry and aristocracy (C.R.S. xxviii, pp. 268, 289, 291) were ordained, although not *alumni*; but this makes little difference to the result.

7. Knox, *Douai Diaries*, pp. 68–80. According to Marie Rowlands, 'The Staffordshire Clergy, 1688–1803', *Recusant History*, ix (1968), p. 221, the secular clergy here were 'almost without exception drawn from the ranks of the lesser gentry families'; but the lists given *ibid.*, pp. 230, 233 (*c*. 1790) do not seem to bear this out, and if true I do not think this was typical. Cf. below, ch. 14, p. 356.

8. It may be noted that what I have said concerns, formally speaking, only the secular clergy; institutions for the training of regular missioners do not seem to have kept similar records. In 1773, so far as I can calculate from the list in Foley, *Records of the English Province*, vii part 1, pp. cxxvi–cxxviii, something less than a third of the Jesuit missioners in England were sons of the gentry. B. Basset, *English Jesuits* (London, 1967), pp. 276 f., says that this was characteristic of the Jesuits throughout, but gives no evidence, and seems to be simply relying on this list. There cannot be much doubt that the Jesuits were more gentlemanly in recruitment during the seventeenth century; e.g. admissions to the English College in Rome were, at least for the early part of the century, to a large degree ultimately admissions to the Society; and cf. above, n. 5. Thus I see no reason to doubt that the pattern of recruitment of the seculars was typical of the clergy as a whole.

and his successors seem to have tried to support all its members on the endowment, and in 1599 it was still assumed that this would support a total of sixty staff, *alumni* and servants. By this time, a period of living above its resources and numerous other difficulties had left the college with a burden of debt which absorbed much of its income, and in 1612 this figure came down to fifty, which left room for hardly more than 30 students. This itself was obviously too optimistic: by 1640 it was regarded as foolhardy for the college authorities to attempt to pay for a dozen, and after that the original endowment rarely seems to have supported so many.[9] This had the effect of filling the college with paying students who had not undertaken to be ordained, and most of whom were not; many of those who had were nevertheless required to pay for much or most of their education. Matthew Kellison, who became head of the college in 1613 and presided over this transition in its fortunes, did his best to counteract it by organising the provision of scholarship funds from England;[10] but this was a long job and had not made much headway before the Civil War, which precipitated another crisis. Except for a permanent scholarship for two students from Lancashire which Kellison had secured in 1628, and which survived the war, few scholarships seem to have been available until towards the end of the seventeenth century, when the vicars-apostolic began to take an interest in the matter. Gradually their efforts bore fruit, and by 1750 the college was comparatively well endowed: at this time, besides seven or eight *alumni* on the papal foundation, between 30 and 40 out of 90–100 students in the lower classes were on scholarship funds; about half of these arose from gentry bequests, the rest were endowed or administered by the vicars-apostolic, former presidents or local clergy associations. Challoner was extremely active in this field. He had himself been supported on one of Bishop Leyburn's burses at the beginning of the century, and from the time of his episcopate he sent a steady stream of scholarship students to the college: in 1751 he was supporting seven. He also persuaded his London colleagues, Benjamin Petre and James Talbot, to follow his example, which they could well afford to do.[11] Here was at least one reason why a Catholic priest in the eighteenth

9. C.R.S. x, pp. 11–15, 118; Guilday, *English Catholic Refugees*, p. 324; C.R.S. xxviii, pp. 272, 289 f.
10. C.R.S. x, pp. 219 ff.
11. Beales, *Education under Penalty*, p. 142; C.R.S. x, pp. 263, 277; xi, pp. 441, 496, 499—note that several of these are for the support of boys from the donor's family; C.R.S. xxviii, pp. 272, 280, 289 f., 296 f, 299; Burton, *Challoner*, i, pp. 8 f.

century was more likely to be the son of a northern farmer or London tradesman than a member of a landowning family.

At this stage I draw no conclusion from these facts, except to repeat the suggestion that this history of clerical recruitment is something like a potted history of the community during this period. Instead I present the views of an eighteenth-century president of Douai, Robert Witham, on how to treat those of his students who were 'engaged in the vocation of the mission':

> He must have an eye to the wants they may be under in any kind, and relieve them as well as it is in his power, without distinction or persons, gentlemen or otherwise, which tis very impertinent for anyone to reflect upon. Virtue and an exact complyance with our dutys, especially joyn'd with learning, are the chief recommendations he must have a regard to. What were the Apostles? and the being a minister of God makes everyone equal or above the condition of being born a gentleman.[12]

12. C.R.S. xxviii, p. 309.

MISSIONARY QUESTIONS

IN the first part of the book, we have seen the Catholic clergy
grappling with the question of whether they formed a mission or a
church. Here we may consider this question as settled in favour of
the first alternative, and proceed to examine their activity and achievements as a missionary body. In doing so, we may bear in mind that a
missionary condition for the clergy was the natural counterpart of a
sectarian condition for the community as a whole: that it entailed a
regime of ecclesiastical *laissez-faire*, in which the relations of clergy and
laity were governed in the first place by the laws of supply and demand.
At this point students of seventeenth-century English history may call
to mind a chapter in Christopher Hill's *Economic Problems of the Church*,
in which the cause of Puritanism and the cause of private enterprise are
found to coincide in the organisational and financial structure of the
Puritan movement.[1] I am not sure whether its author would welcome a
successful application of his scheme to the operations of the Catholic
mission. But, challenged by his example, and also by a good deal of
contemporary metaphor, I propose in the first place to consider the
mission, somewhat abstractly and over the long term, as one might
consider a business from the point of view of its board of directors.
Whether its operations, as a business, are to be construed as intrinsically
dissolvent of the seigneurial constitution of the lay community prevailing in this period, is a question in historical theory which I think we
may leave in suspense: I hope to show that they were, if only in the
very long run, destructive of it in practice. I take successively four
questions which arise. First, given that the traditional ecclesiastical
structure was excluded, who ran the mission, how, and how efficiently
did they run it? Second, how many priests did they have at their
disposal? Third, how effectively were those priests deployed? Fourth,

1. Oxford, 1956; chap. xi, 'The Feoffees for Impropriations', esp. pp. 263 ff.; cf.
Society and Puritanism, pp. 489, 492.

how was the whole operation paid for, and what in general was the financial structure of the mission? In the next chapter I shall try to approach the missionary profession at a more human level.

(i)

ORGANISATION

The chief conditions for successful missionary organisation in England would seem to have been to ignore ecclesiastical precedent, keep bureaucracy to a minimum and stay in touch with the problems of the working priest. On these criteria, and ignoring an initial period of confusion, the mission started fairly well, went through a bad patch after 1600, had recovered itself before the end of the century and continued to be competently run until the close of our period. The first effective regime was that of Henry Garnet, who was superior of the Jesuits in England from 1586 until his arrest after the Gunpowder Plot, and acted for much of that time as organiser of the mission as a whole.[2] None of his predecessors had had time to do more than get a rough idea of the problems; Garnet, during his long period of office, in conditions that were unpromising from a number of viewpoints, constructed a working organisational machine which proved a model for his successors, whether they appreciated this or not.

Although Garnet instituted, from 1590, the practice of meeting his own (Jesuit) missioners once or twice a year, his was not a participatory type of government; he exercised effective control over a large number of secular-clergy missioners, but they do not seem to have had a voice in the making of any central decisions of missionary policy.[3] Problems of distribution and finance, decisions as between mobility or stability for priests, or about the disposition and role of lay volunteers—all these were essentially settled by the Jesuit superior as an individual, either

2. P. Caraman, *Henry Garnet* (London, 1964), pp. 102 ff., 127 ff. My discussion of Garnet is almost wholly dependent on Caraman's work, though I do not always agree with his conclusions.
3. Caraman says (*Garnet*, p. 127) that seminary priests always joined with the Jesuits at the biannual meetings. It is true that there were two unnamed secular priests at the meeting at Baddesley Clinton in 1591, but they seem to have played a minor role. The statement in my text may be a little exaggerated, but seems essentially true.

on the spot or after reference to his own superior abroad; in this respect
Garnet's intimacy with Acquaviva, the Jesuit general throughout his
regime in England, gave him a virtually free hand.[4] This is not to
suggest that Garnet took no advice. He stuck firmly to the periodic
assembling of Jesuits although it might well have been felt that this
was not in the circumstances a very good idea; at one meeting at
Baddesley Clinton in 1591, well known through John Gerard's graphic
description of it, he had been having a 'consultation' with his most
experienced men—Robert Southwell, Edward Oldcorne and Gerard
himself—the night before they were all very nearly arrested at one
stroke.[5] None the less, it is evident that the Jesuit belief in unfettered
individual decision-making was carried over into his government of
the mission as a whole.

It was scarcely possible to run the mission, as a whole, except from
London or somewhere nearby, and though Garnet was never able to
establish a secure and permanent headquarters there, he moved
steadily in this direction: after 1600 he was a fairly permanent fixture at
White Webbs, a house belonging to the Vaux sisters on Enfield Chase.[6]
His preference in local organisation was to give wide regional responsibilities to men whose competence he was sure of and, within generally
agreed guidelines of activity, leave them to get on without interference.
Their business was to provide a rational framework of operations, not
so much for other Jesuits, since until quite late in Garnet's regime there
were hardly enough Jesuits in the country to man a full complement of
such regional posts, as for those among the seminary priests who were
willing to avail themselves of it and accept the degree of Jesuit direction
which it entailed; by the mid-1590s this was probably a majority of
them. The best instance of a regional organiser under the Garnet
regime was Richard Holtby, whose work in the North-east we have
already noticed;[7] two secular priests, John Mush and Thomas Bell,
seem to have had a similar position in other parts of the North, until
Bell turned informer and Mush fell out with Garnet after he had applied
to enter the Society and been turned down.[8] John Gerard looked after
East Anglia until he was sent elsewhere by Garnet after his arrest and

4. Caraman, *Garnet*, pp. 34 ff., 45 f., 80, 226 f., 246, etc.
5. *ibid.*, pp. 131 ff.
6. *ibid.*, pp. 57, 68, 164, 242 f., 264, 299.
7. Above, pp. 87 f.
8. Aveling, *Northern Catholics*, pp. 151, 159, 167; Caraman, *Garnet*, pp. 53 f.

subsequent escape from the Tower; his place seems to have been taken by the secular John Bavand.[9] For some years Garnet tried to supervise the east Midlands himself, spending part of the year there and part in London until the task of central administration became too heavy. In the west Midlands, his settling of Edward Oldcorne at Hinlip Hall in Worcestershire in 1589 marked the beginning of a period of effective local organisation which ended when Oldcorne and himself were arrested at Hinlip in January 1606.[10] Farther west, in response to successive requests from both Parsons and Garnet for Welshmen, Robert Jones was established about 1598 and proved equally successful along the south Wales borders.[11] Elsewhere there were gaps. South of the Thames Garnet's organisation does not really seem to have got off the ground. There is no sign of anybody in the South-east until Richard Blount, later one of Garnet's more distinguished successors, was received into the Society in the late 1590s; in west Sussex and Hampshire he does not seem to have done much more than rely on Southwell's extensive family connections as a basis for intermittent visits; in the South-west promising efforts broke down after the arrest of a potential local organiser, John Cornelius, and a subsequent breach in relations between his patrons, the Arundell family, and the missionary organisation. The North-west, Lancashire included, seems to have been another gap; Garnet complained that his organisation failed to penetrate into some areas because of obstruction from established priests, and it would be unrealistic to suppose that he could have achieved a complete coverage of the country.[12]

The Jesuits claimed that they were not exercising authority or jurisdiction over the secular missioners, but offering them services which they were free to accept or refuse. This was true enough, though it begged one or two questions. Aveling seems to have got the measure of the relation in describing their regime as a system of clientage. It functioned by a purely empirical mixture of means: partly through spiritual direction and the anxiety of many secular priests to become Jesuits; partly through the power of the purse; and partly because, through a system of more or less country-wide connections with the

9. e.g., *Autobiography of John Gerard*, pp. 23, 29 f., 32.
10. Caraman, *Garnet*, pp. 64, 91, 331 ff.
11. C.R.S. xxxix, p. 108; Caraman, *Garnet*, pp. 100, 247 and above, p. 97.
12. *ibid.*, pp. 95, 159, 164, 189, 216, 315; B. Basset, *English Jesuits* (London, 1967), pp. 157 f. (Blount); C. Devlin, *The Life of Robert Southwell* (London, 1956), pp. 111 f., 127 f.; and see above, chap. 5, p. 104.

laity, they were able to match supply with demand and get priests into places. Garnet was particularly keen to keep an eye on the intake of newcomers from the seminaries, and much of the funds at his disposal seems to have gone on maintaining them quietly in London until there was somewhere definite for them to go.[13]

A decade after his assumption of office, when rumbles of opposition were becoming clearly audible, Garnet sent an account of his steward-ship to Acquaviva in which he claimed, by and large, to have produced order out of chaos and ensured that most of the seminary priests had a steady job to do.[14] This claim seems to me justified: in twenty years of first-hand experience, Garnet became familiar with the full range of problems and choices which were to frame the activity of those who ran the mission during the next two centuries. His solutions were in part an emergency response to an overwhelming situation, but they possessed two virtues which outlasted it and them: they were totally empirical, and they functioned with an absolute minimum of formal jurisdictional authority in the superior. Considered on grounds of pure efficiency, Garnet's regime gives a convincing impression of economy and crispness which, for the secular clergy, were not achieved again before the late seventeenth century. The mission would certainly have functioned a good deal better if it had been continued. But we cannot be surprised that its virtues were not appreciated by those who did not share the Jesuit idea of the Church.

Erected in 1598, and functioning in circumstances which have already been discussed, the archpriest regime was, I think it is clear, intended in the first place to modify Garnet's regime by devolving authority within it to members of the secular clergy, but not to change it funda-mentally. The more important date is 1602, when it was converted into a separate system, Garnet's remaining in existence alongside it. The organisation George Blackwell was given in 1598, a series of twelve regional 'assistants' chosen from the secular clergy, resembled the Jesuit regime in that it was intended to give more weight to effective organisational services than to jurisdictional authority, though one

13. Aveling, *Northern Catholics*, pp. 164 f.; John Bennet, in P. Hughes, *Rome and the Counter-Reformation in England* (London, 1942), p. 289; Devlin, *Southwell*, pp. 151 f.; Caraman, *Garnet*, pp. 34, 45 f., 216, 318, etc.; William Gifford, in Law, *Archpriest Controversy*, i, p. 11; and especially Parsons in Tierney-Dodd, *Church History*, iii, p. cxviii.

14. See his long letter to Acquaviva, 16 April 1596, in Caraman, *Garnet*, pp. 45, 215 ff.; cf. *ibid.*, p. 35 f., and Devlin, *Southwell*, p. 161.

would have scarcely suspected this from Blackwell's operation of it. His powers did contain a jurisdictional element absent in Garnet's: he had power to wield over priests the threat of reducing, suspending or withdrawing their missionary faculties. But this, in intention, did no more than put some extra weight behind the same powers of practical supervision: the power to send priests where they could serve most usefully, and to summon and preside at assemblies of missioners.[15] It is possible that the six assistants who were appointed by name in 1598 (Blackwell was to appoint the other six himself) had already been doing the job under Garnet.[16] Nor does Blackwell's elevation seem to have disturbed existing arrangements in regions where the local organiser was a Jesuit: Blackwell was instructed to keep in touch with Garnet in the exercise of his duties, and I take this to mean that where a Jesuit clientage existed Blackwell would not give instructions to seminary priests who belonged to it unless he had Garnet's agreement to do so. Finally, though he passed some money on to Blackwell, Garnet still kept control of at least one important instrument of general influence, the funds and arrangements which he had developed for receiving new arrivals until they could be accommodated on the mission.[17] He may well have thought that Blackwell was not competent to run a delicate operation like this; if so, he was probably right. As a whole, the experiment was a failure: partly because there was too much opposition, partly because Blackwell was the wrong man to choose and partly, I suspect, because Garnet began to withdraw from the general oversight of the mission as soon as Blackwell was appointed. I doubt if it came as much of a shock to either of them when they were instructed to cease collaboration in 1602.[18]

Besides bringing unitary organisation of the mission to an end, this decision inaugurated a long period of confusion in the organisation of the secular clergy. The Jesuits survived it much better, as Garnet had perhaps foreseen they would: it made possible the building up of so

15. Text of brief of appointment in Tierney-Dodd, *Church History*, iii, pp. cxix–cxxiii (faculties at cxx–cxxi); see in general J. H. Pollen, *The Institution of the Archpriest Blackwell* (London, 1916), and above, chap. 2, pp. 46 f.
16. They were: John Bavand (Norfolk), Henry Henshawe, Nicholas Tyrwhitt (presumably Lincolnshire), Henry Shaw, George Birkhead, James Standish (?Lancashire): Tierney-Dodd, *Church History*, iii, p. cxxi.
17. Caraman, *Garnet*, p. 255; the power is specifically reserved in Garnet in the papal brief revising the archpriest's instructions in October 1602: below, n. 18.
18. I get this impression from Caraman, *Garnet*, p. 241 and thereafter; Brief *Venerunt nuper*, 5 October 1602, in Tierney-Dodd, *Church History*, iii, p. clxxxi.

much of the missionary organisation as remained in his hands into a specifically Jesuit mission greatly expanded. This was achieved almost entirely through a more liberal policy in accepting applicants from among the secular missioners. Garnet continued to press for this until the end of his administration, and Acquaviva, who was in general extremely cautious on this subject, must have been persuaded to agree. In 1598 there had been eighteen Jesuits in England; the effective body of missionaries was not much more than ten, and a number of these were newcomers. In 1607 the number was 43, and thereafter it shot up rapidly to the figure between 150 and 200 at which it remained, more or less, for a century and a half.[19] The organisation of this large body elaborated the framework Garnet had laid down. By 1623, when the body of English Jesuits had grown sufficiently to be erected into a Province under the government of Richard Blount, it covered the country in twelve districts; about half of these had been roughly in existence in Garnet's day, though vast regions like Holtby's had been divided, and there was to be some further division after the Restoration. The duties of a local superior were much as Garnet had envisaged them: apart from seeing that the priests in his district behaved according to their rule, got on with their job and spent a week every year doing the Spiritual Exercises, he was to see to their physical and spiritual needs, assemble them twice a year for days of recollection and move them about as the needs of the mission might require. The provincial, with whom the local superiors were instructed to keep closely in touch, continued to live in or around London except in times of extreme crisis, and possessed a small staff; its most important member was the procurator of the province, who handled the finances. This organisation remained practically unchanged for 150 years: judging by its results— its success, for example, in riding disasters like the Popish Plot—it continued to operate at the high level of economy and effectiveness on which Garnet had launched it.[20]

In contrast to this smooth development, the other and larger half of Garnet's legacy suffered from acute organisational growing pains which well outlasted the archpriest regime itself, abandoned in 1623. It suf-

---

19. Caraman, *Garnet*, pp. 247, 318; Guilday, *English Catholic Refugees*, pp. 146 f.; Aveling, *Northern Catholics*, pp. 236 f.

20. Foley, *Records of the English Province*, vii part 1, p. xc and *passim*—see Map 6 for boundaries of districts; Basset, *The English Jesuits*, pp. 167–168, 195–197; a good insight into the workings of the organisation in the late seventeenth century will be found in John Warner's Letter-Book, C.U.L. Ms. Ll.i.19.

fered from a variety of handicaps. Whether or not one may consider the breach with the Jesuits as justified on other grounds, it was a crippling blow to the organisation of the secular mission; at the same time the haemorrhage of secular priests into the Jesuits, and the obsession of many of the others with abstract questions of jurisdiction and ecclesiastical structure, made patient organisational construction practically impossible. It was probably in any case futile to try to make a 'Jesuit' structure work without the cement of Jesuit spirituality. Control of the localities was extremely patchy, and depended on the influence of the archpriest's assistants, an oligarchy of powerful individuals whose prestige often exceeded that of the archpriest himself. Conflict between it and the Jesuit system was bound to mean competition for the favours of the gentry, and there was a good deal of local infighting between the two; as one might have anticipated, the Jesuits had the better of it.[21] Meantime, to add to the complication, a missionary body of Benedictine monks was being constituted which rose fairly quickly to about half the size of the Jesuit one. For some time the Benedictines were too worried as to whether they should be on the mission at all to make much contribution to its administrative development. In the long run they may have helped to encourage the trend from monarchy towards consultative oligarchy, since their mission was ultimately run by a predominantly self-perpetuating General Chapter meeting periodically abroad; they showed, as in their decision to divide the mission-field into provinces of Canterbury and York, archaeological tendencies which were to emerge in more striking form among the secular clergy. To hindsight, the history of their mission may suggest that a sizeable body of missioners could get on well enough with a minimum of attention to organisational matters, though it may well be that as a consequence it was something of a shambles until after the Civil War.[22]

The lesson was in any case not to the taste of the secular leadership. For nearly half a century after the arrival of William Bishop in 1623, the organisation of the secular clergy was dogged by an obsession with hierarchical order which got in the way of practical adjustments to the

---

21. Report of Richard Button, archdeacon of Staffs. and Leicester, 7 March 1633 (from Archives of St Edmund's College, Ware, kindly communicated to me by Dr A. F. Allison); *V.C.H. Leicestershire*, ii, pp. 59, 67 f.
22. Aveling, *Northern Catholics*, pp. 240, 242; D. M. Lunn, 'The Origins and Early Development of the English Benedictine Congregation, 1588–1647' (Cambridge Univ. Ph.D. thesis, 1970), pp. 271 a–b, 217–218. Dr Lunn is preparing a book on the subject which will supersede the sketchy indications given here.

missionary task. Bishop and Smith constructed a system which had three tiers—vicars-general, archdeacons and rural deans—and required at least fifty people to operate it. To this they added the Chapter, which consisted of a dean and eighteen canons: its membership was not identical with the local officers of the mission, and it was not originally intended to exercise pastoral functions. Considered as a system of governing the secular clergy, of whom there were probably not as many as 400 at this time, this was an absurdly elaborate structure, but it is doubtful whether it was genuinely so considered; it became a missionary organisation by default, since there was no Catholic bishop in England for fifty years after 1631.[23]

During this time the Chapter formed the government of the secular clergy in England, so far as there was one. Its constitution evolved to meet the task: its membership expanded to include all the vicars-general and archdeacons, besides ten other canons; since this was an unwieldy body, and most of the chaptermen now lived out of London, it could not govern by itself. It became a General Assembly meeting in theory once every three years and in practice a good deal less often; its authority was exercised by a small cabinet or Consult consisting of the officers (dean, secretary, treasurer) and one or two other members living in London. In principle this was quite an attractive system, an attempt to find a workable regime for the secular clergy in the opposite direction to that explored by the Jesuits: in its later years it proved that it could do a capable job. But for most of the time it hardly seems to have done so: it was the victim of party conflict; it seems to have fallen to pieces during the 1640s; its most influential figures, like John Sergeant, were commonly men who had less than half an eye on the running of the mission. Only in 1667, when Sergeant's regime was overthrown, does one get the impression that it acquired a leadership which had a real concern for pastoral problems and something like an overall policy for the mission. During the following years there seems to have been a thorough overhaul of the system, dealing with the reception of priests from the seminaries, their distribution to districts and residences, and the conduct of local superiors; these were required to make frequent

23. Hughes, *Rome and the Counter-Reformation in England*, pp. 323, 326 f.; Tierney-Dodd, *Church History*, iv, pp. cclxxiv–cclxxv, cclxxx, cclxxxii–cclxxxiv; A.A.W., John Kirk, Ms. 'Continuation' of Dodd, Documents, Art. IV, no. 7—names of vicars-general and archdeacons, with areas of competence, 1623; position after 1660 in Williams, *Wiltshire*, p. 241.

visitations of the priests in their districts, and later to call them all together for a yearly meeting. Much attention was paid to the creation, expansion and security of endowed funds, whose functions will be discussed in due course. Altogether one has the feeling that the work of this period provided, at last, a foundation for real progress.[24]

After 1685 it was up to the vicars-apostolic to see that progress was continued, and by and large they managed to ensure that it was. The most immediately striking difference between their regime and its predecessor was that they made do with practically no institutional structure at all. Hardly one of them possessed so much as a secretary, and looking back on their work Wiseman complained bitterly of their failure to observe proper procedures, keep records or stay in the same place: 'the whole episcopal regimen seems to have led a sort of nomadic life, wandering about in stage-coaches and gigs from place to place'.[25] They abandoned the idea that they should set up chapters themselves, and relied for the supervision of their districts very much on their own efforts, generally lightened by the assistance of a coadjutor with right of succession. The archdeacons withered away, except as honorary figures and guardians of funds, and the vicars-general, reduced to four by Leyburn on his arrival and abolished when their territories were given a bishop each, seem to have survived thereafter only in the North, where they were certainly necessary.[26]

From 1688 the secular mission, and to a slowly increasing extent the mission as a whole, was run by four individuals operating in four large districts (London, Midland, Northern and Western), with about half-a-dozen assistants between them. At first sight, the vicars-apostolic do not look a very dynamic body. Several of them were old and feeble, like Bonaventure Gifford, an old chapterman who lived 92 years and was London vicar-apostolic in succession to John Leyburn for the last 31 of them (1703–1734), or paralysed with painful ailments like George Witham (Midland, 1703–1716; North, 1716–1725). Other weaknesses

24. Williams, *Wiltshire*, pp. 95–113 *passim*; Hemphill, *Early Vicars-Apostolic*, pp. 161 ff.—decrees of General Assembly of the Chapter, 1676; Kirk, 'Continuation', Documents, Art. IV, no. 8—officers and territorial divisions, 1694. Cf. above, chap. 4, pp. 60 ff, and below, p. 245. I should add that though I have drawn heavily on Williams's account, the interpretation is my own.
25. Ward, *Sequel to Catholic Emancipation*, ii, p. 6.
26. Hemphill, *Early Vicars-Apostolic*, pp. 47–49, 91, 129 f.; 128, 130 (northern vicars-general); 164 ff. (district chapters). Leyburn's vicars-general and arch-deacons in Kirk, 'Continuation', Documents, Art. IV, no. 9. Rowlands, 'Catholics in Staffordshire', p. 43.

they brought upon themselves. Taken together, their understandable anxiety to keep out the regulars, their lack of control over clergy funds, and an instinct for survival in an aristocratic world, led them sometimes to ask for men as their successors who had little qualification except private means and relatives in the magnate class. Hence there were two Petres and two Talbots among them, none of whom would probably have stood much chance on their own merits. The worst case was the appointment of Benjamin Petre as coadjutor to Gifford in the London district in 1721. Petre knew no theology, as he was the first to confess, and little Latin either; the prospect of exercising his office tortured him with anxiety. A year later he sent to Rome to resign, only to receive from the clergy's agent there a masterpiece of equivocation whose bluff dismissal of formal qualification ('You cannot but know something, more or less . . .') would have made Richard Smith turn in his grave. But this tribute to the aristocracy, however deplorable in itself, was not typical. Only two of fourteen other appointments made before 1770 fell into the same category: one was Benjamin Petre's nephew Francis, who was a competent if not memorable bishop in the North between 1752 and 1775, and the other was John Stonor, who ran the Midland district from 1716 to 1756. Stonor was a Talbot on his mother's side and a protégé of his uncle the Protestant Duke of Shrewsbury; his appointment was a political one; he had had difficulty in making up his mind to a priestly career, and kept the instincts of a *grand seigneur* and a taste for intrigue. It was probably just as well that he failed in his efforts to be appointed to the London district. Nevertheless he turned out to be one of the best and most energetic of the eighteenth-century bishops. Even Benjamin Petre justified his appointment when, having found in Richard Challoner just the man for his job, he got him for his coadjutor and promptly retired to farm in Essex, leaving him to get on with it.[27]

The full range of Challoner's services to the community can only be appreciated on a larger time-scale than we are dealing with at the moment. During forty years he was a model vicar-apostolic in London; as he practised them, the duties of the office were those of a missionary priest on a wider scale, though he also did what was necessary or pos-

27. Hemphill, *Early Vicars-Apostolic, passim*; pp. 69–77 (Benjamin Petre—letter quoted at p. 74), 118 f., 173 f. (Witham's aliments), 147–149 (Petre and Challoner); for Stonor, *ibid.*, pp. 49 ff., 58–66 and R. J. Stonor, *Stonor*, pp. 280–286. Cf. also Hemphill, *op. cit.*, pp. 67 f., for an attempt to get a Howard as London vicar-apostolic in 1721, which failed because of his death; by all accounts it would have been quite a good appointment.

sible in the way of planning for the future. It may be that he casts too favourable a light on the regime as a whole. There is certainly one blot on the record, the dereliction of duty on the part of the Benedictine Philip Ellis which left the Western district without a bishop for twenty-five years after 1689;[28] the earlier decades of the regime look on the whole less satisfactory than the later ones, and there was in particular a sticky period around 1720 when Gifford and Witham were past it and Stonor had hardly found his feet. Still, apart from Stonor, at least four of the bishops of this period had something of Challoner's quality: James Smith, the founding father of the Northern district (1688-1711); the Franciscan Matthew Prichard, effectively the first bishop in the West (1713-1750); Edward Dicconson, Stonor's vicar-general before his appointment to the North, unfortunately at the age of 71, in 1740; and John Hornyold, who succeeded Stonor in the Midlands in 1756.[29]

Cardinal Manning described their regime as one of 'organic dissolution'. One may see what he meant, but ask whether it mattered; Challoner showed at least as good a grasp as Manning of the inwardness of episcopacy when he wrote to Hornyold that 'prelacy in our circumstances has nothing in it to be coveted but the benefit of more labour and trouble and the opportunity of serving a greater number'.[30] What their administration lost by its lack of institutional structure it gained by personal contact. A vicar-apostolic who remained at his post for any length of time, as most of them did, must have known his clergy fairly well and have met a high proportion of his flock. Some organised regular meetings with their missioners: Challoner met his priests who worked in London once a week. Nearly all of them made at least one tour through his district, which might take several months, when he administered confirmation in the congregations, preached, received reports from the priests and met the gentry.[31] Certainly there were several who had time to pursue an interest in things like agricultural improvement, turnpikes or cattle-breeding; but, with the exceptions

28. cf. Williams, *Wiltshire*, pp. 124 ff.
29. Hemphill, *Early Vicars-Apostolic*, pp. 27-30, 38 f. (Smith); 44 f. (Prichard); 119 f., 141 f. (Dicconson: see also his letter-books in Lancs. C.R.O. RCWB, no. 5); Rowlands, 'Staffordshire', pp. 10 ff. (Hornyold). For Challoner, E. H. Burton, *Life and Times of Bishop Challoner* (2 vols., London, 1909).
30. Burton, *Challoner*, i, p. 304; Ward, *Dawn of the Catholic Revival*, i, p. x, for Manning's view.
31. Kirk, 'Continuation', Documents, Art. IV, no. 24 (Smith); Burton, *Challoner*, ii, pp. 9, 27; example of a visitation (1741-1742), *ibid.*, i, pp. 137 ff., 174-215.

already indicated, they were not amateurs. As one may see from their reports to Rome, they knew their districts inside out,[32] and if they were apt to put the gloomiest construction on their knowledge they were percipient and active enough to ensure that their predictions were falsified by the outcome.

Looked at as a whole, the organisational history of the mission is one of successful adaptation of means to the missionary task; not surprisingly, in view of the respective traditions they represented, this adaptation was achieved rather quickly by the Jesuits and rather slowly by the seculars, but it was substantially complete by 1685. We should therefore expect the second half of our period to give more general evidence of efficiency and purpose than the first, and I hope to show that it did. It would however be unreasonable to expect too much. Leaving aside external obstacles posed by the law or the gentry, we still cannot treat the missionary organisation as a freely functioning machine. Nobody was ever in charge of it as a whole, not even those who came nearest to being in this position and would have filled it best, Garnet at the beginning of our period and Challoner at the end. The existence of separate missionary organisations and the lack of formal superiority among the vicars-apostolic ensured that there would always be different sources of authority. In any case, compliance with instructions on the part of the ordinary priest was always in effect voluntary. Among the regulars, and notably among the Jesuits, a superior had a context of religious obedience and a tradition of availability to work in: the individual Jesuit on the mission was required 'at the nod of obedience to remove from place to place, where the greater service of God, the salvation of [one's] neighbour, and each one's greater perfection demanded'.[33] In the circumstances we cannot take this literally, but on the whole the English Jesuits seem to have lived up to their principles in this respect, even to have overdone them. The comparable text from the secular clergy is the modest resolution of the General Assembly of the Chapter in 1676 that 'no priest is to enter a residence, nor to sleight a residence recommended unto him if indifferently convenient, nor to desert it without first acquainting his

---

32. See their returns to Propaganda, 1773, printed by J. H. Whyte, *Recusant History*, ix (1968), pp. 206–214—reports from Challoner, Francis Petre, Walmesley (West) and Hornyold. Petre is markedly vaguer than the others; admittedly, he had the largest flock to deal with.

33. Foley, *Records of the English Province*, vii part 1, p. xc—Instructions of 1659.

superiors'; the vicars-apostolic were in a somewhat stronger position, but not much so.[34] All this will indicate that a search for missionary policy will not lead us to sharp decisions or bold schemes, but rather to an anonymous instinct burrowing to enlarge a space too confined for comfort.

(ii)

NUMBERS

It is not too difficult to discover, at any stage in this period, roughly how many priests the mission authorities had at their disposal, and certainly easier than finding out how many Catholics they had to serve. It may help to confirm the suggestions already made on this point if we realise that the volume of missionary labour available remained comparatively stable throughout. Thus it seems reasonably certain that when Queen Elizabeth died there were about three hundred missionary priests in England; in 1773 there were rather less than four hundred. For most of the intervening period, we have detailed and frequent returns of numbers from the Jesuit sector of the mission; these show that from the time the English province was established in the 1620s until it was dissolved in form in 1773, and excluding occasional periods of crisis, its missionary strength fluctuated between about 120 and 170 members, but was substantially the same at any time. So, by and large, was that of the Benedictines.[35]

So it seems mistaken, in discussing the numerical strength of the mission, to put the emphasis on its ups and downs, as contemporaries usually did and most historians have done; all the same it would be misleading to suggest that there were no ups and downs at all. A graph

34. Hemphill, *Early Vicars-Apostolic*, p. 161; cf. C.R.S. ix (1911), p. 111; Rowlands, 'Staffordshire', p. 24.
35. The nearest thing to an accurate estimate of the number of priests on the mission in 1603 is in Aveling, *Northern Catholics*, p. 243—c. 330-355 in 1609, of which 70-75 regulars; rather lower figures than those suggested by Hughes, *Reformation in England*, iii, p. 396 and McGrath, *Papists and Puritans*, p. 299; cf. above, chap. 8, p. 190. For 1773, below, n. 38. The Jesuit statistics are given in Foley, *Records of the English Province*, vii part 1: see especially the 'Analytical Catalogue' at p. clxviii, from which Table II (below, p. 419) is derived. A table of Benedictine numbers throughout the period will be found in Aveling, 'The Education of 18th-century English Monks', *Downside Review*, lxxix (1961), pp. 135-136.

representing them would have a fairly simple wave-like shape. The 300 priests of 1603 composed a body which had been expanding rapidly for twenty-five years, and was to go on expanding for another thirty or more, until at least the eve of the Civil War. During the 1630s estimates were made by two men with reasonable access to information, the Benedictine Leander Jones and the papal agent Gregorio Panzani. In 1634 Jones reported to Cardinal Barberini that there were roughly 1,000 priests on the mission; 500 to 600 seculars and about 450 members of religious orders. This was an exaggeration, since he greatly over-estimated the number of Jesuits and Benedictines; a total of 300 regular missioners at this date seems on the generous side. Panzani got this figure and its components about right, so his own estimate of about 500 seculars inspires a certain confidence. Nevertheless he acknowledged that he could not get a proper list of secular clergy, and those compiled by the Chapter at about the same time suggest a rather lower figure. Altogether we may assume that, between the death of Elizabeth and the eve of the Civil War, the number of priests on the mission rose from 300 or so to about 750.[36] The increase in secular-clergy numbers, though considerable, had not been so large as the increase of regulars; we should of course remember that much of the Jesuit mission had been recruited from secular missioners.

As far as one can see, the total membership of the mission remained at or about the level reached in 1640 until towards the end of the century. In so far as there was a general trend, it was downwards; but the clergy remained buoyant enough to weather three serious crises between 1641 and 1689 with, numerically speaking, only superficial damage. The Jesuits, reduced to 90 by the onslaught of the Popish Plot, were back to 150 at the beginning of the eighteenth century; the

36. Leander Jones, 'Apostolici missionis status in Anglia', in State Papers Collected by Edward Earl of Clarendon (3 vols., Oxford, 1767–1786), i, pp. 199 ff.; for Panzani, W. M. Brady, The Episcopal Succession in England and Ireland, iii (Rome, 1877), p. 90; Aveling, Northern Catholics, p. 243; Benedictine figures in Aveling, 'Education of English Monks', p. 135, and (rather higher) C.R.S. xxxiii, pp. 263–266. There is also a note by John Southcote, secretary of the Chapter, dating from the early 1630s (A.A.W., series B, xlviii, no. 4: kindly communicated to me by Dr A. F. Allison), and possibly prepared for Panzani. His figures for regulars resemble Panzani's, but he only gives 260 seculars. This was apparently the number of individual priests entered in his records from names supplied by the archdeacons, and for reasons connected with administrative confusion and clerical unemployment one may assume that his list was defective. But it does suggest that 500 is too high for seculars, and 750 rather an outside limit for the total.

Benedictines declined a little after the Civil War, but had a revival in the 1680s, and more missioners than ever before (70 or so) around 1700; other orders like the Dominicans and Franciscans developed small-scale missions during this period, keeping the total of regular missioners at about 300. We are not very well informed about numbers of secular clergy at this time: an estimate made in 1667 of a total missionary body of about 800, perhaps a little exaggerated, suggests that they maintained their pre-Civil War numbers through to the Restoration; by the end of the century they seem to have been beginning to decline. Aveling suggests 350 seculars as an absolute minimum for this time: I should think it unlikely there were more, and prefer the lower to the higher end of his generally plausible figure of 650–700 priests for the mission as a whole about 1700.[37]

Seventeenth-century estimators tended to exaggerate, eighteenth-century ones to minimise. In 1706 Dr John Betham, an ex-missioner then chaplain at the émigré court of Saint-Germain, offered a substantial underestimate of the effectives of the mission. He thought there were 400 priests serving on it altogether, of whom 250 were seculars, 70 Jesuits, 40 Benedictines and about as many other regulars. There were certainly twice as many regulars, and probably a good deal more seculars, than he supposed; he was in fact predicting fairly accurately, except in one respect, the situation seventy years later. In between there was a period of considerable though not catastrophic decline, but this took place very largely in the numbers of secular clergy. In 1773 the total of regulars returned by the vicars-apostolic to Propaganda was 217, 121 Jesuits, 44 Benedictines and 52 others. Both Jesuits and Benedictines returned rather higher figures than this: the number of regulars on the mission had fallen, though not drastically. The number of seculars had fallen much faster, and by this date they formed well under half the total: according to the bishops, 175 out of a total of

---

37. Aveling, *Northern Catholics*, p. 340; Meyer, *England and the Catholic Church*, p. 64, from Brady, *op. cit.*, iii, p. 107, for the 1667 estimate. The figure given by the Roman emissary Agretti, two years later, of about 500 priests all told, 230 of them seculars, is such an obvious underestimate that one wonders if Brady misread the figures (*ibid.*, iii, p. 109), but 800 was probably a little exaggerated. For the Jesuits, see Table II. Aveling's estimate for seculars seems to be a guess based on numbers for Yorkshire at this period. Returns to the secretary of the Chapter in 1692 reported about 80 'brethren' in 9 of the 19 archdeaconries; admittedly some of the returns are given as 'imperfect', and neither Lancashire nor London was among them; but here again 350 looks like a maximum rather than a minimum.

392.[38] This decline seems to have occurred mainly during the earlier decades of the century, and obviously reflected the reduction in recruitment to the seminaries, especially from the gentry, which has already been noticed. By the 1730s the vicars-apostolic were sending up signals of distress. In 1735 Dicconson, after checking with the records of the Chapter, concluded that since 1715 at least 148 secular missioners had died; two years later he had another twenty deaths to add. This was probably more than twice the rate of new arrivals; during the same twenty-two years Dicconson calculated that Douai had sent over only 60 new missioners, while the other seminaries provided very few indeed. At much the same time Stonor was explaining to Rome that he had recently had seven mission stations fall vacant, hitherto filled by secular priests, which he had had to supply with 'regulars and foreigners (i.e. Irishmen)'. Challoner and others were already beginning to attack the problem at the seminary end, and their efforts were ultimately to prove successful; but, on the mission there is little sign that the tide had turned before 1773.[39] Looking back on the whole period, we may come to a reasonably firm conclusion. Considered as a whole, the number of priests on the mission rose steadily, during the 75 years or so following its inauguration, to reach a peak of about 750 by 1640. It remained at this figure for some decades, and had not come down very much by 1700, when it was about 650. A long-term decline began at about this date, and by 1770 the figure was somewhat less than 400.

At this point it seems necessary to confront these figures with those already suggested for the size of the lay community, for while they confirm one another in some respects they seem contradictory in others. Judging only by the number of its priests, the community would have reached a peak about 1640, declined a little by 1700, and a great deal more by 1770; in fact, if our conclusions are somewhere near the truth,

38. Hemphill, *Early Vicars-Apostolic*, p. 102 (Betham, from A.A.W. xxxviii, 271); 1773 figures from Brady, *op. cit.*, iii, 169, 212, 263, 301, the first as corrected by Burton, *Challoner*, i, p. 171; cf. J. H. Whyte, 'The Vicars-Apostolics' Returns of 1773' (see above, n. 32), pp. 205 ff. For Jesuits, see Table II. Dicconson's 1737 figure of 156 seculars (Hemphill, *op. cit.*, p. 139), is another obvious underestimate; cf. T. G. Holt, 'A note on some 18th century statistics', *Recusant History*, x (1969), pp. 6, 8.
39. Hemphill, *op. cit.*, p. 101; also Dicconson Papers (Lancs. C.R.O. RCWB, no. 5), i, pp. 77, 97—Dicconson to his brother William, 14 July 1735, with additional comments made two years later; to Stonor, 20 September 1735; *ibid.*, p. 31: Stonor to Mayes, agent in Rome, 15 May 1736; cf. Hemphill, *op. cit.*, p. 98, for Irishmen. For Challoner, see above, chap. 9, p. 201.

and ignoring the period before 1600 where estimation seems futile, it went up modestly but steadily, except during the second half of the seventeenth century. For the seventeenth century as a whole, the two sets of figures tell a not dissimilar story, though if they are correct the general trends in the size of the community were greatly exaggerated among the clergy; it increased faster than the community at large up to the Civil War and had fallen back perceptibly by 1700, while the community remained stationary or, if it fell back, did so only a little. But after 1700 they go their own ways entirely: marked decline of the clergy, respectable increase, apparently, of the community as a whole.

These discrepancies would be reconciled if it were found that the missioners of the seventeenth century were a good deal less intensively employed than those of the eighteenth. I think it is clear that this was the case, and much of what follows might be adduced in support of it; but to provide some solid ground for these indications it is worth citing some direct evidence. There was in the first place a general consensus that, during the first half of the seventeenth century, the volume of missionary manpower outran the volume of missionary work which, given the accepted limits and available resources, existed to be done; complaints about clerical under- or unemployment were general. The earliest had already been voiced in 1609, and though these were premature they would certainly have been justified during the following decades.[40] Leander Jones had no doubt, in 1634, that far too many priests were being sent on the mission. Admittedly he thought that there were more in the country than there were, and the reasons he gave were slightly melodramatic: he thought that both the seculars and the Jesuits were pumping priests into the country and duplicating effectives in order to support claims to run the entire mission themselves; and also that the quality of missioners was declining as men without property entered it as a profitable career and, failing to find a suitable place, drifted about on its fringes disturbing those already settled. It would have been simpler, though it would rather have spoilt his argument, to point to the floods of sons of the gentry entering the seminaries. All the same, his description of the consequences remains instructive: 'whence it happens almost of necessity that these missioners, who have no proper place of residence, are forced either to wander about in other people's, or to fall into want. So they become contemptible, and are

40. 'Rationes pro moderando ingressu sacredotum': A.A.W. ix, no. 117; also C.R.S. xli (1948), pp. 53, 103, 123.

considered practically as paid servants; and somebody is always trying to squeeze somebody else out of the place he possesses.' His solution was to raise the qualifications for entry to the mission, in age and intellectual capacity, and to introduce a means test which, except for very brilliant students, would exclude anyone whose family was not rich enough to support him. He also wanted Propaganda to lay down maximum numbers for each branch of the clergy, corresponding to their financial resources and the volume of work they had, and to stop them bringing in new priests except to fill specific vacancies.[41] It would obviously have been possible to take a less deflationary view than Jones's but his evidence is substantially confirmed from the other side of the clerical fence. Richard Smith's supporters also believed that the inflation of missioners meant competition for places and unemployment, and gravely disadvantaged the clergy in the effort to maintain their status against lay patrons; one of his archdeacons said in 1633 that a third of the existing missioners, if they were all of one order—whichever order it was—would make a better showing than was being made at the time.[42] John Donne would apparently have agreed.

During the half-century after the Restoration such complaints slowly began to die down. On the eve of the Popish Plot John Warner, from Liège, told his General that 'many' Jesuits in England had nothing to do: he thought they should spend their time usefully translating foreign books of devotion into English.[43] In 1667 the Chapter had spoken of clerical unemployment and its consequences in terms more or less identical with those used thirty years earlier: priests, it said, were going into trade because they could not find work as priests. In 1708 Bishop Gifford still spoke of 'overstocking', though he seems to have meant only in London; elsewhere secular-clergy superiors were beginning to find that 'the hands were too few for the work'.[44] With the regulars, who recruited more strongly in the late seventeenth century, this point was reached a little later: shortly after 1700 the Benedictine

41. 'Apostolici status missionis in Anglia', above, n. 36.
42. Hughes, *Rome and the Counter-Reformation in England*, pp. 409 f.; Aveling, *Northern Catholics*, pp. 243, 340; Richard Button to John Southcote, 7 March 1633 (above, n. 21).
43. Warner to Jesuit General, 10 June 1678: C.U.L. Ms. Ll.i.19, f. 3.
44. J. A. Williams, *Bath and Rome: the Living Link* (Bath, 1963), p. 46, quoting Hughes, 'The Return of the Episcopate to England' (*Clergy Review*, x (1935), pp. 194 f.); Hemphill, *Early Vicars-Apostolic*, p. 99; Dicconson to Stonor, 20 September 1735 (above, n. 39)—the last remark relates to four unidentified counties, possibly including Lancashire; Dicconson said the same was true of Yorkshire.

superior in the North had permanent lodgings in York for unemployed priests to live in; judging by the exceptionally large numbers of Jesuits returned from London in 1710 and 1720, they were having the same trouble. Yet by the 1730s both were beginning to complain of a shortage of men: in 1735 the Jesuit provincial got the length of the tertianship reduced in order to keep more available.[45] Altogether the suggestion of Figure I (below, p. 422) that surplus became deficiency somewhere after 1715 seems to present the position very much as it appeared to contemporaries.

One other point may be made here. Despite the evidence given above, it seems probable that the surplus of the middle and later seventeenth century was mainly accounted for not by unemployment but by under-employment. The period when it was largest was also the period when the single-house chaplaincy became generally adopted among the gentry. It seems obvious that it was the surplus which had made this possible; the process must also have done a good deal to absorb it. This was, of course, a most inefficient way of deploying the clergy, and it had other drawbacks as well; but it seems at least to have done some good in this respect, and to have helped to create towards the close of the seventeenth century a period of rough equilibrium between clerical supply and demand which may do something to account for the improvement of intra-clerical relations. The demand for gentry chaplains declined during the eighteenth century, but so of course did the numbers of the clergy.

It is harder to cite witnesses for an increasing work-load among missioners after 1700, but there can be little doubt that, though patchy, it was real. In 1735, Dicconson concluded his account of the decline of the secular clergy by reporting that the most recent deaths 'obliges some to help at more than one place; sometimes above 1,000 souls, which is work enough for double the hands'.[46] As the century wore on it became increasingly normal for a country priest to have more than one mission to serve. These were usually seculars; among regulars the increase in activity came rather from the expansion of seigneurial congregations and the emergence of relatively well-attended chapels in

---

45. Aveling, *West Riding*, p. 265 and 'Education of English Monks' (see above, n. 35), pp. 136–137; Table II; Archives of the English Province, S.J., Generals' Letter-Books III (2)—Letter-Book 1720–1744, f. 283; General to Turberville, 17 April 1734; f. 288v: General to Browne, 30 April 1735.
46. Above, n. 44.

towns. The implication of Figure I, that between 1640 and 1770 the ratio between missioners and laity in the community rose from 1:80 to 1:200 seems perfectly acceptable. One can only speak of an eighteenth-century shortage of missioners in a very relative sense, and there was certainly no problem here that redistribution could not solve; but it was precisely in the distribution of their manpower that missionary authorities encountered their most formidable difficulty.

(iii)

DISTRIBUTION

The problem had been with the mission from its earliest days, and Parsons had seen it fairly clearly. 'At my first entry into England,' he wrote in 1581, immediately after his return to France, 'I cast my eyes around so far as I could to determine which portion of the kingdom was in greatest need of our help, and which portion as time went on would be best able to further our cause.' Except for his pertinent conclusion that something ought to be done about the university of Cambridge and the region which lay within its sphere of influence, what he said set out the terms of the problem as it was to persist for a century and more. In great tracts of Wales and the northernmost counties, where the people, despite or because of their 'spissa ignorantia', were most likely to respond to missionary efforts, seminary priests, he thought, simply had not ventured.[47] He tried to do something about this, but five years later there was much the same story to tell: Southwell said that there were several counties which had plenty of Catholics but no priests at all; missioners tended to ignore them and make for one or two favoured areas, or else hang around London without going anywhere.[48]

These comments partly suggest lack of organisation, and Garnet during the next decade was able to do a good deal about that; but they also raised by implication the problem of the influence of the gentry on the distribution of the mission. In so far as this was a financial problem, it will be considered shortly: at the moment I want to try and express it in simple geographical terms. The problem was to prevent an exces-

47. C.R.S. xxxix, pp. 98, 108.
48. Caraman, *Garnet*, p. 35.

sive number of priests accumulating in the South and the Midlands, where there were Catholic gentlemen and Catholic money, but relatively little opportunity for missionary work; and to ensure that an adequate number functioned in the darker corners whose denudation Parsons had deplored, where there were plenty of opportunities but relatively little money, and other conditions discouraging to a missionary priest. By and large, a priest was likely to be more effective in the North than in the South and, at least before 1680, in the West than in the East. For convenience I shall take the boundary laid down in 1688 between the Northern and Western districts on the one hand, and the London and Midland districts on the other, as roughly dividing the regions of greater and lesser missionary possibilities, and interpret in the light of it the distribution of priests throughout this period, so far as it is known. It can in fact be known about as accurately as the number of missioners: we know fairly exactly how the whole clergy was distributed in the 1770s, and how the Jesuit sector of the mission was distributed at any date after 1620. I present in turn our knowledge on these two points, and proceed to a more hypothetical discussion of the secular clergy, with the object of constructing a distribution of the mission on the eve of the Civil War. With this knowledge we shall be able to get a general idea of what was going on throughout our period, and detect any differences between different bodies of clergy.

Of the 392 priests returned by the vicars-apostolic in 1773, 181 were working on the farther and 211 on the nearer side of the dividing line. There were 137 in the Northern district, 44 in the Western district, 120 in the London district and 91 in the Midland district. Distribution inside the districts was uneven. Half the northern priests were working in Lancashire (69), half as many as that in Yorkshire (36) and again half as many in Northumberland (18). In the West, there were no more than nine priests in the whole of Wales, and most of these were on the fringes of the country; the rest were scattered through south-west England. Half the priests in the Midland district were working in the western counties of Warwick, Staffordshire and Worcester: Warwick had the most priests, Staffordshire the largest number of missions; none had as many as Northumberland. About seventy of the priests in the London district lived in the metropolis itself, the rest in the home counties. Apart from Hampshire, no other county except those mentioned maintained as many as ten priests.[49]

49. References as above, n. 38. See Map 4 (below, p. 410).

It will be helpful in interpreting these figures to distinguish between London and the rural lowlands, and also between the North and the West. The distribution will then be: London, 70; rural South and Midlands, 141; North, 137; West, 44. It is fairly clear that, two hundred years after Parsons's discovery of the problem, some kind of denouement had been reached. In Wales the mission had collapsed. There were still a lot of priests in London, but since London was now rapidly developing as a missionary field they cannot all be regarded as surplus labour, and had probably better be ignored. Apart from this, a reasonable balance had been struck between North and South, though the effects of the distribution of lay wealth were still evident. Though it had failed in Wales and the West, the mission had otherwise gone a long way towards achieving the kind of rational distribution which Parsons had aimed at.

To find out what had happened in the interval we start with the distribution of the Jesuit mission from the eve of the Civil War to 1770.[50] The districts into which it was divided did not fit exactly into the districts governed by the vicars-apostolic; but we can achieve comparability by dividing them also between London, the remainder of the South and Midlands, the North and the West including Wales. As before we had better leave London out of account. Here there were normally about twenty Jesuits—twenty-four in 1621, twenty in 1770— who included the provincial, his staff and the unemployed; during the seventeenth century Jesuits had also worked in the city, notably of course during the reign of James II, but they do not seem to have done so thereafter.

London apart, there were at the outbreak of the Civil War 140 Jesuits on the mission in England: sixty of them were working to the north and west of the dividing line (thirty in the North, twenty-eight in Wales and the West), and eighty in the South and Midlands. Including those in London, there were then about twice as many Jesuits in the South as in the North and West. Thirty years later, in 1672, the general position had hardly changed: again excluding London, there were forty-seven on the farther side of the dividing line and sixty-seven on the nearer.

50. See Table II, and Maps 6 and 7 (below, pp. 416–419). Cf. Basset, *English Jesuits*, p. 164 (figures for 1620). It should be noted that the districts into which the Jesuit mission was divided do not fit exactly into those governed by the vicars-apostolic: Staffordshire is included in the North until 1661, and Wiltshire and Dorset with the South, not the West. For 1640 these should roughly cancel each other out.

The one obvious difference was that the decline of the Welsh and Western missions had already become apparent: they now employed only seventeen Jesuits. The process of this decline has been traced already, and it was not reversed; by the end of the century the Jesuit districts of the West were practically extinct, and though an effort was made to revive them, they contained no more than sixteen missioners in 1771. But this century of decline in the West was also a century when the balance between North and South was reversed. The figures tell their own story: 1672, sixty-seven (South) and thirty (North); 1700, fifty-four and forty-five; 1771, forty-five and fifty-seven. This distribution could no doubt have been improved, but it was reasonably healthy. So was that of the Benedictines, who had gone through exactly the same process: twice as many men in the South as in the North during most of the seventeenth century; concentration on the North during the boom period around 1700, bringing numbers to equality about 1700; increasing predominance of the North thereafter.[51]

We come to the secular clergy, and had better begin with what we know, their distribution in 1773. At that date, according to the vicars-apostolic, there were 175 secular priests in the country, 97 on the near side of the line (London district 55, Midland district 42), 78 on the far side (Northern district 67, Western district 11). Redistributed as before, the figures would be: London itself, 25–30; South and Midlands, about 70; North, 67; Wales and West, 11.[52] Their distribution was then roughly the same as that of the Jesuits, and looks about as effective. It may appear a little less so, but one should remember that the Western district was by now more or less a preserve of the regulars, and that many if not most of the secular clergy in London were now engaged in solid missionary work. Jesuits and seculars were therefore deployed in much the same way in 1770: had they been so during the previous century and a half, and had their deployment similarly improved in this time?

The answer appears to be roughly yes, but that during the seventeenth century the distribution of seculars had possibly been even more unbalanced than that of the Jesuits. It does not seem possible to trace it, as we can for the Jesuits, from 1640 to 1770; but enough information was collected by the Chapter during the 1630s to enable one to make a

51. Aveling, *Northern Catholics*, p. 239; 'Education of English Monks', p. 137.
52. *loc. cit.*, above, n. 38; my figure for seculars in London itself is a guess based on the information there given.

reasonable conjecture about the distribution of the secular clergy on the eve of the Civil War. We start from the information already given, that there were then perhaps 450 secular priests in England. Beyond the demarcation line, there seem to have been roughly 130–140 secular missioners—something over 70 in the North and probably about 60 in Wales and the West.[53] The Chapter found that there were about 40 in London, some in prison. This leaves a total of about 270 for those who were working in the rest of the country and those who had simply got lost. Allowing a good deal for the last category, we may suppose that getting on for 200 secular missioners were working in the South and Midlands at this time.[54] We cannot treat these figures very confidently, but I think we are entitled to conclude that the geographical imbalance of the Jesuit and Benedictine missions at this time was repeated, if not exaggerated, among the seculars. One example may help to drive the point home: the Chapter found that in the four northernmost counties of England—Northumberland, Durham, Cumberland and Westmorland—there were then a total of thirty-three priests. Two of them were Scots friars labouring among the heathen in Northumberland; apart from them, there were sixteen secular missioners and fifteen regulars working in this large and uninviting area.[55] It does not seem a very convincing contribution on anybody's part.

Some conclusions may be drawn. Maldistribution of the clergy was more or less inevitable in the community during the period of gentry supremacy, and does not seem to have affected one set of missioners much more than another. It was serious for most of the seventeenth century; before the end of the century a slow but steady progress was being made towards doing something about it, though it was far from eliminated in 1770. On the whole, the regulars seem to have made more of an effort on the problem until about 1700, the seculars thereafter. Although they had made their peace with the gentry, the Jesuits were in some degree buttressed against the pressure of their environment by

53. For the North, C.R.S. i (1905), pp. 97 ff., and Aveling, *Northern Catholics*, pp. 236, 240, 245; my figure for the West is a hypothetical one based on a list of secular clergy supporters of Richard Smith in the area, 1631, in A.A.W., main series, xxiv (transcribed by Dr A. F. Allison, whom I must once again thank for passing his transcription on to me): total, 39.
54. cf. lists of secular clergy compiled by John Southcote in the 1630s (A.A.W. Main series, xxvi–xxvii *passim*, and above, n. 21): 41 seculars in London, 78 in nine Southern and Midland counties.
55. *loc. cit.*, above, n. 53.

a competent organisation and some sort of overall policy. Relatively lacking in both until rather late in the day, the secular clergy give the impression of being more directly vulnerable. Certainly there were seculars like the Yorkshireman John Marsh who, as his archdeacon wrote in 1692, 'has been in good places in the South' but, evicted in consequence of the Popish Plot, 'humbly betook himself to the most desolate and laborious place in this district [Egton Bridge] . . . to assist a great number of poore in the moores'. But others were likely to echo the feelings of one of his eighteenth-century successors: 'From the Moors in Yorkshire, good Lord deliver us'—I think he meant the people as well as the place.[56] The enthusiasm of volunteers was hardly, in the long term, a sufficient answer to the problem, and it does not seem to have been effectively taken in hand until the time of the vicars-apostolic. Signs of a new determination in the North appear with the arrival of James Smith in 1688, though his efforts were not always a success;[57] it is visible in the efforts his successors made to impose an obligation that priests, when ordained, should go on the mission in the district from which they originated. This was mainly designed for the benefit of the North; but Stonor seems in general to have supported it, which was self-denying of him since his own Midland district had become a consumer rather than a producer of priests as vocations among the gentry declined.[58] The idea was not pushed, on the grounds that it would upset the gentry by interfering with their freedom of choice; but the maintenance of secular-clergy numbers in the North during a period when they were in rapid decline elsewhere points to some *de facto* enforcement of the obligation as the century proceeded. It might still be said that changes in missionary distribution were less the result of intention than a simple response to the changing geography of the community. Perhaps we may postpone an answer to this question until we have investigated the finances of the mission.

56. C.R.S. ix (1911), p. 110; Leys, *Catholics in England*, p. 162.
57. Cf. C.R.S. ix, p. 111; case of Mr Calvert.
58. Rowlands, 'Staffordshire', pp. 20 f.; Hemphill, *Early Vicars-Apostolic*, p. 100.

(iv)

FINANCE

At this point I borrow, via Christopher Hill, a text from the Puritan activist Richard Sibbes:

> It were to be wished that there were set up some lights in all the dark corners of the kingdom . . . One way is, *To have a competent maintenance*: to devise it for the poor ministry, that they might live by the gospel that preach the gospel.[59]

This was also the case for Catholic priests; but in the long view their position was perhaps a more complex one than that of the preachers of the Protestant word. Reduction to their 'prime condition' of dependence on the 'voluntary contributions of men' was an incident of their missionary state; but an effective missionary activity was probably, for the Catholic clergy, impossible without some degree of financial independence. A solution to this conundrum was to take a long time to achieve. Our first information about these matters dates from the early years of the Jesuit mission, and in particular from the regime of Henry Garnet; much of it emerged as a by-product of the Archpriest controversy, which obliged the Jesuits to defend themselves against charges of money-grubbing and malversation. From Garnet's own references, from those of other Jesuits like Gerard, and from an account of the missionary practice of Parsons and Campion, we get a fairly clear impression of the two main areas in which financial problems arose on the mission, and of the policy adopted by the Jesuits in meeting them. One concerned the maintenance of the individual priest, and the other the creation of general funds which could be used for the advancement of the mission as a whole.

Individual Jesuits, Garnet explained, lived on what he called 'regular alms', a reliable income made up from covenanted contributions from a small group of families. This appears to have been Garnet's method of meeting a principle which the Jesuits at that time were anxious to preserve, that none of them should be dependent on an income provided directly by an individual patron, since this would reduce him to the status of a chaplain and inhibit his freedom of speech and action. It

59. C. Hill, *Economic Problems of the Church* (Oxford, 1956), p. 245.

may represent a weakening of the principle, which certainly became impossible to maintain later.[60] Garnet also had at his disposal a general fund or funds. This came, partly from a scheme of general subscription broached to some of the gentry in 1585, which did not prove successful in the long run; partly from the property of young men of wealthy families who wished to become Jesuits and to convey their property to the Society when they did so; and partly from donations. We have an example of the second source in the case of Thomas Wiseman, son of John Gerard's convert William, who left Garnet some £3,000 before departing to join the noviceship abroad; and we hear of sizeable contributions of one kind or another made by penitents of Gerard and Southwell, like the Countess of Arundel.[61] Garnet's critics were probably quite right in suspecting that all this amounted to a fund of considerable size;[62] he, on the other hand, could claim that it was not a private fund for the Jesuits but a general reserve for the mission as a whole. According to his account it was spent, partly on supporting the seminary at Douai, partly on financing the reception of new missioners and partly in providing for the needs of Catholics other than the gentry by supporting priests in poor areas and helping in general to create a system of circulating missioners.[63]

In the present context Garnet's efforts are perhaps less important for what they achieved at the time, than as a guide to the future: the financial history of the mission for the next two centuries may be read as a commentary on them. In the first place they cover most of the sources from which a priest's income might be derived, which apart from payments for individual services like Mass-stipends or baptism-fees fell into three categories. He might have a private income; he might depend on a payment for the general use of his services, which according to the number of people who contributed to it would resemble more

60. Caraman, *Garnet*, p. 217; C.R.S. xxxix, pp. 321 f., 331 f. It is not entirely clear whether Garnet meant that all the Jesuits were being supported together by regular contributions from a group of laymen, or each one; the second interpretation seems more likely.

61. Caraman, *Garnet*, pp. 34, 45 f., 104, 173, 216; *Autobiography of John Gerard*, pp. 25 f., 179 f., 182. It seems to have been envisaged that Jesuits would encourage people to contribute to a general fund of this kind (C.R.S. xxxix, pp. 322, 332), though Parsons seems to have hoped that it could be managed by lay assistants rather than by the Jesuits themselves.

62. e.g. William Gifford, in Law, *Archpriest Controversy*, i, pp. 11–14—extracts nos. 34, 36, 38, 51, 54.

63. Garaman, *Garnet*, pp. 45 f., 215 f., 217; *Autobiography of John Gerard*, pp. 26 f.

or less a salary, a subscription or a congregational collection; or he might be supported on an endowment or fund. The boundaries between these categories were sometimes indistinct: death or impending death of laymen and priests alike tended to convert revenues of the second type into revenues of the third; on the other hand, the complicated system of trusteeship involved in the administration of endowments which were in principle outside the protection of the law often, if it did not lead to the loss of them altogether, made it hard to distinguish income arising out of them from a simple salary. Nevertheless the distinction was an important one, and the clergy were at all times anxious to maintain it. Further, Garnet's experience, as in other cases, exposed what was to become the essential financial problem of the mission: to see that funds which derived almost exclusively from the aristocracy and gentry were not exclusively devoted to serving their own spiritual convenience.

One or two additional points may be made before proceeding. Financially speaking, the mission was an indigenous growth: continental subsidies, so far as they existed, were confined to the support of continental institutions and did not, except in the early days, make a predominant contribution even there; the mission properly speaking paid for itself at all times. It did this without extravagance. During the seventeenth century its authorities worked on the assumption that a priest would cost £20–25 a year to maintain; during the eighteenth, this went up to some £30–40. Considering that the clergy of the Church of England had claimed £20 a year as a decent living in 1563, when the sixteenth-century price-rise was only halfway through—admittedly a Catholic priest did not have a wife and children to support—these were modest expectations. Despite some assertions to the contrary, and allowing for some Elizabethan exceptions which may perhaps be regarded as special cases, there was no difference in the standard of living assumed for a secular priest and for a member of a religious order, Jesuit or not.[64]

64. For Jesuit assumptions about the cost of maintaining a priest in the seventeenth century see, e.g., Richard Blount's account of the terms of the Petre foundation in Foley, *Records*, ii, pp. 396 f.: 'cui dotando praeter reditum annuum perpetuum quasi mille scutorum, summam capitalem sexdecim mille scutorum in parata pecunia seposuit: quae si ad nummum dumtaxat decimum quintum exponatur, ad alendas vigenti (*sic*) quinque personas omnino sufficiet'. That is, an annual rent-charge of about £250, plus £4,000 invested at 7% equals £280 p.a.: total £530 p.a., quite sufficient for 25 priests. The sum may be compared with the total of £6,361 6s. 1d. subscribed to the Puritan Feoffees for Impropriations between 1625 and 1633: Hill,

It is convenient to begin by pursuing the financial fortunes of the Jesuits, since from the 1620s onwards the English province furnished periodic financial states to Rome, and while these require some interpretation they provide a remarkable degree of insight into the resources and problems of a large portion of the missionary clergy.[65] It seems best to begin with the last return made by the Province before the outbreak of the Civil War, in 1636: a time when it had settled down into its system of local organisations, which were to bear the weight of its financial arrangements for the next century and a half, and from many points of view a prosperous one. Since Jesuits did not, in principle, possess individual incomes, the Jesuit mission depended for its regular income, as in Garnet's day, on the two other sources described, which they referred to as 'funds' and 'alms'—distinguishing, if one reads between the lines, such income from alms properly speaking by describing it as 'regular' or 'ordinary' alms. They also refused to accept benefactions which could only be employed for a particular purpose in a particular neighbourhood,[66] which meant that financially speaking the unit of the Jesuit mission was the local district or 'college'; each made a separate return of its income, in which the distinction of funds and alms was more or less preserved. We are thus able to discover how the income of the province was distributed throughout the country, and roughly speaking where it came from. With a little adjustment we can divide the country into the regions already used to investigate the deployment of personnel: in 1636 the distribution of income was as follows.[67] The Northern districts had an income of £621 10s. and the

Economic Problems, p. 254. For the secular clergy, see W. Vincent Smith, 'The Maintenance of the Clergy of Northumberland and Durham in Penal Days', *Ushaw Magazine*, xlvii (March 1937), p. 4; Rowlands, 'Staffordshire', p. 30; Aveling, *West Riding*, p. 265.

65. Most of the evidence for the financial history of the Jesuit province will be found in Foley, *Records*, vii part 1, pp. cxxxix–clxvii: see Table III. Reference will be made by 'College' or 'Residence' and date.

66. General ruling by Jesuit General Piccolomini, 1651, in T. Hughes, *History of the Society of Jesus in North America: Documents*, i part 1 (London/New York, 1908), pp. 38 f.; examples in Archives of the English Province S.J.: College of St Aloysius —Billington mission: benefaction refused on these grounds, to be handed to a secular, 1736; English Province Correspondence, iv (1746–1856), p. 28—Carteret (provincial) to Beaumont (Lancs. superior), April 1755: benefactions cannot be accepted with conditions attached, though Mass-stipends may.

67. See Table III; I assume income whose source is not specified to be alms, not funds; and that four of the Roman *scudi* in which the sums were originally expressed, equal £1 sterling.

Western districts of £514 a year, making a total for North and West of £1,135 10s. The income of the Southern and Midland districts was practically twice as large: £2,178 10s. The income of the London Jesuits, amounting to £717, brought the entire reliable income of the mission to £4,031. Since there were not more than 170 Jesuits to divide it into, the mission as a whole had rather more funds than it needed in order to survive; but the income was not distributed evenly throughout the country and the southern districts were very much better off than the rest.

Rather less than half the total came from endowed funds—£1,816, compared with £2,215 from 'alms'; but here again there was a marked difference between different parts of the country. Endowed income accounted for just about half the income in the South and Midlands, and for just under a third in the North and West. We know the sources from which most of these endowments came. The southern funds came from two large benefactions, one from William, second Lord Petre, and the other apparently from Mrs Eleanor Brooksby and perhaps also from her sister Anne Vaux, the two being daughters of the Lord Vaux of Harrowden who had been closely connected with the earliest period of the Jesuit mission. The Petre foundation was made between 1632 and 1635, and represented a capital sum of £8,000, half of which was paid in cash, and the other half probably secured on lands of which the trustee-ship remained in the family. At a rate of 7%, this sum was to produce an annual income of about £500. In 1636, when it was not quite fully launched, it was producing £458; later it produced £570.[68] The other foundation provided an income of £625 a year, implying a capital sum of £9,000. Eleanor Brooksby had died in 1624, though her sister was still alive; the fund seems to have been in the possession of the Jesuits from about 1630, though there was some difficulty, no doubt from relatives, in securing it. Unlike the Petre bequest, it seems to have been entirely in the hands of trustees.[69] Taken together, these two funds provided the Jesuit mission with over a quarter of its regular income; they were intended to support 55 priests, 25 on the Petre foundation and 30 on the other. They were almost certainly the largest bene-

68. See above, n. 64, and College of Holy Apostles, 1636 and after. There is no sign of this endowment in the account of Petre finances given by C. Clay in *Recusant History*, xi (1971), pp. 87–116, which suggests that it was handed over fully to the Society.
69. Foley, *Records*, ii, pp. 311 f.; College of the Immaculate Conception, 1636 and after; *V.C.H Leicestershire*, ii, pp. 67 f.

factions received by any body of clergy on the mission throughout these two centuries.

Other endowments, amounting to about £730 a year, existed in three other districts—in Wales, Lancashire and London; we know most about the fund of the Welsh college of St Francis Xavier. Of its funds of £200 a year, £80 came from an endowment of £1,200 made by Lady Frances Somerset, daughter of the fourth Earl of Worcester and wife of William Morgan of Llantarnan. She was a penitent of Robert Jones, and 'reflecting that most of her husband's estate consisted of Church livings, dealt with him about making some satisfaction for the same'. The bequest was made in her will, about 1620, and executed by her husband and later by her son, Sir Edward Morgan, though he did it without much enthusiasm; it provided for the support of four Jesuits, two in north and two in south Wales. The rest of the funds of the district were not the result of direct benefaction, but had been accumulated by successive superiors from alms received, principally no doubt from the fourth and fifth Earls of Worcester and other members of the family, and laid out in the purchase of the house at The Cwm, near Monmouth, and a number of adjacent farms whose rents or mortgages brought in the remaining £120 or so.[70] The Lancashire fund seems to have been the income of the estate of Southworth Hall, near Warrington, which certainly belonged to the district by the 1650s and had probably done so before the Civil War; its passage to the Jesuits had something to do with the Gerard family, but it seems more likely that they had bought it than received it as a gift, and that in constitution the Lancashire fund resembled the Welsh.[71] Where the London fund came from we do not know: put together, the three of them only amounted to about two-thirds of the Petre and 'Vaux' foundations.

The trouble about large benefactions was that the wishes of benefactors and the constitution of the Society prevented them from being used outside the region where they originated. Naturally enough, benefactors were rarely anxious to support priests who would be working in some part of the country totally remote from their own interests; besides, in order to set the funds on a proper footing, and to maintain the theory of religious poverty, it was necessary to erect the mission operating in the region in question into a fictitious college, situated in a

70. Foley, *Records*, iv, pp. 333–336; College of St Francis Xavier, 1625 and after.
71. Archives of the English Province: College of St Aloysius—Croft mission.

fictitious place, and extending in fact over a defined area. Thus the Petre bequest became the property of the College of the Holy Apostles, formally established at, of all places, Chelmsford and actually covering the counties of Essex, Suffolk, Norfolk and Cambridge.[72] The other bequest became the property of the College of the Immaculate Conception, whose territory was Derbyshire, Leicestershire, Nottinghamshire and Rutland. A list of eight counties where Jesuit missionary effort was likely to offer the least return would have included most of these; yet a quarter of the province's funds were tied up there. Leaving aside all other sources of income, these two colleges had funds for an establishment of 55 Jesuits, and at no time contained much more than 30, some of whom were engaged in teaching grammar to the children of the gentry. As a result of the Petre bequest, the number of Jesuits in East Anglia went up from six to eighteen; there were seventeen in the College of the Immaculate Conception in 1632, though it settled at somewhat less than this. Asked for more, the provincials pleaded shortage of men; it seems likely that they were simply unwilling to send priests to districts which were overstocked already.[73] At a time when there were not more than fourteen Jesuits in Lancashire they may be felt already to have gone farther than they ought to have in meeting the wishes of large benefactors.

For while, in large areas of the South and Midlands, the Jesuits had more money than they knew what to do with, they were in even larger areas of the North and the West hindered by poverty from exploiting to the full missionary opportunities of an altogether more promising order. This was probably not true of Wales and the Welsh border, where after thirty years of hard work and wise management the College of St Francis Xavier had reached what seems an admirable equilibrium between its resources and its opportunities; it kept twenty men fully occupied on an income which was just about adequate, half of it a return for present labours, the other half provided by Lady Frances Somerset's bequest and past economies invested in Monmouthshire land and used to serve regions and classes of the population which had no means of paying for its services.[74] It was only partially true in the

---

72. Hughes, *History of the Society of Jesus in North America: Documents*, i part 1, pp. 38 ff., for correspondence on the subject between the Jesuit General and the English Provincial, 1650–1651; Foley, *Records*, ii, p. 396.
73. See Annual Letter of College of Holy Apostles, 1638 (Foley, *Records*, ii, p. 566).
74. Foley, *Records*, vii part 1, p. cxlii; iv, pp. 334 ff.

Lancashire district: the College of St Aloysius had much the same resources as the College of St Francis Xavier, supported about the same number of priests, and could even spare one to teach grammar; but it could certainly have found work for more men if it had had them.[75] The regions which really suffered were the North-east, from Yorkshire to Northumberland and including Cumberland, and the extreme South-west. They possessed no funds at all, and had therefore not been constituted as colleges; the twenty-nine priests who worked in these two vast regions lived on 'alms' amounting to not quite ten pounds a head. This was not of course their whole resources: the ten Jesuits working in Yorkshire, who returned a steady income of just over £100, said that they had enough for seven, meaning presumably that they estimated their casual receipts at about £40 a year: two of them lived with individual patrons and had 'very small' annual salaries. But when all allowances are made they cannot have been exaggerating when they reported, a little tartly, that they had a 'special opportunity of practising religious poverty'.[76] Farther north things were even tighter: partly, it would appear, because they had discouraged a sizeable bequest from Dorothy Lawson on the grounds that it would impoverish her children, the eleven Jesuits of Northumberland and Durham lived at an altogether different level from those of the well-endowed districts in the South. They seem in fact to have done very largely without money, sharing the meal and roof of the poor Catholics whom they visited in the course of long circuits made on foot across the northern uplands. In 1636 they said they could make do with what they had, but during the Civil War they seem to have been in real want; it was not for another half-century that their economic condition began to approach that of most of their brethren in the South.[77]

The economic problems of the Jesuit mission in the 1630s arose neither from inadequate nor, as its opponents often alleged, from excessive resources, though there was justification for taking either view; they were essentially problems of distribution. The Jesuit superiors seem to have been aware of them: they kept priests back from rich districts, and sent to poor ones more than there was reliable support

75. *ibid.*, vii part 1, p. cxlii—'nowhere a greater need of active missioners'.
76. *loc. cit.*, n. 75, and *ibid.*, iii, pp. 257 ff.—Annual Letter of 1635; Aveling, *Northern Catholics*, p. 237.
77. *loc. cit.*, n. 75; and Foley, *Records*, ii, pp. 91 ff., 101; Palmes, *Life of Mrs Dorothy Lawson*, pp. 45 f.

for; and they seem to have made some attempt to redistribute resources more profitably. Apart from the district funds, there was some money at the general disposal of the provincial; in 1649 this was being used to subsidise the mission in Lancashire, Yorkshire and the North-east, and again in the early eighteenth century in Lancashire and the South-west. But there was very little of it: in 1711 the subsidy amounted to £40 and was meant, no doubt with 'alms', to support three missioners. John Warner complained in the 1680s that there was no proper provincial fund, and one never seems to have been created.[78] Here we may probably detect the consequences of an important change of policy which had occurred since the Garnet regime. Garnet's funds had been designed for use in any part of the country which might need them, irrespective of their place of origin: devolution of financial control to the districts seems to have been a feature of the subsequent regime of Richard Blount and Henry More and one of the concessions to the gentry which marked their period of government. The anxieties of bene-factors were certainly important in the formal erection of the province in 1622–1623, and one may suspect that they carried equal weight in determining its structure.[79] As a result, the Jesuit mission in England was for at least half a century seriously hampered by an excessive con-centration of its resources in the South.

Like the distribution of priests, the distribution of Jesuit income did not greatly change between the outbreak of the Civil War and the Popish Plot. Like the gentry on whom they depended, the Jesuit districts which had established funds before the war, though they often drew no income for long periods during the troubles and confiscations which followed, seem to have kept their capital more or less intact. The Petre fund, despite a loss from fraud, was still returning something like its original income during the 1680s; the 'Vaux' fund, probably less well protected, suffered from the Commonwealth sequestrations, but about half of it survived into the Restoration. The local Jesuits seem to have got the capital out of the hands of its original trustees, and reinvested part of it in an estate at Ashbourne in Derbyshire, held in the name of

78. St John (North-east) and St Michael (Yorkshire), 1649, 1651; St Aloysius (Lancashire), St Stanislaus (South-west), 1711. It appears that the provincials were trying about 1650 to expand funds under their own control for this purpose (Hughes, *History of the Society of Jesus in North America: Documents*, i part 1, pp. 39 f.), but they do not seem to have had much success. For Warner, C.U.L. Ms. Ll.i.19, f. 50v.
79. cf. Basset, *English Jesuits*, p. 166.

Rowland Eyre of Hassop; the fund was producing £340 a year in 1672. The Welsh fund lost about £50 worth of land during the Civil War, but made this up from savings; the district was not getting much out of the estate at The Cwm in the 1670s, but this seems to have been because the income was being ploughed back into improvements. In Lancashire the Southworth estate had been bought, or more probably bought back, in 1654 through the collaboration of William Blundell's Protestant cousin Sir Richard Bradshaigh; the trusteeship arrangements seem here again to have given rise to some difficulty, and this estate also was conveyed to the Eyres of Hassop, Thomas Eyre purporting to purchase it in 1674 for £5,000. Despite contrary indications in the financial states returned from the district, it may well be that nothing much had been lost: when the College of St Aloysius was divided at the Restoration by the hiving-off of Staffordshire, the two districts had the same total endowment as before the War. The London fund also had serious difficulties with its trustees, but emerged from the Interregnum with something less than two-thirds of its income intact.[80] Altogether, then, the crisis did not much affect the financial imbalance of the mission, and the southern districts continued to attract the largest benefactions. During the 1650s the London College of St Ignatius was in hopes of £3,000, which seem to have been disappointed; at the same time a bequest of £1,000 fell in dispute between the Colleges of St Aloysius and the Immaculate Conception. This would suggest that it originated in Staffordshire, from the Gerards or Fitzherberts; the problem was probably solved by the erection of the Staffordshire mission into a separate district in 1661. During the 1670s the districts of Lincoln, Hampshire and Staffordshire accumulated sufficient funds to be erected into colleges; the Residence of St George, which covered Worcestershire and Warwick, acquired property in and around Worcester, though it was disappointed of further expectations in the 1690s. At the same date the Jesuits in the South-west revealed that they

---

80. Holy Apostles, 1658, 1672, 1685. Immaculate Conception, 1655, 1658, 1672; R. Meredith, 'The Eyres of Hassop (ii)', *Recusant History*, ix (1967), pp. 9–13—Ashbourne estate bought for £2,478 in 1667–1668, six tenants with three-life beneficial leases; income apparently about £100 p.a., collected by Eyre's bailiff; the College seems to have had another estate at Holbeck Woodhouse, Notts., which served as its headquarters. St Francis Xavier, 1658, 1672; Foley, *Records*, iv, p. 335. St Aloysius, 1645, 1658, 1672; Archives of the English Province, College of St Aloysius: Croft mission, for Southworth estate. St Chad, 1672. St Ignatius, 1658, 1672.

were eagerly anticipating a death which would bring them in £6 a year.[81]

Although the largest new benefactions did not materialise, the disproportionate endowment of the southern and midland districts evidently persisted in fairly acute form throughout most of the seventeenth century. What reduced it to at least more manageable proportions was, first of all, the crises of the Popish Plot and of 1688–1689. The Popish Plot agitation, and the hunt for superstitious trusts which it inspired, did indeed fall impartially on uplands and lowlands since, among other discoveries, it exposed the complete financial arrangements of the colleges of St Francis Xavier in Wales and the Immaculate Conception in the Midlands, including the estates at The Cwm and Ashbourne; something may have been saved from the wreck in both cases, but neither district flourished after this.[82] The fall of James II acted more selectively, since the period of open activity had given those districts which had hitherto had more money than they could use the opportunity to invest heavily in town schools and chapels: two in London, one at Bury St Edmunds, one at Stafford and one at Wolverhampton, besides the Northern ones at Pontefract, Wigan and Durham. The destruction of these in the rioting which followed James II's flight abolished at a blow the surplus wealth of the Southern and Midland districts.[83] The imbalance could hardly, while the structure of the Province remained unchanged, be prevented from reappearing to some degree: by 1711, when the dust had settled, three of the four most heavily endowed missions, apart from London, were still in the South —Hampshire, where the Jesuit connection with the Arundell family was

---

81. St Ignatius, 1658—trouble from relatives; St Aloysius, 1658; St Hugh, St Thomas, St Chad, 1685—the last erected in 1672, the first two in 1676; St George, St Stanislaus, 1696. T. G. Holt, 'The Residence of St George', *Worcestershire Recusant*, no. 20 (1972), pp. 45–78, is a good account of the situation of one of the smaller Jesuit districts; financial details at pp. 54, 64, 67.

82. Foley *Records*, iv, pp. 462 ff.; St Francis Xavier, 1690, 1693, 1696, which imply that something was saved in 1678, but all lost after 1688–1689; Meredith, 'The Eyres of Hassop' (*loc. cit.*, above, n. 80); Immaculate Conception, 1685; Warner, in C.U.L. Ms. Ll.i.19, ff. 29, 31, 43*v*, 54. See also W. A. Shaw (ed.), *Calendar of Treasury Books, 1679–80* (1913), pp. 85, 114; *1681–85* (1916), pp. 349, 615, 786—concerning a sum of £2,550 apparently lent on mortgage to Henry Neville of Holt, Leicestershire, by the College of the Immaculate Conception, in the name of Viscount Carrington and others, which would appear to represent a portion of the district fund not invested in estates.

83. St Ignatius, Holy Apostles, St Aloysius, St Hugh, St Michael, 1690; cf. above, chap. 4, p. 72.

by now firmly established, East Anglia and Lincolnshire, which continued until 1740 at least to have more money than it could use. But though it remained unsatisfactory that the Jesuit mission should be more heavily endowed in Wiltshire and Hampshire than in Lancashire, the immense disparities of the earlier period had been ironed out.[84]

Of the remoter regions, while there was now little hope in the West, the North was growing modestly richer. In Northumberland Jesuit fortunes tended to follow those of the Haggerston family, and one may see the repercussions of rising prosperity in the endowments which successive generations of the family found it possible to make. In the 1660s Thomas Haggerston had been able to raise only a rent charge of £6 a year for the support of a Jesuit on his estates; in 1710 Jane, mother of the extremely well-endowed Sir Carnaby, left a total of £680 to various pious purposes, half of which went to provide £20 a year to keep a Jesuit in the district 'and not elsewhere'. By 1740 the junior branch of the family, now settled at Ellingham, could manage a benefaction of £500. From the records of the Newcastle lawyer with whom they dealt, we discover that the Jesuits in the North-east were able, in one year (1713), to lay out £1,000 mainly in loans to Catholic landlords of the region, though their total funds did not produce more than £100 a year until after 1740.[85] But no part of the northern mission was ever in a position to maintain all or most of its priests from such endowments; altogether, the annual income from the funds of the three northern districts in 1711 did not amount to more than £8 10s. for every Jesuit working there, compared with £15 for the southern and midland districts.[86] Nevertheless, the expansion of the Jesuits in the North went on steadily up to 1773. A little of the deficiency was, as we have seen, made up by direct subsidy from provincial funds, but it was chiefly overcome from two other sources. The first was an improvement in the scale and organisation of 'alms'. In most country districts

84. See Table III, 1711; for the Arundells and the Jesuits in Wiltshire, see Williams, *Wiltshire*, p. 148.
85. Northumberland C.R.O. Z HG xii, 27 April 1710; Z HG i, nos. 43, 46a, 49; Archives of the English Province, Generals' Letter-Books III (2), f. 333v: General to Boult, 16 July 1740. Northumberland C.R.O. Z MD 130, p. 147—cf. W. V. Smith, in *Transactions of the Arch. and Arch. Society of Durham and Northumberland*, xi, parts v–vi (1965), pp. 423–424. As a good deal of the money was lent to George Collingwood of Eslington, who was improving his estates (*Northumberland County History*, xiv (ed. M. H. Dodds, 1935), p. 518), it may have been lost when the estate was forfeited after Collingwood's participation in the 1715 rising.
86. See Table III, 1711.

this still usually meant direct salaries from individual gentry patrons, but arrangements for congregational support were spreading, especially in Lancashire where there were congregations of adequate size, and it was one advantage of the growing shortage of priests that superiors could now threaten to remove a priest from a rural congregation which could afford to make them, but did not.[87] In several towns, again notably in Lancashire, missions were coming into existence which depended, in effect, exclusively on such support: in Liverpool in 1734 there was a fund of only about £2, which seems to have been the usual subsidy paid by Jesuit districts to a country priest to serve occasionally in a neighbouring town; in spite of this there was a permanent priest and an organised monthly congregational subscription bringing in £21 2s. a year.[88] Under the uninformative heading of 'alms' or 'charity', the Jesuit financial returns of the eighteenth century record a development of great importance in the relations of priests and their congregations.

Continued expansion in the North was also assisted by what appears at first sight another concession to the gentry. The Jesuit rule forbade the possession of a private income; but gentry families found it more congenial, and probably safer, to provide annuities for sons entering the order than to contribute to the funds of the Society at large. By 1680 such *peculia* had come to be tolerated, but according to Warner they had to be paid by the provincial, who thus acquired control of money which could in some degree make up for the lack of a provincial fund. In the difficult years after 1689 the practice seems to have become more common, but to have been used to correct inequalities of distribution in the province. What happened in the eighteenth century was that the family of an intending Jesuit would, where possible, make him an endowment which could effectively be controlled, locally or nationally, by the Province, could be used inside the mission with some degree of flexibility, and would be amalgamated with the funds of the Province or the district when the priest in question died.[89] In 1711 nearly £700

---

87. Archives of the English Province: College of St Aloysius, Bedford Leigh mission, case of 1758; English Province Correspondence, iv, f. 102, for an agreement between a priest and the congregation at Linstead Lodge, Kent.

88. T. Burke, *Catholic History of Liverpool* (Liverpool, 1900), pp. 9 f.; and see below, chap. 14, p. 338. Similarly in Bristol: Oliver, *Collections* (see above, chap 5, n. 51), pp. 108 f.

89. Warner, in C.U.L. Ms. Ll.i.19, ff. 48*v*, 50*v*—to General, 23 April, 27 May 1683; Archives of the English Province: Generals' Letter-Books III (2), p. 256—

of the Province's income was coming from this source, over a third of the revenue provided by endowed funds; the northern and western districts accounted for £300 of this, and the north-eastern 'Residence of St John', with £125, had the highest figure for any district.[90] The decision may very likely have had a socially restrictive effect on the recruitment of the Jesuit mission; but it was certainly not applied as a general rule in the way that Leander Jones had earlier suggested, and used with moderation it seems to have done a reasonable amount of good. It happens that we possess an account of the Jesuit mission in Durham and Northumberland, dating from the close of our period, which enables us to grasp the progress which had been made. In 1750 the district contained eleven Jesuits; they reported themselves as serving some 2,000 Catholics, and though there may have been a few more than this they were not likely, as in Lancashire, to raise significant congregational subscriptions from a clientele of this size. Five of them were chaplains who received salaries from individual gentlemen: £10 besides their keep in every case except Haggerston, where the priest had £15 and another £8 from the district funds; most of them had sizeable seigneurial congregations to look after, as at Callaly and Haggerston, and some did work elsewhere. The other six, with one partial exception, were supported on the funds, which must have included the patrimony of individual Jesuits as well as benefactions from the gentry. In fact, if not in theory, most of the gentry endowments were earmarked for particular country missions, and the rest of the funds went to maintain priests in Durham and Newcastle, to increase inadequate endowments in the country stations, and to provide the usual small payment for a country priest to visit periodically towns like Alnwick and Morpeth,

---

General to Turberville, 12 March 1729: Jesuits with individual pensions or annuities cannot dispose of them at their own pleasure, but must deposit fund either with their superiors or with the procurator of the province, 'et in faciendis expensis ab ipsius annutu dependeant'; also English Province Correspondence, iv, f. 28, concerning 'annuitants of Mrs Prov.': their 'peculium' to become property of the province after their death.

90. See Table III, 1711; an example, Mr Parker, with an annuity of £23 p.a., moved from Plowden in Shropshire to Alnwick in 1746: Price, 'Three Jesuits at Plowden Hall', *Recusant History*, x (1969), p. 170. A further motive may have been that individual property of this kind was easier to protect at law; cf. the case of the Staffordshire bequest of Joseph Gerard, 1705 (Rowlands, 'Staffordshire', pp. 141 f.), which was successfully disputed by his brother-in-law; the Jesuits seem to have tried to prove that the land was the property of his younger brother Philip, a Jesuit novice.

which had as yet no permanent priest themselves.[91] Altogether, this looks a creditable achievement. While maintaining close and friendly relations with a group of gentry families, the Jesuits of the North-east had by 1750 succeeded to a large extent in recovering their freedom of action, and appear to have been using it in an intelligent and forward-looking way. There seems enough evidence to indicate that, in this, their eighteenth-century experience was typical enough of the Jesuit mission as a whole.

It would never have been possible to draw up reports of the financial state of the secular clergy comparable to those compiled by the Jesuits. They were late in acquiring an effective organisation, and it was in the nature of the secular as against the regular vocation that income should belong to individual priests or missions, rather than to larger bodies or districts; qualifications to this position did not assume much importance before the late seventeenth century. Yet in the special conditions of the English mission the formal distinction of vocations made less difference than it might have done elsewhere; in essentials, all branches of the clergy were financially speaking in much the same boat.

The seculars too had failed to set up a general fund for the mission at large. Richard Smith had probably tried to do this, and in 1630, before retiring to France, he and the leading members of the Chapter jointly contributed to setting up a Chapter fund. The original contributions amounted to about £2,000. Others were made by friendly priests and some by laymen: they cannot have come in very fast, since during the 1630s the secretary of the Chapter was trying to increase the fund by offering 8% on loans. Despite the usual losses and difficulties, the capital appears to have risen to a nominal £10,000 or so by 1662, though only about half of this was actually in the hands of the Chapter; thereafter it seems if anything to have declined. Some of it was money held in trust for particular missions, but there was never more than a handful of these; such funds, like those which was held for the colleges abroad, were distinguished from the 'particular' or 'proper stock' of the Chapter. It is not clear that this was used for anything except to support the officers of the Chapter itself, and to finance the agents who were sent to Rome to lobby for the appointment of bishops. Little or none of it seems to have been used for missionary purposes; if this had ever

91. Smith, 'Maintenance of the Clergy of Northumberland and Durham in Penal Days' (above, n. 64), pp. 8 ff. (from Foley).

been intended, the intention must have been abandoned by the 1670s.[92]

Meanwhile some secular priests, like some Jesuits, lived on endowed funds, some on salaries from patrons, some on congregational collections; the main difference was that it was proper for a secular priest to retain a private income if he had one, and it is probable that throughout the period a fairly large number did so. Confronted by complaints about the size of their benefactions, the Jesuits were inclined to allege that many of the secular clergy had large private incomes; it is doubtful if this was true of many of those actually engaged in the mission, though it applied in some other cases.[93] At best, those who were younger sons of gentry would possess modest annuities; as we have seen, the Jesuits were not above making use of this resource themselves. The difference was perhaps less in the source of income than in the relative facility which the Jesuit organisation gave them of applying it with some regard to the overall needs of the mission; at their least flexible, Jesuit resources could be redistributed within an area of some size. Benefactions to the secular clergy were, however, usually donated for the support of a priest in a particular neighbourhood, whose services were often earmarked for the use of a particular class of people—the tenants, for example, of a small number of gentlemen. Other local funds accumulated as the result of a large number of small bequests and donations from independent farmers, the natural outcome of a long period of peripatetic ministration in a district. The most common situation seems to have been a combination of both. Sometimes permanent and successful missions arose on these foundations, like that centred at Marton in Holderness which originated before the Civil War and was settled on reliable foundations by a mixture of congregational contribution and gentry endowment towards the close of the seventeenth century. The Rider fund for the support of a priest in Coverdale, already noticed in another context, seems another successful instance. But often enough these attempts broke down, and one's impression is that more of such funds disappeared than survived. Where the trustees were local gentry,

92. M. Havran, *The Catholics in Caroline England* (London, 1962), pp. 78–79; Old Brotherhood Mss. iv, nos. 1 (Chapter fund, 1630–1662), and 114–119 (state of the fund in the mid-eighteenth century). For a mission endowment of £1,000, dating from 1677, held in trust by the Chapter, see M. Hodgetts, in *Worcestershire Recusant*, no. 16 (1970), p. 12.
93. e.g. Caraman, *Garnet*, p. 174; cf. Aveling, *West Riding*, p. 242; Havran, *The Catholics in Caroline England*, p. 78.

the money was apt to disappear when the family ran into difficulties, or was washed away in a general deluge like the Civil War. Few individual priests were strong enough to insist on adequate security, much less to badger a gentleman into making over the capital as the Jesuits were often able to do; it was hardly before the eighteenth century that the secular clergy possessed in the vicars-apostolic authorities of a standing to keep the gentry to their obligations, or that the endowment of local missions went forward in any large and permanent sense.[94]

Though it proved incapable of doing much about these problems itself, the Chapter did in the end contribute to solving them; it encouraged the growth of funds belonging to local clergy associations or brotherhoods which gave them something of the corporate strength and stability, and the flexibility in the use of resources, of the Jesuit districts and Colleges. Like other notable advances in the missionary efficiency of the secular clergy, these financial improvements seem to date from the shake-up of the Chapter after 1667;[95] we are lucky to possess a full account of the origins of one of them, the fund for the secular clergy of Hampshire, otherwise known as the Hampshire Hog.[96] The rules of the fund were drawn up in their full form in 1683, though the fund had been in existence a little earlier: they began by citing the examples of community of property to be found in the Acts of the Apostles and the primitive Church to warrant the creation of a 'Common Stock', described how difficult it was to operate successfully without one, and explained what they hoped a fund would achieve. 'More priests in every county would be maintained, their externall labours lessened, their internall retreats more frequent: all people, the poor espeacially in all places whatever would be more duely observed, every Priest be completely provided for, nor would there be any cause for fear of want in old age.'[97] The last point raised a welfare problem of particular concern to the secular clergy, who could not, like the regulars, fall back on their order if they became sick or incapable or, if they had nowhere else to go

94. See the Yorkshire examples in Aveling, *East Riding*, pp. 33, 43, 53–55; *West Riding*, p. 242; *Northern Catholics*, p. 242 (a Benedictine fund, but suggestive of the general situation), 245 f., 343, 345 f.; Rowlands, 'Staffordshire', for a local fund lost at law in the 1720s.
95. Hemphill, *Early Vicars-Apostolic*, pp. 162–163—Chapter regulations of 1676; cf. also Miller, 'The Catholic Factor in English Politics, 1660–1688' (see above, chap. 4, no. 19), p. 9, citing a Yorkshire priest on the need of a 'good purse' for the mission there. I assume he meant a common fund rather than an individual income.
96. C.R.S. xliii (1949), pp. 9–17.
97. *ibid.*, p. 11.

to, retire to a continental house at the end of their missionary service. Although this dual purpose of the local funds must always be taken into account, we are here concerned with their relation to the priest at work; and here the Hampshire priests were above all concerned to see that Catholics in their district who were too poor to maintain priests themselves should get adequate attention. Having surveyed the needs of the district, they hoped to be able to divide it into manageable circuits which would ensure that all Catholics had regular access to a priest, and use the fund to subsidise priests who would then be left with a clientele which had not the resources to maintain them properly.[98]

The fund itself had been accumulating since about 1670: much of it was subscribed by the clergy themselves, as the Chapter had pressed them to do; it also attracted donations from the laity, including one of £600 given by John Caryll of Harting in 1672 to 'help the poore in Sussex or Hantshire'.[99] Other benefactions were made during the eighteenth century, when most of the capital was invested in New South Sea Annuities or local mortgages. The fund does not seem to have been, on the whole, much of a success: it never seems to have reached a very high figure—in the middle of the eighteenth century its capital was still apparently less than £2,000; it seems to have been mismanaged, and a good deal of the capital invested in mortgages was lost; money intended to support rural missions appears to have been diverted to maintaining a priest and chapel in Winchester, which may help to explain the decline of rural Catholicism in the district which seems to emerge from Challoner's eighteenth-century visitations.[100]

In other districts the picture looks a good deal brighter. In Staffordshire and three neighbouring counties a Common Purse was established in 1676: its earliest foundation was to provide for an itinerant priest to supply temporary vacancies and emergencies throughout the region; and while it accumulated funds for welfare provision, its most substantial endowments were, before the end of the century, being used to develop permanent secular missions, first in Wolverhampton, then in the countryside. The Staffordshire clergy seem to have been wealthy: most of the endowment probably originated as the property of in-

98. ibid., pp. 16 ff.—note the clergy's anticipation that this will cause problems with the gentry.
99. ibid., pp. 18 ff.
100. ibid., pp. 1–3; Burton, Challoner, i, pp. 155–159; ii, p. 171; Whyte, 'The Vicars-Apostolics' Return of 1773', p. 207.

dividual priests. The fund was a substantial one, invested mainly in London stocks, and amounted by the end of the eighteenth century to some £10,000; though it too seems to have been administered rather badly and without much regard for the interests of the other counties it was formally intended to serve, it nevertheless succeeded in overcoming to some extent the bane of excessive local restriction, and provided most of the funds for missionary expansion in those parts of the west Midlands where, during the eighteenth century, industrial development was altering the balance of population and the distribution of social weight.[101] Much the same would seem to be true in the North-east, though here we can only judge the history of the fund from its effects, and it is likely that, as the northern clergy complained generally in 1731, their funds were 'smaller than in other parts'. During the 1740s, when Edward Dicconson investigated the income of the eleven secular priests in Durham and Northumberland, their posts consisted of two or three gentry chaplaincies, three country missions endowed partly by the gentry and partly by former priests, and five town missions in Durham, Sunderland, Stockton, Newcastle and Hexham. These last, though they also had specific endowments, were the particular concern of the general fund, which had already been supporting priests in Durham and Newcastle in 1700; this received a fillip from Lady Mary Ratcliffe, aunt of the Earl of Derwentwater executed in 1715, who left it her entire fortune when she died in 1724, and the money seems to have been wisely spent in building up the resources of town missions and helping the rural ones through the teething troubles which were apt to accompany financial independence.[102]

The growth of these local funds made a great deal of difference to the secular clergy; in some parts of the country at least—and certainly in parts where success was to be crucial for the future—they enabled them to catch up with the Jesuits in matters of distribution and finance, and in some respects to surpass them. There is certainly little to choose

---

101. Rowlands, 'Staffordshire', pp. 44 ff., 29–31, 181 ff.; M. Greenslade, 'The Association of Staffordshire Clergy, 1686', *Staffs. Catholic History*, no. 2 (1962), pp. 13–18.
102. Smith, 'The Maintenance of the Clergy in Northumberland and Durham', pp. 5–8; Hemphill, *Early Vicars-Apostolic*, p. 130; A.A.W. Main series, xxxviii, no. 2, for priests maintained by clergy funds *c*. 1700. The Ratcliffes seem originally to have been supporters of regulars but had fallen out with the Jesuits by 1715: C.R.S. lxii (1971), p. 317; Lady Mary had also endowed the secular mission in York in 1696: Aveling, *Recusancy in York*, pp. 99, 385.

between Jesuit and secular distribution in the North-east in the 1740s, and in the matter of independence from the gentry the seculars seem to have gone ahead. Yet the system had its flaws: apart from the fact that they may not have administered their funds with the greatest competence, the local clergy associations remained in principle benefit societies of narrow membership and horizons, and the last thing they were concerned with was the redistribution of funds between districts; as between one another, they too reflected local wealth rather than local need, and where the need for them was in some ways most pressing, in Wales and the South-West, they never seem to have existed at all.

Progress beyond this point depended upon the exercise of wider powers and a wider vision by the vicars-apostolic. Some of them were willing to promote the local funds as providing at least a more satisfactory guardianship for endowments than lay trustees: James Smith took this point of view in the North. But even where they did not regard independent funds as an affront to episcopal supremacy they took the view that future endowments must be retained under their own control, and saw that funds were built up and administered with a view to the needs of their districts as a whole. Financially, their main contribution was to impose on all the clergy in their districts the obligation to pay into a central fund one-third of all payments received for particular services, like Mass-stipends. The idea, for which Richard Smith offered some precedent, seems to have been put into practice by James Smith in the North in 1697, and taken up by his brethren four years later. Presumably it did not apply to regulars, and it can hardly have functioned in the Western district. It seems to have achieved the ideal of being both relative painless and relatively profitable: by 1794 the Midland district fund amounted to £21,000, though all of it cannot have come from this source; with the revenue of the Common Purse or clergy fund, which after 1760 was effectively at the bishop's disposal, it was then producing an income of about £1,000 a year. In London the district fund grew fast enough for Challoner, besides a variety of other charitable works, to be able to pay a living wage of £20–40 a year to a number of priests who, away from the fashionable quarters served by embassy chapels, ministered to growing popular congregations in the east and south of the city, 'in situations and places,' wrote Milner, 'where there was the greatest prospect of doing good'.[103] By 1773, when

103. Aveling, *Northern Catholics*, pp. 344 f., 383 f.; Rowlands, 'Staffordshire', pp. 48–60; Burton, *Challoner*, i, p. 360; ii, p. 31; Ward, *Dawn of the Catholic*

the Jesuits were knocked out of the race, the secular clergy were probably already outdistancing them along the trail they had been the first
to blaze. All in all, they had jointly done their best to overcome the disabilities imposed upon them between 1600 and 1750 by the social constitution of the community they served. In the meantime, many opportunities had certainly been lost; but the community which finally
emerged was equipped with a clergy which had very largely overcome
the problems of distribution and finance which had dogged it for so
long; and if we compare their situation with that of the Church of
England, we may well conclude that the Catholic clergy had by the
close of the eighteenth century achieved an organisation of men and
resources, however limited they were, which gave practical substance
to the formal advantages of a missionary over a traditional order, and
enabled it to manage a good deal more successfully the great transition
on which the country was embarking.

Revival, i, p. 24. Particular difficulties arose about the control of clergy funds when
the bishop appointed was a regular: G. Anstruther, 'The Appointment of Bishop
Williams', *Archivum Fratrum Praedicatorum*, xxx (1960), pp. 314 ff. But this was the
only case outside the Western district. The Chapter fund also helped out in
London: Old Brotherhood Mss., iv, nos. 114, 119 for three endowments to 'assist
the poor' in London, one for the parish of St Giles.

11

THE PRIEST IN THE COMMUNITY

T HE mission required competent leadership, appropriate organisation and adequate resources; but what mattered in the end was the individual priest, his perseverance in the 'spiritual harvest and workmanship' to which he was called.[1] Seen as a whole, the missionary enterprise was an engine bogged down in a sticky terrain where it eventually found sufficient purchase to move forward; we need finally to explore these conditions and this impulse as they are revealed in the experience and activity of the priest on the ground. Until recently the working life of the missionary priest has not been a matter of much interest to historians. At the time his life was normally thought worth recording, as in Challoner's *Memoirs of Missionary Priests*, only if it had ended on the scaffold, and a hasty reader of Challoner would hardly suppose that the priests of whom he wrote did very much of note between the day they arrived in England and the day they were arrested. Since then, the martyrological perspective has remained the predominant one. Here, although we do not need to question the appropriateness of this perspective in itself, we must be concerned with the priest in so far as he survived to get on with his ministry, and in the first place with the novel conditions in which that ministry was conducted. Seen in the long term, and from our present point of view, the cult of martyrdom which characterised the early phase of the mission looks almost like a necessary aid in the transition from the high clerical condition of the pre-Reformation Church to the situation of the missionary priest.

The abandonment of clerical dress by secular priests of graduate status or religious, was in itself a dramatic representation of the change; Allen had been obliged to defend it from traditionalists, and did so with good humour.[2] From the Elizabethan bravery of John Gerard and the

1. Knox, *Allen Letters*, p. 32.
2. *ibid.*, p. 36.

country dress of Ambrose Barlow, with his battered hat and 'a pair of scurvy old slip-shoes', to the long curls of the Restoration, the brown coat and breeches of the eighteenth century, and indeed to the ruffles and short hair of the Regency, the missionary priests in England dressed as laymen, and moved among them with little sense of segregation.[3] A certain freedom of social manners, by comparison with continental clergies, went with a conception of their office which was professional rather than mysterious, though not necessarily any the less dedicated for that, and certainly appropriate to the circumstances in which their ministry would be placed.

For the conditions of the clerical life were more various than has commonly been supposed. Aveling has remarked on the insufficiency of the traditional picture of the Elizabethan missioner, 'living furtively and more or less permanently in some great house, supplied liberally with ingenious "priest's holes" ',[4] and it is clear that in the early decades priests accommodated themselves to a wide variety of external situations, and that a high proportion of them had no permanent home at all. By the beginning of the seventeenth century, when the confusion had abated somewhat, it had become possible to take stock of the situation, and the Jesuits made in 1616 the first general survey of the priestly *modus vivendi*. This divided missioners into three sorts: those who lived in the large households of magnates, and were more or less immune from interference; those who, in the familiar manner, lived a concealed, restricted and rather lonely existence in gentry houses, 'sitting like sparrows upon the housetop'; and those who circulated.[5] The Jesuits gave no indication what proportion of their numbers existed in any of these conditions in 1616, but the first was obviously the privilege of a few, and there were probably still at this date more in the third than in the second. We can now be fairly sure that most priests in the early decades of the mission were peripatetic; the wholly travelling priest did not disappear until about 1700, and the partially travelling or 'riding'

3. Mathew, *Catholicism in England*, p. 59: the instructions to Parsons and Campion require 'moderation' in dress: C.R.S. xxxix, pp. 319 f.; cf. *Autobiography of John Gerard*, pp. 17 f.; 'The Apostolical Life of Ambrose Barlow', *Downside Review*, xliv (1926), p. 237—a reference for which I am greatly indebted to Dr D. M. Lunn; Rowlands, 'Staffordshire', p. 31; Aveling, *West Riding*, p. 265. For portraits of Jesuits at various dates, see Basset, *English Jesuits*, pp. 208, 240, 304.

4. Aveling, *West Riding*, p. 217.

5. 'Modus vivendi hominum Societatis', 1616, with later comments probably by Henry More dating from the 1640s, in Foley, *Records*, ii, pp. 3–6; a better translation *ibid.*, vii part 1, pp. xvi f.

missioner succeeded him. The secular clergy tended to find this condition irregular, as it was natural they should; but a degree of mobility was as appropriate to the missionary state as a certain blurring of the distinction between clergy and laity, and between one sort of priest and another.[6]

As the Jesuit survey described him, the travelling priest moved continually about on foot or on horseback, though he normally had some kind of base. He went from one house to the next, staying overnight and passing on in the morning, adapting his behaviour to the circumstances of the household, assuming a different name, changing his dress and the direction of his movements from one house to another. Twenty-five years earlier, fresh from the experience of his own missionary tours, Parsons had given more details. He would arrive at a house towards the end of the afternoon; spend the evening hearing confessions and giving spiritual direction; say Mass, with a sermon, first thing in the morning; stay in the house and write until dinner (i.e. midday); and then ride off towards the next house, thinking out his sermon in the saddle. Such, the survey implied, were the truly active missioners, and they were certainly an admirable illustration of the Jesuit doctrine of mobility. The Jesuits had thought a good deal about the problems involved and were, for example, keen to provide bases or rest-centres which the travelling secular missioner might envy his Jesuit colleagues. But in essentials his way of life was the same, and we may find illustrations of it from any branch of the clergy and any part of the country. It would be hard to find a more evocative case than that of George Napper, who arrived one evening in 1610 at a house in a Berkshire village; he was observed going in and 'having assisted the family, and performed his devotions [said Mass] very early, . . . took his leave and was making the best of his way through the enclosures, supposing all quiet at that early hour', when the village constable and his posse arrested him. The Benedictines had a hankering for stability, but in Lancashire up to the Civil War Ambrose Barlow spent a week on circuit for every three at home, going 'on foot with a long staff on his back like a countryman . . . sometimes to several places in a morning to say Mass, and after that to another I know not how far off that night'. In the Jesuit district of St Thomas of Canterbury, which covered the south of England from Dorset to Sussex, all the priests seem to have been itinerants in the middle of the

6. cf. 'A way to deal . . .', C.R.S. xxxix, p. 332, on the importance of priestly mobility in avoiding the nexus of patron and client.

century, and one was reported to have a circuit of two hundred miles which he went round on foot once a month; on one such journey into Dorset in 1647 the then superior of the district, Thomas Bennet, riding a pack-horse and dressed in a smock-frock, had an encounter with an Independent cavalry officer and three troopers which would not be out of place in *Don Quixote*.[7] At this time gentry were still to be found among the custom of such itinerants, but their chief service was to poorer Catholics; by 1700, when their range had probably somewhat narrowed, they were regarded as suitable to the needs of farming households worth one or two hundred pounds a year.[8]

For the same reason they were specially characteristic of the upland regions. William Anlaby and Thomas Atkinson worked in Yorkshire. Anlaby started in 1578, tramping with his kit in a bag, then bought a horse and joined up with Atkinson, with whom he served an extensive territory running from Richmond to Hull. Anlaby was arrested in 1597, and so apparently was the horse, for Atkinson thereafter went the round on foot until his own arrest and execution in 1616. The Jesuits of Northumberland and Durham lived much the same way until late in the century, trudging to homely dinners across the northern hills. One has a good view of Ralph Corby 'with a little staff in his hand, which he called his horse, desiring those in the house where he came to "set by his horse for him" '; and of Thomas Gascoigne returning from his monthly tour in the depth of winter, and chopping wood for a fire in the outhouse he lived in between times.[9] After the Restoration Jesuits and Benedictines still took this way of life for granted in the North, though conditions were becoming less spartan, and there were still two 'laborious itinerants' among the secular clergy in Yorkshire in 1692, one of whom had been at it for forty years. It was probably a few years after this that the northern vicar-apostolic was trying to organise with the help of the north Yorkshire gentry the means to provide a 'roving missioner in the moorlands'.[10]

7. Foley, *Records*, ii, p. 5, and iii, pp. 404, 407, 411–420; C.R.S. xxxix, p. 83; R. Challoner, *Memoirs of Missionary Priests* (ed. J. H. Pollen, London, 1924), p. 308 —for another case, John Sugar in Warwickshire, pp. 275 f.; 'Apostolical Life of Ambrose Barlow' (see above, n. 3), pp. 240–241.
8. Aveling, *West Riding*, pp. 240 f.; *Northern Catholics*, p. 242; A.A.W. Main series xxxviii, no. 2, printed by J. A. Williams in *Recusant History*, xii (1973), pp. 42 ff.
9. Aveling, *East Riding*, p. 22; Challoner, *Memoirs*, pp. 232, 339; Foley, *Records*, vii part 2, pp. 1111–1112, and iii, pp. 91 ff., 101.
10. Aveling, *Northern Catholics*, p. 242 (Benedictine constitutions, 1661), 346; Foley, *Records*, ii, p. 537 (Jesuit annual letter, 1671); C.R.S. ix, pp. 106, 108.

As in the North-east, so on the Welsh border. According to Challoner, the Appellant priest Roger Cadwallader spent some sixteen years
tramping the uplands of Monmouthshire and adjacent parts of Wales;
'he was'—he probably needed to be—'a very zealous reformer of evil
manners'. His Jesuit rival Robert Jones reported in 1613 that several
of his men were at the primitive stage of perpetual motion, and that he
was still looking for the base of operations which he was shortly to
establish at The Cwm. Except as refugees in the aftermath of Charles I's
defeat, the Welsh Jesuits never penetrated the heart of the mountain
country, but they seem to have done their duty in the borderlands
faithfully enough until the destruction of their mission at the time of the
Popish Plot.[11] By this time the mobile missioner was in any case on the
way out. Horses were coming in, and as a general rule it seems fair to
say that the more priests rode, the less genuinely available they became.
In the backwoods a priest on foot had a wider social range, and argu-
ably a wider geographical range, than a priest on a horse. Horses fitted
the trend towards a more gentlemanly standard of life, partly explained
by the increasing gentility of the missionary body, which went ahead
during the seventeenth century. The point may seem perverse: in any
event, a spirit of heroic dedication could not be expected to last for ever,
and declining mobility was to some extent simply a consequence of
settling the mission on permanent foundations. As these foundations
settled, it became clear that the missionary priest was destined to one
of two conditions, which differed in most respects but both provided
him with a permanent roof over his head.

The way of life of the family chaplain is a more familiar one, and had
been a feature of the missionary scene since the earliest days. The position is provided for, though reluctantly, in Gilbert's notes on the
mission of Campion and Parsons. It is illustrated, among Elizabethan
priests later executed, by Cuthbert Mayne in the household of the
Tregians, John Payne with the Petres and John Cornelius with the
Arundells: Cornelius, though a protégé of the Arundells, chafed in the
situation, and wanted to go to the North, or to Ireland, where he felt he
would have more scope. Robert Southwell, partly by mistake, assumed
something like this position in the household of the Countess of
Arundel, though he went on missionary tours as well. John Gerard was
never quite in it himself, though his experience of the inside of the

---

11. Challoner, *Memoirs*, p. 300; Foley, *Records*, iv, p. 385 and v, pp. 447, 472.

Catholic gentry household was unrivalled, and it is noticeable that several of the places he stayed in had permanent chaplains as well.[12] But by the time the Jesuits surveyed the mission in 1616 this kind of stability was obviously growing more common. The large households of the nobility, where superiors commonly lived—Henry More with the Petres during his time as provincial; among seculars, Richard Smith with Lady Montagu at Battle, and elsewhere—often contained more than one priest, and were a special case.[13] According to the Jesuits, few heads of houses, even large ones, had yet sufficient confidence in their neighbours or their servants to ignore the statute-book to this degree. Usually the priest lay low in an attic room which contained a bed, a table and an altar, and was told to walk along the beams so that the floor would not creak and to be careful about opening windows and showing lights; he was not allowed to go about the house, might only slip out for a walk after dark, and must not come back until the servants were at supper, or in bed. In an otherwise bustling household he might spend weeks or months alone, seeing only those who came to Mass, the maid who brought his dinner, and with luck after meals one of the children, or their mother, 'look[ing] in to apologise for not having been able to pay him a visit sooner'.[14] From a servant's point of view it was all very queer;[15] from a priest's, particularly when he had been trained for a life of activity, it must have been frustrating in the extreme. Perhaps this led the Jesuits to exaggerate a little; in any case, as the seventeenth century proceeded, the position of the private chaplain was obviously becoming less of a nightmare, and a more generally accepted feature of domestic life. Benedictines especially took to it with some aplomb, as an invitation to the meditative life. Augustine Baker's friend Robert Haddock 'in his ordinary residence, that offered him no impediments to it . . . gave himself to dayly recollection by exercise of mental prayer, and vacation from exterior distractive solicitudes, and in so doinge spent the space of a fortnight, to his much comfort in soule'; Leander Jones spoke of such monk-chaplains as living, singly or in

12. Above, n. 6; Rowse, *Tudor Cornwall*, pp. 346, 357; Challoner, *Memoirs*, p. 39; Foley, *Records*, iii, p. 438; Devlin, *Southwell*, pp. 132 f., 181 f.; *Autobiography of John Gerard*, pp. 24, 29, 145 f.
13. Foley, *Records*, ii, pp. 5 f.; Southern, *An Elizabethan Recusant House*, pp. 39 f.
14. Foley, *Records*, ii, pp. 4 f.
15. Examples in J. Leatherbarrow, *The Lancashire Elizabethan Recusant* (Chetham Society, 1947), p. 86; C. Howard, *Sir John Yorke* (London, 1939), pp. 29 f.

pairs, 'tanquam in cellis suis'.[16] By the Civil War family chaplaincy was well enough established to have given rise to a problem which was to dog the mission for more than a century: after the royalist defeat, the Lancashire Jesuits reported that most of the substantial Catholic families had temporarily gone to seek refuge in other districts, and taken most of the local Jesuits with them. Twenty years later John Sergeant's 'Dialogue' about the clerical condition could assume that almost all the problems to which it gave rise were problems between house-chaplains and their patrons.[17] This was not entirely the case, but it was to be a defensible view for some time to come.

This missionary calling was difficult to reconcile with this degree of domestication, but it was possible to envisage it, in a limited way, as a task of household reform. This had been a theme of the early missioners, who complained of the easy-going ways and superficial spiritual guidance of the old priests, and put down to it the lack of vigour in the Catholicism of their patrons. Gerard, who was a specialist in the matter, showed a strong hand in reforming the households of William Wiseman and Elizabeth Vaux. Among the Jesuits, the movement reached its peak in the early seventeenth century, touching something like the sublime with the achievement of James Pollard at Osgodby, and something like the ridiculous with that of Ferdinand Palmer in Lancashire, who tried to persuade married couples to take vows of chastity—which Gerard had done his best to discourage—and forced one gentleman to get rid of a large collection of play-books. Richard Smith exercised similar authority in the household of Lady Montagu, and needed all of it to moderate her penitential enthusiasm.[18] At this level of intensity, the

---

16. Augustine Baker, 'Treatise of the English Benedictine Mission': C.R.S. xxxiii, p. 185; Leander Jones, 'Apostolici Missionis Status in Anglia' (1634): *Clarendon State Papers*, i, p. 199. G. Dolan, 'Chapters in the History of the English Benedictine Missions', *Downside Review*, xvi (1897), p. 64, prints a charming passage from William Cowper which appears to portray Dom William Gregson, chaplain at Weston Underwood, Bucks, in the eighteenth century, as he

> 'Walks forth to meditate at eventide
> And think on them that think not for themselves.'

17. Foley, *Records*, ii, pp. 8 f.; the 'Dialogue' is in Old Brotherhood Mss., ii part 2, ff. 528–539 (incomplete). This is to be dated to 1667; date, style and content convince me that Sergeant was the author, though there seems no direct evidence.

18. C.R.S. xxxix, pp. 329 ff., 339 ff.; *Autobiography of John Gerard*, pp. 28 ff., 145 ff.; Foley, *Records*, ii, pp. 18 ff. and, for Osgodby, above, p. 128; Southern, *An Elizabethan Recusant House*, pp. 49 f.

spiritual government of seventy or eighty people was no sinecure; in so far as the job of a domestic chaplain tended to become one, it was not because the typical gentry household was a great deal smaller than this, as because it was unthinkable, in the long run, that heads of households should allow the clergy a predominant voice in determining their domestic arrangements.

William Watson's claim, in 1600, that 'a priest his place in civil conversation' was somewhere between a knight and a baron, and Milner's eighteenth-century story of the chaplain who was not allowed a silver candlestick to go to bed with as these were reserved for members of the family, no doubt imply equally exaggerated estimates of the household precedence of the clergy at their respective dates; but the general trend they indicate can hardly be doubted.[19] From about the middle of the seventeenth century, when the practice of private chaplaincy was becoming most widespread, the clergy began to complain that they were not being treated with due respect by their patrons. Sergeant's 'Dialogue' of 1667 spoke bitterly of domineering behaviour by heads of households, and of the poor conditions, mean and shoddily furnished rooms, which chaplains were expected to put up with; he told a story of a Protestant maid who said she knew he was a priest because he was respectably dressed but slept in a garret. There was also a drone of complaint about cavalier treatment of the priest at Mass. Richard Lascelles's *Little Way How to Hear Mass*, written in 1644 as a book of household instruction, was eloquent on the subject, and particularly hostile to wives who treated the chaplain's duty as falling within the general province of the kitchen. 'It's a shame to hear women that can hardly read the petitions of the Jesus Psalter undertaking to teach priests to wipe their chalices etc.': he complained that ladies were apt to speak out if they felt the priest was getting through Mass too slowly.[20]

If the 'Dialogue' is anything to go by, this reversal of roles was complete by the 1660s. Patrons, it said, would tell a new priest that they did not expect to be contradicted in conversation; 'and if he happens to meddle in the ordering of their families, their deportment towards their kindred and neighbours or their dealing in bargains and the like (in

19. William Watson, *A Decacordon of Ten Quodlibetical Questions* (London, 1602), p. 53: cf. my own 'Character of Elizabethan Catholicism', in T. Aston (ed.), *Crisis in Europe, 1560–1660* (London, 1965), p. 239; Burton, *Challoner*, i, p. 142.
20. 'Dialogue', ff. 533 f., 534 ff.; Aveling, *Northern Catholics*, p. 252. Price, 'Three Jesuits at Plowden Hall', pp. 165 f., 168, 171, gives a good idea of the 'nervous strain' which might exist between a priest and the family.

which God knowes his duty too oft obliges him to enterpose), O that's a nice and tender poynt, there he intrenches upon their temporalls, a thing contrary, as they suppose, to his function'.²¹ There was no doubt an element of caricature in this: at about the same time William Blundell was asking the advice of the clergy on problems of tenant right. But Charlotte Jerningham's reaction to the chaplain's intrusion in the making of her father's will—'What a pity it is that these good Priests cannot confine themselves to Spiritual Matters!'—was probably more typical than this, and increasingly so during the eighteenth century.²² And there was hardly a genuine contradiction between this point of view and the requirement commonly made by patrons that chaplains should occupy their leisure time with duties of a useful nature in the household or on the estate. In the earliest years of the mission, it had been a standard form of concealment for a priest to adopt the disguise of one or other of the more important household offices; thereafter the actual exercise of such functions became more common, though this was usually over the protest of the priest. Augustine Baker, who happened to be a skilled common lawyer, complained that his patron 'expected that he should despach much of his secular businesses for him', and said 'he was not a priest for his purpose' when he proved 'backward' to do this. Two eighteenth-century Benedictines in a similar case were Bede Potts, who was required to act as agent at Everingham for the absentee Sir Marmaduke Constable, and Anselm Bolton, who was left in charge of the Fairfax estate at Gilling during a minority in the 1780s. The Jesuit Francis Anderton ran the Haggerston estate while the young Sir Carnaby was abroad on the grand tour, though here the arrangement was agreeable to both parties. An active landlord like Nicholas Blundell would not expect such services, and they were perhaps exceptional; but occupations of this kind, if only as tutor, played some part in the life of all chaplains of the period, and within limits were probably acceptable to priests who might have little else to do.²³

21. 'Dialogue', f. 534r and f.
22. Above, chap. 7, n. 80, for Blundell: there is also the mildly comic case of Dorothy Lawson, who insisted on taking advice on agricultural problems from her priest, William Palmes, who knew nothing whatever about them and had hastily to consult others: William Palmes, *Life of Mrs. Dorothy Lawson*, p. 37; *Jerningham Letters*, i, p. 344.
23. Rowse, *Tudor Cornwall*, p. 346; C.R.S. xxxix, p. 332; Leys, *Catholics in England*, p. 79; Aveling, *Northern Catholics*, pp. 384 ff.; P. Roebuck, 'Absentee

We need to know how far this domestic situation inhibited a priest from exercising his ministry outside the household to which he belonged. The charge that patrons prohibited such activity became a commonplace during the Restoration, and was most forcibly expressed in the Dialogue from which I have already quoted. They made, it claimed, 'conditions that [chaplains] shall not stir abroad without leave', or that 'they must help nobody, but their own household, nor meddle with assisting sick, converting Protestants, etc. (all contrary to the intent of their mission)'.[24] There was certainly a contradiction of principle between the roles of a domestic and a missionary or congregational priest, and it had several practical consequences. Families which had come to assume that spiritual ministration would always be available in their houses, would expect this convenience to accompany them wherever they went, and a priest who travelled around with his family would not be a satisfactory minister to a congregation.[25] Even if they stayed put, gentlemen were obviously inclined to feel that if they paid for a priest they were entitled to the exclusive use of his services. Yet in practice the position was less cut-and-dried.

The service of a gentry family was normally considered to cover all who might in some way be regarded as the gentleman's private responsibility, whether they were members of his household or not; the actual condition of a domestic priest was not so much that of a private chaplain as that of a priest serving a proprietary church whose limits were roughly defined by the boundaries of an estate. This was very much the case at Little Crosby, where the priest could retire from the house to the village without in any way changing the character of his congregation. It was the case with John Gother at Warkworth, the house of the Holmans in Northamptonshire to which he retired after 1688, much as he might have appreciated a wider sphere of activity; and with the Benedictine and Jesuit chaplains at Gilling who fought a brave rearguard to defend the tenants from the selfishness of successive Lords Fairfax. Mission records after 1750 show that an estate congregation of anything

---

Landownership in the late 17th and early 18th Centuries: a Neglected Factor in English Agrarian History', *Agricultural History Review*, xxi (1973), pp. 1–17 (Everingham); Northumberland C.R.O. Z HG vii, 1; Rowlands, 'Staffordshire', p. 29.

24. 'Dialogue', ff. 534r and ff.; cf. 532r. Cf. Philip Hughes, 'The Return of the Episcopate to England', *Clergy Review*, x (1935), pp. 194 f., based on a text of 1667 very close to the 'Dialogue'; also quoted in Williams, *Bath and Rome*, pp. 46 f.

25. Aveling, *Northern Catholics*, p. 384; *East Riding*, p. 56.

up to three hundred people was by then not uncommon, and one may point to the comments left by the Benedictine John Fisher, who served the Langdales at Holme-on-Spalding-Moor, as showing that the concerns of many priests who were formally private chaplains were in fact congregational rather than domestic.[26] For those patrons who were rich enough to afford it, and whose responsibilities were large enough to make it realistic, it was convenient to divide domestic and congregational functions between two priests. In Yorkshire, at various times after 1630, the Constables, Gascoignes and Fairfaxes maintained both a domestic priest and a tenant missioner, though these arrangements usually broke down in periods of economic difficulty and retrenchment, and none survived beyond the end of the seventeenth century. From this date however we have a charming picture of two secular priests, William Pegg and Henry Harnage, who 'live together in a very honourable residence'—apparently Madeley Court in Coalbrookdale, belonging to the Brookes—'the one for the family, the other for the country . . . great painetakers in the harvest'. Throughout the eighteenth century the Lords Arundell maintained a similar establishment of two Jesuits at Wardour; it is noticeable that they paid their chaplains more than their missioners, and were on a much closer social footing with them.[27]

The question remains, how far domestic priests were able or willing to serve Catholics who had no dependence on their patrons—to 'assist the poor' as the phrase went. Early in the seventeenth century Richard Smith had complimented Lady Montagu on her willingness to receive all comers to Mass in her house, as if this was uncommon. The implication that outsiders would normally be refused admission seems too strong: certainly by the eighteenth century some acquaintance in the locality or, for a stranger, a certificate of Catholicism would ensure access to a family chapel even if there was a mission nearby.[28] We also know that, even in the depths of the domestic regime, a family priest would not necessarily wait for the outsider to come to him. Returns to the Chapter in 1692 show that there were a number of them who 'made excursions' or 'assisted the poor'. Mention of such cases implies that

26. *Great Diurnal*, i, pp. 163, etc.; Burton, *Challoner*, i, pp. 4 f.; Aveling, *Northern Catholics*, p. 384; and see below, p. 300, for Fisher.
27. Aveling, *East Riding*, p. 54; *West Riding*, p. 239; *Northern Catholics*, p. 384; C.R.S. ix, p. 114; Williams, *Catholic Recusancy in Wiltshire*, pp. 151–164.
28. Southern, *An Elizabethan Recusant House*, p. 44; 'Four Catholic Congregations', *Recusant History*, ix, pp. 97 ff.; *V.C.H. Leicestershire*, ii, p. 60.

they may have been unusual, and clerical reports betray an anxiety to prove that domestic chaplaincy did not exclude missionary zeal. One feels more confident that this was true in the North than in the South. Thus a Yorkshire secular, Augustine Smithson, arrived in 1660 to reside with Sir Solomon Swale at Stainley, was taken under the wing of the established priests of the district, and 'wanted no assistance that could animate the tolerable diligence and endeavours of a young missioner'; they invited him to preach at their own houses and others in the surrounding country, and generally encouraged him to take an active view of his function.[29] One can certainly exaggerate the restrictive effects of the domestic system, but it does seem obvious that it involved a degree of clerical underemployment which contrasts both with the age of the circulating missioner and with that of the settled congregational mission into which it was beginning to evolve from about 1700.

From the priest's point of view, the distinctive feature of a congregational way of life was that it gave him a permanent and independent home. In the most favourable case, which the author of the 'Dialogue' regarded as the only proper condition for a secular priest, he became a 'householder', able to keep a servant or housekeeper, to set, in theory, an example of economy or hospitality to his flock, and in practice to entertain his neighbours, the landlord, even the parson to dinner or a drink. But not many were in this agreeable condition by 1770: the solidly-built priest's house with adjacent chapel, fitting snugly and unobtrusively into the northern landscape, would only have become common during the next half-century. Before he acquired one the congregational priest was normally more or less of a lodger, living with farmers and small landowners, like the Yorkshire priests Richard Frank of Holderness, who lived for thirty-six years in the same house and 'hath always paid for his diet', and John Marsh of Egton Bridge, who 'takes some rooms and keeps house of himself'. After his move from Little Crosby Hall, Robert Aldred was effectively in this position, though he still received a salary from his landlord; so were an increasing number of priests during the eighteenth century.[30]

Given this freedom, the great majority were keen to justify their

29. C.R.S. ix, pp. 108, 111, 112, 113, 114; Aveling, *Northern Catholics*, pp. 349 f.
30. 'Dialogue', pp. 533v and ff.; *Great Diurnal*, ii, p. 38 and i, p. 185; Rowlands, 'Staffordshire', p. 32; priest's houses illustrated in F. O. Blundell, *Old Catholic Lancashire* (3 vols., London, 1925–1941), i, p. 131 (Brindle) and B. Little, *Catholic Churches since 1623* (London, 1966), p. 48 (Netherton, Lancs.); C.R.S. ix, pp. 109–110; above, n. 26.

existence by a life of unspectacular service to their flocks. As Joseph Berington fairly said, they were 'open, disinterested, religious and laborious; steady in the discharge of their duties; fond of their profession and emulous of supporting the character of primitive clergymen'; and if they were not as much men of the world as he would have liked them to be, it was just as well for the congregations they served.[31] The density of its Catholic population made Lancashire a favoured terrain of the congregational priest, and two examples from the county, one early and one late, may suffice. The first was the Benedictine Ambrose Barlow, who ministered to the Catholics at Leigh for twenty-three years before his execution at Lancaster in 1641. He was of a gentry family in the neighbourhood, and had some private means, but chose to live on an endowment of £8 a year which had been given by an old lady of the Tyldesley family, who owned land and an 'old hall' in the parish, to support a priest for the poor Catholics there. To put himself on a footing with his flock, he chose to lodge in the house with an 'honest country farmer' as his host, to wear country dress, to walk instead of ride, and to live mainly on a meatless diet of 'whitemeats and garden stuff'; though, as he said, 'if God should send a venison pastie, he would not refuse to eat of it'. His idea of the priestly function was in several ways a traditional one, in which hospitality and the rituals of charity figured largely. Three times a year, at Christmas, Easter and Whitsun, he issued a general invitation to his flock and all comers, and on the eve, to quote Challoner, 'the Catholics resorted to him from distant places, and passed the night after the manner of the Primitive Church, in watching, prayer and spiritual colloquies; whilst for his part he was employed almost all the night in hearing confessions. On the next day he treated them all with a dinner, where he, and some of the more honourable sort of the flock, served them that were poor . . . When he sent them home, he gave each of them a groat in alms; and when he had dined, he distributed what remained to the poor of the parish.' Otherwise he said his daily Mass, preached, heard confessions and performed a variety of other services in the community, as we shall see. His is one of the few cases where we can see a congregational priest at work in the earlier phase of the mission.[32] In Lancashire the type was presumably to be found throughout the seventeenth century, as it was

---

31. *State and Behaviour of English Catholics* (Birmingham, 1780), p. 174.
32. Challoner's account is in *Memoirs*, pp. 392-400; it is obviously based on the 'Apostolical Life' (above, n. 3), from which I quote, p. 240.

in Yorkshire,[33] but we do not get so close a view of it again until the
eighteenth, when we can find it illustrated in some comments of the
secular priest Simon Bordley of Aughton. Bordley wrote to his bishop
in 1789 to complain that things were not as they had been when he
came on the mission fifty years before. His neighbour Mr Caton of
Formby was upsetting his congregation by refusing to hear confessions
except on Saturday evening, when people could not come either because they had to get to market at Liverpool or because they could not
spare the hours from domestic work; and also by putting up the Mass-
offering from a shilling to half-a-crown. 'The people of Formby are
very religious in getting their parents etc. prayed for; they used to come
to me with a shilling in their hand saying, I desire you for God's sake
to say a Mass for my father and accept of this. Which pleased me well,
as they did not ask for a Mass for a shilling as the price of it, but for
God's sake.' Mr Caton also rode around the country at a gallop, and did
not preach, which Bordley thought a grievous lapse from the standards
of the old missioners 'who think it our duty to preach to our people, and
not content ourselves with reading a bit out of a book. Any old woman
can do that.'[34] Bordley was seventy-nine, and a *laudator temporis acti*,
but he gives a clear impression of the secure status, down-to-earth concerns and unforced conscientiousness of a country priest as the type was
becoming common at the close of our period. 'The utmost extent of my
ecclesiastical ambition from my infancy,' wrote another Lancashire
man, 'was to be the pastor of a country congregation . . . I think it the
happiest of lives.'[35] However liberal the seigneurial regime, and however much country congregations may have prospered under the wing
of a concerned and sensible landlord like Nicholas Blundell, the restoration of freedom was a tonic for the priesthood. As it became more widespread during the eighteenth century, the missioner began to recapture
the buoyancy of earlier years, and was able to find in two centuries of
experience the resources to confront a drastically changed environment
with, by and large, a notable degree of energy and devotion.

It would be possible to peer into the spiritual life of the clergy, and

33. See the case of Nicholas Postgate of Egton Bridge, in Aveling, *Northern Catholics*, p. 348.
34. Hemphill, *Early Vicars-Apostolic*, pp. 94-96: for Bordley (1709-1799; son of a Lancashire farmer; also had an important role as a schoolmaster), see Gillow, *Bibliographical Dictionary*, i, pp. 272 f.; in Staffordshire the mass-offering was 2s.: Rowlands, 'Staffordshire', p. 30a.
35. Ward, *Eve of Catholic Emancipation*, iii, p. 197 (Robert Gradwell).

the topic is an important one, since it was in the practice of interior recollection that a priest would find a recourse from the pressure of his external situation and the strength to transcend it in the exercise of his missionary function. But to pursue it fully would be difficult, and might tend to distract us from our subject. It is enough to suggest that a close relation between prayer and the active service of one's neighbour, such as was generally characteristic of counter-Reformation Christianity, would seem to have been a condition of the vitality of the mission, as it had been of its existence in the first place. During the first half of our period this was most likely to be found among Jesuits and those whom they influenced; some features of the Benedictine tradition were hard to adjust to it, but this was diverse enough to unite contemplative spirituality to the missionary vocation in a way which could certainly enrich the latter. The secular clergy, in freeing themselves from Jesuit supremacy, may well have lost contact during much of the seventeenth century with any spiritual doctrine at all, but managed in the end to find one in the tradition of St François de Sales as revived by Challoner in the early eighteenth century. This did not differ greatly from the Jesuit ideal, but since it was less controversial—and since the latter had probably by now lost a good deal of its flexibility and conviction—it seems to have provided a generally acceptable framework for the interior life of the clergy at the close of our period.[36] It probably does something to account for the shift towards a more active position in the community which was characteristic of the time. I conclude by examining some features of this active role.

The duties of the Catholic priest in relation to the laity are no doubt in some sense eternally the same: to perform the sacrifice of the Mass and to administer the sacraments through all changes of exterior circumstance. But historically his activities have altered a great deal in response to the requirements of the societies in which he has operated, and at least two important changes may be observed in England during the period with which we are concerned. We can see, in the first place, that non- or para-sacramental aspects of the priestly function which had been taken for granted before the Reformation remained important in

36. For the Jesuits, one may consult Foley, *Records*, vii part 1, p. xc; ii, p. 5; vii part 2, p. 1102. For the Benedictines, Lunn, 'English Benedictine Congregation' (see above, chap. 1, n. 30), pp. 321-325; C.R.S. xxxiii, pp. 104 f.; Aveling, *Northern Catholics*, pp. 385 f. and 'Education of English Monks' (below, n. 40), p. 140. For the seculars, Rowlands, 'Staffordshire', pp. 44 ff.; Burton, *Challoner*, i, pp. 82 f., 118-120, 346 f., 352 f.

the earlier phase of the mission, but subsequently withered away. We can also observe, coinciding with changes of sacramental practice and emphasis, the effects of the counter-Reformation idea that what should figure centrally in the activity of priests were the tasks of conversion and instruction which, if adequately carried out, would convert a predominantly social mode of religion into a predominantly individual one. This was the doctrine of the Elizabethan Jesuits, or most of them, and also of the anonymous secular priest who complained around 1600 that many of his colleagues could do no more than perform their sacramental functions, and were incompetent to give spiritual direction or instruction to individuals.[37] Our main attention must be directed to the second of these changes; but the first was an essential preliminary to one aspect of it, and cannot be ignored.

The first of the non-sacramental functions which may be regarded as a hangover from the pre-Reformation Church was that of arbitrator in feud. The Jesuit reports of the early seventeenth century put a good deal of emphasis on this topic, though not so much as they did in Ireland, a difference no doubt corresponding to the relative standards of civility prevailing at the time in Irish and north English society. Ambrose Barlow, according to Challoner, 'had a great talent in the composing of differences, and reconciling of such as were at variance'. Relics of this activity may still be found in the eighteenth century, but there is little sign that the clergy regarded it as an essential part of their vocation after the Civil War. Perhaps the habit had not been lost but transmuted: at the end of the century Gother did his best to point it in a direction better suited to the needs of the age and the community, saying that the priest should give his peace for his flock 'by drawing upon himself the difficulties, calumnies and insults of men by those unwelcome truths which his duty obliges him to speak'. Certainly in its primitive form it seems more relevant to the pastoral situation of the pre-Reformation (or indeed of the Anglican) clergy than to that of the missionary priest.[38] The same might well be said of an activity which

37. Letter from an unnamed priest to Thomas More, clergy agent in Rome, 1611–1612: Aveling, *Northern Catholics*, p. 251.
38. Foley, *Records*, vii part 2, pp. 1104, 1106, 1114; Challoner, *Memoirs*, pp. 392 f.; *Great Diurnal of Nicholas Blundell*, i, p. 107; Leys, *Catholics in England*, p. 128. Gother's views in M. Norman, 'John Gother and the English Way of Spirituality', *Recusant History*, xi (1972), p. 315 and (more traditional) in Eamon Duffy, 'Joseph Berington and the English Cisalpine Movement, 1772–1803' (Cambridge Univ. Ph.D., 1973), p. 23. For the background to the problem, see Thomas, *Religion and*

has recently received some attention, that of exorcism, and of physical and psychic healing in general. It has become clear from the massive evidence presented by Keith Thomas that this subject is an important one, and lies not on the periphery but somewhere near the centre of a consideration of the role of the Catholic priest in England until, say, 1650. It was a characteristic feature of the regime of William Weston as superior of the Jesuits in England during the 1580s to emphasise such miraculous powers as a principal skill of the missionary priest. A spectacular campaign beginning with the personnel of the large households of the southern gentry was claimed as a cause of numerous conversions, and the Jesuit mission reports continued to draw attention to this aspect of the priestly role until the Civil War, reporting for example sixty exorcisms from Lancashire in 1626. Except for Weston, the Jesuits do not seem to have taken this aspect of their work more seriously than other priests. From among the secular clergy we have the (admittedly Jesuit-influenced) John Cornelius, who managed to extract parts of a knife and a complete sandbag from the stomach of a possessed woman; and a group working around Wolverhampton about 1620 who were involved in the case of the 'boy of Bils[t]on', a spurious victim of witch-craft and diabolic possession who was allegedly induced to cough up knitting-needles. Among the Benedictines, Ambrose Barlow had a reputation as an exorcist, though his approach seems to have mingled scepticism with conviction. Confronted with a man who was 'troubled', he 'conceiv[ed] that it might be he was not possest, but obsest with the spirit of covetousness' and got him to confess that he had hidden a piece of gold in a meal-chest; going to look for it, 'he found a thing in shape most like a toad, having downe upon the backe like unto a gosling', picked it up with a pair of tongs and threw it on the fire, causing an explosion which set light to the dunghill in the yard, but apparently solving the case. Similar cases may be found until the end of the century, but as a regular activity the casting out of devils seems to have gone out with the pacification of feuds.[39] It was, in some degree,

---

the Decline of Magic, p. 154, and my own 'The Counter-Reformation and the People of Catholic Ireland, 1596–1641', in T. D. Williams (ed.), Historical Studies VIII (Dublin, 1971), pp. 158 f.—more generally in 'Blood and Baptism', in D. Baker (ed.), Studies in Church History, x (Oxford, 1973), pp. 129–143.

39. Thomas, Religion and the Decline of Magic, pp. 488–492 (with numerous references to Foley's Records), 76, 202, 485; P. Caraman (ed.), William Weston: The Autobiography of an Elizabethan (London, 1955), pp. 24–27; Challoner, Memoirs, p. 198, also 364, 395; Staffordshire Catholic History, no. 11 (1971)—a facsimile

artificially induced for motives of competitive missionary propaganda; but in some parts of England at least, and notably in Lancashire, it was evidently a simple response to a popular need which continued to be felt after the Church of England had come to the conclusion that it could not conscientiously pander to it. As such, it did not represent a novel departure, but a persistence of the tradition that healing of one kind or another was a function which the priesthood was expected to perform for the community; it had an equally traditional social aspect which related it, more or less intimately, to the pacifying role of which I have already spoken. Priests seem to have thought highly of it, at least until the Civil War; and it is probably not too much to say that for many of their clientele outside the gentry it was the least dispensable of their services. In a mainly illiterate community this would not be very surprising.

The point may be disputed, and it would certainly be wrong to give the impression that missionary priests had not been inspired from the beginning by the more strenuous conception of their role propagated, at its best, by the church of the counter-Reformation. What may I think be said without too grossly over-schematising the facts is that, as an activity directed to transforming the Christian awareness of the community by works of conversion and instruction, the ministry of the missionary priest went through two distinct phases. Roughly speaking, during the seventeenth century it concentrated on the practice of confession and was mainly aimed at the gentry; during the eighteenth century it concentrated on catechising the community at large. Priests of course had other instruments of enlightenment at their disposal: they 'held forth', as Nicholas Blundell put it, a good deal. But without disparaging their skills in this field one can fairly say that by comparison with Puritans and Anglicans preaching was not their forte. It was partly that until the eighteenth century the external circumstances of their ministry militated against it, and partly that they lacked the sense of urgency to communicate Scripture which gave its edge to the Protestant preaching ministry. The point can be exaggerated: there was not much wrong with the advice being given to Benedictine missioners in the 1760s, that their sermons should be 'such as suit the Genius of the English People, that is, let them be wrote in a rational, concise manner,

reprint of 'The Boy of Bilson'; 'The Apostolical Life of Ambrose Barlow', *Downside Review*, xliv (1926), p. 242.

pathetic, and keeping close to the subject', and that they should 'carefully avoid the French verbosity'. By this time the clergy had come largely to identify preaching with simple instruction; earlier they seem to have seen it more as a means of testifying to the existence of the community in general (' "Our fathers have sinned, and are not, and we have borne their iniquities" . . . How wonderful is God in all his ways that any of us should survive to this day at all.') than of affecting the lives of its members in particular. One seventeenth-century priest went so far as to give up preaching altogether, on the grounds that confession was a superior instrument of reform and instruction; his was an exceptional case, but it seems sensible to take the hint.[40]

For the gentry, the priest was probably always in the first place a confessor, and it was typical of the evolving function of the sacrament of penance in the practice of the counter-Reformation that it became extremely difficult to distinguish the sacramental relation as such from the more general relation of spiritual counsel. This was particularly obvious in the earlier decades of the mission, when political problems arose for the gentry which were also problems of conscience: in the most famous instance, it is not easy to tell whether Henry Garnet and the Gunpowder plotters were engaged in a sacramental relation or not.[41] The point could no doubt be determined in practice by discovering whether the layman was on his knees, though there is evidence that this was not general practice during the seventeenth century, except for the act of absolution, and one can conceive that kneeling would not have come too easily to some of the gentry.[42] What went on between penitent and priest is naturally not easy to discover, though there are probably enough manuscript notes and confessional manuals in existence to make a thorough study possible. Short of this, we may accept the evidence that the arrival of the Elizabethan Jesuits provoked a painful revolution in the penitential customs of the gentry, stirring them out of a comfortable habit of annual confession at Easter, and forcing them to attend to the improvement of their daily lives and to consider the sins of the mind as well those of the body; John Gerard's autobiography is

40. *Great Diurnal of Nicholas Blundell*, i, pp. 47, 53 and *passim;* Aveling, 'The Education of English Monks', *Downside Review*, lxxix (1961), p. 150 and *West Riding*, p. 266; Challoner, *Memoirs*, p. 353; Rowlands, 'Education and Piety of Catholics in Staffordshire in the 18th Century', *Recusant History*, x (1969), p. 75.
41. Caraman, *Henry Garnet*, p. 410.
42. Gother, *Instructions for Confession*, etc. (London, 1744), p. 45; Aveling, *West Riding*, p. 251; Rowlands, 'Education and Piety', p. 67.

a mine of particular instances. These were often general confessions covering a lifetime, and Gerard's method was to insist, sometimes in the face of panic-stricken demands by people who felt they could not afford to wait, on a period of intensive preparation which normally took several days and involved a systematic examination of conscience. This was clearly a novelty, and penitents required guidance on how to do it, as in the case of Sir Thomas Langton, whom Gerard recommended to get a friend to read him Luis de Granada's *Explanation of the Commandments*:

> After each Commandment I suggested that he should spend a little time in reflection, and try to recall the ways and the number of times he had offended against each, and make an act of sorrow before passing on to the next . . .[43]

Although the Jesuits were regarded as specialists in confession, and probably had a more considered and uniform approach to it than other missioners, it does not seem that differences were very material. We find a milder version of Gerard's practice in Richard Smith's account of a misunderstanding with Lady Montagu, who thought he was accusing her of concealing her sins when he appears to have been trying to get her to confess them in a more orderly way; and a more lurid one in Challoner's memoir of William Webster *alias* Ward. He seems to have worked in London, mainly among the gentry, in the years before the Civil War, and had the reputation of a 'rigid ghostly father'. He believed that the fear of hell-fire was a tonic for the worldly, and thought that the rich should be treated more rigorously than the poor; 'and however his roundness and plain language did not always please them, yet his spirit was so good, that he made impressions on their souls, even then when they would scarce lend him patient ears'. Outspokenness of this degree was probably uncommon, and might obviously be counterproductive: Ambrose Barlow was alleged to be so severe that sinners were afraid to come near him. Most priests were probably inclined to follow Allen's advice and make allowance for the difficulties in which people were placed.[44] Yet altogether there can be no doubt that confession, at least among the gentry, involved a stiff examination of the

43. 'A way to deal . . . ', *C.R.S.* xxxix, p. 330; *Autobiography of John Gerard*, pp. 20 f., 32, 34, 166 f., 169, 175 f., 178 ff., 186 f., 190 f.
44. Southern, *An Elizabethan Recusant House*, p. 27; Challoner, *Memoirs*, pp. 382 ff., 395; Knox, *Allen Letters*, p. 34.

penitent's way of life and promoted a serious and spiritual view of the practical consequences of being a Christian.

So far as one can penetrate the practice of missioners in matters of 'satisfaction', or 'penance' narrowly speaking, it was inspired by the same motives. There are some traces of ancient usage, like the case of the servant at Little Crosby who 'should have set up in the night with [her] Sweet-heart', but was prevented and sent off on a pilgrimage to Holywell instead;[45] but they seem to be rare. Gerard gives no hint that he thought such impositions of any reformative value, and it is not clear that he imposed penances in the conventional sense at all; given a reformed life, and the settlement of practical matters like debt, he seems to have felt that the 'satisfactory' element in the sacrament was sufficiently met by almsgiving and donations for pious purposes. It is unlikely that the large benefactions which often followed upon his hearing the confessions of the wealthy, and caused ill-feeling among members of the secular clergy, ought strictly to be regarded as penitential; but it would seem that almsgiving was felt throughout this period to be an appropriate element in the satisfaction for sin, and so long as it was treated as part of a continuing process of personal reform the practice does not seem open to objections of laxity.[46] There were certainly more rigorous ways of achieving the end, like the Borromean and 'Jansenist' method of deferring absolution until repentance had been proved by a period of amendment, which was certainly in use among the secular clergy at a later date.[47] If we wish to see the results of a century and a half of pressure we may consult the exhaustive questionnaire composed for himself by Peter Gifford about 1740, and used for his daily examination of conscience:

How do you spend your time, and how far do you render it serviceable to your last end? . . .

45. *Great Diurnal*, ii, pp. 62, 65, 66. Peter Fitton said he knew of a Benedictine who smacked his female penitents' bottoms, 'perhaps on the pretext of giving them a penance': report cited above, chap. 7, n. 23, f. 116r.

46. *Autobiography of John Gerard*, pp. 25, 179 f., 182; cf. the thoughts of Sir Thomas Gascoigne, apparently about distributing his alms in Masses for the dead according to the advice of his confessor: Aveling, *West Riding*, p. 254.

47. Below, p. 272; some nineteenth-century editions of Challoner's *Garden of the Soul* (Croshaw, York, 1839, p. 261; Duffy, Dublin, 1846, p. 202) contain a 'Prayer after Confession, when absolution has been deferred'. Cf. M. Greenslade, 'The Association of the Staffordshire Clergy, 1686', *Staffordshire Catholic History*, no. 2 (1962), p. 16, for what looks like the same thing in the seventeenth century.

What self-denials do you practice, and what fruit of penance do you bring forth in satisfaction for your sins? . . .

What care and endeavour do you use for being faithful to the covenant you make with God every time you sue to him for pardon for your sins in the Sacrament of Penance?[48]

I do not know what conclusions are to be drawn from the fact that Gifford later abandoned his religion.

Comments from Allen and Gother suggest that it may have been some time before anything like these standards were brought to bear on 'the common Catholic people's confession'; and it seems to have been understood that meditation and self-examination were things they would have little time for. No doubt there was more emphasis on simple satisfactory penances, as in the case of the girl at Little Crosby, or the Yorkshire servant who was required 'to say every day three Ave Marias, three Paters and one Creed, and to give three pence to three poor folks'.[49] By the end of the seventeenth century, as the discipline of the eight indulgences became established, they were at least going to confession with some regularity; by then it was usual to go to confession the evening before a feast on which communion was to be received, or else in the morning before Mass. There might certainly be objections to the second of these practices: Gother complained that to confess on a feast day was a 'Solecism of Devotion', and 'greatly disapprove[d]' of those who '[ran] from the confession seat to the communion table'; but from rural congregations who had little leisure and a distance to travel to a priest, or indeed from priests who might have more than one congregation to serve, it was unreasonable to expect more. The result was not necessarily hasty or superficial, if we may judge by the picture we get of a congregation in Staffordshire, which had its monthly Mass in a room at the top of a farmhouse, waiting on the stairs or walking in the fields until confessions were finished.[50] In town congregations there was more flexibility, or so one would gather from Challoner's insistence on staying at home every evening 'that he might be in the way to hear

48. Rowlands, 'Education and Piety', p. 78.
49. Knox, *Allen Letters*, p. 34; Gother, *Instructions for Confession*, etc., pp. 85 f.; *Autobiography of John Gerard*, p. 32; Aveling, *East Riding*, p. 33 and *West Riding*, p. 251; above, p. 270.
50. Rowlands, 'Education and Piety', p. 67; Gother, *Instructions*, pp. 81–83; *Catholic Magazine*, v (1834), p. 308—on the other hand, the Jesuit Francis Mannock, in Aveling, *Recusancy in York*, p. 156, on carelessness of priests over confessions of the poor.

confessions'; William Mawhood normally visited him to 'do the necessary' on Saturday evenings. A couple of entries in Mawhood's diary, which reveal an instance where Challoner deferred absolution, show that the eighteenth century was a time of searching confessional investigation for others than the gentry.[51] Perhaps this was not typical; it would certainly have been impossible to extend these standards to the community at large unless there had been a notable improvement in their level of religious instruction since the seventeenth century. Here as elsewhere the barrier to the progress of counter-Reformation Catholicism was a barrier of education.

Catechising in the more general sense had always been an activity of the missionary priests; in the narrower sense of the religious instruction of children, the chaplain at home, and schools and convents abroad, performed the duty adequately for the gentry, whose level of instruction seems to have been consistently high. But the gentry's gain was the rest of the community's loss: the advent of the domestic regime may well have led to a falling-back from whatever progress had been made in the early decades of the mission. The problem had never really been lack of material.[52] Lawrence Vaux's *Catechism* of 1568, though wordy and old-fashioned, provided a reasonable basis but had gone out of circulation fairly early in the seventeenth century; English versions of the more usable catechisms of Canisius and Bellarmine existed from about 1600, and the latter seems to have established itself as the means of instruction for children. All the same there is little sign of urgency until towards the end of the seventeenth century. The main catechism used by the secular clergy had been produced by the Douai priest Henry Turberville in the 1640s, and it was large, complex and expensive; some forty years seem to have passed before a more practicable version was produced. Then, during or just before the reign of James II, an *Abstract* of it was made, possibly by Gother, 'for the use of children and ignorant people'; at the same time there was a penny reprint of Bellarmine, and

51. Burton, *Challoner*, i, pp. 82 f.; *Mawhood Diary*, pp. 61, 91, 118 f.—18 December 1777: 'did some part of the necessary'. Mawhood did not communicate at Christmas but on 4 January, having gone to confession again on the 3rd and evidently been absolved this time.
52. For my account of Catechisms I have relied a great deal on Stephen Marron, 'Bishop Challoner and our Catechism', *Douai Magazine*, ix (1936), pp. 111–120; also T. G. Law's ed. of Lawrence Vaux, *A Catechisme of Christian Doctrine* (Chetham Society, new series iv, 1885: with useful introduction) and A. F. Allison and D. M. Rogers, *A Catalogue of Catholic Books in English, 1558–1640* (*Biographical Studies*, iii, nos. 3 and 4, 1956; repr. 1968), pp. 157 f., 35 f., 76, 16 f.

others followed. Seconded as it was before long by Gother's various *Instructions*, this burst of activity seems significant, and the momentum gained was not lost thereafter. From now on it was continually reinforced by the pressure on the clergy of an imperative characteristic of the period. Gother insisted on the theological motives for associating instruction with observance, 'desiring [Catholics] ever to remember that the Sacraments work their Effects, according to the disposition and preparation of the Receiver'. In the course of time there was a tendency for some of the clergy to consider their function as primarily to teach, and only secondarily to administer the sacraments.[53] In the abstract one may think this deference to the spirit of the Enlightenment overdone, but in the circumstances it was a necessary reaction and a sign of life. Most priests, in any case, seem to have maintained a reasonable balance.

On the ground, we can see the effects of the new spirit operating at Little Crosby. Early in 1707 Nicholas Blundell, after a disappointing experience with his incumbent chaplain, wrote to the Jesuit superior of the district to ask for a man who 'is willing to take Pains amongst the Poore Catholicks, of whom we have a great many', and with the arrival of Robert Aldred serious work seems to have begun. On the first Sunday in 1708, which was presumably the beginning of the new dispensation, Blundell 'counted 32 Boyes and Girles at Catechismey after Vespers'; five years later, no doubt with the elder members of the congregation in mind, Aldred 'began to explicate the Mass after Benediction and designes to continew explicating it and other things'.[54] This was evidently not an isolated instance; by the 1720s the demand for cheap catechisms was growing briskly, and publishers were doing their best to meet it: from this point a third version of the Douai catechism was on the market, price twopence, 'exceedingly abbreviated and simplified', and intended for the use of very young children. For this purpose it seems to have supplanted Bellarmine, no doubt because Challoner took it up when he came to London a few years later. Challoner was a dedicated catechist in person, and he made various contributions in print, striking after some experiment the happy mean with

53. Gother, *Instructions*, p. 98, and in Norman, 'John Gother' (see above, n. 38), p. 315; Duffy, 'Joseph Berington' (see above, n. 38), pp. 23–24, where the point is admirably made and put in context; Aveling, 'Education of English Monks', p. 147 f.
54. *Great Diurnal*, i, pp. 129, 159; ii, p. 46.

his *Abridgement of Christian Doctrine* which seems, properly enough, to have come out in the year (1770) with which our present period closes. This was a rather expanded version of the small catechism already mentioned, containing 250 questions and answers instead of a hundred; its stiff, sensible phrases were to become embedded in the minds of English-speaking Catholic children for almost two centuries to come.[55]

Meantime his fellow-bishops had been busy as well. In June 1741 he had a letter from Edward Dicconson, recently appointed to the North and staying with Stonor at Heythrop on the way to his district. Stonor had told him that 'in order to remedy the ignorance of several kinds in many among the poorer sort', he had 'modelled a Book of Prayers and Exhortations, in which the Readers and Hearers will have their minds instructed and memorys refreshed with not only the principal Points of Faith, but also with what concerns the theological and moral virtues, etc.: in short with the whole contents of our Catechisms, in a very intelligible and moving manner. As much at least as seems possible in a Tract of so small a bulk as it will make.' The originality of Stonor's effort was to put to use in a catechetical context the custom of reciting psalms and litanies which was well established in English Catholic tradition. Dicconson was impressed by it, and he and Stonor hoped that all the vicars-apostolic would give it their blessing, 'for that will embolden us to make the experimental use of it'.[56]

The draft did not meet with this general approval: Challoner must have preferred the conventional question-and-answer catechism and probably had reservations about Stonor's doctrine. But it did get into print the following year, and shortly afterwards the Midland clergy were leaving money in their wills and providing out of their Common Fund for the distribution of an English Catechism to the poor; in 1747 they did the same for the English Scriptures, presumably in Witham's 1730 edition of the Douai version, shortly to be superseded by Challoner's.[57] All this suggests that by this time the Midland clergy were working hard on the catechetical front. In the Western district, Charles Walmesley was requiring his clergy in the 1770s to give catechism and instruction to 'both children and the upgrown people', and advising his

---

55. Marron, 'Bishop Challoner and our Catechism', p. 118; Burton, *Challoner*, i, pp. 94, 100 ff.; ii, p. 160 ff.

56. Dicconson to Challoner, 1 June 1741 (Lancs. C.R.O. RCWB, no. 5: Dicconson Letter-Books, ii, p. 241); published in 1742 as *An Exercise of Devotion*, cf. above, p. 130.

57. Rowlands, 'Staffordshire', p. 35; 'Education and Piety', p. 74.

coadjutor to see that the poor were provided with Catechisms (Challoner's, no doubt), and that the gentry did their duty by providing them for their own poor and servants.[58] In spite of the evidence from Little Crosby, things may have been more backward in the north. Illiteracy was almost certainly higher than elsewhere, and there was probably not much action during the regime of Francis Petre, who succeeded Dicconson in 1752. Simon Bordley implies that the Lancashire congregations were fairly well instructed, but the evidence from Yorkshire is not impressive. At York in 1737 the Jesuit Francis Mannock was denouncing the ignorance of poor Catholics in the city, and testifying that the Rosary was still recommended as the best method of hearing Mass for 'rusticis qui legere non possunt'; in 1772 the Benedictine John Fisher was contemplating a rural flock 'mean and indigent as to worldly substance, illiterate and ignorant as to Religion notwithstanding the pains taken by my predecessor . . . Such as I found them, such I believe I shall leave them.' Ullathorne, who was born in the same part of the country in 1806, remarks that he did not imagine that his parents were aware that there was a Catholic bible in English; he got his own education at a local Church of England school, and knew the Anglican Catechism by heart, though he was excused from learning it.[59]

The general sense of effort is unmistakable, and suggests a favourable comparison with the contemporary endeavours of the Church of England in this field.[60] But as the effort began to be felt on the ground, it met obstacles in the condition of popular elementary education and in the attitude of the gentry. Until the ordinary Catholic was literate he was not going to make a great deal of the attempt to instruct him; and short of a system of interdenominational education—which did to some extent exist after 1750, but only in towns[61]—it devolved upon the community to make sure that he was. For middling Catholics the problem was solved by places like the boarding school at Sedgley Park in

58. Williams, *Bath and Rome*, p. 52 and *Wiltshire*, p. 137; also Duffy, 'Berington', p. 23.

59. Aveling, *Recusancy in York*, pp. 156–157, 162 and *West Riding*, p. 266; S. Leslie (ed.), *From Cabin-boy to Archbishop: the Autobiography of Archbishop Ullathorne* (London, 1941), pp. 4–6.

60. cf. Norman Sykes, *Church and State in England in the Eighteenth Century* (Cambridge, 1934), pp. 243–246; M. G. Jones, *The Charity School Movement* (Cambridge, 1938), 35 f., pp. 62 ff.

61. W. R. Ward, *Religion and Society in England, 1790–1850* (London, 1972), p. 13 (Manchester); Aveling, *Recusancy in York*, p. 148 (York).

Staffordshire launched in 1762 by Stonor and Hornyold; town children would probably have access to charity schools, Catholic or not. The education of the rural poor would have to depend on the efforts of the priest and the landowner. Priests, by and large, saw the problem clearly and were anxious to do something about it: thus the Midland clergy who left money for catechisms also left a foundation of £20 a year and some books to teach poor children to read and write. But the hint of a popish school was enough to stir the Anglican authorities to action, and the Catholic gentry was highly sensitive to threats of trouble if they allowed one on their estates; under such pressure, the Fairfaxes removed from Gilling a Benedictine who seems to have set up a school there.[62]

This was an instance of a general difficulty: on the whole the gentry were not very enthusiastic supporters of intensive religious instruction for everyone. A few were simply irresponsible; others seem to have felt that their duty extended to ensuring prompt and regular religious observance, but no further.[63] There were certainly exceptions: Nicholas Blundell was one, and so was Stephen Tempest of Broughton, who was an enthusiast for Catechisms and thought they would be good for the nobility and gentry 'as well as for servants and people of the lowest rank'. No doubt, had he been so placed, he would have taken Walmesley's hint and bought them for his dependants. But Walmesley does not sound confident that many would do this, and he was probably right. One landowner in Co. Durham was persuaded to make a foundation of £500 'in favour of the poor Catholicks in the parish of Chester-le-Street, namely for the support of a priest to . . . instruct the people there and bring up their children in the fear of God'; he died shortly after, and his brother tried to keep the money for a family chaplain, though he finally paid up in 1760. After an interview with the Archbishop of York in 1765 Sir Henry Lawson dismissed his Jesuit priest for being too 'busy' at Brough, an offence which probably included an

---

62. Rowlands, 'Education and Piety', pp. 72-75; Aveling, *Northern Catholics*, pp. 385, 379.
63. For example, on the Clavering estate at Callaly in Northumberland about 1780 there was a congregation of nearly 300 which seems to have been very diligent in its religious practice but contained a high proportion of illiterates: cf. my 'Four Catholic Congregations in rural Northumberland', *Recusant History*, ix (1967), pp. 93 ff., 95-97, 110 f., 114 with Northumberland C.R.O. Z CO viii, 8/6 (wages for haymaking at Callaly, 1784)—of 55 men, women and children who acknowledged payment, 43 made marks, 3 had somebody else sign for them, and 9, all male, signed for themselves.

excess of catechetical zeal.[64] I see no evidence for supposing that the Catholic gentry objected on principle to the instruction of the poor. But many of them gravely hampered it by insisting on their prior claim to the services of the priests they maintained, and those who did not were harassed by the difficulty of drawing a line between the instruction of Catholics, which was no doubt laudable, and proselytising among Protestants, which they considered suicide. Changes of religion through tenancy, employment and marriage were one thing; parsons might grumble, but they were a fact of life. Proselytising by the Catholic clergy was another matter: it is clear that, with or without prodding from the Church of England, the gentry were anxious to prevent it. It is also clear that from about 175c they were finding the clergy hard to hold.[65] The discovery of a catechetical vocation was what had been needed to revive the missionary temper, and it had profound implications for the future of the community. Challoner may not actually have predicted, when colleagues complained of the conduct of the gentry, that there would be a 'new people',[66] but something like this Brechtian notion was surely in his mind. Exterior circumstances were to help in making it a reality sooner than anyone can have anticipated.

64. Stephen Tempest, *Religio Laici* (?1764), pp. 18, 122, 143; E. Walsh and A. Forster, 'The Recusancy of the Brandlings', *Recusant History*, x (1969), pp. 54 f.; Aveling, *Northern Catholics*, pp. 379, 38c.
65. See, e.g., Aveling, *loc. cit.*, n. 62; Rcwlands, 'Staffordshire', p. 34; Williams, *Wiltshire*, p. 179; cf. above, p. 260.
66. Burton, *Challoner*, ii, p. 212.

12

RETROSPECT, 1600–1770

APERIOD of 170 years is a long time in the history of a community; a great deal happened in England between the death of Queen Elizabeth and the accession of George III. I have tried to see the period as a whole because it did not seem to me possible to penetrate the community at any depth without giving the elements of which it was constructed a measure of undistracted attention; hence what has been an analytical or structural description, more circular than progressive in direction. I would be prepared to justify the method adopted by the results achieved; yet it has of course evaded the duty of the historian to present the results of his enquiry in the sequence of time, and something should be done, even in a small way, to make up for this.

Again, in looking separately at aspects of the community's life, I have concluded that important changes, evolutions, turning-points are to be found in most of them. In some cases the relation between different sorts of change may be obvious, in others less so; sometimes there may be no causal relation at all. Even so, we must try to see them as happening to a body of people whose existence was continuous in time, contributing to the collective experience of those who lived through them from one year, one decade, one phase in the country's history to the next. It may be that the result of this retrospect will be to suggest that another method of approach might have been more useful than the one adopted; if so, I plead guilty, but reply that I do not see any other way of finding out.

I am sure that the key to any satisfying construction of the chronology of the Catholic community in the period we have traversed lies in the simple statistical sequence presented in chapter 8. The implications of this were that, defined as I have defined it, the post-Reformation Catholic body in England continued to expand from the launching of the Elizabethan mission until somewhere a little short of the mid-seventeenth century; that during the next half-century or so it ceased to grow and may possibly have contracted; and that from somewhere about 1700 it resumed an expansion which was still in progress in 1770. Uncertain as the figures may be in which this sequence has been expressed, I am satisfied of its general correctness, and prepared to take it as the primary datum in the chronology of the community between 1600 and 1770, as that which requires to be explained. We may look in turn at the three periods which have been outlined.

The first period of expansion was roughly identical with the reigns of James I and Charles I. It obviously depended, in the first place, on a persistence of the enthusiasm generated in clergy and laity by the Elizabethan mission, a factor impossible to ignore though difficult to pin down, and one which was evidently on the decline by 1640. The clearest quantifiable element of expansion was the steady growth of missionary forces in the field: some 300 in 1600, some 750 in 1640. A less obvious one was the improvement in organisational structure of the mission which had been launched by Henry Garnet in the 1590s and was perfected, as far as the Jesuits were concerned, by 1623. The secular clergy, though less happily placed in this respect, had certainly made *some* organisational progress between the appointment of the first archpriest in 1598 and the departure of Richard Smith in 1631; 1623, the date of William Bishop's arrival, would also be a date of some importance here. During the 1620s the consolidation of the Catholic fraction of the English landowning classes was reaching its conclusion with the abandonment of the church-papist position, the establishment of domestic conformity and the habit of continental schooling. By this time also the Elizabethan conflicts between clergy and gentry were moving towards a settlement, already achieved by the regulars by about 1620, postponed for the seculars by the issue of prelacy which came to the fore in the next decade; the increasing predominance of gentry in clerical recruitment must also by about 1620 have been beginning to produce an assimilation of points of view. The immediate consequence of this for the community at large was to provide the mission with adequate funds; it also helped to maintain the supply of priests and to complete the organisational network. Outside the gentry, the community was able to make some progress through the extension of the circulating mission and penetration into at least some of the dark corners of the land. It benefited from a persistent demand among ordinary people for traditional and quasi-magical services which a Catholic priesthood was able to provide.[1]

There were also, during this period, some external factors of a favourable kind, though how much effect they had is open to dispute: the attitude of early Stuart administrations was certainly the most important of them. Admittedly there were periods of revived hostility, one after the Gunpowder Plot which produced a series of statutes attempting to undermine the structure of the community, as well as difficulties about the oath of allegiance; there was another during the foreign and parliamentary crises of the late 1620s. But by and large the administrations of James I and Charles I moved steadily in the direction of an accommodation with the Catholic gentry: a *modus vivendi* was reached over the financial aspects of recusancy after the introduction of Wentworth's compounding system in 1626, and with the church courts over matters like marriage and burial during the 1630s. For Catholics other than the gentry, and indeed for the gentry themselves, the traditionalist attitude adopted by the crown in such matters as sports must have had something of the same relaxing effect. The tendency of foreign-inspired versions of Catholicism to become respectable or notorious at Court, illustrated by Charles I's marriage, was a factor of more uncertain import. Such favourable effects as it may have had seem temporary or restricted in their scope; it is difficult to see it as having any clear connection with the growth of the community in the country, except that it may possibly have encouraged one or two Catholic magnates to emerge as more active supporters of the mission than they had been hitherto. Any benefits were almost certainly outweighed by the popular and parliamentary reaction which it provoked. Similarly, and despite some good intentions, one cannot see that the papacy did much during this period which was likely to encourage the growth of the community: rather the reverse.

To relate these influences to the actual growth of the community we may resort, with due diffidence, to the Jesuit missionary reports of the time, which show traces of most of them. For most years between the establishment of the Jesuit province in 1623 and the outbreak of the Civil War we have the figures which they sent to Rome of the converts they claimed to have made: an over-sensitive index, perhaps, of under-

1. I have discussed this period in somewhat greater detail in 'The English Catholic Community, 1603–1625', in A. G. R. Smith (ed.), *The Reign of King James VI and I* (London, 1973), pp. 91–105.

lying trends, but usable none the less. In 1623 they reported 2,630 converts, in 1624 something over 750; in 1625, a difficult year, 379; during the 1630s their figures remained fairly stable at between 400 and 550.[2] These figures were compiled from what was returned to the provincial from the local districts, and allowing for a desire to make a good impression I think one may attach some credence to them: for a body whose effective missionary strength was somewhere between 100 and 150 they are not extravagant, and the element of distortion was presumably the same throughout. One can imagine that they were specially anxious to make a good showing at the beginning, and that their figure for 1623 contained converts who had been saved up from previous years. Granted this, the figures tell a plausible enough story: boom conditions prevailing, or still continuing, in the early 1620s; a set-back due to unfavourable political circumstances in the late 1620s; a revival from 1630 which did not reach the level of the earlier period but maintained itself very steadily until the Civil War.

Such as it is, this information gives substance to the view that the community continued its first phase of comparatively rapid expansion until about 1620 and, though it continued to grow from then until the Civil War, did so more by acquired momentum than otherwise and was tending to level off. The calling of the Long Parliament, and the prolonged political crisis to which it gave rise, was certainly a blow to the community in many ways: it disorganised the mission and the seminaries, gave the gentry a difficult time financially and otherwise, and stimulated, particularly in the early years, a recurrence of popular phobia about Catholics. It is surely correct to conclude with it the first phase in the community's history. Yet, seen in perspective, it looks as if this massive incursion of the outside world did little more than precipitate a change of fortunes which was already on the way.

The long-term factors which were operating to bring this about seem fairly clear. The first would seem to me to be the division of the mission in 1602. Aveling has properly observed that we ought not to be misled by its prevalence in the documentary evidence into overrating the degree to which intra-clerical conflict associated with this division impinged on the community at large.[3] But the division itself, with the confusion and duplication which resulted from it, must I think be taken

---

2. Foley, *Records of the English Province*, vii, part 2, pp. 1098–1144 *passim*.
3. *Northern Catholics*, p. 164; cf. my own review article, 'The Yorkshire Catholic Community, 1558–1791' (above, p. 3).

as a factor tending to restrict the expansion of the community; and the same must be said of the preoccupation among leaders of the secular clergy with problems of ecclesiastical order which prevented them from giving their undivided attention to the cultivation of the mission field. At the same time, the concordat with the gentry, which advanced the community's fortunes in the short run, implied that the objectives of the mission were shifting from expansion in the direction of stability; it meant a decreasingly economic use of men and resources, a decline in the circulating mission, a slackening of effort in the dark corners of the land. It also tended to reinforce a division between the quality as well as the quantity of ministration offered to the gentry and to the rest of the community: the gentry, and to some extent their immediate dependants, received the full impact of the reformed Catholicism of the counter-Reformation, while the rest of the community, short of instruction and sacramental provision, was allowed to tick over at the level of traditionalist practice suitable to a pre-literate mentality. Equipment provided by the Elizabethans for the popular mission, like Parsons's *Book of Resolution*, fell into other hands and was used in the service of Protestant evangelism. Thus the expansion of missionary numbers outstripped the expansion of the community, and a 'surplus' of missioners appeared not because there was nothing for them to do but because nobody was willing or able to see that it was done. If I were asked to choose a single incident to illustrate the turn of the tide I would suggest the rejection of the ideal and practice embodied in Mary Ward's *Institute of Mary* which became final in 1631. Here, I think, the community had been offered the opportunity of a second wind, which could have carried its phase of primitive expansion on through the seventeenth century. In rejecting it, it registered its determination to play safe, and missed the boat for a couple of generations.

Roughly speaking, the recession occupied the second half of the century, though one would date it rather differently according to what aspect one had primarily in mind. Factors of revival were certainly present from about 1680, but it may be that they did not make much lasting difference until somewhere after 1700; in the present state of knowledge it is difficult to be sure. Missionary numbers did not decline after 1650, but clerical un- or under-employment established itself as a structural feature of the community. But the most unpromising aspect of the clerical scene was the persistence, for decades after its harmfulness had been demonstrated, of the church-nostalgia embodied in its most negative form by the Chapter in the age of John Sergeant. The years of Sergeant's supremacy in the Chapter (1650–1667) were probably not quite the nadir of the community's fortunes, which I would be inclined to date between 1660 and 1680, but they are near enough for one to point with some confidence to a connection between them. Not only was Sergeant's leadership, from a missionary point of view, misguided in itself; it threw the secular clergy into a state of prolonged schism and disarray in which it was difficult for it to attend to the needs of the community. From the point of view of the laity, aristocratic supremacy had now reached its peak, with all the restrictions on clerical activity which this implied; after 1650 the single-house chaplaincy absorbed an increasing, and finally an overwhelming proportion of priests, who were themselves more uniformly drawn from the gentry than at any other time. As the drift towards introversion continued, the circulating mission was largely, though never entirely, abandoned and the community suffered a decisive decline in one 'dark corner' where it had made real progress, the Welsh borderlands. There were certainly counterbalancing features to landlord government; it was important, and perhaps essential, to the process of congregational formation; and it seems clear that a more systematic oversight exercised over the dependants of the gentry ensured that the community did not actually decline in numbers, or at least did not decline very much. All the same, it does seem to have come rather close to losing its momentum altogether. It got through the Interregnum in tolerable shape, but gained little or nothing from the relatively favourable climate of the Restoration;[4] had it been faced with a Whig regime after the blows of the Popish Plot, it might have found it difficult to recover.

The period may be envisaged from another, and perhaps more fundamental point of view. It seems to me now, more clearly than it did when I embarked upon this description, that what happened to the community in the later seventeenth century was not simply a phase of numerical stagnation and declining activity, but also a phase of transition, during which it was undergoing a distinct change in character. The community which emerged from this obscure crisis was in many ways qualitatively different from the one which entered it. Here I feel that particular attention needs to be paid to the evolution of the men-

4. Miller, 'The Catholic Factor in English Politics, 1660–1688' (see above, chap. 4, n. 19), p. 10, remarks appropriately that 'by Charles II's reign, the English mission was carried on in a minor key'.

tality of Catholics suggested in chapter 6: a shift in attitude to some fundamental features of life between what may roughly be called traditionalist and modernist instincts.[5] Without overdoing the contrast, or eliminating the differences which still seem to me to exist between English pre- and post-Reformation Catholicism in general, one might suggest that the community which was expanding up to the Civil War was still, taken all in all, a traditionalist community, while the community which began to grow from somewhere about the close of the seventeenth century was a 'modernist' one, in the sense that it shared the essential secular values of the society it lived in. In the interval Catholics had become reconciled to their environment. It may be said—as Dr Cowgill's figures would suggest—that Englishmen in general were 'traditionalist' up to the Civil War, or nearly; but traditionalism was certainly in question to a degree which gave Catholics a position at the extreme of what was acceptable; fifty years later, their state of mind was far more clearly part of a national consensus, and the subsequent expansion of their body did not threaten it. For Catholics, then, the later seventeenth century was a difficult passage, when they had lost contact with some older certainties and not yet acquired some new ones; when its first wind was exhausted and its second had not arrived; when it was unlikely to make much headway or to present itself to the outside world as standing for anything very persuasive.

Evidence from the statistics of conversion is admittedly even scrappier for these decades than for those before the Civil War, since a full series of Jesuit reports is not available. Around 1670 they were offering an annual figure of about 600, somewhat higher than during the 1630s; around 1700 it was 300. They apologised continually for the poverty of their harvest, blaming the restrictions of the domestic regime as well as exterior obstacles.[6] One continuous series that we possess comes from the Franciscans, who had a circulating mission around Birmingham from 1657, and for the next forty years kept a register of how many people they had converted. Given by decades, the figures were: 1650s (two years only), eleven, implying that in a full decade they might have converted fifty; 1660s, thirty-seven (very few after 1662); 1670s, fifteen; 1680s, thirty-nine (almost all between 1684 and 1686); 1690s, fifty-seven (mainly 1693–1696: the register stops in 1698). Over the whole period they had an average of nearly four converts a year;

5. Above, p. 147, etc.
6. Foley, *Records*, i, pp. 270–272; v, 91, 161–162.

between 1663 and 1683, of a little over one.[7] Given more such instances, it would be possible to relate the very general terms of this discussion more closely to what was happening on the ground. Those that we have give reason to believe that the community had a difficult river to cross during these decades, and was not guaranteed to make it.

We have seen that it did make it, and by 1770 had made a good deal of progress on the farther shore. David Mathew has written that it is only from about 1700 or a little earlier that the Catholic community can be regarded as 'homogeneous', its history as having 'a certain unity'.[8] This seems to overdo the point a little; but perhaps I am right in believing that Mathew had in mind something not unlike the processes of psychological and congregational formation which, I feel, reached their denouement somewhere about this date. It was appropriate that the principal agent of this denouement, seen from a spiritual point of view, was John Gother, since it was certainly among the secular clergy that the first signs of revival appeared, and in a general sort of way it may be said that, while in its first expansive phase the community was largely indebted to the religious orders (and notably to the Jesuits), the second was dominated in spirit, if not in numbers, by the secular clergy. Hence the crucial importance of the final reconciliation of the secular clergy with its role as a missionary body which was first evident at the Chapter meeting which threw over John Sergeant in 1667 and made possible the solution of the community's ecclesiastical problems in 1685. The burden of church-nostalgia which had dogged the secular clergy through so much of the seventeenth century was lifted, and they got down to brass tacks at last.

From this point of view James II gave the community a fillip just at the point where it could prove most valuable: his reign was probably the only instance where external intervention contributed to the community's revival, but it was an important one. It ensured that the new episcopal regime was successfully launched; it showed, I think, that missionary labour undertaken in a realistic spirit could produce results that were modestly encouraging; it revealed that the community could have a future in towns. James's failure meant that the benefit of these new conditions would be postponed, though it had the advantage of freeing the bishops from court patronage, which might otherwise have

7. J. McEvilly, 'Worcestershire Entries in a Franciscan Register, 1657–1824', *Worcestershire Recusant*, no. 13 (1969), pp. 10 f.; no 14, pp. 34 ff.
8. 'The Approach to Recusant History', *Dublin Review* (1959), pp. 29, 31.

become a millstone round their neck; but the community had undoubtedly been helped to orientate itself towards a more hopeful future. The pause which followed the Revolution was put to good use by Gother, whose retirement to Warkworth gave him a chance to reformulate the Catholic way of life in terms appropriate to an age whose values were regularity, rationality and work. It was he above all who provided a satisfying answer to such queries as had bothered William Blundell in 1683;[9] who ensured the success of the transition to modernity, and gave the community solid spiritual ground to stand on during the eighteenth century. The decade after 1700 is certainly more important for the first publication of his *Instructions* than for the enactment of new hostile legislation. By this time the growth of congregations which had been going on under the regime of the gentry had reached a point where a revival of vigour among the clergy would find something substantial to work on.

That this revival occurred seems to me unquestionable. It was probably not unconnected with the shift in recruitment to the clergy by which it shed its character of a refuge for unemployed sons of the gentry, a process which I have found hard to date but seems to have been well under way by 1700.[10] It was made possible by the progress towards financial independence which, so far as the secular clergy were concerned, had been begun by the local clergy associations in the latter years of the Chapter regime, and went on steadily under the vicars-apostolic: a necessary condition for the slow improvement, visible among both seculars and regulars, in the relation between the distribution of priests and the needs of the community. It was given the edge which managerial improvements could not provide as the clergy rediscovered in the catechetical field a stimulus which they had not possessed since the first half-century of the mission. Their experience under James II, the example and influence of Gother and the instruments he provided, the experiments of Stonor; more generally, the spread of an active spirituality among the secular clergy, French examples, and the wider climate of eighteenth-century opinion: all these contributed to a state of mind among the clergy which found an admirable, if prudent, interpreter and guide when Challoner became London vicar-apostolic in 1740.

Certainly the early decades of the eighteenth century were a difficult

---

9. See above, p. 119; and in general Miller, *Popery and Politics* (see above, chap. 4, n. 19), pp. 239–249.   10. See above, chap. 9, pp. 198–200.

period in some ways: the clergy was declining rather rapidly in numbers, though this was no bad thing; from Dicconson's comments on their death-rate it looks as if their average age may have been unusually high. Decline in the numbers of Catholic gentry families gave rise to difficulties, though its causes were often wrongly diagnosed and its effects usually exaggerated; the Land Tax was a minor encumbrance, the persistence of Jacobitism perhaps a more serious one. All the same I do not share Mathew's conviction that this was the weakest period in the community's history; it must have possessed a good deal of vitality to maintain or increase its numbers at a time when factors of decline were undoubtedly present.[11] The pessimistic view is surely over-influenced by what was happening among the gentry. At a time when, even in the rural environment, the growth of a farming interest was altering the social balance of the community, this seems a doubtful emphasis; nor does it sufficiently take account of the determination rising among the clergy to close the gap between the levels of religious experience and understanding available to the gentry and to the rest of the community, which had been so visible in the seventeenth century. Challoner's efforts on this front were distinguished and of lasting value, but they had been preceded by half-a-century of attention to the problem, and among his predecessors were men who approached it in a more imaginative frame of mind than he did; though they lacked his ability or opportunity to shape an ideal into a widely practicable programme. In any event, during the three decades of Challoner's regime with which our period closes, the ideal was at least coming within measurable distance of realisation, and in this sense the community was certainly becoming more homogeneous as well as more expansive. In other respects, of course, it was becoming more diversified: the rise of missions in towns and manufacturing districts testifies to the managerial achievements of the period, but also the fact that the lower orders of the community had, in many cases at least, acquired a level of religious culture which would stand them and the community in good stead as processes of economic and demographic transformation began to gather speed after the middle of the century. In 1770 the community would seem to me to have had some three-quarters of a century of modest growth behind it, and it was certainly in a condition to face the future with reasonable confidence.

11. See above, p. 219; below, p. 324; Mathew, 'The Approach to Recusant History', p. 31.

Before proceeding to see what the future had in store, I think it is worth pausing for a moment to see what contribution a knowledge of the vicissitudes of this small constituent of the population of Europe may make to the understanding of the European experience as a whole during the period with which it deals. One point may attract attention. I have argued that the central feature of the chronology of the community was a period of recession occupying roughly the second half of the seventeenth century and occurring between two expansive periods, the first of which may be broadly dated 1570-1640, the second 1700-1770. This is a conclusion which will awaken echoes in the mind of anyone recently concerned with the history of seventeenth-century Europe, since a consensus has been emerging that in various respects the middle of the century was a time of unusual difficulty and strain, of contraction or transition between two more confident and expansive epochs, of 'general crisis'. Wide agreement about the existence of this situation has been accompanied by much controversy about what was ultimately the matter, and since the subject here examined would seem to present another, if minor, instance of it, it is natural to wonder what points of view it would support.

One thing is obvious. The recession in the English Catholic community will not fit happily any of the views in the field whose immediate intention is to account for the prevalence of conflict, and notably of political conflict within states, in the years around 1650. It would be an exaggeration to say that there *was* no conflict inside it, but conflict was certainly on the way out. Hence a view like Trevor-Roper's, intended to explain why England and other countries suffered simultaneously from political upheaval at this time, cannot apply directly to its case. That is not to say that it is wrong or irrelevant. Transposed into ecclesiastical terms, a flowering of 'parasitic bureaucracy' was very much what had been nipped in the bud by the Catholic gentry in the 1620s; a crisis in 'relations between society and the (ecclesiastical) state' had been averted or solved a decade before Charles I and Parliament went to war. The transition from something like the Renaissance to something like the Enlightenment could take place without breaches of continuity.[12]

It could not, or did not take place without intervening recession. Hence a historian of English Catholicism will feel more directly ad-

12. H. R. Trevor-Roper, 'The General Crisis of the Seventeenth Century', in T. Aston (ed.), *Crisis in Europe, 1650-1660* (London, 1965), pp. 59-95.

dressed by views of the mid-seventeenth century which envisage it, in
the first place, as a bottleneck rather than a crisis, a time of contraction,
a trough in the graph of human activity. Such is Hobsbawm's presentation of the case, and returning to his essay after some years I have been
staggered by the degree to which it provides a larger analogy for my
own. There was, he says, in the middle of the seventeenth century a
'social crisis of consumption'; the flame of capitalist enterprise burned
low in the atmosphere of a 'feudal' society which was constitutionally
incapable of providing an adequate demand for its products; 'expansion
was possible and took place, but so long as the general structure of
rural society had not been revolutionised it was limited, or created its
own limits; and when it encountered them, it entered a period of crisis'.
Read 'missionary' for 'capitalist' enterprise and the description fits very
well. The English mission was indeed afflicted with a social crisis in the
consumption of its products, and confined within the narrow possibilities of a luxury trade. If the seminaries had been factories they
would have gone bankrupt through over-production; the price of
priests, like the price of everything else, must have been at rock bottom
between the 1640s and the 1670s.[13]

In itself Hobsbawm's model may have its shortcomings, but I think
it is sufficiently apposite to make the analogy worth exploring. If we are
to fathom its meaning we shall need the help of historians who are
prepared to consider Christianity an autonomous feature of European
life but are none the less able to approach it in the frame of mind which
makes analogy fruitful. One such, in principle, is Pierre Chaunu, who
has attempted to describe seventeenth-century Christianity in the con-
junctural or wave-like terms of a 'temps long de la Réforme de
l'Eglise'.[14] For various reasons his attempt is less useful for our
purposes than it might have been. For one thing, his view would seem
to be that, by and large, fluctuations in Christianity ought to be regarded as contrapuntal to, not synchronous with, fluctuations of an
economic or demographic kind: the seventeenth century was a 'temps
dur, temps difficile, *donc* temps fertile, temps de l'esprit'. This position
seems related to his rigorously otherworldly or Barthian view of genuine
Christianity, which obliges him to dismiss the humanist or Jesuit

13. E. J. Hobsbawm, 'The Crisis of the Seventeenth Century', *ibid.*, pp. 5–58,
especially pp. 14–17.
14. *La Civilisation de l'Europe Classique* (Paris, 1970), pp. 394, 457–508, esp.
463 f., 480–502.

tradition as a Pelagian aberration which has no place in the history of Christianity as such. If the point of view is correct, this book is more or less superfluous: Chaunu's reconstruction of the rhythms of seventeenth-century Christianity seems to have nothing to offer to a historian of English Catholicism I say 'seems', because it may be that all we need to do is to read the graph upside-down. A Catholic phase of the long wave of Reformation taking off, in France, in the first decades of the seventeenth century and running away into the sand somewhere after 1680 is just about the exact opposite of the situation here. And this is not accidental, for the Catholicism of Bérulle, Saint-Cyran and Arnauld, eminent as its virtues were in many respects, was not designed for conditions across the Channel, and I would regard its presence in the background as a significant contributor to the difficulties of English Catholicism at this time.

Whatever may be the case with established Catholicism, a minority community in a *pays de mission* requires for its progress a certain insistence on the virtues of the active life; its vitality is therefore more likely to fluctuate with than against the rhythms of the world in general. The Elizabethan mission depended for its existence on a revaluation of the active virtues which sustained the sixteenth-century counter-Reformation in general by reinterpreting Catholicism in the light of values characteristic of Renaissance Europe as a whole. The recession in the English Catholic community exemplified a wider inability in Catholicism to sustain these values in the face of a renewed assertion of the primacy of order which was likewise general in seventeenth-century Europe and does much to account for its unexciting performance as a whole.[15] The revival of the community may need to be seen in a different light: it appears to contradict the general experience of Catholicism and indeed of Christianity in this period, to run counter to the assumption that during the eighteenth century the ways parted between renewed secular growth and religious decline.

It may indeed simply do so, and if it does we should need to emphasise the transition in English Catholicism of which I have spoken, its reconciliation with the general ethos of English society, as a process tending to insulate the community from the rhythms of continental experience and ensure it a stake in the extraordinary vitality of eight-

15. For this point of view in general, see my edition of H. O. Evennett, *The Spirit of the Counter-Reformation* (Cambridge, 1968), e.g. pp. 41 f., 137–142.

eenth-century England. Probably this is more or less what was happening; though it must also be said that the conventional appreciation of eighteenth-century Christianity in general and Catholicism in particular may need to be revised. If we can see in the eighteenth century, as as Delumeau has seen, a qualitative, minority Catholicism expanding while the quantitative Catholicism of universal conformity decayed, we shall not need to overdo the parting of the ways between English Catholicism and its continental hinterland. *Minoritaire* from the start, and by now consentingly so, the English Catholic community was better placed to do justice to the prospects this situation might offer.[16] Attractive as it is, I think this point of view is at the moment a little too speculative to be relied on, and will assume that the revival of the Catholic mission in eighteenth-century England does represent a certain divorce from the experience of the Catholic continent. That assumed, it is possible to return to the analogy between business and missionary enterprise provided by Hobsbawm, and to make use of it to illuminate both the decay and the revival of English Catholicism.

We may ask what it implies. It may, for example, imply that in early-modern Europe Christian activism should be considered a branch of entrepreneurial activity in general, modelled upon a pre-existing economic structure, dependent upon it for its vitality, and suffering directly from its deadlocks. It may also imply the reverse: that, as Weber was inclined to think, business enterprise should be considered a branch of Christian activism in general, dependent upon it for its motivation, though no doubt in the long run acquiring a momentum of its own. Without proposing to solve a perennial controversy, I would suggest that there is something in both these interpretations of the analogy, but that the first will apply more readily in Catholic, the second in Protestant Christianity. If that is so, we may see the English mission as drawing for the vigour of its primary phase on an entrepreneurial substructure which was continental and Catholic and which failed to provide it with support much after 1600. As it settled into stagnation, activist Protestantism gathered its energies to their climax, transforming English society and helping to launch it upon its own entrepreneurial career. By the close of the seventeenth century the new structure was sufficiently well developed for the forces of Catholic

16. Jean Delumeau, *Le Catholicisme entre Luther et Voltaire* (Paris, 1971), p. 307.

activism to begin to derive from it—from, to put the point at its crudest, the London stock market[17]—the sustaining power without which they do not seem to have been able to go forward.

17. For a comparable situation, though not one which supports the distinction of Protestant and Catholic suggested above, see the discussion of joint stock benevolence in M. G. Jones, *The Charity School Movement* (Cambridge, 1938), pp. 3, 12.

PART THREE

BIRTH OF A DENOMINATION, 1770–1850

'Bred in another form of religious observance I stand aside, unbiased, from the trivialities with which controversies are mostly informed; whatever differences exist there remains the clear, wide and refreshing Christianity, desired by all men, but obscured by the little darkness of their own imperfect vision. To the better understanding of such broad Christian feeling I am thankful to have been permitted, in a small way it is true, to exercise my art.'

Edward Elgar to Archbishop Randall Davidson,
27 February 1927: Percy M. Young, *Elgar*
(London, 1955), p. 230.

13

THE ROAD TO WIGAN

THE span of some eighty years which I propose to examine in these concluding chapters may seem either too long or too short. Too short for anyone who, noting the word 'denomination', may have in mind the advance of a Catholic community to the status of one among a plurality of bodies of roughly equivalent weight and standing, mutually accepted and accepting, and forming between them a polygon of forces on which much of the structure of a plural society may rest.[1] It would be difficult to pretend that this was the state of affairs in England in 1851: it might be said, in defence, that the remarkable events of the mid-nineteenth century were such as to ensure the acquisition of this status at some future date, but in the short run their effect was perhaps to retard this development rather than to promote it. On the other hand, the period may seem too long for anyone whose sights are trained on the legal, external conditions within which an English Catholic community existed: the substantive abolition of penal restraint on the exercise of the Catholic religion in England dates from 1791, the substantive removal of civil disabilities—more significant, at least in the short run, in an Irish than in an English context—from 1829. Such dates have traditionally formed a *terminus ad quem* for historians concerned with the post-Reformation Catholic community, or at least a line of division between its two major phases. It would indeed have been possible to present these eighty years as an 'age of emancipation', beginning with the first relief act of 1778, and passing the milestones already mentioned to conclude with the closure of the missionary ecclesiastical regime in 1850—'restoration of the hierarchy'

---

1. cf. two recent sociological discussions of the problem: Will Herberg, *Protestant, Catholic, Jew* (Garden City, N.Y., 1960 edn); and D. A. Martin, 'The Denomination', *British Journal of Sociology*, xiii (1963), 1–14. Neither of these analyses is readily applicable to situation described here, though aspects of both of them are relevant.

or 'papal aggression'—treated as an act which 'emancipated' the clergy from historical shackles in somewhat the same way that the laity had been emancipated by parliamentary statute. This last position is that indicated by Bernard Ward in his classic history of the community between 1780 and 1850,[2] to whose numerous volumes I think he would have regarded this theme as supplying the unifying force. This justification would not apply here. Anyone who tries to grasp the history of the English Catholic community *as* a community—as a body of people, at the junction of two larger wholes, with its own internal structure and way of life—must, I think, be struck by the relatively small part which external enactments, whether they emanated from the political or the spiritual sovereign, had in accounting for its existence, forming its characteristics, or altering the course of its progress; the same, if we are considering the enactments of the English or British Parliament, must I think be said for the beneficial legislation of this period as for the repressive legislation of an earlier one. What has been attempted in this book is precisely to write the history of the community as a community. I may possibly, in the interests of clarifying my subject, have pushed the point farther than a disinterested spectator might find acceptable, but if the choice was worth making in the first place it is worth pursuing to the end.

What follows, then, is not a study of Catholic emancipation in any received sense of the word: it is an attempt to see how, to what degree and with what modifications, a traditional religious community maintained its continuity through an age of unprecedented upheaval. And it is essentially from this point of view that the dates have been chosen. 1770 may not be a date of any great significance in the history of the industrial revolution in England; but it will do very well for the point at which the general transformation of the conditions of English life began to make itself felt in a transformation of the English Catholic community and to break up the relatively stable structure within which it had existed for something like a century and a half. 1850 may also not be a particularly significant year in the history of England at large; but it may be taken to represent a point beyond which the community here studied—what, from the present point of view, one may reasonably term the old English Catholic community—may be said, if not to have ceased to exist, at least to have been transformed beyond recognition.

2. Bernard Ward, *The Sequel to Catholic Emancipation* (2 vols., London, 1915), i, p. 7.

It is important for the argument of this book that the period indicated should be treated as a conclusion, if only a partial conclusion, as well as a beginning. I have argued that the history of the post-Reformation Catholic community in England is not to be envisaged as process of continuous decline reaching its nadir in the eighteenth century, but as a patient and continuous process of construction from small beginnings in which the eighteenth century represents a phase of modest progress and of careful preparation for the future. The reader can hardly be expected to accept this revision unless he is given some account of what these preparations subsequently achieved; still less to take on trust a conviction that the early nineteenth century was in many respects a period of take-off for English Catholicism, the period in which, perhaps for the first time, the mission evoked a response commensurate with the effort put into it; and for the community as such an age of quantitative expansion and qualitative maturity, when it managed to combine fidelity to its tradition and openness to its environment with a rare, and certainly so far unequalled, measure of success. In offering support for this conviction, which may be found unusual, I am also concerned to cast doubt on two sets of *idée reçue* about nineteenth-century English Catholicism, which are more or less directly the converse or complement of the erroneous idea mentioned above. The first is the notion propagated by Newman, Wiseman and others around the mid-century, and thenceforth part of the folklore of English Catholicism, of a 'Second Spring', a miraculous rebirth dating from somewhere around 1840. The second, more commonly accepted by historians, is that for all serious purposes the Catholicism of modern England may be taken as a cutting from the Catholicism of Ireland transplanted by emigration into an alien land which had long ceased to have anything worth mentioning to offer in the way of an indigenous Catholic tradition. Both these notions seem to me unacceptable, if in different degrees. I shall hope to demonstrate that the first is a piece of tendentious ecclesiastical propaganda; the second is a respectable historical opinion—one indeed to which I hope I have done adequate justice by concluding the book at the point I have chosen—which requires to be modified in important and historically significant respects.

I have not made these remarks for argument's sake, or to provide the book with a central thesis which it might otherwise appear to lack. The purpose of historical polemic is to delimit, in Toynbee's phrase, intelligible fields of study: in concluding the book as I have done I have aimed at completing an intelligible whole. The case for this intelligibility on chronological grounds has already been put. On topical or structural grounds one might add that an account of how the community extricated itself from the mediaeval (presented in Part I) invites as complement an account of how it adjusted itself to the modern; and that we may pass a safer judgment on the calibre of a body formed in circumstances of stability (the subject of Part II) when we have seen how it responded to a world once again decidedly on the move.

During these eight decades, in any event, the community underwent a radical transformation in almost every respect. In numbers it multiplied about ten times: the criteria which have been used to give a figure of 80,000 Catholics in England in 1770 would give something like three-quarters of a million in 1850.[3] Its local distribution was also transformed, though less radically; partly because it implanted itself in parts of the country which had been barren of Catholics since the Reformation—in the industrial belt of the West Riding of Yorkshire and south-east Lancashire, in the east Midlands, in south Wales, one might almost add in London; partly because, in the regions of its traditional strength—the rest of Lancashire, the North-east, the west Midlands—its centres of gravity shifted from the countryside to towns and manufacturing districts. This numerical and local transformation brought, inevitably, an occupational and social transformation: congregations of labourers, handicraftsmen, tradesmen, the simply poor, their wives and children, topped by a stratum of business and professional families, replaced in the centre of the scene congregations of gentry, farmers, agricultural labourers and rural craftsmen.

This transformation, I repeat, was in the first place a transformation of the *English* Catholic community; it would, though their arrival of course made a great difference to the numbers involved, have occurred if no Irishmen had set foot in the country. If we stand at the year, 1770, which we have taken as its starting-point, there are two relevant points

---

3. J.-A. Lesourd, 'Les Catholiques dans la société anglaise de 1765 à 1865' (Thèse de l'Université de Strasbourg, 1974), i, pp. 9–10—Catholic population on basis of Registrar-General's figures for Catholic marriages, 1850: 762,120; the Mass-attendance figures given by the Religious Census of 1851 (252,783), multiplied by the figure of 2·5 suggested below (note to Table IV), would suggest something rather lower, in the region of 650,000, but a slightly more liberal multiplier would probably be appropriate at this date. Cf. Philip Hughes, 'The English Catholics in 1850', in G. A. Beck (ed.), *The English Catholics, 1850–1950* (London, 1950), pp. 42 ff.; though some of Hughes's calculations seem rather doubtful.

about the community which need to be borne in mind. The first has already been made: it was not contracting, but expanding, partly because of the general facts of English rural demography in the eighteenth century, and partly because of the efforts which the Catholic clergy, despite the limitations placed on their activity, had been putting into the work of popular catechising since about 1700. The second is that its social and occupational characteristics were already in process of change. An analysis of the returns of papists of 1767, on which we mainly rely for our knowledge of the size of the community at this time, has indicated that even then, of those Catholics in active employment, considerably more were occupied as non-agricultural labourers and handicraftsmen than in agriculture and domestic service combined: to be exact, of those whose occupations were given, 51% were in the first category and 34% in the second and third together. In most parts of Lancashire, well over half the Catholics in employment were non-agricultural workers of one kind or another.[4] It would be possible to jump to excessive conclusions from these figures: no information is available for 30% of the Catholics in employment, and a predominance of non-agricultural workers is not necessarily inconsistent with a community still predominantly rural. Nevertheless they should be taken very seriously. What they reveal is, in the first place, only the reverse image of an expanding rural population, the consequences of a pressure which would affect Catholics just as it affected other Englishmen. Yet they were perhaps specially responsive to it: by comparison with other religious bodies, they were disproportionately concentrated in parts of the country where the process was most intensive; they may well have had special reason to be attracted to occupations where legal and customary restraints and discriminations did not apply; their clergy, taken as a whole, were enthusiastic to build up congregations which would be free of landlord control. These factors, it may be suggested, were shifting Catholics more rapidly than other Englishmen out of the ways of their forefathers;[5] we must now try to follow their footsteps on the ground, bearing in mind that their movement, in so far as it did not lead them to abandon their religion, must tend of itself markedly to accelerate the growth of the Catholic community.

4. Lesourd, thesis cit., ii, pp. 93–229, especially pp. 102, 115, 121.
5. Lesourd, thesis cit., ii, pp. 115 f.; cf. Rowlands, 'Staffordshire', p. 179, and my own 'More Northumbrian Congregations', Recusant History, x (1969), pp. 20–22 and n. 31.

If we wish to look at the rural end of this process, we may first take note of some remarks jotted down at about the time the papist returns were being compiled by a working missionary priest: the Benedictine John Fisher, who served a seigneurial congregation at Holme in the East Riding of Yorkshire.

There seems little prospect [he wrote, reflecting on the circumstances of his flock] of any great Increase to the Catholick Religion in this place. As there are no Manufactures, the country has no Employment for the people that may be bred in it above the old number; and thus the young ones of both Sexes when 14 or 15 Years of Age will continue to go off and seek a Livelyhood elsewhere, where intermarrying with parties of a different perswasion and gaining Settlements and being also it's likely depriv'd of the opportunity of practising the Cath: Religion, they or their Descendants will drop off...[6]

Other parts were more fortunately placed in this respect than the East Riding of Yorkshire. Staffordshire, which had two rapidly expanding centres of manufacture, the Potteries in the North and the metal-working Black Country in the South, was one of them. It had also a relatively large body of Catholics, whose history during the eighteenth century has been fully investigated by Marie Rowlands, and provides a model of the general development which has been suggested. The 1767 returns show that Staffordshire Catholics were not the stable body, clinging faithfully to the same piece of soil from generation to generation which a Gothic view of English Catholic history might lead one to suppose. One of the items of information required about individual Catholics was how long they had resided in the parish where they lived, and from this the fact emerges that none of the fifteen congregations in the county contained a majority of people who had been born in the parish or parishes where they were now to be found; the average length of residence was ten years. The Catholics of rural Staffordshire were evidently willing to move to places where work was to be had. Since the

6. Aveling, *West Riding*, p. 266; other remarks by Fisher in K. M. Longley, *Heir of Two Traditions: the Catholic Church of St John, Holme-on-Spalding-Moor* (privately printed, 1966), p. 12. The date of the passage quoted by Aveling appears to be 1766, not 1745. Compare this and the evidence for the clearing of poor tenants from the neighbouring Everingham estate (P. Roebuck, in *Agricultural History Review*, xxi (1973), p. 6) with the growth of Catholic congregations in York and other Yorkshire towns: Aveling, *Recusancy in York*, pp. 122 f., and *West Riding*, p. 264.

1720s there had been a well-established chapel in Wolverhampton, a town where the Catholic gentry, and notably the Gifford family, carried a good deal of weight; a number of rural Catholics had been moving there, mainly to work in various branches of the metal-working trade. 265 were returned from the town in 1757; we can detect from the length of residence given a movement gathering way from small beginnings. 84 of them had been born there, 70 had come from outside more than ten years before and 113 had arrived since 1757. We can only presume that the movement continued, since by 1830 the Wolverhampton congregation had about 1,000 members, and there were sizeable congregations in several of the Black Country towns and villages nearby. The local clergy showed energy and imagination, and there does not seem to have been much 'dropping off'. There were few Irishmen either here or in the Potteries, where the same thing had been happening on a smaller scale, until after about 1825.[7]

Conditions were equally favourable for the transformation in the North-east, where there were overgrown rural congregations like that on the Clavering estate at Callaly in Northumberland, and a strong demand for labour on Tyneside and in the mining districts around. Two substantial mining enterprises were in Catholic ownership in 1767, one at Stella-on-Tyne and another at Felling near Gateshead; together, the parishes in which they were situated returned over 600 Catholics, most of whom were employed in the industry. Many of them were no doubt rural immigrants; others must have settled in the lower reaches of Tyneside, but they do not seem to have got much attention from the clergy until the arrival of James Worswick as priest in Newcastle in 1795. During the next twenty years—the first of fifty he spent at the task—Worswick had remarkable success in building up congregations in Newcastle itself and in North Shields, where he started a new chapel in 1817. This was a tribute to his own unremitting labours, but he was presumably helped by currents of emigration from the rural congregations; by the end of this period Irishmen do not seem to have constituted more than about a quarter of his flock, though the proportion increased rapidly after about 1820. In so far as one can see it as a

7. Rowlands, 'Staffordshire', pp. 102 ff., 109, 181 ff., and the edition by Miss Rowlands and others of *Roman Catholic Registers: Chillington, Wolverhampton, etc.* (Staffordshire Parish Registers Society, 1958–1959), from which I deduce the statement about Irish immigration; *Catholic Magazine*, v (1834), 307—'not less than 650' communicants at that date. For the activity of the clergy, and congregations in the Black Country, see below, pp. 317 f.

whole, the position in the North-east looks much the same as in Staffordshire, though one has the impression that the transformation occurred rather later, and was rather less successfully managed and more dependent on assistance from Ireland.[8]

Taken together, the number of Catholics undergoing this change of life in the west Midlands and the North-east cannot have amounted to more than a fraction of those who underwent it in Lancashire. This makes it particularly unfortunate that no attempt seems to have been made to investigate it here, though David Mathew drew attention to the subject twenty years ago, and to the fact that town congregations in Lancashire represented the double effect of English and Irish migratory movements working at their highest pressure. In a general way it is clear from their baptismal registers that most rural Catholic congregations were feeling the effects of the intense demographic growth of the county, and that their members, like everyone else, were being attracted by higher wages and booming conditions in the manufacturing towns.[9] But so far the records of these congregations have yielded only one precise illustration of the point, and it is not a very representative one. Between 1811 and 1850 John Lingard, the historian, was the priest of a small congregation at Hornby, at the northern end of the county, ten miles from Lancaster on the edge of the Forest of Bowland. In the intervals of his historical work Lingard kept a regular list of his Easter communicants, in which he noted what had happened to communicants of the previous year who had failed to reappear in the current one. His congregation of farmers and farm labourers, hatters and weavers, never contained much more than 100 communicants at any time, and was declining, but during this period 133 of them went away, and 62 of these told Lingard where they were going. Nine were only moving to local villages, but 42 were off to the towns of the North-west, from Kendal

8. 'Four Catholic Congregations in rural Northumberland', *Recusant History*, ix (1967), pp. 88 ff.; A. M. C. Forster, 'Catholicism in the Diocese of Durham in 1767', *Ushaw Magazine*, lxxii (1962), pp. 74–76; E. Walsh and A. Forster, 'The Recusancy of the Brandlings', *Recusant History*, x (1969), p. 45, etc.; *Catholic Registers of the Secular Mission of Newcastle-on-Tyne* (C.R.S. xxxv, 1936), pp. 198 ff. See also the map of Catholicism in the North-east in J. D. Gay, *The Geography of Religion in England* (London, 1971), p. 280.

9. Mathew, in *The English Catholics, 1850–1950*, pp. 224 f.; Lesourd, thesis *cit.*, ii, pp. 326 f., and above, n. 4 and 5: the Lancashire rural registers are in C.R.S. xv (1913), xvi and xxiii (1922). Cf. A. H. Redford, *Labour Migration in England, 1800–1850* (Manchester, 1926), pp. 11, 16 f., 59 f.; and Gay, *Geography of Religion in England*, pp. 93, 278.

to Manchester; one was off to London, four to other parts of the British Isles and six to America.[10]

Taken from the point of arrival, in the congregations of the Lancashire towns, the view becomes clearer; it seems simplest to confine oneself to the four Lancashire industrial towns with the largest Catholic congregations—Preston, Wigan, Liverpool and Manchester—and to begin with the crude facts of their numerical growth. I have assembled these in the form of a table (Table IV); how the figures have been arrived at I explain in an accompanying note. What follows is a commentary upon them.

According to the 1767 returns there were about 4,000 Catholics in the three English towns in whose rural hinterland they were most thickly concentrated—Preston, Wigan and Liverpool; this was something over twice as many as there had been forty or fifty years before. There were few in Manchester, which is not surprising as it had no tradition of Catholicism and there were few congregations within a reasonable distance of it. The Liverpool congregation was already the largest of the three, and growing more rapidly than the others though, unlike those of Preston and Wigan, its history did not go back before 1700. In 1783 the local vicar-general, John Chadwick, estimated 2,600 communicants in the three congregations, suggesting roughly the same total, along with 400 (or a total congregation of 600) for Manchester, where a chapel had been established in the interval. Chadwick's figures seem on the conservative side, which may possibly be explained by the fact that the three larger congregations were served by Jesuits. It would certainly seem from its baptismal registers that the Liverpool congregation had expanded a good deal since 1767, though its religious practice may well have suffered from the shattering conflict which had just broken out inside it.[11] For the next thirty years, for which I know of no direct estimates of congregational strength for any of these congregations, we are reduced to somewhat risky calculations based on the baptismal registers (Table IV(a)). What these appear to show is that the Wigan congregation remained stable until 1800, but had doubled by 1810 when it stood at over 2,000, while those at Liverpool and Man-

10. Lancashire C.R.O. RCHy: Easter Communicants, 1811 ff. The northern towns migrated to were: Lancashire (12), Preston (9), Kendal (8), Blackburn (5), Manchester (4), Liverpool (3), Ashton-under-Lyne (1).

11. There were 132 baptisms in 1767 (C.R.S. ix (1911), pp. 205 ff.), compared with 260 in 1788 (Table IV(a)); cf. below, chapter 14, pp. 341 f.

chester increased sharply and continuously, and amounted at the latter date to some 9,000 and 6,000 people respectively. By then there were four chapels in Liverpool and two in Manchester. Preston would shortly have two as well: I have not examined its baptismal register, but the congregation had certainly increased very considerably,[12] and in size it would have come somewhere between those of Wigan and Manchester, probably amounting to some 4,000 people. If we accept that figure, we find that in 1810 the Catholic congregations of the four towns—there were now eight of them—contained a total of some 22,000 members, compared, on Chadwick's figures, with 4,500 thirty years before. In 1819 we reach reasonably firm ground once again. In, presumably, 1820, some Catholic source which I am so far unable to identify published a booklet detailing 'The Catholic chapels and chaplains, with the numbers of their respective congregations, in the county of Lancaster, as taken at the end of 1819'. I do not know the circumstances in which it was compiled, but it was clearly an attempt to do directly what has been attempted here, that is, to calculate actual congregations, and its figures in general inspire confidence, though in some cases the criterion of membership used may have been somewhat more liberal than those used here. The figures were: for Preston, 6,000 members in two chapels with four priests; for Wigan, 3,000 in two chapels with three priests; for Liverpool, 18,000 in four chapels with six priests; for Manchester, 15,000 in two chapels with four priests. The figures for Liverpool and Wigan are much what would have been given by using the baptismal calculation (as described in the note to Table IV) for this date, though on this basis one may suspect a little exaggeration in Liverpool and more than a little in Manchester.[13] However, we can be fairly sure that in 1819 the effective congregations of the four towns would not amount to less than 33,000 people, and they were probably rather larger than this. The next set of figures that I know of was compiled in response to a parliamentary enquiry in connection with the emancipation act of 1829; for present purposes it is a good deal less satisfactory, since in most cases it was obviously not a count of congregational members, and was apparently the result of

12. In December 1817 the priest, Joseph Dunn, said that the congregation had multiplied five or six times since his arrival, which was in 1775: Archives of the English Province S.J.—College of St Aloysius: Preston.
13. See Table IV(a): the figures suggested by this calculation are about 14,500 for Liverpool and about 10,000 for Manchester.

estimates given by the Catholic clergy who were finding the task of computation beyond their powers and were in some cases giving way to a spirit of exaggeration which was once again abroad. Fortunately most of their figures can be checked against baptismal registers, and against a good deal of helpful information about the genuine size of their congregations elicited five years later, when most of them were called to give evidence to the parliamentary enquiry into the state of the Irish poor in Great Britain, whose results were published in 1836. Of the figures given in 1829—Preston, 10,900; Wigan, 5,000; Liverpool, 31,800; Manchester, 51,180—the last is wildly exaggerated and should be reduced to something less than 30,000, giving a total for the four towns of something like 75,000 Catholics, perhaps a fifth of their population. Since Catholic immigration had certainly much intensified since 1820, this is not an implausible figure in itself, but it is certainly not acceptable as an estimate of the number of people who actually frequented the dozen Catholic chapels which now existed in these towns. The evidence given by some of the Liverpool priests to the Poor Enquiry in 1834 is particularly enlightening in this respect: it implies that, at a time when there were about 40,000 baptised Catholics in the town, their five chapels had all told about 13,000 communicants, and effective congregations, including children, amounting to about 20,000.[14] If the same applied in Manchester, there would have been about 18,000 chapel-goers in a total Catholic population of 35,000. In Wigan, according to the evidence given, things were much the same in 1834 as in 1829, though there had perhaps been some decline due to hard times in the weaving trade. For Preston, where the Enquiry is not much help, we have a count of Mass attendance on 9 January 1834: at three Masses in the two chapels 3,557 attenders were counted, which implies an effective congregation of some 8,000. All this would give a total upwards of 50,000 chapel-going Catholics in the four towns in 1834, a body which had multiplied about twelve times during the previous fifty years.

From that date until 1850 it was to multiply at least as fast. At the religious census of 1851, which for our purposes was a census of Mass attendance on 30 March in that year returned by the clergy, the chapels in the registration districts which centred on the four towns returned a total of 57,979 attenders, implying effective congregations totalling about 145,000 members. The figure is exaggerated because, except in

14. See Table V.

the case of Manchester, the districts covered a wider area than the towns themselves; it included returns from thirty-five chapels, while there were only eighteen within the town boundaries. But these would have possessed most of the large congregations, and we shall be fairly safe in assuming for these a total of about 120,000 members in 1851; something like 15,000 in Preston, 8,000 in Wigan, upwards of 50,000 in Liverpool and upwards of 40,000 in Manchester. If we include all those returned from the four registration districts, these towns now contained nearly a quarter of the church-going Catholics in England and Wales.

In these dry figures the transformation of the Catholic community in England is recorded, the launching of a new phase in its history with which it is not the purpose of this book to deal. But, as I have argued, the transformation itself is also part of the history which is properly to be dealt with here: how much a part we can only discover by subjecting to interpretation the crude statistics of urban growth. The most pressing task of interpretation is to distinguish its English constituent from its Irish one; but before we attempt this, one preliminary comment seems called for. If we plot on a graph, as has been done in Figure II, the figures for all four towns from 1783 to 1851, we get a curve which is comparatively smooth, showing indeed an accelerating rate of growth, but not, even perhaps in the 1840s, the sudden change of scale which would reveal a genuine breach in continuity, and could only be caused by the intervention of some wholly external factor. Further, it is not at all clear that the points at which the rate of growth appears to increase can always be correlated with periods of intensified Irish immigration. This does not seem to have been a very continuous movement, but to have occurred in waves of increasing size: one around 1790, another after 1820 and another in the 1840s.[15] Even if we suppose that a change of gear in the late 1840s has been concealed by the imperfections of the graph—which may well be true but is not borne out by such baptismal figures as I have seen—it gives no clear sign that anything very striking happened to the rate of growth either about 1790 or about 1820: rather the contrary, in fact. Considering the conjectural character of much of the material the graph is based on, it would be unwise to press too far arguments which might be drawn from it; but at least it offers *prima facie* evidence for a solid foundation of continuous and self-generating

15. A. H. Redford, *Labour Migration in England*, pp. 114 ff.; Sheridan Gilley, 'The Roman Catholic Mission to the Irish in London', *Recusant History*, x (1969), p. 124.

growth underlying what was added by recruitment from outside. With this possibility in mind we may look at the direct evidence of English and Irish participation in the congregations of the four towns. I select two points of enquiry, fifty years apart: 1783 and 1834.

In 1783 the Irish constituent may be regarded as more or less negligible. In Liverpool, where it must have been largest, and an Irish merchant community had certainly played a part in the congregation's growth, only about 20% of the baptisms, and probably a smaller percentage of the active congregation, was Irish, and indeed the proportion seems to have declined somewhat during the previous half-century.[16] In 1834 a serious attempt on the problem was made by the priests who gave evidence to the Enquiry on the Irish Poor. In Liverpool they indicated that, as a whole, about 30% of their congregations were English-descended and about 70% Irish-descended; of their 13,000 communicants, about 4,000 and 9,000 respectively. The proportion varied between the chapels: as one might expect the congregation at St Patrick's, built in 1821 specifically for the purpose, was more or less wholly Irish; the oldest-established chapel, St Mary's, had a congregation which was between a third and a half English; at the others two-thirds were given as Irish or Irish-descended.[17] In Manchester, as one would have anticipated, the congregations were a good deal more homogeneously Irish in character, but even here not wholly so. As in Liverpool, St Patrick's, recently opened and serving the quarter of the city known as Little Ireland, had a purely Irish congregation, and its priest, Daniel Hearne, who was also Irish, thought that Irishmen and their descendants formed 90% of all the Catholics in Manchester; the English priests at the other chapels thought the ratio was about five to one.[18] It seems reasonable to split the difference, and assume an English

16. These are my conclusions from the Liverpool baptismal register (C.R.S. ix, pp. 205 ff.) which, as published, covers the period 1741–1773.
17. See Table V, which I have constructed from the information given in the *Report on the Irish Poor in Great Britain*, Appendix, pp. 8, 22–25.
18. *ibid.*, pp. 42–43. It may be worth while offering the result of an attempt made to arrive at some conclusion on the subject by distinguishing English and Irish in the baptismal register of St Chad's, Rook Street, where the priest gave the estimate mentioned in the text (Lancs. C.R.O. RCMc/1–5: registers, 1772–1847). Of 665 children baptised in 1835, I deduced on the basis of surnames that 300 had two Irish parents, 119 two English parents and 234 were of mixed parentage; of the parents of children in the last category, I deduced that at least 99 were of mixed religion, since both godparents appeared to be Irish. If accurate, this calculation would give an Irish percentage in the congregation of about 70%. I have little doubt that it exaggerates both the English and the mixed element, though I have tried to

constituent of about 15%, or 2,700 out of an effective congregation of 18,000. At Wigan, on the other hand, Irishmen were in a minority: the English proportion was given as between 50 and 60%, or some 3,000.[19] There were very few Irish in Preston: the priests' estimates varied between a couple of hundred and a thousand, a negligible proportion of a congregation of eight or nine thousand.[20] This will give us in 1834 a total for the four towns of 19,200 English and 31,800 Irish or Irish-descended, in a total of 51,000; or 38% English and 62% Irish.[21]

What stage this represented in the progress of the relation between English and Irish congregational membership is not easy to say. If we were to assume that the growth of the English membership proceeded at a constant rate between 1783 and 1851, the point of equilibrium between English and Irish members would have been passed about 1818, and by 1851 the English proportion would have fallen to about 20%. The first of these deductions is probably fairly accurate—it certainly fits very well with what will be suggested later about the importance of the years around 1820 in the history of the community; the second probably underestimates the English proportion, since the growth of Preston as a whole accelerated markedly between 1834 and 1851, and two new chapels were built during this time, though there was little Irish immigration until later.[22] Altogether, a ratio of three Irish-descended to one English-descended Catholic in the four towns in 1851 seems likely. All this is however extremely conjectural, and for the time being it seems safer to stick to the relatively well-attested proportions of 1834, and to offer some conclusions on the basis of them.

In so far as these towns offer an accurate model of what was happening in the country at large, and I see no reason why they should not, we

---

be as careful as possible; it does at any rate suggest that the conclusion drawn in the text is, if anything, an underestimate of the English constituent. It may be compared with that made by the priest of St Anthony's, Liverpool, from his baptismal register for 1831, 1832 and 1833; he concluded that the percentages of children baptised during these years who were of Irish extraction were respectively 62, 68 and 66 (*Report on the Irish Poor*, Appendix, p. 8).

19. *ibid.*, p. 89.

20. *ibid.*, pp. 90 f.; cf. Redford, *Labour Migration*, p. 140.

21. Table VI.

22. cf. K. S. Inglis, *Churches and the Working-Class in Victorian England* (London/ Toronto, 1963), p. 125—6,000 attenders at three Masses at St Wilfrid's, 1851; though he seems to assume that this was due to Irish immigration; H. Clemesha, *History of Preston-in-Amounderness* (Manchester, 1912), pp. 322 f., etc. See Figure II.

may conclude that English Catholics were, as one would have anticipated, in a minority in the movement which led to the transformation
of the community; but it was a very considerable minority. Over fifty
years they had multiplied their numbers four or five times; if we add
the congregations of smaller towns like Lancaster, Blackburn and
Warrington, they were probably by now slightly more numerous than
the Catholics of the Lancashire countryside, whose occupations were in
any case, as we have seen, not primarily agricultural.[23] If there had been
no Irish immigration, the transformation of Lancashire Catholicism
would have been less rapid and less massive, and the final result somewhat different in character; but in essentials what happened would still
have happened. A large and interesting book might be written on the
relations of English and Irish Catholics in the nineteenth-century
Lancashire towns. They were, initially at any rate, divided in some
degree by language, by a contrast of economic status—which should not
be exaggerated, since both elements contained people of a wide variety
of incomes and occupations—by differing social *mores*, political instincts, attitudes to the clergy, assumptions about the running of chapels
or simple mutual dislike. They were to be unified by intermarriage, by
a common schooling and by the inevitable processes of assimilation
which applied in particular to the children of immigrants who had been
born in Lancashire: several of the priests who gave evidence in 1834,
Irish as well as English, remarked how rapidly those processes were
operating, even at that date.[24] Except in the purely Irish congregations,
like those of the two St Patrick's, chapel-going was no doubt in itself an
agent of assimilation. To attempt to describe this process would take
us beyond the scope of this book; some comments about it may be left
until we have seen what was happening in towns where, as in Manchester, there was little or no indigenous Catholicism to assimilate to.

Purely Irish communities, with Irish priests, and a self-consciousness
which kept them from any real contact with English Catholicism until
well after 1850, arose in Cardiff and industrial south Wales, in Cumberland, in the West Riding of Yorkshire and elsewhere.[25] But they were
on the whole a marginal phenomenon; what was more usual, par-

---

23. Compare the figure in Table VI with those for rural Catholics in *Parliamentary Papers*, 1830, xix, *passim*.
24. *Report on the Irish Poor*, p. xix; Appendix, pp. 21, 22, 26 f., 61–63.
25. One of these, in Cardiff, is investigated in John Hickey, *Urban Catholics* (London, 1967).

ticularly in the larger cities, was the mixed and stratified community where a minority of English Catholics of relative wealth and position united more or less imperfectly with a more or less large body of poor Irishmen, and where segregation by chapels commonly resulted from congregational growth.

The Birmingham congregation suggests what Manchester Catholicism might have looked like if Irish immigration had been a fraction of what it was. In its relation to a background of west Midland rural Catholicism its position resembled that in Wolverhampton, though by all accounts it was a prosperous body containing a number of wealthy businessmen as well as Catholics in industrial employment. It built its first chapel (St Peter's) in 1786, and its second (St Chad's) in 1809, though this was not primarily a result of expanding numbers; in 1834 the number of English Catholics in Birmingham was given as about a thousand. Birmingham did not receive much Irish immigration during the nineteenth century: there seem to have been virtually no Irish Catholics there until about 1820; in 1834 the priests thought there were about 6,000, half of whom did not come to church. By this time there seems to have been some degree of segregation between the chapels: St Chad's had the larger, and predominantly Irish, congregation, St Peter's the smaller, more respectable and more English one.[26] In these respects it provided a small-scale model for the progress of Catholicism in London.

The Catholic population of London was of very mixed origins, later distinguished by Charles Booth with a good deal of finesse. He distinguished two indigenous elements: one aristocratic, consisting of the nobility, the gentry and their relations, the other an element of professional people, merchants and tradesmen, middle and lower-middle class, London-born and immigrants from the provinces or from abroad. He thought there were traditional Catholics and converts in both milieux; except for some people of mainly German origin in the middle-class element, they were all English. Besides these, there was a large working-class element almost wholly immigrant in character, mainly poor Irish and poor Italians.[27] The social geography of London, if nothing else, would have ensured that these different elements should have practised their religion, from an early date, in separation from one

---

26. *Catholic Magazine*, v (1834), p. 314; *Report on the Irish Poor*, Appendix, pp. 1–7; J. A. Jackson, *The Irish in Britain* (London/Cleveland, 1963), p. 15; and see below, pp. 319 f. and chapter 14, p. 347.
27. Quoted in J. A. Jackson, *The Irish in Britain*, p. 145.

another. In the West End were the chapels of the aristocracy, often taken over during the late eighteenth century from the foreign embassies which had until then maintained a sort of protectorate over them; during the first decades of the nineteenth century the smartest of these was the chapel in Warwick Street, near Piccadilly, originally the Bavarian embassy chapel.[28] Catholics of the business and professional classes lived mainly immediately to the west and north of the City, in Clerkenwell and in Holborn; since the middle of the eighteenth century, they had had two chapels, one in Moorfields and the other, originally the Sardinian embassy chapel, in Lincoln's Inn Fields. Of their congregations, William Mawhood, the Smithfield woollen-draper whose diary, kept for the last decades of the eighteenth century, we possess; Thomas Langdale, the Holborn distiller whose large and inflammable plant was burnt down in the Gordon Riots; and John Milner's father, who was a tailor in Clerkenwell, seem reasonably typical examples. All of them, one may remark, had come from the North, though this was largely a migration of people who were relatively prosperous when they arrived, and quickly became more so. On this ground it was they who attracted most attention from the rioters of 1780. Most of the London vicars-apostolic felt more at home with this sector of London Catholicism than with the aristocracy in the West: from Challoner's time until well after 1800 they lived in a modest house in Castle Street, off Theobald's Road. In his lifetime, and for some time afterwards, the Lincoln's Inn Fields chapel was in effect the vicar-apostolic's own congregation; by the end of the century it had been overtaken in importance by that at Moorfields, where St Mary's, a large chapel built in a severe classical style in 1820, acted for some time as a kind of cathedral for the London district and in some sense the showpiece of the Catholic community to the country at large.[29] Below this level London Catholicism was certainly, as Booth supposed, almost wholly Irish in origin. Irish settlement in London was a fact of long standing, and had traditionally been concentrated in the parish of St Giles, west of Holborn. This was a notoriously rough area: its in-

28. Ward, *Dawn of the Catholic Revival*, i, pp. 24 f., 189 f.; *Jerningham Letters*, i, p. 155.
29. E. E. Reynolds (ed.), *The Mawhood Diary* (C.R.S. l, 1956) *passim*; F. C. Husenbeth, *The Life of the Right Rev. John Milner, D.D.* (Dublin, 1862), pp. 4 f.; George Rudé, 'The Gordon Riots', *Transactions of the Royal Historical Society*, v series, vi (1956), pp. 93–114, especially pp. 96, 98; Burton, *Challoner*, i, p. 117; ii, pp. 258 ff. and *passim*; Ward, *Dawn*, i, p. 29; *Eve*, ii, pp. 158 f.

habitants do not seem to have had much time for religion, and the English clergy seem to have fought shy of them for a long time. Challoner was the first to take them seriously as a missionary problem, and he and the priests he left to get on with the task seem to have ensured that they had a reasonable provision, outside the framework of the English congregations and chapels, until they finally got a congenial chapel with the foundation of St Patrick's, Soho, in 1793. Meanwhile new immigrants were accumulating in larger quantities in the east and south of the City, and Challoner by his efforts and example had ensured that they got fairly prompt attention; priests were provided to serve them, and three new chapels—in Wapping, Bermondsey and Southwark—built between 1770 and 1800.[30]

Within this tripartite structure Catholicism grew in London after 1800 not much less rapidly than it did in Lancashire. Its eight or nine chapels of 1800 had become thirty-five in 1851, their total congregational strength grown from an undetermined percentage of the 10,000 people returned as papists from the metropolis in 1767 to about 100,000 in 1851:[31] still a good deal smaller than the combined congregations of the four Lancashire towns, but of comparable weight in the economy of the transformed community. How many of them were of Irish origin we can do no more than conjecture. From the distribution by parishes of Catholics returned in 1767 and 1780, it seems obvious that more than half of them, though perhaps not much more, were Irish; whether they formed a majority of practising Catholics seems much more doubtful. Over the next seventy years the Irish-descended

---

30. For the Irish in eighteenth-century London, see M. Dorothy George, *London Life in the Eighteenth Century* (London, 1966 edn), pp. 120–131; Jackson, *The Irish in Britain*, pp. 42 ff., etc. For missionary efforts, Burton, *Challoner*, i, pp. 79, 130; ii, p. 86; Ward, *Dawn*, i, pp. 26, 194, 302; *Eve*, i, p. 192; ii, p. 156; B. W. Kelly, *Old English Catholic Missions* (London, 1907), p. 74 (Bermondsey); T. R. England, *The Life of the Rev. Arthur O'Leary* (London, 1822), pp. 190, 232 f. The most recent discussion of the problem, which takes a less favourable view of English efforts than that presented here, is Sheridan Gilley, 'The Roman Catholic Mission to the Irish in London', *Recusant History*, x (1969), pp. 122 f.; it deals mainly with the nineteenth century.

31. Lesourd, thesis *cit.*, ii, p. 182 (1767): cf., for 1773, J. H. Whyte, 'The Vicars-Apostolics' Returns of 1773', *Recusant History*, ix (1968), p. 207—'De numero plebis Catholicae Londini nihil certe affirmare possumus . . . Credimus autem . . . Catholicorum numerus . . . non excedere viginti millia'; for 1780, the analysis of the Papist Returns of that year in Rudé, 'The Gordon Riots', pp. 108–109 (13,379). For 1851, *Parliamentary Papers*, 1852–1853, lxxxix, pp. clxxxiv, 1–9 (35,994 attenders in thirty-five chapels, of which four made no return).

proportion of London Catholicism must have risen very steadily, yet the upper and middle reaches were also growing, no doubt to a lesser extent, by the means that Booth indicated, and it would be foolish to neglect the effects of mixed marriage and conversion at every level. In 1843 Bishop Griffiths guessed that three-quarters of his flock were Irish;[32] he was not much of a hand at figures, but this—somewhat less than in Manchester, somewhat more than in Liverpool—seems about right, or not more than marginally on the low side. If we suppose that of the 100,000 Londoners who practised the Catholic religion in 1851, some 80,000 were of Irish descent (many of them, one may add, by now rather remotely), some 20,000 of English, or at least of non-Irish, I do not think we shall be exaggerating the native contribution. Here, as elsewhere, we have also a transformation of the English Catholic community to deal with.

At this point a problem calls for discussion which is relevant both to the statistical argument as so far conducted, and to a final factor in the process of transformation which we have yet to consider. It is sometimes supposed that religious practice, in the conventional sense of the word, was universal among Irish Catholics in the early nineteenth century, and continued to be so among those who emigrated to England—or would have so continued had adequate facilities been provided.[33] We have already seen that this was not quite how the position appeared to men who might have their prejudices but were all the same in the best position to observe: Vincent Glover, a Liverpool priest who had had eighteen years' experience of the problem when he gave his evidence in 1834, said that the 'good' and the 'bad' among the Irish in the city divided about 50–50, and suggested that this was something to do with the state of religious instruction at home, which he thought was good in the south of Ireland and execrable in the north. One of the priests in Birmingham remarked more roundly that half the immigrants were 'scum', who had come to escape trouble at home, and would not have anything to do with him. If we ignore their pejorative form, the observation that about half the immigrants effectively practised their religion when they came to England seems to be fairly generally borne out.[34]

32. Gilley, 'The Roman Catholic Mission to the Irish in London', p. 131; cf. Ward, *Sequel*, i, p. 177.
33. Thus Inglis, *Churches and the Working-Class*, pp. 121 f.
34. *Report on the Irish Poor*, Appendix, pp. 2, 22. Cf. Inglis, *op. cit.*, pp. 122 f.; Gilley, *art. cit.*, p. 131 (Griffiths); Jackson, *The Irish in Britain*, pp. 145 f. (Booth).

This degree of 'dropping off', as it had been known in the eighteenth century, or 'leakage', as it came to be termed, not very elegantly, in the nineteenth, has been variously interpreted, and how one interprets it is of some significance to a judgment about the transformation of Catholicism in England. On one view, popular in the mid-nineteenth century and recently supported by a study of the Irish Catholic community in London, it was primarily the fault of weaknesses of imagination and organisation on the part of the vicars-apostolic and the English Catholic clergy during the last decades of the missionary regime, as well as of exclusiveness on the part of English Catholic congregations.[35] There is certainly some truth in both these points. In regard to the first, we have already seen that the English clergy in London do not seem to have taken much notice of the Irish in their midst until the middle of the eighteenth century, and it would not be surprising to learn that some of Challoner's successors were less devoted than he was to making up for lost time. We shall be noticing in due course aspects of English congregational structure which bring some support to the second.[36] But on the whole I do not think that the English Catholic community of the early nineteenth century shirked its responsibilities in this matter, and although this is not the place to pursue the question at length it seems important to draw attention to some considerations which point in the opposite direction.

In the first place, there seems to be a degree of universality about the 50–50 division which transcends the particular explanation given. It appears to be fairly general among Catholic immigrants everywhere, irrespective of region or type of congregation. In Liverpool, for example, it seems to have applied as much to the purely immigrant congregation at St Patrick's, which had been built relatively promptly, and had an Irish priest and no paid sittings, as it did in the more mixed congregations elsewhere in the city. Across time, it seems to apply fairly universally throughout the whole period of substantial Irish immigration, and apparently does so at the present day.[37] It also seems to transcend differences of community and denomination: possibly, as I have suggested, the degree of 'dropping-off' among English Catholic

35. Gilley, *art. cit.*, pp. 124 f. *passim.*
36. Above, pp. 311 f; below, p. 353.
37. *Report on the Irish Poor*, Appendix, pp. 24 f. (St Patrick's); Owen Chadwick, *The Victorian Church*, ii (London, 1970), p. 402; Jackson, *The Irish in Britain*, p. 148.

migrants was somewhat less, but the signs are that it was not very significantly so; it was certainly as high, to say the least, among Englishmen of the Church of England who migrated from the country-side to towns and manufacturing districts.[38] One is inclined to deduce that this degree of detachment from religious observance has been a more or less universal incident of uprooting and migration in these con-ditions, and that it cannot primarily be understood within the context of any particular religious body.

It is often, on the other hand, assumed that the Irish had a peculiar intensity of attachment to the Catholic religion which, if reasonably provided for, would have ensured, by comparison with other com-munities, a far lower incidence of detachment in the circumstances of migration. The supposition may well be true in some respect, but does not necessarily support the argument constructed upon it. It should be remembered that we are here dealing, not with some general sense of self-identification as Catholic, but with a habit of participation in the complex of religious acts and observances which has, since the counter-Reformation, formed the backbone of Catholicism as a type of Christian life. Even—or perhaps particularly—in Ireland, the sense has not always implied the habit. Although the subject has not yet been fully clarified, it appears to be true that formal and regular religious practice was far from universal among Catholics in early nineteenth-century Ireland; how far, we have yet to learn, but we certainly cannot assume that 50% of religious observance among immigrants in England is to be com-pared with 100% at home.[39] The chief explanation for this will prob-ably not be that Irish Catholicism in this period was riddled with religious indifference; but that for a considerable proportion of Irish

---

38. Chadwick, *The Victorian Church*, i (1966), pp. 325 ff.; a specific example, from Liverpool, *ibid.*, ii, p. 229; for English Catholics, cf. note to Table IV, p. 423.

39. cf. Emmet Larkin, 'The Devotional Revolution in Ireland, 1850–1875', *American Historical Review*, lxxvii (1972), pp. 625–652, who argues that 'the great mass of the Irish people' did not become 'practising Catholics' until after 1850: see esp. pp. 625, 630, 635 f., 639, 651. I am greatly indebted to Dr David Miller, of the Carnegie-Mellon University, Pittsburgh, Pa., for letting me see his unpublished essay 'Catholic Religious Practice in Pre-Famine Ireland' (referred to by Larkin, p. 635), where a general figure of between 33 and 40% Mass-attendance, higher in English-speaking than in Irish-speaking areas, is suggested on the evidence of the Report of the Commissioners of Public Instruction, Ireland, 1834. It is difficult to compare Dr Miller's figures with my own (see notes to Table IV), but I would hazard a guess that a figure for religious practice in Ireland strictly comparable to my 50% would be somewhere about 70–75%.

Catholics their religion was still a folk-religion, barely touched by the counter-Reformation, short on formal instruction, and unfamiliar with the obligations of regular religious observance and sacramental practice.[40] When this factor has been fully weighed, the difference in attitude between Irish Catholics and English Protestants will probably appear less marked; and we may develop a measure of respect for the activity of the English Catholic clergy in their 'mission to the Irish', and come to consider a success of 50% as an achievement rather than a failure.

From this discussion of the crude demographic facts relevant to the expansion and transformation of the Catholic community in England between 1770 and 1850 two points may be remembered. First, that during this period Irish immigration was rarely responsible for the creation of town congregations, and accounts for their expansion to a degree which was subject to the widest regional variations, but taken as a whole does not appear to exceed about 70%. Second, that in discussing the expansion of these congregations one must try to maintain a balance between the simple facts of immigrant demography, which are not in themselves directly relevant to the issue, and the missionary efforts of a predominantly English clergy; when we have tried to weigh the impact of purely demographic factors it remains true that they would have had no effect had not the opportunities they offered been seized by a clergy with a missionary vocation strong enough to respond to them. This response was, it seems to me, forthcoming; it was indeed only one instance of a more general resolve to apply to industrial England the instincts of the missionary life.

Coinciding as it did with the abolition of legal restraints upon their activity, the industrial revolution was a blessing to the Catholic clergy. It helped to shake up the Catholic community to a degree which made a continuance of gentry rule impossible, and abolished the interior restraints on their action which had probably for a long time been more important than the exterior ones. It also created among those whose lives had been transformed an audience more genuinely prepared to listen to what they had to say than any which had existed in England since the foundation of the mission. 'In manufacturing districts,' wrote one of them, 'there is found a greater spirit of enquiry, and a greater free-

40. Cf. Gilley, 'The Roman Catholic Mission to the Irish in London' pp. 139 f.; George, *London Life in the Eighteenth Century*, pp. 129 f. (wakes).

dom of thought and expression, than in the less populous parts of the country, and consequently the pastor who avails himself of this opportunity is sure to find his zeal rewarded with many conversions, and an abundant harvest of souls.'[41] They were relatively few in number, and they were hampered for several years by the problem of extracting the college at Douai from revolutionary France and erecting its successors on English soil. But this translation, once made, gave a distinct fillip to the industrial mission, since two of the three sites on which new colleges now rose—Ushaw, near Durham, and Oscott, near Birmingham—were in or adjacent to industrial territory. All in all, the priests who emerged from the new establishments had for the first time a really free field in which to practise their vocation; they were not all equally enthusiastic, but many of them give the impression of having fallen upon industrial England like men who had not eaten a solid meal for a very long time. In Lancashire, in London, the claims of the Irish were shortly to monopolise, more or less, their attention on this front, and to obscure the enterprise for the historian. In the Midlands, where Irish immigration did not occur on a large scale during this period, we can see it in its purest form.

Francis Martyn was one of the first priests to be ordained at Oscott, and for twenty-four years he worked as a missioner in the Black Country. In 1807 he was sent to a recently settled mission in the village of Bloxwich, some five miles from Wolverhampton and two from Walsall. Since the mid-eighteenth century it had been visited once a month by a circulating priest from Wolverhampton, and in 1800 funds had been put to buying a house and shop in the village, where two French émigré priests had resided in turn until Martyn's arrival; they had used the shop as a chapel for a congregation of some fifty communicants. Martyn built a proper chapel, and in thirteen years of work had gathered a congregation of several hundred. Most of its members now came from Walsall; in 1821 Martyn hired an assembly room in the town and used it as a second chapel. In 1825 he replaced the assembly room with a 'beautiful Grecian chapel', and in 1829 the two chapels were split, Martyn moving house to Walsall, while a new priest came to take his place at Bloxwich; in 1834 they had 550 communicants between them. Relieved of Bloxwich, Martyn looked for new opportunities and found them in West Bromwich, a place 'scarcely acquainted with Catholicity'; by 1832, West Bromwich had a Catholic chapel and priest's

41. *Catholic Magazine*, v (1834), p. 310.

house, a congregation of some 300, 'rapidly increasing', and a resident priest in the person of the Hon. and Rev. George Ignatius Spencer, who in this properly down-to-earth environment 'entered upon his missionary career with alacrity and zeal'.

When Martyn was finally transferred to Wolverhampton in 1831, he left behind him three thriving congregations containing something more than a thousand Catholics, where a quarter of a century before there had been a small handful. From his experience we can see how, at this time and in regions of this kind, a small deposit of traditional Catholicism could, given vigorous attention, serve as a basis for expansion which at its own level was as impressive as that of a Lancashire town congregation. Traditional Catholicism provided the original nucleus. It also provided Martyn with an *entrée* at Walsall, in the person of Joseph Bagnall, probably a manufacturer of some kind and member of a Catholic family which had made its money in the Potteries: Bagnall helped to finance the 'Grecian chapel' and may well have had to do with some of the conversions. A mixed marriage and a tolerant Protestant husband gave Martyn his chance at West Bromwich. These opportunities would now be exploited, with a freedom impossible hitherto, in the service of an appeal to the public in general and a curious and disorientated working class in particular. Sunday evening lectures in the assembly rooms and courses of public instruction infallibly attracted a keen and regular audience; interest could be pursued to the point of conversion through the individual contacts and deathbed conversations which were the traditional stock-in-trade of the missioner in England. Such converts formed the bulk of the congregations which Martyn left behind him: seventy, for example, out of a hundred people confirmed at West Bromwich in 1833. The rest were probably children of Irishmen working in the iron foundries; there do not seem to have been many Irishmen in the other congregations.[42]

For a slightly later example of the same thing, we may go to Coventry, where the Benedictine William Ullathorne arrived as priest, after a spell among the Australian convicts, in 1841. The mission had its roots in the eighteenth century, but does not seem to have had much success until about 1800, when the Benedictines took it over; after this, according to Ullathorne, it had one hardworking priest who built up the congregation, another who let it run down, and by 1841 consisted of some hundreds of dissatisfied people. Ullathorne was only in Coventry for

42. *ibid.*, pp. 307 f., 310–313; *Report on the Irish Poor*, Appendix, p. 163.

about five years; after this he became a bishop, and later the first Roman Catholic Archbishop of Birmingham. He was not a specially imaginative or enterprising man, and his idea of what a missionary priest should do in these circumstances, beyond his sacramental functions, was no different from anyone else's: go his rounds, preach, give Sunday evening lectures and courses of instruction, and try to put up a decent chapel. He was however exceptionally successful: in 1851 the chapel returned a Mass attendance of 900, which implies a congregation of over 2,000; an afternoon—presumably Catechism or Sunday school —attendance of 300; and an evening attendance of 1,000, probably at some kind of lecture or instruction. Its morning attendance was 13% of the whole attendance in the town, and about one-third of the attendance of the Church of England; it had the largest individual attendance of any chapel. Ullathorne thought the rate of conversion was about 100 a year. He had two advantages that other missioners lacked. The first was the help of Margaret Hallahan, whom he brought to keep house for him, a London-born Irishwoman with a good deal of experience teaching in the school attached to the London mission of Somers Town. In Coventry she started a girls' school and made herself acquainted with the factory girls, who were Methodists; on Sunday evenings she held open house in the schoolroom, where people came to meet Ullathorne and he gave an instruction. Her influence no doubt accounts for the family atmosphere in the congregation which Ullathorne felt so nostalgic for later. His other gift was an uncomplicated, acute pleasure in finding himself with these 'simple and pious people who have gone through great temporal hardships' and were looking for a 'word to live upon', and in the response they gave to his efforts. Twenty years after he left, he came back to Coventry on a visitation and had a reunion with them which moved him deeply. 'They are an English people of converts,' he wrote, 'and yet they have the deep Irish faith together with the English quality of good works. It has been a feast to be among them.'[43] In these matters at least, and whether he quite appreciated the fact or not, Newman was Ullathorne's pupil and the continuator of a vigorous tradition; his own work and that of the community with whom he settled in 1849 in a disused gin-distillery in the heart of industrial Birmingham was not more and not less dedicated than that of others. His congregation at Alcester Street was formed by

43. C. Butler, *Life and Times of Bishop Ullathorne, 1806–89* (2 vols., London, 1820), i, pp. 117–134; *Parliamentary Papers*, 1852–1853, lxxxix, p. 77.

the same methods and from the same sort of people as Ullathorne's at Coventry; the chapel where he sat for hours in a bug-ridden confessional seems above all to have represented a source of help, warmth and meaning for factory girls who had lost contact with any other. From it, too, sprang a body of English converts whose entrance into the community may perhaps have meant more to it than that of Newman himself.[44]

Outside the Midlands this industrial mission was before long obliged to adapt itself as principally a mission to the Irish. Yet this was never entirely the case, and it is worth adding a final instance to help prove this point and others made in this chapter. It comes from County Durham. In 1830 two country missions stood along the Pennine fringes, one at Esh, some five miles from Durham near the new seminary at Ushaw, and another at Brooms, eight miles to the north-west, near what was to become the iron town of Consett; all this was then still wild and bleak upland country. Both missions had roots in the manors of the northern gentry, though these were by now a little remote: one belonged to the Smythe family, who had not lived there for nearly two centuries, and another had descended to Thomas Eyre, the first president of Ushaw and a man who put much of his considerable wealth behind the Catholic mission in the North-east. A family of minor gentry, called Smith, lived at Brooms. Shortly after 1800 Eyre had made an endowment for a priest to serve both missions; a chapel and priest's house had been built at Esh, and a chapel at Brooms, on land provided by the Smythes and the Smiths of Brooms respectively. The resident priest in 1830 was William Fletcher, who is described as an 'indefatigable missioner', and had need to be, since he served some 400 square miles of Pennine country, from all of which he drew a congregation of perhaps three hundred farming people. In December 1834 he started a Sunday school at Brooms, which functioned fortnightly, since he only came on alternate Sundays; at the same time, collieries, the railway and ironworks were beginning to transform this corner of his territory, while the rest remained untouched. To everyone's surprise, the school, and the Brooms congregation, began to grow: one Sunday in March 1836 John Smith of Brooms counted fifty-four children at communion, of whom 'a third at least . . . are of Protestant parents, yet voluntarily send and seem quite pleased that Mr Fletcher

44. Meriol Trevor, *Newman: the Pillar of the Cloud* (London, 1962), pp. 455 f., 504 f., 517, 583.

should teach their children'. The chapel became too small, and a gallery was added in the summer. In December, Smith wondered at the contrast between what was going on at Brooms and the immobility of the congregation at Esh. 'It is becoming so fashionable to attend the chapel that we are never without some of the neighbouring Protestants, with all of whom, so far as I can learn, Mr Fletcher is in high favour . . . He is just now attending two persons on their deathbeds, neither of whom, I think, have ever been in a Catholic chapel, yet they or their friends have sent for Mr Fletcher.'[45] This unanticipated success encouraged a new venture in a more southerly part of the region which had never been able to support a regular mission and was now in the throes of the same transformation. In 1842, the *Catholic Directory* carried an appeal for support for a new mission at Bishop Auckland:

> In consequence of the numerous coal mines opened in this neighbourhood, and the establishment of several public works, the influx of population has been very great, and many of the new residents are Catholics. These, with the Catholics who for years have been scattered among the villages of this mining district, amount to not less than 400 souls. They are all of the labouring class. There is no provision for the priest, except what may arise from the contributions of these poor people; but their great distance from any Catholic chapel, the frequency of accidents among the coal mines, and the spiritual destitution of an extensive tract of country around Bishop Auckland have induced [Bishop Mostyn] to attempt the establishment of this mission.[46]

Given this degree of activity, Catholicism was able to compete on not unfavourable terms, during the social upheavals of the first industrial age, for the interest of people whose inherited assumptions had been upset, who had often lost touch with the Church of England and who responded to anyone who proved, from whatever point of view, to be genuinely interested in their lives. Numerically speaking the effect of this industrial mission on English Protestants was no doubt small beer

45. 'H.H.', 'A description of the Catholic Missions in the County of Durham', *Catholic Magazine*, ii (1832), pp. 114, 117 f.; letters of John Smith of Brooms to Miss Taylor of Cannington, 11 March, 2c September, 16 December 1836 (Papers of the Smiths of Brooms, Ushaw College: extracts communicated to me by the kindness of Rev. W. Vincent Smith); for Thomas Eyre, see David Milburn, *A History of Ushaw College* (Ushaw College, Durham, 1964), pp. 37–114 *passim*.
46. *Catholic Directory* (1842), p. 38.

compared with its effect on Irish Catholics, but it is misleading to ignore it since it was responsible for a growth of the community, in parts of the country scarcely touched by Irish immigration, as impressive in its own way as what was going on in Lancashire or London.

To conclude. What English Catholicism underwent between 1770 and 1850 was a process, not a cataclysm; more exactly, it underwent several processes at once, working together towards the creation of a complicated whole, which historians should not be content to dismiss in a single formula. If we are looking for formulae, at least three seem equally legitimate, though they would refer to somewhat different periods. We may speak of an age of transformation of the English Catholic community, beginning about 1750; of an age of the Irish deluge, beginning about 1790; we are equally entitled to speak of a golden age of the English mission, lasting from perhaps 1800 to its formal closure in 1850.[47]

47. The reader may like to contrast my treatment of this subject with the admirable, though unfinished, paper of Raphael Samuel, 'The Catholic Church and the Irish Poor' (Past and Present Conference on Popular Religion, 1966, typescript), which deals mainly with the second half of the nineteenth century.

14

HIERARCHY RESTORED

IT is obvious that a transformation of the kind and scale indicated must have upset the balance of power in the community as it had stood in 1770; and it is easy to see, generally speaking, in what direction this balance was changed. In 1770 the community was still dominated by its secular aristocracy; in 1850 it was dominated by its clergy. The 'restoration of the hierarchy' of 1850 was an expression and a confirmation of this change; from one point of view it represented the accomplishment of the clerical programme of the sixteenth and seventeenth centuries, the close of a long and patient effort to undermine the constitution of lay supremacy which had emerged from the conflicts of the earlier period. But, simply because the England of 1770–1850 was not the England of 1570–1650, this process could not be simply a copy of the earlier process, in reverse. We have not only to enquire why, how and when the gentry lost supremacy and the clergy gained it: we have also to keep an eye open for developments specific to the age, for modifications of the traditional regime by which it might have mastered the transformation of the community, for the outlines of an alternative denouement. The issue is perhaps not purely an historical one. Now that the regime of 1850 has ceased to satisfy even those who have succeeded to its places of authority, the moment may have come to explore what other prospects offered at the time, even if it should turn out that, at the time, there was no feasible alternative.

A 'decline of the gentry', in the general sense of a loss of the pre-eminence in the community which it had held since at least 1650, did without question occur in the period we are now dealing with. There is so little question about it that it seems reasonable to take many aspects of it for granted, and confine oneself to making some necessary distinctions and drawing attention to some particular points. It should for example be understood that the power of the English Catholic aristocracy, like that of the English aristocracy in general, depended on a combination of demographic or biological, economic, social and—applying the term within the Catholic community—political constituents. These were not necessarily all weakening at the same time, and some of them became stronger during these decades; indeed the weakening of some aspects of their position is explained by a strengthening in others, and vice versa.

In the first place they were not, numerically speaking, declining towards extinction. Some gloomy comments made in 1780 by Joseph Berington, in his *State and Behaviour of English Catholics*, might be taken to indicate that this was so; but although Berington was no fool, and had some serious points to make, he also had an interest and found a kind of satisfaction in exaggerating their importance.[1] Of the 'twenty' causes which, he hazarded, would be found to be 'work[ing] their diminution', we may confine ourselves for the moment to the first two: conformity to the Church of England, and biological extinction of families. The years between 1715 and about 1760 were those in which the worldly prospects of a Catholic landowner were in many respects least promising, and conformity seems to have been more common than usual, particularly among the southern gentry. During these years the most important group of Catholic landowners in the south of England, whose territory lay in west Sussex and east Hampshire, disintegrated: the Lords Montagu of Cowdray, the most persistent Catholic magnates in Sussex, conformed in 1742; so did the important gentry families of Gage and Shelley. It is not easy to find parallels for this case elsewhere: according to Aveling there were half a dozen cases of conformity in the West Riding during the century, but nothing resembling a landslide.[2] The position may have been rather worse in the South than in the North, but I cannot detect anything more than a fairly steady drift of individual conversions, which slowed down as the century proceeded and had stopped by its close: in Lancashire, the Molyneux, later Earls of Sefton (1768), in Yorkshire Sir Thomas Gascoigne of Barnborough (1780), in Staffordshire Peter Gifford of Chillington (1786), in Northumberland Sir John Swinburne of Capheaton, also in 1786. Except the last, these were all landowners of considerable importance and influence, but they brought no families of lesser gentry with them, and indeed the

1. *State and Behaviour of English Catholics* (Birmingham, 1780), pp. 116, 93; pertinent comments by Eamon Duffy, 'Ecclesiastical Democracy Detected: i, 1779–87', *Recusant History*, x (1970), p. 199.
2. Burton, *Challoner*, ii, p. 171; Aveling, *West Riding*, p. 261.

first two of them went to some lengths to limit the effects of their conversion on the rest of the community.[3] In fact it seems clear that biological difficulties were thinning the ranks of the eighteenth-century Catholic gentry more effectively than changes of confession: Aveling's investigation of the West Riding has turned up sixteen heads of Catholic gentry families who failed to produce male heirs during the century, compared with six who conformed; such difficulties do not seem to have been confined to Catholics, but it is not necessary to be a professional demographer to notice, as one follows the fortunes of families, the effects of a 'lurking rigoristic strain' and of intermarriage within a narrowing group.[4] The Weld family may serve as an example. In the 1730s Edward Weld's wife sued him for divorce on the grounds of impotence, though after her death he married and had children. The eldest son, Edward, died childless after two marriages, at the age of forty-seven; Thomas, who succeeded him, said he did not find the idea of marriage attractive, though he had four wives and fifteen children. His eldest son, likewise Thomas, appears to have wanted to be a priest from the start, and finally became one, indeed a cardinal, after his wife's death. Nineteen years of marriage to Lucy Clifford had given him one fragile daughter who married her second cousin and died at thirty-two.[5] It may be inadvisable to attempt any exact figures, but there were probably about 400 Catholic heads of landowning families in 1700, and about 200 in 1770.[6] After this the number does not seem to have changed much until the close of our period; it probably increased a little, owing to a reversal in the flow of conversions, after about 1830.

There is another lesson to be drawn from the case of the Welds; for while the family was certainly going through a difficult time, bio-

3. F. O. Blundell, *Old Catholic Lancashire* (3 vols., London, 1925–1941), i, pp. 68 ff.; Aveling, *West Riding*, pp. 260, 262; Rowlands, 'Staffordshire', p. 175; B. Charlton, *Recollections of a Northumbrian Lady* (London, 1949), pp. 194 f., 124.
4. Aveling, *West Riding*, p. 261; *Northern Catholics*, pp. 396 f.; *East Riding*, p. 50.
5. Oliver, *Collections illustrating the history of the Catholic Religion* (see above, chap. 5, n. 51), p. 46; A.A.W. Main series, xxxviii, nos. 166 f.; S. Leslie, *Mrs Fitzherbert* (London, 1939), pp. 7 f.; Leys, *Catholics in England*, p. 189; J. Kirk, *Biographies of English Catholics in the Eighteenth Century* (eds. J. H. Pollen and E. Burton, London, 1909), p. 246; *D.N.B.*, Thomas Weld.
6. For 1700: A.A.W. Main series, xxxviii, no. 2—list of some 260 Catholic gentry maintaining priests; cf. Magee, *English Recusants*, p. 186—814 Catholics of gentry rank and above in 1715, which together suggest the figure given in the text. For 1770: Berington, *State and Behaviour*, p. 120; probably based on Catholic peers and gentry who signed the petition for relief in 1778, given as 207 in Burton, *Challoner*, ii, p. 196.

logically speaking, it was also getting richer and richer. In this it was only a particularly striking example of what was true of the Catholic gentry as a whole. During the earlier decades of the 18th century they had suffered from additional taxation at a time when the burden of taxes was a problem for small landowners in general; but except for a special levy in the 1720s, this had never presented a very formidable problem, and after the middle of the century it scarcely mattered. In 1780 Berington complained that rising standards of conspicuous consumption were wreaking havoc with the incomes of men who did not have the opportunities which enabled their Protestant neighbours to support them. The standards of the Catholic gentry were certainly rising, and instances may be found of difficulty or failure for these reasons among smaller landowners in the north; but there is no real evidence of a general problem.[7] On the contrary, everything indicates that after 1750 they were, as a whole, well able to support the rising expectations of the time, and continued to do well for a century or more. Here they were in the first place simply the beneficiaries of a general wave of landowning prosperity in England: he was a poor landowner who could not make a good living during this booming period, and at least before 1800 it seems likely that a shortage of other occupations tended to keep the mind of the Catholic gentleman profitably fixed upon his estate. Though unfortunately they cease to be useful after about 1780, the land tax returns of the preceding period show a healthy upward trend in incomes, with a doubling of receipts over the previous twenty or thirty years nothing very unusual. At the end of the century well-endowed families like the Welds and the Arundells were doing very nicely, as one may judge from a spate of large-scale building on their part; the Jerninghams' letters are full of references to wealth among members of 'the Body'.[8] Besides, the reduction in numbers of the Catholic gentry, in so far as it was due to problems of reproduction, went to increase the

7. Aveling, *West Riding*, pp. 259–261; Rowlands, 'Staffordshire', pp. 117–130, 146–153 and 'The Iron Age of Double Taxes', *Staffs. Catholic History*, no. 3 (1963), pp. 30–46; Berington, *State and Behaviour*, pp. 116 f., 122, and similar comments by Vicar of Woolhampton, Berks., in Leys, *Catholics in England*, p. 200; a case of difficulty in the North in Bossy, 'Four Catholic Congregations', *Recusant History*, ix (1967), pp. 93 f., 107 f. (Claverings of Callaly), but such cases do not seem to support the pessimistic general description of Edward Hughes, *North-country Life in the Eighteenth Century: the North-East, 1700–1750* (Oxford, 1952), pp. xvi f.
8. Rowlands, 'Staffordshire', pp. 165 f.; Aveling, *East Riding*, p. 52; Williams, *Wiltshire*, pp. 187 f.; Mathew, *Catholicism in England*, p. 142; *Jerningham Letters*, i, pp. 38, 43, 218.

wealth of those who survived: as families died out, or ended in heiresses, estates amalgamated. The Welds had acquired five separate estates in this way by the close of the eighteenth century. The Stourtons, who in 1700 possessed a poverty-stricken peerage and a small estate in Wiltshire, progressed to affluence through marriages which gave them the Walmesley estate in Lancashire, and those of the last Lord Langdale (died 1777) in Yorkshire and Staffordshire. Sir Clifford Constable, who died in 1823, was the grandson of a fourth son of the 3rd Lord Clifford of Chudleigh who had picked up Tixall in Staffordshire from one of two heiresses of the last Lord Aston of Tixall, a Chichester estate in Devon and the large property of the Constables of Burton Constable in Yorkshire. 'Nothing,' as Aveling remarks of the Everingham branch of the Constables, to whom much the same occurred, 'could prevent them emerging with vigour, their position in the county unimpaired, into the Victorian Age.'9 In a time of unprecedented agricultural prosperity, habits of intermarriage were a recipe for affluence; the tide did not begin to turn until after 1870.

In so far as the position of the landed aristocracy in the Catholic community depended on their capacity to contribute to its institutions and enterprises, it was in the early nineteenth century stronger than it had ever been, and they did contribute according to their means. Yet—to take a striking example—the munificence of the 16th Earl of Shrewsbury in launching his own church-building operations and assisting those of others, indeed in rescuing the Midland district from bankruptcy, did not secure him a real voice in the reconstruction of the community which occurred in 1850.10 Wealth, and a tradition of active concern with its affairs, seemed to go for nothing when real decisions were come to: what had happened was that wealth had become detached from social influence.

The exodus of rural Catholics, the growth from this and other sources of the town and industrial congregations, were movements which were likely of themselves to dislodge the landowning gentry from their predominance in the community; and bound to do so in so far as these congregations were formed of Irish immigrants or of converts who had

9. Ward, *Dawn*, i, p. 235 (Welds); Williams, *Wiltshire*, pp. 207 f. and Kirk, *Biographies*, pp. 147, 182 (Stourtons); *ibid.*, pp. 46–56 and *Jerningham Letters*, i, p. 38 (Clifford); Aveling, *East Riding*, p. 52.
10. cf. E. S. Purcell and E. de Lisle, *Life and Letters of Ambrose Phillipps de Lisle* (2 vols., London, 1900), i, pp. 321–327.

no personal or family background in the traditional community. This goes almost without saying. But even a numerically much inferior rural Catholicism would probably have been able to support the Catholic gentry in a more impressive rearguard than it proved capable of conducting, had they not also failed to maintain an effective ascendancy in this sector of the community. By 1770, as we have seen, the rise of an independent farming interest, and the spread of non-agricultural occupations among rural Catholics, had made possible the emergence of a network of rural missions independent of gentry influence, and given the clergy a new confidence in their dealings with the gentry. The seigneurial congregation, though it too had in some respects an Indian summer in the last decades of the eighteenth century, was no longer the model of the rural Catholic community; and it was suffering, and bound increasingly to suffer, from changes of habit and attitude among the gentry themselves. In 1780, despite his qualms about the inroads of fashionable life, Berington could still point with reasonable confidence to a hard, if diminishing, core among them who were still country-dwellers, spending the income from their estates in the neighbourhood, 'their doors . . . encompassed with the blessings of their neighbours'.[11] Fifty years later an observer equally typical of her own time could present for general recognition the picture of a Catholic gentleman returning home incognito after decades of absence and neglect. An old coachman sits by the door of the closed chapel, explaining that the last priest died fifteen years ago, and no creature has entered it since but the rats and the birds. The Catholics of the estate have fallen off, children have grown up without instruction, and married Protestants, and *their* children have no religion and may not even be baptised. There is a chapel five miles off, but it is too far for those who have to walk, and for children, and there is no warmth or food when you get there: not like the days of old Sir William, the visitor's father, who gave breakfast to everyone who came to Mass, and left a name for charity and virtue in the neighbourhood.[12] In the manner of her generation, the unidentified 'Female' was laying it on with a trowel; but the general drift of her remarks was reasonably accurate. Since about 1750 it had become true that a family of Catholic gentry was more likely to be found living off its estates than on them. This was partly a direct consequence of the

11. *State and Behaviour*, p. 122.
12. Extract from 'Alton Park; or, Conversations on Religious and Moral Subjects', by 'A Female', in *Catholic Magazine*, i (1831–1832), pp. 118–122.

accumulation of estates in the hands of a single family: in Staffordshire, for this reason, there were several substantial estates owned by Catholics but practically no resident Catholic landlords at the end of the eighteenth century. It was also the effect of the drift away from country living which Berington and others had deplored. Gravitating in the first instance to provincial centres like York or Durham, they moved through seasons at Bath and similar resorts, towards the acquisition of town houses and settlement for much of the year in London. After 1815 a number of them took to living on the Continent, and the more aristocratic began to intermarry with the aristocracies of Catholic Europe. One may partly judge the extent of the shift from the relative ease with which it became possible to accommodate in English country houses the numerous bodies of English religious, male and female, expelled from their continental settlements in the aftermath of the French revolution.[13]

It is true that after 1830 there was a movement of reaction, inspired by the Gothic revival; but all things considered this was chiefly mediaeval play-acting, and far from reversing the decline of seigneurial Catholicism, showed how inescapable the process was.[14] It was arguable of the Catholic members of the English aristocracy, as of the class as a whole, that they were 'tending more and more to a separation of themselves from those whom nature, providence and law have placed beneath them', and that they had lost the key to 'those means of communication that in former days knit all orders of the people together'.[15] This was written in 1820: a date by which the social influence of the gentry had, as has been convincingly suggested, ceased to be of real significance in the composition and activity of the Catholic community at large.[16] Against this background, the politics of the community during the decades around 1800 deserve a short discussion.

13. Rowlands, 'Staffordshire', pp. 173 f. Examples of the trend towards living abroad in Kirk, *Biographies*, p. 56 (Sir Clifford Constable); W. Ward, *Life and Times of Cardinal Wiseman* (2 vols., London, 1897), i, pp. 69, 73 (Arundells); Purcell and de Lisle, *Life and Letters of Ambrose Phillips de Lisle*, i, pp. 64, 80 (Earl of Shrewsbury); and at a lower level, 'Frideswide, O.S.B.' [M. W. F. Stapleton], *Reminiscences: the life story of a Victorian Catholic Family* (East Bergholt, 1938), p. 129; Barbara Charlton, *Recollections*, pp. 163 f., 184.

14. The classic example is in Purcell and de Lisle, *Life and Letters of Ambrose Phillips de Lisle*, i, pp. 103–114; some general comments in Mathew, *Catholicism in England*, p. 219.

15. Quoted in Harold Perkin, *The Origins of Modern English Society* (London, 1969), p. 183.

16. Bernard Ward, *The Eve of Catholic Emancipation* (3 vols., London, 1911–1912), ii, p. 155.

During the half-century between 1778 and 1829, when the structure of anti-Catholic legislation in Great Britain was being dismantled, there came into existence a series of bodies intended to represent the interests of English Catholics in the consequent negotiations. A glance at their changing composition and policy will confirm what has been suggested about the changing balance of power in the community as a whole. The first Catholic Committee[17] was set up in 1778 and organised a petition for relief, on the basis of which an act was passed giving Catholics access to the armed forces and abolishing some of the penal legislation against priests. The Committee itself, and those who petitioned, were exclusively from the aristocracy and gentry, and the clergy were intentionally not consulted, 'the English Roman Catholic gentlemen being quite able to judge and act for themselves in [temporal matters]';[18] only as an afterthought was Challoner invited to comment on the oath of loyalty embodied in the act. The second Committee, set up in 1782 after an interval during which the Gordon Riots had done something to justify Challoner's fears about legislation, was also entirely composed and representative of the aristocracy and upper gentry, and predominantly of those whose interests lay in the South and Midlands; its weightiest member was an anti-clerical magnate, Lord Petre. In 1787, when the way was becoming clear for a more comprehensive relief act, something was done to widen the basis of the Committee, and three clerical members were elected: James Talbot, vicar-apostolic of the London district since Challoner's death in 1781, Charles Berington, brother of Joseph and coadjutor in the Midland district, and Joseph Wilkes, the Benedictine priest of the chapel at Bath. But the concession was more apparent than real, since all three were as much representative of the aristocracy and gentry as of the clergy, Talbot and Berington because of their family position, and Wilkes because he shared the views of his aristocratic congregation; besides, it was hardly pure geographical convenience which ensured that all three of them came

17. The history of the Catholic Committees is narrated in Burton, *Challoner*, ii, pp. 181–212, and Ward, *Dawn of the Catholic Revival*, i, pp. 87–185, 240–296, 339 f.; to which should now be added the valuable commentary in Eamon Duffy, 'Ecclesiastical Democracy Detected: i, 1779–87; ii, 1787–96', *Recusant History*, x (1970), pp. 193–209, 309–331. Dr Duffy's thesis, 'Joseph Berington and the English Cisalpine Movement, 1772–1803' (Cambridge Ph.D., 1973), is excellent on the ideological side of the problem and adds considerably to Ward's narrative for the period with which it deals.

18. Burton, *Challoner*, ii, p. 190.

from the South and Midlands. There was thus plenty of room for the emergence of an opposition in which regional, class and clerical elements would unite; its first spokesman was a northern landowner, Sir William Lawson of Brough, but it soon coalesced under the clerical leadership provided by the northern and western vicars-apostolic, William Gibson and Charles Walmesley, and found an untiring and intransigent voice in John Milner, at this time a young priest in charge of the chapel at Winchester.

Two mutually antagonistic parties thus confronted one another when Pitt's government finally launched the relief bill in 1791, which was in effect to bring full religious toleration for English Catholics. As introduced, the bill reflected the views of the Committee, with some of whose members the government was in close relations, notably in requiring those who were to benefit from it to take a long oath which among other things included a condemned passage from James I's oath of allegiance of 1606 and a declaration against papal infallibility; it also failed to give any legal protection to ecclesiastical endowments. It soon emerged that these views were not shared by a majority of the community, and the bishops—united, with one rather feeble exception, in opposition to the Committee—were now confident enough to take direct political action themselves.[19] A well-judged appeal for episcopal solidarity to their Anglican counterparts in the House of Lords secured amendments to the bill which gave the bishops most of what they wanted and made the Committee, which had assured everybody that only its own scheme could possibly get through Parliament, look silly and evasive. Altogether the Catholic gentry and aristocracy had suffered a defeat on what they might have regarded as their own ground, and although it would be premature to suppose that this marked the end of their predominance in the community, it was obvious that they could no longer successfully claim to determine its relations with the outside world.

On the passage of the Act the Committee dissolved, and nothing replaced it for sixteen years: for most English Catholics the degree of toleration now achieved was perfectly sufficient, and they were not represented in the abortive attempts at further legislation which followed the Irish Act of Union of 1801. Finally, under Whig auspices, a new Board of British Catholics[20] was formed in 1808, with the purpose of

19. cf. Duffy, *art. cit.*, p. 316, on the emergence of 'militant episcopacy'.
20. For the history of the Board, which is less well-known than that of the Committee, see Ward, *Eve of Catholic Emancipation*, i, pp. 99–157, ii and iii *passim*.

agitating for political rights and of formulating the concessions which might make the enactment of them acceptable to Protestant opinion. What is immediately relevant is the changes in its composition which indicate what had been going on in the community since the dissolution of the Committee. It was the organ of an Association, membership of which was open to all who paid a moderate subscription; its board was elective, and consisted of the four vicars-apostolic—not apparently *ex officio*—and eight lay members. Its president was Lord Stourton, a peaceable man much under the influence of John Lingard, and at least one of its members, the intelligent and liberal George Silvertop, could be regarded as a representative of the general state of lay opinion in the North. In the fact that the gentry still predominated in it, while the bishops participated and had something resembling a veto on decisions, the Board fairly represented the balance of power within the community at the time it was instituted; in the fact that divisive issues were dealt with in a spirit of compromise and negotiation, it successfully embodied a state of mind then widely prevailing within it. Milner, who had been a bishop since 1803, campaigned against it as a replica of the old Committee, but though it had its shortcomings it was certainly not that. It was hardly its fault that the balance on which it depended turned out to be a precarious one, or that events had made it superfluous before its object was achieved in the Act of 1829.

In the internal affairs of the community one theme dominated the history of the Committees and the Board: whether laymen—meaning in effect the aristocracy and gentry—were entitled to a voice in the appointment of bishops, and if so how that voice was to make itself heard. Claims of this nature, which were governed by the need felt, in an age of statutory freedom, to find a more formal expression for the informal controls which had operated in the past,[21] were doomed to failure by the internal evolution of the community; but, if only as an index of that evolution, it is worth noticing how, between the 1780s and the 1820s, they were progressively reduced and finally abandoned altogether. The Committee, which strikes one as rather insensitive to the history of the question, saw its enemy in Rome rather than in clericalism as such. It wished to turn the vicars-apostolic into bishops-in-ordinary, who were to be elected by a panel composed of diocesan clergy and laymen and would perhaps have been subject to its supervision thereafter. This was the proposal which drew from the opposi-

21. cf. Duffy, *art. cit.*, p. 197.

tion the *Ladies' Address* to the Committee requesting, if the scheme were adopted, votes for women, in the hope that bishops so elected would issue more practical regulations about fasting and abstinence.[22] Something like it was tried when both the London and the Northern districts fell vacant during 1790, but Rome and the North united to ensure that the attempt was a fiasco, and the following year the rout of the Committee was completed by its defeat over the terms of the Relief Act.

By the time the Catholic Board was constituted in 1808 the Revolution in France and the Irish Act of Union had altered the terms of the controversy. The gentry, as far as the Board represented them, no longer questioned the missionary regime or the right of Rome to appoint the vicars-apostolic; in so far as they hoped to exercise any influence at all, they looked for no more than a negative voice: a voice, moreover, which was to be listened to not for its own sake but because it spoke for the Crown.[23] The controversies which arose out of attempts to complete the process inaugurated by the Act of Union were more relevant to Ireland than to England; but if some of the schemes had been enacted which proposed to grant civil equality to Catholics in return for a royal veto on episcopal appointments they would have had a considerable effect upon the balance of power within the English Catholic community. As amended by Canning, Grattan's bill of 1813 would have vested the veto in a royal commission consisting of Catholic peers and gentry, a position not unlike that claimed by the Catholic Committee in 1790. The Catholic Board proved in general favourable to the idea of a Commission, and subsequent discussion revolved mainly around the composition of its members. William Poynter, vicar-apostolic of the London district and chief representative of the clergy in the Board's deliberations, objected to lay influence in theory but was prepared to negotiate about it in practice. In 1813 he took the view that a Commission composed of an equal number of laymen and bishops would be acceptable, and was prepared to 'submit to', though not to 'concur in', something less. This submission proved unnecessary, since the bill was withdrawn, and further lobbying ensured that the next proposal, Plunkett's bill of 1823, was for a Commission of which

22. Ward, *Dawn*, i, p. 229.
23. It is notable that as early as 1794 Lord Petre was trying to recruit the influence of the Crown to maintain aristocratic influence in episcopal appointments: Duffy, *art. cit.*, p. 325.

bishops formed a majority; here the position remained until Peel withdrew the final veto scheme in 1829, and left the appointment of Catholic bishops to Rome.[24]

The figure who dominated the later stages of this phase of community politics was John Milner, and he is worth attention here because he rose to prominence in the community as an unqualified opponent of aristocratic predominance within it, and may fairly be regarded as a prophet of its later social constitution.[25] His life—he was born in 1752 and died in 1826—coincided with the Indian summer and final decay of the Catholic gentry as a governing power. He was a fairly typical product of the eighteenth-century clerical revival: the son of a London tailor who had migrated from Lancashire, he had been sent to Douai on a scholarship by Challoner, and after his ordination worked in London as one of Challoner's own missioners before being sent by him to Winchester, where he remained as priest from 1779 to 1803. His position as the foremost defender of hierarchical claims in the government of the community was established between 1787 and 1793, when he emerged as a dangerous opponent of the Catholic Committee and its ideas of an elective episcopate: from this period date his two hierarchicalist manifestos, *The Divine Right of Episcopacy* and *Ecclesiastical Democracy Detected*, his important part in the movement which obtained the modification of the 1791 relief bill, and his construction at Winchester of the first Catholic chapel (St Peter's) built in the Gothic style, which was a manifesto in itself.[26] Hard feelings prevented his promotion for some time, but in 1803 he became Midland vicar-apostolic, and remained in this position for twenty-three years, living in Wolverhampton, with expeditions to London, to Rome and to Ireland. As bishop in his district, he seems to have been energetic and successful, and also prepared to temper his high clerical principles where these might interfere with congregational concord or missionary

24. Ward, *Eve*, ii, pp. 32–40; iii, pp. 62–65.

25. F. C. Husenbeth's *Life of the Right Rev. John Milner, D.D.* (Dublin, 1862) is an informative though hagiographical biography which should be read in conjunction with Ward's temperate commentary in *Dawn*, i, pp. 47–49, 94, 228, 257, 309, and *Eve, passim*. Joan M. Connell, 'The Roman Catholic Church in England, 1553–1850' (Chicago Ph.D. thesis, 1969), is rather slight, but provides material (chaps iv and v) for an unflattering view of Milner. None of these writers takes much notice of Milner's work as a bishop, and a proper study of this would probably enable his career to be seen in a better perspective.

26. B. Little, *Catholic Churches since 1623* (London, 1966), pp. 49 f.; illustrations, p. 41.

expansion; in the politics of the community at large his conduct was more questionable, though whether it was less successful may be a matter of opinion. On the negative side he was as invincibly hostile to the Catholic Board as he had been to the Catholic Committee; his opposition rested partly on the formal grounds that such organs of lay initiative were contrary to the divinely-instituted hierarchy of the Church and to what he called 'Catholic Principles', and partly on the practical grounds that they perpetuated the tradition of aristocratic leadership in the community. He regarded Poynter and the rest of the vicars-apostolic, who were prepared to negotiate with and through it, as men willing to betray their order in exchange for aristocratic patronage and financial support.[27] He also thought them willing to surrender essential items of Catholic doctrine and discipline in order to make it easier for the Whig magnates to sponsor proposals for Catholic emancipation which would bring no benefit to anybody except the Catholic gentry. On the positive side he claimed to stand for all those members of the community who were not either gentry themselves or subject to aristocratic influence: a proportion he estimated variously at 99·9% or more conservatively at 80% of the whole.[28]

If one allows for exaggeration, this was in broad outline a not unimpressive interpretation; if it was correct, one might well be entitled to speak of Milner as the father of the modern English Catholic community. In some respects Milner certainly did stand for elements in the community which were hostile to aristocratic tradition. This was notably true of the Irish element. As we have seen, Irish Catholic immigrants had been accumulating in England in considerable numbers since about 1790: it seems likely that Milner had inherited from Challoner a sense of their potential significance for the future of the community; and he was certainly the first vicar-apostolic to see that the community's politics could no longer be conducted on the assumption that they did not exist. Soon after his appointment he became agent in

---

27. It was in fact true that at least two of the vicars-apostolic of the period were largely dependent on subscriptions raised from the gentry and aristocracy: for Douglass, Ward, *Eve*, i, 173 ff., and cf. the remarks of Thomas Penswick on his over-familiarity with the gentry in David Milburn, *History of Ushaw College* (Ushaw College, Durham, 1964), p. 38; for Collingridge, J. B. Dockery, *Collingridge* (Newport, Mon., n.d. [?1954]), pp. 90 f. Douglass's dealings with Berington and Milner receive a sympathetic and convincing treatment in Duffy, 'Joseph Berington', pp. 255 ff., 269, 287–290.

28. Ward, *Eve*, ii, pp. 53, 182.

England for the Irish Catholic hierarchy, and after some delay came to see that a campaign for an unconditional grant of political rights, without any of the concessions which the Catholic Board was anxious to negotiate and the other vicars-apostolic prepared to admit, would be extremely popular among Catholics resident in England but of Irish birth or blood. Thus his petition for unqualified emancipation, circulated in 1819–1820 in opposition to one sponsored by the Catholic Board, was widely supported in Manchester, Liverpool, Bristol and London, where there was a growing immigrant population, and in some cases provoked a schism between the clergy and a majority of their congregations.[29] Apart from acquiring the Irish vote Milner was able to reach a certain amount of popular support by agitating for the restoration of the Jesuits in England, against the opinion of his episcopal colleagues and the instincts of the Catholic Board; he was evidently, for this reason, a good deal more attractive to the Wigan congregation than their own bishop, Gibson.[30] Finally his own record as bishop was good enough to ensure that he was supported in his own Midland district.

There is however some distance between admitting that Milner was often, outside the ranks of established authority, a popular figure in the community, and accepting his claims to represent the whole body with the exception of the gentry and their dependants. After 1803 I should have thought it most improbable that he had as much as half the community on his side: though it is of course highly significant of what was going on within it that even a substantial minority of its members should have been attracted to so intransigently anti-aristocratic a programme. I should also be extremely doubtful of the view, which has gained support among historians, that Milner was a spokesman, against the traditional governors of the community, for a growing Catholic middle class. In so far as this body existed, its congregational instincts, which we shall be exploring shortly, were alien to him, and while he supported them in particular cases he seems to have done so for tactical reasons which are hard to reconcile with his extreme hierarchical principles. On political questions men of this kind seem to have supported him half-heartedly in his own district, and to have taken the opposite

---

29. *ibid.*, p. 234; Husenbeth, *Milner*, pp. 356 f.; Dockery, *Collingridge*, p. 156. For details of the dispute in Manchester, see *Orthodox Journal*, vii (1819), pp. 113, 163 f., 184 f., 217 f., 249 f.

30. See below, p. 346; also Connell, 'Roman Catholic Church in England' (see above, n. 25), p. 183.

side in Lancashire, where they were most numerous, and elsewhere.[31] The alternative to the traditional regime which Milner had in mind was patently not bourgeois but clerical and—for all his attacks on 'democracy', ecclesiastical and civil—demogogic in character. Hence his attraction to what he understood of Irish Catholicism, and the ambition, which governed the last twenty years of his activity, to remodel the English Catholic community on Irish lines. Whether this was a practicable project may be a matter of opinion: it was certainly a little premature. What is perhaps most interesting about Milner's activity is that, though it was primarily directed against the influence of the gentry, effective opposition to it came increasingly, not from them, but from the other vicars-apostolic; and their differences with him lay in matters of personality, tone, timing and procedure rather than in matters of substance. By the time Milner died in 1826 it was already obvious that the Catholic gentry and aristocracy were no longer going to present any genuine obstacle to the exercise and extension of Roman and episcopal jurisdiction.

What was not quite so obvious was whether the only alternative to aristocratic supremacy was clerical supremacy. The transformation of the community had entailed one further consequence than has so far been discussed; despite frequent assertions to the contrary, there emerged within it, during the eighteenth and early nineteenth century, something which one may term a third estate: the rise of a farming interest, which has already been discussed, had been followed at a slightly later date by the rise of a business interest in the towns.[32] Its importance, relative to other denominations, is not easy to determine; at a guess, I should think it was a good deal less important than among most branches of Old Dissent, but relatively speaking a good deal more important than in the Church of England. Its affinities certainly lay with the first of these bodies rather than with the second.

The alternative to clerical government which was offered by the emergence of this sector of the community may be described as a type of congregationalism: its viability depended on the existence of constitutional forms at the congregational level. These, as we shall see,

31. Mathew, *Catholicism in England*, pp. 155 f.; Ward, *Eve*, iii, pp. 63 f.; *Orthodox Journal*, vi (1819), pp. 154 f.
32. Above, p. 113; besides the evidence in local studies like Aveling, *East Riding*, pp. 56 f. and Rowlands, 'Staffordshire', pp. 178 ff., see the comments about Lancashire, dating from the 1790s, in Milburn, *History of Ushaw College*, pp. 50, 68.

came into operation during this period on a scale which may be found surprising to anyone acquainted only with later or earlier phases of the community's history. It proved, indeed, impossible to maintain them against clerical attack, and with them the prospects of an alternative to clerical absolutism disappeared. In the circumstances, and particularly in the circumstances of Irish immigration, this failure was practically inevitable, but it does not follow that the subject is of marginal interest. The rise and fall of congregational and allied institutions were events as important in the history of the community as any which have so far been discussed in this book, and I propose to deal with them in some detail.[33]

As town chapels began to be built during the latter half of the eighteenth century, a system emerged which was not uniform, but had certain common characteristics. The clergy were maintained by a regular congregational subscription which entitled those who paid it to a sitting or bench in the chapel. The administration of these arrangements might be in the hands of the clergy alone, or of a group of trustees or committee representative of the congregation, or of a body representing both. Where such bodies undertook the building or rebuilding of a chapel, the money was usually also raised by subscription, and the body might continue to manage the temporal affairs of the chapel after it was built.[34] Lancashire was the original home of the system, and we can see how it functioned in several of the Lancashire towns. The Jesuit priests who had worked in Liverpool since the early eighteenth century had been maintained, except for a small endowment from the district funds, by a congregational subscription, payable monthly according to income. When the mission acquired a chapel these arrangements were adapted accordingly, and in 1758, probably in connection with a rebuilding of the chapel which had been burned down in a riot, a set of formal regulations was agreed between the congregation and the local Jesuit superior, John Mansell. They provided that the bench-holders—there seem to have been about a hundred of them—should elect five trustees, and that these should assess and collect the bench-rents, pay the priest or priests, and generally take over the financial side of the mission. The trustees were to be men of property, to serve for three years under an

---

33. For interesting comparisons with the situation in the United States, see J. T. Ellis, *American Catholicism* (Chicago, 1956), pp. 44–46, 183.
34. See *Catholic Magazine*, iii (1833), pp. 5 f., for an illuminating general discussion of the subject.

annual president, to meet once a quarter, and to act by majority vote; there seems to have been a lower limit on the size of subscription which would entitle a bench-holder to a voice in choosing them.[35] This was a more detailed, as well as a more strictly 'congregationalist' constitution than seems to have existed in the chapels of neighbouring towns; all of them had some arrangement of this kind, though at Wigan and Preston, which were also Jesuit missions, evidence about their composition and operation does not seem to exist before the chapel-building operations of 1785 and 1793 respectively. Both had bodies of trustees, which at Wigan consisted of the two priests and three lay members of the congregation, at Preston simply of three laymen. At Preston the arrangements were least like those at Liverpool, in that the chapel remained the property of the Jesuit district, and the trustees were trustees for it, not for the congregation; whoever actually collected the bench-rents, the financial control of the chapel remained in the hands of the priests, and the renting of a bench implied no property right in the chapel. After 1800 there was some agitation for a more 'congregational' system, but it does not seem to have been successful.[36] The position at Wigan was nearer to what it was at Liverpool: the trustees, though they included the priests, represented the congregation, and resorted to general meetings when important decisions had to be taken. The meetings were not however meetings of bench-holders, and seem to have been called for practical reasons rather than because of any legal obligation.[37] This was probably much the same position as at Lancaster, the only secular-clergy mission of the four, after the construction of the chapel in Dalton Square in 1797; at that time the congregation elected four trustees, including the priest, and arrangements for the future were that the priest for the time being was always to be

---

35. Thomas Burke, *Catholic History of Liverpool* (Liverpool, 1900), pp. 9 f.; R. J. Stonor, *Liverpool's Hidden Story* (Wigan, 1957), p. 34; Raymond Hormasa *alias* Harris, *An Appeal to the Public: or, a candid narrative of the Rise and Progress of the differences now subsisting in the Roman Catholic Congregation of Liverpool* (Liverpool, 1783), pp. 144–149.

36. Archives of the English Province of the Society of Jesus—College of St Aloysius: Preston (volumes and pages not numbered): Statement of John Dalton, William Talbot and John Blundell, trustees, 5 May 1794, and *passim*.

37. *loc. cit.* above, n. 36: Wigan—especially notice of meeting called by trustees, 21 April 1814, and resolution passed at meeting, 11 November 1817, with list of signatories; lists of bench-holders and -rents in 1785, in F. O. Blundell, *Old Catholic Lancashire* (3 vols., London, 1925–1941). ii, pp. 73–75, and in 1819 in Lancashire C.R.O. RCWJ 1/4.

one of them, and that when one of the lay trustees died the others would co-opt another layman from the congregation.[38]

Few other parts of the country had town congregations as populous, as wealthy and as well established as those of Lancashire, and congregational institutions rarely reached this degree of elaboration elsewhere. In London, where Challoner had seen to it that most chapels were controlled by the clergy, there were two exceptions. In 1787 the former Bavarian embassy chapel in Warwick Street, which was to be for some decades the centre of aristocratic Catholicism in the metropolis, was taken over by a committee of trustees consisting of Lord Petre, Sir John Throckmorton, the Earl of Shrewsbury and his brother James Talbot, the London vicar-apostolic. The committee was to undertake the entire temporal management of the chapel, including the payment of the priests; all 'spiritual regulations' remained the province of the bishop, who was to appoint the clergy while taking account of the Committee's recommendations.[39] The other exception was St Patrick's, Soho, founded in 1793 by a group of businessmen of Irish extraction and 'run until 1813 by a lay committee which hired the priests and defied diocesan efforts to cast them down'.[40] More typical was the case of Moorfields chapel, whose financial arrangements one can discover from the diary of one of its attenders, William Mawhood. The subscription, which in Mawhood's case amounted to 2 gns. a year, was paid direct to the priest, and there was no lay committee or trustees; on the other hand there was a 'Chapel Society', with subscription membership and elected stewards, which undertook the congregation's charitable work.[41] Elsewhere fairly vigorous congregational institutions can be found in the chapel at Bath, in Birmingham and probably in Bristol;[42] further research would presumably reveal others, though there do not seem to have been any in

38. R. N. Billington and J. Brownbill, *St. Peter's Lancaster: a History* (London/ Edinburgh, 1910), pp. 83 ff.

39. Ward, *Dawn*, i, pp. 191–192.

40. Sheridan Gilley, 'The Roman Catholic Mission to the Irish in London', *Recusant History*, x (1969), p. 126; T. R. England, *The Life of the Reverend Arthur O'Leary* (London, 1822), pp. 236 ff.

41. *Mawhood Diary*, pp. 38, 135, 145 *passim*; however, the 'lay leaders' of the congregation were in a position to prevent the sale of distasteful literature in the chapel in 1796, which suggests that the 'Chapel Society' had some control over what went on inside it: Duffy, 'Joseph Berington', pp. 253 f.

42. For Bath, see J. A. Williams, *Bath and Rome: the Living Link* (Bath, 1963), pp. 55 f., 70 ff., 77 ff.; Ward, *Sequel*, i, pp. 36–38; for Birmingham, see below, p. 347; for Bristol, Dockery, *Collingridge*, pp. 161 ff.

the towns of the North-east, where the clergy was wealthy enough to resist them, and the Birmingham chapel may have been the only case in the Midlands. It should of course be remembered that, whether they were built and owned by the congregation or by some branch of the clergy, all town chapels put up in the decades after 1791 were to a greater or lesser extent supported by the rent of sittings; a congregation so constituted was likely to take a proprietorial interest in its chapel and to feel entitled to a voice in what went on there.

None the less in the long run congregational instincts could hardly persist in the absence of any formal institution to embody them; and the crucial test for the viability of such institutions was bound to take place in the congregations of the Lancashire towns. Hence the significance for the evolution of the community at large of the congregational conflicts which occurred in Lancashire between about 1780 and 1820.

The first and fiercest of them broke out in the Liverpool congregation in 1778,[43] when the two ex-Jesuits serving the mission were Joseph Gittins *alias* Williams and Raymond Hormasa *alias* Harris, a naturalised Spaniard. It had two main causes. There was in the first place a constitutional conflict between the congregation as constituted by the arrangements of 1758 and the Jesuits of the Lancashire district: William Molyneux, the next superior, had decided that the chapel was Jesuit property, appointed a trustee, revoked the 'regulations' and put the collection of bench-rents into the hands of the senior priest, Williams. It is hard to say what the rights and wrongs of the case were, and so far as one can see matters were brought to a head less by the congregation than by a ferocious dispute between the two priests. Harris accused Williams of depriving him of his due share of the income, and began to support agitation for a return to congregational control on the grounds that, if the purse-strings were held by a committee, he would get a better share of the bench-rents than he was getting at the moment. There was probably something more to it than this. Harris, who besides his work at the chapel served as some kind of official interpreter at the port—the Spaniards having become involved, on the other side, in the American war—had close relations with the Liverpool merchant

43. My account depends mainly on the *Appeal to the Public* (above, n. 35), and I hope I have made due allowance for the partisan nature of this production; earlier attempts to make sense of the dispute will be found in Burke, *Catholic History of Liverpool*, pp. 14–24; C.R.S. ix, pp. 183 ff.; Stonor, *Liverpool's Hidden Story*, pp. 34 f.

community, and became popular with its members by defending in print the scriptural warrant for slave-trading. The core of his support in the congregation seems to have consisted in men of this kind, and they were likely to have had a predominant voice in a chapel run according to the 'original regulations'. In any event a meeting of bench-holders was held in September 1779 which demanded their reinstate-ment and elected a body of trustees in accordance with them. This started a schism in the congregation and a complicated and occasionally violent conflict which went on for several years.

Although Harris does not inspire much confidence as a priest, the congregation seem to have had a good case, and it was accepted by the northern vicar-apostolic, then Thomas Walton, to whom they appealed; he thought it was up to them to make such arrangements as they saw fit for the payment of their subscriptions, and that the priests would do best to leave financial matters to them and get on with their proper work. After some two years' argument the Jesuits accepted this system for the future, but a settlement was held up by argument about what appear to be trivial matters. By this time there was a new and less con-ciliatory bishop, Matthew Gibson, who suspended Harris from his functions for obstructing the settlement in December 1781. Another year or so of conflict followed. The congregational trustees began opera-tions without waiting for a settlement, tried to take possession of the chapel in March 1782, and were sued for trespass at Lancaster Assizes; the suit was withdrawn when the congregational trustees threatened to bring evidence that Thomas Clifton of Lytham, the Catholic landowner who had brought the suit, had no title to the property himself and was only acting on behalf of the Lancashire ex-Jesuits. This action seems to have persuaded the latter that they had better come to terms, and after a series of meetings held at Lancaster, at Preston, where Gibson appeared, and finally at Wigan in February 1783, they agreed to hand over the chapel property to two other local gentlemen, to hold in trust 'for the use of the Roman Catholic congregation of Liverpool'; the 'original regulations' would then come into force, and the existing congregational trustees would act as 'managers or Acting Trustees'. It was in addition agreed, in a matter which had come to the forefront since Harris's suspension, that the trustees—presumably the 'Acting Trustees'—would acquire the right, hitherto exercised by the Jesuits, to nominate priests to the chapel, who would not be admitted unless they promised to abide by the regulations; if a priest proved unsatisfactory they would be entitled to present reasons to the bishop why he should be dismissed, though the bishop's decision would be final.

This agreement never came into effect either. One reason was the untimely death of the original trustee for the Jesuits, Thomas Clifton, without whose consent a legal transfer of the property could not be made. Another, and probably more important reason, was a division among the Lancashire ex-Jesuits. The relevant fact was that after the formal suppression of the society in 1773, the property arrangements of the former colleges and districts remained as they had been before, while the spiritual arrangements passed into the hands of a vicar-general appointed by the bishop—in this case Joseph Emmott, the ex-Jesuit serving the Molyneux estate at Gilmoss, just outside Liverpool. Emmott appears to have taken the view that his brethren might do what they liked with the property of the Liverpool chapel, but had no business to interfere, as they appeared to have done in their agreement with the congregation, in the appointment of its priests. He persuaded Williams to retire, got Gibson to suspend both him and Harris from exercising their functions in Liverpool, and offered the mission to the Benedictines, who sent two men to take over the priests' house and chapel in April 1783.

This was hardly a step towards congregational concord, though in the end it possibly did more good than harm. It was a successful coup, because it was popular with a considerable part of the congregation, especially with those who were disfranchised under the 'original regulations' because they did not pay enough for their sittings, or who had no sitting at all;[44] at a time when the congregation was expanding rapidly, as we have seen, such members must have been increasingly numerous. (Perhaps it should be added that a congregational split on these lines, which later on would often have involved antagonism between English and Irish members, cannot be supposed to have done so at this time.) It thus proved possible for the senior Benedictine priest, Archibald Macdonald, to call a successful meeting of the congregation which confirmed him in his right to collect the bench-rents himself and elected a new and amenable set of 'chapel wardens' whose functions are not clear, but do not seem to have amounted to very much. With this support behind him, Macdonald was able to ride the storm which followed, including a great deal of disturbance in the chapel, some mild rioting outside, and another lawsuit, launched this

44. cf. *Appeal*, pp. 159 f., 283 f., 312.

time by the trustees against Williams for unlawfully putting Macdonald in possession of their property. One of his more vigorous steps was to ban from the chapel any member of the congregation who did not accept the new regime and, when the consequent exclusion of bench-holders from their benches seemed likely to get him into further trouble with the law, to have their benches taken out of the chapel and dumped in the yard outside. The Benedictine regime survived; the lawsuit against Macdonald failed, so apparently setting a precedent against the recognition of Catholic congregational institutions which was followed in England, though not in the United States; and Bishop Gibson finally intervened in October 1783 with a pastoral letter 'to the Catholics of Liverpool', in which he denounced resort to common-law remedies in a matter which he now held to fall entirely within ecclesiastical juris-diction, rejected all congregational claims to a voice in choosing pastors and affirmed in the most explicit terms that the Church was a hierarchical society in which the clergy commanded and the laity obeyed.

This was an unrealistic position to take up in the English Catholic community as it then stood, and in the end a compromise seems to have been worked out. The Benedictines remained in possession of the original chapel, and maintained their new regime; presumably, in the end, the Jesuits conveyed their property to them. But it was in any case becoming too small for the Liverpool congregation, and instead of en-larging it two new chapels were started in 1788; one by the Benedictines in Seel Street, which Macdonald was sent to take charge of, and another by the ex-Jesuits. It looks as if the Jesuit chapel took over the supporters of the 'original regulations', and they may have brought their regula-tions with them; twenty-five years later, when the priest died and the Jesuits had no one else to send, a new chapel (St Nicholas's, Copperas Hill) was built in 1815, with trustees and congregational control of a similar kind.[45]

From this date until 1850 the Catholic population of Liverpool ex-panded with gathering speed; but of the numerous new chapels which were built, St Nicholas's remained the only one with full congregational institutions. Yet the poverty of the new immigrants made it necessary to find some way by which the resources of those Liverpool Catholics who had wealth to spare could be applied to making provision for their needs; and despite earlier conflicts it remained until practically the end

45. Burke, *Catholic History of Liverpool*, p. 79.

of this period a generally accepted axiom that this could be most successfully done if men of this type were entrusted with some measure of congregational responsibility. Apart from St Nicholas's, lay committees drawn from the Catholic *bourgeoisie* of Liverpool were erected in connection with four chapels. They did not serve as permanent bodies of congregational representatives, and though they had other functions their main task was to build or rebuild chapels. They were answerable to a 'Society' of subscribers, and responsible for raising funds, for the planning and design of the buildings—a fact reflected in their preference for classical or 'methodistical' architecture against the tide of clerical Gothic—and probably for managing the chapel until the accounts were settled and debts paid off; thereupon the chapel was intended to be handed over as a going concern to the bishop, or to the religious order for which it had been built. After St Nicholas's, the first of these bodies built St Patrick's in 1821, which was designed as a large immigrant chapel with no paid sittings on the ground floor, though there were presumably some in the gallery; in 1832 another rebuilt St Anthony's, a small and insecure chapel founded in 1810 by a French émigré priest. These were both secular-clergy chapels; two more were built for religious orders. The 'St Francis Xavier Society' was launched in 1840 to carry out a gentlemen's agreement made with the Jesuits at the building of St Nicholas's in 1815, and re-establish the Society in Liverpool. Frightened no doubt by their earlier experience, the Benedictines resisted intervention almost to the last, with the result that by 1840 they served two fifty-year-old chapels which must have been hopelessly inadequate for their congregations. It was probably Jesuit competition which finally persuaded them to launch, in the original chapel, a 'St Mary's Society' which built a new one in 1844–1845.[46]

I have dealt at some length with the history of congregational institutions in Liverpool because it provides a test for the prospects of a Catholic 'third estate' as successor to the social predominance exercised for so long by the landed gentry, and suggests that this was not an entirely implausible proposition. It also suggests some of the difficulties a body of this kind would meet in making headway against the current of Catholic tradition. Both these points may be supported by a glance

---

46. *ibid.*, pp. 33–79 *passim*; for St Patrick's, an example of 'methodistical' architecture, see B. Little, *Catholic Churches since 1623* (London, 1966), p. 63 and ill. p. 64; St Anthony's however was Gothic, *ibid.*, p. 69, ill. p. 72.

at two other town congregations in which constitutional conflicts arose, those of Wigan and Birmingham. By about 1815, the Wigan chapel which had been erected thirty years before had become too small for a congregation which by now ran into some thousands. The Jesuits, in conjunction with the chapel trustees, proposed to rebuild it on a larger scale but ran into opposition from the bishop, William Gibson. This was inspired, partly by hostility to congregational pretensions, partly by the irritability of extreme old age in a man who had never found it easy to work with others, and partly by a dispute about the status of the new Jesuit establishment at Stonyhurst, and of the Society of Jesus in England, after its general restoration by the pope in 1814. Gibson appears to have obstructed any rebuilding of the old chapel, and authorised his vicar-general to start collecting for a new one, to be served by the secular clergy. In November 1817 the trustees of the existing chapel called a well-attended congregational meeting which resolved to defy the bishop by boycotting his scheme and launching one of their own. They failed to stop the secular chapel going forward, but with the support of a large majority of the congregation proved extremely successful with their own; as a result, from the beginning of 1818 two large Catholic chapels—the secular and Gothic St Mary's and the Jesuit and classical-baroque St John's—began to go up some hundred yards distant from one another, to the accompaniment of a brisk flow of repartee from all sides. The trustees claimed that the congregation was entitled to rebuild its own chapel without asking leave from the bishop; the secular clergy accused them of criminal insubordination to lawful superiors; the trustees suggested that their 'venerable prelate' had 'lost his mental faculties'; the vicar-general, who was priest at Chorley, proposed that St John's be laid under interdict. Finally, apparently through the good offices of Milner, a settlement was arrived at: Gibson agreed to authorise both chapels so long as his rights in the appointment of priests to St John's were recognised. This result was on the whole a victory for congregationalism: the secular chapel does not seem to have been much of a success at first, but a continuing increase in the Catholic population of Wigan ensured both St Mary's and St John's a plentiful congregation in future.[47]

47. Ward, *Eve*, iii, pp. 33 f.; Archives of the English Province of the Society of Jesus, College of St Aloysius: Wigan, *passim*—quotation from Charles Walmesley to Richard Thompson, 27 February 1818; Little, *Catholic Churches*, pp. 56 f. and ill. between pp. 72 and 73.

Duplication of chapels, though in a more convenient form and a less embittered climate, proved also the solution at Birmingham. The Franciscans had traditionally served the mission here, and with the help of a local subscription they had built the first chapel (later St Peter's) in 1786. By 1800 this had become too small, and there was agitation among the wealthier members of the congregation for rebuilding under the auspices of a lay committee. The position was complicated by the fact that the Franciscans were running out of men, and negotiating with the bishop to provide an incumbent for the chapel. When Milner became Midland vicar-apostolic in 1803 he was faced by what the Franciscans termed 'a party of upstart purse-proud puppies' claiming a voice in the appointment. When the Franciscans proved able to resist this intrusion on their rights, the opposition formed a committee to build a second chapel. Milner, when appealed to, accepted this solution and the new chapel (St Chad's) was started in 1807 and finished two years later: it was owned and managed by lay trustees until some date before 1826, when they sold the property to Milner. St Peter's remained in the hands of the Franciscans, and in 1824, when the last of them died, was handed over to Milner. Again, there was a demand from the chief members of the congregation, who thought it was time for the Catholics of Birmingham to 'take that station in the town, to which their increasing numbers, wealth and respectability entitled them', to be consulted about the new priest. Milner was accommodating; an able and energetic man, T. M. McDonnell, was appointed amid general satisfaction; and provision was made for continuing congregational participation of an informal kind. Some time later this became embodied in a 'Society of the Sacred Heart', which provided McDonnell with strong congregational support when he fell foul of the next bishop, Thomas Walsh.[48]

By about 1820 the tension between the clergy and the third estate over congregational institutions had reached a point of balance. With a few exceptions, the full nonconformist pattern of formal and permanent lay control of chapels, with congregational property in the fabric, responsibility for improvements, payment of priests and claims to patronage had not established itself in face of clerical opposition. But in other respects the level of congregation participation and activity remained high. We have seen it expressed in the chapel-building operations of committees in Liverpool, and examples of the same thing could

---

48. *Catholic Magazine*, v (1833), pp. 313 ff.; Dockery, *Collingridge*, pp. 47, 58 ff.

be adduced from London, Birmingham and elsewhere.[49] Meetings at which such bodies were set up, or answered for their conduct to subscribers or congregations were large, vigorous and frequent; even in places where the clergy was always in undisputed control, like Manchester, congregational meetings were held to discuss new projects and organise the raising of funds.[50] In matters outside the strict running of chapels, congregational bodies had a freer rein, and during this period they undertook a wide range of charitable and educational activity: they were particularly involved with the erection, maintenance and supervision of charity schools. In London the 'Chapel Society' at Moorfields was running a school for the children of poor Catholics by 1770; William Mawhood was a subscriber, and both he and his son Charles were elected as stewards.[51] After this, the London vicars-apostolic seem to have discouraged lay intervention in education; but it developed rapidly in those Northern and Midland towns where congregational instincts were stronger. In Liverpool, charity schools were founded at the same time as the Seel Street chapel (1789), St Nicholas's and St Patrick's. St Nicholas's school, which was certainly run, like the chapel, by a lay committee, had 300 children in it by 1821 and was rebuilt in 1830. Those who were responsible for these schools also collaborated with William Rathbone and others in the 'Benevolent Society of St Patrick', an interdenominational body devoted to the education of Irish immigrant children, which had established its 'Hibernian Schools' in 1807; after 1835, when Rathbone and his fellow-liberals had a majority on the reformed Corporation, it was possible to absorb some of the rising tide of immigrant children in the Corporation schools, whose regime was modified so as to admit the children of Catholics and Dissenters, but this policy was reversed when the Corporation changed hands again in 1841, and a massive expansion of Catholic Charity Schools became necessary. In the years immediately following, St Patrick's school was expanded to take 1,000 children, and the St Mary's Society, while rebuilding the original Liverpool chapel, set up a new

49. D. Gwynn, *Lord Shrewsbury, Pugin and the Catholic Revival* (London, 1946), pp. 23, 59 f., 78, 123: the Birmingham project was not a success.
50. *Catholic Magazine*, iii (1833), pp. 90 f.: 'Meeting of Manchester Catholics' reported to by Henry Gillow, priest at Mulberry Street, who needs money to pay off chapel debt and to provide income for a third priest; committee elected, some £1,000 raised.
51. *Mawhood Diary*, pp. 38, 165, 217, 266, 278. Cf. the history of the undenominational bible-schools in London in Ward, *Eve*, ii, pp. 160–165.

school as well.[52] On a smaller scale, the same was happening elsewhere. The Lancaster congregation built a school in 1805; Wigan resolved to build one in 1814, and seems to have postponed rebuilding the chapel until it was completed. In Birmingham the opening of St Chad's was followed by the foundation of a pair of charity schools, one for boys and one for girls, by the two congregations in conjunction; by 1830 they had 400 children in them.[53]

Thus by 1840 the weight of congregational participation, restricted in the management of chapels, had come to rest in the two associated and by now overwhelmingly urgent activities of chapel-building and elementary education. It remained to be seen whether this compromise with hierarchical traditions would leave a lasting imprint on the conduct of the community. Whether or not it did so depended very largely on the attitude and resources of the bishops; by 1850 it had become clear that the bishops were unwilling to maintain the compromise and capable, at a pinch, of doing without it. The sequence of events by which this decision was made and enforced remains rather obscure; but it is clear that the issue was brought to a head by the foundation in 1838, through the initiative of Charles Langdale, son of the Lord Stourton who had been president of the Catholic Board, of a 'Catholic Institute'. So far as one can see this was intended as a kind of super-committee which would support and guide the fund-raising efforts of bodies up and down the country in respect of chapels and schools, ensure that money was got to where it was most needed and in general sort out the increasingly chaotic finances of the community. Its president was the Earl of Shrewsbury, and its central committee was aristocratic in composition; but it also had branches in provincial cities, notably in Liverpool, which represented the *bourgeoisie*. The combination did not prove a very successful one.[54]

Probably because some of them were in serious financial straits,[55] the

52. Burke, *Catholic History of Liverpool*, pp. 26–79 *passim*; J. Murphy, *The Religious Problem in English Education: the Crucial Experiment* (Liverpool, 1959); *Catholic Directory, 1839*, p. 84; *1843*, p. 36.
53. Billington and Brownbill, *St Peter's Lancaster*, p. 88; Archives of the English Province, S.J.—College of St Aloysius: Wigan—Meeting of 21 April 1814, etc.; for Birmingham, *Catholic Magazine*, i, pp. 384, 570; iv, pp. xxii–xxiii; v, p. 316; and *Report on the State of the Irish Poor in Great Britain*, pp. 1–2.
54. Ward, *Sequel*, i, pp. 194–198; Burke, *Catholic History of Liverpool*, pp. 57 f.; E. Lucas, *The Life of Frederick Lucas, M.P.* (2 vols., London, 1886), i, p. 121.
55. For the financial problems of the Midland district, see Gwynn, *Lord Shrewsbury, Pugin and the Catholic Revival*, p. 27; *Catholic Magazine*, iii (1833), p. 484,

bishops contented themselves at first with pouring cold water on the scheme, on the grounds that the task would be 'too intricate and various to be successfully managed by a general committee'. But in 1844 Bishop Brown of the newly-created Lancashire district brought its operations to a halt in what was no doubt the most important region of its activity. He issued a pastoral letter in which all existing fund-raising machinery for churches and schools was declared to be abolished and replaced by a district board which contained no lay members; in future, the Lancashire laity was to contribute by individual donation, or in church, or in specified conditions in connection with church-collections; how the money was to be spent became a matter for the clergy to decide. Whether this dramatic intervention came into effect immediately, and whether it was accompanied by similar action on the part of other bishops, do not seem clear. But there can be little doubt that this was a fairly effective death-blow to the church-building operations of lay committees. The action had possibly been precipitated by a crisis which blew up on the educational front in 1843, when the committee of the Institute expressed agreement with a government proposal for the compulsory non-denominational education of factory children, to be supervised by the Church of England, but failed to get a *quid pro quo* in the form of a grant for Catholic schools. This discredited it in the provincial branches, and by 1847 the Institute had fallen into disarray; the bishops had little difficulty in replacing it with a Poor School Committee consisting of two laymen and eight representatives of themselves; the local school-committees seem to have been got rid of at the same time.[56] The logical conclusion of the whole process, the abolition of surviving proprietary rights of congregations in their chapels, followed—or was at least widely understood to have followed—in the papal brief erecting a new hierarchy in 1850.[57]

This abortive attempt to incorporate congregational institutes and lay committees into the structure of the English Catholic community raises a number of problems which deserve discussion. The only interpretative comment about it which I know of was made by Bernard

---

where Walsh suggests a solution similar to that later adopted in Lancashire; Wilfrid Ward, *The Life and Times of Cardinal Wiseman* (2 vols, London, 1897), i, p. 343.

56. Ward, *Sequel*, i, p. 196; Burke, *Catholic History of Liverpool*, pp. 79–80, 93; Lucas, *Life of Frederick Lucas*, i, pp. 114 ff., 151 f., 280 ff.; Ward, *Wiseman*, ii, pp. 359, 450.

57. See below, p. 362.

Ward, who thought it a transplantation into town chapels of habits of gentry patronage inherited from the countryside.[58] While not entirely off the point, this seems a misleading view, which may be explained by the almost exclusive attention paid in Ward's history of the community to what was going on in London and the South. It is obviously applicable to two aristocratic congregations, one in London (Warwick Street) and the other in Bath; but it should have emerged from what has been said that these were untypical. Some confusion may have arisen in the use of the term 'trustee'. It may refer either, in the sense traditional in the history of the community, to laymen who acted on behalf of a body of clergy in the ownership of mission property, like Thomas Clifton for the Jesuits in Liverpool, or to representatives of a congregational body. Trustees of the first kind were invariably local landowners and rarely, if ever, members of the congregation; trustees of the second kind were always members of the congregation, and rarely gentry. The trustees at Liverpool were originally, so far as I can see, all Liverpool merchants, and later manufacturers and professional men as well. The most prominent family among them, the Rossons, who provided three generations of members to bodies of this kind and, in John Rosson, the leader of the Liverpool Catholic *bourgeoisie* in the 1820s and after, were successively occupied in trade, soap-manufacture and the law; of the original Lancaster trustees, Robert Gillow was the proprietor of a furniture factory and Richard Worswick the principal banker of the town.[59] Two of the trustees at Wigan during the dispute with Bishop Gibson came from gentry families, but the most prominent of them, Charles Walmesley, certainly lived in Wigan, though whether he exercised a business or profession is not clear. The congregational forces in Birmingham were clearly led by substantial businessmen and manufacturers; they included John Hardman, who had a firm specialising in decorative metalwork and seems to have made a fortune out of the Gothic revival.[60] The main force behind congregational self-assertion

58. Ward, *Dawn*, i, p. 191.
59. C.R.S. ix, p. 190; for the Rossons, Burke, *Catholic History of Liverpool*, pp. 15 f., 47, 58, 65, etc.; *State of the Irish Poor in Great Britain*, p. 32; *Catholic Directory, 1842*, p. 131; J. Murphy, *The Religious Problem in English Education* (Liverpool, 1959), p. 10; for Gillows and Worswicks, Billington and Brownbill, *St Peter's Lancaster*, pp. 83 f., 101 f.
60. M. Haile and E. Bonney, *Life and Letters of John Lingard* (London, ?1911), p. 336; Gwynn, *Lord Shrewsbury, Pugin and the Catholic Revival*, pp. 59, 61, 136; Ward, *Wiseman*, i, pp. 350, 435.

came from those who paid for and occupied the benches of town chapels, and except in the cases already mentioned very few of these were members of the landed gentry.

The point is worth insisting on because it helps to place the movement in a wider context of English social and political development and to indicate one reason why it failed. In its strictly congregational aspect it may be regarded as an attempt to adapt for the Catholic community a model which had served the Protestant dissenting bodies since 1689. In its wider implications it drew upon the mutual understanding between Catholics and Dissenters which, if one ignores the doubtful precedent of James II, may be traced back at least as far as the 1780s. What had begun as an intellectual flirtation of Joseph Berington with Priestley and the rational dissenters grew into something more solid in the friendship between Lingard and Henry Brougham, the collaboration between Catholics and Unitarians among the Liverpool *bourgeoisie*, and the participation of priests in movements like the Birmingham Political Union.[61] In its heyday in the 1820s this was a good deal more than a tactical alliance in the political field: it represented a similarity of status and background and a genuine approximation of views about the practical implications of Christianity and the means to be adopted for achieving them. Catholics of what were coming to be called the 'middle classes', and often the town clergy who ministered to them, fitted without much difficulty into the 'benevolent system' of association for general improvement which had sprung from the undenominational enthusiasms of the later eighteenth century. They found it as reasonable as others of their station that the principles of the system should be extended into other fields, as they were, politically speaking, in the years around 1830.

It was this vigorous contemporary environment, rather than the weight of an aristocratic history, that gave its weight to congregational or associational developments in the community. Their decline coincided with a change in the general climate. By 1829 it had become clear that the sympathetic elements in Dissent were precariously placed in relation to a hostile rank-and-file; in the situation in which it was achieved the removal of Catholic disability stimulated a return to cruder polarities;

61. Duffy, 'Joseph Berington', pp. 95 ff., 142 ff.; Ursula Henriques, *Religious Toleration in England, 1787–1833* (London, 1961), pp. 168 f.; Haile and Bonney, *Lingard*, pp. 240 ff., 230; above, p. 348 (Liverpool); *Catholic Magazine*, iii (1833), pp. 238, 332, and *Report on the Irish Poor*, p. 1 (McDonnell in Birmingham).

after 1832 dissenting politics floundered towards an uninspired sectarianism.[62] In these circumstances it was difficult for the non-conformist model to retain much attraction for Catholics, and those who hankered for it were in a weaker position than they would in any case have been to resist the combination of pressures building up against them within the community.

As in most other communities, the congregational system was always in some degree oligarchical, and tended to become more so. At Lancaster the trustees recruited by co-optation, thought his does not seem to have been usual; the electoral body of bench-holders was in any case far from the whole congregation. Thus in Wigan the total number of communicants in 1785 was given as 600, and the number of bench-holders was 114; in 1818, when the whole congregation was given as 3,000, it was 156.[63] As we have seen at Liverpool, this tendency towards oligarchy could prove the undoing of congregational claims at moments of crisis. It ought not however to be exaggerated: at £1 a year, which seems to have been the standard rent for a cheap sitting, a man with a family consisting of five persons would be paying no more per head than the 1d. a week which was being collected from the Irish poor in the 1840s; and congregational institutions were not in principle incompatible with arrangements of the latter kind. If Wigan is anything to go by, trustees with important decisions before them showed themselves anxious for the approval of all the 'regular Catholics' in the congregation, whether they were bench-holders or not. Many complaints against the system were demagogic, and there is certainly a case for saying that an oligarchical system was better than no system at all. All the same, it must be confessed that it was not well designed to ensure effective representation in an age of galloping growth, and less so when most of the growth was supplied by extremely poor people divided by all kinds of barriers from those who sat on the benches in front of, or above them, and who found congregational arrangements not so much expensive as alien and 'Protestant'.

This immediate problem, more than anything else, ensured the rapid success of the episcopal reaction. But there is at least one reason for looking at this in the perspective of 200 years of the community's

62. Henriques, *op. cit.*, pp. 146–147; N. Gash, *Reaction and Reconstruction in English Politics* (Oxford, 1965), chaps. iv–v; W. R. Ward, *Religion and Society in England, 1790–1850* (London, 1972), pp. 177–205.
63. See references above, n. 36.

history. Against this background the hostility of bishops and secular clergy to congregational institutions will not cause much surprise; it was also, as we have seen, less uniform than might have been anticipated. What is more intriguing is the position of the religious orders. They had, after all, hitherto stood out as defenders of the ecclesiastical rights of the laity, and it may be felt that this was the moment to discover whether they had really meant what they said. The answer remains ambiguous. I do not think it is accidental that most of the congregational institutions which have been discussed emerged out of missions which had been served by the regular clergy—Jesuit, Benedictine and Franciscan; and in some cases, as at Wigan, claims to congregational autonomy were closely involved with claims on the part of a religious order. Yet it would clearly be impossible to interpret these congregational conflicts, as a whole, as reviving in a new environment the confrontation which had taken place in the days of Richard Smith. When it came to the point the regulars proved too concerned with their own property rights to follow a consistent policy of fostering congregational self-government in temporal matters. It may be that they had grown too close to the gentry; or that things would have turned out differently had not their suppression left the Jesuits, at the critical period, without overall direction and in disarray. In any case their failure and that of the other religious orders to adapt their traditional position to the circumstances of a new age was certainly an important reason why congregational institutions proved to have shallow roots. They disappeared from the Catholic community without much struggle, and left almost no trace; a final judgment on their record will probably remain a mixed one, even when it has made full allowance in the criticisms they incurred for ecclesiastical dogmatism, Irish emotions and Gothic bigotry about anything that smacked of Dissent. Earlier historians of the community, in so far as they have noticed them, have not found them attractive. Perhaps it is only now possible, with the hindsight of a century and more, to guess that in the long run what was lost by their suppression was a good deal more worth having than what was gained.[64]

The powers in the community which one sector of the laity had abandoned and another failed to acquire, fell necessarily to the clergy, and in the so-called 'restoration of the hierarchy' of 1850 they received the particular institutional shape which has survived. Taken as a whole,

---

64. cf. the pertinent comments of K. S. Inglis, *Churches and the Working-Class in Victorian England* (London/Toronto, 1963), pp. 135–136.

the last century of the old regime was a period of clerical revival; by about 1820 independence had been achieved, and during the next decades independence began to turn into supremacy. Most of the foundations of this supremacy have already been exposed: the clergy had nursed the instinct for it through ages of frustration; they had prepared for a better future by modest but pertinacious activity during the eighteenth century, and seized the opportunities given them by demographic growth, migration and social transformation, and by the freedom from external restraint secured by the Act of 1791. After 1820 they went forward on a rising tide of poor immigrants, on the momentum of their own dedicated activity, and against an opposition—if that is not too strong a word—undermined by the revolution in sensibility ravaging the English upper classes, and in particular by a mediaevalism which counselled surrender to clerical claims.

It is worth remembering that this process of clerical revival, though it went faster and farther in the Catholic community than elsewhere, was by no means confined to it. Writing of the wider arena of the Church of England, Geoffrey Best has spoken of the emergence around 1820 of a clerical 'confidence in the reviving strength and *esprit de corps* of their order', of a growing sense of separation from and independence of the laity, of the widening range of social functions which fell to them in an age of improvement.[65] The same—even I think on the last point— could have been said of the Roman Catholic clergy before the Oxford Movement began to imply that they and their counterparts in the Church of England had even more in common than might have been supposed. Best has also remarked on the tensions which began to accumulate, in the Church of England, between the episcopal hierarchy and the clerical rank-and-file as reform and missionary expansion altered the balance of power between them in favour of the former;[66] and here also the historian of the Roman Catholic community finds himself on familiar ground. Indeed it may reasonably be said that, given its tradition and circumstances, the establishment of a clerical supremacy, in general, was a probability so banal as scarcely to need discussion. It none the less remained to be seen whether this access of power would actually accrue to the Catholic clergy as such, or rather to their episcopal superiors: whether, in short, the clerical regime of the future

---

65. G. F. A. Best, *Temporal Pillars* (Cambridge, 1964), pp. 245, 258 ff., 268, etc.; cf., for the Methodists, Ward, *Religion and Society in England*, pp. 236 ff.
66. Best, *op. cit.*, p. 262.

was to be oligarchical or monarchical in character, and it was essentially this question, rather than the more fundamental issue which had already been settled, which was answered by the papal act of 1850.

Taken in 1820, a snapshot of the English Catholic clergy would have shown a body with well-defined characteristics.[67] It was a small body, a little over 400 strong, or scarcely more than it had been fifty years earlier; this despite an influx of French émigré clergy during the revolutionary decades, a number of whom settled permanently as missioners in England. The dearth of clergy was not surprising, in view of the disintegration of the whole structure of continental training-establishments which began with the suppression of the Jesuits and ended among the after-effects of the French Revolution. Three secular-clergy seminaries —at Ware in the London district, Ushaw in the Northern and Oscott in the Midland—were now functioning in England; but difficulties of transplantation and the loss of funds meant that they were as yet unable to supply more than a trickle of new priests.[68] They had also probably had some effect in restricting the classes in the community from which the clergy was drawn. As secular opportunities expanded, recruitment from the gentry had dried up altogether; at the same time the disappearance of the scholarship funds which had been patiently built up in eighteenth-century Douai had probably restricted recruitment at the lower level. As a result, the majority of the clergy seem now to have been drawn from the ranks of the prosperous third estate.[69] A more marked difference from the position in 1770 was that, due in particular to the shrinkage of the Jesuits but also probably to a general decay of enthusiasm for the religious life, the regular clergy, which had been in a sizeable majority on the mission fifty years before, was now a

---

67. See, e.g., the report of Robert Gradwell to Propaganda, 1818, in W. M. Brady, *The Episcopal Succession in England and Ireland*, iii (Rome, 1877), pp. 191, 235, 270, 311; a series of clerical statistics for the period 1800–1840 will be found here. Annual lists of missions and totals of missionary priests are given in the *Catholic Directory* from 1838 onwards; see also those given for 1851 by Philip Hughes in G. A. Beck (ed.), *The English Catholics, 1850–1950* (London, 1950), pp. 48–50, from the religious census of that year.

68. Thus the college at Ushaw, opened in 1808, reached a total of 125 students (not all clerical students) in 1811 and remained practically stationary in size until 1850: Milburn, *History of Ushaw College*, p. 367.

69. A very high proportion of the more prominent clergy had been educated at the school at Sedgley Park near Wolverhampton, specifically a foundation for the commercial classes: *Catholic Magazine*, iii (1833), pp. 31 ff.; cf. Rowlands, 'Education and Piety of Catholics in Staffordshire in the 18th Century', *Recusant History*, x (1969), pp. 72 f.; Milburn, *History of Ushaw College*, p. 50.

dwindling minority. By the 1830s secular priests formed about 70% of the whole body. The very great majority of them were English: French émigrés had never amounted to much more than 10% of the clergy, and were now certainly a smaller proportion than that; there was as yet no significant Irish constituent, except for a certain number of priests of Irish descent who appear to have been born in England, and totally Anglicised.[70] They were probably younger, and more energetic, than their forebears of fifty years before, and they had need to be, considering the changes which had occurred in the circumstances of their ministry. The priest serving in a closely-knit country congregation under the benevolent eye of a Catholic landlord was by now a practically extinct figure, and the duties of a family chaplain were becoming a tiresome chore to be undertaken only by the apprentice or the superannuated. Despite what is often said, rural missioners were frequently busy men, with more than one congregation and a wide area of country to serve.[71] But an active priest could expect to rise before long to the responsibilities of a strenuous ministry in the towns and manufacturing districts of Lancashire, the North-east or the Midlands, or in London; by 1820 many of these priests were men of considerable standing in the local community at large, wielding patriarchal authority over large congregations which they had often built up from small beginnings, building chapels, supervising schools, raising funds, preaching to large audiences of mixed denominations, coping with congregational ambitions, national dissension or labour agitation in their flock.[72] In the local associations of secular clergy which administered the clergy funds they possessed a vehicle for the collective expression of their views, which were marked by a consciousness of caste, a flexible paternalism towards the laity, and no excessive deference towards higher ecclesiastical authority. The shortage of priests, now progressing from the relative

70. T. M. McDonnell in Birmingham was an example but not apparently his namesake Charles, born in London and working there 1819 according to Ward, *Eve*, ii, p. 156, born in Castlebar according to J. McLoughlin, *Essex Recusant*, xiv (1972), p. 39.
71. See, e.g., the case of William Birdsall, in my 'More Northumbrian Congregations', *Recusant History*, x (1969), p. 20.
72. Examples: Rowland Broomhead in Manchester: B. W. Kelly, *Old English Catholic Missions* (London, 1907), pp. 267 f. and C. Hadfield, *A History of St. Marie's Mission, Sheffield* (Sheffield, 1889), pp. 23 f.; James Worswick in Newcastle: C.R.S. xxv, pp. 205 ff. Ward, *Religion and Society in England, 1790–1850*, p. 120, has an attractive description of Broomhead: 'Much loved, he was more of a public figure than any Manchester Catholic priest has been since.'

to the absolute, tended in itself to enhance their importance, just as excessive numbers had helped to diminish it during the seventeenth century.

It may well be true, as Bernard Ward suggested, that the formulation of precise clerical demands was set off by the Act of 1829 and reflected a desire on the part of the clergy to achieve an enhancement of their status and opportunities comparable to what the higher ranks of the laity had then achieved.[73] Like earlier programmes it took the form of an agitation for a return to 'ordinary' ecclesiastical government, a 'restoration of the hierarchy'; what was special about it was that it envisaged this primarily as improving the position of the ordinary clergy in relation to their bishops. Two precise advantages were expected to accrue to the clergy when the missionary regime was abolished: they would acquire security and stability in their appointments through the erection of a local parochial structure, and cease to be tenants-at-will, movable at the discretion of the vicars-apostolic; and they, or their senior members, would receive electoral rights in the appointment of bishops, which would ensure them promotion according to what they felt to be their merits and get rid of the 'hereditary' system of recruitment by co-optation which obtained among the vicars-apostolic.

Formal agitation for these ends began among the clergy of the London district in the early 1830s, at the annual meetings of the London Secular Clergy Fund; they were also relevant to the inauguration in 1831 of the *Catholic Magazine* as the voice of the secular clergy. By 1837 the movement seems to have had the support of a large majority of the clergy in the London and Northern districts, and at least of an influential minority in the Midlands. John Lingard gave a good deal of useful advice in the background, notably against trying to revive the claims of the old Chapter as an instrument of clerical promotion. The most prominent figure in the movement—perhaps because he had time on his hands—was the Duke of Norfolk's chaplain, Mark Aloysius Tierney, whose invaluable if partisan re-edition of Charles Dodd's *Church History of England* was something like a collective manifesto of the party. By the time this began to appear, in 1839, the movement was already some two or three years past its peak. In 1837 the London and Midland vicars-apostolic, Griffiths and Walsh, had been to Rome to see what changes in ecclesiastical structure would be

73. Ward, *Sequel*, i, p. 7.

acceptable to the Curia; in the following year all of them, at a general meeting, agreed to propose a small concession to the senior clergy on the question of stability and a rather larger one on the question of electivity. They also proposed, not before time, that the number of bishops and districts should be increased from four to eight. This did admittedly meet one of the demands of the clergy, especially in the North; but it also reflected a concern for those more pressing problems which had already made the essentials of their programme obsolete. The proposal was carried out, amid a good deal of episcopal infighting, in 1840[74].

Whatever their failings, the vicars-apostolic of the 1830s—Bramston and Griffiths in London, Walsh in the Midlands, Penswick and Briggs in the North, Baines in the West—were likely to have a clearer view of the general necessities of the Catholic community than a body of clergy whose attitude, in this context, resembled that of a trade-union rather than, as Wiseman alleged, that of the Anti-Corn Law League.[75] They were aware that the time was one of unprecedented tasks and opportunities; however self-interested their opinion that this was no time to surrender the flexibility of the missionary regime in favour of parochial freehold, it was undoubtedly correct. They may be accused of responding too slowly to the pressure of events, of clinging for too long to attitudes which were out of date; but at least they did respond.

It had in particular become obvious that the English secular clergy, which for the past sixty years had been moving steadily towards a monopoly of missionary forces, could no longer retain this position without grave damage to the Catholic community; if the clergy was to expand at anything like the rate required, it would have to draw on the religious orders, the clergy of Ireland and any other source which offered. To recognise this went against the grain for men who, with the exception of the Benedictine Baines, had all grown up in the English secular tradition; but by 1840 most of them had come to accept it. At that date there seem to have been about sixty Irish priests working in

---

74. Ward, *Sequel*, i, pp. 54–56, 122–134; Haile and Bonney, *Lingard*, p. 274; W. B. Ullathorne, *History of the Restoration of the Catholic Hierarchy in England* (London, 1871), pp. 18–20. There is a good account of the reorganisation of 1840 in Connell, 'Roman Catholic Church in England' (see above, n. 25), ch. vi, where a view less favourable to the vicars-apostolic is taken.

75. R. J. Schiefen, 'The Organisation and Administration of Roman Catholic Dioceses in England and Wales in the mid-nineteenth Century' (London Ph.D. thesis, 1970), p. 50.

England, most of them in London and the North.[76] Resistance to
English regulars proved harder to overcome. Naturally enough, the first
signs of change came from the Western district, from Collingridge,
who had restored the Jesuits to Bristol in 1828, and especially from
Baines. Walsh in the Midlands seems to have come round by 1838,
when he issued an invitation to the regulars to come and evangelise
Birmingham; Briggs in the North must have done so before 1840, when
the Jesuits returned to Liverpool and started expanding in Preston.
Bramston and Griffiths kept the Jesuits out of London until well into
the 1840s, though Griffiths maintained that this was because they wanted
a superfluous West-End mission and were not prepared to go to the less
attractive parts of the metropolis where they were needed.[77] Aided by
recruits from the clergy of the Church of England, and from abroad, the
number of priests working in England rose from 500 in 1840 (certainly
a modest advance on thirty years before) to 700 in 1850.[78] This was far
from sufficient, as is shown by the dramatic increase in the following
decade, but it does suggest that the vicars-apostolic had a better sense
of priorities than the more vocal members of their clergy, who give the
impression of wanting to institute a closed shop.

Since 1835 from outside and after 1840 from within the body of
vicars-apostolic, as coadjutor to Walsh in the Midlands, the leading
propagandist for unrestricted missionary expansion, and the chief
supporter of regular aspirations, had been Nicholas Wiseman. Wiseman
was of course not a man who had centuries of English Catholic experience in his bones. His personal rise to power, completed in 1850,
marked a breach in continuity quite as distinct as that effected on the
level of ecclesiastical structure by the 'restoration of the hierarchy' with
which his name is associated.[79] Yet this event was a conclusion as well
as a beginning. In the form in which it was achieved, and the contrast
between this form and what had been envisaged by the clergy which had

76. This is my own deduction from the list of clergy published in the *Catholic
Directory* (1840), pp. 39–42.
77. Ward, *Eve*, ii and Dockery, *Collingridge*, pp. 320 f. (Bristol); Ward, *Sequel*, i, pp.
154 f. (Birmingham); for Lancashire, above, p. 345 and H. Clemesha, *History of
Preston-in-Amounderness* (Manchester, 1912), p. 323; for London, Ward, *Sequel*, i,
pp. 57 f. and Gilley, 'The Roman Catholic Mission to the Irish', pp. 130 f.
78. *Catholic Directory* (1840), pp. 39–42; (1851), pp. 85–105—lists of clergy.
79. For the narrative of events leading up to the 'restoration', see Ullathorne's
History (above, n. 74), which forms the basis of the account by G. Albion, in G. A.
Beck (ed.), *The English Catholics, 1850–1950* (London, 1950), pp. 88–97; Ward,
Sequel, ii and Ward, *Wiseman*, i, *passim*.

launched the agitation for a 'restoration', we reach a paradoxical yet practically inevitable denouement of the clerical revival. We also reach the conclusion of the whole complicated process, extended over something like a century, through which the transfer of power in the community was accomplished. The 'restoration' as such lies beyond the purview of this book; but one feature of it requires to be mentioned in this context.

The 'restoration' was in the first place designed, in direct opposition to the intentions of its early promoters, to reinforce the monarchical authority of the bishops over their clergy. The concessions which the vicars-apostolic had been prepared to offer in 1837–1838 never came into effect; by 1845 they had been persuaded by Wiseman that the best way to secure their authority over the clergy was to ask Rome to institute a diocesan episcopate while leaving the ecclesiastical status of the English mission unchanged in other respects: for, as Griffiths put it, a 'restoration of the hierarchy in so far as changing the vicars-apostolic into titular bishops in England'. When Wiseman went to Rome to negotiate the change in 1847, one of his principal arguments was that a diocesan episcopate was essential to bring law and order into the Catholic community, and to instil a proper spirit of obedience among clergy as well as laity. These arguments bore fruit in the terms of the act of 'restoration' itself. The vicars-apostolic were transformed into an autonomous body of bishops with power of legislation in synod, and except for a certain degree of supervision from Propaganda all inhibitions to their action were removed. All customs, laws or privileges claimed to derive either from the pre-Reformation English Church or from the missionary period were declared to be abrogated in principle, and the new hierarchy was given a free hand to conduct itself with them as it saw fit. At the same time all rights and powers hitherto belonging to the vicars-apostolic were expressly transferred to the new bishops, who thus acquired all the advantages of a traditional episcopate while retaining the freedom of action characteristic of the missionary regime.[80]

This transference did not affect the clergy alone. Read as it stood, the act of 'restoration' submitted to the discretion of the new bishops, not only all legal rights which might be claimed by the inferior clergy, but

80. Ullathorne, *History*, pp. 20 f.; Albion, *art cit.*, pp. 88, 91 f., 122 f. For what the new hierarchy did with its powers, see now the admirable thesis of R. J. Schiefen, cited above, n. 75.

all ecclesiastical rights which, during the missionary age, had been claimed and exercised by the laity also. The point was made before the parliamentary committee set up in the excitement following the papal act:

> 'Do you conceive that the brief, if legal, will, directly or indirectly, affect the temporal rights of patrons and incumbents and other subjects of the Queen of this country?'
> 'Yes—and of the congregations in the temporalities of their chapels.'
> . . .
> 'Then at this moment the Roman Catholic Church in England has not the protection of any bye-laws whatever?'
> 'No.'[81]

This was admittedly a hostile view, reflecting the ethos both of the English Common Law and of English Catholics, lay and clerical, who had campaigned against Wiseman. The new hierarchy appears to have prudently avoided putting its powers to the test. It had however little need to do so, since almost every claim that mattered had already been made good in the years before 1850. In any event, the undisputed government of the Catholic community now fell to the Cardinal-Archbishop and twelve suffragans, assembled in synod at Oscott, before whom Newman preached on the 'second spring'. This was an eloquent sermon, but a misleading contribution to English Catholic history. What had happened was less the 'revolution in the moral sphere' of which he spoke, than a counter-revolution in the social sphere. It certainly did not restore, as Newman hopefully affirmed, an English Church which had been in abeyance since the Reformation. On the other hand it is possibly a little extreme to dismiss the event, as an experienced canon lawyer has done, as a 'polite fiction'.[82] A sociologist of religion might suggest that it brought to a close the history of a sect and inaugurated that of a denomination. This description, appropriate enough in itself, would need some qualification if it implied, in the life of the community described, an opening to wider horizons of what had hitherto been closed in upon itself. On the contrary, the 'denomi-

---

81. *Select Committee on the Law of Mortmain* (Parliamentary Papers, 1851, xvi), p. 277—T. C. Anstey and Francis Trappes, 5 June 1851.
82. J. H. Newman, *Sermons preached on Various Occasions* (London, 1908), p. 169; M. V. Sweeney, 'Diocesan Organisation and Administration', in G. A. Beck (ed.), *The English Catholics, 1850–1950*, pp. 116–150—comment at p. 116.

nationalism' of which it was both a victim and a vehicle illustrated that more general hardening of lines and narrowing of sympathies which had helped to bring to a disappointing close an age of experiment in the institutional arrangements of the country.[83]

83. cf. Ward, *Religion and Society in England, 1790–1850*, pp. 1–6 and *passim*.

15

THE HEART OF THE MATTER

I HAVE tried already to present some aspects of the religious life of the community in so far as they reflected the process by which it came into existence, or as part of the relationship, inside it, of clergy and laity. It is time to confront the subject more directly, since it is after all, even for a historian in a sociologically-minded age, the heart of the matter. This historian may find good reason to leave his attempt until this stage, since it may be claimed that in its devotional life between roughly 1750 and 1840 the community arrived at an interior synthesis of its collective experience and brought the history of its formation to a close. It achieved a comprehensive devotional structure which maintained the continuity of tradition while it renewed and adapted its data into forms appropriate to the situation. For this renewal, it drew partly on the general resources of counter-Reformation Catholicism, partly on those of its plural and Protestant milieu and a good deal on its own judgment and powers of invention. In investigating this synthesis, we shall be dealing mainly with prayer, and frequently with 'prayers' in the colloquial sense; with prayer both private and public, individual, domestic and congregational. We shall also be dealing with the implications of Christianity as they were felt to concern the Catholic in his daily life and his relations with his fellow-men; and we shall finally be exploring how, for reasons which have already been sufficiently indicated, the synthesis dissolved.

Almost everything we need to know about the private devotion of English Catholics during these decades can be discovered by consulting Challoner's *Garden of the Soul*. This was first published in London in 1740, and intended to supersede the community's traditional standby, the *Manual of Devout Prayers*, which it did. Its characteristics emerge clearly from a comparison with the older work: its view of devotion was individualist and meditative, as opposed to collectivist and quasi-monastic; it contained a strong dose of instruction. In its fusion of the meditative and the instructional with the sacramental and liturgical it was a normal product of the counter-Reformation; its most obvious debt was to St François de Sales. What also made it characteristically of the counter-Reformation was that it was not primarily world-escaping but activist in its orientation: hence its alternative title—*A Manual of Spiritual Exercises and Instructions for Christians, who (living in the World) aspire to Devotion*. But Challoner seems to have been anxious not to push either of these characteristics too far: in the second case particularly he implied a good deal that others might make more of than he did. There was much that was conservative in the *Garden of the Soul*, though the main burden of it may be regarded as 'progressive'; it was thus excellently calculated to provide the community with its devotional backbone during the following century.[1]

It begins with a very short 'Christian Doctrine', expounding 'What every Christian must believe', and 'What every Christian must do, in order to life everlasting'. This is unpolemical, except in those parts of the first section which deal with the Church and the sacraments. Even here, there is no attack on contrary opinions; in the second section, which is little more than an exposition of the ten commandments, there is nothing specifically 'Catholic' at all. Finally there is a catena of scriptural passages—'Gospel-lessons to be pondered at leisure by every Christian soul'—resembling in general effect the *Imitation of Christ*; they affirm the need to choose between a Christian and a worldly life, and the obligation of love.

Devotionally, the theme of the *Garden of the Soul* is the spending of the day in the presence of God. It begins with a 'Morning Exercise': make the sign of the cross at waking; 'take care . . . to rise early, that you may gather the manna of Heaven'; after dressing and washing, 'kneel down in your oratory, or by your bedside' and say the Our Father, Hail Mary, Apostles' Creed and *Confiteor*. There follows a longish 'form of morning prayer', expressing adoration and thanks-

---

1. Burton, *Challoner*, i, pp. 127–137; a sympathetic account of the *Garden of the Soul* in Horton Davies, *Worship and Theology in England*, [iv] (Princeton, N.J., 1962), p. 22. For the counter-reformation background, H. O. Evennett, *The Spirit of the Counter-Reformation* (Cambridge, 1968), pp. 23 ff., 126 f.; and L. Cognet, *La Spiritualité moderne: i, L'Essor: 1500–1650* (Paris, 1966), pp. 274 ff. The earliest edn I have seen is apparently the second, Meighan, London, 1741; the one I have mainly used is Hall and Elliott, Newcastle, 1789, which does not significantly differ. For the *Manual of Devout Prayers* I have used the edn published by Meighan, London, 1728.

giving to God; offering to him 'all the thoughts, words and actions of this day, that they may be all consecrated to thee, by a pure intention of thy greater glory'; and asking for mercy on the Church, the country, relatives, friends and enemies, superiors and dependants, the suffering and the faithful departed. The tone of the prayer is one of restrained emotion; it concludes with a brief invocation of Our Lady, the saints in heaven and the angel guardian. At this point, as if to avert the formalism lurking in the recitation of written prayers, and to ensure that aspirations are put to practical effect, Challoner reminds his reader of the psalmist's injunction to 'meditate on thee in the morning', and enjoins a period of mental prayer. He explains what this means, and produces from St François de Sales's *Introduction to the Devout Life* guidance on how to go about it and ten meditations 'which may serve as examples of this exercise; and are very proper to bring to a resolution of serving God'. Here Challoner might have been advised to rely more on himself: the sober injunction to 'lay up in your mind such points of your meditation as have touched you most, and oftentimes in the day reflect on them' did not gain much force from a comparison with 'the gathering . . . of a nosegay in the garden of devotion, to smell at all the day'.

Between now and his evening devotions, the Catholic will be occupied in his worldly business, for which Challoner provides him with guidance in a pithy review 'Of the ordinary actions of the day, and the spirit with which they ought to be performed'. Work is good in itself, since idleness is the 'mother of all mischief'; those who are not obliged to earn their own living should nevertheless take up some occupation. It is also an obligation of religion, though Challoner seems uncertain whether to treat it as a positive Christian calling or a necessary curse. 'God Almighty most certainly appoints to everyone in his family his respective employment . . .; offer up both yourself and your work . . . to him, in union with the works in which your Saviour was employed in his mortal life . . . Submit yourself to the labours of your calling, as to a penance laid upon you by the Almighty.' It ought to be done well but should not become an obsession: 'take care to mortify that overgreat eagerness with which you sometimes find yourself set upon your work, and do all with calmness and peace, if you would have God to be with you'. Meals should begin and end with grace, and be approached in a spirit of modest, even furtive, asceticism: 'let not a meal pass without offering up to God some bit which you have most inclination to . . .

but take care to do this so as not to be taken notice of'. Recreations should be moderately engaged in, as necessary for the health of the body and the relaxation of the mind. In conversation, the Catholic should practise the presence of God, talk soberly and seriously without being ostentatiously pious or exposing 'what passes in your interior'. He should never contradict others without good reason: 'be as civil as you can, but without flattery, or condescending to anything that is evil; and be modestly cheerful, with the fear of God'. Challoner does not suggest that it is part of a Christian's duty to spend much time in study or general reading: he is to spend 'at least one quarter of an hour' in reading a spiritual book, and go to sermons as often as he can, taking care to draw appropriate consequences for his own behaviour. 'Remember that the word of God, heard or read, and not put into practice, will one day rise in judgment against you.' At the end of these instructions, and as if to embody the lesson they convey, Challoner places two hymns to the Holy Ghost, including Dryden's translation of the *Veni creator spiritus*, with the prayer which follows them in the breviary:

O God, who hast taught the hearts of thy faithful by the light of thy Holy Spirit, grant that we may by the gift of the same spirit be always truly wise . . .

The day's work done, the Catholic retires for his evening devotions, which may take a more public or a more private form: in private he will say the Our Father and other prayers as in the morning, and follow these with an examination of conscience which balances the morning meditation and 'ought never to be omitted'. He places himself in the presence of God, gives thanks for His benefits, and asks for light to see his sins; he examines the events of the day, 'endeavour[s] to be heartily sorry' for faults revealed, and resolves to amend, making particular resolutions for the following day. When he has finished his devotions, he may do his spiritual reading. While undressing, he should prepare the morning's meditation; in bed, he should think about death, and 'offer up to God [his] sleep . . . that by this repose of nature [he] may recover new vigour to serve him'.

In the various editions of the *Garden of the Soul*, the form of evening prayers changes a good deal,[2] and this reflects an uncertainty as to whether these should properly be said individually or collectively.

2. Compare *Garden of the Soul* (1789), pp. 181 ff., with edn published by Haydock, Manchester, 1799, pp. 170 f.

Challoner's heading is 'Evening Devotions for Families, or for Particulars'; and while the examination of conscience and related instructions could scarcely have been carried out in a group—some of them,
indeed, seem rather ill-suited to married people—most of the remaining
devotions would be performed more suitably by a domestic unit
assembled together. They consist of the Litany of the Saints and a number of prayers and responses taken from the offices of vespers and com-
pline, plural in form. Thus in particular the prayer following the com-
pline hymn *Te lucis ante terminum*, given in translation:

> Visit, we beseech thee, O Lord, this habitation, and drive far from it
> all snares of the enemy; let thy holy angels dwell therein, to preserve
> us in peace; and may thy blessing be upon us for ever . . .

In other contemporary manuals, which contain forms of evening
prayer similar to Challoner's, *habitaculum* is translated 'house and
family', and this was to prove the more popular version.[3] During the
later decades of the eighteenth century, the long and complex family
devotions of the *Manual of Devout Prayers*, with their exhausting
litanies for every day of the week, were evidently falling into disuse,
though they probably survived in some gentry households. Attempts to
replace them by something more liturgical—in particular by an English
translation of the daily office of vespers—did not prove successful either
with the gentry or with the 'well-disposed Christians in low circumstances of life', for whom a shorter and cheaper version was published
in 1770.[4] *The Layman's afternoon devotion . . . with litanies and night
prayers usually said in Catholic families*, which appeared in Preston in
1778, drew heavily on Challoner, and it was essentially the evening
devotions in the *Garden of the Soul* which fixed the form of family
prayers for the following decades. It was presumably their relative
brevity which gave them the advantage over older forms. Admittedly,
one child's eye view of them, as practised in a household of the mid-
nineteenth century, was that they were 'tedious and long' and 'seemed
never to end'; and it may be that in more leisured households devotions

3. So in *The layman's afternoon devotion* (Preston, 1778: see below), p. 173.
4. *The Complete Catholick Manual: containing Morning and Evening Prayers for the Use of Catholic Families . . .* (n.p., 1770), preface; according to this *The Divine Office for the Use of the Laity* had been published in 4 vols. in 1768. I have seen a 2 vol. ed. by B. Rayment, Haydock, Manchester, 1806. The compiler of *The layman's afternoon devotion* found the Preston congregation more attracted to an evening service out of the *Garden of the Soul* than to one taken from the liturgical office.

were extended with matter drawn from elsewhere in the book. It is also obvious that the increasing accessibility of chapels was tending to remove both morning and evening prayers, except in so far as they were purely individual, from the domestic scene. The liturgical manual of domestic prayer of 1770 was offered especially for domestic use by those who could not get to public vespers: William Mawhood, whose practice must presumably reflect Challoner's own direction, became during the 1780s a regular attender at Sunday vespers in the chapel at Lincoln's Inn Fields, but makes no reference to family praying in his diary. Challoner and others put emphasis on the religious functions of the family, and as late as 1860 it could be assumed that a Catholic's worship was divided into the public, the domestic and the personal; but the domestic community as a subject of worship was certainly losing importance, its functions divided between the individual and the congregation.[5] Challoner had established the forms of individual prayer before the outset of our period; it is in congregational prayer that the most vigorous signs of activity and experiment appear.

For an eighteenth-century English Catholic Mass was 'prayers' *par excellence*, and though the use of this term was partly the consequence of a legal taboo, it also represented with some accuracy what an average Catholic would expect to be doing when he came to Mass. As we have seen in the commentaries of Gother, 'devotional' and 'liturgical' traditions were in conflict in the Catholic's attitude to Mass, and the former more deeply ingrained; it is not clear how much headway Gother's liturgical approach had made by the beginning of this period. In the *Garden of the Soul*, at any rate, Challoner offered a conflation of the two approaches which, if one takes the liturgical attitude as the ideal, fell somewhat short of Gother. In his Mass instructions he put a good deal less emphasis than Gother on the congregation as the true offerers of the sacrifice; he did not print the ordinary of the Mass or even, like Gother, a full translation of it. This was certainly available elsewhere, but the popularity of the *Garden of the Soul* must have ensured a preponderance of the 'devotional' tradition. The Catholic was advised, when entering the chapel, to 'chuse, as much as you can, a place to kneel in, where you may be most recollected and least disturbed'. He was then presented with a detailed commentary on what was taking place on the altar, and with a series of meditative prayers appropriate to

5. 'Frideswide', *Reminiscences*, p. 29; *Mawhood Diary*, pp. 160 f., 188 f., 248 ff.; *Garden of the Soul* (Richardson, London, etc., *c*. 1862), preface.

successive moments of the action. Those at the beginning, as at the *Confiteor*, and at the end, at the communion, were free-standing private devotions in the first person singular; those in the middle, from the offertory to the *Pater Noster*, were in the plural form and closely related to the action of the Mass. The individual was exhorted to join with the priest, verbatim, at the Kyrie, Gloria, Creed, Preface, Pater Noster and Last Gospel, though not at the consecration, the words of which were not given. Prayers of a general kind stood in for the Proper of the Mass, which was not given either.[6]

The congregational element was thus distinctly limited in the form of Mass-participation propagated in the *Garden of the Soul*; and although it may be said that this was natural enough in a manual of private devotion, it does seem to have reflected a general attitude on Challoner's part. During Mass itself, it seems clear that Challoner's advice was followed; hence there was little demand for the Mass in English. But it was not entirely acceptable among either the clergy or the laity, and particularly not in the town congregations which began to flourish with the general opening of chapels. Their attitude to collective worship, as to congregational institutions, was influenced by the nonconformist environment into which they emerged, and their attitude to uniformity of service was that it would 'preclude that desire of variety, and of making improvements, so congenial to the human mind'.[7]

The traditional practice of the community gave scope for such improvements, since it had been customary to use the opportunity of assembling at Mass as an occasion for collective prayer, and Catholics had been encouraged to perform services of prayer and instruction when priests were not available. As chapels became established, priests and congregations built upon this foundation to compose their own forms of prayer for recitation before Mass, and several of these were printed. They were invariably in English. I propose to consider three of them, which cover the period between 1791 and 1840 and cast a great deal of light on the attitude of Catholics to public worship during the half-century which followed its formal legalisation.

The earliest of these represents practice in the Midland district, and

6. *Garden of the Soul* (1789), pp. 65–100.
7. [N. A. Gilbert], *The Method of Sanctifying the Sabbath Days at Whitby, Scarborough, etc.* (2nd edn by G. L. Haydock, York, 1824), preface. For the English liturgical background of the period in general, see Horton Davies, *Worship and Theology in England*, [iii] (Princeton, N.J./London, 1961).

was first printed in 1792 though no doubt in use before this date; it probably originated in the Wolverhampton chapel, for which we have an expanded version printed in 1801 and apparently composed by John Carter and John Kirk, priests at Wolverhampton and Lichfield respectively.[8] It begins, after the sign of the cross, with a free version of psalm 94 (*Venite exultemus*), simplified and rationalised, for recitation by the priest with congregational responses: a declaration of intention to worship God in the service of the Church. This is followed by the Our Father, and congregational 'acts' of faith, hope, charity and contrition; these are in the first person plural, and in the original form seem to have been meant to be spoken by the congregation; in the second form they are given to the priest, with congregational responses added at the end of each. A litany is then recited: in the original form, there is one for ordinary Sundays, and special ones for Easter, Christmas and Whitsun; in the later form different ones are also given for every quarter, following, it may be noted, the calendar, not the liturgical, year. The practice of composing litanies had a long and flourishing history in the community; they had formed a considerable part of the collective domestic devotions of the *Manual of Devout Prayers*, which provided a stock from which composers of litanies for public congregational use were able to draw. Unlike the traditional Latin litanies translated in the *Garden of the Soul*, these gave scope for originality: as collective petitions for God's mercy and assistance in the particular circumstances of the praying community, they could properly be composed, modified or rearranged as these circumstances altered. In the general climate of liturgical experiment then prevailing in England, it was natural for Catholics to make use of such resources of this kind as their own tradition provided; in their use of the litany they came nearest to the practice of extemporary and occasional prayer characteristic of some branches of the English Protestant tradition. One should not exaggerate the resemblance: Catholics were the last people likely to countenance

8. *Prayers before and after Mass, first published for the use of the Middle District* (Coghlan, London, 1792); *Prayers before and after Mass said in the Catholic Chapel at Wolverhampton* (Wolverhampton, 1801); Husenbeth, *Life of Milner*, p. 109; J. Gillow, *Bibliographical Dictionary of English Catholics*, i (1885), p. 412. Husenbeth ascribed the second version to Joseph Berington: there seems no evidence for this, but Carter and Kirk were both friends and followers of his, and their improvements certainly reflect his influence: cf. Duffy, 'Joseph Berington', pp. 279 f., 294, 299; M. Rowlands, 'The Staffordshire Clergy'. *Recusant History*, ix (1968), esp. pp. 238 ff. It will be noticed that there were prayers after Mass as well as before it, but these were shorter and less variable and for simplicity's sake I have neglected them.

effusions of 'enthusiasm'; but priests at least had the opportunity, in cultivating the genre, to exercise their own imagination and sense of relevance. A couple of examples may illustrate the interplay of tradition and experiment in the Wolverhampton litanies. The *Manual* had contained, as part of the litany for Wednesday morning, petitions

That it may please thee to preserve the Catholics of this land from all sin and wickedness, and so to adorn their lives with solid piety, that others seeing their good works, may glorify thee our heavenly Father

and

That it may please thee to grant us the Grace of improving such Restraints and temporal Disadvantages as we fall under, into an occasion of Retiredness and Christian severity, supplying our want of publick Assemblies by a greater Diligence in private Devotions.[9]

The first of these petitions retained its actuality throughout changes of regime; it was reproduced in the single litany of the earlier Wolverhampton form, and also in the later one, where it formed part of the litany for the autumn quarter. The second obviously required some adjustment: the earlier litany, no doubt predating 1791, has

That under the most severe restraints, we may, with the exactest fidelity, perform all our duties.

In the later litany for the winter quarter, the petitions are for thankfulness, and for proper use of opportunities now available; they reach a conclusion which reflects the 'enlightened' views of Joseph Berington but was no less appropriate for that:

That we may be ever thankful for whatever opportunities thou art pleased to give us of meeting in thy worship,
That we may lay hold of all such opportunities for thy greater glory, and the good of our souls . . .
That as to us, thou hast mercifully enlarged the liberties of thy worship, so throughout the world all restraints may be removed;
We beseech thee, hear us.

After the litany comes the reading of the epistle and gospel of the Sunday (in English) and the instruction or sermon; these are preceded and followed by realistically phrased prayers for understanding—

9. *Manual of Devout Prayers* (1728), pp. 167 ff., 172.

Give us a diligent and obedient spirit, quickness of apprehension, capacity of retaining, and the powerful assistance of thy holy grace . . .

—and for fruitful application

. . . that as we have now heard what our duty is, we may be enabled to accomplish it, through Christ our Lord.

Finally the priest recites a translation of a prayer from the Canon of the Mass, *Unde et memores*, identifying the sacrifice of the Mass with that of the Cross, and asking the Father to accept it, as he did those of Abel, Abraham and Melchisedech; like all the prayers of the Canon, it draws attention to the participation of the congregation as offerers of the sacrifice. Mass then begins, the congregation no doubt doing its best to follow the instructions in the *Garden of the Soul*.

The second set of prayers was composed by the Jesuits Joseph Dunn and Nicholas Morgan, priests at Preston, and William Dunn, brother of the former and secular priest at Blackburn, for the use of their respective congregations. Its first edition, so far as I know, dates from 1805, a second from 1823; since Joseph Dunn had been priest at Preston for some thirty years before the first of these dates, it presumably reproduces earlier practice.[10] It avoids the impression sometimes given by the Wolverhampton form, of setting itself up as something like a substitute for the Mass: the whole ordinary is given in English, and divided usefully into five parts, with instructional headings ('Part I—The Preparations of the offerers; by Acts of Humility, Praise, Faith, etc. . . .'). The counterpart of this is that the prayers before and after Mass rather lack direction. The two forms have a good deal in common: the second edition of the Preston prayers, though not the first, also begins with the psalm *Venite exultemus*, on which it attempts no improvements; it contains, in the singular form, similar acts of faith, hope, charity and contrition, and prayers for the sick and the dead; a prayer for keeping the Sunday holy ('O Almighty and Eternal God, who hast appointed us six days, in which we may labour and do all our work, and hath consecrated the seventh to thyself . . .') is identical with that which follows the Wolverhampton spring litany. There are three main changes. Instead of

10. *Prayers to be said before and after Mass . . . in the Catholic Chapels of Preston and Blackburn* (Manchester, 1805; Preston, 1823). For Joseph Dunn, see above, p. 304; he was possibly also the compiler of *The layman's afternoon devotion* (above, n. 3). For William Dunn see Duffy, 'Berington', pp. 195 f.

a litany, there is a sequence of psalms and canticles; immediately before Mass there is a long prayer in which the congregation, through the priest, explains its object in offering it, and prays for the Church, for the spread of truth and light, for the king, secular authorities and nation, and for its own members, living and dead; the sermon comes after Mass, not before it. Formally speaking, it is not very satisfying. It gives the impression of having grown by accretion rather than been constructed with any particular purpose in mind; there is some duplication; the congregation is not always kept clearly in view as the subject of the prayers; and some of the psalms do not seem specially relevant. On the other hand, the Mass achieves greater prominence, and the whole service feels lived-in, as if people liked it the way it was.

The last of these forms was composed by John Lingard in the early 1830s. His intention was partly to produce a form of public prayer which would be attractive to potential Protestant converts; but he was also concerned, for its own sake, with the reform of Catholic worship and instruction, much of whose language he considered incomprehensible to ordinary people. To this end he composed a new catechism, and retranslated the psalms and gospels. His *Manual of Prayers for Sundays and Holydays* was the principal fruit of all this activity: it was printed in 1833, but the version I have used was published in 1840 by his friend Robert Tate, and contained additions and alterations of which Lingard did not approve.[11] It is thus possible that some of what follows is not by Lingard, though it seems to me unlikely that there has been any tampering with his prayers before Mass, which have the stamp of authenticity.

After the sign of the cross, and a statement of intention to devote the holy day to divine service, they begin like the others with the psalm *Venite exultemus*, of which Lingard offers alternative versions, one resembling the Preston form and retaining the text of the psalm itself, though a good deal is left out, the other the Wolverhampton form. Both are said with congregational responses, and they are followed by three short prayers, the first two rather heavily historical, about the keeping of the Sabbath. The priest and congregation say in turn the two halves of the Our Father. A prayer 'that we may deserve to obtain what thou promisest' makes a suitable passage to the acts of faith, hope and charity,

---

11. Gillow, *Bibliographical Dictionary*, iv, p. 274; Haile and Bonney, *Life and Letters of Lingard*, pp. 239 f., 266 f.; *Catholic Magazine*, i (1831–1832), p. 546, etc.; iii (1833), p. 457; *Manual of Prayers for Sundays and Holydays* (Croshaw, York, 1844).

which are adopted, with the congregational responses, from the Wolverhampton form, but simplified. The remainder consists of a series of short sequences, each comprising a statement of intention, a psalm, a brief litany (omitted in two cases) and a concluding prayer or prayers. In these the congregation, through the mouth of the priest, prays for forgiveness of sins; in thanksgiving for blessings; for God's future protection on themselves and others; for the sick; for the faithful departed; and for grace to offer Mass worthily.

Formally speaking, Lingard's first object was obviously to combine the virtues of the litany-tradition with those of the psalm-tradition, and he could only do this by subjecting both of them to drastic reconsideration. His use of psalms is extremely free: they are all retranslated, with a view to simplicity and comprehensibility; archaisms of language are removed, and Hebrew obscurities simply omitted; considerable liberties are taken in rearrangement, and the sequence of thought from one verse to the next is pointed by means which sound as if they might not recommend themselves to a Hebrew scholar. At the expense of the mysterious and the specific, Lingard achieves compression, a plain, even tone and continuous relevance. He begins with psalm 50 (*Miserere* —the repentance of David), which would have been fairly well known to congregations, omitting a difficult half-verse. His psalms for the second and third sequences (Thanksgiving; Trust in God as helper and protector) are artificial constructions from a variety of different psalms; surprisingly, they sound rather convincing. The fourth, for the sick, is a very truncated and rearranged version of psalm 30 (*In te, Domine, speravi*); the fifth, for the dead, inevitably paslm 129 (*De profundis*); the sixth, in preparation for Mass, psalm 83 (*Quam dilecta tabernacula tua*), uncut.

The litanies which follow the psalms are skilfully composed: brief, pertinent and well integrated both within each sequence and with each other; they are also properly congregational. The first contains an invocation of the Trinity, and three affirmations of guilt, with the response *Have mercy on us*; the second, three affirmations of thanksgiving (for creation, redemption and sanctification, to the three persons of the Trinity) with the response *Praise and glory be to thee, O God*; the third an affirmation of trust in God and petitions for the congregation itself, for the Church, for the country ('That it may please thee to pour out thy mercies on this nation, to free it from ignorance, error and vice, and to make all its people virtuous and happy'), and for personal relations, with the response *We beseech thee, hear us*. There are no litanies attached to the prayers for the sick and the dead; presumably Lingard thought them redundant. The last litany consists of four petitions related to the sacrifice of the Mass: to God the Father speaking by the prophet Malachi of the passage of acceptable sacrifice from the Jews to the Gentiles; to Christ as high priest, as sacrificial lamb, and as he who has made Christians into priests of the new sacrifice ('Thou who hast made us kings and priests to God, a holy nation, a purchased people . . .')—with the response, *Hearken to our petitions*.

The concluding prayers are simple enough, but draw attention to some theological or practical implications of what has been done. The first prayer, for forgiveness of sins, emphasises that this is expected only through Christ's merits and promises; the thanksgiving prayer contains a passage which some might have found risky—'Let our souls magnify the Lord, and our spirits rejoice in God our Saviour'; the third and fifth draw attention to a particular obligation which rests upon the congregation to pray for its own members, and for 'those with whom it hath been thy pleasure to connect us by the ties of kindred, religion and society'; the fourth draws attention to the fact that the object of prayer for the sick is not primarily the restoration of health. The prayers for the offering of Mass conclude the whole appropriately with a reminder that Christ instituted the sacrifice at the Last Supper, is really present as victim, and that it is only through him that the congregation can offer it. In a final prayer, the priest asks God not to consider their or his own unworthiness, but the worthiness of what is offered, so that 'through the merits of Christ's death we may be cleansed from sin, and be admitted hereafter to see him face to face in his eternal sanctuary in Heaven'.

Lingard's service would have taken something under half an hour to perform. A liturgical scholar would no doubt find it deficient in one respect or another: looked at by a layman, it gives an impression of considerable formal beauty and appropriateness, and it strikes me personally both as a genuine creative achievement in its own right, and as the successful culmination of a phase of liturgical experiment. Lingard clearly knew the other forms which have been discussed, and no doubt others which have not come to light; he had learnt from both of them, avoided their respective drawbacks and come up with something which was at once boldly experimental and deeply grounded in the experience of the community. In the shorter view, his prayers before Mass gave an adequate liturgical expression to the congregational bent in late eighteenth- and early nineteenth-century English Catholicism; in the longer view they indicate the achievement of a maturity of spirit towards which the community had striven through the two and a half centuries of its history. I know of no evidence to suggest how far they were used outside Lingard's own congregation at Hornby, whether indeed they were used at all. By 1840, in any case, ecclesiastical authority had come to frown on such efforts, and the liturgical trend was setting in a very different direction.

As we have seen in the instructions of the *Garden of the Soul*, the Catholic was expected, beyond his private or formal prayer, to worship God by cultivating the intention of serving him in the acts of his secular life. Formed in the circumstances of the earlier eighteenth century, Challoner's view of the secular obligations of the Catholic was probably in practice a somewhat restricted one. He certainly maintained, and transmitted in the community, a strong view of the antagonism between Christianity and 'the world'. Yet his teaching was capable of different interpretations, and during the period we are now considering it was the more expansive interpretation which came to the fore.[12] The changing exterior circumstances of the community were in themselves likely to promote a difference of tone: contacts multiplied; Catholics came to consider themselves, and to be widely considered, as members of one of a variety or more or less equivalent communities; and the 'secular' trend of eighteenth-century Christianity created a climate of opinion concerned to emphasise the ideals of behaviour which united Christians and play down the doctrinal and ecclesiastical factors which divided them. It was therefore natural that a 'secular' view of Christianity should make headway among Catholics, who could in any case find a good deal of warrant for it in their own counter-Reformation tradition. The most obvious place for it was a part of the public worship of the community which we have so far neglected, the sermon; we may look at the sermons of the most popular Catholic preacher of the period, James Archer. Most of Archer's preaching, it is true, was done at a comparatively early period: it reflects the particular circumstances of the 1780s and 1790s, and also of the metropolitan congregations who were his principal audience. But although he had ceased to preach by 1820, and had come under criticism from Milner, his published sermons, which

12. Some relevant comments, not directly concerned with Challoner, in Aveling, *West Riding*, pp. 261 f.

had begun to appear during the 1780s, remained popular and were last reprinted in 1845. We may therefore take his doctrine as representative of an attitude widespread in the community at least until this date.[13]

The tone of Archer's preaching activity is given in the preface to his main collection of sermons, written in 1785. He rejects controversy and polemic, claims that the principles of Christian morality, which he is concerned to expound, are effectively identical in all denominations, and affirms that God must approve all honest seekers. Charity is the first obligation of Christians. 'I wish to see all men, however various their religious creed, mutually loving, cherishing and assisting one another, and walking through the chequered paths of this mortal life in harmony and peace.'[14] We may wonder, after this, what precisely Archer has to contribute as a preacher of Catholic Christianity, and whether he is not about to jettison the specific characteristics of his community in favour of generalised exhortations of a fashionably enlightened kind, carrying a strong undercurrent of political apologetic. This seems to have been roughly Milner's view, and as usual there was something in it; but it did not take account of Archer's concern to ground his doctrine in Catholic spirituality, notably in that of Challoner, of whom he was in some ways a more faithful disciple than Milner.

For this reason, although Archer is mainly concerned with the relations of the Catholic and the world, it is necessary to begin with an account of his views on devotion as such. With some marginal additions of a rationalising kind, as that 'fasting must naturally abate the ardour of the passions, by depriving them of their fuel', these are essentially Challoner's, and conventional enough: what matters is not the devotional act but the 'disposition of the heart', and Catholics may prove by their lives that their practice is not superstitious. He agrees that there are plenty of Catholics, 'particularly among the lower order of those who are natives of a neighbouring island', who 'may attach too much importance to external practices, and render them ridiculous by their

13. *Sermons on various moral and religious subjects* (4 vols., London, 1785–1786; 2 vols., London, 1817—I have used both edns); *Sermons on various moral and religious subjects, for some of the principal festivals of the year* (London, 1789); *Sermons on Matrimonial Duties* ... (London, 1804); these will be referred to as *Sermons*, i, ii and iii, with references to individual sermons by number in each series. Ward, *Dawn of the Catholic Revival*, i, pp. 28 f.; Husenbeth, *Life of Milner*, p. 228. For Archer's career, see Gillow, *Bibliographical Dictionary*, i, p. 55—he was born of a poor family in London, and his mother at least was Irish or London-Irish; Duffy, 'Joseph Berington', pp. 176 f., 214, 222, 272.
14. *Sermons*, i (1785), preface, p. 5.

manner of using them'; when engaged in by people who never come to confession or communion, they are 'insults and mockeries'. More generally, he draws attention to the probable presence of self-regard and sensible pleasure in those who multiply devotional acts. All this is to clear the way for his positive doctrine, again perfectly in tune with Challoner's, that devotion is simply 'that habitual disposition of the soul which is formed by divine love', 'a continual sense of the presence of God', and is therefore not a retreat from or an alternative to worldly activity. 'Devotion is not so properly any particular act, as a spirit which is to animate and dignify all our actions.'[15]

'All your employments, my brethren, are properly religious exercises.' What is needed to make the conduct of temporal affairs into a way of sanctification is not extraordinary behaviour, but purity of intention towards God, order and regularity, a concern to 'redeem the time' and to be serviceable to one's neighbour. We 'are called upon by Almighty God to exert ourselves in our respective stations, that we may promote his honour and glory, at the same time that we become useful to ourselves and our fellow-creatures'. This is what the saints did: 'they were saints, because they discharged all the duties of their station, and discharged them well'; sanctity is perfectly compatible with a 'cheerful enjoyment of our situation in the world'.[16]

Among those employments which are 'properly religious exercises', the care of the family has a high place: Archer preached a series of sermons on 'Matrimonial Duties'. 'Home . . . should be the seat of your comforts, the scene in which you exercise your virtues.' Husbands should not avoid it; wives should devote themselves to it, not putting their responsibilities on to others so as to enjoy the delights of society, and spending their spare time in the improvement of their minds. The authority of parents is an emanation of the divine authority: it must be exercised for the same end, in the service of care and love. What is taught to children must come within a framework of parental example and instruction; parents should teach religion themselves, 'recommend[ing] your instructions by seasonable caresses', adducing God from the night and the stars, taking their children to chapel and explaining the services to them. The family should come together before the altar, as

15. *Sermons*, i, 8 ('Of Exterior Devotion and Religious Ceremonies'), 9 ('On the Sacred Name of Jesus'), 18, 27 ('On Devotion').
16. *Sermons*, i, 6 ('On the value and employment of time'), 7 ('On Regularity in the Conduct of Life'), 12 ('On Purity of Intention'); ii, 1 (All Saints).

well as in prayer and spiritual reading at home; hence mixed marriage is to be discouraged. In considering their children's future, parents should be neither authoritarian nor over-ambitious, but respect their freedom, discover their natural abilities, and 'assist them in the choice of a state of life, in which they may become useful to themselves and beneficial to the community'.[17]

Besides what is required by work and family, the Catholic has 'civil duties' to fulfil. The primary obligation on the Christian is that of charity, and charity is to be exercised within the bounds of the civil community to which he belongs. He is to love his fellow-countrymen; he may not withdraw his participation from them for sentimental reasons (such as Jacobitism), nor on the grounds that the community does not grant him full civil equality. The 'present constitution' is 'happy', because it is the guardian of political and moral liberty; and there is a suggestion that exclusion from a political career, as such, may help the Catholic to be a more, rather than a less, free and useful member of society. Failure to serve one's neighbour on the grounds of difference of religious belief must above all be condemned, as contrary to the law of charity, specifically denounced in the parable of the Good Samaritan and particularly to be avoided by Catholics, who are generally understood to act with severity towards those who dissent from them. 'Remember, that notwithstanding the varieties of customs and opinions, all your fellow-creatures have a claim on your benevolence; all should be dear to you: because all are made after the image of God, all are redeemed by [Christ's] blood . . . Let then, my beloved friends, let your active and spirited exertions, your honest industry, contribute to public happiness . . .'[18]

By twentieth-century standards, Archer's view of what constitutes public happiness is a restricted one, in that he lacks any notion that the unimpeded exercise of constructive social activity may require some alterations in the framework of the society within which it seeks to operate. In this sense, Archer's secular gospel is the reverse of a social gospel: in seeking to demolish religious barriers, he remains a prisoner of social ones, and this not merely through inattention. After a sermon in which he has asserted the beneficent effects of public worship in

17. *Sermons*, iii, 1–6 *passim*, 7; i, 6, 15.
18. *Sermons*, i, 11 ('On the Civil Duties of a Christian'), 43 ('On Fraternal Charity'); ii, 6 ('On Forgiving Injuries'), 7 ('On the Excellence of the Christian Dispensation').

inspiring enthusiasm for the common good and 'lead[ing] the minds of men to a consideration of the natural equality of the human species'—it was admittedly a fund-raising sermon, appealing to a mixed audience for subscriptions for a new chapel—it is depressing to find him concluding with a recommendation of the gospel as having 'so blessed an influence in preserving the order, subordination and comforts of civil society'.[19]

This is perhaps simply to say that as a preacher Archer does not quite measure up to the standard set by Challoner as a devotional guide or by Lingard as a composer of congregational prayers. For this very reason, we are entitled to take him as a representative figure, formulating, justifying and promoting instincts which were widespread in the community.[20] In drawing attention to deficiencies in his view of the Christian's duty in the world, one is at the same time indicating deficiencies in the community, which do not need to be defended. By the same token, both he and it deserve credit for what, taken as a whole, is a not unworthy attempt to discover the implications of the gospel in the circumstances of a particular environment. It is obvious enough that, at various points and in various ways, it was affected by influences deriving from a Protestant milieu and an interdenominational audience ('To almost every Protestant library,' Charles Butler remarked, 'and to many a Protestant toilet, Mr Archer's sermons have found their way'[21]); without assuming that such influences were invariably beneficial, one may at least claim that in this case their effect was to enforce a concentration upon essentials. Archer's doctrine, by its adherence to Challoner and through him to the masters of counter-Reformation spirituality, marked a successful recovery and reformulaton of ideals and attitudes which had been present at the birth of the community but which had inevitably been repressed by the conditions in which the community had been obliged to exist in the meantime. Though it may in principle be open to the objection of underplaying some necessary

19. *Sermons*, iii, 15.
20. As examples of this representativity I would suggest: Stephen Tempest, *Religio Laici* (1764), pp. 7 f.; *Mawhood Diary, passim*, e.g. the frequent occasions where Mawhood records having gone to non-Catholic services and sermons, pp. 87, 161, 193, etc.; George Silvertop, in Ward, *Eve*, ii, pp. 235 f.; William Ullathorne, *From Cabin-boy to Archbishop*, pp. 4 ff. Mawhood was friendly with Archer, and heard him preach quite often (*Diary*, see index under *Archer*); his sermons were regularly read to Ullathorne's congregation at Scarborough (*op. cit.*, p. 9).
21. Gillow, *Bibliographical Dictionary*, i, p. 55.

tensions between Christianity and 'the world', it was both a recall to the sources and a tract for the times. It probably deserves some credit for the buoyancy of the community during the following decades; were there no other evidence to adduce, it would be a sufficient answer to the claim which became current from the 1840s that the traditional Catholic community was a *gens lucifuga*, lurking in the catacombs and unwilling to venture into the world outside.

This complex of attitudes to God, to prayer and to Protestant England provided the bony structure of the community's way of life until about 1830. At that date, despite some appearances to the contrary, it was perhaps at its greatest maturity: the last volume of Lingard's *History of England*, which was—barring the works of Edward Elgar—its most characteristic and enduring product, appeared in that year.[22] After this the structure began to disintegrate. How quickly and how completely it disintegrated, how much of it survived the final phase of transformation of the traditional community, are questions which it is difficult to answer with assurance, and would certainly carry us beyond the scope of this book. What may be said with confidence is that, when Lingard died in 1851, the state of mind and the way of life which he had embodied were in retreat, a defensive minority opinion in a community which was being inwardly as well as outwardly transformed.

From about 1830 the foundation-stone of the whole structure, the *Garden of the Soul*, began to crumble. The first notable blow was struck in an edition published in Birmingham, in 1830, under the aegis of Thomas Walsh and no doubt inspired from Oscott. The next quarter of a century was a period of extreme confusion in the publishing history of the *Garden of the Soul*. What was happening, in general, was that those who were responsible for successive re-editions were losing sight of the idea of devotion as taught by Challoner and developed by Archer, and undermining the book's coherence as a handbook of daily Christian living in the world. In some hands it became more like a missal, a liturgical guide to attendance at Mass and the reception of the sacraments, much of it in Latin; in others, a compendium of occasional prayers and peripheral 'devotions'. Under Wiseman, the latter tendency predominated. Challoner's guidance in spirituality, his insistence on the entrenchment of prayer in the circumstances of everyday living, lost its

---

22. *A History of England, from the first invasion of the Romans . . . [to 1688]* (1st edn, 8 vols., Mawman, London, 1819–1830).

centrality, suffered mutilation and was finally omitted altogether.[23] This process does not seem to have been completed before 1850, and the editions I have seen suggest that there was a good deal of resistance to it; but it is clear that during the previous twenty years a serious breach in the continuity of the community's inner development had occurred. I am not suggesting that, in a choice between the old and the new devotional regimes all the arguments were on one side: a new regime was clearly required in a mass community whose circumstances were poor and standards of instruction low. It will have been noticed that, to convey its message fully, the *Garden of the Soul* required not only a high standard of education and instruction, but a secure social position and a good deal of leisure. The pity was not that it was superseded, but that what superseded it failed to take adequate notice of what it had achieved. What was wanted, as Lingard saw, was to recast its contents in such a way as to make them accessible to an audience which had by now become too remote from the one Challoner had envisaged. 'I am sure,' he had written in 1829, thinking of the farmers and labourers of his congregation, 'that whoever will compose a prayer-book for the poor so simple, so easily intelligible, that they may perfectly comprehend what they repeat, will render an unostentatious but most praiseworthy service to religion.'[24] Unhappily the following decades were not a time when unostentatious services were in vogue, and the opportunity was neglected.

What was happening in the field of public worship was rather similar, and equally antipathetic to Lingard's ideals. The first step towards the restriction of improvements to the standard liturgy had been taken by Milner shortly after he took over as Midland vicar-apostolic in 1803. Since the Wolverhampton form of congregational prayer had been compiled by priests of whose orthodoxy he was suspicious, it is not surprising that he should have wished to see it abolished in what now became in effect his own chapel. In 1804 he had it replaced by a revised form of his own composition, and this he recommended for general use throughout the district.[25] It was the same general shape as the earlier

23. Burton, *Challoner*, i, pp. 135 f. I have not seen the Birmingham edition: the process described may be followed in the editions published by Croshaw, York, 1839; Duffy, Dublin, 1846; Richardson, London, etc., *c.* 1862; and Thomson, Preston, 1880 (first approbation dated 1858).

24. Haile and Bonney, *Lingard*, pp. 239 f.

25. *An Exercise, for Sanctifying Sundays and Holydays, and for preparing to Assist at Mass profitably* (Wolverhampton, 1804; new edn 1817); Husenbeth, *Life of Milner*,

form, centred on a litany, and concluding with a sermon; but Milner
replaced the existing litanies by a single litany of the Mass, a grindingly
theological composition which looks as if its main object was to ex-
tinguish errors on the subject surviving from the previous regime. It
proved unpopular in Wolverhampton. This was not a very felicitous
effort; all the same, Milner remained within the tradition he disliked.
He added to his form of prayers an interesting preface, in which he discussed the history and present condition of public prayer in the community. As one would have expected, he was not enthusiastic about the
liturgical private enterprise then obtaining; he complained that most
existing forms had had no ecclesiastical approval, and that some of them
—the reference is probably to the later Wolverhampton form, and it
would be illuminating to know what Milner had in mind—'have even
been borrowed from the publications of sectaries'. However, he went on
to say that he did not intend to impose his own form or to prohibit any
other forms except those drawn from heterodox sources: the implication, I think, was that the earlier Wolverhampton form was acceptable
though the later one was not. He had also a good deal of sense to say
about the desiderata for composition in the genre, which he reasonably
described as a difficult one. His objection to the singing of psalms in
English indicates that he would also have liked to replace existing forms
of evening prayer by a Latin vespers, but there seems no sign that he
tried to do this.[26]

Milner's action was presumably effective in his own district, but so
far as I can see it had no effect elsewhere. So long as congregational
instincts and institutions retained any vitality such interference was
unlikely to be welcome; the next decades were, as we have seen, a time
of considerable activity in the field of congregational prayer. I have no
evidence to suggest that Milner's distaste was shared by his contemporary vicars-apostolic, though it was probably transmitted to his
successor Thomas Walsh; but as the movement for liturgical revival
gathered way and the autonomy of congregations and clergy retreated
in face of episcopal monarchy, the end of the age of private enterprise
in congregational prayer could be foreseen. Twelve years after Milner's

---

pp. 108 f. It is obvious from the resolutions of the meeting of vicars-apostolic in
1803, after Milner's consecration, that he tried to persuade his colleagues to impose
a uniform set of prayers before Mass, and failed: Bernard Ward, *History of St.
Edmund's College* (London, 1893), p. 319.
26. Husenbeth, *Life of Milner*, p. 110.

death, in 1838, the vicars-apostolic finally fell in with his wishes by enacting a uniform order of prayers before and after Mass for use throughout the country, and prohibiting evening prayers in English.[27] Whatever the form of Mass-prayers imposed, the effect was certainly to extract most of its meaning and vitality from the tradition, which subsequently fell into disuse. The unadorned Latin Mass was left as the only act of Catholic morning worship, its collective character concealed from view; English hymn-singing survived, and may have flourished better under the new regime than it had under the old, but it did so in the context of a Latin evening service of Vespers and Benediction. Coming as it did sharply on the heels of the publication of Lingard's *Manual of Prayers*, this action must be regarded as the effect of a conscious decision to reject the English language as a vehicle of public prayer in the community. Here again was a grave breach in the development of the community's tradition; it would prove difficult, perhaps impossible, to repair.

This may strike one as a perplexing decision, and one which can scarcely, as in the case of the *Garden of the Soul*, be explained as a response to the changing composition of the community. Its explanation is ideological rather than social: a determination to get rid of anything which might suggest that the Catholic community in England was a sectarian body, a branch of the English dissenting tradition; to get rid, indeed, of the idea that there was properly speaking such a thing as a Catholic community in England at all; to revive the claim whose abandonment, it has been argued, was the first condition of the existence of this community, that there was and always had been one church in England, which was Roman and Catholic. This renunciation of the community's actual past was inspired from a number of disparate sources—romantic-mediaevalist, Roman-ecclesiastical, ex-Anglican—which do not require to be disentangled here. I shall only be concerned to draw attention to some ways in which it had been making progress during the last decades of the traditional community's history, as evidence of a transformation of the religious imperatives governing the community's attitude to the world outside.

It is simplest to discuss the transformation in terms of the relationship between Catholics and Protestants, though what was finally at issue was a more fundamental or more existential question about the relationship between Catholics and English society at large. It may be

27. Ward, *Sequel*, i, p. 133.

illustrated by a glance at problems which arose for Catholics concerning their obligations in the conversion of other Englishmen to their belief. Some of them were problems of canon law: conditional rebaptism of Protestant converts for example, disapproved of by Challoner, half-heartedly adopted by the vicars-apostolic in 1803, but apparently not normal practice until the 1830s; or the discipline of mixed marriage, imposed in its modern and rigorous form—no full ceremony, formal agreement by the non-Catholic party that all children should be brought up Catholics—on the repeal of the Hardwicke Marriage Act in 1836.[28] But here we are primarily concerned, not with enactments of law, but with general attitudes, and though one must tread more warily here, the signs and general direction of change are clear enough. I hope it has been shown that early nineteenth-century Catholics did not regard the conversion of their fellow-countrymen with indifference: the days when the gentry were concerned and in a position to put a ban on 'proselytism' were over. Nevertheless, one may gather from Archer's sermons that they approached the topic from a different point of view than later prevailed. Most of them accepted plurality of religious belief as a natural consequence of historical development and the exercise of rational choice; the fact that there was an established church in England which was doctinally in error might be regarded more as a consequence of history than of reason, but it was a fact of life, and they had no particular quarrel with it. They hoped that the country would become more Christian, but did not identify this hope with the expansion of their own community. They felt modestly confident that this expansion would come through the removal of what they considered irrational prejudice, and believed that Christian living on their part and patient work—not necessarily, as Lingard's *History* shows, directly apologetic in character[29]—were the best ways of removing it.

For some, and notably for Milner, this was too tepid, and conflict had already broken out in 1810 when the Catholic Board, on whose proceedings Archer was an important influence, had launched itself with a set of five resolutions. The last of these affirmed that it 'concurred with [the government] in its desire to make adequate provision for the mainten-ance of the civil and religious establishments of this country'; which meant that it was not advocating civil concessions to Catholics as a

28. Ward, *History of St. Edmund's College*, p. 319; cf. C.R.S., i (1905), p. 186; Ward, *Sequel*, i, pp. 191–193.
29. cf. Haile and Bonney, *Lingard*, p. 96.

means of overthrowing the Church of England. Milner thought that
Catholics could not conscientiously 'concur' in the support of the
Protestant religion, and took the resolution to imply an undertaking not
to proselytise.[30] This was to stretch the meaning of the resolution very
far; but if Milner meant to say that it was wrong for Catholics to be
contented with their position as one among a plurality of bodies in a
national community which maintained a Protestant establishment, he
was putting his finger on the central issue. This was precisely what the
Board did mean, and the community as a whole would certainly have
agreed with them; despite Milner's opposition, it continued to do
so.[31]

Among the various factors which had brought about the change of
climate noticeable by about 1830, one must certainly attach full weight
to the influx of Irishmen with different instincts about Protestantism,
established or unestablished, and to the rise of a more intransigent
spirit among Protestants themselves. But what brought the question to
a head was the influx of the particular type of convert from the gentry
and clergy of the Church of England which began to appear in the
community about 1830; men who brought with them an inherited dislike for the ethos of dissenting bodies and a messianic faith in an impending general conversion of England to Catholicism which would
put an end to sectarianism once and for all, and restore order to a dis-
integrating country. Wiseman, though he scouted some of the more
extreme manifestations of this state of mind, found it in general congenial, and through his rise to power a watered-down version of it
became part of the public ideology of English Catholicism.[32]

It can be said in favour of this outlook that, if the older attitude of
English Catholics towards the society they lived in was to be abandoned,
something more suitable to the new devotional and liturgical climate
had better be devised to take its place. But it is not surprising that it
should have been greeted in the traditional community with irritation,
scepticism and distaste. What brought these feelings to a head was the
progress of a movement to secure the conversion of England, understood as above, a prominent if not a predominant place in the public

30. Ward, *Eve*, i, pp. 112 ff., 127 ff.; Husenbeth, *Milner*, pp. 173, 181, 209.
31. See for instance the Wolverhampton litany of 1801 (above, p. 327); the Newcastle resolution of 1815 (Ward, *Eve*, ii, p. 237); the resolution of the Catholic
Association, 1826 (*ibid.*, iii, p. 174).
32. Ward, *Sequel*, i, pp. 203 ff.; Purcell and de Lisle, *Life and Letters of Ambrose
Phillips de Lisle*, i, pp. 50 f.; Ward, *Wiseman*, i, p. 406.

worship of the community. It was led by two converts, Ambrose Lisle Phillips and George Spencer, but had encouragement from Walsh and Wiseman, the authorities in the Midland district where they lived. The movement provoked at Easter 1840 a devastating pastoral letter from the western vicar-apostolic, Peter Baines, in which he explained why he was refusing to allow this 'novel and extraordinary project' to get a footing in his district.[33] Since Baines's pastoral was probably the last full-scale public manifesto of traditional English Catholicism, and since it touched on most of the topics which have been discussed in this chapter, it is worth a little attention. Baines offered two reasons for his refusal, the first spiritual, the second practical. In terms closely reminiscent of Archer's, he insisted that the primary obligation upon English Catholics in relation to their Protestant fellow-countrymen was the obligation of charity. This required that Protestants should not be arbitrarily treated as 'heretics', and that Catholics should not cultivate devotional or dogmatic excesses (like the Immaculate Conception) which a well-intentioned Protestant would be unable to stomach, or which (like the prayers for the Conversion of England) would give unnecessary offence. At the root of such conduct he diagnosed devotional externalism. On the practical side, he pointed sourly to the statistics of conversion in his own district during the previous year: 'if we suppose [the rate of conversion] to become thirteen times as great as it is at present, still the conversion of the Western District will require above a thousand years. This does not look much like an immediate national conversion.'[34] Hence the Conversion of England, as Phillips and Spencer—and by implication Wiseman—saw it, must be regarded as 'morally impossible, and therefore not to be made an object of public prayer'. In so far as they assumed miraculous divine intervention, and supported the assumption with dubious prophecy (as they did), he dismissed them as promoters of superstition and victims of 'old wives' fables'; and he concluded by affirming, prosaically but reasonably enough, that what was needed to promote the Catholic religion in his district was not an ill-considered campaign of prayer, but more work, more money and more priests. Despite its testy tone, this was an im-

---

33. Peter Augustine Baines, *A History of the Pastoral Addressed to the Faithful of the Western District* (not published, ?1841): consisting of the pastoral itself and of the 'Letter to Cardinal Fransoni' in its defence.
34. This arithmetic was not in the pastoral itself, but in the 'Letter to Fransoni', p. 30.

pressive statement of the accumulated experience of two and a half centuries.

On the face of it the argument between Baines and the conversionists was an argument about forms of public prayer, and since prayer is what we have here been principally concerned with, it will be appropriate to conclude by seeing exactly what, in terms of prayer, the issue was. As we have already noticed, the old community had not neglected its duty to pray for the country at large: the old *Manual of Devout Prayers* had contained a 'Litany of Intercession for England', and this had been drawn upon by compilers of congregational prayers. It had been modified for the single litany in the earlier Wolverhampton prayers before Mass, where it was followed by a prayer that God would 'forgive the sins of our forefathers, deliver the people from ignorance, and all of us from the spirit of contradiction, licentiousness and error'; as such it was presumably current in the Midland district. An expanded 'Litany in behalf of our Country' formed part of the additions made to the *Garden of the Soul*, apparently for the use of the London district, in the edition of 1818. Like the earlier forms, this was not directly a litany for the conversion, but for the general reform of the country:

Bless this people, O Lord, and be thou their inheritance.
And sanctify us, and make us a holy nation . . .
Grant that all obstinacy and blindness be removed from the hearts of this people, and that being reformed according to thy holy will, they may serve thee in holiness and truth.
Hear us, O Lord.[35]

All this was in the tradition which Baines represented. The change came during the 1830s, and originated in the Midland district; whether Walsh or Wiseman was responsible for it, and how precisely it related to the activity of Phillips and Spencer, I am not sure. In any event, versions of the *Garden of the Soul* began to appear containing a revived 'Litany of Intercession for England' which was specifically a conversion-litany and very different in tone from the current versions:

From the spirit of pride, rebellion and apostacy,
Deliver England . . .

35. Above, n. 9; *Prayers before and after Mass* (Wolverhampton, 1792), p. 8; *Garden of the Soul* (Dolman, London, 1840; repr. of enlarged 1818 edn, for which see Burton, *Challoner*, i, p. 124), pp. 342 f.

That it may please thee to hasten the conversion of this our miserable country, and reunite it to the ancient faith and communion of thy church,
We beseech thee, hear us.

The concluding prayer was that God should deliver the nation from the 'spirit of contradiction, licentiousness and discord: that instead of so many divisions and changes in religion, under which they labour, they may be again restored to that unity of mind, steadiness of faith and tranquillity of conscience, which is nowhere to be sought but in the communion of thy church'.[36] The relation of this prayer to the one attached to the earlier Midland litany is obvious; the differences between them will repay a good deal of attention.

Baines was no doubt successful in preventing the public recitation of this litany in the Western district; Griffiths in London achieved much the same result by authorising a reissue of the 1818 version of the *Garden of the Soul* and its 'Litany in behalf of our Country'; in his own version, Briggs in the North seems to have attempted compromise by printing the other litany in a toned-down form, though the final prayer remained.[37] Wiseman's rise to power did away with such shillyshallying, and by 1850 the litany was generally restored among the prayers of English Catholics. Whether the sentiments it expressed were as yet imprinted on their hearts, I cannot pretend to relate. In so far as they were to become so, the community would have to learn a second time much that it had succeeded, painfully, in learning once already.

36. The second petition and prayer will be found in edns of the *Manual of Devout Prayers* from about 1700; I am not sure how long it continued to include them. The first edn of the *Garden of the Soul* in which I have found the litany is that of Duffy, Dublin, 1846, pp. 281–285, but it was certainly in circulation before 1839 (cf. following note).
37. See the London, 1840 and York, 1839 edns of *Garden of the Soul* (above, n. 35 and 23), in the latter case pp. 402 f.

VARIETIES OF NONCONFORMITY

S INCE I have undertaken to situate the history of the English Catholic community within the more general history of nonconforming bodies in England, it seems incumbent upon me to offer, in conclusion, some view of the history of English nonconformity into which a Catholic community would fit. If my point is sound, the usual notion of what is meant by nonconformity must be to some degree revised: one cannot just balance the Catholics on top of a pile of other nonconformists, or squeeze them in at the bottom, and leave the matter there. I believe it is possible, even with limited knowledge and in a limited space, to do a little better than this.

I start from three assumptions on which I think it may be possible to secure agreement. The first is that the primary fact of English Christianity since the Reformation is the Church of England, and the primary division is between those who have found its fare satisfying and those who have not. The second is that it is a mistake to apply to this situation metaphors derived from modern political history; that only confusion and misunderstanding can come from thinking of Christian communities in terms of left and right and assuming, for example, that bodies of dissidents may be located on the 'left' or 'right' wings of a Church of England situated in the middle. Probably we cannot think of the situation at all without some such local collocations, but at least we should try to cleanse them of overtones of a political kind. Finally, and most to the point: the assumption that the term 'Dissent' in English history is to be understood with the qualification 'Protestant' in front of it seems to me incorrect. If the word 'Protestant' is to have any serious meaning it must surely entail a belief, explicit or implied, in some version of the three primary doctrines of the Reformation: the prime authority of Scripture, justification by grace through faith, and the priesthood of all believers. If these conditions are felt to be, historically speaking, too stringent, one can surely not expect less of a Protestant than belief in two of these; and one may add, as a qualifica-

tion which underlies them all, a belief in the divinity of Christ. Apart
from the Catholics, and leaving aside the Jews, there were two important English religious communities in this period which did not fulfil
these conditions; one was a product of the seventeenth century, the
other of the eighteenth. It so happens that both of them have some
special historical link with the Catholic community.

The first was the Quakers. While I am aware that the theological
position of Quakers is a matter of some dispute, it seems clear that if
Protestantism is defined as above Quakers cannot be considered
Protestants. The doctrine of the indwelling Spirit leads certainly to an
extreme version of the priesthood of all believers, but is not compatible
either with the principle of *sola scriptura* or with the doctrine of justification by faith: the point seems to have been as clear to George Fox
as it was to his Presbyterian critics. It also tended to make the divinity
of Christ an optional belief, as it seems to have been for William Penn.
It may be historically somewhat artificial, but it is surely correct in
principle, to relate the belief of Friends to pre-Reformation types of
'spiritual' or mystical religion, transmitted perhaps by bodies like the
'Family of Love'. Since the Toleration Act of 1689 applied in principle
only to Protestant Dissenters, it was necessary to make special provision in it for Quakers; an attempt was made to get them to make
declarations of belief in the Trinity and in the Scriptures as the revealed word of God, but these proved acceptable only with qualifications which reveal that Quakers were unwilling to be pinned down to
either doctrine. The point was not lost on the Society for the Propaga-
tion of the Gospel, which made the conversion of Quakers a principal
object of its activity.

It is of course true that, historically speaking, the Quaker community emerged out of a background of Protestant sectarianism during
the period of the Civil War and Interregnum; that tendencies in the
direction they took can be discovered in popular Puritanism; and that
the language and habits of Quakers were indelibly marked by this inheritance. In this sense it is no doubt correct to regard Quakerism as 'a
natural extreme of the whole spectrum of English Puritan thought'.
But I do not think this position would have satisfied George Fox, whose
universal condemnation of all 'notions' and 'professions' is surely to
be understood as a secession from Protestantism as such; the unique
persistence of the Quaker community among the proliferating religious
groups born during the 1650s testifies to some important difference,

and I should have thought that this was it. The fact that Fox recruited widely, though not invariably, from sectarian Protestant communities which were disheartened or in disarray would seem to support the case rather than to weaken it.

I am not suggesting, as did Prynne, Baxter and others, that Quakers were Catholics in disguise, though in so far as Baxter meant to say that what Quakers were preaching was the opposite of Protestant Christianity, I think he was right; the Irish Franciscan who said that 'none came so near him as the Quakers' was certainly talking some kind of sense. But the relations between Catholic and Quaker communities do bear some reflecting on. Geographically, the Quaker community was a product of the northern uplands, and it has already been suggested that the success of Fox's mission here may be seen as a consequence of the failure of the Catholic clergy to take advantage of its missionary opportunities in this region. The Quakers, it may be argued, were the body which most successfully filled the vacuum created by the geographical and social indrawing of Catholicism during the seventeenth century. In some areas, as in Cleveland, Catholics and Quakers existed side by side; more commonly, their strongholds were separate but adjacent. Quakers were thick on the ground in north Lancashire, the far north-west and Craven, but made little impression in south Lancashire or Northumberland; the fact may no doubt be partly explained by differences in the local predominance of gentry. Perhaps it would be going too far to claim on this evidence that Catholics and Quakers were complementary rather than conflicting communities; yet there are surely essential features of the Quaker way of life—the language, the attitude to the *rites de passage*, the concern about peace, the idea of 'friendship' itself—which have an archaic character more reminiscent of pre- than of post-Reformation Christianity, and seem to have their roots in traditional northern society. The same might be said of the early Quaker cult of miraculous healing. I should also be inclined to argue that Quaker doubts about the Scriptures reflect a more general lack of esteem for the bible in the North. Finally, one may cite evidence that Catholics and Quakers got on rather well together. In upland Yorkshire they seem to have lived amicably side by side; in Lancashire, William Blundell was exploring the mind of Quaker neighbours in 1665, and with Nicholas the relation seems to have grown into a genuine attraction. In April 1710 he 'went to Liverpool in expectation to have seen a great meeting of Quakers', but got there too late; finally he managed to get to one in London. Altogether it does not seem surprising that a Quaker should have been the first disinterested Englishman to write and act systematically on the assumption that Catholics might be regarded as members of a dissenting community among others, and that it would be good for the country if they were. It can certainly be maintained that William Penn's judgment of James II was politically at fault; but I do not think he was an opportunist, and otherwise it is hard to see how he could have arrived at these convictions unless there were something between Quakers and Catholics of the kind suggested here.[1]

The affinity of Quakers and Catholics may strike one, on the whole, as consisting more in a degree of complementarity than of actual likeness; if we are looking for the dissenting body whose history is most like that of the Catholics, I think we shall find it in the Presbyterians. Their origins in the clerical discontents of Elizabethan England were more or less contemporaneous, and the programmes on which they launched themselves had at least a number of external similarities: a high, rigorous, universalist notion of the Church, a concern for godly discipline, clerical activism were common to both. Their differences, of course, are equally obvious: they stood, at this time, at opposite ends of the theological range; the lay support to which they appealed was different both in its social composition (though the difference can be exaggerated) and in its religious instincts; the Catholic clergy stood out for a rigorous separation from the Church of England, while the 'Presbyterian' clergy sought to act upon it from within, and objected to the separation of some of their brethren.

As this policy gained some success, the ways of Catholics and 'Presbyterians' divided: indeed 'Presbyterians' disappeared into the Church of England at the same time as Catholics devoted themselves, *faute de mieux*, to the construction of a separating community. Certainly

---

1. I have drawn essentially on the classic studies of W. C. Braithwaite, *The Beginnings of Quakerism* and *The Second Period of Quakerism* (2nd edns by H. J. Cadbury, Cambridge, 1955 and 1961); for the more Protestant view of Quakers which is widely held nowadays, see H. Barbour, *The Quakers in Puritan England* (New Haven/London, 1964) and Cadbury, in Braithwaite, i, p. 544. Elizabeth Isichei, *Victorian Quakers* (Oxford, 1970), seems an admirable study of a later phase of the community, particularly interesting here on the conflict between evangelical and non-evangelical appreciations of Quaker tradition. See also K. Thomas, *Religion and the Decline of Magic* (London, 1971), p. 127; Aveling, *Northern Catholics*, pp. 343 f.; Gibson (ed.), *A Cavalier's Notebook*, p. 113; *Great Diurnal of Nicholas Blundell*, i, p. 251; iii, p. 115, and index under Quakers.

their experience in the early seventeenth century had some common features, notably in their difficulties with prelatical episcopacy; but they were at this time far apart, divided by the gulf between those who belonged to the Church of England and those who did not—a division which became the more pronounced when the establishment itself adopted a form of Presbyterian order, and Presbyterian doctrine, in 1646. Even at this point, though, when it would seem that Presbyterian and Catholic traditions had least in common, we discover in Richard Baxter, by any standard the greatest figure in English Presbyterianism, a man who was both the recipient and the vehicle of influences which link them: recipient of some central features of the spiritual doctrine of the counter-Reformation as conveyed to Englishmen by Robert Parsons; transmitter of an ideal of 'catholicity' which was certainly not the opposite of Protestantism but did all the same begin the process of detaching English Presbyterianism from its Calvinist roots; father of a rational and humanist 'Arminianism' which was in the end to bring the two communities very near to each other indeed.

First of course there had to be a Presbyterian community, something which seemed as inconceivable to Baxter as a Catholic community would have seemed to, say, Reginald Pole. But what Catholics had done already, Presbyterians were obliged to do after 1662. Ejected from the establishment, 'condemned to denominationalism' and to an assimilation with the ways of the congregational separatists which they had always deplored, they were henceforth, inwardly and outwardly, in much the same boat. And just as, in the person of John Gother, a Presbyterian inheritance was to help the Catholic community to shape its tradition fruitfully for the new age, so the 'catholicity' of Baxter, before the eighteenth century was far advanced, had led most Presbyterians to a renunciation of Calvin, and indeed of Protestantism as such, and to the adoption of a view of the Christian life which the masters of counter-Reformation spirituality, and English Catholics brought up on the *Garden of the Soul*, could have found little reason to quarrel with. Admittedly, they had moved at the same time towards a unitarian view of God; but the effect of this, in the circumstances, was to break the final link which bound them to their Protestant origins and to establish them as something like a more rationalistic and more liberal version of 'catholic' nonconformity. Further, if we look at the Presbyterians as an organised body, we find a distinct resemblance to the Catholic community in two respects. Like the Catholics, and unlike other Protestant dissenters, their doctrine of the Church prevented them from developing a congregational theory; like the Catholics, they were obliged to develop a congregational practice and did so in a hand-to-mouth sort of way. The results were practically identical: 'a vague aggregation of trustees and principal subscribers' seems a description equally applicable to the arrangements of either community; the spiritual dominance of the pastor was much the same in either case; the bulk of a congregation was as likely to become dissatisfied with the conduct of a ruling minority. There also seems an obvious parallel in the growth of general funds, their application to the ministry of poor congregations, and the importance of controlling them for effective leadership in the community. United by benevolence and a distaste for enthusiasm, Catholics and Presbyterian-Unitarians attended sermons in one another's chapels; it seems likely that the liturgical experiments of Catholics at the end of the century drew on Presbyterian examples. No wonder that by 1800 the leading members of the two denominations in Liverpool or Birmingham were on such excellent terms; or that Unitarians played much the same role in the removal of Catholic disabilities in the nineteenth century as Quakers had attempted to do in the seventeenth.[2]

On this showing there seems a good case for dividing English Dissent into a Protestant and a non-Protestant segment. In the first one would place the offspring of Puritanism—earlier Presbyterians, Congregationals, Baptists—and of Methodism. There have been different interpretations of Methodism as of Quakerism, but in the Methodist case the weight of the argument seems to come down firmly on the Protestant side;[3] for the purposes of the discussion I take Methodists to be dissenters. In the second category one would place Catholics, Quakers and Unitarians. It is obvious that the second group does not have the unity of the first, and may be regarded as a Cave of Adullam; but this description itself is not a bad guide to the character of non-Protestant dissent

2. My debt here is above all to C. G. Bolam, J. Goring, H. L. Short and R. Thomas, *The English Presbyterians* (London, 1968); to Patrick Collinson, *The Elizabethan Puritan Movement* (London, 1967) and 'The Godly: Aspects of Popular Protestantism in Elizabethan England' (Past and Present Conference on Popular Religion, 1966, typescript) for the earlier period; and to B. L. Manning, *The Protestant Dissenting Deputies* (ed. O. Greenwood, Cambridge, 1952) for the later—note especially the Unitarian view of Dissent, pp. 55, 68 f. On Baxter and the counter-Reformation, see my 'Postscript' to H. O. Evennett, *The Spirit of the Counter-Reformation* (Cambridge, 1968), p. 132.
3. R. Davies and G. Rupp (eds.), *A History of the Methodist Church in Great Britain*, i (London, 1965), notably the 'Introductory Essay' by Gordon Rupp.

in England. Bearing this division in mind, we may try a rough sketch of religious movements in England from the sixteenth century to the nineteenth.

In the beginning was the Church of England: Cranmer's, Elizabeth's, Grindal's, Hooker's. Whether it was or is a Protestant institution is a question which it does not seem necessary to try and answer here. What matters is that it has been thought not to be so, or adequately so, by successive generations of Protestant Englishmen; and also perhaps that, by comparison with the pre-Reformation Church, it has been by nature a rather rigid institution, with a limited capacity to absorb autonomous movements. Since, between the sixteenth century and the nineteenth, Protestant convictions provided the spur to every large-scale movement or revival of religious feeling in England, there has been a recurring tension between the institution of the English Church and the religious opinions predominant in the nation, and where the institution has been insufficiently accommodating the result has been separation and the emergence of Protestant dissenting bodies. In any case, Protestant convictions as powerful as those which have recurrently taken hold of Englishmen, unmediated by any institutional frame, were likely of themselves to inspire a fissiparous sectarianism. Threatened or confronted by the consequent confusion, other Englishmen have felt the need to reaffirm the values of unity in Christianity. For most of these the Church itself has provided a congenial home; for others, its institutional character has been felt as a barrier to the cultivation of a 'unitarian' spirituality which would meet something like the spiritual demands accommodated in autonomous Protestantism. Hence movements of reaction, which have periodically strengthened the element of authority in the Church of England, have also tended to give birth to separating communities of non-Protestant dissent: Catholics in the later years of Queen Elizabeth, Quakers in the mid-seventeenth century. In their case as in others, it was the fate of unity-seekers to end by increasing the proliferation of competing bodies which they had set out to transcend. With Presbyterians the case is somewhat different, in that their stand for unity and their secession from Protestantism occurred at different times and in different connections; though there is probably something to be said for regarding the Unitarians at the end of the eighteenth century as refugees from Protestant enthusiasm. During the next half-century, as the Protestant awakening multiplied Methodists, revived the Protestant dissenters, and spread Evangelical-

ism through the Church of England, it seems clear that the major
benefits of reaction went to the Catholic community, which was now
for the first time since the early seventeenth century in a condition to
take permanent advantage of it. Leaving Irish migration out of account,
a modest but significant expansion of Catholicism took place, dwarfed
as it was by the wave of Protestant revival. Although I am not thinking
primarily of the Oxford movement, it does seem a reasonable deduction
from its history that here, as in the reign of Elizabeth, there was a connection between the larger event and the smaller. Before the nineteenth-
century immigrations the non-Protestant dissenting communities were
never large, perhaps because the fear of unbridled Protestantism has
never been quite borne out by the event. Their role in enlarging the
national experience beyond what could be accommodated within the
frame of the Church of England has been the minor one, but without
them the whole experience would have been markedly poorer. Taking
the three together, their contribution has been fairly distinguished: the
Catholics may well have been the least distinguished of the three, but
they do have the credit of being the first.

Something may also be said about the place of the Catholic community, not simply in a tradition of non-Protestant dissent, but in the
dissenting universe as a whole. In some degree the dissenting situation
made its own conditions; as we have seen in comparing Catholics and
Presbyterians, they might impose a similar history on communities of
opposite theological standpoints. Among the topics which come up for
consideration in this context, the history of the itinerant ministry seems
the most obvious.[4] Perhaps it is unhistorical to trace the Methodist
itinerancy back, via the Quakers and early Baptists, to the priests of the
Elizabethan mission; but itinerancy was not an idea which had much
warrant in Protestant tradition, and it was specially difficult to reconcile
with congregational principles. To Catholics, at least to Catholics of a
Jesuit frame of mind, with their craftsmanlike notion of the ministry
and their inheritance from the friars, it came fairly readily; it is not so
much less likely that the Jesuits should have converted Protestants to it,
than that they should have converted the Catholic secular clergy. No
doubt it would be safer to put the suggestion in a less specific form. For

4. Another would be the history of counter-reformation spirituality in England,
on which see J. Orcibal, 'The Theological Originality of John Wesley and Continental Spirituality', in Davies and Rupp, *op. cit.* above, n. 3, pp. 83 ff., and above,
n. 2.

the Jesuits itinerancy was a particular application of the idea of the Church as a missionary institution, and it will generally be conceded that, in discovering the missionary or apostolic idea of the Church, Protestants were heavily indebted to the Catholicism of the counter-Reformation. That the missionary urge should nevertheless have been so recurrent a feature of English Protestant communities in an age when apostolic Protestants were hardly common in the rest of Europe, may be supposed to owe something, by imitation or competition, to the illustration of missionary Catholicism to be found on their own soil. A prudent fidelity to its missionary vocation was sufficient to enable the Catholic community to overcome the tendency to numerical atrophy which dogged the other communities of non-Protestant dissent and to emerge as an expansive force in the age of the Industrial Revolution. It may reasonably be said to have helped to provide Protestants with the equipment to ensure that by 1850 the multitudinous constellation of Dissent and the solar system of the Church of England were roughly equivalent elements in the national universe.

If at this point I give the impression of trying to prove too much, it may be because I have reached the limit of what a historian can do. In exploring the function of a Catholic community within a general corpus of Dissent I may have been looking for contiguity, or historical relations, where all that can or need be shown is similarity, or formal ones. It would be possible to fall back on the position that in the binary universe of Dissent relations of contiguity are effective within its Protestant and non-Protestant segments, while relations of similarity—in household and chapel, in itinerancy and financial structure, in the phenomena of the church-become-sect and the sect that would be a church—range freely across the divide. The position seems a sound one, but I suspect that more than this may be said. If it is to be said, it seems however necessary to accept the implications of a terminology which somehow creeps up on one, and take ship from the familiar shores of history, hoping to strike land somewhere in the Americas of structural anthropology.

Let us suppose for a moment that a people practising the various forms of Christianity which were current in England from the reign of Elizabeth to the reign of Victoria had been discovered by a structural anthropologist on a trip through the Brazilian jungle.[5] What reflections

5. In what follows I have been helped by the essays in Edmund Leach (ed.), *The Structural Study of Myth and Totemism* (London, 1968 edn), especially by that of K. O. L. Burridge, pp. 91 ff.

might he have come to? There would I think have seemed to him, as to
us, to be a primary division between those whose belief and practice
were conducted within the forms of an institution identified with the
organs of political authority, and those whose belief and practice had
inspired the creation of communities which were not so identified.
Among the latter he would have noticed a rich diversity, and suspected
the workings of a collective religious mind seeking to exhaust its *a priori*
possibilities. Proceeding further, he would no doubt have recognised
something like the division we have made among them, though it would
probably have seemed appropriate to him to express it in other terms.
He would have had in mind, no doubt, a fundamental distinction
between nature and culture, and distributed these communities into
those whose relation to Divinity was mediated through some channel of
communication which might be regarded as part of the natural equipment of man, and those for whom it was mediated through a cultural
artefact or text. He might probably have extended this observation
into the more general view that those in the first category seemed to
think of the divine as being in some way continuous with the human, to
appeal to an authority which was in some way immanent in the world;
while those in the second category viewed the divine as being by its
nature discontinuous with the human, transcendent and other. Looking
at the two categories in turn he would have noticed that they were
asymmetrical in various ways, yet symmetrical in another. The communities in the second category—those who believed in a transcendent,
'culture'-revealed God—were much larger than those in the first,
possibly ten times as large; they also possessed a unity which the others
did not, in that the text in which all of them placed authority was the
same, and that they construed its meaning in roughly the same way.
They differed about the social and organisational forms which a community faithful to this meaning should adopt. Some believed that it
should embrace all in a unity, though they were not in a position to put
their belief into practice; others that it should consist of a relative few
gathered here and there out of the world, and that those so gathered in
any place were set free from the authority of those gathered in other
places; others again, that it should consist of many, who would be
maintained in the correct path by a circulation of qualified teachers (the
hope had not been fulfilled). In this pattern he would no doubt have
observed a dialectical process which had exhausted the possibilities in
this particular line, though it might be preparing the way for some

further transformation. The communities on the 'nature' side of the division had no common view about where to look for messages from the Godhead; one looked for them to tradition, another to a voice within the soul, another to the rational mind. These too might seem to have exhausted their possibilities, but to have done so in a formal rather than a dialectical way which indicated that their role was in some sense a negative or passive one and—rightly or wrongly—did not suggest much capacity for transformation in the future. Distributed along this scale, the communities of Dissent could be presented as a series showing Unitarians at one end and Particular Baptists at the other; Catholics would come somewhere between Unitarians and Quakers.

Such speculations may or may not have value in themselves. To the historian, they will present a multitude of imperfections, and if there is any gold waiting to be extracted by this method, they certainly do no more than scratch the surface of it. I offer them, let me repeat, merely to try to substantiate a belief that the history of the Catholic community has something to contribute to the history of the country at large.

MAPS, TABLES AND FIGURES

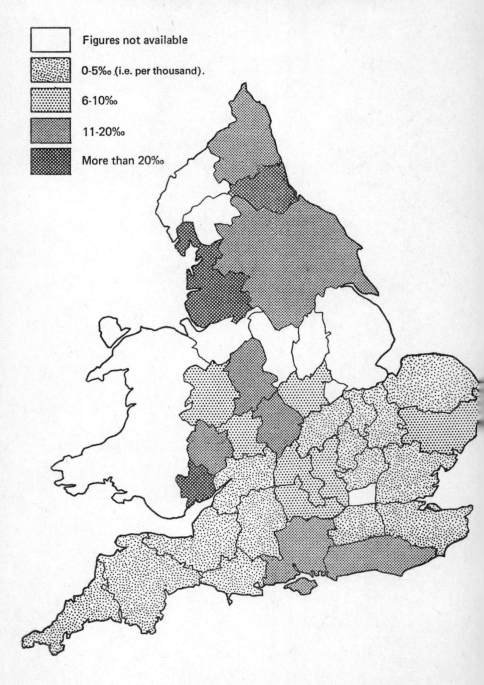

MAP 1   DISTRIBUTION OF CATHOLICS 1641-2

Proportion of Recusant Households to All Households, by Counties

Figures not available

0-5‰ (i.e. per thousand).

6-10‰

11-20‰

More than 20‰

A

THE DISTRIBUTION OF THE COMMUNITY, 1641–1829

Note to Map 1

I have constructed this map from the data in Magee, *English Recusants*, p. 201, where the recusant totals for 1641–1642 (see above, chap. 8, pp. 186 f), divided by two, are compared with the total number of houses per county given by John Houghton in 1693 ([W. Cobbett,] *Parliamentary History of England, v : 1688–1702* (London, 1809), Appendix, p. cvi). Since in the text I take the number of Catholics at that date to be about twice the number of recusants returned, I have felt it better to divide by 2·5 in order to arrive at a (very notional) number of households. This rough and ready procedure is open to various objections, but it does produce a result which makes sense and can, if not pressed too far, be meaningfully compared with Map 3. Its main virtue is the pattern of distribution which it suggests, which seems to me extremely plausible: compare the diocesan map of Catholics in the province of Canterbury, based on the Compton census of 1676, in A. Browning (ed.), *English Historical Documents, viii : 1660–1714* (London, 1953), p. 415, as well as Map 3.

The actual figures for the counties showing the highest proportion of Catholics are, per thousand: Monmouth, 94; Lancashire, 90; Durham, 25; Hereford, 20; Warwickshire and Sussex, 18; Yorkshire and Northumberland, 16; Hampshire, 14; Staffordshire, 11; Worcestershire, Shropshire and Oxfordshire, 10. In the case of Lancashire the figure is based on the larger of the two totals mentioned in the text, in the case of Staffordshire on the smaller; taking the other totals would not change the categories into which these counties fall.

Readers should beware of assuming that northern counties for which returns are not available would have shown proportions comparable to those of neighbouring counties; on the contrary, it seems likely that there are no figures for Cumberland, Westmorland and Cheshire because the number of recusants in these counties was insignificant (compare following maps).

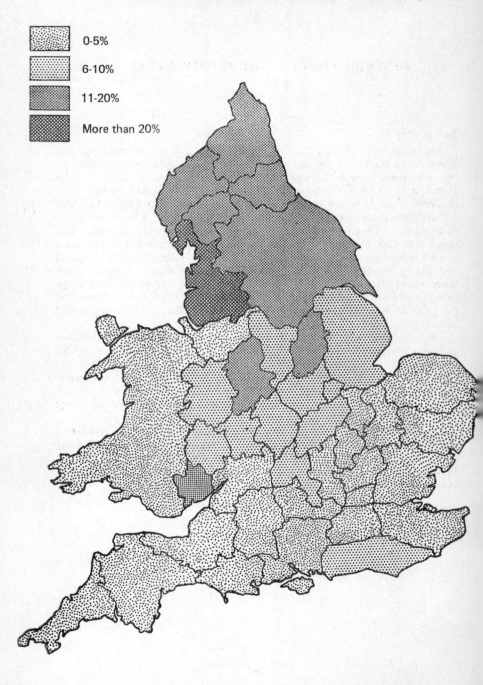

MAP 2   DISTRIBUTION OF PROPERTY HELD BY CATHOLICS, 1715-20

Percentage by Value of Landed Property in Catholic Possession, by Counties

0-5%

6-10%

11-20%

More than 20%

Note to Map 2

I have adapted this map, with some misgivings, from that in Magee, *English Recusants*, frontispiece, using the data provided on p. 199 (cf. pp. 176 ff.). Magee constructed it by taking the annual rental of the landed property of Catholics as registered under the act 1 George I, c. 55, in 1715–1720 (detailed in E. E. Estcourt and J. O. Payne (eds.), *The English Catholic Nonjurors of 1715* (repr. Farnborough, Hants., 1969)) and comparing it with the total assessment of each county for the Land Tax in 1700; he appears to have added 50% to the income registered to allow for various deficiencies in registration. It would be unwise to take this as more than a rough guide to the absolute weight of Catholics among the rent-receiving classes, but I think it gives a fair idea of their proportional distribution, provided one remembers that people did not necessarily live where they drew their rents from (e.g. in Cumberland, where the figure is probably also exaggerated by a low assessment). The surprisingly large figure for Nottinghamshire is mainly due to two families, Howard (Dukes of Norfolk) and Clifton. One may note: (1) the general conformity of the distribution here to that of the community as shown on Maps 1 and 3, very striking in, e.g., the South-east and South-west, or the sequence Lancashire–Cheshire–Staffordshire; (2) a difference in the order of magnitude of something like ten times between the representation of Catholics among the rent-receiving classes and among the population as a whole, since a distribution per cent here produces a result markedly similar to the distribution per thousand of Maps 1 and 3 (the difference was probably somewhat less than this, cf. Magee, p. 168, 7 or so per cent of Catholics among the gentry in 1680, compared with roughly 1% of the population; a reason for believing that Magee's percentages of property held by Catholics are too high, though not very much so); (3) the strong negative correlation between this (and the previous) map and the distribution of wealth in the South and Midlands indicated by the maps in *English Historical Documents*, viii, pp. 458–459; (4) the favourable prospects of a community which possessed anything like the suggested proportion of the landed property of Lancashire in the early eighteenth century.

The actual figures given by Magee for the counties with the highest proportions of Catholic property are: Lancashire, 35%; Durham-and-Northumberland, and Staffordshire, 20%; Cumberland-and-Westmorland, 18%; Yorkshire, 15%; Nottinghamshire and Monmouthshire, 11%. A single figure of $4\frac{1}{2}$% is given for Wales.

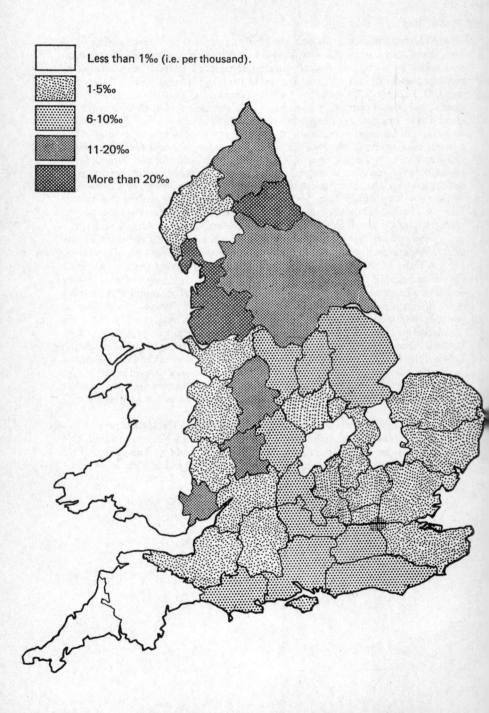

MAP 3   DISTRIBUTION OF CATHOLICS IN 1767

Less than 1‰ (i.e. per thousand).

1-5‰

6-10‰

11-20‰

More than 20‰

Note to Map 3

This map has been constructed by M. J.-A. Lesourd from the Returns of Papists of 1767, using for comparison the average of the estimated population of counties given by P. Deane and W. A. Cole, *British Economic Growth, 1688–1959* (Cambridge, 1969), p. 103, for 1751 and 1781. It is certainly the nearest thing to an accurate map of Catholic distribution so far achieved for any date in this period, and I am most grateful to M. Lesourd for allowing me to use it. The reader will note the marked conformity of pattern in the distribution to that given in Map 1, the indications of stability (even, here and there, of growth) in the North and the West Midlands, of marked decline in the Welsh borders, and rather less marked decline in the South-Central area (where, however, signs of the influence of the Catholic gentry and aristocracy may still be detected), and of growth in London. The distribution of missions given in Map 4 confirms the accuracy both of the Returns and of M. Lesourd's reconstruction.

MAP 4   CATHOLIC MISSIONS IN 1773

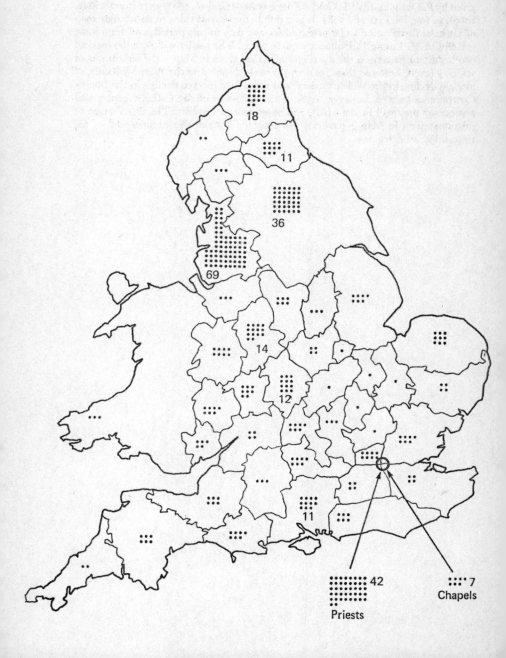

18

11

36

69

14

12

42
Priests

7
Chapels

11

Note to Map 4

Constructed from the vicars-apostolics' Returns of 1773 printed by J. H. Whyte in *Recusant History*, ix (1968), pp. 206–214. This is intended as a map of missions, though the numbers returned were sometimes of missions or 'residences', sometimes of priests. The only place where this makes much difference is in London, where the figure for priests is composed of thirty-four priests with missionary faculties attached to embassy chapels, and eight other missionaries (I ignore the thirty or so priests given as living in private houses in London, without missionary faculties) and the figure for chapels is that given in Ward, *Dawn of the Catholic Revival*, i, p. 24. The figures for Cheshire and Westmorland, which are not given in the returns, are supplied from the vicar-general's report of 1783 (Ushaw Mss. ii, 129): the two for Cumberland make up the 137 given for the North as a whole. Monmouthshire was included in Wales, for which nine missionaries were returned: there seem to have been five or six missions in the county at this time (J. B. Dockery, *Collingridge* (Newport, Mon., [1954]), p. 133). I have amended the figure of '5 or 6' missions given by the vicar-apostolic for Co. Durham in the light of the description given by A. M. C. Forster, *Ushaw Magazine*, lxxii (1962), pp. 71 ff.: it is possible that this includes as missions one or two centres which would not have been returned as missions elsewhere.

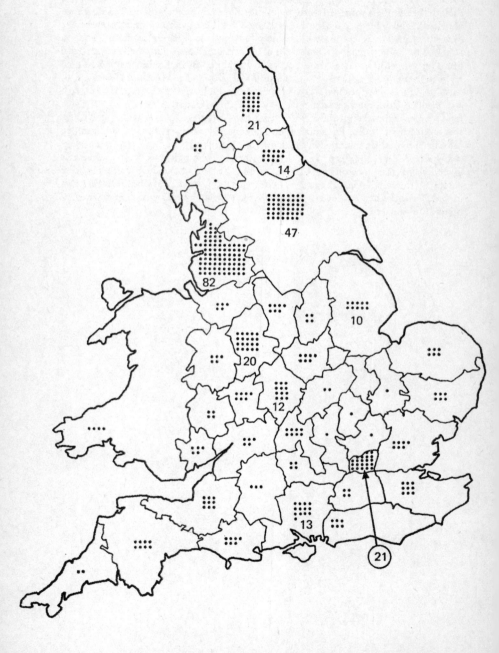

MAP 5   CATHOLIC MISSIONS IN 1829

Note to Map 5

Taken from the map made by Bishop Baines for Propaganda in 1829 and printed in Bernard Ward, *The Sequel to Catholic Emancipation*, i, facing p. 26. London missions are included in Middlesex: the comparable figure in 1773 would therefore be fifteen.

This was probably about the latest date at which the distribution of the mission would have reflected the distribution of the indigenous community without too much adjustment for immigration to be useful for purposes of comparison with earlier periods. One may note: (1) the continuing stability of pattern during half a century of radical change; (2) the significant if unsensational expansion (330 missions in 1773, 383 in 1829); (3) the fact that this expansion had occurred in areas where the community had been well-established in the eighteenth century (Lancashire, the North-east, the west Midlands, London); (4) that, on the whole, it had become weaker in areas where it was weak already, e.g. the counties north of London and the Welsh borders; in the far North-west it had been preserved from extinction by Irish immigration into Cumberland. By contrast the south-western counties were beginning to show some return for a good deal of effort, and the growth of seaside resorts was reflected in the missions of the south coast. What the map does not show, of course, is the drastically altered size and character of many of the congregations which these dots represent, or the shift from rural to town missions within counties.

B

THE CLERGY AND THE COMMUNITY, 1600–1770

TABLE I. *Social Origins of Clerical Students at the Colleges of Douai,
Rome and Valladolid, 1590–1750.*

(Sources: see above, chap. 9, n. 2)

   I   Total number of students of known origins
  II Percentage of sons of gentry
 III Percentage of sons of commoners

	Douai			Rome			Valladolid			All		
	I	II	III	I	II	III	I	II	III	I	II	III
1592–1600				29	52	48	115	48	52	144	49	51
1601–1610				95	45	55	107	50	50	202	48	52
1611–1620				86	70	30	54	63	37	140	66	34
1621–1630	[46]	[67]	[33]¹	65	58	42	21	62	38	86	59	41²
1631–1640	[79]	[79]	[21]¹	69	67	33						
1641–1650				81	65	35						
1651–1660				64	73	27						
1661–1670				29	38	62						
1671–1680				24	46	54						
1681–1690				12	17	83						
1691–1700	27	41	59³									
1701–1710	38	32	68									
1711–1720	26	65	35									
1721–1730	31	42	58									
1731–1740	41	39	61									
1741–1750	39	15	85									

1. All students admitted to the college: of the eighteen known to have taken the mission oath, 11 (61%) were gentry, and 7 commoners.
2. Excludes Douai students.
3. This and the later figures are for *alumni* only and exclude those ordained as convictors.

The earlier figures may be compared with those given in Joan Simon, 'The Social Origins of Cambridge Students, 1603–1640', *Past and Present*, no. 26 (1963), pp. 60–63.

MAP 6   JESUIT DISTRICTS; 1623-1773

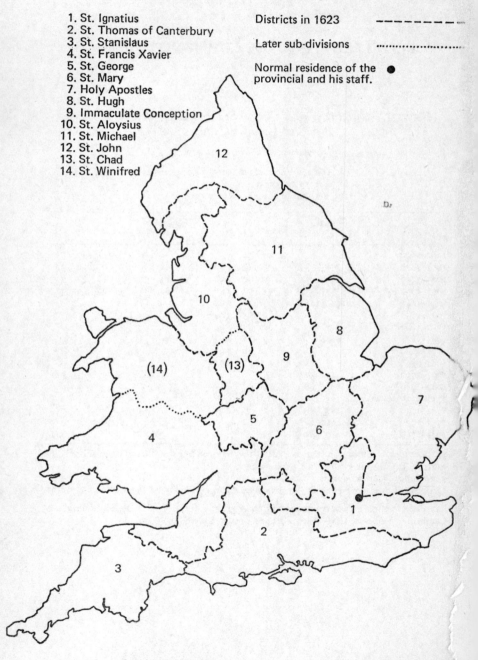

1. St. Ignatius
2. St. Thomas of Canterbury
3. St. Stanislaus
4. St. Francis Xavier
5. St. George
6. St. Mary
7. Holy Apostles
8. St. Hugh
9. Immaculate Conception
10. St. Aloysius
11. St. Michael
12. St. John
13. St. Chad
14. St. Winifred

Districts in 1623

Later sub-divisions

Normal residence of the
provincial and his staff.

Note to Map 6

Constructed from Foley, *Records of the English Province*, vols. i–iv. Foley gives no attribution for Shropshire or Huntingdonshire, but Shropshire certainly belonged to St Winifred in the eighteenth century and there were probably never any Jesuits in Huntingdonshire anyway. The separation of Staffordshire from the Lancashire district took place in 1661, that of St Winifred from St Francis Xavier in 1667.

One thing worth noting is the tendency to choose for the original districts titles with an international, contemporary and often aggressively Jesuit flavour: to St Stanislaus, St Francis Xavier and St Aloysius one may add the original titles of the Lincolnshire and East Anglian districts—St Dominic and Bl. [Francis] Borgia respectively. By contrast titles which reflect local or historical patriotism appear in the smallest district of the original distribution (St George), in new names given when districts were erected into colleges (St Hugh for St Dominic in Lincoln; one may add, if only in a negative sort of way, the Holy Apostles for the Bl. Borgia in East Anglia) and in the new districts hived off from larger ones during the Restoration (St Chad, St Winifred). Such titles evidently reflect the loyalties of the gentry, and their appearance is some indication of the growing influence of the gentry and their benefactions on Jesuit organisation during the seventeenth century.

MAP 7 DISTRICTS OF THE VICARS APOSTOLIC, 1688-1840

1. London District
2. Midland District
3. Northern District
4. Western District

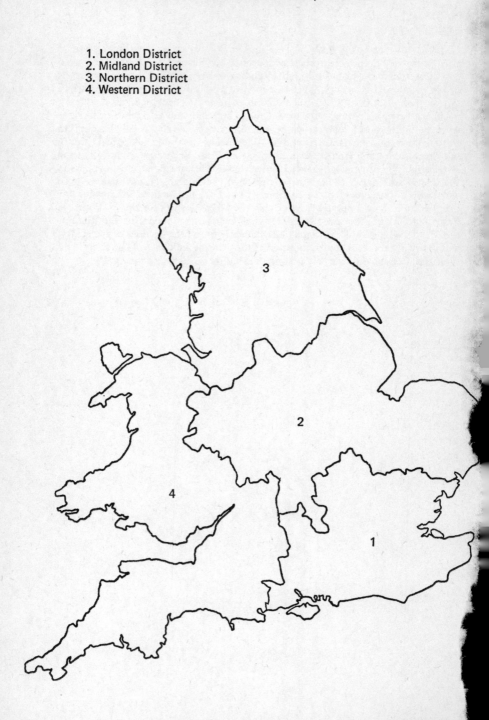

TABLE II. *Distribution of Jesuits in England, 1621–1771.*

(Source: see above, chap. 10, n. 35)

	1621	1641	1672	1700	1720	1750	1771
North	(28)[1]	40[2]	30	45	46	48	57
Wales and West	(10)[3]	28	17	13	17	14	16
South and Midlands	42[4]	72[4]	67	54	59	52	45
London	24	31	23	16	32	21	20
TOTAL	(104)	171	137	128	154	135	138

North: Lancashire, Yorkshire, Durham, Northumberland, Cumberland, Westmorland, Cheshire.
Wales and West: Wales and Monmouthshire, ?Shropshire, Herefordshire, Gloucestershire, Somerset, Devon and Cornwall.
South and Midlands: Rest except for St Ignatius (i.e. London, Kent, Surrey, Middlesex, Hertfordshire, Berkshire).
London: St Ignatius.

1. Includes Staffordshire; no return from St John.
2. Includes Staffordshire.
3. No return from St Stanislaus.
4. Excludes Staffordshire.

Seven Jesuits were returned from St John in 1625, five from St Stanislaus in 1632 and eleven from Staffordshire in 1661.

Below I give the figures as percentages, adding seven priests for St John and five for St Stanislaus to the totals for North and West respectively in 1621, and transferring five, for Staffordshire, from North to South in 1621 and 1641.

	1621	1641	1672	1700	1720	1750	1771
North	26	20	22	35	30	36	41
Wales and West	12	16	12	10	11	10	12
South and Midlands	41	45	49	42	38	39	33
London	21	18	17	13	21	16	15

By comparison with the table of crude numbers, this helps to make clearer the rise as well as the decline of gentry dominance of the mission, and also points to the 1715 rebellion as a cause of temporary setback to the progress of the northern mission in the second half of the period.

TABLE III.   *Financial State of Jesuit Mission, 1636 and 1711.*

(Source: see above, chap. 10, n. 65)

(a) 1636

Region	Scudi	Annual Income Sterling	Funds	Sources Alms	Uncertain	Priests	Income per Priest
		£ s.	£	£ s.	£ s.		£
North	2,486	621 10	206	415 10	—	44	14
Wales and West	2,056	514	200	210	104	27	19
South and Midlands	8,714	2,178 10	1,083	500	595 10	77	28
London	2,868	717	327	200	190	39	18
TOTAL	16,124	4,031	1,816	1,325 10	889 10	187	21 10

Staffordshire is included with the North. St Stanislaus and St Thomas of Canterbury made no return in 1636; I have used the figures they gave in 1642. In the returns sums are given in Roman scudi; I have converted these into sterling at 4 scudi to the pound. The income whose nature is uncertain came from St Stanislaus, St George, St Mary, St Thomas of Canterbury and St Ignatius. The first four of these described themselves in and after 1645 as living entirely on alms, so the two upper figures in this column should probably be regarded as alms. In London (St Ignatius) it is clear from a comparison with the returns of 1625, 1628, 1642 and 1645 that there was a fund and regular alms producing the income given in these columns; the additional £190 returned in 1636 cannot have come from a fund, since it does not reappear, and looks like a non-recurring item of some kind. The number of priests is that given in the financial returns of 1636, with some gaps filled by recourse to the personnel figures of 1641; it seems a little exaggerated. Finally, the figures seem to have been intended to represent (notionally) reliable and regular income and so would exclude casual gifts and payments.

(b) 1711

Region	Income Scudi	Sterling	Funds	Sources Alms	Private Income	Provincial Subsidy	Priests	Income per Priest
		£	£ s.	£	£ s.	£ s.		£ s.
North	2,879	720	420	29	246	25	53	14 10
		1,260		*569*				*24*
Wales and	1,043	261	189	—	55	16 10	18	14 10
West		*401*		*140*				*22*
South and	5,264	1,316	908	125	283	—	63	21
Midlands		*1,576*		*385*				*25*
London	2,383	596	429 10	54	112 10	—	22	27
		776		*234*				*35*
TOTAL	11,569	2,892	1,946 10	208	696 10	41 10	156	18 10
		4,013		*1,328*				*26*

Staffordshire included with the South. The figures do not necessarily add up exactly because of the conversion from scudi.

The unitalicised figures are those given in the return of 1711, but they are obviously not a full record of the province's annual income, notably in the matter of alms. It looks as if what was recorded under 'alms' here were long-established regular payments for local priests which had not acquired the status of endowments. Other forms of income (congregational subscriptions, and possibly chaplain's salaries as well as occasional receipts for Mass-stipends, etc.) do not seem to have been counted. We get some light on the situation from the returns of 1714, which report the number of Jesuits living on 'alms' or 'charity' (i.e., I take it, on this sort of income) as follows: North, 27 (including 14 in the Lancashire district); West, 7; South, 13; London, 9. Assuming that each priest must have accounted for an income of £20 a year, I have added the appropriate sum in italics to the figures for 'alms', total income and income per priest. This is a crude procedure, and may involve a little duplication, but it does make it possible to offer something like a general breakdown of the province's income at this date; the results look fairly credible, and capable of bearing comparison with the figures for 1636.

Of the income of St Ignatius, £118 was a fund for the support of the provincial and his staff.

FIGURE I

THE SIZE OF THE COMMUNITY AND THE NUMBERS OF THE CLERGY 1600-1770

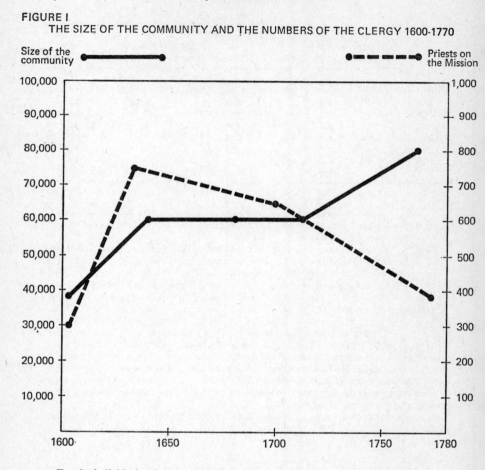

For the individual estimates on which this figure is based, see above, chapter 8 *passim*, and chapter 10, § (ii); I have simply drawn straight lines between them.

Of the figure of 392 priests returned by the vicars-apostolic in 1773, 30 were described as living privately in London without missionary faculties, and should therefore not be counted (see note to Map 4); but the number of regulars was somewhat underestimated. Hence the figure of 380 priests at this date given here.

Some of the growth which seems to have occurred between 1710 and 1767 must have been due to an influx of Irishmen notably into London; but this would not appear to account for much more than a quarter of it (see above, pp. 307, 312).

C

THE GROWTH OF THE COMMUNITY IN LANCASHIRE, 1770–1850

Notes on Tables IV and IV(a)

Table IV has been compiled from a variety of heterogeneous sources (detailed below), and a number of comments about it require to be made:

1. It is intended to give totals of congregational members, not of all the inhabitants of the town in question who were in some sense Catholics: I have reconstructed the information available to me with this in mind. There was at all times a considerable gap between the number of people who had been baptised as Catholics, and the number of genuine congregational participants, and estimates or censuses of Catholics were frequently attempts to give a figure for the larger rather than the smaller category. The gap between the two populations almost certainly increased during these eighty-four years, but I have made a conventional assumption that the second was at all times 50% of the first. Where estimates refer to the actual size of congregations, they are normally either figures for Easter communicants (as in 1773 and 1783) or figures for Mass attendance on a particular Sunday (as in 1851, or Preston, 1834). To figures for Easter Communicants I have added 50% to give the effective congregation including children; to figures for Mass attendance I have applied a conventional multiplier of 2·5. The scale of conversion between figures of these various kinds will therefore be:·

Baptised Catholics	100
Effective Congregation	50
Easter Communicants	33
Mass attendance on an average Sunday	20

Objection might be made to all these assumptions; I can only say that they are all reasonably defensible in themselves, and produce reasonably coherent results. More than rough accuracy is not claimed.

2. Where populations have had to be calculated on the basis of baptismal figures (as in Table IV(a)) I have had to make an assumption about the birth-rate. It is impossible to produce a single figure which would apply satisfactorily to all four towns throughout the period; according to the *Report on the Irish Poor* (Appendix, p. 8), at different times, in different towns and in different congregations within a single town, the birth-rate varied between about 1 in 30 and about 1 in 15—an enormous rate reached for a time in some of the Irish immigrant communities. For the period when I have had to depend on baptismal figures a figure at the lower end of this scale would probably be correct: I have used a rate of 1 in 30, based, where possible, on an average of five years' baptisms. This will probably give a somewhat high estimate of the baptised population; but, for the same period, the assumption that the effective congregation was 50% of the baptised population (see above) is probably too severe, and these errors may roughly cancel out. These assumptions do at least, for the period between 1783 and 1819 when nothing better seems to be available, provide a series of figures which are credible, consistent with each other, and reasonably consonant with the direct estimates available for both these years.

TABLE IV. *Catholic Congregations in Four Lancashire Towns, 1770–1850.*

	Preston	Wigan	Liverpool	Manchester	Estimated total
1767	1,043	1,194	1,743	351	4,431
1773	1,500	900	2,250	[400]	5,050
1783	1,200	900	1,800	600	4,500
1790	[2,000]	1,200	3,900	1,700	8,800
1800	[3,000]	1,200	5,700	4,000	13,900
1810	[4,000]	2,100	9,300	6,300	21,600
1819	6,000	3,000	18,000	⟨15,000⟩	37,000
1829	⟨10,900⟩	5,000	⟨31,800⟩	⟨51,200⟩	
1834	8,892	7,000	20,000	18,000	54,000
1851	⟨19,420⟩	⟨12,767⟩	⟨69,125⟩	44,105	*120,000*

Figures in square brackets are conjectures of my own.
Figures in diamond brackets I assume to be seriously inflated.
Figures in italics, in the totals column, have been revised downwards to take account of exaggeration in individual estimates; I have not felt able to offer a plausible reduction for the figures given in 1829.

Sources

1767   Returns of Papists, as in Lesourd, thesis *cit.*, ii, pp. 192, 198, 204. The Manchester figure includes Salford.

1773   Vicars-Apostolics' Returns of 1773: see J. H. Whyte, in *Recusant History*, ix (1968), 210: communicants plus 50%. Manchester is not mentioned in this return.

1783   Return of John Chadwick, vicar-general, to Bishop Matthew Gibson, 3 February 1783: Ushaw College Collection, Ms. ii, 129.

1790–1810   Figures constructed from baptismal registers, given to nearest hundred: see Table IV(a). Those for Preston are conjectural.

1819   *The Catholic Chapels and Chaplains, with the number of their respective Congregations, in the county of Lancaster, as taken at the end of 1819* (Liverpool, no date, presumably 1820. Copy in the Gillow library at the house of the Jesuit fathers, Farm Street, London).

1829   *Returns of Papists, 1829* (Parliamentary Papers, 1830, xix): figures given by priests, Manchester and Preston figures cover area wider than the town; probably meant to include all baptised Catholics. A census of Catholics in Wigan in 1829 gave a total of 6,369, but it is not clear what criteria were being used: *Report on the Irish Poor*, p. 8.

1834   *Preston* From census of Mass attendance, 9 January 1834 (total at 3 Masses in two chapels, 3,557), multiplied by 2·5: P. Whittle, *The History of the Borough of Preston*, ii (Preston, 1837), pp. 147–148.
   The remainder are my own figures for effective congregations based on evidence in *Report on the State of the Irish Poor in Great Britain* (Parliamentary Papers, 1836, xxxiv), Appendix, pp. 8–84 (Liverpool and Manchester), 87 f. (Wigan). The Liverpool figure is a communicant figure of 13,000 plus 50%; total baptised Catholics (baptismal figure times 18), *c.* 40,000. For details, see below, Table V. For Manchester, *ibid.*, pp. 43 f.: census of St Patrick's, Livesey Street, 1834: 11,009, of which 5,397 children (baptismal rate of 1 in 15·4). Remaining baptisms in Manchester, 1833: 1,303—multiplied by 18 = 23,454. Total 34,463. There were 2,237 baptisms in Liverpool in 1833, compared with 2,017 in Manchester; hence I assume the total of baptised Catholics in Manchester to have been, as all other serious evidence shows, less than in Liverpool, and the rough estimate of 40,000–50,000 given *ibid.*, pp. 42, 61 to be exaggerated.

There was probably some connection between this estimate and the inflated figure given in 1829. I have followed the Liverpool evidence, and the assumptions explained in note 1 above, in dividing the baptismal estimate by two in order to arrive at the communicant congregation, including children.

1851 *Religious Census of 1851* (Parliamentary Papers, 1852–1853, lxxxix): Mass attendance in registration *district*, multiplied by 2·5. Except in the case of Manchester, these include returns from more than the town chapels: 2 of Preston (district) chapels not returned.

TABLE IV(a). *Baptismal Estimates for Three Congregations, 1790–1820.*

		Wigan	Liverpool	Manchester
1790	Base Figure	82	260	112
	Estimate	1,230	3,900	1,680
1800	Base Figure	83	382	269
	Estimate	1,240	5,730	4,035
1810	Base Figure	138	619	423
	Estimate	2,070	9,285	6,345
1820	Base Figure	184	965	[662]
	Estimate	2,760	14,475	[9,930]

Except in the case of Liverpool 1790 and 1800, which are based respectively on baptisms for 1788, and an average of those for 1797–1800, and of Manchester 1820 (see under Sources), all these figures are based on an average of five years' baptisms ending on 31 December in the year stated. The assumption is of a birth-rate of 33 per thousand, or a multiplier of 30; divided by 2 on the assumption made above, note 1: i.e. base figures are multiplied by 15. I have not examined the Preston registers, or found any published totals derived from them, and the figures given in Table IV for Preston are therefore pure conjecture; their general drift is however well supported by the reference in the text, chap. 13, n. 12.

Sources: Wigan—baptismal registers in Lancs. C.R.O. RCWJ (St John's) and RCWM (St Mary's); Manchester—*ibid.*, RCMc, nos. 1–3 (St Chad's, Rook Street, 1772–1821, and annual totals for St Mary's, Mulberry Street, 1795–1810 and 1816–1818, given on flyleaf of no. 2)—the figure for 1820 is constructed from the average for St Chad's, 1816–1820 (280), St Mary's, 1818 (282), and a conjectural hundred for St Augustine's, Granby Row, which opened in 1820, though its registers do not appear to begin until January 1821; Liverpool, from *Report on the Irish Poor*, Appendix. p. 8.

TABLE V. *Congregations of the Five Catholic Chapels in Liverpool, 1834.*

	Total Catholics	*English*	*Irish*	*% Irish*
St Mary's	9,000	3,000–4,500	4,500–6,000	*50–67*
St Peter's	7,500–10,000	2,000–3,000	5,000–7,000	*67*
St Nicholas's	[*?7,500*]	[*?2,500*]	[*?5,000*]	[*?67*]
St Patrick's	6,000	*?nil*	6,000	*100*
St Anthony's	7,500[1]	2,500	5,000	66
TOTALS	37,500–40,000	10,000–12,500	25,500–29,000	*67–75*

	Communicants	*English*	*Irish*	*Effective Congregation*
St Mary's	3,000	1,000–1,500	1,500–2,000	*c. 4,500*
St Peter's	2,500–3,000	800–1,000	1,700–2,000	*c. 4,000*
St Nicholas's	[*2,500*]	[*800*]	[*1,700*]	[*c. 4,000*]
St Patrick's	2,000[2]	nil	2,000	*c. 3,000*
St Anthony's	2,500	800	1,700	*c. 4,000*
TOTALS	12,500–13,000	3,400–4,100	8,600–9,400	*c.* 19,500

Constructed from evidence in *Report on the Irish Poor*, Appendix, pp. 8, 22–25. Figures in
Roman type are those given by the priests of the respective congregations to the enquiry;
figures in italics are constructed from these by using the assumptions made in note 1 to
Table, above. Figures for St Nicholas's are conjectural, since none were given; the priest
said that 'by far the greater number' of names in his baptismal register were Irish.

1. On the basis of 430 baptisms in 1833, multiplying by 18: *ibid.*, p. 8.
2. On the basis of a 'Sunday congregation' of 'at least 1,200': *ibid.*, p. 25.

It may be remarked that the total of 40,000 Catholics in Liverpool at this date, arrived at
by the method used above, is very much the same as would be given by calculating on the
basis of baptisms in 1833, using the multiplier of 18 suggested *ibid.*, p. 8: 2,237 times 18 =
40,266. On the basis of the percentage of Irish baptisms given by the priest at St Anthony's,
the *Report on the Irish Poor* assumed that 60% of Catholic baptisms in Liverpool were Irish,
and that the Irish Catholic population of the city in 1833 amounted to 24,000 (*ibid.*, p. vii,
and Appx. p. 8, where 'two-fifths' is clearly an error for 'three-fifths'); I take this to be an
underestimate.

TABLE VI. *English and Irish in the Catholic Congregations of Four
Lancashire Towns, 1834.*

	English	*Irish*	*Total*
Preston	7,500	500	8,000[1]
Wigan	3,000	2,000	5,000[1]
Liverpool	6,000	14,000	20,000
Manchester	2,700	15,300	18,000
	19,200	31,800	51,000

1. I have adopted conservative totals for the congregations of Preston and Wigan in order to
avoid exaggerating the English element; it seems probable that the figure offered for Wigan
in Table IV was somewhat exaggerated.

FIGURE II

ENGLISH AND IRISH IN THE GROWTH OF CATHOLIC CONGREGATIONS
IN FOUR LANCASHIRE TOWNS' 1783-1851

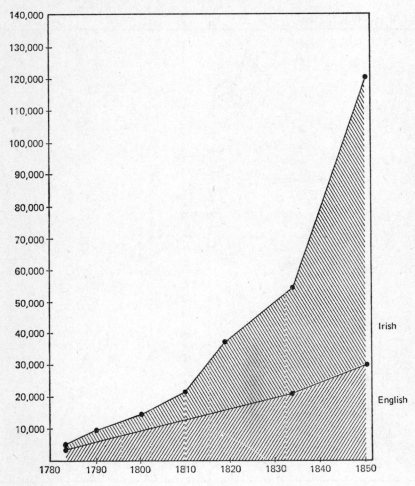

Based on the figures in Tables IV and VI, but treating the English element a little more generously than I do in Table VI. In trying to give an idea of the growth of the English element in these congregations, I have simply drawn a straight line between the figure for 1783 (taking a small percentage off for Irish at that date) and that for 1834, and projected it onwards with some allowance for an increase in the rate of growth. I do not claim that the result is perfect (e.g. it seems likely to exaggerate the English predominance around 1800–1810), but I suggest that it gives a reasonable idea of the actual situation. The implications that the balance of the two groups changed between 1810 and 1820, and that in 1851 about ¼ of the practising Catholics in these towns were of English origin, seem credible enough. See above, pp. 306–309.

MAP 8. *Places Mentioned in the Text: (a) the North; (b) the South.*

MAP 8(a)   THE NORTH

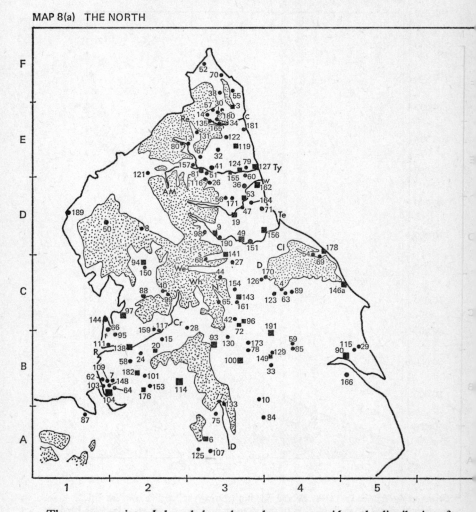

These maps are intended as a help to the reader, not as a guide to the distribution of Catholicism in England: some places (e.g. Otterburn (131)) are mentioned precisely because there were few or no Catholics there. However, they may serve as a rough guide to this distribution, and since some geographical suggestions about the incidence of Catholicism in the North have been made in chapter 5 (pp. 79ff) I have thought it useful to sketch on the northern map some features of the landscape which may help to illuminate the discussion. The dotted areas represent the extent of moorland at the present day (from D. P. Bickmore and others, *Atlas of Britain*

MAP 8(b) THE SOUTH

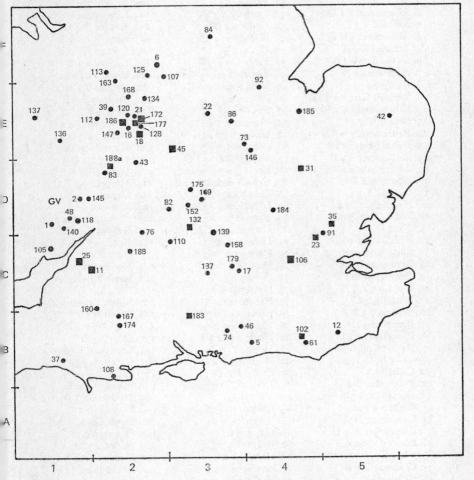

and Northern Ireland (Oxford, 1963), p. 41): no doubt it was somewhat wider during the period covered by this book. Note the extreme dearth of places with Catholic connections in the far North-west, and (bearing in mind the point about Otterburn made above) the signs of alternating allegiance in the dales on the eastern side of the Pennines (above, p. 88). The greater density of places mentioned in the North than in the South is slightly obscured by the fact that I have used a larger scale for the northern map than for the southern.

Key to Maps 8 (a) and (b)

151. Sockburne a 3 D
152. Somerton b 3 D
153. Southworth Hall
     a 2 B
154. Stainley a 3 C
155. Stella a 3 E
156. Stockton a 4 D
157. Stonecroft a 3 E
158. Stonor b 3 C
159. Stonyhurst a 2 B
160. Stourton b 2 C
161. Studley a 3 C
162. Sunderland a 4 E
163. Swinnerton b 2 F
164. Thornley a 4 D

165. Thropton a 3 F
166. Thornton a 5 B
167. Tisbury b 2 B
168. Tixall b 2 E
169. Tusmore b 3 D
170. Upsall a 4 C
171. Ushaw a 3 D
172. Walsall b 2 E
173. Walton a 3 B
174. Wardour b 2 B
175. Warkworth b 3 D
176. Warrington a 2 B
177. West Bromwich b 2 E
178. Whitby a 5 D

179. Whiteknights b 3 C
180. Whittingham a 3 F
181. Widdrington a 4 E
182. Wigan a 2 B
183. Winchester b 3 B
184. Wing b 4 D
185. Wisbech b 4 E
186. Wolverhampton
     b 2 E
187. Woolhampton b 3 C
188. Wootton Basset b 2 C
189. Workington a 1 D
190. Wycliffe a 3 D
191. York a 4 B

Districts

Alston Moor	AM	Golden Valley	GV	Swaledale	S
Cleveland	Cl	Nidderdale	N	Wensleydale	We
Craven	Cr	Redesdale	Re	Wharfedale	Wh
Fylde	F				

Rivers

Coquet	C	Ribble	R	Tyne	Ty
Derwent	D	Tees	Te	Wear	W

SHORT LIST OF ABBREVIATIONS AND FULL TITLES

A.A.W. Archives of the Archbishop of Westminster.

AVELING, HUGH[J.C.H.], *Post-Reformation Catholicism in East Yorkshire, 1558–1790* (East Yorkshire Local History Society, 1960).

AVELING, HUGH [J.C.H.], *The Catholic Recusants of the West Riding of Yorkshire 1558–1790* (Proceedings of the Leeds Philosophical and Literary Society, 1963).

AVELING, HUGH [J.C.H.], *Northern Catholics : the Catholic Recusants of the North Riding of Yorkshire* (London, 1966).

AVELING, JOHN[J.C.H.], *Catholic Recusancy in the City of York, 1558–1791* (C.R.S. monograph series ii, 1971).

BLUNDELL, M., *Cavalier: Letters of William Blundell to his Friends, 1620–1698* (London, 1933).

Blundell, Nicholas. See below under Tyrer.

BOSSY, JOHN, 'The Character of Elizabethan Catholicism', in T. Aston (ed.), *Crisis in Europe, 1560–1660* (London, 1965), pp. 223–246; originally in *Past and Present*, no. 21 (1962), pp. 39–59.

BOSSY, JOHN, 'Four Catholic Congregations in Rural Northumberland, 1750–1850', *Recusant History*, ix (1967), pp. 88–119.

BURTON, EDWIN H., *The Life and Times of Bishop Challoner, 1691–1781* (2 vols., London, 1909).

CARAMAN, PHILIP (ed.), *John Gerard : the Autobiography of an Elizabethan* (London, 2nd edn, 1956).

CARAMAN, PHILIP, *Henry Garnet (1565–1606) and the Gunpowder Plot* (London, 1964).

CASTLE, E. (ed.), *The Jerningham Letters, 1780–1843* (2 vols., London, 1896).

C.R.S. Catholic Record Society.

C.R.S. i (1905): *Miscellanea* (J. H. Pollen (ed.), *The Notebooks of John Southcote, 1628–1636*).

C.R.S. ii (1906): *Miscellanea* (J. H. Pollen (ed.), *Memoirs of Robert Persons, S.J.*).

C.R.S. iv (1907): *Miscellanea* (Lord Burghley's Map of Lancashire (frontispiece); *Memoirs of Robert Persons*, continued).

C.R.S. ix (1911): *Miscellanea* (P. Ryan (ed.), *Some Correspondence of Cardinal Allen*; Liverpool Registers).

C.R.S. x–xi (1911): E. H. Burton and T. L. Williams (eds.), *The Douay College Diaries, 1598–1654*.

C.R.S. xiv (1914): *Miscellanea* (Registers, including that of Monox Hervey).

C.R.S. xv–xvi, xxiii (1913–1914, 1922): J. P. Smith and others (eds.), *Lancashire Registers*.

C.R.S. xxii (1921): *Miscellanea* (R. Stanfield (ed.), *The Archpriest Controversy*; Narrative of John Bennett; Chalcedon Papers).

C.R.S. xxvii (1928): E. H. Burton and E. Nolan (eds.), *The Douay College Diaries, 1715–1778*.

C.R.S. xxx (1930): E. Henson (ed.), *Registers of the English College at Valladolid, 1589–1862.*

C.R.S. xxxiii (1933): J. McCann and H. Connolly (eds.), *Memorials of Father Augustine Baker and other Documents relating to the English Benedictines.*

C.R.S. xxxv (1936): *Miscellanea* (Newcastle Registers).

C.R.S. xxxix (1942): L. Hicks (ed), *Letters and Memorials of Robert Persons, i : to 1588.*

C.R.S. xl (1943): W. Kelly (ed.), *The Liber Ruber of the English College, Rome: i,* Nomina Alumnorum, *1631–1783.*

C.R.S. xli (1948): L. Hicks (ed.), *The Letters of Thomas Fitzherbert, 1608–1610.*

C.R.S. xliii (1949): R. E. Scantlebury (ed.), *Hampshire Registers* (Hampshire Secular Clergy Fund).

C.R.S. xlvii–xlviii (1953, 1955): T. A. Birrell (ed.), John Warner, *History of the English Persecution of Catholics and the Presbyterian Plot* (2 vols.).

C.R.S. l (1956): E. E. Reynolds (ed.), *The Diary of William Mawhood.*

C.R.S. li (1958): P. Renold (ed.), *The Wisbech Stirs.*

C.R.S. liii (1961): C. Talbot (ed.), *Miscellanea: Recusant Records* (includes H. Aveling (ed.), *Papers of the Northern Commission for Compounding with Recusants, 1626–1632*).

C.R.S. liv–lv (1962–1963): A. Kenny (ed.), *The* Responsa Scholarum *of the English College, Rome, 1598–1685.*

C.R.S. lvi (1964): *Miscellanea* (H. Aveling (ed.), *Recusancy Papers of the Meynell Family*).

C.R.S. lvii (1965): H. Bowler (ed.), *Recusant Roll no. 2, 1593–4.*

C.R.S. lx (1968): A. G. Petti (ed.), *Recusant Documents from the Ellesmere Mss.*

C.R.S. lxii (1971): G. Holt (ed.), *The Letter-book of Lewis Sabran, 1713–1715.*

C.R.O. County Record Office.

D.N.B. L. Stephen and S. Lee (eds.), *Dictionary of National Biography* (21 vols., London, 1908–1909).

FOLEY, H. (ed.), *Records of the English Province of the Society of Jesus* (7 volumes, London, 1875–1883).

Gerard, John. See *Caraman.*

GILLOW, J., *A Bibliographical Dictionary of English Catholics* (5 vols., London/New York, n.d.: vol, 1, 1885).

HEMPHILL, B., *The Early Vicars-Apostolic of England, 1685–1750* (London, 1954).

H.M.C. Historical Manuscripts Commission.

KNOX, T. F. (ed.), *Letters and Memorials of William Cardinal Allen* (London, 1882).

LAW, T. G. (ed.), *The Archpriest Controversy: Documents relating to the Dissensions of the Roman Catholic Clergy 1597–1602* (Camden Society, 2 vols., 1896, 1898).

MATHEW, DAVID, *Catholicism in England. The Portrait of a Minority: its Culture and Tradition* (London, 1948 edn used here: 1st edn 1936).

LEYS, M. D. R., *Catholics in England, 1559–1829. A Social History* (London, 1961).

MAGEE, B., *The English Recusants* (London, 1938).

Mawhood, William. See C.R.S. l.

P.R.O. Public Record Office, London.

ROWLANDS, M., 'Catholics in Staffordshire from the Revolution to the Relief Acts, 1689–1791' (Birmingham University M.A. thesis, 1965).

TIERNEY, M. A. (ed.), [*Charles*] *Dodd's Church History of England* (5 vols., London, 1839–1843).

TYRER, F. (ed.), *The Great Diurnal of Nicholas Blundell*, i : *1702–1711 ; ii : 1712–1719 ; iii : 1720–1728* (Record Society of Lancashire and Cheshire, 1968, 1970, 1972).

V.C.H. Victoria County History.

V.C.H. Lancashire, vol. ii (eds. W. Farrer and J. Brownbill, 1908).

V.C.H. Leicestershire, vol. ii (eds. W. G. Hoskins and R. A. McKinley, 1954).

V.C.H. Oxfordshire, vol. ii (ed. W. Page, 1907).

V.C.H. Staffordshire, vol. iii (ed. M. W. Greenslade, 1970).

WARD, BERNARD, *The Dawn of the Catholic Revival in England, 1781–1803* (2 vols., London, 1909).

WARD, BERNARD, *The Eve of Catholic Emancipation : being the History of the English Catholics during the first 30 years of the 19th Century* (3 vols., London, 1911–1912).

WARD, BERNARD, *The Sequel to Catholic Emancipation* (2 vols., London, 1915).

WILLIAMS, J. A., *Catholic Recusancy in Wiltshire, 1660–1791* (C.R.S. monograph series, i, 1968).

INDEX

I have tried to make up for the fact that this book does not, on the whole, deal with events in chronological sequence by grouping the main references for particular periods under the heading of the reigns of individual kings or queens (or the Interregnum). Names in italics are those of modern scholars; subject headings are given in capitals. Italic figures indicate major references.